Recommended Reference Books for Small and Medium-sized Libraries and Media Centers

RECOMMENDED REFERENCE BOOKS

for Small and Medium-sized Libraries and Media Centers

2004
EDITION

Dr. Martin Dillon, Editor in Chief
Shannon Graff Hysell, Associate Editor

A Member of the Greenwood Publishing Group

Westport, Connecticut • London

LIBRARIES UNLIMITED
A Member of the Greenwood Publishing Group, Inc.
88 Post Road West
Westport, CT 06881
1-800-225-5800
www.lu.com

Library of Congress Cataloging-in-Publication Data

Main entry under title:

Recommended reference books for small and medium-
    sized libraries and media centers.

    "Selected from the 2004 edition of American
reference books annual."
    Includes index.
    I. Reference books--Bibliography. 2. Reference
services (Library)--Handbooks, manuals, etc.
3. Instructional materials centers--Handbooks,
manuals, etc. I. Dillon, Martin   II. Hysell, Shannon Graff
III. American reference books annual.
Z1035.1.R435   011'.02   81-12394
ISBN 1-59158-168-0
ISSN 0277-5948

Contents

Introduction

Recommended Reference Books for Small and Medium-sized Libraries and Media Centers (RRB), now in its twenty-fourth volume, is designed to assist smaller libraries in the systematic selection of suitable reference materials for their collections. It aids in the evaluation process by choosing substantial titles in all subject areas. The increase in the publication of reference sources in the United States and Canada, in combination with the decrease in library budgets, makes this guide an invaluable tool.

Following the pattern established in 1981 with the first volume, RRB consists of book reviews chosen from the current edition of *American Reference Books Annual*. This nationally acclaimed work provides reviews of reference books, CD-ROMs, and Internet sites published in the United States and Canada within a single year, along with English-language titles from other countries. ARBA has reviewed more than 58,000 titles since its inception in 1970. Because it provides comprehensive coverage of reference sources, not just selected or recommended titles, many are of interest only to large academic and public libraries. Thus, RRB has been developed as an abridged version of ARBA, with selected reviews of resources suitable for smaller libraries.

Titles reviewed in RRB include dictionaries, encyclopedias, indexes, directories, bibliographies, guides, atlases, gazetteers, and other types of ready-reference tools. General encyclopedias that are updated annually, yearbooks, almanacs, indexing and abstracting services, directories, and other annuals are included on a selective basis. These works are systematically reviewed so that all important annuals are critically examined every few years. Excluded from RRB are regional guides in the areas of biological sciences, travel guides, and reference titles in the areas of music and fine arts that deal with individual artists. All titles in this volume are coded with letters, which provide worthwhile guidance for selection. These indicate that a given work is a recommended purchase for smaller college libraries (C), public libraries (P), or school media centers (S).

The current volume of RRB contains 548 unabridged reviews selected from the 1,570 entries in ARBA 2004. These have been written by more than 200 subject specialists throughout the United States and Canada. Although all titles in RRB are recommended acquisitions, critical comments have not been deleted, because even recommended works may be weak in one respect or another. In many cases reviews evaluate and compare a work in relation to other titles of a similar nature. All reviews provide complete ordering and bibliographic information. The subject index organization is based upon the 22d edition of the *Library of Congress Subject Headings*. Reference to reviews published in periodicals (see page xxi for journals cited) during the year of coverage are appended to the reviews. All reviews are signed.

The present volume contains 37 chapters. There are four major subdivisions: "General Reference Works," "Social Sciences," "Humanities," and "Science and Technology." "General Reference Works," arranged alphabetically, is subdivided by form: bibliography, biography, handbooks and yearbooks, and so on. The remaining three parts are subdivided into alphabetically arranged chapters. Most chapters are subdivided in a way that reflects the arrangement strategy of the entire volume: a section on general works and then a topical breakdown. The latter is further subdivided, based on the amount of material available on a given topic.

RRB has been favorably reviewed in such journals as *Booklist*, *School Library Media Quarterly*, *Journal of Academic Librarianship*, *Library Talk*, and *Reference Books Bulletin*. For example, *Library Talk* (Jan/Feb 2002, p. 54) states that RRB is "the answer to the prayers of librarians of small to medium-sized facilities who need to buy reference materials." The editors continue to strive to make RRB the most valuable acquisition tool a small library can have.

In closing, the editors at Libraries Unlimited would like to express their gratitude to the contributors whose reviews appear in this volume. We would also like to thank the staff members who have been instrumental in the preparation of this work.

Contributors

Gordon J. Aamot, Head, Foster Business Library, Univ. of Washington, Seattle.

Stephen H. Aby, Education Bibliographer, Bierce Library, Univ. of Akron, Ohio.

Anthony J. Adam, Reference Librarian, Prairie View A & M Univ., Coleman Library, Tex.

January Adams, Asst. Director/Head of Adult Services, Franklin Township Public Library, Somerset, N.J.

Michael Adams, Reference Librarian, City Univ. of New York Graduate Center.

James W. Agee Jr., Library Acquisitions, Central Missouri State Univ., Warrensburg.

Donald Altschiller, Reference Librarian, Boston Univ.

Frank J. Anderson, Librarian Emeritus, Sandor Teszler Library, Wofford College, Spartanburg, S.C.

Charles R. Andrews, Dean of Library Services, Hofstra Univ., Hempstead, N.Y.

Alan Asher, Art/Music Librarian, Univ. of Northern Iowa, Cedar Falls.

Susan C. Awe, Asst. Director, Univ. of New Mexico, Albuquerque.

Christopher Baker, Professor of English, Armstrong Atlantic State Univ., Savannah, Ga.

Mark T. Bay, Electronic Resources, Serials, and Government Documents Librarian, Hagan Memorial Library, Cumberland College, Williamsburg, Ky.

Leslie M. Behm, Reference Librarian, Michigan State Univ. Libraries, East Lansing.

Carol Willsey Bell, Head, Local History and Genealogy Dept., Warren-Trumbull County Public Library, Warren, Ohio.

George H. Bell, Assoc. Librarian, Daniel E. Noble Science and Engineering Library, Arizona State Univ., Tempe.

Laura J. Bender, Science Librarian, Univ. of Arizona, Tucson.

John B. Beston, Professor of English, Santa Fe, N.Mex.

Barbara M. Bibel, Reference Librarian, Science/Business/Sociology Dept., Main Library, Oakland Public Library, Calif.

Adrienne Antink Bien, Medical Group Management Association, Lakewood, Colo.

Terry D. Bilhartz, Assoc. Professor of History, Sam Houston State Univ., Huntsville, Tex.

Richard Bleiler, Reference Librarian, Univ. of Connecticut, Storrs.

Daniel K. Blewett, Reference Librarian, College of DuPage Library, College of DuPage, Glen Ellyn, Ill.

Edna M. Boardman, Bismark, N.D.

Polly D. Boruff-Jones, Asst. Librarian, Indiana Univ.—Purdue Univ. Indianapolis, University Library.

Christopher Brennan, Assoc. Director, Drake Memorial Library, SUNY, Brockport, N.Y.

Georgia Briscoe, Assoc. Director and Head of Technical Services, Law Library, Univ. of Colorado, Boulder.

Janet Dagenais Brown, Assoc. Professor and Education and Social Sciences Librarian, Wichita State Univ., Kans.

Jana Brubaker, Catalog Librarian, Northern Illinois Univ., De Kalb.

Patrick J. Brunet, Library Manager, Western Wisconsin Technical College, La Crosse.

John R. Burch Jr., Director of Library Services, Cambellsville Univ., Ky.

Frederic F. Burchsted, Reference Librarian, Widener Library, Harvard Univ., Cambridge, Mass.

Joanna M. Burkhardt, Head Librarian, College of Continuing Education Library, Univ. of Rhode Island, Providence.

Hans E. Bynagle, Library Director and Professor of Philosophy, Whitworth College, Spokane, Wash.

Diane M. Calabrese, Freelance Writer and Contributor, Silver Springs, Md.

E. Wayne Carp, Professor of History, Pacific Lutheran Univ., Tacoma, Wash.

Joseph Cataio, Manager, Booklegger's Bookstore, Chicago, Ill.

Boyd Childress, Reference Librarian, Ralph B. Draughon Library, Auburn Univ., Ala.

Hui Hua Chua, U.S. Documents Librarian, Michigan State Univ. Libraries, East Lansing.

Dene L. Clark, (retired) Reference Librarian, Auraria Library, Denver, Colo.

Erica L. Coe, Reference and Digital Initiatives Librarian, Univ. of Dayton, Ohio.

Donald E. Collins, Assoc. Professor, History Dept., East Carolina Univ., Greenville, N.C.

Jeannie Colson, Reference and Electronic Resources Librarian, Columbia International Univ., Columbia, S.C.

Barbara Conroy, Career Connections, Santa Fe, N.Mex.

Rosanne M. Cordell, Head of Reference Services, Franklin D. Schurz Library, Indiana Univ., South Bend.

Kay O. Cornelius, (formerly) Teacher and Magnet School Lead Teacher, Huntsville City Schools, Ala.

Paul B. Cors, Catalog Librarian, Univ. of Wyoming, Laramie.

Gregory A. Crawford, Head of Public Services, Penn State Harrisburg, Middletown, Pa.

Mark J. Crawford, Consulting Exploration Geologist/Writer/Editor, Madison, Wis.

Gregory Curtis, Director, Northern Maine Technical College, Presque Isle.

Joseph W. Dauben, Professor of History and History of Science, City Univ. of New York.

Melvin Davis, Asst. Professor, Interlibrary Loan Librarian, Middle Tennessee Univ., Murfreesboro, Tenn.

Dominique-René de Lerma, Professor, Conservatory of Music, Lawrence Univ., Appleton, Wis.

R. K. Dickson, Professor of Art History and Studio Art, Wilson College, Chambersburg, Pa.

Scott R. DiMarco, Director of Library Services, Herkimer County Community College, N.Y.

Tara L. Dirst, Technology Coordinator, Abraham Lincoln Historical Digitization Project, Northern Illinois Univ., De Kalb.

Margaret F. Dominy, Information Services Librarian, Drexel Univ., Philadelphia.

G. Kim Dority, G. K. Dority & Associates, Castle Rock, Colo.

David J. Duncan, Reference Librarian, Humanities, Wichita State Univ., Ablah Library, Kans.

Joe P. Dunn, Charles A. Dana Professor of History and Politics, Converse College, Spartanburg, S.C.

Bradford Lee Eden, Head of Cataloging, Univ. of Nevada at Las Vegas.

Marianne B. Eimer, Interlibrary Loan/Reference Librarian, SUNY College at Fredonia, N.Y.

Patricia A. Eskoz, (retired) Catalog Librarian, Auraria Library, and Asst. Professor Emeritus, Univ. of Colorado, Denver.

Lorraine Evans, Instruction and Reference Librarian, Auraria Library, Denver, Colo.

Elaine Ezell, Library Media Specialist, Bowling Green Jr. High School, Ohio.

Judith J. Field, Senior Lecturer, Program for Library and Information Science, Wayne State Univ., Detroit.

Jerry D. Flack, Professor Emeritus, Retired.

James H. Flynn Jr., (formerly) Operations Research Analyst, Dept. of Defense, Vienna, Va.

Michael A. Foley, Honors Director, Marywood College, Scranton, Pa.

David K. Frasier, Asst. Librarian, Reference Dept., Indiana Univ., Bloomington.

Susan J. Freiband, Assoc. Professor, Graduate School of Librarianship, Univ. of Puerto Rico, San Juan.

David O. Friedrichs, Professor, Univ. of Scranton, Pa.

Thomas K. Fry, Assoc. Director, Public Services, Penrose Library, Univ. of Denver, Colo.

Sandra E. Fuentes Riggs, Librarian, Montgomery Library, Cambellsville Univ., Campbellsville, Ky.

Jeanne D. Galvin, Chief of Reference, Kingsborough Community College, City Univ. of New York, Brooklyn, N.Y.

Ahmad Gamaluddin, Professor, School of Library Science, Clarion State College, Pa.

Zev Garber, Professor and Chair, Jewish Studies, Los Angeles Valley College, Calif.

Susan J. Gardner, Collection Development Coordinator—Leavey Library, Univ. of Southern California, Los Angeles.

Denise A. Garofalo, Director for Telecommunications, Mid-Hudson Library System, Poughkeepsie, N.Y.

John T. Gillespie, College Professor and Writer, New York.

Lois Gilmer, Library Director, Univ. of West Florida, Fort Walton Beach.

Caroline L. Gilson, Coordinator, Prevo Science Library, DePauw Univ., Greencastle, Ind.

Harold Goss, Jr., Librarian I, Auburn Univ. Libraries, Auburn, Ala.

Anthony Gottlieb, Asst. Clinical Professor, Univ. of Colorado School of Medicine, Denver.

Ravonne A. Green, Library Director, Brenau Univ., Gainesville, Ga.

Richard W. Grefrath, Reference Librarian, Univ. of Nevada, Reno.

Laurel Grotzinger, Professor, Univ. Libraries, Western Michigan Univ., Kalamazoo.

Linda W. Hacker, Reference Librarian, SUNY Brockport, Brockport, N.Y.

Patrick Hall, Director of Libraries, State Univ. of New York at Kenton.

Deborah Hammer, Head, History, Travel and Biography Division, Queens Borough Public Library, Jamaica, N.Y.

Joe Hardenbrook, Reference Librarian/Instructor, Newton Gresham Library, Sam Houston State Univ., Huntsville, Tex.

Marvin K. Harris, Professor of Entomology, Texas A & M Univ., College Station.

Maris L. Hayashi, Asst. University Librarian, Florida Atlantic Univ., Boca Raton, Fla.

Lucy Heckman, Reference Librarian (Business-Economics), St. John's Univ. Library, Jamaica, N.Y.

David Henige, African Studies Bibliographer, Memorial Library, Univ. of Wisconsin, Madison.

Mark Y. Herring, Dean of Library Services, Winthrop Univ., Dacus Library, Rock Hill, S.C.

Joseph P. Hester, SRO-Learning, Claremont, N.C.

Ladyjane Hickey, Head of Cataloging and Business, Management and Marketing Bibliographer, Newton Gresham Library, Sam Houston State Univ., Huntsville, Tex.

Susan Tower Hollis, Assoc. Dean and Center Director, Central New York Center of the State Univ. of New York.

Sara Anne Hook, Assoc. Dean of the Faculties, Indiana Univ., Purdue Univ., Indianapolis.

Shirley L. Hopkinson, Professor, Div. of Library and Information Science, San Jose State Univ., Calif.

Mihoko Hosoi, Public Services Librarian, Cornell Univ., Ithaca, N.Y.

Shannon Graff Hysell, Staff, Libraries Unlimited.

Charmaine Ijeoma, Asst. Professor of English and African and African American Studies, Penn State Abington College, Pa.

David Isaacson, Asst. Head of Reference and Humanities Librarian, Waldo Library, Western Michigan Univ., Kalamazoo.

D. Barton Johnson, Professor Emeritus of Russian, Univ. of California, Santa Barbara.

Richard D. Johnson, Director of Libraries Emeritus, James M. Milne Library, State Univ. College, Oneonta, N.Y.

Thomas A. Karel, Assoc. Director for Public Services, Shadek-Fackenthal Library, Franklin and Marshall College, Lancaster, Pa.

Edmund D. Keiser Jr., Professor of Biology, Univ. of Mississippi, University.

John Laurence Kelland, Reference Bibliographer for Life Sciences, Univ. of Rhode Island Library, Kingston.

Christine E. King, Education Librarian, Purdue Univ., West Lafayette, Ind.

Lori D. Kranz, Freelance Editor, Chambersburg, Pa.

Betsy J. Kraus, Librarian, Lovelace Respiratory Research Institute, National Environmental Respiratory Center, Albuquerque, N.Mex.

Marlene M. Kuhl, Library Manager, Baltimore County Public Library, Reisterstown Branch, Md.

Natalie Kupferberg, Biological Sciences/Pharmacy Library, Ohio State Univ., Columbus.

George Thomas Kurian, President, Encyclopedia Society, Baldwin Place, N.Y.

Robert V. Labaree, Reference/Public Services Librarian, Von KleinSmid Library, Univ. of Southern California, Los Angeles.

Sharon Ladenson, Social Sciences Bibliographer and Reference Librarian, Michigan State Univ. Libraries, East Lansing.

Linda L. Lam-Easton, Assoc. Professor, Dept. of Religious Studies, California State Univ., Northridge.

Elaine Lasda, Librarian, Health Care Association of New York State, Rensselaer.

Rob Laurich, Head of Reference and Collection Development, The City College of New York.

Martha Lawler, Assoc. Librarian, Louisiana State Univ., Shreveport.

Charles Leck, Professor of Biological Sciences, Rutgers Univ., New Brunswick, N.J.

John A. Lent, Drexel Hill, Pa.

Michael Levine-Clark, Reference Librarian, Univ. of Denver, Colo.

Tze-chung Li, Professor and Dean Emeritus, Dominican Univ.

Charlotte Lindgren, Professor Emerita of English, Emerson College, Boston, Mass.

Koraljka Lockhart, Publications Editor, San Francisco Opera, Calif.

Jeffrey E. Long, Editor of *SoutteReview* Newsletter, Univ. of Massachusetts Medical School Library, Worcester.

Glenn Masuchika, Senior Information Specialist, Rockwell Collins Information, Iowa City, Iowa.

John Maxymuk, Reference Librarian, Paul Robeson Library, Rutgers Univ., Camden, N.J.

George Louis Mayer, (formerly) Senior Principal Librarian, New York Public Library and Part-Time Librarian, Adelphi, Manhattan Center and Brooklyn College.

Dana McDougald, Lead Media Specialist, Learning Resources Center, Cedar Shoals High School, Athens, Ga.

Glenn S. McGuigan, Reference Librarian, Penn State Abington, Abington, Pa.

Peter Zachary McKay, Business Librarian, Univ. of Florida Libraries, Gainesville.

Robert B. McKee, Professor, Mechanical Engineering, Univ. of Nevada, Reno.

Lynn M. McMain, Instructor/Reference Librarian, Newton Gresham Library, Sam Houston State Univ., Huntsville, Tex.

Michael G. Messina, Assoc. Professor, Dept. of Forest Science, Texas A & M Univ., College Station.

G. Douglas Meyers, Chair, Dept. of English, Univ. of Texas, El Paso.

Elizabeth M. Mezick, CPA/Asst. Professor, Long Island Univ., Brookville, N.Y.

Robert Michaelson, Head Librarian, Seeley G. Mudd Library for Science and Engineering, Northwestern Univ., Evanston, Ill.

Ken Middleton, User Services Librarian, Middle Tennessee State Univ., Murfreesboro.

Bogdan Mieczkowski, Cocoa Beach, Fla.

Seiko Mieczkowski, Cocoa Beach, Fla.

Bill Miller, Director of Libraries, Florida Atlantic Univ., Boca Raton.

Terri Tickle Miller, Slavic Bibliographer, Michigan State Univ. Libraries, East Lansing.

Jim Millhorn, Head of Acquisitions, Northern Illinois Univ. Libraries, De Kalb.

Paul A. Mogren, Head of Reference, Marriott Library, Univ. of Utah, Salt Lake City.

Janet Mongan, Research Officer, Cleveland State Univ. Library, Ohio.

Terry Ann Mood, Professor Emeritus, Univ. of Colorado, Denver.

Craig A. Munsart, Teacher, Jefferson County Public Schools, Golden, Colo.

Valentine K. Muyumba, Monographic Cataloging Librarian, Indiana State Univ., Terre Haute.

Madeleine Nash, Reference Librarian, Spring Valley, N.Y.

Rita Neri, Health Sciences Librarian, Long Island Univ., Brooklyn Campus, N.Y.

Deborah L. Nicholl, Asst. Professor, Elizabeth Huth Coates Library, Trinity Univ., San Antonio, Tex.

Christopher W. Nolan, Asst. University Librarian, Elizabeth Huth Coates Library, Trinity Univ., San Antonio, Tex.

Carol L. Noll, Volunteer Librarian, Schimelpfenig Middle School, Plano, Tex.

Herbert W. Ockerman, Professor, Ohio State Univ., Columbus.

James W. Oliver, Chemistry Librarian, Michigan State Univ., East Lansing.

John Howard Oxley, Faculty, American Intercontinental Univ., Atlanta, Ga.

Harry E. Pence, Professor of Chemistry, State Univ. of New York, Oneonta.

Anna H. Perrault, Assoc. Professor, Univ. of South Florida, Tampa.

Phillip P. Powell, Asst. Reference Librarian, Robert Scott Small Library, College of Charleston, S.C.

Jack Ray, Asst. Director, Loyola/Notre Dame Library, Baltimore, Md.

Patrick J. Reakes, Journalism/Mass Communications Librarian, Univ. of Florida, Gainesville.

Nancy P. Reed, Information Services Manager, Paducah Public Library, Ky.

Allen Reichert, Electronic Access Librarian, Courtright Memorial Library, Otterbein College, Westerville, Ohio.

Robert B. Marks Ridinger, Head, Electronic Information Resources Management Dept., Univ. Libraries, Northern Illinois Univ., De Kalb.

John M. Robson, Institute Librarian, Rose-Hulman Institute of Technology, Terre Haute, Ind.

Deborah V. Rollins, Reference Librarian, Univ. of Maine, Orono.

John B. Romeiser, Professor of French and Dept. Head, Univ. of Tennessee, Knoxville.

Jill Rooker, Assoc. Professor and Program Coordinator, Instructional Media, Univ. of Central Oklahoma, Edmond.

Patricia Rothermich, Reference/Business Librarian, Courtright Memorial Library, Otterbein College, Westerville, Ohio.

Nadine Salmons, Technical Services Librarian, Fort Carson's Grant Library, Colo.

Diane Schmidt, Asst. Biology Librarian, Univ. of Illinois, Urbana.

Willa Schmidt, (retired) Reference Librarian, Univ. of Wisconsin, Madison.

Ralph Lee Scott, Assoc. Professor, East Carolina Univ. Library, Greenville, N.C.

Colleen Seale, Humanities and Social Sciences Services, George A. Smathers Libraries, Univ. of Florida, Gainesville.

Karen Selden, Catalog Librarian, Univ. of Colorado Law Library, Boulder.

Susan K. Setterlund, Science/Health Science Librarian, Florida Atlantic Univ., Boca Raton.

Shikha Sharma, Coordinator of Library Instruction, SUNY College at Brockport.

Deborah Sharp, Head Librarian, Lexmark Information Center, Univ. of Kentucky, Lexington.

Susan Shultz, Librarian, Michigan State Univ., East Lansing.

Esther R. Sinofsky, Coordinating Field Librarian, Los Angeles, Calif.

Kennith Slagle, Asst. Director for Collection Management, Jackson Library, Univ. of North Carolina at Greensboro.

Richard Slapsys, Umass Lowell Reference Coordinator, Fine Arts Librarian, Umass Lowell, Mass.

Mary Ellen Snodgrass, Freelance Writer, Charlotte, N.C.

Kay M. Stebbins, Coordinator Librarian, Louisiana State Univ., Shreveport.

Martha E. Stone, Coordinator for Reference Services, Treadwell Library, Massachusetts General Hospital, Boston.

John W. Storey, Professor of History, Lamar Univ., Beaumont, Tex.

William C. Struning, Professor, Seton Hall Univ., South Orange, N.J.

Timothy E. Sullivan, Asst. Professor of Economics, Towson State Univ., Md.

Philip G. Swan, Head Librarian, Hunter College, School of Social Work Library, New York.

Paolina Taglienti, Head of Acquisitions, Long Island Univ., Brooklyn Campus Library, N.Y.

Martha Tarlton, Head, Reference and Information Services, Univ. of North Texas Libraries, Denton.

Marit S. Taylor, Reference Librarian, Auraria Libraries, Univ. of Colorado, Denver.

Mary Ann Thompson, Asst. Professor of Nursing, Saint Joseph College, West Hartford, Conn.

Linda D. Tietjen, Senior Instructor, Instruction and Reference Services, Auraria Library, Denver, Colo.

Bruce H. Tiffney, Assoc. Professor of Geology and Biological Sciences, Univ. of California, Santa Barbara.

Vincent P. Tinerella, Asst. Professor/Reference Librarian, Northern Illinois Univ., De Kalb.

Bradley P. Tolppanen, History Bibliographer and Head of Circulation Services, Eastern Illinois Univ., Charleston.

Gregory M. Toth, Reference Librarian, State Univ. of New York, Brockport.

Elias H. Tuma, Professor of Economics, Univ. of California, Davis.

Diane J. Turner, Science/Engineering Liaison, Auraria Library, Univ. of Colorado, Denver.

Robert L. Turner Jr., Librarian and Asst. Professor, Radford Univ., Va.

Arthur R. Upgren, Professor of Astronomy and Director, Van Vleck Observatory, Wesleyan Univ., Middletown, Conn.

Nancy L. Van Atta, Dayton, Ohio.

Leanne M. VandeCreek, Social Sciences Reference Librarian, Northern Illinois Univ., De Kalb.

Vang Vang, Reference Librarian, Henry Madden Library, California State Univ. Fresno.

Dario J. Villa, Reference Librarian/Bibliographer, Ronald Williams Library, Northeastern Illinois Univ., Chicago.

Graham R. Walden, Professor, University Libraries, Ohio State Univ., Columbus.

Adalyn Smith Watts, Librarian, San Joaquin Valley College, Calif.

J. E. Weaver, Dept. of Economics, Drake Univ., Des Moines, Iowa.

Kathleen Weessies, Maps/GIS Librarian, Michigan State Univ., East Lansing.

Amy K. Weiss, Coordinator of Cataloging, Belk Library, Appalachian State Univ., Boone, N.C.

Andrew B. Wertheimer, Asst. Professor, Library and Information Science Program, Univ. of Hawai'i—Manoa, Honolulu.

Lucille Whalen, Dean of Graduate Programs, Immaculate Heart College Center, Los Angeles, Calif.

Christine A. Whittington, Head, Reference Services and Asst. Access Librarian, Raymond H. Fogler Library, Univ. of Maine.

Robert L. Wick, Asst. Professor and Fine Arts Bibliographer, Auraria Library, Univ. of Colorado, Denver.

Agnes H. Widder, Humanities Bibliographer, Michigan State Univ., East Lansing.

Mark A. Wilson, Professor of Geology, College of Wooster, Ohio.

Terrie L. Wilson, Art Librarian, Michigan State Univ., East Lansing.

Glenn R. Wittig, Director of Library Services, Criswell College, Dallas, Tex.

Julienne L. Wood, Head, Research Services, Noel Memorial Library, Louisiana State Univ. in Shreveport.

Neal Wyatt, Collection Management Librarian, Chesterfield County Public Library, Va.

Courtney L. Young, Social Sciences Librarian, The Pennsylvania State Univ. Libraries, University Park.

Diane Zabel, Endowed Librarian for Business, Schreyer Business Library, Pennsylvania State Univ.

Louis G. Zelenka, Jacksonville Public Library System, Fla.

L. Zgusta, Professor of Linguistics and the Classics and Member of the Center for Advance Study, Univ. of Illinois, Urbana.

Anita Zutis, Adjunct Librarian, Queensborough Community College, Bayside, N.Y.

Journals Cited

AG	*Against the Grain*
BL	*Booklist*
BR	*Book Report*
Choice	*Choice*
JAL	*Journal of Academic Librarianship*
LJ	*Library Journal*
RUSQ	*Reference & User Services Quarterly*
SLJ	*School Library Journal*
TL	*Teacher Librarian*
VOYA	*Voice of Youth Advocates*

Part I
GENERAL
REFERENCE
WORKS

1 General Reference Works

ALMANACS

C, P, S

1. **Chase's Calendar of Events 2004.** New York, McGraw-Hill, 2004. 752p. illus. index. $54.95pa. ISBN 0-07-142405-9. ISSN 0740-5286.

There is a lot to be said for tradition and *Chase's Calendar of Events* proves the point. The 2004 edition retains all the features of the previous versions presented in the same format and still remains a fascinating and useful record of holidays and special events.

The directory is international in scope. National and religious holidays of many countries are included, along with special events sponsored by organizations and days designated by presidential proclamations. In total, there are 12,000 entries listed by month and day. Each is accompanied by a brief annotation explaining the day's significance, history, or purpose. When appropriate, contact information is given. The "Spotlight" section features milestones in several categories—the past, the world, and education to name a few. In addition to the monthly lists there are a lot of informative treasures that will be useful at the reference desk. There is a perpetual calendar, hurricane names for several years, presidential facts, and state information (including symbols). Awards and prizes of all types are listed. And again this year the winners of the Webby Award appears. Even the subject index can be used as an information resource. For example, all the space missions are listed by name and date. Travelers can check their destination and find all the holidays and special events in that area. *Chase's* is available online by subscription, but the print version remains as interesting and valuable as ever.—**Marlene M. Kuhl**

P, S

2. **New View Almanac.** 3d ed. Bruce S. Glassman, ed. Farmington Hills, Mich., Blackbirch Press, 2003. 607p. illus. maps. index. $49.95. ISBN 1-56711-674-4.

For those who shrink at the thought of dense, small print statistical tables accompanied by extensive source and explanatory notes this is the book to choose. More than 2,000 charts, graphs, maps, and other visuals in color and black-and-white cover statistics from 12 broad subject areas. The variety of subtopics within these areas gives an entertaining and informative glimpse into life and culture in the United States. Among the topics covered are health, lifestyles, politics, demographics, crime, and sports. Each section opens with a short overview of the subject accompanied by a "Fingertip Facts" sidebar. The sidebar offers interesting tidbits of information such as how many gallons of soft drink the average American consumes in a year. The charts and graphs report on such things as the most popular beverages, the growth of digital camera sales, and the states with the highest Internet use. Demographic information covers accidental deaths (1998 figures) as well as states with the highest populations of African Americans, Asians, and Hispanics. Sports records cover high school, college, and professional teams as well as participation in individual sports. Sources are cited for the statistics only. Some charts have no date (i.e., Latinos with diabetes) and no sampling or interpretative information is provided. The almanac will be popular with young students who will welcome the attractive, easy-to-understand graphics and who are not concerned about source details. [R: LJ, 15 Oct 03, pp. 58-60]—**Marlene M. Kuhl**

BIBLIOGRAPHY

Bibliographic Guides

C

3. **H-NET Reviews in the Humanities and Social Sciences. http://www2.h-net.msu.edu/reviews/.** [Website]. Lansing, Mich., University of Michigan, 1998- . Free. Date reviewed: 2003.

H-NET Reviews is an online, scholarly review journal within H-NET, "an international inter-disciplinary organization of scholars teachers dedicated to developing the enormous educational potential of the Internet and the World Wide Web." H-NET resides on computers at MATRIX: The Center for Humane Arts, Letters, and Social Sciences OnLine at Michigan State University, but scholars worldwide participate in its intellectual activity, which includes e-mail discussion lists, a job guide, announcements of upcoming conferences and workshops, calls for papers, funding opportunities, and publications. *H-NET Reviews*' editors solicit reviews from scholars who have registered as reviewers. The reviews have no print equivalent. Because they reside on the Web, *H-NET Reviews* can be published more quickly than print reviews; can be more substantive because they do not have to adhere to page budgets; and can be interactive, with authors invited to submit comments on reviews. The audience and writers come from an international community; both books reviewed and the reviews themselves include some written in German and French.—**Christine A. Whittington**

National and Trade Bibliography

C, P

4. **The Small Press Record of Books in Print 2002-2003.** 31st ed. [CD-ROM]. Paradise, Calif., Dustbooks, 2003. Minimum system requirements: 386, 486, or Pentium processor. CD-ROM drive. Windows 3.1, 95, or NT 3.5.1. 4MB RAM. $55.00. ISBN 0-916685-93-4.

Now in its 31st edition, *The Small Press Record of Books in Print* provides more than 46,000 individual entries of books currently in print published by approximately 5,000 small, independent publishers worldwide conveniently published on CD-ROM. Since the volume of publishing provided by small presses continues to expand, the editors estimate that the number of items listed will continue to grow 10 to 25 percent annually.

This CD-ROM edition is actually a compilation of pdf documents representing an author index, a subject index, a title index, and a publishers listing. Full information on each book is included in the author and subject indexes. The title index provides only the title and author(s). Full information includes author(s), title, publisher, width and height, pagination, type of binding, price, publication date, ISBN, and a very brief descriptive comment. The publisher listing gives the publisher name, address, telephone number, e-mail address (if available), and contact names.

Although easy to use, the pdf files are very large. For example, the subject index is 3,227 pages long and is almost 15 megabytes in size. This can cause problems for some computers, especially older ones, even though they match the minimum system requirements of a 386 processor and 4 megabytes of RAM. Also, depending on the processor speed, searching using the Adobe Acrobat find command can be slow since each page must be searched sequentially. The subject index uses fairly generic subject terms, although the use of bookmarks helps the user find relevant books on a topic fairly quickly.

As a collection development tool, especially for libraries that seek to purchase materials from small publishers, this work is well worth the cost.—**Gregory A. Crawford**

BIOGRAPHY

International

C, P

5.   **Advocates and Activists, 1919-1941: Men and Women Who Shaped the Period Between the Wars.** David Garrett Izzo, ed. West Cornwall, Conn., Locust Hill Press, 2003. 664p. $85.00. ISBN 0-9722289-5-0.

This superb work of scholarship features individually authored biographical essays about 35 people who were witnesses to one of the most turbulent and important times in recorded history and who changed the world in profound ways. All but two are Americans. The biographies have been organized into seven categories: "Labor, Social, and Political Activists" (e.g., Margaret Sanger, William Z. Foster); "Educators, Philosophers, Cultural Theorists and Critics" (e.g., V. F. Calverton, Joel E. Springarn); "Stage and Film Professionals" (e.g., D. W. Griffith, Orson Welles); "Artists" (e.g., Thomas Hart Benton, Aaron Douglas); "African-American Advocates and Activists" (e.g., Arthur Alfonso Schomburg, Alain Locke); "Writers and Poets" (e.g., Jack Conroy, Meridel Le Sueur); and "Journalists" (e.g., Albert J. Nock, George Seldes). Concluding each essay is a bibliography of both primary and secondary sources. While each essay emphasizes the people themselves, taken as a whole this fine book also illuminates the entire world-changing period between World War I and World War II, reflecting how these individuals both influenced and were influenced by it. The focus, scope, and scholarship of this book make it worthy of inclusion in academic and public collections alike.—**G. Douglas Meyers**

P, S

6.   **Biography Today: Profiles of People of Interest to Young Readers. 2002 Annual Cumulation.** Cherie D. Abbey, ed. Detroit, Omnigraphics, 2002. 471p. illus. index. $58.00. ISBN 0-7808-0510-0. ISSN 1058-2347.

Biography Today (see ARBA 2002, entry 15, for a review of the 2001 edition) is the annual accumulation of the 24 people profiled in the three soft cover issues published throughout the year. This series is designed and written for young readers age 9 and up. The individuals selected have received media attention, but they are also personalities that young people want to know about. The personalities included are from a wide range of occupations, age groups, and countries. Those included range from writer J. R. R. Tolkien and former Mayor Rudolph Giuliani to student and poet Mattie Stepanek and pop singer Aaron Carter. The entry on Osama bin Laden includes a list of related terms to assist the reader in understanding his background and culture.

Alphabetically arranged, the lengthy articles provide information on the person's early years, education, employment, family, career highlights, hobbies, and honors and awards. Each entry is easy to read, and the articles are interspersed with black-and-white photographs, quotations, and related information, which makes the articles appealing. Each profile has a bibliography of resources for further reading or research as well as a current mailing address and list of Websites. Each annual volume has a cumulative index that includes names, occupations, nationalities, and ethnic and minority origins of all individuals profiled since the series began in 1992. A "Places of Birth Index" and a "Birthday Index" follow this index. This volume is recommended for school and public libraries.—**Elaine Ezell**

C, P

7.   **Current Biography International Yearbook 2002.** Patrick Kelly and others, eds. Bronx, N.Y., H. W. Wilson, 2002. 570p. illus. index. $115.00. ISBN 0-8242-1017-4. ISSN 1538-3296.

In an era dominated by an emphasis on computer products, H. W. Wilson has introduced a new print annual focusing on people "making history and headlines outside the U.S." (only two persons from the United States are listed). In style, approach, and appearance this product is an extension of the more than 60-year-old H. W. Wilson title *Current Biography*. It is to be issued each January, with approximately 200 profiles ranging from 2 to 6 pages. Details of the individual's life and career are provided, along with quotations and notes from journalists and those who know the person. A short bibliography concludes each entry. Usually a photograph is included (these are of the same black-and-white variety found in *Current Biography*, which are too frequently disappointing).

Indexing is by name entry, and separately by profession category. Oddly, no index by country is included; the "List of Biographical Sketches" as part of the front matter usually lists the country with which the person is associated, but sometimes only lists the organization. An analysis of the countries listed by this reviewer (and a check of the entries for those listed by organization) shows that 69 countries are represented. The following eight countries had more than five entries each: Argentina, Brazil, China, France, Germany, India, Japan, and the United Kingdom. The United Kingdom had the most entries, with 16 in total. No specific selection criteria are to be found in the front matter, leaving the reader a little unclear as to why sports personalities dominate the entries for certain countries.

Quoting H. W. Wilson literature, the entries are written in a "lively, entertaining style" (entries are written by staff writers whose initials appear at the end of entries). Entries are both useful for reference, as well as being rich in various details, and are presented in an easy-to-read style. Each profile has been "written specifically" for this new product, so none have previously appeared in *Current Biography*. Listings are for living persons. At $115 this title costs no more than many large monographic reference titles, and provides access to information not easily found elsewhere. Should locations that already subscribe to *Current Biography* purchase this new title? Clearly the *International* volume greatly expands the world scope of the original set. No other product provides the level of detail for such a range of personalities; many cover similar territory, but in significantly abbreviated formats. This resource is highly recommended for large and small academic and public libraries.—**Graham R. Walden**

C, P

8.   **The Houghton Mifflin Dictionary of Biography.** New York, Houghton Mifflin, 2003. 1661p. $48.00. ISBN 0-618-25210-X.

The Houghton Mifflin Dictionary of Biography provides a broad overview of historically significant as well as contemporary figures from all walks of life. The single-volume reference guide covers more than 18,000 reliable, alphabetic entries on politicians, artists, musicians, scientists, writers, and criminals (among many others). While most entries are no longer than one paragraph, the text features 300 prominent individuals more extensively. For example, the entry on William Shakespeare is 13 paragraphs and includes a chronological list of his plays and nondramatic works. However, the volume does not list specific criteria for the selection of prominently featured individuals, and, consequently, it is unclear why some particularly noteworthy figures, while included in the text, are not highlighted. For example, the dictionary provides a more extensive, featured entry on U.S. suffragette Elizabeth Cady Stanton, but devotes only short paragraphs to significant contemporary U.S. women's movement leaders, such as Gloria Steinem and Betty Freidan. While an introductory essay describes the text as an Americanized version of the standard British reference work, *Chambers Biographical Dictionary* (see ARBA 2000, entry 12 and ARBA 87, entry 30), the content and organization of the 7th edition of *Chambers* is very similar to the *Houghton Mifflin* text. Consequently, this volume is recommended for public, academic, and school libraries that do not already own the 7th edition of *Chambers Biographical Dictionary*.—**Sharon Ladenson**

P, S

9.   **1000 Years of Famous People.** New York, Kingfisher, 2002. 255p. illus. index. $24.95. ISBN 0-7534-5540-4.

Proclaiming itself a stylish reference for the whole family, *1000 Years of Famous People* declares a number of world leaders excellent; gives the Spice Girls more room than Anne Frank and Thomas Aquinas and slightly less than Albert Einstein and Nelson Mandela; and is biased toward recent and more photogenic individuals. It does include highlights of famous and infamous people before the 1,000-year cutoff and overall the entries provide a good faith effort toward inclusiveness. Every person listed can be located by name through the index, and subject groupings such as "World Leaders" and "Movers and Shakers" (which oddly includes serial killers) are helpful. Within each section the entries are chronological and include dates, a brief biography, a chronicle of accomplishments, and a one-line summary of notable achievements. This is an entry-level biographical source, but one that could kindle interest in younger readers and spark further discussion and research.—**R. K. Dickson**

United States

C, P

10.   **American National Biography. http://www.anb.org.** [Website]. New York, Oxford University Press. Price negotiated by site for institutions; $250.00 (secondary schools); $89.00 (individuals). Date reviewed: Aug 03.

The *American National Biography* (ANB), first published in 1999 (see ARBA 2001, entry 17), was a landmark publication and winner of several prestigious awards, including the 1999 Dartmouth Medal Award. It has since been launched as a searchable Web database and now features more than 17,400 biographies of significant Americans in politics, scholarship, science, sports, business, and now actors and activists. The biographies have been written by more than 2,000 contributors and provide an overview of each person's personal and career highlights. Often compared to the *Dictionary of American Biography* (DAB; Charles Scribner's Sons), this product differs in several ways, the most significant is that DAB only provides biographies of people who died up to 1980, while ANB provides updates quarterly.

The online edition of this valuable resource offers several features useful in a reference library setting. New biographies are added quarterly in January, April, July, and October, and many of those include illustrations or photographs. A typical update provides about 30 new biographies. Past biographies are updated with new information. Biographies online also often include hyperlinks to related biographies within the database as well as Websites of interest outside of the site—more than 80,000 in all. The site is searchable by subject name, occupation, gender, birth date, birth place, death date, contributor name, or full text keywords.

Access to this site is highly recommended for large public and academic libraries. The fact that it is updated so regularly is a strong selling point, as is the fact that at 25 volumes the print version will take up quite a lot of space and become dated fairly quickly.—**Shannon Graff Hysell**

C, P

11.   **Current Biography Yearbook 2002.** Clifford Thompson, ed. Bronx, N.Y., H. W. Wilson, 2002. 671p. illus. index. $115.00. ISBN 0-8242-1026-3. ISSN 0084-9499.

C, P

12.   **Current Biography Illustrated. http://www.hwwilson.com/Databases/cbillus.htm.** [Website]. Bronx, N.Y., H. W. Wilson. Price negotiated by site. Date reviewed: May 03.

The latest edition of *Current Biography Yearbook*—now entering its seventh decade of publication —follows true to form to its predecessors (see ARBA 98, entry 22 and ARBA 93, entry 37). Indeed, the current volume is a bit more expansive than earlier editions in that it boasts more than 200 entries. There is a simple alphabetic arrangement of subjects, and all are currently living (or at least, were at time of publication). Although a high proportion of the biographical sketches are devoted to entertainment and sports figures, there is also a generous sprinkling of business, political, artistic, and intellectual leaders. The index by profession toward the end of the volume allows a quick overview of the range of endeavors pursued by the subjects. The sketches are generally limited to around 2,000 words, yet certain political figures, such as Harvey Pitt and Donald Rumsfeld, are given more in-depth examination. The individual portraits are not meant to court controversy, and each of the contributors clearly tries to be as even-handed as possible. As in earlier editions, the individuals being portrayed are allowed to speak in their own voice as much as possible.

The online version of this product, *Current Biography Illustrated*, provides more than 25,000 articles and obituaries provided from past issues of *Current Biography*. The biography's remain unchanged, but more than 19,000 illustrations are included on those profiled. Each year nearly 450 new biographies are added. Users can search by name, profession, place of origin, birth or death date, ethnicity, gender, or popular works. A bibliography provides users with new resources for further study. Building on its solid reputation, *Current Biography Yearbook* remains an essential purchase for reference collections at all levels.
—**Jim Millhorn**

Latin America and the Caribbean

C, P, S

13. **Contemporary Hispanic Biography: Profiles from the International Hispanic Community. Volume 3.** Ashyia N. Henderson, ed. Farmington Hills, Mich., Gale, 2003. 242p. illus. index. $80.00. ISBN 0-7876-7150-9. ISSN 1541-1524.

Contemporary Hispanic Biography contains highly readable profiles of "influential persons of Latino heritage" (p. ix). This is volume 3 of a cumulative set, so those who have purchased previous volumes will likely want to continue the series. The volume contains four cumulative indexes that provide access by nationality, occupation, subject, and name.

The indexes are all useful, although the subject index has redundant and inconsistent elements. For example, there is a "Baseball" subject heading listing the entries to all profiles on people associated with baseball teams, whether players or managers. In addition, there are independent subject headings for every baseball team: "Colorado Rockies Baseball team," "Florida Marlins Baseball team," "Montreal Expos Baseball team," and so on. On the other hand, there is a subject heading for the "Women's National Basketball Association (WNBA)," but no heading for the "New York Liberty Basketball team." Lisa Lobo, profiled in this volume, played for both the New York Liberty and the Houston Comets. There is a heading for the "Houston Comets Basketball team," but Lisa Lobo is not under it.

Entries contain an "At a Glance . . ." highlighted box, a biographical profile, and a source list that includes books, periodicals, and online resources. Some personalities require the addition of a discography or selected writings list. Online resources are surprisingly stable, and in a random testing of 20 links, none were broken. The main site name is given in the citation, along with the more specific page URL.

There is one drawback to the selection of online resources. Links to Gale databases, such as *Biography Resource Center* and *Contemporary Authors Online*, are included, but there is nothing to suggest that they are not public Websites. If your library does not subscribe to the database, users may become frustrated by lack of access. Also, the links to the Gale databases are not as specific as the links to Websites. A link to the Gale database will only take the user to the main search page, so he or she will have to run a name search to get the article.

The book structure is copied from Gale's successful Contemporary Black Biography series (see ARBA 2000, entries 283-285). One surmises that this copying is done from template to template, because several index pages have "Contemporary Black Biography" at the top. This is very sloppy proofreading.

Also, this error reminds librarians that Gale products can be very similar to each other, and overlap content and audience age. Before purchasing this work, librarians may wish to review other Gale products, such as the U*X*L Hispanic American Library series (2d ed.; see entries 127-130), to find the most suitable reference addition.

Having given these warnings, this reviewer still recommends *Contemporary Hispanic Biography*. The style has the fluid feeling of a magazine interview, making it a very enjoyable reading experience. Indeed, the reading level seems about equivalent to most popular entertainment magazines, suggesting a potentially wide audience. However, I suspect that high school and public libraries will be the most interested in utilizing this resource. Academic libraries may give this title more careful consideration.—**Sandra E. Fuentes Riggs**

DICTIONARIES AND ENCYCLOPEDIAS

C, P, S

14.   **E.encyclopedia.** New York, DK Publishing, 2003. 448p. illus. maps. index. $39.99. ISBN 0-7894-9869-3.

The *E.encyclopedia* is a unique and fascinating book created by Dorling Kindersley and Google. The book has its own Website, which users of the *E.encyclopedia* can use to obtain current and interactive content on any subject of their choice. The links in the Website include animations, videos, sound, virtual tours, interactive quizzes, databases, timelines, and real-time reports. The topics researched by this reference work are divided into nine subject areas: Space, Earth, Nature, Human Body, Science and Technology, People and Places, Society and Beliefs, Arts and Entertainment, and History.

As an additional benefit, users also have access to an extensive selection of downloadable images from DK Publishing's image library. This reference work, geared toward almost all age groups, is an interesting combination of both the print and electronic worlds, where the user can go back and forth between book and Website to collate and obtain information. This reference work is highly recommend for the K-12 age group, and it is a welcome addition for most higher education reference collections as well.—**Bradford Lee Eden**

P, S

15.   **Encyclopedia Americana.** international ed. Danbury, Conn., Grolier, 2003. 30v. illus. maps. index. $999.00/set. ISBN 0-7172-0136-8.

This new edition of *Encyclopedia Americana* marks the 174th year this encyclopedia has been in print. Presented in 29 volumes plus one index volume, *Encyclopedia Americana* continues to provide tens of thousands of entries on thousands of subjects. The articles are written in a style that will be easily understood by high school students, college students, and the educated layperson. Each year new articles are added to the set and hundreds of articles are updated by the original author or the editors of the encyclopedia.

One of the features that makes this encyclopedia stand out is the publisher's attempt to be as comprehensive as possible when covering large subject areas. For instance, significant historical documents are given their own entry (e.g., the Declaration of Independence, the U.S. Constitution), the books of the Bible are given separate entries, and many important works of literature and art are discussed in separate entries. This allows for more in-depth coverage of significant topics. Cross-references are provided between entries, which will help users know when related topics are treated separately in the set. Entries also include a bibliography that can be used for further research. Maps, illustrations, photographs, charts, and sidebars are used frequently throughout the text. The majority of these, however, are in black and white, with very few in color. The preface states that population statistics for the United States are based on the U.S. Census Bureau's 2000 census results.

This encyclopedia continues to be a worthwhile addition to school, academic, and public libraries. It is more in-depth than *The World Book Encyclopedia* (see ARBA 2003, entries 41 and 42), although not quite as visually appealing. Libraries will want to update their edition every three to five years to ensure timeliness and accuracy.—**Shannon Graff Hysell**

P, S

16.   **The Firefly Visual Dictionary.** By Jean-Claude Corbeil and Ariane Archambault. New York, Firefly Books, 2002. 952p. illus. index. $49.95. ISBN 1-55297-585-1.

The Firefly Visual Dictionary claims to be the successor to a popular visual dictionary published a decade ago by Macmillan. This latest version contains 35,000 terms, 6,000 color illustrations, and an index that lists each term in the book. Its 17 chapters are organized into categories such as "Astronomy," "Earth," "Human Being," "Clothing," "Personal Adornment and Articles," "Arts and Architecture," and "Sports and Games." Illustrations include both the modern (parts of a computer, for example) and ancient (a Greek temple plan), with the preponderance of entries being associated with everyday objects of the current time.

The art work in *The Firefly Visual Dictionary* is exceptionally clear and detailed. However, the print used throughout the text and index is almost microscopic. The six-pound weight of the volume also somewhat limits its usefulness as a ready reference.

Those for whom English is a second language will probably find this *The Firefly Visual Dictionary* a valuable resource. While trivia devotees will enjoy the wealth of somewhat esoteric information contained in some entries, most native English speakers will find the illustrations in a standard dictionary to be quite sufficient. [R: LJ, 1 Sept 02, p. 162; SLJ, Nov 02, p. 95]—**Kay O. Cornelius**

P, S

17.   **Grolier Student Encyclopedia.** Danbury, Conn., Grolier Educational, 2004. 17v. illus. maps. index. $249.00/set. ISBN 0-7172-5865-3.

This attractive, new 17-volume encyclopedia set is aimed at primary school children. Each slim volume is exactly 64 pages, making it lightweight and easy for children to handle. Every volume features a comprehensive set index in the back, making it extremely convenient to look things up. The roughly 700 alphabetically arranged entries vary in length from a few paragraphs ("Twain, Mark") to four pages ("Medicine") . Each entry is accompanied by at least one illustration, often in color and including photographs, diagrams, or maps. The text is straightforward and factual, and each entry begins with a brief summary or definition of the topic in large blue print. Longer entries are divided into subheadings. There are cross-reference aides within the main entry listings (i.e., "crocodile, *see* reptile") as well as cues to "look in the index for" a certain word. There are *see also* references at the end of each entry (i.e., "mercury, *see also* astronomy") , where applicable. Despite these efforts, the index could be more detailed or there could be more cross-references, as in the case, for example, where there is nothing listed under "Harry Potter" in the index yet there is an entry on J. K. Rowling that discusses these books.

The emphasis is on North America, including coverage of every U.S. state and president, as well as all Canadian provinces. Other countries are also covered in entries like "Turkey and the Caucasus" and "Countries of the World." Further topics include planets, the natural world, modern technology, and important people in academic fields such as art, science, music, and literature (but excluding most popular culture figures). There are occasional sidebar listings of "key facts" or "amazing facts."

This encyclopedia is geared toward younger children than Grolier's *New Book of Knowledge* (see entry 20), and likewise it is for a younger group than the nine-volume *The Oxford American Children's Encyclopedia* (Oxford, 2002), which covers more material (over 2,000 entries). It is most similar to the 13-volume *World Book Student Discovery Encyclopedia* (see entry 23), also aimed at primary and middle school students and featuring even larger print, pronunciation aids, and more entries (over 2,000), including people from popular culture like Shaquille O'Neal. This *Encyclopedia* is recommended for public or school libraries, especially those not owning the World Book set, and for home use.—**Susan J. Gardner**

C, P

18.   **Merriam-Webster's Collegiate Dictionary.** 11th ed. Springfield, Mass., Merriam-Webster, 2003. 1623p. $25.95. ISBN 0-87779-809-5.

C, P

19.   **Merriam-Webster Collegiate.com. http://www.merriam-webstercollegiate.com/.** [Website]. Springfield, Mass., Merriam-Webster. $14.95; One year free with purchase of book. Date reviewed: Sept 03.

Some 10 years have passed since the last edition of *Merriam-Webster's Collegiate Dictionary* was published in 1993 (see ARBA 94, entry 1076), and in that time the world and the English-language have changed dramatically. The most obvious change has come in the form of the technological boom but changes have also occurred in the areas of science, business, and slang and popular culture. The 11th edition provides more than 165,000 entries and 225,000 definitions, 10,000 of which are new to this edition. In all, the book boasts more than 100,000 changes since the last edition.

The basic format of the *Dictionary* remains much the same. The work begins with a preface, an explanatory note and chart, a guide to pronunciation, a list of abbreviations used in the work, and pronunciation symbols. The work concludes with a six-page list of foreign words and phrases; biographical names; geographical names; signs and symbols used in astronomy, biology, business, chemistry, computers, and mathematics; and a style guide. The most significant changes occur within the bulk of the volume—"The Dictionary of the English Language." Here users will find new words in the areas of technology (e.g., *dot-commer, DSL*), business and finance (e.g., *identity theft, fast-track*), science (e.g., *Little Ice Age*), health and medicine (e.g., *LASIK*), and slang (e.g., *dead presidents, phat*), just to name a few. The editors have taken care to update definitions as well and provide cross-references, etymology, and example phrases.

The online edition of *Merriam-Webster's Collegiate Dictionary* allows users to research the meaning and etymology of words, find rhyming words and words of opposite meaning, or browse words beginning or ending with the word. The *Dictionary* also provides a thesaurus, encyclopedic entries, a Spanish-English dictionary, a style guide, and a selection of word games. Users can bookmark, print, or e-mail selected word definitions.

Two factors make this *Dictionary* a valuable addition to any academic, public, or school library: the reputation of the publisher and the publication and the accessibility of the reference tool in print, CD-ROM, and Internet formats. Individuals buying this product are provided with a CD-ROM at the back of the volume as well as free access to the *Dictionary*'s Website for one year. This work is highly recommended. [R: Choice, Jan 04, pp. 873-874]—**Shannon Graff Hysell**

P, S

20.   **The New Book of Knowledge, 2003 Edition.** Danbury, Conn., Grolier Educational, 2003. 21v. illus. maps. index. $699.00/set. ISBN 0-7172-0535-5.

What makes *The New Book of Knowledge* unique is that it is designed specifically for children and young adults grades K-12. Unlike other encyclopedias, such as *Encyclopedia Americana* (see entry 15) and *Encyclopaedia Britannica*, *The New Book of Knowledge*'s entries were selected by teachers, children's and school librarians, and cultural specialists who know school curriculum and the educational needs of students. This 2003 edition provides an A to Z listing of entries presented in 21 volumes. Each entry is written by a specialist in the field and includes the name of the author, while many also include the name of an article reviewer as well. The articles are written to be easily understood by young children, although those entries that are more technical in nature will most likely only be understood by young adults. Illustrations, photographs, maps, charts, and informational sidebars accompany nearly every entry and the publisher stresses that each has been double-checked for accuracy and readability. More than 13,000 illustrations are presented in this set.

This encyclopedia is designed to be easy to search by including guidewords at the bottom of each page. Most of the entries also provide cross-references and *see also* references at the end of entries. The set also features "Wonder Questions," which are designed to grab the interest of students and inspire further research. As an added feature the encyclopedia provides a paperbound "Home and School Reading and Study Guides" volume that provides a bibliography to thousands of topics covered in the encyclopedia. Each recommended title is grouped by reading level—primary, intermediate, and advanced.

What makes this encyclopedia so outstanding are the full-color illustrations, the well-written text, and the fact that the information provided works well with current curriculum standards. This work is also available in an online edition from Grolier at http://go.grolier.com (see ARBA 2002, entry 33, for a review). This encyclopedia will be an ideal addition to school and public libraries. Compared to that of many other comparable encyclopedias, the price is quite reasonable.—**Shannon Graff Hysell**

C, P

21.   **Shorter Oxford English Dictionary on CD-ROM.** [CD-ROM]. New York, Oxford University Press, 2002. Minimum system requirements: PC with 200 MHz Pentium processor. 16-speed CD-ROM drive. Windows 95, 98, ME, NT, XP, or 2000. 32MB RAM. 290MB hard disk space. SVGA monitor. 16-bit sound card. $109.95. ISBN 0-19-860613-3.

This second version of the *Shorter Oxford English Dictionary on CD-ROM* can be installed easily. Unlike some other recent Oxford dictionary products on CD-ROM, this CD-ROM contains extensive background material of various kinds, including the prefaces to the 1st and 5th editions of the printed work, a list of lexicographers, a guide to the use of the dictionary, a pronunciation guide, a transliteration guide, and a list of abbreviations and symbols. There is a complete history here of the genesis of this particular CD-ROM product, and how it relates to and differs from the various print products. This version of the SOED is everything the printed version is, and more, given its search features.

Without extensive discussion of the printed SOED itself, one need only say that it concentrates on English words from 1700 onward, with attention also to older words that have continuing relevance to current English or that appear in the works of major authors like Milton, Shakespeare, and Spenser. The content of this CD-ROM product is essentially identical to that of the printed version, although updated.

The standard word entries include the headword in bold type; a standard British pronunciation rendered in the International Phonetic Alphabet (and a sound-recorded pronunciation for 100,000 of the words); parts of speech (in italic type); date of first use, expressed as "e" (early), "m" (middle), or "l" (late) plus the century, such as "e19"; etymology (in square brackets); and a definition section. The definitions are sometimes enhanced by one of 83,000 illustrative quotations. Also included in each entry, where applicable, are phrases containing the headword; compounds including the headword; derivatives containing the headword plus a suffix; usage labels; variant spellings; and grammatical and other information. Entries are based on existing OED entries, rewritten and augmented with the latest in scholarly inquiry. The entries are much easier to wade through than those in the full OED, owing in part to the typography and organizational principles used here.

The heart of the dictionary, of course, is the alphabetic list of headwords, which one can scroll through in the left-hand column of the screen. Clicking on any word brings up the basic entry. Looking at "Poulter," for example, one sees immediately that it is an archaic, "ME" (Middle English) term, and one immediately sees the compound term "poulter's measure," a "rare prosodaic measure consisting of alternating lines of 12 and 14 syllables." The primary term means "an officer of a noble household, a monastery, etc., in charge of the purchase of poultry and other provisions." The user learns that the term is "obsolete exc. HIST LME" (historical in Late Middle English).

At the top of the screen, there are two buttons. Clicking on the "pronunciation" button will generate a recording of someone speaking the word (in standard British English). Clicking on the "etymology" button provides etymological information. There are two tool bar lines at the top of the screen. The top one includes several buttons with options, settings, search history and entry history, bookmarks, and a "find" button to enable one to search for specific words within a long entry. The second line at the top of the screen contains the button for "Advanced Search." The "Advanced Search" button enables one to do a variety of power searches. Other power search options include case-sensitive searching, exact character searching, and a variety of proximity searches extending out to words within 10 words of each other. One can also filter out material on particular parts of speech. Other buttons on the second line include an "i" button which takes one to the extensive background information referred to at the start of this review; a printer page that formats the printing of definitions with a header stating where the material comes from; a button for saving definitions to the hard drive; and a "?" button that provides extensive help, with many topics listed, from how to search to uninstalling the software. The second line also contains a "find word" box to enter any word for a simple search.

This new version of the SOED is a highly professional and powerful tool that merits the respect and attention of all who are interested in serious study of the English language. It is reasonably priced for home use as well. [R: LJ, 1 May 03, p. 164]—**Bill Miller**

C, P, S

22.   **Wikipedia. http://www.wikipedia.com.** [Website]. Free. Date reviewed: Dec 03.

Wikipedia is an open content encyclopedia that was initially launched on the Web in January 2001. The English-language edition currently has over 192,000 articles. In addition to English, *Wikipedia* is available in a number of languages, among them German, French, Polish, Swedish, Japanese, and Chinese. It is a collaborative effort of volunteers managed by a nonprofit organization, the Wikimedia Foundation.

Articles can be accessed by using the search box on the top or bottom of the screen or by browsing the general list of topics under the heading "encyclopedia." Search instructions are available under "Readers' FAQ." As a general rule, articles tend to be fairly brief, and they include hypertext links. By creating an account, virtually anyone with Internet access can anonymously contribute articles and edit content as a "Wikipedian." The "Page History" link allows the reader to view revisions of the article but does not provide information on the credentials of those who wrote or edited content. As a result, it can be difficult to determine whether the article was prepared by an authoritative source. While the quality of the content varies considerably, the intention is that the frequent editing by "Wikipedians" will result in continual improvements. The home page provides instructions and information for potential contributors. Another feature of *Wikipedia* is a current events section, which includes links to external news sites from around the world.

Since *Wikipedia* is a work in progress, it will be interesting to see how it evolves over the next few years. In the mean time, it does not serve as a substitute for more traditional print and electronic encyclopedias. [R: AG, Nov 03, p. 101]—**Martha Tarlton**

P, S

23.   **The World Book Student Discovery Encyclopedia.** 2003 ed. Chicago, World Book, 2003. 13v. illus. maps. index. $359.00/set. ISBN 0-7166-7400-9.

Encyclopedias are often a starting point for a student's research, and *The World Book Student Discovery Encyclopedia* provides an entry-level reference source, whether searching for facts or browsing for fun. *The World Book Student Discovery Encyclopedia* is a 13-volume children's encyclopedia, aimed toward an audience of kindergarten through fourth grade. *Student Discovery* offers age-appropriate information on basic subjects of interest, including animals, insects, biographies of U.S. presidents and Canadian prime ministers, inventors, artists, and other famous people, and geographical and factual information on the states and countries around the world. It includes 2,150 articles (300 of which are new or revised), over 3,500 photographs, drawings, maps, and other illustrations.

Entries are presented in alphabetic order, with an index and atlas in volume 13. A typical page of *Student Discovery* will have two entries, with a paragraph or two about that specific entry, accompanied by a photograph or illustration. Other features include phonetic spellings for hard to pronounce words, cross-references to guide users to specific entries, and information and history for every letter of the alphabet. In addition to the basic entries, there are several types of color-coded articles: two-page, blue bordered articles on the states; two-page, red-bordered articles for Canadian provinces; and one- to four-page, green-bordered articles for world countries. Each of these articles includes maps, facts, important dates, and historical and cultural information. Several dozen feature articles, on topics such as dinosaurs, automobiles, paper, and clothing, give expanded information and more illustrations. The colored backgrounds used on these four-page entries distinguish these articles from the basic articles in each volume.

Interspersed throughout volumes 1-12 are "Hands-On!" activities children can complete, such as creating a height growth chart (with the "Child" entry) and making print blocks (with the "Printing" entry). Volume 13 is a combination atlas/index, with 24 pages of world and continent maps as well as a country index. Cross-references within the index guide users to the appropriate index entry; illustrations of specific items or concepts within articles are also indicated.

Minor criticisms include dated photographs and occasional fuzzy graphics, and tight margin binding in the index volume that makes the middle portion of the world maps difficult to read. Also, having all "Hands-On!" activities listed in the index with page references would be helpful to parents, teachers, and crafty children. Simple language, basic facts, and appropriate photographs and images make *Student Discovery* a fine source to introduce young children to the organization, presentation, and usefulness of an encyclopedia.—**Caroline L. Gilson**

DIRECTORIES

C, P

24. **Encyclopedia of Associations: National Organizations of the U.S.** 40th ed. Alan Hedblad, ed. Farmington Hills, Mich., Gale, 2003. 3v. index. $615.00/set. ISBN 0-7876-7120-7. ISSN 0071-0202.

This 40th edition of the *Encyclopedia of Associations* is much like earlier editions—it serves as a directory for finding contact information for organizations within the United States. Gale offers a separate two-volume directory for those looking for international organizations (37th ed.; see ARBA 2002, entry 42). This volume provides information on more than 22,000 nonprofit organizations, including 500 organizations new to this edition. The editor also claims that more than 40 percent of the entries have been updated since the last edition. Organizations include are: national nonprofit membership organizations, international organizations set up in the United States, local and regional associations with a national interest, nonmembership organizations, for-profit organizations, and defunct organizations.

The work is organized first by broad subject areas (e.g., "Trade, Business, and Commercial Organizations"; "Educational Organizations"; "Veterans', Hereditary, and Patriotic Organizations") and then alphabetically by specific category. Each organization listed is assigned an entry number and provides the following information: full title; address, telephone and fax numbers, and e-mail and Website address; year founded; membership; budget; language; a brief description; libraries; awards; publications; and conventions or annual meetings. Organizations are made accessible by a name and keyword index found in volume 3 as well as a keyword list found at the beginning of volume 1.

This work remains a valuable addition to large public and academic libraries. This product is available in electronic format on CD-ROM from the Gale Group, or it can be purchased online from DIALOG and Lexis-Nexis or through Gale's InfoTrac.—**Shannon Graff Hysell**

C, P

25. **Headquarters USA, 2004: A Directory of Contact Information for Headquarters and Other Central Offices of Major Businesses & Organizations in the United States and in Canada.** 26th ed. Detroit, Omnigraphics, 2004. 2v. index. $185.00/set. ISBN 0-7808-0649-2. ISSN 1531-2909.

Headquarters USA, 2004 is much more than even the title suggests. Some of the organizations that *Headquarters USA* provides information on are educational institutes, state and county government offices, trade organizations, and political action committees. While it is true that one could access much of this information through other means (databases, the Internet, and CD-ROM directories), the amount of information contained in this two-volume set is striking. It quickly proves itself to have the kind of added value that makes for an indispensable reference work. Everything is very clear. Volume 1 is a simple alphabetic list, by organization name. Volume 2 is classified by subject, much like a telephone directory. It is surprisingly fast to locate information in this paper resource, and Website addresses are provided for those that prefer to go online.

Good attention is paid to small details. When a fax number is given that is not a main number, the institution section is given. For example, in several listings for hospitals, an asterisk indicates that the fax number given is for admitting. Even when checking a company site on the Web, it can be notoriously difficult to find a toll-free number. Databases that provide company profiles do not often have the toll-free number for headquarters. This directory provides toll-free numbers in the majority of entries. This directory is highly recommended for a variety of library reference settings—academic, public, and special libraries.—**Sandra E. Fuentes Riggs**

GOVERNMENT PUBLICATIONS

C
26.   Hernon, Peter, Harold C. Relyea, Robert E. Dugan, and Joan F. Cheverie. **United States Government Information: Policies and Sources.** Westport, Conn., Libraries Unlimited/Greenwood Publishing Group, 2002. 430p. index. (Library and Information Science Text Series). $70.00pa. (w/CD-ROM). ISBN 1-56308-978-5.

This handbook provides the user with a comprehensive overview of the information policies of the U.S. government. Outlining the vast resources that the U.S. government disseminates, the authors illustrate how to locate this information while providing a tutorial, tracing the history of these policies from the eighteenth century to today's electronic government materials. Of critical importance to the flow of government information, this handbook describes changes in government policies since the terrorist attacks of September 11, 2001, with particular emphasis on the impact of the Patriot Act. Designed to serve a wide research clientele, this handbook is supported by a companion CD-ROM with study questions, key documents, tutorials, and exercises. In addition to covering most branches of the federal government, the authors explain key terminology and offer sources likely to provide information on important issues, such as presidential communications, declassified records, intellectual property, freedom of information, statistical sources, and much more. Although much of this information can be found through a standard Internet search, this work does bring together a compendium of policy information not easily found in one title. This volume is a must for library collections with a strong government information component.—**Patrick Hall**

HANDBOOKS AND YEARBOOKS

P, S
27.   Ash, Russell. **The Top 10 of Everything 2004.** New York, DK Publishing, 2003. 256p. illus. index. $19.00pa. ISBN 0-7894-9659-3.

For $19 this work is a true treat! Who does not want to know the top 10 habitable buildings in the world, or the top 10 Tom Cruise films, or history's top 10 worst tsunamis? These lists, and more, are provided in this must-have paperback volume now in its 15th edition. In fact, there are over 700 lists drawing from what the author says is a "diversity of quantitative superlatives"; not the "10 best," but only things that can be measured are included.

From a library perspective, each list has a complete source citation following the entry, most often from government, the United Nations, or topical organizations. In the after matter there is an excellent list of top Websites for finding further information. Ten large subject categories, such as "the universe and the earth," "culture and learning," "sports and leisure," and "town and country," group the various lists. A fine index is also provided.

Sure, this information is available elsewhere, and sure, librarians can probably pull the information for patrons from other sources, but this volume is so compact, colorful, concise, loaded with photographs, and so easy to read, that libraries really ought to have this work—probably each edition. It is especially fun to see how things change in superlatives from year to year. Librarians will not want to put it down either. It is a good read and just right for information hounds. [R: LJ, 15 Nov 03, p. 57]—**Paul A. Mogren**

C, P

28. **The Europa World Year Book 2003.** Florence, Ky., Europa Publications/Taylor & Francis Group, 2003. 2v. index. $920.00/set. ISBN 1-85743-227-4. ISSN 0071-2302.

C, P

29. **Europa World Online. http://www.europaworldonline.com.** [Website]. Florence, Ky., Europa Publications/Taylor & Francis Group. Price negotiated by site. Date reviewed: Nov 03.

The 44th edition of *The Europa World Year Book* carries on the tradition of earlier editions (39th ed.; see ARBA 99, entry 36) by presenting timely, accurate information on political, economic, and commercial institutions around the world. Volume 1 begins by listing 1,650 international organizations, including the United Nations and the European Union. It then provides an alphabetic survey of countries, from Afghanistan to Jordan. Volume 2 carries on the surveys, listing Kazakhstan to Zimbabwe. For each country the following information is provided: an introductory survey on the country's history, government, defense, economic affairs, education, and holidays; statistical survey on area and population, health and welfare, agriculture, industry, external trade, transportation, tourism, and education; and directory information for government, legislature, diplomatic representation, religious centers, the press, finance, and trade and industry. The set concludes with a three-page index of territories.

The online version of this work is *Europa World Online*, which provides the same information but in an easy-to-search database format. The online edition also provides additional statistical surveys and is updated on a regular basis to ensure accuracy of information. Links to related sites are also made available with this database, saving the user much time in their research. The print and online editions of this valuable resource continue to be worthwhile investments for public and academic libraries.—**Shannon Graff Hysell**

PERIODICALS AND SERIALS

C, P

30. **Periodical Contents Index. http://pci.chadwyck.com.** [Website]. Alexandria, Va., Chadwyck-Healey. Price negotiated by site. Date reviewed: 2003.

Periodical Contents Index in an electronic database with more than 200 years of fully indexed articles from journals in the arts, humanities, and social sciences providing access to more than 10 million citations. It provides abstracting and indexing for 3,035 journals from their inception to 1991. The overall dates of coverage are 1770-1991 with separate records for over 10 million journal articles. More than one million records are added each year. Users can search for articles by words or phrases in the title, by author, and by journal title. The search can be restricted to the language of the article, the journal's subject, the year of publication, or a range of dates. In addition, researchers can access a list of issues for each journal and a table of contents for each issue. The broad coverage of this index provides researchers access to originally published materials and to articles on historical topics.

For many of the citations in the *PCI*, UMI's *American Periodicals Series Online, 1741-1900* provides full text. The American Periodicals series were microfilm projects begun in the 1970s: *American Periodicals I, 1741-1800*, and *American Periodicals II, 1800-1850*. The first microfilm series contained 89 titles, such as Benjamin Franklin's *General Magazine* and Tom Paine's *Pennsylvania Magazine*. The 911 titles in the second series covered the issue of slavery and events leading up to the Civil War. The titles are now available in full text in the APS Online, which contains 89 journals published between 1740 and 1800, and 118 periodicals published during the Civil War and Reconstruction. Many women's and children's magazines are contained in the collection. Because the database contains digitized images of the magazines pages, researchers can see the original typography, drawings, and layouts. Together, the *Periodicals Contents Index* and the *American Periodicals Series Online* provide easy access to a broad range of periodicals important in American history. These products cover the eighteenth and nineteenth centuries up to the period in which the *Readers' Guide* began. There is overlap with the indexing provided by the *19th Century Masterfile* Web database. Researchers will be wise to utilize both databases.—**Anna H. Perrault**

QUOTATION BOOKS

P

31.   **America in Quotations.** Bahman Dehgan, ed. Jefferson, N.C., McFarland, 2003. 217p. index. $35.00pa. ISBN 0-7864-1586-X.

This collection brings together quotes about the United States by Americans and non-Americans —the famous and the not so famous. The selections are categorized by subject to include the nation, the American people, places, the individual, relationships, social life, culture and the media, politics, the military, international relations, and business and the economy. The entries are listed chronologically and range from the humorous to the serious. For example, we hear Auguste Bartholdi, the sculptor of the Statue of Liberty, say "America is an adorable woman chewing tobacco." One is struck by how constant our national character has remained over time. Alexis de Tocqueville (1805-59) stated "America is a land of wonders, in which everything is in constant motion and every change seems an improvement." He also noted, "Every problem in America turns into a legal problem." The editor's choices are often cynical. This is particularly evident in the section describing American cities. There are very few positive comments. This is surprising given our country's beauty and physical diversity. Even cities usually considered attractive receive no positive comments. This tendency for the negative carries over to politics. We read Theodore Roosevelt saying Jefferson was "Perhaps the most incapable executive that ever filled the presidential chair." This is not the usual remark we expect about this Founding Father. Another example comes from Henry Kissinger regarding Watergate: "The illegal we do immediately, the unconstitutional takes a little longer." Even so, the editor succeeds in catching the essence of the American spirit. The reader sees this in a quote from Mary McCarthy: "The happy ending is our national belief."—**Adrienne Antink Bien**

C, P

32.   **The Concise Oxford Dictionary of Quotations.** rev. 4th ed. Elizabeth Knowles, ed. New York, Oxford University Press, 2003. 547p. index. $15.95pa. ISBN 0-19-860752-0.

The user looking for a quotation from the Koran, William Shakespeare, or Bob Hope need look no further than the revised 4th edition of *The Oxford Concise Dictionary of Quotations*. Based on the 5th edition of *The Oxford Dictionary of Quotations* (Oxford University Press, 1999), this publication consists of a similarly diverse (although obviously smaller) collection of quotations organized alphabetically under the name of the source. A keyword index comprised of the most significant words in each quotation allows the user to find quotations on a particular subject. The final section of the book, entitled "Sayings and Slogans," contains an entertaining collection of quotations organized into categories such as advertising slogans, cartoon captions, last words, and misquotations. It is this section that has been expanded from the 4th edition of *The Concise Oxford Dictionary of Quotations* (Oxford University Press, 2001) to include additional quotations and categories. If you already own the 2001 publication, this relatively minor enhancement may not justify the purchase of the revised edition.

The paperback format, while conveniently sized, also has the disadvantage of small print. Nevertheless, this book of quotations would be a fine addition to any library collection.—**Jana Brubaker**

C, P

33.   **Contemporary Hispanic Quotations.** Daniel E. Stanton and Edward F. Stanton, comps. Westport, Conn., Greenwood Press, 2003. 251p. illus. index. $55.00. ISBN 0-313-31464-0.

Contemporary Hispanic Quotations is a straightforward, well-organized book providing approximately 1,000 quotations from notable Hispanics. According to the introduction, in this work "Hispanic" is interchangeable with "Latino" or "Latina." The book's subjects "have roots in the continental United States, Mexico, Puerto Rico, Cuba, the Dominican Republic, Guatemala, El Salvador, Nicaragua, Costa Rica, Panama, Colombia, Venezuela, Peru, Ecuador, Bolivia, Chile, Argentina, Spain, Portugal and the Philippines" (p. xi). Entries are in alphabetic order. The name, place, and date of birth are bolded in the entry heading. A brief biographical note of one to three sentences follows the heading. The quotes are listed next, with the source and date included.

There is an author index and a subject and keyword index. There are also two appendixes. The first is the most interesting, and is all too brief. The appendix of "Anonymous Graffiti, Quotations and Proverbs" is a collection of anonymous sayings, such as "ojos que no ven, corazón que no siente." This saying is defined in the appendix as the equivalent to the English proverb "Out of sight, out of mind." While the meaning-for-meaning translation makes sense, it would have been a nice touch to include word-for-word translations as well, since they give a unique sense of cultural distinctiveness. For example, note that it is the heart and not the head that is affected by the absence in this proverb. The second appendix, "Fields of Professional Activity," is a simple list by career of those quoted in the book.

This well-organized work would be a good resource for libraries with Hispanic and Latino collections. This book should be useful in both public and undergraduate academic settings and is recommended.
—**Sandra E. Fuentes Riggs**

C, P

34.   **The Oxford Dictionary of Modern Quotations.** 2d ed. Elizabeth Knowles, ed. New York, Oxford University Press, 2002. 483p. index. $35.00. ISBN 0-19-866275-0.

The 2d edition of *The Oxford Dictionary of Modern Quotations* is truly a joy to read, and I mean "read" as one reads a joke book. As one makes their way through this extremely eclectic collection of sayings from the modern world's politicians, artists, and pop celebrities, one cannot help but marvel at what an utterly creative time we are living in to produce this panoply of witticisms, malapropisms, and flights of humorous illogic. If one needs a clever, ice-breaking quote to begin an after-dinner speech before the Rotary Club, this is the book to seek out. Although there are legitimate, intellectual uses for this book beyond amusement, I cannot fathom any. It is too sporadic, too noncomprehensive for sociological research and analysis, which is no fault of the editor since quotes are mere snapshots in a historical narrative, a timeline that often is not immediately apparent to the reader. Yet, it is this haphazard, disjointedness of aphorisms, leaping in and out, that is the strength of this tome. It has the serendipitous nature to titillate the imagination, to trigger within the memory of the reader stages, scenes, and landscapes from the past that have gone dark. This reviewer read with startling laughter the quotations of Monty Python's Flying Circus, and the daffy world of English humor came flooding back from my youth, complete with "silly walks, dead parrots," and the Spanish Inquisition, who no one expects (p. 230). The book can also frighten. I reread the comment by the American physicist J. Robert Oppenheimer as he witnessed the first atomic bomb explosion: "I remember the line from the Hindu scripture, the Bhagavad Gita? 'I am become death, the destroyer of worlds' " (p.246) and I remembered the fear of living a childhood under the threat of the "Bomb."

Being one of the "The Oxford Dictionary of" series, this book is naturally heavily saturated with the sayings of English politicians and celebrities who are relatively unknown to Americans, but that is not a disadvantage. However, a distinct disadvantage is its Anglo-American emphasis. It could have been more international in scope and included much more quotations from people of other nations. The book ends with a keyword index and a selected thematic (e.g., administration, age, American, art) index. Both tools are helpful to the after-dinner speaker. I can strongly recommend this book to be included in the collection of any library. [R: LJ, 15 May 03, pp. 80-82; SLJ, Oct 03, pp. 104-105]—**Glenn Masuchika**

Part II
SOCIAL SCIENCES

2 Social Sciences in General

GENERAL WORKS

Catalogs and Collections

C, P

35. **Inter-University Consortium for Political and Social Research. http://www.icpsr.umich.edu.** [Website]. Ann Arbor, Mich., Inter-University Consortium for Political and Social Research. Free. Date reviewed: 2003.

This is the official Website of the Inter-University Consortium for Political and Social Research (ICPSR). ICPSR is a not-for-profit, membership-based organization that provides access to the world's largest archive of computerized social science data. In addition, ICPSR assists member colleges and universities by providing training in basic and advanced techniques in qualitative social analysis. This organization was founded in 1962 and serves more than 325 colleges and universities in North America. There are also several hundred members outside the United States and Canada. ICPSR has four general goals: to acquire social science data, to preserve the data, to provide open and equal access to the data, and to promote the effective use of social science data. Data relate to a wide range of social science disciplines: sociology, demography, political science, history, economics, criminal justice, public health, foreign policy, and law. This detailed Website explains ICPSR's mission, provides information for members, and includes the searchable database of archived ICPSR data. There are also links to other data sites. This site is an essential source for all academic libraries with social science librarians.—**Diane Zabel**

Dictionaries and Encyclopedias

C

36. **Encyclopedia of Community: From the Village to the Virtual World.** Karen Christensen and David Levinson, eds. Thousand Oaks, Calif., Sage, 2003. 4v. index. $595.00/set. ISBN 0-7619-2598-8.

The *Encyclopedia of Community*, in four volumes, combines the organizational and editorial expertise of Karen Christensen and David Levinson with the knowledge of 399 contributors from 18 countries to create a research tool that contains 500 entries, 266 extensive primary-text sidebars, 4 major appendixes of 150,000 words, more than 100 visuals, and an index. Entries range in length from 500 to 6,000 words, each complete with references, compiled by visible scholars from many major institutions. Of interest is appendix 1, "Resource Guides," which prepares the student and scholar for additional research. This appendix is topically divided; cross-referenced with encyclopedia entries; and lists books, Websites, journals, and community organizations.

The *Encyclopedia of Community* accomplishes its objectives by addressing four fundamental questions: "How have people experienced community, throughout history and around the world?"; "How are communities different from other kinds of groups and associations?"; "Are we really 'bowling alone,' or have we found new forms of community thanks to widespread mobility and the Internet?"; and "Have cars and television destroyed our sense of community?" The scope of this work ranges from community in ancient history to community in popular culture (e.g., television shows, movies). Topics include various types of communities, biographies, case studies, human development, and social capital, to mention a few. The 237 pages of appendixes and article resources make it a valuable tool for the serious researcher, the student of "community," and the teacher or college professor.

The *Encyclopedia of Community* is sociologically technical; for example, the entry on "Conflict Theory" states "Conflict theory tries to classify and describe the types of conflicts that exist (for example, in terms of whether they are productive or destructive). It then attempts to explain the ways in which conflict proceeds or is structured (both by internal and external forces) and how it can be managed or resolved" (p. 323). Because the writing is clear and direct and the volumes have a textbook style to which students have grown accustomed, the *Encyclopedia of Community* is a major resource for high school through college and graduate students. Consider the explanation contained in the following statement: "Even those who generally approve of conflict resolution processes are concerned that the animating principles of conflict resolution may be distorted, as when, for example, a voluntary and consensual process such as mediation or arbitration becomes mandatory. (This can happen when a contract requires people to use a particular dispute resolution process or when courts require disputants to go to mediation before getting a trial.)" (p. 322). The extensive list of entries, many sidebars using primary references, the reader's guide, the comprehensive introduction, and resources give the *Encyclopedia of Community* completeness and depth, and provide the student, social scientist, and historian an essential tool for many and multiple uses. [R: LJ, 15 Nov 03, p. 58]—**Joseph P. Hester**

P
37.   Hirsch, E. D., Jr., Joseph F. Kett, and James Trefil. **The New Dictionary of Cultural Literacy.** rev. ed. New York, Houghton Mifflin, 2002. 647p. illus. index. $29.95. ISBN 0-618-22647-8.

One could quarrel with the authors' subtle distinction between patriotism (a love of country that embraces diversity and harbors no fear of different cultures) and nationalism (a tribalistic presumption of cultural superiority that looks askance at things foreign), but their contention that a sense of community requires a shared body of knowledge is indisputable. Thus, this 3d edition of a national bestseller, compiled by 3 Virginia professors whose respective disciplines are English, history, and physics, focuses on that common knowledge "every American needs to know." This common knowledge is what the authors call "cultural literacy," and it demands at least some familiarity with the Bible, American and world literature, history, geography, the social sciences, the fine arts, business and economics, the physical and life sciences, and technology. Regardless of one's religious persuasion, for instance, a culturally literate American must have some grounding in the Bible to understand references to a David and Goliath battle, the wisdom of Solomon, the patience of Job, extending an olive branch, a doubting Thomas, or the parables of Jesus. Likewise, how could any American participate in the national culture without knowing something of the Boston Tea Party, Benedict Arnold, the Bill of Rights, the Bronx, the Bible Belt, Cape Canaveral, Gallup polls, and DNA?

Included herein are some 7,000 clearly written entries, of which numerous ones have been updated and about 500 are new. Technology and science dominate the latter, reflecting the enormous changes in those fields since the second publication, when a Web page was unheard of. A sensible organization and an exhaustive index simplify access to this treasure trove of information. Beginning with "The Bible" and ending with "Technology," the work is divided into 23 sections, with relevant terms, events, and people alphabetically subsumed under each. A "Pronunciation Key" is also helpful. Since this is a work for a popular audience, it would be a suitable purchase for public libraries. [R: LJ, 1 Nov 02, pp. 78-80]—**John W. Storey**

3 Area Studies

GENERAL WORKS

Dictionaries and Encyclopedias

P, S

38. **World Book Encyclopedia of People and Places.** Chicago, World Book, 2003. 6v. illus. maps. index. $289.00/set. ISBN 0-7166-3750-2.

The present work is the 9th edition of the *World Book Encyclopedia of People and Places* to appear since 1992 (see ARBA 02, entry 84; ARBA 01, entry 343; and ARBA 92, entry 490, for reviews of previous editions). Multivolume encyclopedias being expensive, when new editions come out so frequently one would like assurance of enough different material to make its purchase worthwhile. Introductory pages and the publisher's Website offer no enlightenment in this regard. As the 2002 edition was unavailable to this reviewer, the 2000 edition was used for comparison.

The alphabetically arranged, multipage country entries seem mostly unchanged, except in some cases where events since 1996 are added on to a current history section. The Afghanistan article adds a whole extra column, whereas Albania receives only two new sentences. Lengthy articles on larger nations appear unchanged, such as the one on Italy, where there is no mention of Berlusconi's return to power. Historical sections for each country seem totally unrevised. This leads to unfortunate falsehood in the case of Afghanistan, where the rise and fall of the Taliban government are documented but the giant Buddha statues it so controversially destroyed at Bamian are still noted as a sight worth seeing. A "Fact Box" offering basic statistics on population, government, and the economy (e.g., Gross National Product, growth rate) has been updated for each entry, and a 3-page list of country Websites has been added after the comprehensive index in volume 6.

Numerous photographs, maps, and charts make this an attractive set for elementary and middle school students, but the publisher would do well to issue periodic online updates instead of frequent print editions. This reviewer recommends purchasing this set only every four or five years, and using almanacs and online resources to stay current in between.—**Willa Schmidt**

Handbooks and Yearbooks

C, P

39. **Nations of the World, 2004: A Political, Economic & Business Handbook.** 4th ed. Millerton, N.Y., Grey House Publishing, 2003. 1614p. maps. $145.00pa.; $180.00 (w/CD-ROM). ISBN 1-59237-006-3.

This book profiles 231 sovereign nations and self-governing territories. For each profile, if complete, key facts are given as well as a map, country overview, key indicators, risk assessment, country profile, and business directory. Both key facts and key indicators in chart format are convenient for quick reference. The bulk of information is in the section of country profiles, which includes a historical profile, political structure, political parties, population, religions, education, health, welfare, main cities, spoken languages, media, economy, external trade, agriculture, industry and manufacturing, tourism, mining, hydrocarbons, energy, financial markets, banking and insurance, time, geography, climate, dress codes, entry requirements, hotels, credit cards, public holidays, working hours, telecommunications, electricity supply, weights and measures, social customs, security, directions for getting there, and transportation. Most articles are signed. The length of the articles varies from 3 pages to over 10 pages. After the "Country Profiles" section is a "Global Profiles" section that is divided by region. Each region consists of a map, overview, currencies, and key indicators. The book ends with "U.S. Embassies," a misleading title. The embassies referred to are foreign embassies (some are not embassies) in the United States, not U.S. embassies in foreign nations.

The book is well compiled and will be particularly useful to anyone in international business and traveling for business. It would enhance its usefulness if in all profile maps the sovereign nation that controls the non-sovereign territory was listed, and criteria for "Risk Assessment" were provided. The book provides rich information in a well-designed format on nations and territories in the world. A companion CD-ROM is available to book buyers. [R: AG, Nov 03, p. 62]—**Tze-chung Li**

UNITED STATES

General Works

P, S

40.   **World Almanac Library of the States Series.** Milwaukee, Wis., World Almanac Library, 2003. 52v. illus. maps. index. $1,383.20/set; $26.60/vol.

This 52-volume set from World Almanac Library offers elementary and middle school students the opportunity to research each state individually. The information compiled here was gleaned from *The World Almanac* (see ARBA 2002, entry 5), *The World Almanac for Kids* (see ARBA 2002, entry 6), and *The World Almanac Encyclopedia*. Each of the 50 states receives its own volume, as well as Washington, D.C. and Puerto Rico. Each volume is 48 pages in length and offers information on the state's history, people, land, economy and commerce, politics and government, and culture. The books use photographs, maps, and many sidebars with "fast facts" to hold the attention of young readers. The volumes conclude with a biography of notable people from the state, a timeline of historical events, a list of yearly festivals, and a concluding page of facts and Websites. Young researchers can use this set to study individual states or to compare the histories, economies, and geography of various states.

Larger school and public libraries that can afford this title will benefit from its easy-to-search pages and wide range of information. For those that find this series too steep for their budgets, they can purchase individual volumes on their state and surrounding states or can opt for the less-expensive but still comprehensive title from Blackbirch titled *The Blackbirch Kids Visual Reference of the United States*, which includes much of the same information but in one volume (see ARBA 2003, entry 81).—**Shannon Graff Hysell**

C, P

41.   **Worldmark Encyclopedia of the States.** 6th ed. Farmington Hills, Mich., Gale, 2004. 859p. maps. $170.00. ISBN 0-7876-7338-2. ISSN 1531-1627.

First published in 1981, this hefty, information-packed reference book basically retains the original format in this most recent edition (see ARBA 2002, entry 94, for a review of the 5th edition). Inside the front cover is a United States map showing states with their capitals and major cities, while the back endpapers present small, color replicas of the 50 state flags. The preface introduces the history of the book. "Notes" cites sources for some, but unfortunately not all, of the data in the volume, and the "Guide to State Articles" explains the book's organization, subject headings, and symbols. The one-page "Conversion Table" provides conventional measures as well as more unusual ones, including the weight of bags of coffee and bales of cotton.

Articles are arranged alphabetically and deal with each of the 50 states, the District of Columbia, Puerto Rico, the U.S. Caribbean Dependencies, and the U.S. Pacific Dependencies. All include facts and statistics arranged under 50 standard, numbered subject headings. Especially noteworthy is the lengthy, concluding chapter devoted to the United States as a whole. Useful and current bibliographies at the end of each chapter yield resources for additional reading, but do not cite the sources used to write the chapter. The text closes with a brief glossary and a table of abbreviations and acronyms. The compilers have used both state and federal Websites and federal agency publications to update the 2001 edition. Population figures reflect June 2002 U.S. Census Bureau totals and the famous person entries are current through July 2003. Students used to Web searching may bypass this book, but it remains a valuable tool for beginning research on subjects ranging from state flora and fauna to government, ethnic groups, and principal daily newspapers.—**Julienne L. Wood**

AFRICA

C

42.   **The African Studies Companion: A Guide to Information Sources.** 3d rev. ed. Hans M. Zell, ed. Lochcarron, Scotland, United Kingdom, Hans Zell Publishing Consultants, 2003. 545p. index. $170.00 (w/online edition). ISBN 0-9541029-1-6.

This somewhat expensive 3d edition of one of the most essential tools in African studies continues the high standard established by the previous 1989 and 1997 editions (2d ed.; see ARBA 98, entry 105). Its length (twice that of the 1997 version) reflects clearly the explosion in online resources related to Africa produced both within and outside the continent. The organization of the work is also marked by major alteration, most visibly a greater number of chapters (expanded from 9 to 23) and extensive reworking of all sections of text, which retain their former titles. New topical chapters cover print and online data on African-language resources; sources of statistical, economical, and financial data; cartographic information sources (including map vendors and CD-ROM products); Africana films and videos; African newspapers; major African academic libraries and national archives; and Africanist documentation and bibliography. The chapter on major libraries and documentation centers with significant Africana holdings in the previous edition has been split into two separate chapters, while the section on major African and international organizations active in the continent has been substantially expanded. Of particular value for librarians involved in regular online searching for African data is chapter 22, "Information and Communication Development in Africa," which, while examining general Internet sources for information on the continent, goes beyond this to consider issues involved in the construction of an effective Internet framework for the continent, electronic communication initiatives, and networked communities, presenting references to literature on these intertwined questions. The amount of new and updated information provided by this work (in particular the number of Internet sites) is so massive that it should be acquired by all college and university reference collections as well as public libraries of all sizes desirous of having one good resource on Africana in their collections. An added incentive to purchase is that password access to the electronic version of this title, available at http://www.africanstudiescompanion.com, is provided to owners of the print edition.—**Robert B. Marks Ridinger**

ANTARCTICA AND THE POLAR REGIONS

C, P

43.   Mills, William James. **Exploring Polar Frontiers: A Historical Encyclopedia.** Santa Barbara, Calif., ABC-CLIO, 2003. 2v. illus. maps. index. $185.00/set; $200.00 (e-book). ISBN 1-57607-422-6; 1-57607-423-4 (e-book).

William James Mills is Librarian and Keeper of Collections for the Scott Polar Research Institute in Cambridge and has written this excellent two-volume encyclopedia of the Arctic and Antarctic. Articles consist of well-written essays on polar topics, together with cross-references to other relevant articles within the encyclopedia, and end with a "References and Further Reading" section. The article concerning "George De Long" (1844-1881) is typical of most entries in the volume. There is a brief introductory paragraph, followed by a three-page narrative of De Long's Jeannette Polar Expedition of 1879-1881. There is an illustration for the De Long article from R. Perry's 1887 book on the Jeannette expedition. What is not clear, unfortunately, is who wrote the three-page narrative. It is assumed that Mills wrote the entire encyclopedia himself, since no other authors are cited as being credited for the text. The title page lists six contributing authors, but it is not clear what if anything they contributed to the work. In the two-page introduction Mills lists 36 people who "assisted in the writing of *Exploring Polar Frontiers*, but I alone bear responsibility for the resulting text." If this is so, then the work is wonderfully done, with each essay telling a fascinating story of Arctic and Antarctic exploration and discovery.

The volume begins with a table of contents that lists each article in the two-volume set, followed by two indexes prior to the actual text: articles listed in chronological order, and articles listed in a classed bibliography order. Before the main text are 20 line maps of the Arctic and Antarctic, followed by an introduction. The work concludes with a glossary, a polar timeline, a comprehensive selected bibliography and index, and a page that contains one sentence: "About the Author." In a large number of cases the works used for illustrations are not cited in the "References and Reading" section. However, in some cases they are, forcing the reader to perhaps sometimes miss additional works that are only cited with the illustration. As noted above, the articles are very well written and the work is an attractive two-volume set. Illustrations are very well placed and complement the text as needed. The work appears to be available as an electronic book for a slightly higher price. The reviewer was not given access to the e-book for this review. Most general reference collections will want to acquire this set. Geology, geography, and polar research special collections will find this a handy compendium.—**Ralph Lee Scott**

ASIA

China

C, P

44.   **The Territories of the People's Republic of China.** Florence, Ky., Europa Publications/Taylor & Francis Group, 2002. 277p. maps. $185.00. ISBN 1-85743-149-9.

This volume on the People's Republic of China is the third country covered in Europa's series of books on territories. The book is divided into three parts. The first part discusses the regional from an economic viewpoint and a political viewpoint. A chronology, country statistics, and a directory of country officials are provided in this section also. Part 2 covers each of the 22 provinces, 5 of the autonomous regions (Guangsi, Nei Mongol, Ningxia, Tibet, and Xinjiang), and 4 special municipalities (Beijing, Shanghai, Chongqing, and Tientsin). Each entry gives an overview of the province, the history, economy, and a directory of leaders. The two new administrative municipalities of Hong Kong and Macao are covered by an overview of their geography, history, and economy. Maps and principal officials of these provinces accompany the overviews. Part 3 is a list of alternative names and provides a gazetteer. An alternative name index and an index of areas are included. An appendix on the Republic of China is discussed in the end chapter.

The information is accurate and current, but concise. If one needs current country information about the People's Republic of China for a student doing a research project or for the business traveler planning a trip to China, this volume will prove to be a handy reference tool.—**Kay M. Stebbins**

Japan

C, P, S

45.   Frédéric, Louis. Käthe Roth. **Japan Encyclopedia.** Cambridge, Mass., Belknap Press of Harvard University Press, 2002. 1102p. index. $49.95. ISBN 0-674-00770-0.

Over the past dozen years, there have been many English-language encyclopedias on Japan, from the multivolume set *Kodansha Encyclopedia of Japan* (Kodansha America, 1983) to many illustrated encyclopedias for popular audiences. None of those, however, are ideal for readers or librarians needing a brief explanation of detailed concepts or important individuals or sites from Japan's long history. This is exactly the need filled by the *Japan Encyclopedia*. The *Encyclopedia* contains about 14,000 entries, most of which are a paragraph long, exploring such key concepts as agriculture or geography. Entries elucidate important biographies, and important places in Japanese history (e.g., shrines, cities, temples, colleges) and even the famous statue of the dog, Hachiko.

Some areas are covered in less detail. For example, there is no entry for World War II, the Pacific War, Unit 731, or the Nanjing Massacre, although there is some discussion of the former in the "History" entry. There is also poor coverage of the next period, with no cross-reference from the "Occupation" to the "Supreme Commander for the Allied Powers," which itself is a short entry. The entries all seem to be by Frédéric (1923-1996), who wrote other works on Japanese art and Southeast Asian studies. Entries do not offer any references, although there is 15-page bibliography at the end. The index is only fair, and also has few cross-references.

As a ready-reference tool or bedside reader's companion this reviewer believes this is a most worthwhile volume. Users should spend time familiarizing themselves with the features of the *Encyclopedia*. The brief "Note on Usage" only explains romanization. One needs to explore the work to discover the excellent chronology and tables of emperors, prime ministers, and even of governor-generals during the years when Japan occupied Taiwan and Korea. Since the guide does not explain this, one also needs to locate key longer entries, such as "Film," "Literature," "Archaeology," and "History" (but not "Religion") , which contain important facts not otherwise explained in the shorter entries. Besides the aforementioned shortcomings, it belongs in the ready-reference collection of most high school, public, college, special, and research libraries.—**Andrew B. Wertheimer**

AUSTRALIA AND THE PACIFIC AREA

P

46.   Nightingale, Neil, Jeni Clevers, Hugh Pearson, and Mary Summerill. **Wild Australasia.** New York, Firefly Books, 2003. 240p. illus. maps. index. $29.95. ISBN 1-55297-855-9.

Australia, the world's island continent, has more unique species than anywhere else. Biodiversity abounds with more than twice the number of species found in Europe and the United States combined. This rich and wonderful natural history of Australia and its nearby string of islands (New Zealand, New

Caledonia, New Guinea, New Britain, and Lord Howe Island) is expertly described and beautifully illustrated with over 200 photographs.

Written to accompany a six-part BBC television series, "Wild Down Under," the book is divided into five sections by ecosystem: Rainforests, Deserts, Gum Tree Country, Oceans, and Islands. The last section, "New Worlds," covers the changes humans brought to this bizarre continent. Each section has two or three concise chapters.

Easy to read and full of startling facts, the book is a treat to browse but can also be comfortably read from cover to cover. The format of each chapter adds to the practicality of the volume. Each chapter begins with a full-page summary in large print. There are "starred" large-print factoids throughout each chapter as well as "triangles," which draw the reader to highlighted information on especially interesting animals or plants. Most chapters also have a two-page spread on "special features" of each chapter, such as fruitbats or koalas. Every page delights the eye with outstanding photographs.

The bibliography, index, maps, and especially the gazetteer, which describes the "authors' personal best places to experience the natural wonder of each region," add to the book's usefulness. It is also easy to handle (9-by-11 inches), yet large enough that the photographs can be fully appreciated.

While *Wild Australasia* is not a comprehensive reference book of natural history, it is a beautiful, excellent reference for gaining a broad understanding of the major concepts that underlie reasons why this part of the globe is so special. It whets the appetite for more. This book is a bargain for the price and most libraries will want to purchase it. This reviewer could hardly set it down!—**Georgia Briscoe**

EUROPE

General Works

C, P

47.   **Central and South-Eastern Europe 2004.** 4th ed. Florence, Ky., Europa Publications/Taylor & Francis Group, 2003. 809p. index. (Regional Surveys of the World). $450.00. ISBN 1-85743-186-3. ISSN 1470-5699.

This volume belongs to the Regional Surveys of the World series, and is full of information in its double-column pages. It is part of an ambitious project that started in 1990 and is already in its 4th edition, indicating the fast pace of change that has characterized the region since the 1989 overthrow of communism. The survey can be used as an insightful guide to the region, its two main subdivisions, or the individual countries. Central Europe includes Poland, the Czech Republic, Slovakia, Hungary, Slovenia, and three former Soviet Republics of Estonia, Latvia, and Lithuania. South-Eastern Europe covers Serbia and Montenegro, Bosnia and Herzegovina, Macedonia, Croatia, Albania, Romania, Bulgaria, and the only nonformer communist country of the entire group, Greece.

The current volume features statistical coverage from 1998 through 2003. In its descriptive parts, European viewpoints are mildly indicated, as in the criticism of a decision to purchase U.S. rather than European equipment. But then most of the 33 contributors are from Great Britain. Even so, the contents are generally objective. The prefatory part of the book contains a long list of abbreviations and international telephone codes for the countries of the area covered. Part 1, the "General Survey," serves as an introduction to common concerns within the area: unification, economic problems, social policy and welfare, religion, minorities, and the environment, plus the special situation of the Baltic region and the former Yugoslavia, as well as the Macedonian question. Part 2 comprises country surveys, with a uniform layout of geography and maps; a chronology that traces a country's history from its beginnings to the more detailed recent period; an essay on the history of the country and another on its economy; a statistical survey that is equivalent to a synoptic statistical yearbook for the individual countries (the section that this reviewer found especially informative); and a "Directory" that compresses information on the legal framework of the country, its national and local government, political organizations, foreign diplomatic representatives within the country, its judicial system, religions, the press, the publishers, telecommunications, financial system, trading and industrial organizations, trade unions, firms engaged in transport, tourism, culture education, social welfare, institutions engaged in environmental work, and defense. The bibliographies that end these country surveys are far from comprehensive, but they allow interested readers to take it from there. Part 3 of the volume profiles some of the leading national political figures. Part 4 provides regional information, beginning with organizations, the main of which is the United Nations and its many related organizations (such as the Economic Commission for Europe, the UN Children's Fund, UN Development Program, and UN Peacekeeping), the World Trade Organization, and others, and continues with foreign research institutes that include Central and South-Eastern Europe in their programs. Two select bibliographies, for periodicals and for books, are up-to-date and absorbing. A guide to pronunciation would have been a useful addition to the contents. The use of circumflexes for the national languages is good, but not perfect or consistent.

This volume is useful for businesses, academia, international organizations, politicians, and individuals who are interested in particular countries of the region. *Central and South-Eastern Europe* is an excellent and helpful project that is well edited, highly informative, and authoritative.—**Bogdan Mieczkowski**

Ireland

C, P
48.   **The Encyclopedia of Ireland.** Brian Lalor, ed. New Haven, Conn., Yale University Press, 2003. 1218p. illus. maps. index. $65.00. ISBN 0-300-09442-6.

This reference work is a huge volume of 1,218 pages packed full of information about Ireland from prehistory to the present. According to the publisher, it is the most comprehensive book to date on all aspects of Irish culture, history, and life. It contains more than 5,000 alphabetically arranged entries by over 900 contributors, as well as more than 700 illustrations and maps, many in full color. Articles on music, literature, politics, religion, and sports, along with biographies and topics such as the role of women in Irish life and the contribution of Irish scholarship to science and philosophy, are just some of the tantalizing entries.

The volume includes both a subject and regular index at the back of the book. This reference work is well researched, and would be an excellent addition to most academic and public library collections.
—**Bradford Lee Eden**

LATIN AMERICA AND THE CARIBBEAN

General Works

C, S
49.   Randle, Janice W. **Issues in the Spanish-Speaking World.** Westport, Conn., Greenwood Press, 2003. 275p. illus. index. $45.00. ISBN 0-313-31974-X.

Unlike many reference books this is not a dictionary or encyclopedia on the Spanish-speaking world; instead, this work examines many of the persistent issues taken up by scholars. The geographical coverage of the book is broad in that Randle addresses both Latin America and Spain.

Each chapter of the book focuses on a controversial issue concerning the Spanish-speaking peoples. Topics covered range from a debate over which Hispanic nation's peoples speak the "best" Spanish and the question of Columbus and his impact on the New World to issues dealing with Catholicism and bullfighting. All of the entries contain background information followed by a discussion of both sides of the issue in question. Each chapter also offers student activities, vocabulary lists, and source lists.

Although it would be impossible to cover every possible controversial question dealing with the unique history and culture of the Spanish-speaking world, the author has chosen some of the most commonly debated and presented them in a coherent and cogent manner. The only criticism here is that this is a single-author work that may have been made stronger in a collaborated project. Nonetheless, this is a useful work that many students will find helpful as they begin to explore the issues unique to Spanish-speaking nations.—**Melvin Davis**

Cuba

C, P

50.   **Encyclopedia of Cuba: People, History, Culture.** Luis Martínez-Fernández, D. H. Figueredo, Louis A. Pérez Jr., and Luis González, eds. Westport, Conn., Oryx Press/Greenwood Publishing Group, 2003. 2v. illus. index. $175.00/set. ISBN 1-57356-334-X.

Ask the average person on the street what the mention of Cuba brings to mind and chances are the answer will include Castro, cigars, and Elian Gonzalez. The 700 articles in this 2-volume set broadens that perspective by looking at a wide range of topics that portray Cuba's rich history and culture.

The information is organized into 12 topical sections, with alphabetic entries within each section. Articles run from a paragraph to several pages. The Castro entry runs three pages. The 1959 revolution and its significance are discussed in a succinct but thorough four-page essay. Post-revolutionary (pre-Castro) Cuba and its politics are of necessity a major focus of the *Encyclopedia* but the colonial and republican periods receive equal attention. In addition to the three political divisions, there are sections on national symbols, geography, popular culture, and the Cuban Diaspora. A significant part of the book is dedicated to the arts. Short biographies of writers, musicians, and visual artists give not only the basic biographical information but also discuss the relevance of their work. Other entries cover political and historical figures. The editors have been successful in presenting an objective view of Cuba. This effort is particularly noticeable in entries on social issues. For example, the articles on education and health care acknowledge the positive changes made in these areas under Castro's rule.

The *Encyclopedia*'s vocabulary makes it accessible to students as young as those in middle school. Cross-references in bold typeface are embedded in the text of articles and a *see also* list appears at the end. References are given after each entry but it should be noted that many of these are only available in Spanish. That problem is offset by a selected subject bibliography of English-language sources that appears as an appendix. Other appendixes include a timeline and excerpts from historic documents, speeches, and treaties.

There is a table of contents, an alphabetic list of entries, and an index. The index can prove frustrating. A search for the date of Cuba's independence from the United States proved elusive. There is no entry for "independence" nor does the word appear as a subheading under "United States." The date actually appears in an article on relations with the United States and in the timeline. This problem may hinder the use of the *Encyclopedia* for quick reference answers. Overview essays at the beginning of each section would have helped to provide a context for the individual entries. This would have been especially useful to readers with little knowledge of Cuban history.

Given the fact that this work is the only resource of its kind, the benefits far outweigh the problems. The *Encyclopedia* presents an honest and interesting view of a country that is often perceived as having no history but that related to communism, Castro, and human rights violations. [R: LJ, 15 May 03, p. 78; SLJ, Aug 03, p. 111]—**Marlene M. Kuhl**

Mexico

C, P

51.   Dent, David W. **Encyclopedia of Modern Mexico.** Lanham, Md., Scarecrow, 2002. 343p. illus. maps. index. $49.50. ISBN 0-8108-4291-2.

This single-volume work focuses on Mexico from the presidency of Lázero Cárdenas (1934-1940) through that of Vicente Fox, whose term began in 2000. The author, David W. Dent, a political scientist, thoroughly covers the major events, people, and issues that have shaped Mexico for almost 70 years.

For the most part, the entries are in depth enough for the reader to gain solid information, yet they are not so overly long that the typical student becomes disinterested. Many entries contain a suggested readings section that directs researchers to more information on the topic. Dent includes a useful timeline, a list of abbreviations and acronyms, as well as a brief narrative introduction to the history of modern Mexico. There is also a section devoted to online resources, which points users to alternative nonprint sources.

This is a solid single-authored encyclopedia that many students and researchers will find useful. Its compact nature, easy accessibility, and clear writing make this an excellent choice for those doing general research. The work is, however, geared toward social scientists; as a result, researchers interested in fields such as science and technology or many aspects of the humanities will find themselves looking elsewhere. [R: SLJ, Feb 03, p. 86]—**Melvin Davis**

MIDDLE EAST

General Works

C, P, S

52.   **Atlas of the Middle East.** Washington, D.C., National Geographic Society, 2003. 96p. illus. maps. index. $19.95. ISBN 0-7922-6460-6.

This brief, colorful, beautifully designed, information-packed atlas is a delightful addition to reference sources on the region. Besides first-class maps of each Middle Eastern country, it includes large, useful city maps of Baghdad, Beirut, Cairo, Damascus, Jerusalem, and Tehran, and many specialized thematic inclusions. The regional theme entries provide maps and charts on climate, population, religion, ethnic and linguistic groups, oil, water, and development indicators. All are bright, inviting, and user-friendly, and the amount of information displayed is exceptional. A historical section includes world heritage sites, a timeline, maps depicting borders and other features at various times during the twentieth century, and a compendium map of regional conflicts (1945-2002). Appendixes include flags; a glossary of geographic equivalents, abbreviations, and conversions; an index; and a listing of reference sources. The inexpensive price allows every library to add this attractive and valuable reference source to their holdings, and they should. [R: LJ, 15 May 03, p. 76]—**Joe P. Dunn**

P, S

53.   **Teen Life in the Middle East.** Ali Akbar Mahdi, ed. Westport, Conn., Greenwood Press, 2003. 266p. illus. index. (Teen Life Around the World). $55.00. ISBN 0-313-31893-X.

A volume in the series Teen Life Around the World, this work aims to present a sociological study of adolescent life in today's Middle East. Following the introduction by the editor titled "Teens, Islam, and the Middle East," the book compares, contrasts, and evaluates everyday living of young people in diversified societies that collectively regard traditional mores of a societal group as essential to its preservation. Eleven countries are surveyed: Iran, Iraq, Israel, Jordan, Kuwait, Lebanon, Palestinian territories, Saudi Arabia, Syria, Turkey, United Arab Emirates, and Yemen. The chapters address the multiple challenges of modernism (e.g., technology, Westernization, new ideas) to tradition-based society and cover questions of behavior, belief, food, entertainment, family, recreation, schooling, and social life. The information gathered (mainly historical and sociological) is generally accurate and balanced, especially the chapters on Iraq and Iran. Not so, however, on the Israelis and the Palestinians, where the subject matter is either inaccurate (no tension between Palestinian Christians and Muslims), selective (no mention of yeshiva-world teens nor Palestinian teen bombers), or politicized (e.g., Zionism and democracy are incompatible, Palestinian uprisings represent moral social rage). Nonetheless, despite a wide spectrum of experiential difference and scholarly interpretation, today's Middle Eastern teens across the spectrum strive for a more peaceful and serene tomorrow.—**Zev Garber**

Afghanistan

C, P

54.   Clements, Frank A. **Conflict in Afghanistan: A Historical Encyclopedia.** Santa Barbara, Calif., ABC-CLIO, 2003. 377p. illus. index. (Roots of Modern Conflict). $85.00; $130.00 (w/e-book). ISBN 1-85109-402-4.

One very fine reference source on Afghanistan, Ludwig W. Adamec's *Historical Dictionary of Afghanistan* (3d ed.; see ARBA 2004, entry 114), already exists, and this new addition to the excellent Roots of Modern Conflict series is another outstanding one. This volume provides nearly 400 entries that cover the history of conflict in Afghanistan from 1747 through the Taliban and Operation Enduring Freedom. Other notable features include a lengthy historical narrative introduction, several useful maps, numerous pictures, an extensive chronology, abbreviations and acronyms, an extensive topical bibliography, Websites, and a useful table of contents and index. Both of these reference works are invaluable. At the expensive price, which is the same for each volume, most libraries will have to choose between the two sources. Adamec's volume may be more scholarly. Clements' volume is visually much more attractive and inviting and the entries are for the most part longer. Each entry has additional reading sources at the end of the essay. For these reasons I recommend *Conflict in Afghanistan* over the *Historical Dictionary of Afghanistan* for most general libraries. But all libraries should own one or the other.—**Joe P. Dunn**

4 Economics and Business

GENERAL WORKS

Bibliography

C, P

55. **Core Business Web: A Guide to Key Information Resources.** Gary W. White, ed. Binghamton, N.Y., Haworth Press, 2003. 325p. index. $49.95; $29.95pa. ISBN 0-7890-2094-7; 0-7890-2095-5pa.

This manuscript points out stable, authoritative Websites in major areas of business and explains relevance to the field, consequently saving much frustration and time in trying to locate information on the Web. The book is broken down into chapters written by authorities in each area and contains resources on the subjects of accounting, banking, business ethics, law for business, business research platforms, business statistics, career information and salary surveys, company information, consumer information, a guide to the best demography sources, economics, e-commerce, finance and investments, hospitality and tourism, human resources development, industry information, insurance, knowledge management, labor and collective bargaining, management, marketing and advertising, operation management/research, real estate, small business, taxation, and an index. The editor and chapter contributors are well qualified to write in these areas. This paperback is on average paper with average size and binding. This is a good guide to business key information resources. It is valuable for anyone searching the Web for business information. It should be in all major libraries.—**Herbert W. Ockerman**

Biography

C

56. Cicarelli, James, and Julianne Cicarelli. **Distinguished Women Economists.** Westport, Conn., Greenwood Press, 2003. 244p. index. $65.00. ISBN 0-313-30331-2.

This book identifies 51 women economists who have made notable contributions to the field of economics in the last 150 years. The entry for each woman averages four pages that include a brief biographical sketch, a somewhat longer discussion of each woman's contribution to the field of economics, a brief bibliography of works they authored, and a short list of articles written about them. The bibliography, in itself, is a time saver for researchers who will be able to directly look for additional information without doing further research. Currently there is nothing else like this in print and it fills an identifiable need for those who need this information. Except for a few big names, finding information on economists, male or female, has always been difficult to locate.

Academic libraries with business or economic units will want to acquire this book. It has the advantage of providing them with new names to showcase during National Women's Month, which is celebrated in March.—**Judith J. Field**

Dictionaries and Encyclopedias

C, P, S

57. **Business and Industry.** William R. Childs, Scott B. Martin, and Wanda Stitt-Gohdes, eds. Tarrytown, N.Y., Marshall Cavendish, 2004. 11v. illus. index. $459.95/set. ISBN 0-7614-7430-7.

Marshall Cavendish has published a new encyclopedia of 11 slim (141 pages) volumes targeted to readers with a 7th grade reading level or higher. The first 10 volumes consist of 375 articles arranged alphabetically, with a thematic outline also available that group the articles into 9 major categories. Each article is signed, 2 to 5 pages in length and includes a bibliography. Contributors consist of 92 teachers from colleges, universities, or high schools, reporters, practitioners, and freelancers. The biographical profiles of 55 men and women, selected for their contribution to the evolution of capitalism, are as diverse as Andrew Carnegie and César Chávez, Donald Trump and Ralph Nader. The 56 profiled companies are representative of various business sectors, and career information is included briefly within sidebars that accompany some of the industry articles. Every topic is amply illustrated with color photographs, charts, and timelines that help clarify complex topics such as "Globalization," "Macroeconomics," "Finance," and "Futures Markets."

The editors' interdisciplinary approach has helped achieve their goal of providing a broad overview of the market-based economy in the United States over the past 200 years. Issues such as opposition to the World Trade Organization, environmental regulations, child labor, the minimum wage, sexual harassment, and business ethics are treated as integral parts of the business-society relationship. Government's regulatory role is exemplified in articles on the "Federal Trade Commission" and the "Securities and Exchange Commission." Access points to information in this set are excellent. Volume 11 includes a detailed comprehensive index for the entire set and six separate thematic indexes; an additional bibliography of further readings (including Websites); a glossary; statistical data; and the text of six landmark documents. It would be helpful to identify the separate indexes with tabs or color edges in any future editions because one can easily check the wrong index, or not realize the thematic ones are available.

This is a unique work appropriate for some junior high libraries and for most high schools and public libraries. There is amazingly little content overlap with a somewhat similar work, Macmillan's two-volume *Encyclopedia of Busine$$ and Finance* (see ARBA 2003, entry 134) published in 2001 and targeted to high schools, undergraduates, and laypersons. Both sets will be useful for basic business questions, but *Business and Industry*'s attractive color illustrations and multiple volumes make it appealing and likely to be used. It is also more current, but twice as expensive.—**Patricia Rothermich**

C, P

58. **The History of Economic Thought Website. http://cepa.newschool.edu/het/.** [Website]. Free. Date reviewed: Dec 03.

The History of Economic Thought Website (HET) was a collaborative effort by two graduate students in economics, Goncalo L. Fonseca (The Johns Hopkins University) and Leanne Ussher (New School University). The HET site was created to be a resource of information and Web links about the development of economic thought for a variety of audiences, from students to the broader public.

Fonseca and Ussher state that this site was a labor of love, and their commitment to the discipline is evident in the sheer volume of information they have collected and carefully provided. The organization of this considerable amount of information is another strength of the site. The content covers more than 500 economists from ancient times to present day. Users can navigate this content in three ways: alphabetically by economist, by school of thought, or by the numerous essays and surveys written about specific economic subjects. There is also a useful search function provided by Picosearch.

The information about the economists includes bibliographies of their major works, links to related Web resources, and a discussion of the individual's role in economics. The schools of thought are categorized as follows: Political Economy (Ancient-1871), Neoclassical (1871-Today), Alternative (Heterodox Traditions and Keynesians), and Thematic (i.e., Business Cycle Theory and Game Theory). The site creators acknowledge that their categories are somewhat "loosely defined," having included time-honored schools as well as some they have identified themselves. Fonseca has written most of the essays and surveys.

To supplement this information, Fonseca and Ussher have provided links to online economic textbooks, and an extensive list of relevant print texts. Additionally, they have compiled valuable lists of links to economic-related professional organizations, archives of primary sources, journals, and glossaries.

While the site itself is hosted by the Economics Department of the New School University in New York, the institution bears no responsibility for its content. Furthermore, Fonseca and Ussher state that the information they have provided "has not been reviewed independently for accuracy, relevance and/or balance and thus deserves a critical amount of caution. As a result, we would prefer not to be cited as reliable authorities on anything." They are comfortable, however, with being identified as a general Internet resource. An additional point of concern is the absence of dates as to when the site was created and last updated. The last item added to the "News" page was dated September 30, 2001. This detail, combined with numerous broken links, leads this reviewer to believe that this site is not being kept current. Therefore, while the depth of this site makes it a good resource to consult when conducting economic research, users should verify the information they find against other sources.—**Susan Shultz**

C

59. **The Oxford Encyclopedia of Economic History.** Joel Mokyr, ed. New York, Oxford University Press, 2003. 5v. illus. maps. index. $695.00/set. ISBN 0-19-510507-9.

This is a substantial and comprehensive reference work that will delight and inform both students and researchers alike. With more than 800 scholarly contributors, this distinctive 5-volume set has more than 875 signed articles that provide authoritative, useful information along with discerning interpretations of events, persons and places, institutions, abstract concepts, and processes over the full range of human history and across all regions of the world. As a reference work it is well organized and superbly edited, ensuring that novices and mature scholars will each be able to find sound and useful information. Entries vary in length from in-depth essays of up to 10,000 words to more concise entries of fewer than 1,000 words that are thoroughly cross-referenced in order to facilitate an awareness and understanding of the inter-relationships that exist between concepts, events, and ideas. There are a considerable number of expertly written entries and articles that contain a number of effective maps, illustrations, and tables. All entries include up-to-date bibliographies or annotated bibliographies.

Another useful feature of this valuable and accessible reference work is the inclusion of a practical topical outline of the articles along with an extensive index. Among the many topics covered in this encyclopedia are histories of countries, regions, and cities, agriculture and tenure systems, industry surveys and industrial organization, business histories, institutional and technological change, demography, banking and finance, international economics, labor markets and working conditions, public finance and regulation, transportation, and natural resources and the environment, along with biographies of a number of inventors, business leaders, economists, and economic historians. This reference work also includes a practical and detailed outline of Websites pertinent to the topics and concepts covered throughout its five volumes. The inclusion of these Internet sites will help to keep this significant reference work timely and practical. This is a reference set that deserves to be on the shelves of every library serving the needs of students and scholars. It provides not only useful information but also helps to organize a diverse array of significant topics and concepts in a sensible and logical manner. [R: LJ, Dec 03, p. 99; AG, Dec 03-Jan 04, p. 62]—**Timothy E. Sullivan**

C, P

60. **The Ultimate Business Dictionary: Defining the World of Work.** Cambridge, Mass., Perseus Books, 2003. 657p. $19.95pa. ISBN 0-7382-0821-3.

This dictionary with over 6,000 entries, while it serves as a supplement to *Business: The Ultimate Resource* (see entry 63), can also be used as a standalone dictionary. An international team of business information specialists contributed to the content of the book. The topics that are emphasized deal with e-commerce, economics, finance, banking and accounting, human relations, personnel, marketing, operations and production, and statistics. Each term also includes an abbreviation to indicate the topic where it is used most frequently. Some slang terms are included, such as "dead cat bounce," "cash cow," and "marzipan." There is also an indication if the term is non-U.S. based. Some of the definitions are fairly lengthy, while others are just a sentence or two. There are some very brief (50 words or less) biographical sketches of well-known management gurus. An interesting feature is the multilingual glossary that follows the dictionary, which includes all of the words from the dictionary and renders them in Chinese, French, German, Spanish, Latin American Spanish, and Japanese words. There is a 20-page section on "Facts and Figures" that might be of some limited use for a short period of time. At the bottom of each page (except for the "Facts and Figures" section) there is a business quotation.

The selection of terms reflects current usage and for this modest price this work should be acquired for all libraries that have business materials. Users do get the added bonus of the multilingual dictionary. Users can also register at their site for free and receive monthly newsletters on management topics that could be used to keep their Web page current.—**Judith J. Field**

Directories

C, P

61.   **Business and Company Resource Center. http://www.gale.com.** [Website]. Farmington Hills, Mich., Gale. Price negotiated by site. Date reviewed: Dec 03.

Gale's *Business and Company Resource Center* is a company directory, an industry directory, a business reference database, and an article index in a single interface. The addition of optional add-ons PROMT, Newsletters ASAP, and Investext Plus gives users the benefit of up to four different databases blended together in one searchable package.

The basic *Business and Company Resource Center* (BCRC) includes electronic access to the content of several must-have business reference sources, including: *Brands and Their Companies*, *Business Rankings Annual* (2000 through present), *Encyclopedia of American Industries*, *International Directory of Company Histories*, *Market Share Reporter*, and *Ward's Business Directory of U.S. Private and Public Companies*. The BCRC journal index includes 3,850 titles (2,823 of those are full-text), plus more than 1,500 images. The PROMT database adds another 566 periodical sources (394 full-text) and Newsletters ASAP contains 486 full-text sources. Investext Plus is a collection of full-text investment analyst reports from more than 1,100 contributors worldwide. Investext Plus offers unique multiple-perspective analyses from sources outside the company or industry under review, providing the researcher with balanced, unbiased evaluations and profiles.

The BCRC home page is simple and uncluttered, making navigation straightforward. The home page provides access to the three main components of the database: "Company," "Industry," and "Articles," plus an "Advanced Search" option. There are links to concise "Search Tips"; a "List of Sources" with product information; "Help" screens that include detailed database searching and navigation hints; and a description of the tools available in BCRC.

There is a basic search option on the home page with a drop-down menu from which the user can choose "Company Search," "Industry Description Search," or "Articles Search." This basic search is the one feature of BCRC that might be considered problematic. This option initiates a search within the BCRC subject headings, but that is not immediately clear and a user might assume a keyword search at this access point. Even more confusing is that, when no subject headings match the search terms, a keyword search is initiated. This can result in more focused, complex search strategies yielding a greater number of results than a broader search that was limited to only subject headings. After completing a search via this option, the search defaults back to "Company Search" and the search type must be reselected when modifying the search or entering new terms.

Selecting from the "Company," "Industry," "Articles," or "Advanced Search" options leads the user to a guided search with labeled search fields and a much better search experience. The user can select to search subject headings, keywords, company names, NAICS codes, or whatever options are available for the particular type of search. Article searches can be limited to peer-reviewed sources, full-text sources, type of publication, or title. Search results include tabs and links for navigating to related information. *Business and Company Resource Center* contains an almost overwhelming amount of business information, but Gale has done an excellent job of integrating multiple databases and providing the search capabilities to make that information accessible. [R: LJ, 15 April 03, p. 135]—**Polly D. Boruff-Jones**

C, P

62. **Hoover's Masterlist of U.S. Companies 2004.** Austin, Tex., Hoover's, 2003. 2v. index. $285.00/set. ISBN 1-57311-087-6. ISSN 1066-291X.

By now the Hoover's products are well known to all business researchers in their various iterations. This product provides brief capsule summaries for 10,050 companies, including both public companies traded on the various American stock exchanges and the largest U.S.-based, privately held companies. Additionally, *Masterlist* covers the largest mutual insurance companies, agriculture co-ops, foundations, universities, sports teams and leagues, not-for-profits, major subsidiaries, and major government-owned enterprises. Its intended audience is sales, marketing, and business development professionals, as well as, by extension, the information professionals who work with them.

Capsules provide standard contact information, names of officers, financials (sales, net income, market value), and number of employees for a five-year period. This data are accompanied by a one-paragraph overview of the company; its products and services; and various tidbits of information about the company's market position, future opportunities, leadership, history, or other interesting details. Although for the most part this is straight business writing, occasionally the contributors inject some personality into the descriptions, which can make for some pretty entertaining reading.

Alternative access points are provided by lists of top 500 companies by sales, by number of employees, by five-year sales growth, and by market value, as well as via indexes by industry, by headquarters location, and by stock exchange symbol. Which raises an interesting question: Does it make more sense to license access to the online Hoover's database, which provides multiple advanced searching options and combinations (i.e., more access points), or purchase this print version? The print directory is well done and reliable, the online resource more flexible and current. The libraries for whom this publication may be of interest—large public libraries, academic libraries supporting business programs, and corporate libraries—will need to consider the options within the context of their budgets and patron preferences.—**G. Kim Dority**

Handbooks and Yearbooks

C, P

63. **Business: The Ultimate Resource.** Cambridge, Mass., Perseus Books, 2002. 2172p. illus. index. $59.95. ISBN 0-7382-0242-8.

The subtitle makes the claim that this volume is the "ultimate" business resource. That is a lot to live up to, but the editors give it their best shot and pack a huge amount of information into its 2,172 pages. The result is a very interesting and useful compilation of short essays, how-to information, book summaries and subject bibliographies, biographical information, and reference information.

The body of the work is divided into 7 sections and authored by over 200 contributors. "Best Practice" consists of 2-page essays on management topics organized into 11 theme sections. Themes include "People/Culture," "Marketing," "Strategy/Competition," "Finance," "IT/Information Management,"

"Systems," "Structure," "Leadership," "Renewal/Growth," Productivity," and "Personal Effectiveness." Each section follows a standard format and bulleted points are highlighted in color. Each essay concludes with a "for more information" section. Most of the authors are consultants, but they also include respected business scholars such as Philip Kotler, Charles Handy, and Warren Bennis. The latter also serves on the publication's advisory board.

"Management Checklists and Actionlists" provides brief information on business activities and functions, from conducting a performance appraisal to calculating earnings per share and is organized by topic. "Business Thinkers and Management Giants" provides short biographical sketches for over 100 well-known business writers and business people, including Warren Buffet and Jack Welch. The work's "Management Library" section offers one-page summaries for 70 classic management books. The volume also includes a 200-page business dictionary, an almanac section providing country and economic information, and a bibliography of business information sources.

The scope of *Business: The Ultimate Resource* is very broad. The tradeoff is that the depth of coverage for the many topics included is relatively thin—as is the paper in this 2,000+ page single volume. It is obviously intended to function as a one-size-fits-all desktop business reference source, but libraries will find it useful too. For $59.95 (that works out to about 36 cents per page or $7.50 per pound) the book is a very good value and is recommended for all libraries serving clientele with business information needs.—**Gordon J. Aamot**

BUSINESS SERVICES AND INVESTMENT GUIDES

P
64.   **Morningstar Funds 500.** 2003 ed. Christine Benz and Scott Cooley, eds. Chicago, Morningstar, 2003. 606p. index. $39.95pa. ISBN 0-471-39971-X.

The *Morningstar Funds 500* annual sourcebook, now in its 2d edition, offers an analysis of the 500 best and most popular mutual funds on the market selected by the fund experts at Morningstar. Introductory material includes brief articles by Morningstar analysts such as "Year in Review," "Lessons from the Bear Market," "Great Funds for the Future," and a discussion of the latest revision to their methodology sector analysis. The main section of the book is devoted to one-page reports for each fund arranged in alphabetic order by fund name. Each stock fund report provides features such as composition information, growth and value measures, history, manager strategy, Morningstar category, Morningstar Rating™ and Morningstar's Take, operations, performance, portfolio manager profile, portfolio analysis, rating and risk, sector weightings, style box, and tax analysis. The bond fund reports include these unique sections: credit analysis, current investment style, yield, and expense ratio. A "User's Guide" at the back of the book provides definitions for terms used in the book. Tables and charts provide a performance summary using Morningstar's categories and lists of the leading and lagging funds, manager changes, and fund name changes. Summary pages provide risk and return data in a table format for all 500 funds divided into domestic equity, international equity, or fixed income funds. Two indexes by fund name and manager name complete the volume. Although detailed explanations are provided, this sourcebook may not be a first choice for brand new mutual fund investors. As a reference tool, it provides an impressive amount of information for a small investment.—**Colleen Seale**

P
65.   **Morningstar Stocks 500.** 2003 ed. Mark Sellers III, ed. Chicago, Morningstar, 2003. 570p. $39.95pa. ISBN 0-471-39966-3.

Morningstar, a global research investment firm, has been a source of investment information and stock analysis for nearly 20 years. The company's annual guide to 500 popular stocks is edited by Mark Sellers. Sellers also edits the newsletter *Morningstar StockInvestor.*

The "Report Pages" are the largest section of *Morningstar Stocks 500.* These are concise, one-page company profiles that feature analyst reviews of the strengths and weaknesses of a stock; estimates of fair value, indicating whether the stock is overvalued, undervalued, or fairly priced; "grades" for evaluating a company's growth, profitability, and financial health; and ratings for risk and long-term competitive advantage, as well as an overall rating for the stock. Company and management profiles; listings of major competitors; valuation ratios, such as price/earnings; and five years of financial history are also given. Specific definitions of data found in the "Report Pages" are available in a "User's Guide." An index and statistical tables are available in the beginning of the book.

Given the volatile nature of the stock market, investors should use the information in the "Report Pages" with caution. Company assessments are only valid as of the date the guide was published. Investors should emulate professional financial analysts, who continuously monitor their valuation models and change them as market conditions warrant, by obtaining the most current information available before making any investment decisions.

The most useful components of *Morningstar Stocks 500* are its insightful articles on how to invest in stocks. They will be of interest to any investor that wishes to discover how to use fair value estimates to make better investment decisions or wants to adopt Morningstar's stock assessment methods when evaluating their own investments.—**Elizabeth M. Mezick**

CONSUMER GUIDES

P
66.   **The Grey House Safety & Security Directory 2003.** Millerton, N.Y., Grey House Publishing, 2002. 2v. index. $225.00pa./set. ISBN 1-930956-71-1.

Formerly known as *Best's Safety and Security Directory* (Best Publishing), Grey House is the publisher of this 2003 edition. This two-volume set is an important resource for accessing OSHA regulations, self-inspection checklists, training articles on state-of-the-industry trends and programs, as well as buyers guides. Changes made in this new edition include organizing each volume into eight alphabetic chapters and alphabetizing the "Buyers' Guides" at the end of each chapter. Headers on each page and color-coded content tabs on the side of pages lead readers quickly to their selected section. A separate chapter on "Fall Protection" covers this important area with two new training articles, a checklist, and new commercial products. In total, 22 new and revised training articles detail information on newly patented protective fabrics and fall arrest equipment, new technologies to secure company records, innovative safety incentives, and how to train the trainers.

The accompanying, easy-to-use Website (www.safetydir.com) provides online access to downloadable .pdf files that managers can store in a laptop and print out on job sites. Six important indexes provide added access points: Geographical Index of Manufacturers and Distributors, Company Profile Index, Brand Name Index, Product Index, Index of Web Sites (of advertisers), and Index of Advertisers. Since the terrorist attacks September 11, 2001, safety and security have been in the forefront for U.S. citizens and businesses. Professionals and businesses will use this guide for OSHA regulations, training, and finding necessary supplies and services.—**Susan C. Awe**

FINANCE AND BANKING

Dictionaries and Encyclopedias

P

67.   **Encyclopedia of Retirement and Finance.** Louis A. Vitt, ed., with others. Westport, Conn., Greenwood Press, 2003. 2v. index. $149.95/set. ISBN 0-313-32495-6.

This *Encyclopedia*, whose 1st edition was published in 1996, is a multidisciplinary, authoritative, and comprehensive mosaic of financial topics, vehicles, services, advisors, costs, structures, programs, institutions, products, investments, issues, and social policies that impact nearly every aspect of people's everyday lives. It represents an ambitious joint effort by scholars and practitioners, with almost 200 contributors, 2 consulting editors, 7 associate editors, and 2 managing editors. The editor in chief is the Director of the Institute for Socio-Financial Studies in Middleburg, Virginia. A list of more than 160 core topics is found in the prefatory part of both volumes, and 4 appendixes on "Chronological Summary of Post-ERISA (Employee Retirement Income Security Act of 1974) Benefit Legislation," "Major Post-ERISA Benefit Legislation," "Organization and Resources," and "Types of Benefits by Tax Treatment and Function" precede the index. In more than 800 pages of text the articles provide references to sources and in some cases offer suggested readings and names of pertinent organizations. They are clear, readable, and contain among other things statistical and institutional information. The *Encyclopedia* is recommended for all public libraries and for educational institutions with programs in social services, gerontology, and financial planning.—**Bogdan Mieczkowski**

Directories

P

68.   **The Directory of Venture Capital & Private Equity Firms, 2003: Domestic & International.** 7th ed. Millerton, N.Y., Grey House Publishing, 2003. 1024p. index. $450.00pa.; $889.00 (online database). ISBN 1-930956-77-0.

P

69.   **The Directory of Venture Capital & Private Equity Firms. http://www.greyhouse.com.** [Website]. Millerton, N.Y., Grey House Publishing. $450.00pa.; $889.00 (online database). ISBN 1-930956-77-0. Date reviewed: April 03.

Despite the decline of the stock market and less fevered investment climate, the 7th edition of this well-made directory has increased in size to slightly over 3,200 entries. Some 1,549 are domestic and 1,843 are international firms, with most of the increase due to the increased number of private equity firms. Its simple purpose is to provide a list of investment or venture capital sources. In that regard, it succeeds admirably. Entries are in alphabetic order and offer name, address, telephone and fax numbers, Website, key executives (including degrees and college attended), fund size, average and minimum investment, founding date, investment criteria (such as funding for seed, bridge, expansion of selected firms), geographic preference, industry group preference, key executives, mission statement, and companies in their portfolio. Five detailed indexes give excellent access, covering executives, colleges and universities attended (useful for alumni and fundraising), geographic, industry preferences, and an alphabetic list of all companies in portfolios. Data are updated by research in daily newspapers, print manuals, fax, telephone,

Internet, newsletters, and the business press. It is updated every two years and an annual version is available online for $889. It lists almost double the number of firms of its main competitor, *Pratt's Guide to Venture Capital Sources*, an annual which costs hundreds more. *Pratt's* has been published for more than two decades and is better known, however. *Pratt's* is also available online and has many short essays on the state of venture capital. *The Directory of Venture Capital & Private Equity Firms* is a better value for most libraries than *Pratt's* and is strongly recommended by libraries needing a list of venture capital firms.—**Patrick J. Brunet**

INDUSTRY AND MANUFACTURING

Handbooks and Yearbooks

C, P

70.   **Plunkett's Airline, Hotel & Travel Industry Almanac.** Jack W. Plunkett, ed. Houston, Tex., Plunkett Research, 2002. 436p. index. $249.99pa. (w/CD-ROM). ISBN 1-891775-74-X.

This 1st edition of *Plunkett's Airline, Hotel & Travel Industry Almanac* provides an overview of the travel and hotel industry and the key players. It is intended to be a general guide and offers many easy-to-use charts and tables. A CD-ROM version accompanies the volume.

Chapter 1 describes the major trends affecting the industry, and also includes "Internet Research Tips." Chapter 2 provides travel statistics from trustful sources such as the World Tourism Organization, trade associations, and government sources. Chapter 3 offers industry contacts, such as associations, publications, and various information sources related to the industry. Chapter 4, "The Travel 300," is the core of this publication, and includes ranking charts and leading company's profiles. There are four different indexes for this chapter. Each profile includes the following: company name; Website address; ranks; types of business; brands/divisions/affiliations; names and positions of top officers; address; telephone and fax numbers; brief financials; executive salaries; benefits; competitive advantage; number of apparent women officers; growth plans; and office locations. There are two additional indexes at the end of the publications: Index of Hot Spots for Advancement for Women/Minorities; and Index by Subsidiaries, Brand Names and Selected Affiliations. The glossary at the beginning the publication is brief.

This almanac seems especially useful for market research, strategic planning, and job hunting. The inclusion criteria of chapter 4, "The Travel 300," are not clear and the information provided is not in depth, but the volume provides a good overview of the travel industry. This resource is recommended for business reference collections.—**Mihoko Hosoi**

C, P

71.   **Plunkett's Biotech & Genetics Industry Almanac 2003-2004.** Jack W. Plunkett, ed. Houston, Tex., Plunkett Research, 2003. 523p. index. $249.99pa. (w/CD-ROM). ISBN 1-891775-28-6.

Plunkett's Biotech & Genetics Industry Almanac 2003-2004 is one more example of the fine publications offered by Plunkett Research. This reference book is particularly timely given the considerable interest in biotechnology and genetics from scientific, investment, and entrepreneurial audiences. Although primarily a detailed directory of companies in this industry, the *Almanac* has many additional features that provide an overview to both the financial and research sides of biotechnology, including genomics, proteomics, biopharmaceuticals, business development, and commercialization. With coverage of the 400 major firms in the sector, the *Almanac* presents a comprehensive source for researchers and the general reader.

There are many special features at the beginning of the *Almanac*. The volume begins with a glossary of commonly used biotechnology and genetics terms. There is a short introduction to the volume that explains some of its special features and the methodology that was used in compiling information. This is followed by a guide to using the book, with details on how to read the individual company listings. Chapter 1 provides an overview of 15 trends affecting the biotechnology and genetics industry that is interesting and well written, while chapter 2 offers a generous number of charts and graphs with statistics on the industry. Chapter 3 lists important industry contacts, including associations, publications, and investment companies and databases, which include mailing address, fax and telephone numbers, Web address, and a brief description. Finally, chapter 4 provides specific information on the 400 companies, including rankings, NAIC codes, and alphabetic and geographic indexes. These indexes are complemented by indexes of firms that are noted for advancing women and minorities, and a comprehensive index of subsidiaries, brand names, and affiliations, which are located at the end of the volume.

Individual company entries comprise the bulk of the *Almanac* and are in Plunkett's usual format of easy-to-use boxes and tables. Even though the amount of information for each entry is considerable, entries are attractively presented and easy to use. There are individual boxes for type of business, brands, divisions and affiliates, top officers, and contact information. A shaded box on the right side of the page provides a concise description of the company. Reading just a few of these company descriptions provides an appreciation for the complexity of the work they do, the amount of technology transfer with government and university-sponsored research, and the fast-changing nature of the industry as a whole. Boxes at the top of the page indicate business activities, which are divided into five categories and rankings. The bottom section of the entries contains financial information, stock ticker, number of employees, and fiscal year date. Another box provides information on salaries and benefits, with additional boxes on the company's competitive advantage, location, and ratings for the company's opportunities for women and minorities. Entries have been artfully designed to provide a considerable amount of detail that is still easy to find and that does not overwhelm the reader.

In addition to the two indexes mentioned in the back of the volume, the *Almanac* also has an appendix on research techniques, along with illustrations of various elements that are significant in research, such as DNA, protein, and adenovirus. These illustrations are beautifully done and are particularly helpful in understanding the kinds of research that is done by the companies featured in the *Almanac*.

Plunkett's Biotech & Genetics Industry Almanac 2003-2004 will be an excellent reference source for nearly any kind of library. Certainly it is appropriate for academic and health sciences libraries, along with corporate libraries that support companies either working in or investing in the biotechnology and genetics industry. Finally, many public libraries may find that this book is a useful volume for patrons interested in either the scientific or the investment side of this industry.—**Sara Anne Hook**

C, P

72. **Plunkett's E-Commerce & Internet Business Almanac 2003-2004.** Jack W. Plunkett, ed. Houston, Tex., Plunkett Research, 2003. 516p. index. $249.99pa. (w/CD-ROM). ISBN 1-891775-58-8.

Plunkett's E-Commerce & Internet Business Almanac is a comprehensive directory and guide to the industry. It is arranged within sections: "The E-Commerce and Internet Industry," an overview of trends (including statistics), a glossary, and a directory of industry contacts including government agencies and industry associations; and the "E-Commerce 400," the directory section of companies. The "E-Commerce and Internet Industry" overview section, other than its narrative of current trends as projections, includes statistics and results of surveys by agencies including Pew Internet and American Life Project Tracking and Nielsen/NetRatings. Among statistical and survey results tables in this section are: "Leading U.S. Internet Providers" (by number of subscribers); "Broadband Access Speeds Compared to Dial-up"; "Average Web Usage at Home"; and "What Internet Users Fear."

The directory section, the "E-Commerce 400" (although only 393 companies are covered), provides information concerning "the largest, most successful, fastest growing firms in e-commerce and related industries in the world." Companies selected must meet the following criteria: U.S. based for profit corporations (also added were 24 foreign-based companies); publicly held companies (although a number of privately held firms were added to "round-out certain niche sets of companies") ; prominence or a significant presence in the industry; and financial data regarding companies must have been available (either from company itself or other sources). Companies did not have to be exclusively in e-commerce and Internet fields. Each company listing provides: Website address; mailing address; telephone number; industry group code (based on NAIC code); type of business; officers; financials; growth plans/special features; locations; and brands/divisions/affiliates. In addition to the directory section, companies are indexed alphabetically by location, by industry group, and by firms with international affiliates. Additionally, there are two additional special indexes: one of firms noted as hot spots for advancement for women and minorities and the other of subsidiaries, brand names, and affiliations.

Plunkett's E-Commerce & Internet Business Almanac is an excellent and thorough source on the industry. It is especially recommended to academic library collections and larger public libraries.—**Lucy Heckman**

C, P

73.   **Plunkett's InfoTech Industry Almanac 2003.** 4th ed. Jack W. Plunkett, ed. Houston, Tex., Plunkett Research, 2003. 646p. index. $229.99pa. (w/CD-ROM). ISBN 1-891775-57-X.

The Plunkett series of directories are well known for providing company and industry information on clearly defined subject areas. The 4th edition of this book on the InfoTech industry focuses on information technology that moves or manages voice, data, or video, whether the mode is wireless, Internet, satellite, fiber optics, traditional copper wire telephony, computer network, or emerging technology. Companies that manufacture or provide products or services in these fields, including relevant computer hardware and software, are included. The layout of the company profile page is similar to that used in the Hoover's company directories. Each one-page company profile includes a rank by industry group code and within the company's industry group; types of business, brands, divisions, and affiliations; contact information of up to 27 top officers; the company's address; annual sales and profits figures for the latest fiscal year; number of employees; some indication of salaries of the top executive and what fringe benefits are available to employees; and a statement of the company's competitive advantage. Some companies will be noted for providing advancement opportunities for women and minorities.

In addition to the profiles of 500 companies, the user will find such information as: a glossary of terms; a discussion of the15 major trends facing the InfoTech industry; 17 industry statistical tables; a list of related associations, government agencies, and Websites; an index of companies noted for advancement of women and minorities; and an index listing subsidiaries and brand names. This material comprises just over 20 percent of the book.

The combination of company profiles and the material related to the industry makes this a very useful acquisition for libraries since information on many of the companies included are not readily available in other sources. The industry information provides a framework in which to locate additional material at a later time. The publisher provides a free CD-ROM of the corporate profiles, enabling a user to export data for such activities as a mail merge.—**Judith J. Field**

C, P

74.   **Plunkett's Real Estate & Construction Industry Almanac.** Jack W. Plunkett, ed. Houston, Tex., Plunkett Research, 2003. 528p. index. $249.99pa. (w/CD-ROM). ISBN 1-593920-03-2.

This first edition of *Plunkett's Real Estate & Construction Industry Almanac* provides an overview of the real estate and construction industry and the key players. It is intended to be a general guide and offers many easy-to-use charts and tables. A CD-ROM version accompanies the volume.

Chapter 1 describes the state of the industry and the major trends affecting the industry. Chapter 2 provides statistics from trade associations and government sources. Chapter 3 offers information on the industry contacts, such as government agencies, associations, publications, job-hunting resources, and various information sources related to the industry. Chapter 4, "The Real Estate 400," is the core of this publication, and includes ranking charts and leading companies' profiles. There are five different indexes for this chapter. Each profile includes the following: company name; ranks; business activities; types of business; brands/divisions/affiliations; names and positions of top officers; address; telephone number; fax number; Website address; financials; salaries/benefits; competitive advantage; number of apparent women officers; growth plans; and office locations. There are two additional indexes at the end of the publication: "Index of Firms Noted as Hot Spots for Advancement for Women/Minorities" and "Index by Subsidiaries, Brand Names and Selected Affiliations." The 12-page glossary at the beginning of the publication covers basic industry terminology.

This almanac seems especially useful for market research and job hunting. The inclusion criteria of chapter 4 are not clear and the information provided is not in depth, but the volume provides a good overview of the real estate and construction industry. This directory is recommended for business reference collections.—**Mihoko Hosoi**

INTERNATIONAL BUSINESS

General Works

Directories

C, P

75.   **International Business and Trade Directories: A Worldwide Directory of Directories and Other Print & Electronic Resources.** 3d ed. Millerton, N.Y., Grey House Publishing, 2003. 888p. index. $225.00pa. ISBN 1-930956-63-0.

C, P

76.   **International Business and Trade Directories. http://www.greyhouse.com.** [Website]. Millerton, N.Y., Grey House Publishing. $225.00pa.; $450.00 (online database). Date reviewed: Sept 03.

The 3d edition of this established reference work (2d ed., see ARBA 99, entry 141; and 1st ed., see ARBA 96, entry 228) increases its coverage to nearly 7,000 directories published in over 150 countries worldwide. The directory listings are arranged by industry (nearly 80 industries are covered), then alphabetically by region and country. The directory listings generally contain contact information, including: address; telephone, fax, and toll-free numbers; editor; e-mail and Website addresses; and a brief description of the work. Circulation, pagination, frequency of publication, and ISSN numbers are also provided for many titles. Separate indexes for title, country or region, and publisher follow the numbered entries. Selected special directory issues of business and trade magazines are also included. In terms of coverage, this directory falls between the smaller *Trade Directories of the World* (Croner Publications, Inc.) and the larger *Directories in Print* (21st ed.; see ARBA 2003, entry 45). The directory information is also available as an electronic database and as customized mailing lists. While the title of this 3d edition emphasizes the inclusion of electronic resources, coverage of these resources is somewhat limited and not unique.—**Colleen Seale**

Handbooks and Yearbooks

C, P

77.   **Trade and Development Report, 2003.** By the Secretariat of the United Nations Conference on Trade and Development. New York, United Nations, 2003. 154p. $39.00pa. ISBN 92-1-112579-0. ISSN 0255-4607. S/N E.03.II.D.7.

This is an annual report by UNCTAD, released in early October 2003, that analyzes the recent performance of the world economy and extent of international trade with special attention to the less-well-off countries in the world. The first part in looking at the performance and prospects of the world economy notes in particular the weaknesses in developed countries' economies and the disparities in growth rates in developing countries and transition economies. A discussion of relevant financial and trade flows between regions and changes in patterns are also in this section. Part 2 concentrates on capital accumulation, economic growth, and structural change. This is done with the knowledge that many countries, especially in Latin America, have undertaken serious economic reform measures but have not yet seen consistently the desired rates of growth or poverty reduction. Industrialization and competitiveness are important concerns. Understanding results of policies can help clarify better policy options for the future. While much of the discussion is done regionally, some individual country data and experiences are noted. This is a good source of data and analysis on recent interaction between the wealthier and less-well-off countries in the world. It included notes and references that can be useful to the reader.—**J. E. Weaver**

C, P

78.   **World Economic and Social Survey 2002: Trends and Policies in the World Economy.** By the Department of Economic and Social Affairs. New York, United Nations, 2002. 325p. $55.00pa. ISBN 92-1-109140-3. S/N E.02.II.C.1.

An annual, published by the United Nations, this volume looks at the state of the world economy in 2002 in the first part and public/private interaction in achieving society's goals in the second part. The world economy experienced a severe slowdown in 2001. This volume discusses its synchronicity across countries, especially the major developed ones. Many developing countries were hurt by the contraction of international trade, the decline of primary commodity prices, and the reduction of capital inflows. The survey also discusses the prospects for recovery and what might derail it. The second part looks at the role of the state in the provision of some goods and services and how this role can be altered by involving the private sector in some areas. There are chapters on privatization, electrical utility reform, agricultural technology, health service delivery, and education. There is an annex of statistical tables and notes and explanations of sources are provided. This is a good source for people who want to lean more about what happened in the world economy and what changes are being considered.—**J. E. Weaver**

LABOR

General Works

Dictionaries and Encyclopedias

C, P

79.   **Dictionary of Occupational Titles with O*NET Definitions.** 5th ed. Baton Rouge, La., Claitor's Publishing Division, 2003. 3v. index. $125.00pa./set. ISBN 1-57980-871-9.

C, P

80.   **O*NET Online. http://online.onetcenter.org/.** [Website]. Free. Date reviewed: Oct 03.

O*NET Online (http://online.onetcenter.org/) is the *Occupational Information Network*, an Internet database of worker attributes and job characteristics. Created by the U.S. Department of Labor's Employment and Training Administration, it replaces the *Dictionary of Occupational Titles*. The database currently contains data developed by job analysts who evaluate the skill requirements of thousands of jobs. It will be supplemented in the future by information from the workers themselves describing the work they do and the skills and knowledge needed for their work. Employers, researchers, career counselors, and job-seekers use the database. The O*NET classification system is used by public employment service centers to classify openings and for job placement. The O*NET codes are keyed to the latest Standard Occupational Classification (SOC) codes adopted by the Bureau of Labor Statistics in 1998.

The *Dictionary* has a brief introduction explaining how to use it. Table I is an alphabetic listing of O*NET-SOC Titles that cross-reference the numerical O*NET-SOC codes. For example, Real Estate Sales Agents are classified in 41-9021.00. Looking up that number in Table II: O*NET Definitions, reveals detailed descriptions of the tasks, knowledge, skills, abilities, work activities, and work context of real estate agents. One of five "Job Zones" is also provided, which gives occupations with similar experience, education, and training requirements. An SVP (Specific Vocational Preparation Level) is assigned. The entries conclude with an evaluation of the interests, work values, and work needs characteristics of the occupation. Related O*NET-SOC codes and titles are listed. Readers are referred to the O*NET database, which provides links to *America's Career InfoNet* (http://www.acinet.org/) to find average pay scales and other information for occupations by state.

Additional tables provide cross-references from O*NET-SOC numbers to titles and alternative occupational titles—a feature called "Crosswalk" that relates the codes in the 5th edition to those in use in the 4th edition. And the entire 4th revised edition of the *Dictionary of Occupational Titles*, first published in 1991, is reprinted in volume III. Although the career information is available for free online, this print directory serves as a useful index and reference to the numerical codes and career descriptions as well as providing cross-reference capability.—**Peter Zachary McKay**

C, P

81.   **St. James Encyclopedia of Labor History Worldwide: Major Events in Labor History and Their Impact.** Neil Schlager, ed. Farmington Hills, Mich., St. James Press/Gale Group, 2004. 2v. illus. index. $260.00/set. ISBN 1-55862-542-9.

This is a well-prepared reference to events in labor history, mostly in the United States and Europe between the years 1800 and 2000. It is organized into 2 volumes containing 300 "events." Each event is presented in synopsis form, with text, time horizon, key players, and references for additional readings. There are also an introduction and two essays, one on the United States' and the other on international labor history. The events are presented in an alphabetical as well as in a chronological order. There is also a general chronology of labor history of the period. A bibliography and an index end the second volume. The text of each event is clear and detailed enough to be of help to the student of labor history. However, it is somewhat misleading to describe these volumes as an "Encyclopedia of Labor History Worldwide." It is more like an encyclopedia of the selected events or labor movements. It falls short of being a history of labor in the United States or Europe, let alone the rest of the world. There are many significant omissions, such as the Histadrut (Jewish Federation of Labor in Palestine/Israel), which pioneered in the Middle East and played a major role in the creation of the state of Israel. It is mentioned only once in passing. Another omission is the labor movement in Scandinavia, which displayed pioneering features early in labor history. However, a history of labor must include not only movements and events, but also the absence of such movement. There is little on the developing world. The reader would have benefited from an essay on why there were no successful movement in the Third World, how did labor function, and under what conditions. Finally, reprinting the introduction and the two essays and including a general chronology add little to the quality of the *Encyclopedia*, while they increase the costs. Even so, this *Encyclopedia* will be most welcome for the excellent coverage and clear presentation of the selected events, and the ease of use that characterizes it.—**Elias H. Tuma**

Handbooks and Yearbooks

C, P

82.   **Occupational Outlook Handbook 2002-2003.** United States Department of Labor, comp. New York, VGM Career Books/McGraw-Hill, 2002. 639p. illus. index. $22.95; $18.95pa. ISBN 0-07-138720-X; 0-07-138721-8pa. ISSN 0082-9072.

This is the latest revision, done every two years, of the *Occupational Outlook Handbook* compiled by the United States Department of Labor. It describes the job duties, working conditions, training and educational requirements, earnings, and job prospects in hundreds of occupations that account for seven of every eight jobs in the U.S. economy. It is focused on the job outlook over a projected 10-year period. It does not address short-term labor market fluctuations or regional differences in job outlook. The vast majority of the handbook is information on specific occupations, such as landscape architect, gaming services occupations, and printing machine operators. It does also suggest where to find additional information on an occupation. The *Handbook* opens with a short, general discussion of labor market outlook for the United States. That is followed by a section that identifies sources of information about career planning, counseling, training, education, and financial aid. Then there is a brief article on finding a job and evaluating a job offer. This is a basic source of information and will be of considerable value to those considering different occupations and those who do career counseling.—**J. E. Weaver**

Career Guides

Dictionaries and Encyclopedias

S

83.   **Career Discovery Encyclopedia.** New York, Ferguson/Facts on File, 2003. 8v. illus. maps. index. $175.00/set. ISBN 0-8160-5469-X.

What makes this 8-volume set distinctive is how comprehensively it covers the world of work. Many such reference sets cover only fairly traditional and well-known professions. Here, over 650 jobs are described. There are high-end jobs requiring years of education (oceanographer), everyday jobs that few people think about (fiber optic technician), various nontraditional health professions (reflexologist), and quaint professions that people might think are no longer around (taxidermist). Also included are jobs that few people aspire to but many people will end up doing at least for a time (bartenders, fast-food workers, refuse collectors).

Careers are listed in alphabetic order (Accountant to Zoologist), with a two-page entry for each one. Each entry describes what people in the profession do, what education and training is required, and what the outlook for the career is in the future, such as whether it is in decline or growing at an average or faster than average rate. The text discusses the negative as well as positive aspects of jobs, listing such things as physical discomforts, stress levels, and fierce competition for jobs in some industries. Realistic salary levels are given for every job as well as school subjects recommended and personal skills required. Much of this information is included in an easy-to-understand chart for every career, which also refers the reader to articles about related careers. Each entry also lists several sources of more information—usually professional societies, government licensing agencies, or schools with unique programs.

The reading level is appropriate for middle school, but not too simplistic for high school or even college students trying to choose a major. Overall, this is an excellent and valuable resource for all levels. [R: SLJ, Dec 03, p. 94]—**Carol L. Noll**

Directories

C, P

84.   Crispin, Gerry, and Mark Mehler. **CareerXRoads: The 2003 Directory to Job, Resume, and Career Management Sites on the Web.** Kendall Park, N.Y., MMC Group, 2003. 456p. index. $26.95pa. ISBN 0-9652239-8-1. ISSN 1088-4629.

The 8th edition of *CareerXRoads* is a comprehensive source for the job searcher or recruiter who wants the most complete and up-to-date view of job-hunting through the Internet. The authors, whose biographies indicate a considerable amount of experience in human resources, began collaborating in 1990 and have a passion for Internet recruitment that is evident in the careful preparation of the volume. There are so many books available on job-hunting that it is difficult to know which ones to include in a library's collection. However, *CareerXRoads* fills an important niche by offering extensive "real world" coverage of the fast-changing world of online job searching and recruiting.

The first few pages of *CareerXRoads* provide a detailed description of how to use the volume, including a sample entry indicating where each piece of information in the entry is located. The volume includes a disclosure statement that explains the authors' methodology for selecting and ranking sites for inclusion in *CareerXRoads*. The first 100 pages of the volume are devoted to chapters on designing corporate staffing sites, which will be helpful for employers, career resources, creating Web-compatible résumés, workforce planning, insights on the behavior of those who search for jobs through the Internet, and important skills for recruiters and employees to have in order to attract and retain quality candidates. These chapters are well written and contain a considerable amount of practical and timely information.

The bulk of the volume is devoted to reviews of what the authors consider the 500 best Websites for job searching and recruiting, with 50 of these Websites deemed the "best of the best." In ranking the sites, the authors looked at ease of access, value of the contents, navigation, business model, real-world marketing strategy, and technology. A typical entry for the Websites listed in *CareerXRoads* is half a page in length. The site name, the URL, and contact information (including postal address, telephone and fax numbers, and e-mail address) are provided at the top of the entry. Each entry has a graphics box that notes whether the posting of open positions and résumés is permitted, whether there is a fee or if this service is free, and how many open positions and résumés are available. This is useful information, particularly for job searchers who can use the ratios of positions to résumés to gauge competition and likelihood of success through using the site.

Additional information includes discipline, location, whether an educational degree or special skills are needed for most of the positions on the site, and whether there is an agent who will push jobs or résumés to a PC. There is a brief description of the site, which provides content, terms of use, price, and evaluative comments about the design and ease of use of the sites. For the top 50 sites, entries are given an entire page in *CareerXRoads*. Although the graphics box is the same as for the other entries, the description of the site is more generous. The bottom half of the page actually shows the main page of the Websites. The layout of the entries in *CareerXRoads* is clear, attractive, and easy to read, and the descriptions of the sites are concise and useful. Interspersed throughout this section of the volume are boxes with helpful tips for job searchers and recruiters.

There are several lists provided in the cross-referenced index at the end of the volume. First, there is a master list of over 2,500 job and résumé sites with their URLs. The sites in bold typeface are among the 500 best sites and are reviewed extensively in the volume and those with a "T" are considered among the top 50 sites. Additional lists are for association sites; the "best of the best" sites; sites for career management resources, colleges, corporation staffing pages taken from *Fortune Magazine*'s annual Fortune 500 list for 2002 with ratings from the authors; and sites that promote diversity. There is also a list of sites where résumés and jobs can be posted, with an indication of whether this is a free service or if there is a fee, a list of sites by geographic location, and a list of sites by specialty and industry. Several of these lists do not include URLs, so the reader will have to search for the site.

CareerXRoads will be an excellent addition to any library collection. Public libraries and academic libraries will be particularly interested in this volume, but corporate and special libraries whose organizations are engaged in ongoing recruitment efforts will also find this useful to have on hand.—**Sara Anne Hook**

C, P

85.   Segal, Nina, and Eric Kocher. **International Jobs: Where They Are, How to Get Them.** 6th ed. Cambridge, Mass., Perseus Books, 2003. 354p. index. $19.95pa. ISBN 0-7382-0746-2.

International Jobs: Where They Are, How To Get Them is a comprehensive, useful, and inspiring resource for anyone with an interest in working in the international arena, either in positions here in the United States or overseas. The book presents a broad overview of the many employment sectors and specialty fields where international positions can be found and provides detailed information on potential employers in for-profit, nonprofit, and government agencies and organizations. The information presented in *International Jobs* is practical and presents the reality of the international job market, while at the same time tempting readers with a fascinating array of career possibilities and work assignments. This is the 6th edition of *International Jobs*, which was first published in 1984, and it has been updated to include new hiring procedures, trends for each field, revised sections on banking and consulting, new Websites, and a chapter on nongovernmental organizations. The author has been a career consultant for the United Nations Secretariat, the Ford Foundation, and the United Negro College Fund and has worked in recruitment and career services in for-profit and academic settings.

The organization of *International Jobs* makes it a particularly easy volume to use. It is divided into two main sections, with part 1 providing an introduction to international career development and part 2 offering a detailed description of the individual facets of the international job market. Within part 1, chapters 1-3 include a wealth of information on career planning, occupational research, graduate schools, joint degrees, conducting an overseas job search, résumés, and interviewing techniques. This information is supplemented with listings for graduate schools, Websites for occupational research, sample résumés and letters, and information on student exchange programs.

Part 2 of *International Jobs* is divided into 7 chapters, covering job opportunities in the federal government, the United Nations and related organizations, international banking and business, nonprofit organizations, international communications, teaching abroad, and international law. Each chapter provides an overview of the employment sector and some practical advice on career preparation, then includes a generous number of potential employers in that sector, including address, telephone number, URL, and a description that includes the focus and projects of the potential employer and the kinds of job openings that might be available. These descriptions present the reality of job opportunities for employers. While the information is usually hopeful, it may also seem harsh to readers who lack the necessary educational credentials, work experience, or other application criteria. This is one of the great strengths of the book; readers are given an accurate picture of the job market in a particular field rather than a rosy but unrealistic view. In addition, these chapters include numerous testimonials from people working in an international setting and their career preparation. *International Jobs* also includes a list of recommended readings and an index. Although many readers may think that the volume only covers jobs overseas, *International Jobs* includes many ideas for jobs and employers located in the United States but where the focus of the work is at the international level. *International Jobs* is an attractive volume and will give readers a clear view of the preparation, planning, investment, and commitment needed to pursue a career with an international component.

This work would be an excellent addition to nearly every library collection, particularly those libraries that serve a clientele likely to be interested in career planning and job searching. It would also be useful for readers who are contemplating a new direction in the middle of their careers or who want to explore opportunities for volunteer work with international organizations and agencies.—**Sara Anne Hook**

Handbooks and Yearbooks

P, S

86.   Echaore-McDavid, Susan. **Career Opportunities in Science.** New York, Facts on File, 2003. 306p. index. $49.50. ISBN 0-8160-4905-X.

In this volume, details are provided for a wide variety of science and mathematics careers. *Career Opportunities in Science* provides basic information for over 82 different professions, presented in a format similar to *Occupational Outlook* (GPO). Arranged by 13 broad classifications, such as "Biological Sciences," "Mathematics," and "Medical Science," each section describes 4 to 12 professions within that classification.

Each entry includes a "Career Profile," which is a summary of basic information about the career. A "Career Ladder" offers a visual representation of a typical career path. Following this introductory information is a more detailed analysis of the profession, beginning with a description that details major responsibilities and duties as well as options available within a profession. Other information includes salary ranges; employment prospects; education and training; experience, skills, and desirable personality traits; unions and associations; and tips for entry into the profession. (For example, what can you do while still in high school to begin preparing yourself for this profession?) Each entry covers approximately three pages. Each section of an entry is set off with bold headings. Guide words at the top of each page indicate the broad area under which the profession is classified.

Six appendixes provide additional resources, such as Internet sources for education and training programs, contact information and Website addresses for professional organizations, Websites for many of the professions described in the book, a glossary, and a bibliography of scientific and technical periodicals and books that will help the reader learn more about science and science careers. There is also a comprehensive index.

Students interested in science and mathematics will find this career guide extremely useful. It will enable them to explore a wide range of options within their primary field of interest. The information provided about each career is realistic and current.—**Dana McDougald**

P

87.   Farr, Michael, and LaVerne L. Ludden, with Laurence Shatkin. **300 Best Jobs Without a Four-Year Degree.** Indianapolis, Ind., JIST Works, 2003. 449p. $16.95pa. ISBN 1-56370-861-2.

This unique approach is directed to the job-seeker without an academic degree looking to identify targets for their job search. From a pool of 605 occupations, 300 were selected on the basis of high annual earning, rapid growth rate, and a large number of job openings per year. These are then identified from a number of perspectives. One-fourth of this volume is composed of lists of occupations from those perspectives. Some 34 lists include "best jobs" for women, men, part-time workers, self-employed workers, and those of various age ranges (including over 55). Even more useful are 26 lists by education levels, work experience, specialized training, interest areas, and Holland personality types. The remainder of the guide describes the identified 300 positions, required skills and education, the training that may be required or useful, and profiles the personality types best suited for the position.

This resource is highly desirable for career organizations and practices serving clientele with specific needs for income and opportunities. The aspects of individual interests and personality type adds a useful dimension that might otherwise be lost from a list-oriented resource. Unfortunately, no explanation of Holland's configuration of types is offered to enable readers to identify their types within a context of understanding.—**Barbara Conroy**

C, P

88.   Farr, Michael, and LaVerne L. Ludden, with Laurence Shatkin. **200 Best Jobs for College Gradu-ates.** Indianapolis, Ind., JIST Works, 2003. 450p. (Best Jobs Series). $16.95pa. ISBN 1-56370-855-8.

The authors indicate a number of possible uses for this book: to identify specific jobs, make long-term employment plans, select a college major or other training, get reliable salary information, and prepare for interviews. The information in this book was collected from the U.S. Department of Labor, the U.S. Census Bureau, and the U.S. Department of Education. The Department of Labor O*NET database provided much of the descriptive material for specific jobs. *The Guide for Occupational Exploration* (3d ed.; see ARBA 2002, entry 219) provided the designations for areas of interest, work group, and related job titles.

The book is divided into two parts. Part 1 consists of more than 50 lists of jobs, based on specific criteria. The first list is "Best Jobs Overall." These jobs were selected because they require at least an associate's degree and they have a combination of high pay, fast growth, and a large number of job openings. The jobs are scored and ranked, with those receiving the highest ranking at the top of the list. Other lists include best jobs for workers in specific categories (age, sex, full/part-time work); best jobs for workers with specific levels of education; best jobs for workers with specific personality types; and best jobs for workers with specific areas of interest (art, plants, transportation, and so on). Each list gives the job title, annual earnings, percent growth, and annual number of openings for that job.

Part 2 lists job titles in alphabetical order. Each listing includes a description of the work, skills needed, *Guide for Occupational Exploration* designations, education and training, related knowledge or courses needed, and personality type. A box summarizing educational requirements, growth predictions, number of job openings, percentage of workers who are self-employed, and percentage of workers who do this job part-time is also provided for quick reference.

This book will be helpful for job-seekers and those planning an educational strategy to get the appropriate training for a particular job. College graduates will find it useful to have jobs requiring lesser levels of education screened out, optimizing the utility of the remaining listings. This work is recommended.—**Joanna M. Burkhardt**

MANAGEMENT

C, P

89.   Applegate, Jane. **The Entrepreneur's Desk Reference: Authoritative Information, Ideas, and Solutions for Your Small Business.** New York, Bloomberg Press/W. W. Norton, 2003. 416p. index. $24.95. ISBN 1-57660-086-6.

Designed for entrepreneurs, present and future, Jane Applegate's *The Entrepreneur's Desk Reference* is a practical, informative guide to various aspects of running a business from financing to advertising. *The Entrepreneur's Desk Reference* is written in an A-Z format for quick reference, plus an index to help readers search for specific topics. The author has much expertise on the topic, being the founder and CEO of Small Business Television and SBTV.com as well as author of *201 Great Ideas for Your Small Business*.

Each entry includes a brief one-sentence definition and a description and analysis of several paragraphs. For instance, the entry for "telemarketing" contains a brief definition ("efficient means of enticing or annoying potential customers") plus a five-paragraph analysis of the pluses and minuses of using telemarketing for a small business. Some entries include tip boxes, presenting helpful hints to readers. For instance, within the "franchising" entry there is a tip boxes concerning how to choose a franchise and key questions regarding the franchise agreement. In addition to entries for terms used in small business, there are definitions of related legislation, including COBRA and Federal Insurance Contributions Act (FICA).

Applegate has also provided a "Resources" section, which includes a bibliography of books related to specific topics in small business such as business planning and finances and a directory of agencies, organizations, and services related to small businesses.

The Entrepreneur's Desk Reference is recommended to both public and academic library collections as well as on the bookshelves of entrepreneurs. It should prove valuable as a resource in academic libraries supporting a program of business administration.—**Lucy Heckman**

MARKETING AND TRADE

Dictionaries and Encyclopedias

C

90.   **Encyclopedia of Advertising.** John McDonough and Karen Egolf, eds. New York, Fitzroy Dearborn, 2003. 3v. illus. index. $385.00/set. ISBN 1-57958-172-2.

This important *Encyclopedia* is the most comprehensive reference work on advertising ever published. Until its publication much of the pertinent information about advertising agencies, major advertisers, the history of advertising, significant brand campaigns, international advertising, and other aspects has been widely scattered in books, journals, trade publications, and inaccessible archives. The *Encyclopedia* is a creative collaboration of the Museum of Broadcast Communications (http://www.museum.tv/index.shtml), *Advertising Age* (http://www.adage.com/), and the Hartman Center for Sales, Advertising and Marketing History at Duke University. Many of the rich illustrations that bring the work to life are from the Hartman Center's free Ad* Access database (http://scriptorium.lib.duke.edu/adaccess/). There are print images of more than 7,000 advertisements appearing in U.S. and Canadian newspapers and magazines between 1911 and 1955 presented in this set.

An opening essay by one of the editors discusses the need for the *Encyclopedia*, the scope of the work, and what influenced the decisions on what to include. Each volume has a handy list of entries in the front matter. Volume 3 has a comprehensive index, appendixes listing winners of the Advertising Hall of Fame Award, leading agencies, and the largest advertisers. Additional information on more than 200 contributors is provided.

The work itself consists of approximately 500 alphabetic entries covering advertising agency histories; major advertisers, brands, and markets; biographical portraits of the most influential leaders; and a mosaic of additional topics ranging from the history of advertising, to theories, methods, practices, demographic groups, and organizations. The scope of the work is international. There are substantial entries concerning advertising in Europe, Asia, Africa, and South America as well as individual countries on every continent. Separate entries chronicle the history of advertising before the nineteenth century, during the nineteenth century, from 1900-1920, then during each subsequent decade of the twentieth century. Major advertisers and major markets are discussed. For example, the U.S. automakers Ford, GM, and Chrysler are each featured, along with important foreign companies like Toyota, Volkswagen, and Volvo. Another entry covers the automobile industry as a whole. The biographies profile industry legends like Leo Burnett and David Ogilvy as well as more contemporary figures such as Charlotte Beers. The agency histories include the contemporary giants Omnicom and WPP as well as those who are historically important but which no longer exist such as N. W. Ayer & Sons. Famous brands like Alka-Seltzer, Bull Durham, and Ivory Soap have illustrated entries. The principal advertising industry associations and research companies merit inclusion as well.

Among the many topics covered are advertising to children, the portrayal of women in advertising, sex in advertising, and the impact of feminism. Key demographic groups include the youth market and seniors. Important concepts and research techniques are considered in articles on demographics, psychographics, and targeting. Military, political, religious, and negative advertising are all dealt with. Advertising in all of the major media including radio, television, newspapers, outdoor, and the Internet have separate entries devoted to them. All of the entries conclude with references to further reading. These references are a valuable bibliographic guide to the literature on advertising.—**Peter Zachary McKay**

Handbooks and Yearbooks

C, P

91.   **International Trade Statistics Yearbook, 2001. Annuaire Statistique du Commerce Interna-tional.** By the Department of Economic and Social Affairs, Statistics Division. New York, United Nations, 2002. 2v. $140.00/set. ISBN 92-1-061201-9. S/N E/F.03.XVII.2.

This two-volume statistical yearbook from the United Nations is the best source of international trade information available. Volume 1 contains 1,150-plus pages of tables with trade information from 179 countries or areas in both English and French. A major portion covers information on each country such as imports by principle countries, exports by principle countries, imports and exports by principle commodities of each country, imports by broad economic categories, and exports by industrial origin. In most cases, each of these categories covers the last five years. The manuscript also has a number of tables that explain how to use this volume as well as a 45-page index that gives further information. Volume 2 contains 600-plus pages. Tables are proceeded by information on how to use this series as well. This area is subdivided into commodity groups and under this, various principle countries or areas are subdivided. In both volumes, compression data for larger categories in countries are also available. Most of the data in volume 2 represents the last five consecutive years. The paper quality and binding are above average and the font size has been improved from previous editions in order to make the manuscript more readable. This is an essential addition to any library that is interested in international trade.—**Herbert W. Ockerman**

OFFICE PRACTICES

P

92.   **The Office Professional's Guide.** Erin McKean, ed. New York, Oxford University Press, 2003. 463p. index. $22.95. ISBN 0-19-516519-5.

Oxford University Press Senior Editor Erin McKean and her staff have put together a valuable resource for the modern workplace. Whether the user manages an office, performs accounting duties, or is responsible for developing presentations, this 463-page reference contains useful information.

The *Guide* consists of 14 chapters that deal with topics as diverse as technology and business ethics to English grammar and tactics for making international and domestic travel arrangements. Chapter 11 discusses effective meetings and parliamentary procedure. Chapter 13 devotes more than 20 pages to accounting principles. There are sections providing tips and strategies to interact with difficult co-workers as well as how to manage one's developing career.

The main thrust of the book, however, is to underscore the need for clear writing in business specifically, and the importance of clear written communication in general. In his foreword, Edward P. Bailey states that the *Guide* can make users aware of problems in their own writing; enable users to make better choices of words and sentence structures; and helps them to keep their audience in mind when writing. Other helpful sections are the appendixes. Appendix A consists of business terms in languages other than English, including German, French, Spanish, Russian, and Japanese. Appendix B is a glossary of business and finance terms. There is an eight-page bibliography followed by a four-page subject index.

New graduates, academic researchers, and corporate veterans will find this book useful for work or study. It is recommended for public libraries and academic ready-reference collections. [R: LJ, 15 June 03, p. 64]—**Laura J. Bender**

TAXATION

C

93.   Burg, David F. **A World History of Tax Rebellions: An Encyclopedia of Tax Rebels, Revolts, and Riots from Antiquity to the Present.** New York, Routledge/Taylor & Francis Group, 2004. 502p. index. $95.00. ISBN 0-415-92498-7.

Taxes are regarded, currently and over centuries past, as unwelcome, even onerous burdens by many of those required to pay them. At times, taxpayer discontent, particularly if taxes appeared to be unfair or oppressive, has led to rebellion. *A World of History of Tax Rebellions: An Encyclopedia of Rebels, Revolts, and Riots from Antiquity to the Present*, by David F. Burg, provides a broad chronology of examples of open discontent. Entries are presented in chronological order from 2350 B.C.E. to C.E. 2002. While most examples are profiled in a page or less, significant events are afforded several pages. Each entry is followed by a brief bibliography of primary sources. An extensive bibliography of broader scope is included in the later pages of the book. The author has not attempted to describe every revolt or rebellion against taxes that has ever occurred, but he has incorporated those that have had the greatest influence or that have attracted the most attention. Locating topics of particular interest in the text is facilitated by a table of contents, a chronological list of entries, a list of events by empire or nation, and a comprehensive index. An introduction provides continuity to the history of tax rebellion. Discussion of pertinent tax terms and strategies, as well as biographies of selected persons associated with tax rebellion, are included. The book will serve as a well-documented reference for those who are interested in the development and history of taxes, particularly of rebellions against taxes. It can also provide interesting and readable vignettes in tax history for more casual readers, who are likely to be taxpayers as well.—**William C. Struning**

5 Education

GENERAL WORKS

Dictionaries and Encyclopedias

C

94.   Guthrie, James W., ed. **Encyclopedia of Education.** 2d ed. New York, Macmillan Reference USA/Gale Group, 2003. 8v. index. $850.00/set. ISBN 0-02-865594-X.

Some 30 years since the 1st edition of this resource was published (1971) users now have a completely new and updated edition of the classic *Encyclopedia of Education.* Included in this 8-volume set are 857 articles on key educational concepts, theories, people, institutions, and organizations, with entries ranging from 500 to 5,000 words in length. The signed essays are accompanied by an extensive number of *see also* references, as well as a bibliography and list of relevant Internet Websites.

The essays fall within a very wide range of subject areas in education, including the foundations of education (e.g., history, philosophy, sociology, comparative education), educational psychology, curriculum and instruction, higher education, educational technology, educational policy, and teacher preparation, among others. There are an extensive number of entries on important educational associations, such as the American Association of School Administrators, the American Association of University Professors, the International Reading Association, the National Council of Teachers of Mathematics, and more. Similarly, there are 121 biographical entries on such historically important individuals as John Dewey, Jane Addams, Aristotle, St. Augustine, Alfred Binet, W. E. B Du Bois, Paulo Freire, Maria Montessori, Lawrence Kohlberg, Horace Mann, Jeanne Chall, Carter Woodson, Jean Piaget, and Mary Bethune.

The last volume includes primary source documents (covering court cases, legislation, and international agreements), a thematic outline of the encyclopedia's entries, a list of widely used standardized tests (with addresses, telephone numbers, and Web addresses for the publishers), a list of state departments of education (with Website addresses), a list of some education Websites, and a bibliography of "classic works" in education. Finally, there is a substantial combined index to names, subjects, and titles.

This is an important and much needed addition to the reference literature in education. The list of contributing authors is sprinkled with distinguished experts, and the writing is good throughout. Overall, this set is an essential purchase for academic libraries supporting teacher education. [R: LJ, 1 May 03, pp. 102-104]—**Stephen H. Aby**

C

95.   Leonard, David C. **Learning Theories A to Z.** Westport, Conn., Oryx Press/Greenwood Publishing Group, 2002. 249p. index. $63.95. ISBN 1-57356-413-3.

Given that a number of divergent and major discipline areas contribute to our understanding of learning theory, it is a wonder that a specialized dictionary on the topic has not been available previously. The psychology or education student will find this to be a handy and useful reference to the terminology of a large field of study. As the title suggests, approximately 500 terms relating to learning theory are presented in alphabetic order. All major theories are included and listed by theory name. Many related terms, including computer programs, training systems, or educational technology tools are also listed. The consequence of including technology terms such as digital library or Web-based training is that these terms will become dated while learning theories are more enduring. While some readers may find the inclusion of these terms distracting, their presence likely reflects both the influence of technology on education and the author's professional background in technology. A few related terms one would expect to find, such as "right brain/left brain" or the Perry Model, are not included.

Terms are linked to one of four categories within learning theory (cognitivism, constructivism, behaviorism, and humanism) or grouped with organizational learning or educational technology. Entries range from a short paragraph to one page. Most descriptions provide more than a definition and attempt to include a lot of information in a short space. Within descriptions, terms used elsewhere are italicized but no formal cross-reference is provided. A related terms or *see also* field at the bottom of each description would have been useful. A further enhancement would be to include notable individuals in the alphabetic listing. Many people search for information on theories using the name of the individual who developed the theory (i.e., Piaget, Vygotsky, and Skinner). While names of individual theoreticians are included in the index, many of these individuals should also have a separate entry, given individual search styles and the magnitude of the individual's contribution.

These are relatively minor criticisms. Undergraduate students in education, psychology, business, and many other disciplines will find this to be a useful source for terms and definitions. An annotated bibliography provides sources for more in-depth information and research.—**Lorraine Evans**

Directories

C, P

96. **Educational Opportunity Guide: A Directory of Programs for the Gifted.** 2003 ed. Durham, N.C., Duke University Talent Identification Program, 2003. 307p. index. $15.00pa. ISBN 0-9639756-9-2.

This directory, published by the Duke University Talent Identification Program (see ARBA 2002, entry 242, for a review of the 2001 edition), provides basic information on more than 400 programs for gifted students of all ages. "Programs" includes those conducted by schools, colleges and universities, and camps in the United States and abroad. No information is provided on how these programs are selected or solicited for inclusion. The guide includes a list of basic questions parents should consider in choosing a program for their children, a "Special Advertisement" section (an option for every program included in the main section), a listing of regional talent searches and cooperative programs, and programs held at multiple locations. The main section is arranged by state, with the state director and state association for gifted and talented and individual programs listed by the city in which they are located. Main entries include a brief description of the program, criteria for attendance, grade level, cost (including the possibility of financial aid), and contact information.

There are some errors within the guide, such as a wrong page reference from the Minnesota section to Northwestern University's Regional Talent Search, and a different telephone number for the Honors Symposium at Harding University listed in the main entry than is listed on their Website. More importantly, a major program in Indiana (the Indiana Academy for Science, Mathematics and Humanities located at Ball State University) is not even mentioned. It is impossible for publishers of guides to guarantee that their work is exhaustive, but information about the selection of entries would be helpful to librarians and users.

Some other guides, such as Bunting and Lyon's *Private Independent Schools* (54th ed.; see ARBA 2002, entry 262), include indexes or tables of gifted and talented programs. This resource is recommended as a place to begin searching for programs of various sorts for gifted and talented students. For public libraries and academic libraries supporting teacher education programs.—**Rosanne M. Cordell**

P, S

97.   **Summer Opportunities for Kids & Teenagers 2004.** Lawrenceville, N.J., Peterson's Guides, 2003. 1587p. illus. index. $29.95pa. ISBN 0-7689-1158-3. ISSN 0894-9417.

Do you remember those movies about summer camp, where kids rowed canoes, played ball, hiked, swam, and generally spent time in nature? Well, those days have changed. The stereotypical summer camp of your childhood has mushroomed, like virtually every other product in American society. Now there are summer camps for acting, chess, space, sports, the arts, academic subject specialties (e.g., mathematics, science, languages), and anything else one might imagine. This guide identifies 3,000 such camps around the United States and abroad, with useful descriptive information and a variety of ways to identify camps of interest.

The guide is organized into chapters arranged alphabetically by state and, following that, by country. Within a state or country, camps are listed alphabetically by name. For each camp one can find an address, general information, program information (i.e., dates, costs, availability of financial aid), contact information, application deadlines, available jobs, Websites, e-mail addresses, and lists of offerings (including arts, sports, wilderness/outdoors, trips, academics, and special interest areas). As with other Peterson Guides, there is an accompanying section of full, two-page advertisements provided by some of the camps; this is noted in the camp's brief entry. These provide much more information on camp offerings, its staff, and its philosophy and background, among other things.

There are supplementary directories that provide alternative means of identifying appropriate camps. The specialized directory lists camps by name, then location, under 12 categories covering academic programs, adventure, arts, bible, community service, cultural, family, outdoor, special needs, sports, traditional, and wilderness. There is also a travel programs directory, a special needs accommodations directory (subdivided by type of need), a religious affiliations directory, a sponsor directory, a substantial primary activity directory (arranged alphabetically by topic), and a program directory arranged alphabetically by program name. An introductory quick-reference chart lists general and program information for camps in each state. This is a wonderful resource for those students who have the time, resources, and specialized interests to pursue the opportunities. Public and school libraries should have this available for families.—**Stephen H. Aby**

Handbooks and Yearbooks

C

98.   Blake, Brett Elizabeth, and Robert W. Blake. **Literacy and Learning: A Reference Handbook.** Santa Barbara, Calif., ABC-CLIO, 2002. 267p. index. (Contemporary Education Issues). $45.00. ISBN 1-57607-273-8.

This intriguing exploration of many facets of literacy is divided into 11 chapters that discuss the meaning of literacy, a chronology of its development, foundations (e.g., the development of writing), consequences (e.g., on family life, on libraries), how we learn to read, literature as a way of knowing, the theory and practice of criticism, and reader response. The last two chapters list organizations and educational associations, and a selected bibliography of print and nonprint resources. The authors are education faculty members who have written extensively on literacy.

More of a monograph than a quick reference in format, this work should be placed in the stacks. For example, one might expect to find a few statistical charts noting literacy rates in a reference book on literacy. There are none here, but there is a lengthy analysis of different definitions, types, skills, contexts, and uses of literacy, which makes it clear that it is difficult to measure or compare literacy between groups using a single set of criteria. There is no mention of Reading Recovery, nor are there entries on the adult literacy tests and readability indexes in use today. Buy *Literacy in America: An Encyclopedia of History, Theory, and Practice* (see ARBA 2004, entry 241) as your basic reference tool for these kinds of inquiries.

Questions at the start of each section serve as the basis for explication: "Why should we be concerned with the idea of two ways of perceiving reality in a consideration of reading?" (p. 104); "Why should we be concerned with the foundations of literacy? If we can read and write passably well, is that not enough?" (p. 33). The chapters on how we have progressed in our view of literature from "a focus on the author's intent" to the text itself to "the individual's personal, intuitive response" (p. xiv) present a number of complex ideas in a clear fashion. Chapters on reader response theory and diverse learners include models for training educators and problems and solutions for applying what we know in the classroom setting. Throughout, the works of Plato, Homer, Dewey, I. A. Richards, Jerome Bruner, Umberto Eco, Stanley Fish, Nicholson Baker, and others are all examined in the context of literacy. This work is recommended for most libraries, but especially those supporting programs in education, psychology, and philosophy.
—**Deborah V. Rollins**

C, P

99.   **Education State Rankings 2002-2003: Pre K-12 Education in the 50 United States.** Kathleen O'Leary Morgan and Scott Morgan, eds. Lawrence, Kans., Morgan Quitno Press, 2002. 416p. index. $49.95pa. ISBN 0-7401-0047-5.

Education is a critical social undertaking and a frequently contentious public policy issue. Charter schools, per pupil expenditures, sources of funding, proficiency test results, school crime, graduation rates, and other topics are of major public interest and generate close scrutiny and debate. Furthermore, how states provide for their students' education has an impact not only on the lives of those students and their families, but also on economic development at the local, state, and national level. Not surprisingly, there are a lot of data on education topics, although these data originate from a variety of providers. This volume assembles some of the most interesting data and presents them in a readable format. Over 400 tables of primarily current data are presented comparing states on topics within seven major areas: districts and facilities; finance; graduates and achievement; safety and discipline; special education; staff; and students. Within each category there are dozens of tables of data on various subtopics. These data compare states by listing their data both alphabetically by state and in descending rank order. The data are drawn from a number of national sources, such as the National Center for Education Statistics, the Bureau of Census, the Centers for Disease Control, the National Education Association, the Federal Bureau of Investigation, the American Federation of Teachers, and more. The alphabetic and rank order listings are made easier to read by both the shading of alternate lines of text and the unabbreviated listing of dollar amounts. A complete list of sources consulted is provided, as is a subject index.

This is a well-presented and surprisingly fascinating source of data on education. Any public or academic library will want this title to complement other basic sources, such as the *Digest of Education Statistics*. [R: LJ, Dec 02, pp. 103-105]—**Stephen H. Aby**

COMPUTER RESOURCES

S

100.   **Educators Guide to Free Internet Resources, 2003-2004: Elementary/Middle School Edition.** 2d ed. Kathleen Suttles Nehmer, ed. Randolph, Wis., Educators Progress Service, 2003. 310p. index. $39.95pa. ISBN 0-87708-379-7.

S

101.   **Educators Guide to Free Internet Resources, 2003-2004: Secondary Edition.** 21st ed. Kathleen Suttles Nehmer, ed. Randolph, Wis., Educators Progress Service, 2003. 302p. index. $39.95pa. ISBN 0-87708-378-9.

Because of the rapid proliferation of Websites of educational value, it was decided last year to divide the *Educators Guide to Free Internet Resources* into two publications, one for elementary and middle grades and one for secondary schools. This year's editions follow the same approach. It should be noted, however, that some sources in each guide are suitable for adult use. The guides have been carefully updated. The *Elementary/Middle School Edition* lists 1,697 Websites, with 1,536 being new. The *Secondary Edition* has 1,242 new items out of a total of 1,614. Each guide follows an identical pattern of arrangement. The body, arranged by title, gives information on the resource, including a short, descriptive annotation, suggested grade level, format, special notes that apply, source, and URL. New items are identified by the label "New." The title index is an alphabetic list of all items appearing in the main section, with page reference. The subject index lists under each subject heading all relevant titles with page numbers. The source index lists, in alphabetic order, the sponsoring organization or producer, with page references to listings in the main section where a complete address is given. A "What's New Index" lists the name of new items in the current editions. Introductory pages tell how to use the guide. A chart shows the number of new, old, and total items in each of the 22 subject areas in each guide. These guides will be of use to teachers and parents as well as to many students and other adults.—**Shirley L. Hopkinson**

ELEMENTARY AND SECONDARY EDUCATION

Directories

C, P
102.   **Directory of Distance Learning Opportunities: K-12.** Westport, Conn., Oryx Press/Greenwood Publishing Group, 2003. 302p. index. $69.95. ISBN 1-57356-515-6.

Although this directory is not unique, it has qualities that make it stand out among the others. This directory is an alphabetic listing of distance learning programs throughout the United States. With sources such as this, its very recent copyright date is a distinct advantage. Where most directories of this type list distance education programs in higher education, this directory has found a very distinct niche with programs from kindergarten through grade 12. Schools offering these programs vary from religious to university-based institutions. Also, for-profit institutions are included. Random perusal shows a significant Web presence for instructional delivery, but also, print materials and satellite instruction are available with some programs. Additionally, the basic information delivered in each entry will include: a description of the institution; its accreditation, enrollment, and tuition information; and credit and grading. Particularly important, and not found in many other directories, are course offerings and descriptions of each institution. It certainly demonstrates the wide range of offerings available online. Perhaps, too, these descriptions give the reader an indication of the school's overall philosophical bent. Indexing covers three areas: courses offered, course level, and geographic. Probably the geographic index could have been eliminated if the entries had been arranged by state. This is an excellent source for people who homeschool their children, or perhaps for people who live long distances from schools that might offer courses beyond the traditional fare.—**Phillip P. Powell**

C, P, S
103.   **Funding Sources for K-12 Education 2003.** Westport, Conn., Oryx Press/Greenwood Publishing Group, 2003. 1021p. index. $49.95pa. ISBN 1-57356-591-1.

School funding is in dire straits, as indicated by both the difficulty of passing school levies and the lawsuits around the country over state school funding mechanisms. Consequently, grants loom large as sources of additional funding in such an austere budgetary environment. Competition for grants is usually robust, but opportunities exist if one is fully aware of all the relevant funding sources.

This directory of 2,300 such sources for K-12 education provides that needed information. The entries are arranged alphabetically by the name of the funding source. For each, there is a paragraph-long description of its focus, as well as a sample of recent awards, the amount of the grant, application deadlines, requirements, restrictions, contact information, the sponsor, and the Internet address. Because the directory is arranged alphabetically, it is especially important that there be detailed indexing to facilitate finding appropriate granting organizations. In fact, this directory has three indexes: a subject index, a sponsoring organization index, and a grants-by-program index. The subject index lists grant sources under an alphabetic list of categories, while the program-type index arranges the sources under such categories as basic research, building construction and/or renovation, capital campaigns, scholarships, training programs/institutes, and many more. The modest difficulty with both indexes is the extensive list of possible grant sources listed under the broad categories. In each index, this could require much additional exploration on the user's part in order to identify appropriate funding sources. A more finely tuned subject or keyword index would save the user time. Nonetheless, the education focus and numerous categories make this a valuable research tool when compared to more general funding source directories. Academic, public, and school libraries should find this an important addition to their collections.—**Stephen H. Aby**

HIGHER EDUCATION

General Works

Bibliography

C

104.   Fusco, Marjorie, and Susan E. Ketcham. **Distance Learning for Higher Education: An Annotated Bibliography.** Westport, Conn., Libraries Unlimited/Greenwood Publishing Group, 2002. 132p. index. $35.00pa. ISBN 1-56308-847-9.

Distance education is an area that is evolving rapidly. It is difficult to stay current when creating bibliographies in the subject. Instead of creating a simple annotated bibliography, the authors have created a volume of annotated references with referenced preface material for each chapter giving a good overview of the topics involved in distance learning. The coverage of distance learning is broad covering all aspects not just the delivery of learning and how students cope with the medium. Other equally important areas covered are: administration, marketing, and faculty; accreditation issues; library resources and problems; and a section on resources such as listservs and discussion groups. The annotations are very well written providing enough information to decide whether or not to obtain and read the entire article. Given many of the references are to Websites, logical with distance learning, the authors do make the caveat in their introduction that URLs are fluid and pages often vanish. While the bibliography is not comprehensive, it does provide an excellent overview of distance learning in higher education and the references selected provide a good representation of the subjects that need to be considered and the resources available. This book is a good addition to any collection on distance learning.—**Leslie M. Behm**

Dictionaries and Encyclopedias

C

105.   **Encyclopedia of Distributed Learning.** Anna DiStefano, Kjell Erik Rudestam, and Robert J. Silverman, eds. Thousand Oaks, Calif., Sage, 2004. 549p. index. $125.00. ISBN 0-7619-2451-5.

Remember about 10 years ago when the moment you said the word "web" most people supplied the word "cob" and shuddered? So much for past history. Today the Web means only one thing and so it was only a matter of time before someone put together an encyclopedia that outlined just how much the Web has affected education. What amazes about this volume is how late it is in coming. Distance education has been around for a long time, although it must be admitted that it impacted very few students until about 15 years ago. If truth be told, most institutions that proffered distance programs were of a dubious quality. For many years, anyone who got his or her degree from an institution that made them available without residency, got them at their own professional peril.

We have come a long way. The editors have chosen, oddly to my mind, to title this work distributed rather than distance or online because they believe that the phrases distributed learning or distributed education are more far-reaching. Perhaps in the confines of those whose lifework is this alone are such terms familiar. But to the many masses the phrase is anything but clear and its presence here will possibly deny the editors some sales. This is a shame because they have produced a most credible work.

Separate entries seek to define the wide parameters of distance or online learning. So, for example, the first entry, "Academic Advising," should be read by anyone involved in academic advising, not just those who work with distance education. Other entries, such as "Online Orientation" and "Virtual Campus," are more obviously focused on online education. The entries range from a few hundred to more than a thousand words. Current bibliographies provide readers with other places to turn after the general overviews provided. All articles are signed and affiliations are listed in the front matter. Administrative process, social and cultural perspectives, student and faculty issues, and more are all covered here in more than 100 articles. The editors have assembled a most impressive array of educators to help them, including Robert Zemsky of the University of Pennsylvania, Richard Katz of EDUCAUSE, and Jason Valee of DeVry. [R: LJ, 1 Feb 04, pp. 74-76]—**Mark Y. Herring**

Directories

C, S

106.   **Four-Year Colleges 2004.** 34th ed. Lawrenceville, N.J., Peterson's Guides, 2003. 3109p. illus. index. $29.95pa. (w/CD-ROM). ISBN 0-7689-1124-9. ISSN 1544-2330.

The Peterson College Guides have now been published for more than 35 years, and during that time they have become standard sources in academic and public libraries. Probably the most often selected is *Four-Year Colleges*, which has become an indispensable source. There are several new features in the 2004 edition including a handy CD-ROM, which allows for searching on both Windows and Macintosh computers. Also, a useful feature made possible by the CD-ROM is that application forms may be downloaded and filled out directly on a computer. In some cases these admissions applications can then be sent electronically to the chosen college or university.

These guides have long been considered the most objective, unbiased, and comprehensive descriptions of more colleges than any other guide. In addition to the in-depth listing of all four-year colleges in the U.S. and Canada, there are many additional sections of use to future college students. Some of these include "The College Admissions Process: An Overview; Options, Options, Options" (which includes information on choosing colleges) and several quick indexes that range from an alphabetic index to majors to an entrance difficulty index. Each college entry includes the name of the college or university; address; support type (state or private); costs to students; type of calendar; degrees offered; endowment level; and additional information such as athletics, student life, financial aid, and who to contact to apply. Each entry contains information concerning what standardized tests and other qualifiers are necessary for admission. One excellent feature of the 2004 guide is the "College Admissions Countdown Calendar," which outlines the pertinent month-by-month milestones of the college admissions process. This feature should make it much easier for students to keep track of what they need to do concerning applications to various colleges and when they need to do it.

A criticism that is often heard from librarians is that the books are of flimsy quality. They are usually in tatters before the new one arrives. But part of the attraction of the Peterson guides is their low price, and if they were hard bound the price would no doubt have to rise, making them less available in smaller libraries, or less affordable for individual purchase. This source is highly recommended for all public and academic libraries (including smaller branch libraries), and should be considered as an individual purchase for students who are planning on applying to a college or university in 2004.—**Robert L. Wick**

C, S

107. **Peterson's Complete Guide to Colleges 2003.** Lawrenceville, N.J., Peterson's Guides, 2002. 1860p. index. $49.95. ISBN 0-7689-1114-1.

Peterson's Complete Guide to Colleges 2003 provides students, parents, librarians, and educators a current and comprehensive source for information on higher learning institutions in the United States and Canada. It is intended for anyone interested in information on two-year and four-year colleges. The guide of course provides the critical information for the institutions but it goes a step a two beyond. Also included is information on the college search and selection process. *Peterson's* also includes strategies for most efficiently navigating one's way through applications, financial aid, and enrollment. The guide goes as far as breaking down the high school junior and senior year calendars to identify key dates and activities that should be accomplished at each point.

The core of the book is the college profile sections. They are separated into two categories: four-year colleges and two-year colleges. The first section covers over 2,100 four-year programs. The section begins with tips on how to use it. It is organized in a logical and easy-to-use fashion. Each entry includes the critical information students and parents will be interested in. Some examples of what users will find in each entry are student body size and make up, tuition costs, degree programs offered, and contact information. The main entries are followed by a majors index, which would be most helpful for the individual focused on specific academic interests.

The two-year programs section includes the same key points the reader will find in the four-year section. It is also followed by a majors index, which alphabetically lists all the associate programs offered at two-year institutions and then at four-year institutions. In addition to the majors index at the end of each section, the reader can also locate entries in the alphabetic listing at the end of each section. The entries in this section then refer the user to the correct page number.

Peterson's is clear in its objective and meets it. In addition, the guide provides insight into other valuable facts that can be of assistance when going through the college application process. Some of the helpful information includes advice on standardized tests, financial aid tips, and a guide for the nontraditional adult student. It does all this in a well-written, easy-to-use, and concise style. This reference book can be a very helpful tool for the individual who is about to go through the process of choosing and enrolling in an institution of higher learning.—**Harold Goss, Jr.**

Financial Aid

Directories

C, S

108. **Peterson's Complete Guide to Financial Aid 2003.** Lawrenceville, N.J., Peterson's Guides, 2002. 1525p. index. $49.95. ISBN 0-7689-1115-X.

This financial aid guide is designed to help students and their families find the right school and higher education financial aid. There is a plethora of financial sources listed in *Peterson's Complete Guide to Financial Aid*, and Peterson's describes federal, state, and national and international gift aid available for higher education costs.

The chapters cover universities and college information in the first half of the guide. The last section of the manual covers more than 2,800 scholarships categorized in 10 broad areas. The areas are academic field/career goals; civil, professional, social, or union affiliation; corporate affiliation; employment experience; impairment; military service; national ethnic heritage; religious affiliation; state of residency; and talent. There are indexes for all of the categories.

There are special worksheets for parents and students to use in calculating college costs. There is a tuition waiver index that defines guaranteed tuition, prepayment, deferred, and installment payments. There are chapters contributed by two directors of financial aid to advise parents and their children with the financial aid process. This guide is highly recommended for public, academic, and secondary school libraries for their scholarships and financial aid collections.—**Kay M. Stebbins**

C, S

109.   **Scholarships, Grants & Prizes 2004.** 8th ed. Lawrenceville, N.J., Peterson's Guides, 2003. 796p. index. $29.95pa. ISBN 0-7689-1229-6.

The purpose of this directory is to identify financial aid available to students from private sources. It is designed to complement Peterson's *College Money Handbook* (21st ed.; Peterson's Guides, 2003), which identifies sources of undergraduate funding from public sources such as the federal or state governments and colleges or universities themselves. Together these two works are supposed to provide a broad picture of the funding sources available for college study.

This work is particularly useful for students whose family financial circumstances make them ineligible for needs-based financial assistance from public sources. It also identifies funding for students who possess special abilities and achievements, have personal qualifications such as church membership, or have specific ethnic backgrounds that fit the criteria of private scholarship sponsors.

The 3,400 scholarships that are included are organized into 10 broad categories based on academic goals or skills, personal characteristics, or background, and include such headings as corporate affiliation, nationality, state of residence, or impairment. The academic fields/career goals section is the largest and is subdivided into 81 subject areas organized alphabetically by the scholarship sponsor. There is a chart of all awards over $2,000 (about 600 of them) arranged from highest to lowest, and extensive indexes to make it easier to find appropriate awards to apply for. Although no scholarship directory can be totally comprehensive, this is a very useful source for students looking for awards that are not primarily need based.—**Christine E. King**

INTERNATIONAL EXCHANGE PROGRAMS AND OPPORTUNITIES

C

110.   **Study Abroad 2004.** 11th ed. Lawrenceville, N.J., Peterson's Guides, 2004. 908p. illus. index. $29.95pa. ISBN 0-7689-1273-3.

Now in its 11th annual edition, this extensive guide to overseas study opportunities is intended primarily for students at U.S. colleges. It provides information on over 1,800 semester- or year-long programs that are sponsored by accredited institutions, accepted for credit at U.S. colleges and universities, and not restricted to students enrolled at the sponsoring school.

The program descriptions, which make up the largest section of the book, are arranged by host country and include sponsoring and host institutions, focus and nature of each program, eligibility requirements, application deadline and term dates, living arrangements, costs, and contact information. The descriptions are well indexed by field of study, sponsoring institution, host institution, and availability of internships.

A "Guidance" section at the front of the volume provides a series of helpful essays addressing such topics as preparing and paying for study abroad, opportunities and considerations for persons with disabilities, internship and volunteer options, and health and safety tips. There are other titles that provide this kind of advice at greater length; even *Study Abroad for Dummies* (Wiley, 2003) and the UNESCO *Study Abroad 2004-2005* (2003) provide more directory listings, although compiled for an international audience. For U.S. students, however, this Peterson's title surely represents the most useful and comprehensive directory.—**Gregory M. Toth**

LEARNING DISABILITIES AND DISABLED

C, P

111.   **Learning Disabilities Sourcebook.** 2d ed. Dawn D. Matthews, ed. Detroit, Omnigraphics, 2003. 598p. index. (Health Reference Series). $78.00. ISBN 0-7808-0626-3.

The 2d edition of *Learning Disabilities Sourcebook* far surpasses the earlier edition in that it is more focused on information that will be useful as a consumer health resource. The book includes an overview of learning disabilities and chapters describing the various types of disabilities and conditions that impede learning. Educational issues, accommodations, and coping strategies are also covered.

This book is intended to be a starting point for people who need to know about learning disabilities. Each chapter on a specific disability includes readable, well-organized descriptions of the particular condition. The section on educational issues covers educational alternatives, including special education programs, charter schools, alternative educational programs, and learning strategies. The description of the Individualized Education Program (IEP) and the information on the legal rights of the learning disabled in the educational system are very thorough.

The section on accommodations includes information about testing accommodations and computer-assisted learning for the disabled. The principles for Universal Design for Learning (UDL) are explained. A chapter on determining the appropriateness of assistive technology for particular situations and defining its inclusion in an IEP is clear and helpful. The section goes beyond educational needs and outlines job accommodations, which may be needed for the learning disabled person to succeed in the workplace. Finally, the book has a section on coping strategies, which focuses on the concerns of parents and other family members as well as the needs of the learning disabled child.

The book is well indexed and includes a glossary. Chapter on using ERIC (Education Resources Information) searches and on organizations and helpful Websites will aid the reader who needs more information.—**Jeanne D. Galvin**

6 Ethnic Studies

GENERAL WORKS

Atlases

P, S

112. **Cultural Atlas for Young People.** rev. ed. New York, Facts on File, 2003. 7v. illus. maps. index. $35.00/vol. ISBN 0-8160-5144-5.

The seven volumes of this attractive series aimed at older elementary and middle school students covers "First Civilizations," "Ancient Egypt," "Ancient Greece," "Ancient Rome," the "Middle Ages," "Ancient America," and "Africa." While in the 1st edition these were published separately, from 1989 to 1994 (see ARBA 91, entries 539-542; ARBA 92, entries 472 and 474; and ARBA 95, entry 571), Facts on File has released the new edition as a set. Author, format, and page length of each volume have not changed, although in several cases an additional name is listed as responsible for updating. All compilers are researchers or teachers connected with universities or other educational institutions, mostly in Great Britain. Although maps and event charts have been consistently updated where appropriate, text and illustrations remain largely unchanged from the 1st edition.

Striking photographs and illustrations will appeal to young readers, with substance added in the form of date tables, charts of events, and the excellent maps anchoring each article. Historical information on a given civilization is enriched by articles on daily life, artistic achievement, education, and archaeological remains. The "Middle Ages" volume, for example, contains information on cathedral building, the Bayeux Tapestry, and Scandinavian stave churches; the "Africa" volume includes sections on a Dogon village and Husuni Kubwa as well as the African slave trade and game parks. A glossary, gazetteer, index, and brief bibliography of suggested reading conclude each volume. Public and school libraries will find this atlas a useful purchase, especially given the reasonable price; those owning the 1st edition may pass on it or select individual volumes as needed.—**Willa Schmidt**

Chronology

P, S

113. **The World Book of America's Multicultural Heritage.** 2d ed. Chicago, World Book, 2003. 2v. illus. maps. index. $69.00/set. ISBN 0-7166-7303-7.

This set, aimed at middle and high school students, marks the 2d edition of *The World Book of America's Heritage* (World Book, 1991). Its title change is indicative of the current emphasis on multiculturalism in U.S. society. In contrast to similarly oriented resources such as the *Gale Encyclopedia of*

Multicultural America (see ARBA 96, entry 387) or *Encyclopedia of Multiculturalism* (see ARBA 95, entry 396), which are arranged alphabetically by ethnic group or topic, *World Book*'s 32 chapters feature a chronological approach. Volume 1 covers the peoples who arrived before 1800, such as Indians, explorers, Pilgrims, and African slaves. Volume 2 continues with the movement westward and the flood of immigration in the nineteenth through early twenty-first centuries. Numerous paintings, photographs, and maps provide attractive visual enhancement to a lively and informative text. An index to topics and illustrations concludes each volume.

Few changes were noted from 1st to 2d edition, particularly in volume 1. Updates in volume 2 are confined primarily to chapters 29-32, covering recent immigrants from Asia and Latin America and undocumented workers. A section on Cubans, for example, has added the 1999 Elian Gonzalez controversy; naming of African Americans such as Colin Powell and Condoleeza Rice to important government posts is also documented. But one might ask why a whole new edition has been issued when an updating supplement would have sufficed. Libraries without the 1st edition and in need of a historical summary of American settlement for young readers will find this set appropriate.—**Willa Schmidt**

Handbooks and Yearbooks

C, P

114.   Aguirre, Adalberto, Jr. **Racial and Ethnic Diversity in America: A Reference Handbook.** Santa Barbara, Calif., ABC-CLIO, 2003. 277p. index. (Contemporary World Issues). $50.00; $55.00 (e-book). ISBN 1-57607-983-X; 1-57607-984-8 (e-book).

Emphasis in this recent contribution to the voluminous Contemporary World Issues series is on U.S. society's shift away from a white, Eurocentric population to one that by the year 2000 consisted of fully one-third nonwhite racial and ethnic minorities. In three introductory essays Aguirre, professor of sociology at University of California-Riverside, summarizes the history of early immigration and marginalization of groups not conforming to the Anglo-Saxon core; the increasing importance and visibility of nonwhite minorities going into the twenty-first century; and finally the impact of this "new" diversity on the social fabric as illustrated by reactions such as racial profiling, hate crimes, and affirmative action, including legal cases relating to the latter. Census tables back up information in the text, and an up-to-date list of references follows each essay. Other chapters provide a chronology of events covering the years 1513 through 2003, biographical sketches of 14 representative scholars of contemporary diversity research, supplemental census statistics, pertinent quotations, and summaries of key provisions of the U.S. Patriot Act. Useful abstracted lists of print resources and films and videos are included, but the "Directory of Organizations" offers only a small sampling, as does the list of "Internet Resources." A glossary and a name/subject index complete the volume.

This is an excellent resource for researchers as well as casual readers looking for a cogent alternative viewpoint on U.S. immigration and diversity today, although it should be noted that its main focus is on African Americans, Asians, and Hispanics, with much less attention given to American Indians and other groups. Because it provides a needed balance to traditional surveys, academic and public libraries alike would do well to add it to their reference shelves.—**Willa Schmidt**

P, S

115.   **Fiesta! 3.** Danbury, Conn., Grolier, 2004. 16v. illus. $289.00/set. ISBN 0-7172-5788-6.

The 16-volume *Fiesta! 3* includes countries from Latin America, Europe, North America, Asia, Africa, and the Middle East. Each volume is as colorful as the series name. A bright photograph beaming with color appears on the cover of each volume; this is usually a photograph of one or more children engaged in a celebration or festival.

Each volume describes the festivals and holidays of a country, along with the songs and traditions associated with those celebrations. Each opens with a two-page spread that provides basic information about the country, along with a map, a picture of the country's flag, and a picture of a globe indicating the country's location in the world. Following is a two-page spread about the country's religions and language.

Descriptions about the major celebrations that are traditional to the culture of the country encompass the rest of a volume, with recipes, songs, crafts, and traditional legends or stories. A final page, "Words to Know," is a glossary of important words from the text. Each 32-page volume is heavily and colorfully illustrated with captioned photographs and artwork.

This set, combined with *Fiesta! 1* (see ARBA 98, entry 1262) and *Fiesta! 2* (see ARBA 2000, entry 66) are welcome library additions for social studies and language students, as well as for readers who want to learn more about holidays and celebrations from around the world. Though the reading level may be upper elementary and middle school, high school students will also find these books valuable for report material when studying the culture and traditions of a country.—**Dana McDougald**

S

116.   **The Newest Americans.** Westport, Conn., Greenwood Press, 2003. 5v. illus. maps. index. (Middle School Reference). $200.00/set. ISBN 0-313-32553-7.

This five-volume series provides a unique survey of current immigrant groups in the United States. Primarily focusing on those new immigrant arrivals since 1965, a wealth of information is discussed concerning the social, historical, political, and other pertinent cultural mores of these newest Americans. Immigrant Ecuadorians, Haitians, Laotians, Russians, Ghanaians, and Nigerians are just a few of the ethnic groups whose backgrounds and cultures are continuingly changing the face of America. Employing pictures, charts, and statistical information, the reader is presented with a concise yet thorough synopsis of these new immigrant groups. For example, in volume E-H population and other demographic statistics about Ghanaian Americans could assist students and academics with vital information on the distribution of Ghanaians in selective states. Customs and festival information of immigrant groups are also easily found in these volumes. Accompanied by an extensive bibliography for further study, this reference work is a must for school, public, and academic libraries. [R: SLJ, Dec 03, p. 97]—**Patrick Hall**

P, S

117.   **World Book's Celebrations and Rituals Around the World.** Chicago, World Book, 2003. 5v. illus. index. $238.00/set. ISBN 0-7166-5010-X.

This five-volume set from World Book is designed for elementary-aged children studying the history behind various rituals and holidays celebrated around the world. The volumes are organized into the following topics: birth rituals, harvest celebrations, national celebrations, New Year's celebrations, and Spring celebrations. Volumes have the same organization, beginning with ancient celebrations and then discussing the various rituals of the Far East, South and Central Asia, the Middle East, Europe and the Americas, and Africa. Each volume concludes with a glossary and a volume index.

After a one-page introduction, each volume presents information in two-page segments. The work relies heavily on the use of illustrations; next to each illustration is a one-paragraph description of the ritual or practice. The text nicely balances both religious rituals (from Christian, Jewish, Hindu, Muslim, and Buddhism) as well as national traditions. Children will enjoy browsing the pages of illustrations and reading the text that is specifically written to their level. It will be an ideal tool for teachers and librarians teaching about other cultures' rituals and celebrations. This set is recommended for the children's collections at public libraries and school library media centers.—**Shannon Graff Hysell**

AFRICAN AMERICANS

Biography

C, P, S
118.   Smith, Jessie Carney. **Black Firsts: 4,000 Ground-Breaking and Pioneering Historical Events.** 2d ed. Farmington Hills, Mich., Visible Ink Press/Gale, 2003. 787p. illus. index. $58.00. ISBN 1-57859-153-8.

Black Firsts is a record of black achievement, aimed to give readers a capsule view of the history of blacks worldwide. It is arranged chronologically under 16 broad chapter headings, such as "Arts and Entertainment," "Business," "Government," and "Sports." The broad headings are further divided into categories; for example, under "Arts and Entertainment" one finds "Architecture," "Cartoons," "Circus," "Dance," and "Drama," just to name a few. Under each category, entries begin with a date in bold type, followed by the person's name, his or her birth and death date (if applicable), and the person's "first" achievement. For inclusion in the book, entries had to be documented, using several sources of information whenever possible. Most entries are several sentences long, and some are more than one paragraph, not merely stating the person's "first" but giving something about the person's background and other accomplishments as well. Following each entry is the bibliographic information of the source or sources of information.

Sidebars provide additional information on items of interest, such as "The First Black Catholic College," "Africa's First Independent Republic," "The Oldest Continuously Published Periodical," or "The Oldest Surviving Black Church." Interspersed throughout the text are black-and-white photographs or illustrations of subjects. A comprehensive index provides quick access to entries, and there is a complete bibliography of books and periodicals used as sources for the entries.

Changes from the 1st edition (see ARBA 95, entry 412) include more "firsts"—there were nearly 3,000 in the 1st edition and nearly 5,000 in this edition—and especially more "firsts" by women. The previous edition had 15 chapters, but this edition has an additional chapter, "Government: International," which was added to account for many of the political accomplishments of blacks worldwide. New subject headings were added for this edition, and some of the information found under one subject heading in the 1st edition has been rearranged and expanded in this edition.

This is an authoritative reference work and a welcome addition to black history. It will be appreciated by researchers and browsers alike. Secondary, college and university, and public libraries should all consider this an essential reference.—**Dana McDougald**

ASIAN AMERICANS

S
119.   **U*X*L Asian American Almanac.** 2d ed. Irene Natividad and Susan B. Gall, eds. Farmington Hills, Mich., U*X*L/Gale, 2004. 268p. illus. maps. index. $58.00; $250.00/set. ISBN 0-7876-7598-9.

S
120.   **U*X*L Asian American Biography.** 2d ed. Helen Zia and Susan B. Gall, eds. Farmington Hills, Mich., U*X*L/Gale, 2004. 2v. illus. index. $105.00/2-volume set; $250.00/set. ISBN 0-7876-7601-2.

S

121.   **U*X*L Asian American Chronology.** 2d ed. Maura Malone and Susan B. Gall, eds. Farmington Hills, Mich., U*X*L/Gale, 2004. 196p. illus. maps. index. $58.00; $250.00/set. ISBN 0-7876-7604-7.

S

122.   **U*X*L Asian American Voices.** 2d ed. Deborah Gillan Straub, ed. Farmington Hills, Mich., U*X*L/Gale, 2004. 315p. illus. index. $58.00; $250.00/set. ISBN 0-7876-7600-4.

The U*X*L Asian American Reference Library presents cultural and historical information on the growing number of Americans who descend from Cambodia, China, the Philippines, Indonesia, Korea, Japan, Laos, Thailand, Vietnam, and native Hawaii. The set is divided into five separate volumes—the *Almanac*, *Biography* (two volumes), *Chronology*, and *Voices*. The volumes are designed with middle to high school age students in mind, and each covers the Asian American cultures from a different angle.

The *Almanac* is arranged into 17 subject chapters. It begins by defining each ethnic group discussed and then goes on to provide in-depth chapters on immigration, civil rights, women and families, education, religion, literature, and military, just to name a few. Numerous sidebars with additional factual information and black-and-white photographs are provided. The *Biography* volumes provide profiles of 150 influential Asian Americans that have contributed in the fields of civil rights, politics, entertainment, sports, and more. Each profile is several pages in length, provides black-and-white photographs, includes information on the biographee's childhood and contributions to the advancement of Asian Americans, and provides sources for further information. The work concludes with a name/subject index and an index by field of endeavor. The *Chronology* volume begins with prehistory and concludes with events from June 2003. Events are broken down first by year and then into months and days. This arrangement will help students grasp the historical context in which events happened and perhaps better explain complex times in history such as World War II. The *Voices* volume provides 20 excerpted speeches, orations, and notable works of Asian Americans on such topics as culture and tradition, ethnic stereotyping, and discrimination. The excerpts begin with an introduction to the speaker and the setting, and sidebars explain difficult concepts and historical events that the speaker refers to. The work concludes with a glossary, a timeline, a directory of speech topics, and an index.

This set would be a valuable addition to school libraries and the children's reference collections of public libraries. Each can be purchased separately, but they work extremely well as a set.—**Shannon Graff Hysell**

CANADIANS

C

123.   Bumsted, J. M. **Canada's Diverse Peoples: A Reference Sourcebook.** Santa Barbara, Calif., ABC-CLIO, 2003. 361p. illus. index. (Ethnic Diversity Within Nations). $55.00; $85.00 w/e-book. ISBN 1-57607-672-5; 1-57607-673-3 (e-book).

This title is from the ABC-CLIO series Ethnic Diversity Within Nations. The story begins with the various aboriginal groups migrating to Canada in the 1500s. It continues with the French, English, and Scottish immigration and the governments these groups set up and immigration policies they invoked on all the peoples of Canada. This book illustrates the exclusionary policies during the eighteenth and nineteenth centuries of Canada, and how modern Canada has evolved into one of the more accepting countries of immigrant groups. The author has provided primary documents, timelines, illustrations and maps, and bibliographies with each chapter. This is highly recommended for academic ethnic studies and history collections.—**Kay M. Stebbins**

INDIANS OF NORTH AMERICA

Handbooks and Yearbooks

C, P, S

124.   Rosier, Paul C. **Native American Issues.** Westport, Conn., Greenwood Press, 2003. 185p. illus. index. (Contemporary American Ethnic Issues). $45.00. ISBN 0-313-32002-0.

In *Native American Issues*, Paul Rosier identifies six issues of contemporary interest and importance related to Native Americans and American society as a whole. It is one in a series on Contemporary American Ethnic Issues. The issues include the arguments over team names and mascots, treaty rights, land claims, repatriation of ancestral remains, gaming, and the conflict between economic development and environmental protection.

Each issue is developed and explained within a historical context, and then the pro and con sides are described in more depth. Rosier illuminates issues that are complex, but where each side often has legitimate claims. The inclusion of the words of the persons directly involved in these disputes is an effective and meaningful device. Native Americans are represented as the different cultural groups that they are, not as a uniform voice. They often are on both sides of a given issue.

This is an excellent resource because of the use of varied sources (e.g., newspaper editorials, Supreme Court decisions, scholarly works), engaging style, contemporary and historical interest, inclusion of many additional reference materials, and discussion questions at the end of each chapter that can be used and built upon while using this text in a classroom setting. The only fault to be found with this book is that other contemporaneous issues could not be included, presumably because of space considerations (and the lack of a pro side), such as the Bureau of Indian Affairs and the mismanagement of Native American trust funds. *Native American Issues* is highly recommended for college, university, high school, and public libraries.—**Tara L. Dirst**

S

125.   **Student Almanac of Native American History.** Westport, Conn., Greenwood Press, 2003. 144p. illus. maps. (Middle School Reference). $80.00/set. ISBN 0-313-32599-5.

The *Student Almanac of Native American History* is a two-volume reference set that is comprised primarily of summary histories of a defined chronological era (Before Contact: 35,000 B.C.E.-1491 to Renewal: Native Americans Today, 1946-Present) and an A-Z list of key people, events, and terms. The A-Z list provides more detailed descriptions than is covered in the summary history.

The organization of the text chronologically may be somewhat challenging to a user unfamiliar with Native American history. Since the A-Z listing also goes by era, users may be more successful searching the index. Each volume has a separate glossary, resources, and selected bibliography that pertain to the eras covered in the volume, but the index that is included in both covers each volume.

An excellent feature of the set is the pronunciation guide for terms throughout the text. Items included in the A-Z list are referenced elsewhere in the text, so users will know that a more detailed description is available. Short primary document additions in the A-Z section offer an excellent opportunity to introduce young students to analysis of eyewitness testimony and legal documents. Additional features include maps, images, census tables, and timelines. The *Student Almanac of Native American History* is recommended for middle school, junior high school, and public libraries. [R: SLJ, Dec 03, p. 98]—**Tara L. Dirst**

LATIN AMERICANS

C, S

126.   Acuña, Rodolfo F. **U.S. Latino Issues.** Westport, Conn., Greenwood Press, 2003. 213p. illus. index. (Contemporary American Ethnic Issues). $45.00. ISBN 0-313-32211-2.

The controversy over who constitutes a "Hispanic" or "Latino" continues unabated and it is likely that it will continue for as long as Spanish-speaking Americans are in competition for political and hence economic recognition. *U.S Latino Issues*, by Rodolfo Acuña, provides the confused reader or researcher with a number of interesting insights and with information that may indeed clarify the identity of the Spanish-speaking members who reside in the United States.

The text is divided into very useful chapters that include discussions and overviews of such topics as "race classification," an issue that even the Spanish-speaking groups in America are not always clear about or simply choose to ignore as a determining factor in race relations. Other chapters on "assimilation," "bilingual education," and "affirmative action," provide the reader with much to work with and much to think about. In many ways, this excellent, advanced introduction can either be classified as pertaining in reference or simply relegated to the circulating stacks so that some enterprising scholar or student can have the luxury of taking the volume home. This reviewer hopes that all the other volumes projected to encompass the Contemporary American Ethnic Issues series are as well done as this volume is. *U.S. Latino Issues* is very much recommended for all libraries. Whether it belongs in reference or in circulation stacks will be the task of the particular bibliographer and the clientele of that library.—**Dario J. Villa**

P, S

127.   **U*X*L Hispanic American Almanac.** 2d ed. Sonia G. Benson, Nicolás Kanellos, and Bryan Ryan, eds. Farmington Hills, Mich., U*X*L/Gale, 2003. 247p. illus. maps. index. $55.00/volume; $210.00/set. ISBN 0-7876-6598-3.

P, S

128.   **U*X*L Hispanic American Biography.** 2d ed. Sonia G. Benson, Rob Nagel, and Sharon Rose, eds. Farmington Hills, Mich., U*X*L/Gale, 2003. 321p. illus. index. $55.00/volume; $210.00/set. ISBN 0-7876-6599-1.

P, S

129.   **U*X*L Hispanic American Chronology.** 2d ed. Sonia G. Benson, Nicolás Kanellos, and Bryan Ryan, eds. Farmington Hills, Mich., U*X*L/Gale, 2003. 216p. illus. maps. index. $55.00/volume; $210.00/set. ISBN 0-7876-6600-9.

P, S

130.   **U*X*L Hispanic American Voices.** 2d ed. Sonia G. Benson and Deborah Gillan Straub, eds. Farmington Hills, Mich., U*X*L/Gale, 2003. 294p. illus. index. $55.00/volume; $210.00/set. ISBN 0-7876-6603-3.

The 2d edition of the U*X*L Hispanic American Reference Library is a collection of four U*X*L titles: *Hispanic American Almanac*, *Hispanic American Biography*, *Hispanic American Chronology*, and *Hispanic American Voices*. While these books can be purchased separately, together they create an engaging and comprehensive multicultural reference work for young readers. Each title in the U*X*L Hispanic American Reference Library includes a table of contents; reader's guide (containing a toll-free number for comments and suggestions); and its own index. Although there are some differences of organization, all the books contain definitions, credits for pictures, and information for further study.

The *U*X*L Hispanic American Almanac* is not filled with tabular data and annual statistics. This *Almanac* is an encyclopedic reference to the Hispanic American experience, including articles on history, geographic distribution, work, education, language, literature, cultural expression, and sports. The *Almanac* contains 14 chapters, further subdivided into sections by time period or topic, depending on the chapter content. Statistics are there, but the reader finds them integrated into the text. The most important historical events or concepts covered in a chapter are condensed into a gray "Fact Focus" box. The "Fact Focus" box appears at the beginning of each chapter, providing a mini-chapter guide. In this Hispanic American Reference Library title, definitions are given both in a "Words to Know" front section and in side-margins directly on the page containing the word. Some librarians will find this redundancy a waste of space, while others may feel that it will avoid reader frustration. Terms that are only used once are defined parenthetically, and omitted from the "Words to Know" areas. The content of the *Almanac* is excellent. The chapter on "The Languages of Hispanic Americans" is one of the most clear and concise explanations of language traits and issues that this reviewer has read, and would be helpful even in an adult-level reference work. The brief section on "The Religions of Hispanic Americans," contained in the chapter "The Pillars of Hispanic American Society," includes information on the rise of Protestantism among Hispanics. The section mentions the importance of Methodism to Hispanics in Texas and New Mexico, and reasons behind the rise of Pentecostalism in Central and South America. These topics are often neglected in other works on Hispanic Americans, which treat Hispanics as uniformly Catholic, even while mentioning a rise in Protestantism. It is a pleasure to see the topics included here.

U*X*L Hispanic American Biography is a collection of 100 articles on notable Hispanic Americans, living and deceased, of various regional backgrounds and fields of experience. Based on the *Almanac*'s description, Hispanic Americans are defined as those who live, or lived, in the United States and Puerto Rico, and descended from Spain, Mexico, Cuba, and Central and South America. In some cases, they themselves are recent immigrants from these places. This reviewer was pleased to see cellist and peace activist Pablo Casals, a hero of mine. As expected, one can find current entertainment stars such as Gloria Estefan, Charlie Sheen, and Jennifer Lopez. However, Selma Heyak, the Mexican actress who now lives in the United States and is widely known for bringing *Frieda* to the screen, is not included. One will find a profile of the singer Marc Anthony, but not one of Ricky Martin. There is no denying the importance of Bartolomé de Las Casas, Juan Ponce De León, and Alvar NúZez Cabeza de Vaca, but the biographies of these historic Spaniards who came to and influenced the Americas seem a little out of place, when the majority of the people profiled lived or live in the twentieth century. No biography compilation will please every librarian or reader—someone is always left out. Spanish terms are defined parenthetically, omitting a "Words to Know" section. Cross-references to other profiles are bolded, and a brief "For More Information" section follows each article. With recent celebrities, the brief section is often made up of articles from popular magazines and Web pages. When Web pages are cited, the date accessed is provided. Books are listed where a biography is available, and for historical figures.

U*X*L Hispanic American Chronology is a straightforward and typical chronology. Picture credits are given at the beginning of the work, just before the introduction. The introduction section provides a quick narrative overview of the whole. A glossary and index are included in the back.

U*X*L Hispanic American Voices is sure to be a favorite in the set. This is a compilation of speeches by Hispanic Americans. Each speech is prefaced by a short article, which gives biographical and historical context. Some Spanish words and English words that may be difficult or new for young people are bolded and defined in the side margins. In addition to a standard table of contents, there is a guide to "Speech Topics at a Glance." Among the 32 topics listed are Affirmative Action, Civil Rights, Education, Labor and Unions, Literature, United Farm Workers, and Voting Rights. The introduction includes a section on "Traditions in Hispanic American Oratory" that is quite interesting.

The U*X*L Hispanic American Reference Library set as one of the best reference works on Hispanic Americans for young people. Gale describes the U*X*L reading level as being 7th grade, making this a good reference work for middle-school grades. Public and school libraries should strongly consider the set. Universities that maintain teacher/educational resource collections may consider it as well.—**Sandra E. Fuentes Riggs**

7 Genealogy and Heraldry

GENEALOGY

Dictionaries and Encyclopedias

P

131.   Thode, Ernest. **German-English Genealogical Dictionary.** repr. ed. Baltimore, Md., Genealogical Publishing, 2003. 286p. $29.95pa. ISBN 0-8063-1342-0.

Thode, a full-time genealogist who specializes in German-American genealogy, has translated over the years numerous documents and, while doing so, has been forced to go to several dictionaries in order to accomplish this. This book grew out of his personal need to have reference sources on Germanic genealogy. It is not intended to supplant a general German-English dictionary, but rather to have at hand a German genealogical dictionary that is specifically for those English speakers who are doing German research. He has accomplished his goal.

This *Dictionary* covers categories of terms that are found in genealogical records, including family relationships; days of the week; map terms; months; legal terms; numbers; Roman numerals; signs of the zodiac; coins; liquid and dry measures; measures of lengths; historical territories; place-names (including the Latin versions of major places); geographical terms; occupations; military ranks; types of taxes and tithes; ecclesiastical terms; illnesses; male and female given names; calendar days; and common genealogical words from Danish, Dutch, French, Latin, and Polish. He has also included some genealogical and cultural literacy terms that a German speaker is likely to understand, but which might be hard for an English speaker to find elsewhere, such as HETRINA, which is an acronym that means "Hessian Troops in North America" and had significance during the U.S. Revolutionary War.

In his introductory pages the author provides a good detailed user guide. He also includes a chart of the German alphabet with script variations that helps the user decipher German script. There is also a suffix index and a reverse suffix index. A key to German dialect pronunciations and a map of the German Empire from 1871 to 1918 are included. This will be a useful resource for Germanic genealogical research.—**Robert L. Turner Jr.**

Directories

P

132.   **Cyndi's List of Genealogy Sites on the Internet. http://www.cyndislist.com.** [Website]. By Cyndi Howells. Free. Date reviewed: 2003.

Howells has furnished researchers and hobbyists more than 100,000 links to genealogy resources on the World Wide Web, making it the largest and most comprehensive of its kind. She has managed to update it on a weekly basis, making it a most dynamic resource. As one might think, there is a large array of categories from which the user can choose ranging in content from "Mailing Lists" to "Female Ancestors" and leading to a vast array of Websites from a broad range of organizations and individuals. Several indexes are furnished to aid access.

Cyndi's List is hosted by *RootsWeb* (see ARBA 2003, entry 337) produced by Genealogical Data Cooperative. *RootsWeb* bills itself as "the Internet's oldest and largest genealogy site" and serves as host to several thousand genealogical Websites, 22,000 mailing lists, and 175,000 message boards. It contains interactive guides and various resources for researching family histories. It offers a "surname list" of one million names with dates and locations as well as e-mail addresses to contact others working on the same name.—**Anna H. Perrault**

P

133.   Kemp, Thomas Jay. **Virtual Roots 2.0: A Guide to Genealogy and Local History on the World Wide Web.** rev. ed. Wilmington, Del., Scholarly Resources, 2003. 311p. $29.95pa. (w/CD-ROM). ISBN 0-8420-2923-0.

Kemp, Chair of ALA's Genealogy and Local History Discussion Group, continues the mission of the earlier edition (see ARBA 98, entry 366) to list more than 1,000 "best and most useful" Internet sites for genealogy. In the first of the volume's three sections, "General Subjects," Kemp gathers sites that focus on various ethnic and religious groups, record types, useful repositories, and other topics of interest. The middle section, "United States Sources," is organized alphabetically by state, with the official state Web page listed first followed by the state library, state archive or historical society, and other important sites of interest to the state's genealogists. The last section, "International Sources," is arranged alphabetically by nation, and includes the national library, archives, and record sites for each. For these last two sections, institutional information includes the name of the facility, postal address, telephone number, fax number, and e-mail and Web address.

Although Kemp ranks sites as "Outstanding," "Extraordinary," "Most Extraordinary," or "The Single Most Important Genealogical Web Site on the Web Today," his criteria for such designations are lacking. Furthermore, the "more than 1,000 sites" designation is misleading. While some sites designed by private persons are included, most are subsections of an official state or national repository previously listed. The work is also a good example of the difficulties inherent in published monographs on the Internet, as some sites have broken links, while others have had their URLs changed. Still, this resource will be a useful starting point for those seeking sources for the usual assortment of vital records (e.g., birth, death, naturalization records) as well as the unknown and the unusual (e.g., inward bound slave manifests for the port of New Orleans).—**Christopher Brennan**

P

134.   **Schlegel's American Families of German Ancestry in the United States.** repr. ed. Baltimore, Md., Genealogical Publishing, 2003. 4v. illus. index. $175.00/set. ISBN 0-8063-1728-0.

This extensive collection of German-American family research contains a total of 1,638 pages in 4 volumes. Each volume has a separate index, although the reader needs to be aware that it is not a complete every-name index. The original set was limited to 200 numbered and registered copies, resulting in few copies being found today.

Each family sketch begins with the German origins, often going into great detail about the background of the homeland and covering history in some depth. Many sketches introduce the family in Germany, giving a detailed genealogy of the immigrant family and sometimes of its ancestral roots. Biographical sketches of members of the family in America are generously illustrated with photographs and coats of arms. As is frequently the case with works produced in this time period, the author does not provide sources of information. For the serious researcher who wishes to verify the data, numerous clues are given allowing one to follow the trail. The studies provided are rich in both genealogical and biographical information, and this newly prepared reprint should be a must purchase for all serious genealogical libraries.—**Carol Willsey Bell**

Handbooks and Yearbooks

P

135.   Croom, Emily Anne. **The Genealogist's Companion and Sourcebook.** 2d ed. Cincinnati, Ohio, F & W Publications, 2003. 454p. illus. index. $19.99pa. ISBN 1-55870-651-8.

This *Companion* features United States research, and concentrates on sources normally found outside the family. Among the topics presented in the table of contents, we find some local sources, state and federal records, special collections, courthouse records, immigration and naturalization, census, and libraries. A very detailed index will further assist the researcher.

Information is presented in a very readable fashion, and the text is highlighted by indicators showing research tips, case studies, warnings, or sources as examples. Two particular topics, African American genealogy and American Indian genealogy, are treated in depth. This work is recommended, and for the small price, the user will get an exceptional value. [R: LJ, 1 Nov 03, p. 68]—**Carol Willsey Bell**

P

136.   **The Handybook for Genealogists: United States of America.** 10th ed. Draper, Utah, Everton Publishers; distr., Cincinnati, Ohio, F & W Publications, 2002. 880p. maps. index. $59.95. ISBN 1-932088-00-8.

This is the 10th edition of this huge reference work since 1947, and it now runs to over 800 pages, 90 percent of which is devoted to U.S. sources of potential genealogical information, and the remaining 10 percent addressing international sources. Following an introduction and list of abbreviations are sections devoted to each U.S. state, listed alphabetically. Within each state, information on societies and repositories and on bibliography and record sources can be found, which encompass court, probate, and wills; emigration, immigration, migration, and naturalization; land and property; military; and vital and cemetery records. The mix varies from one state to the next. The sections for each state include colored maps of counties. Finally, postal addresses, telephone numbers, and e-mail addresses for each county are included. Not surprisingly, southern states seem best represented: Georgia, North Carolina, Texas, and Kentucky each has more than New York or California. However efficient such search engines as google.com are, this compilation is more so. Well organized and comprehensive, it mimics information that could be extracted from a search engine only laboriously. Nor is it likely to fall out of date quickly, since e-mail addresses of government agencies tend to be less volatile. The international sections are strongest for Western Europe, a tradition that needs updating. Unfortunately, Mexico is the only Latin American country represented. An index of counties (Washington being the most common name) completes the work.

In short, this is a model reference work—it is thorough, intuitive, and current. As such it is an embarrassment to many other reference works. Note as well that it costs less than seven cents per large format page, bringing it easily within the pocketbooks of even semi-serious genealogists, who will be able to consult it with confidence.—**David Henige**

P

137.   Rose, James M., and Alice Eichholz. **Black Genesis: A Resource Book for African-American Genealogy.** 2d ed. Baltimore, Md., Genealogical Publishing, 2003. 422p. index. $24.95pa. ISBN 0-8063-1735-3.

This 2d edition in many ways is nearly a completely new work. Whereas the 1st edition was more of a bibliography (see ARBA 80, entry 452), this edition has more of a "guide to" emphasis. The authors' purpose is to help the novice in African American family researcher have success. The world of genealogical research has changed greatly since 1978 thanks to the Internet. This work reflects some of those changes.

The book is divided into two parts. The first part is an overview that discusses such topics as the history of African American research, important dates in U.S. African American history, oral history, the National Archives and federal records, military records, migratory patterns, and slavery. The second part is titled "Survey of the States." Here, unlike the 1st edition that divided the United States into regions, each state is listed in a separate chapter along with a chapter on Canada and one on the West Indies. This approach works better. In each of the chapters the state's resources on African American research are listed in the following categories: "Important Dates," "State Archives," "Census Records," "State and County Records," "Cemetery and Church Records," "Military Records," "Newspapers," "Manuscript Sources," "Internet Resources," "Research Contacts," and "Bibliography." Obviously, coverage is widely different in different states. Many Web addresses are included, where available. The 1st edition included more specific items that were available for each area. This edition does a better job of summarizing what kinds of records are available and then encouraging the reader to search those resources. This will be outdated very soon as more resources become available. For example, this book most likely was already in editing in October 2002 when the United States Census for 1880 and other censuses were made freely available at www.familysearch.org and so the only reference in this work is to the CD-ROM product that was then available. There are also some minor errors in the indexing. However, this will be a tremendously helpful guide to those interested in African American research. [R: LJ, 1 Nov 03, p. 72]—**Robert L. Turner Jr.**

HERALDRY

S

138.   Howe, Randy. **Flags of the Fifty States and Their Incredible Histories.** New York, Lyons Press, 2002. 200p. illus. maps. $16.95. ISBN 1-58574-603-7.

Flags of the Fifty States is a high quality, beautifully illustrated book. Each of the 50 states is included, in order of the state's admittance to the Union. A full color illustration of a flag begins each entry, with two or three pages of text following. Each entry contains a concise history of the state, along with a more detailed history of its flag. Each entry also contains the state's nickname, motto, date of admittance to the Union, and a map highlighting the location of the state in relationship to the rest of the United States. Callout boxes in each entry call attention to interesting facts about the state and its flag.

The quality of the book, and the author's love of flags, is evident when the book is first opened. An obvious amount of effort went into the preparation of this book, making it fitting to represent flags that command respect. However, it probably is not particularly useful as a reference book. The order of the entries makes it difficult to find wanted information, unless the reader happens to know the order in which states were admitted. Also, this information is readily available from many other sources. Besides, most libraries do not get many questions that would necessitate such a resource. Although not much use as a reference book, it would be a great book for the general collections of school libraries and possibly public libraries. Unless one's library's patron base contains a lot of budding vexillologists (people who study flags), a decent atlas or almanac should meet the needs this book seeks to meet.—**Mark T. Bay**

PERSONAL NAMES

P

139.   **Dictionary of American Family Names.** Patrick Hanks, ed. New York, Oxford University Press, 2003. 3v. $295.00/set. ISBN 0-19-508137-4.

The *Dictionary of American Family Names* is an extremely comprehensive 3-volume collection of 70,000 surnames that should be especially helpful to genealogists as well as to those with a more casual interest in the history of their family moniker. Highlighting the most common names in the United States in alphabetic order, each name is analyzed in a variety of ways. The relative frequency of the name is expressed numerically, based on the number of people with the name in a sample of 89 million Americans. Thus, Smith is listed as 831,783 and Smulski, on the next page, as 72. The language of origin is then listed, along with variant spellings, regional predominance, as well as typological and etymological histories. Cross-references to related names are given, along with statistical information on the most common given names associated with the surname. If a name is connected in some way to a significant figure in U.S. history, a brief explanation is provided. The first volume begins with introductory texts. There is an excellent general introduction that covers a variety of topics, from the inconsistencies of spelling to a general history of the origins of family names. This is followed by a section that gives an explanation for the statistical methods used in selecting the surnames and their relation to particular given names. A final section consists of articles written by regional experts on the relation of surnames to particular languages and cultures, including those of European, Jewish, Middle Eastern, and Asian origins. [R: LJ, Aug 03, pp. 68-70; AG, Nov 03, p. 60; SLJ, Dec 03, p. 95]—**Philip G. Swan**

8 Geography

GENERAL WORKS

Atlases

S

140. **The Kingfisher Student Atlas.** New York, Houghton Mifflin, 2003. 128p. illus. maps. index. $24.95 (w/CD-ROM). ISBN 0-7534-5589-7.

This atlas features physical and political maps of the world. Organized by continent, the computer-generated maps are colorfully and crisply rendered. Place-names are printed in easy-to-read block print. Continents and the United States are divided into sections for larger and easier viewing. Maps are presented in two-page spreads, with text that describes the physical, historical, and cultural background of the region represented. For many of the regions there is a discussion of the environmental problems and their causes. A locater map with each region map places that region within its global context. In the margin of each two-page spread are color pictures of the flags of each country depicted on the map.

An introduction to the atlas discusses topics such as climate, the natural world, and the world's population. Beginning maps depict both the physical world and the political world. An index lists all the place-names and features found on the maps with the atlas. An accompanying CD-ROM includes 40 maps that are ready to print; however, most are physical maps without any place-names, which limits their use. This is an attractive, serviceable, and inexpensive atlas that elementary through high school students will enjoy using because of the colorful maps and easy-to-read print.—**Dana McDougald**

C, P

141. **Oxford Atlas of the World.** 11th ed. New York, Oxford University Press, 2003. 1v. (various paging). maps. index. $80.00. ISBN 0-19-521986-4.

This annually revised atlas continues to be a valuable addition to public and academic libraries needing the most up-to-date geographical information. The work is organized into six sections. "World Statistics and Images of Earth" provides statistical information on each country, including area in miles and kilometers, population, capital city, and annual income. It also provides geographical information on Earth's oceans, mountains, rivers, lakes, and islands. Following this is a page with maps of "Regions in the News": the India/Pakistan border, Iraq, Afghanistan, Israel, and Colombia are featured this year. The next section is "The Gazetteer of Nations," which includes: an image of each country's flag; information on their geography, politics, and economy; and a sidebar with the country's area, population, capital, government, ethnic groups, languages, religions, and currency. Following this is a 47-page section titled "Introduction to World Geography," which provides maps and charts on the solar system, weather, population, family, minerals, and standards of living, just to name a few. A section of "City Maps" follows that includes detailed maps of 67 major cities; this section has its own index.

The bulk of the volume is the section containing the world maps organized by continents. These maps include physical relief maps, political maps, and large-scale maps of specific regions as well as heavily populated areas. The work concludes with a geographical glossary and a 125-page index. New to this edition are new and renamed provinces in Canada, the former Yugoslavia, and the Democratic Republic of Congo; new statistics from the 2000 U.S. Census; and a complete revision to "The Gazetteer of Nations" section.

The *Oxford Atlas of the World* is one of the most well-executed and accurate atlases available. It should be in all academic and large public libraries.—**Shannon Graff Hysell**

Dictionaries and Encyclopedias

P

142.   **The Encyclopedia of World Geography.** Berkeley, Calif., Thunder Bay Press/Publishers Group West, 2002. 512p. illus. maps. index. $29.98. ISBN 1-57145-871-9.

This beautiful, color-illustrated encyclopedia of world geography contains detailed individual country profiles for the current 193 nation-states of the world (as of the time of publication). The book is divided into 22 regional sections. Dependencies of countries are also given space. Each regional section includes a high-quality topographic map showing key physical features, national boundaries and country names, plus major cities and towns. Individual entries are provided for every country in the world, divided into three major parts: "Geography," "Society," and "Economy." "Geography" describes the physical landscape of the country, "Society" puts the people of that country into the context of their environment by providing a historical chronological review, while "Economy" provides information on how the people have utilized the land and its resources to build an economy that funds (or fails to fund) their nation's requirements. There are many feature panels that appear throughout the volume focusing on items of interest related to each country. Facts and statistics are available throughout the book. A glossary, further reading section, and index round out this well-researched and affordable reference work.—**Bradford Lee Eden**

S

143.   **Junior Worldmark Encyclopedia of Physical Geography.** Karen Ellicott and Susan B. Gall, eds. Farmington Hills, Mich., U*X*L/Gale, 2003. 5v. illus. maps. index. $225.00/set. ISBN 0-7876-6265-8.

This new 5-volume set from U*X*L is devoted to physical geography of nearly 200 countries and is impressive and comprehensive. The encyclopedia is specifically designed for students in grades 5-12, although anyone having an interest in a country's physical geography can use it. The entries are arranged alphabetically and each volume has an appendix with facts and figures on the different countries of the world that many students will find useful and fascinating. For example, Appendix N and O are on the Seven Wonders of the Ancient World and the Seven Wonder of the Natural World. The set is nicely organized. Although the cumulative index is located in only volume 5, it is easy to access and to locate any of the subjects mentioned the other 4 volumes. Each volume contains a detailed glossary known as the "Words to Know" section that students will find helpful and easy to understand. More importantly, the "Further Reading" section after each entry also contains periodicals and reliable Websites to sources like National Geographic. The photographs, illustrations, maps and tables are appealing and generally of high quality; however, one would prefer them to be in color instead of black and white. Nevertheless, *Junior Worldmark Encyclopedia of Physical Geography* is a valuable reference tool for any student.—**Vang Vang**

S

144.   **The Kingfisher Geography Encyclopedia.** New York, Houghton Mifflin, 2003. 487p. illus. maps. index. $39.95. ISBN 0-7534-5591-9.

When opening this book users will begin to explore the world. They will find concise overviews of the historical, cultural, and geographic highlights of 193 independent nations and their dependencies. They will first read informative chapters that explain how the world was formed and how weather and climate continue to reshape the earth we inhabit. Users will then begin to move across the globe continent by continent to learn about the countries within each and how each nation is unique and interesting. A sampling of the nuggets to be discovered along the way is that San Marino has the oldest defined boundaries, dating back to C.E. 301; East Timor is the youngest entry into the world community; back in the 1667, the Netherlands traded New Amsterdam (later to become New York City) to the British for English territories in Suriname (then Dutch Guiana); unlike most South American countries, Argentina has strong Italian-Argentine, British-Argentine, and Jewish communities; and the Bologna University in Italy is the oldest continuing university in Europe, dating back to 1080. At the end of the reference users will find summary material discussing the world's major biological habitats, distribution of water resources, wind and ocean currents, and the effect of pollution on our globe as well as health, economic, energy, trade, telecommunications, industrial production, and educational statistics. Square mileage and population data are also provided for the states, provinces, and regions for each nation. School librarians will want to share this beautifully illustrated resource with students to give them a context in which to understand world events and to begin their work on school research projects.—**Adrienne Antink Bien**

Handbooks and Yearbooks

P, S

145.   Ciovacco, Justine, Kathleen A. Feeley, and Kristen Behrens. **State-by-State Atlas.** New York, DK Publishing, 2003. 128p. illus. maps. index. $19.99. ISBN 0-7894-9257-1.

This colorful atlas is divided into 8 sections: "The Northeast States," "The Southeast States," "The Midwest States," "The Plains States," "The Southwest States," "The Rocky Mountain States," "The Pacific States," and "Washington, D.C. and Outlying Regions." This is really more of a state factbook than an atlas. While there are maps for regions and the individual states within the regions, they are not detailed.

An introduction to each section provides a brief overview of climate, landscape, lifestyle, economy, and a map that shows the states for that region. A timeline running across the bottom of the page provides key dates throughout the history of the region. Following the introduction are two-page spreads for each state within the region. An inset on the first page provides basic information, such as state bird, flower, tree, capital, population, statehood date and rank, largest cities, and land area. There is a brief history of the state; a map with key cities, lakes, and rivers noted; and captioned photographs and drawings that provide information on a variety of facts such as important residents or historical figures, key industries, recreation, historical events, and so on. The majority of the state maps are regrettably spread between the two pages, leaving a part of each of those maps in the gutter. The final section covers Washington, D.C., Puerto Rico, the U.S. Virgin Islands, American Samoa, and Guam. While Washington, D.C. is given a two-page spread, the outlying regions are given only brief coverage. As with other DK publications, this atlas offers a visual playground of colorful photographs and drawings, as well as wide array of facts about each state that readers will find both informative and interesting.—**Dana McDougald**

C

146.   Short, John Rennie. **The World Through Maps: A History of Cartography.** New York, Firefly Books, 2003. 224p. illus. maps. index. $40.00. ISBN 1-55297-811-7.

This reference work focuses on the history of maps from ancient times to the present. It discusses the craft of cartography, and how maps are important statements about the ownership and control of territory and property. Sidebars present historical and background information to specific cultures, important individuals, and time periods. This book is lavishly illustrated; some of the historically significant maps included in this book are the aboriginal "Dreamtime" map, the Madaba mosaic map, the Mappa Mundi, the

Theatrum of the Renaissance, early maps of the New World, and modern maps produced by satellite and remote sensing techniques. Many other interesting subjects regarding the creation, evolution, and history of cartography are presented as well. A bibliography and index are provided.

This is a very concise and well-written reference work on the history of cartography, generally geared toward the high school to undergraduate audience. The many color illustrations and photographs of important maps throughout history make this an essential reference work for many colleges and universities. —**Bradford Lee Eden**

PLACE-NAMES

C, P

147.   **Getty Thesaurus of Geographic Names Online. http://www.getty.edu/research/tools/vocabulary/tgn.** [Website]. Free. Date reviewed: Jan 04.

This online gazetteer is one piece of several Getty structured vocabularies. The purpose is to provide standardization in name use by noting preferred names within a hierarchical structure. It contains over 1,000,000 place-names including populated places ranging from continents to small villages and other features (such as geysers, ghost towns, and glaciers) around the world. The entries provide latitude and longitude coordinates, variations on the name, and a hierarchy such as which county, state, nation, and continent the place is found. Some entries have historical notes. Sources include the 1961 *Columbia Lippincott Gazetteer*, the NIMA GEOnet names server, the USGS Geographic Names Information Service, the *Oxford English Dictionary*, and a number of other resources including Spanish, French, and Italian dictionaries. The thesaurus is strictly in the Roman alphabet with diacritics, and all the source documents originate in the United States and Western Europe.

The *Thesaurus* notes the preferred form of a name, usually being the one in most use at that place; for instance, Nihon is the preferred name for Japan. "English-P" notes the name preferred for English users, which is Japan for Nihon. The thesaurus also provides the ISO (International Standards Organization) 2-letter code, the ISO 3-letter code, and the FIPS (Federal Information Processing Standards) Code. It also lists other variations on the name, such as "Giappone" for Japan, and cites the source of each name.

The search interface is very simple, searching only by place-name. The database will return any name in the database whether it is a preferred form or not. The searcher may also specify a feature type and nation to narrow the results. The thesaurus must have employed some sort of screening process to limit entries since the GEOnet Names Server alone contains 3.6 million entries. It also does not provide complete historical information for every place. For researchers seeking out small villages, the GEOnet names server will continue to be more comprehensive, and localized gazetteers will continue to have more historical information. The value in the thesaurus, however, is the standardization as a controlled vocabulary and its hierarchical structure. At this time, the thesaurus grows through solicited contributions, but an online submission form for the public is in development.—**Kathleen Weessies**

9 History

ARCHAEOLOGY

P, S

148. Fagan, Brian. **Archaeologists: Explorers of the Human Past.** New York, Oxford University Press, 2003. 191p. illus. index. (Oxford Profiles). $40.00. ISBN 0-19-511946-0.

Archaeologists is the latest title in Oxford Profiles, a respected series that provides short biographies of major contributors who helped define a select time period or area of achievement. The author, Brian Fagan, is widely respected for his expertise and writings in archaeology, including *The Oxford Companion to Archaeology* (see ARBA 98, entry 428).

This book includes profiles of 33 archaeologists who made substantial contributions to the field between the seventeenth century and 1960. These highly readable profiles provide details of their life and work and include drawings, illustrations, and photographs to enhance the text. Each entry is approximately four pages in length. Several outline maps are included to show the general locations of the sites mentioned. The book is divided into five sections, each with a three-page introduction that puts the contributions of the archaeologists in context. Section 5 lists and provides a brief paragraph for some prominent archaeologists that are or were currently active.

At the back of the book there are two general timelines of major events in the history of archaeology and events in prehistoric times. These will be of some value to people who are casually interested in archaeology. There is also a five-page glossary of archaeological sites and terms and a short listing of readings and Websites. This set of readings is in addition to the 4 to 6 suggested readings at the end of each profile. Again, both will have some value to someone new to the field. This book will be most appropriate for acquisition by middle school and high school libraries and public libraries.—**Judith J. Field**

AMERICAN HISTORY

General Works

S

149. Outman, James L., and Elisabeth M. Outman. **Industrial Revolution: Almanac.** Edited by Matthew May. Farmington Hills, Mich., U*X*L/Gale, 2003. 242p. illus. index. (U*X*L Industrial Revolution Reference Library). $58.00/vol.; $159.00/set. ISBN 0-7876-6513-4.

S

150. Outman, James L., and Elisabeth M. Outman. **Industrial Revolution: Biographies.** Edited by Matthew May. Farmington Hills, Mich., U*X*L/Gale, 2003. 218p. illus. index. (U*X*L Industrial Revolution Reference Library). $58.00/vol.; $159.00/set. ISBN 0-7876-6514-2.

S

151.　Outman, James L., and Elisabeth M. Outman. **Industrial Revolution: Primary Sources.** Edited by Matthew May. Farmington Hills, Mich., U*X*L/Gale, 2003. 212p. illus. index. (U*X*L Industrial Revolution Reference Library). $58.00/vol.; $159.00/set. ISBN 0-7876-6515-0.

The Industrial Revolution is a time period that changed the world, yet few of us really understand the triumphs and sacrifices that it brought. The three-volume set by James and Elisabeth Outman entitled Industrial Revolution Reference Library does an excellent job of explaining this critical time period and its impact on human history.

The first volume presents a timeline and delves into the origins of the Industrial Revolution, its major technologies, and the social and political impacts. Volume 2 consists of 22 biographical sketches of important people. Volume 3 is a collection of writings from participants and observers that discuss a variety of subjects, including economics, technology, working conditions, politics, and law.

This three-volume format is a good way to tackle such a complex and far-reaching time period as the Industrial Revolution, especially for the middle school or high school reader. The text is well written and straightforward; however, a little more personal narrative in the first two volumes would have captured more of the drama of the time. The volumes are well illustrated and contain interesting sidebars and glossaries. Chapters end with useful "Additional Reading" sections, which includes books, periodicals, and Websites. Each volume has a thorough index; a cumulative index also covers all three volumes. The Industrial Revolution Reference Library is a great reference source for any student interested in researching this fascinating period of world history. [R: SLJ, Dec 03, pp. 97-98]—**Mark J. Crawford**

Bibliography

C

152.　**America: History and Life. http://sb2.abc-clio.com:8080/.** [Website]. Santa Barbara, Calif., ABC-CLIO. Price negotiated by site. ISSN 1528-3437. Date reviewed: 2003.

The main index for the field of U.S. history is *America: History and Life*, which began publication in 1964. This publication broadly covers U.S. and Canadian history, area studies, popular culture, genealogy, multicultural studies, women's studies/gender studies, anthropology, and the history of science, economics, business, education, music, art, and law. As well as the print edition, *America: History and Life* is available for online searching from 1964 to the present as an online database and also from the publisher in a CD-ROM format. The capacity to combine two or more terms or descriptors makes searching in the electronic versions superior to using printed index volumes. The database indexes over 2,000 journals published worldwide, including state historical society journals. In addition to articles, 6,000 citations of book and media reviews and abstracts of dissertations are included. Also included in the electronic database are "CLIO Notes," a research guide that has concise overviews of 22 major historical periods designed to help identify major issues and events; detailed chronologies to give context to those issues and events; and suggestions for papers and class discussions. Search strategies and guided searching using selected index terms assist the beginning researcher as well as a simple searching option. All research in U.S. history or interdisciplinary topics in the social sciences and the humanities should begin by searching the topic in this database.—**Anna H. Perrault**

C

153.　Perrault, Anna H., and Ron Blazek. **United States History: A Multicultural, Interdisciplinary Guide to Information Sources.** 2d ed. Westport, Conn., Libraries Unlimited/Greenwood Publishing Group, 2003. 661p. index. $70.00. ISBN 1-56308-874-6.

This reference guide to U.S. history sources updates a 1994 edition of the same name (see ARBA 95, entry 529). Since many changes in historical research have transpired during the past decade, particularly the rapid increase in the number of electronic sources, this 2d edition is a useful supplement to the original. About 25 percent larger than the 1st edition, this single-volume work contains 1,250 major entries, plus hundreds of additional minor entries contained within the annotations of the major entries. In additional to providing bibliographic data for each entry, the 85- to 250-word annotations describe the scope and coverage, and occasionally assess the utility of the reference tools included in the volume. The work is divided into two parts: general U.S. sources (141 entries) and U.S. history topics and issues (1,109 entries). It is user friendly, with over 100 pages of author/title and subject indexes. The editors have largely succeeded in their attempt to include within the volume wide coverage of the political, economic, diplomatic, military, social, and cultural experiences of Americans of all genders, creeds, and colors.

The writing is intelligible but bland, concise yet uninspiring. Students of history will not pick this book off the shelf for a good read, but scholars will appreciate accessing the wealth of information that is contained within it. This resource is recommended for college and university libraries.—**Terry D. Bilhartz**

Dictionaries and Encyclopedias

C, P, S

154.   **Encyclopedia of the Great Depression.** Robert S. McElvaine, ed. New York, Macmillan Reference USA/Gale Group, 2004. 2v. illus. index. $240.00/set. ISBN 0-02-865686-5.

For years, with hyperbolic extravagance, parents have cited the negligence of their children as the singular reason their households must too often furnish heat and light for their entire neighborhoods. It is not necessarily that they cannot afford the few cents it cost to power an unused reading lamp or to pay for the heat escaping from an open door. As children of the Great Depression, these families learned from their parents the harsh lessons gained from the fear and uncertainty of living through those hard times; life is precarious and waste is immoral. That one remarkable decade in America's history has left an indelible mark on this nation's culture and its legacy continues to shape the attitudes of succeeding generations of Americans.

As one of the most profound crises the United States has ever faced, there is no shortage of reference books written about the Great Depression. Credit Editor in Chief, Robert S. McElvaine, and the publishers at Macmillan Reference for providing a unique addition to the literature with their superb two-volume, A to Z reference, *Encyclopedia of the Great Depression*. Using a multidisciplinary approach from the fields of history, political science, social science, literature, and art, and a conscious effort at presenting a global perspective, this comprehensive work provides 540 signed articles written by subject experts. Entries are informative and engaging and cover a wide variety of topics, notably including in-depth coverage of key issues, analysis of important developments, and biographies of significant individuals. Technically this is a first-rate production covering all the reference bases; included are useful and interesting bibliographies at the end of articles, a good index, and *see* and *see also* cross-references. The set's best feature is its collection of photographs, maybe worth the price alone, and perhaps as compelling as those of any A to Z reference available.

This work will make an ideal companion volume for libraries that already own James Climent's more thematic *Encyclopedia of the Great Depression and the New Deal* (see ARBA 2002, entry 435), and it will serve as a welcome addition to any undergraduate, high school, or public library collection.—**Vincent P. Tinerella**

C, S

155.   Woodger, Elin, and Brandon Toropov. **Encyclopedia of the Lewis and Clark Expedition.** New York, Facts on File, 2004. 438p. illus. maps. index. (Facts on File Library of American History). $65.00. ISBN 0-8160-4781-2.

The 200th anniversary of Lewis and Clark's epic exploration of the upper Midwest and Northwest of the vast Louisiana Purchase lands is now upon us. There are already hundreds of books and monographs about this astonishing journey and its scientific and cultural achievements, and many more will appear to mark the bicentennial, but until now there has been no systematic source of information on the topic. The authors of this volume had the wonderful idea of assembling an encyclopedia on the expedition, making it very easy to look up hundreds of details on the expedition, including the events that led to it and the aftermath. Any library with an American history collection will want this book on its shelves.

One of the most important parts of this volume is its thorough introduction. In a few pages the authors outline the basic story and provide an essential commentary placing the expedition in its political and social contexts. This is followed by a chronology, which starts with Sir Francis Drake on the Pacific coast and ends with the official closing of the western frontier in 1890. Detailed maps are provided showing routes and important villages and landmarks along the way.

There are over 350 encyclopedic articles, from Agency Creek in Idaho to York, who was William Clark's slave and a full member of the Corps of Discovery. Many of the entries are illustrated with black-and-white photographs and drawings, many of the latter from journals of the expedition. Most articles have a "further reading" section, often including Web addresses. The entries themselves are well written, even for a reader only roughly acquainted with the narrative. The range of topics deemed relevant is very large, including brief biographies of each member of the company and in some cases their family members. Items of equipment are covered down to the paper they wrote on and the ink they used. Indian tribes and leaders are covered with special detail, including fascinating stories of their contributions to the expedition's success and, in some cases, their deleterious effects on equipment and morale. There is even a section on "sex during the expedition." I cannot think of a single relevant topic that is not covered by these entries. The two appendixes include a list of the Indian tribes the expedition met (48 of them), and detailed maps of the route. An extensive, categorized bibliography and an index finish this superb volume. [R: LJ, Dec 03, p. 102]—**Mark A. Wilson**

Handbooks and Yearbooks

P, S

156.   **America in the Twentieth Century.** 2d ed. Tarrytown, N.Y., Marshall Cavendish, 2003. 13v. illus. index. $399.95/set. ISBN 0-7614-7364-5.

The 2d revised and expanded edition of *America in the Twentieth Century* is marked by 2 additional volumes to the 11 original ones published in 1995 (see ARBA 96, entry 499). These volumes contain primary sources from 1900 to 1999—approximately 10 for each decade—treating the themes of civil rights, war, culture and society, economics, the environment, and government. There are no primary sources representing the Clinton administration, and the "Culture and Society" section is superficial. The editors have made no effort to correct the original reviewer's criticism that religion is not discussed until volume 6 (1950). Although *America in the Twentieth Century* may be of little use for scholars, it is intended primarily for a general audience. With its integrated discussion of politics, family life, media, sports, technological change, the environment, health and medicine, literature and the arts, race, and women's issues, and its hundreds of biographical sketches and inclusion of scores of colored photographs, this comprehensive social history of the United States is highly recommended for public and high school libraries. [R: SLJ, Aug 03, p. 109]—**E. Wayne Carp**

C

157.   **American Decades: Primary Sources.** Cynthia Rose, ed. Farmington Hills, Mich., Gale, 2004. 10v. illus. index. $895.00/set; $95.00/vol. ISBN 0-7876-6587-8.

This carefully crafted new offering from Gale is sure to be a worthy heir to the discontinued classic documentary American history reference source, *The Annals of America* (Encyclopaedia Britannica,

1968-1987), which is available in print in limited quantities after Britannica sold its inventory of remaining sets to World Book. Gale's latest contribution to the field is intended to serve as a companion to their popular series, American Decades (Gale Group, 1994-2001) and would complement many of the publisher's other prominent reference works in American history, notably the two-volume stand-alone *Gale Encyclopedia of Multicultural America: Primary Documents* (see ARBA 2001, entry 271). This work will also make an ideal companion set for the many libraries that already own *The Annals*, as this new work offers limited coverage, its entries usually provide essays about and excerpts from primary sources rather than the full text of the sources themselves, it is more comprehensive, and despite some inevitable overlap, its selections are generally different.

This informative 10-volume set covers the 20th century, arranged by decade starting in the year 1900, and furnishes more than 2,000 entries in all. Individual volumes are organized topically, with specific entries subdivided within each subject area chronologically, and tied together with a good index with main entries displayed in bold text, facilitating each volume's ease of use. Individual entries begin with a brief synopsis; include basic information about the source and its author; provide separate essays introducing the source and another explaining its significance; furnish excerpts; and end with bibliographies of books, Websites, and audio and visual material (divided by category). The majority of entries include a drawing, photograph, table, chart, graph, document, cartoon, advertisement, catalog page, or some other accompanying high-quality illustration, serving to make the entry more relevant and interesting, and the set as a whole, a delight to browse. Produced by a team of historians, the writing itself is first-rate, offering various perspectives, counterpoints, and diverse ideas and opinions. The selection of sources provides good variety, and historically significant entries tend to show up in different subject areas, allowing the user to judge a source's importance from different perspectives.

American Decades: Primary Sources is certain to become the centerpiece of many serious American history reference collections. This new work is so innovative and well done that it may become a classic itself, and at its advertised price of less than $100 for each sturdy, well-designed volume, well worth the investment.—**Vincent P. Tinerella**

C, S

158.   Bullock, Steven C. **The American Revolution: A History in Documents.** New York, Oxford University Press, 2003. 205p. illus. index. (Pages from History). $32.95. ISBN 0-19-513224-6.

Bullock succeeds quite well in making history important and vital to today. His chronological arrangement of documents gives the reader a sense of growing unrest, building urgency, and inevitability of war. In the documents, one can see both famous players and the not so famous. John Adams is here, as well as Abigail Adams. Patrick Henry and Benjamin Rush play their part, as do Mercy Otis Warren and Benjamin Franklin. Documents such as legislative resolutions, petitions, newspaper columns, and broadsides figure in this book, as well as excerpts from such well-known writings as the Federalist Papers, the Declaration of Independence, the Constitution, and pamphlets such as Thomas Paine's *Common Sense*. But also included are extracts from diaries and letters of the unknown merchants and workers and wives and mothers whose lives will be disrupted by war. Numerous illustrations populate the book, while a timeline gives a quick look at the major events of the time.

Bullock's final chapter, "The Living Revolution: The Revolution Remembered" takes a look at how the Revolution has been represented and remembered in popular culture and in history books, from the romantic and glorious (the painting of "Washington Crossing the Delaware" and Longfellow's poem of "Paul Revere's Ride), to the commercial and materialistic (a 1932 map of "The Principal Events in the Life of George Washington put out by the Standard Oil Company in 1932 in commemoration of the bicentennial of Washington's birthday). It also discusses how the Revolution influenced subsequent political movements in which people struggled for increasing liberty, such as the abolitionist movement and the women's rights movement of the nineteenth century, and, beyond our borders, the French Revolution. Bullock has managed to breathe new life into what for many are dry and dusty documents of a bygone time.
—**Terry Ann Mood**

P, S

159. Heidler, David S., and Jeanne T. Heidler. **Manifest Destiny.** Westport, Conn., Greenwood Press, 2003. 241p. index. (Greenwood Guides to Historic Events, 1500-1900). $45.00. ISBN 0-313-32308-9.

Most of us have a vague impression of "manifest destiny" as being some sort of political philosophy that underlies the expansion of the territory of the United States from the Atlantic to the Pacific in the nineteenth century, but attempts to find out more about it often lead to a diffuse literature where it is mentioned but rarely analyzed. This book addresses the topic directly and in considerable detail, finally providing in one place a comprehensive view of the movement. The result is an enlightening and sometimes surprising book that is easy to read yet scholarly in tone.

The authors make the initial point that while the phrase "manifest destiny" was coined in 1845, the concept that Providence predestined the United States to stretch from coast to coast predates even the American Revolution. It was at times a driving force of American domestic and international politics, and just as often it was itself driven by these forces. One interesting insight in this book is how thoroughly the American system of slavery contaminated international relations, from fears (and hopes) that bordering territories would become refuges for escaped slaves to competition between slave and free states over new lands. The Mexican-American War is treated especially well in this book. The parallels between this war and the present conflict in Iraq are intriguing. As today, the domestic opposition to the war with Mexico questioned how much of it was threat abatement and how much was expansionism. History again proves instructive to the present.

This book begins with a chronology of American territorial acquisition from 1785 to 1850. This is followed by seven chapters starting with a historical overview and including the complicated histories of Florida, Indian policies (basically "Indian removal") , Texas, Oregon, and the Mexican-American War. There are also short biographies of important people associated with expansionism, texts from primary documents (such as treaties and legislation), a short glossary, and an annotated bibliography. A few historical drawings in the center of the book provide some evocative images.

Manifest Destiny is part of the Greenwood Guides to Historic Events, 1500-1900 series. Libraries that own this series will certainly want to add this book. Libraries without the series may wish to begin acquiring it. This is an accessible, well-referenced history series that will serve any reading audience.
—**Mark A. Wilson**

S

160. Howes, Kelly King. **Mexican American War.** Farmington Hills, Mich., U*X*L/Gale, 2003. 237p. illus. maps. index. $52.00. ISBN 0-7876-6537-1.

The Mexican American War (1846-48) barely gets mentioned in most U.S. history books, but deserves attention because it gave the United States Texas, New Mexico, Arizona, California, and parts of Nevada and Utah. It defined our southern border, was the first war the U.S. fought on foreign soil, the first war in which battles were photographed and covered first-hand by newspaper correspondents, and illustrates the effectiveness of Polk's presidency. This war was the training ground for the officer corps that went on to lead both sides of the Civil War and included many individuals who later became president —Robert E. Lee, Ulysses S. Grant, Jefferson Davis, Lew Wallace, George Gordon Meade, Albert Sidney Johnston, Stonewall Jackson, George Pickett, George McLellan, Zachary Taylor, and Franklin Pierce. It was a controversial war in which Lincoln, Emerson, and Thoreau were among the dissenters. It also set in place resentments that still mark American-Mexican relations. Mexico paid a heavy toll in lives and lost about 50 percent of its territory, leaving the country with feelings of shame and in political chaos.

This junior high text has two sections. It begins with a chronological account of the political forces and important battles that shaped the conflict. Woven into the narrative are brief biographies, newspaper cartoons from the time, source documents (e.g., Declaration of War), and excerpts from Thoreau's "Civil Disobedience" essay. The second part offers more extensive profiles of the key players. There is also a timeline, glossary, and activity ideas. This reference not only gives readers a better understanding of Manifest Destiny and southwestern expansion, it also gives insights into the Civil War and the United States' current political relationship with Mexico.—**Adrienne Antink Bien**

C, P, S

161.   **Library of Congress Civil War Desk Reference.** Margaret E. Wagner, Gary W. Gallagher, and Paul Finkelman, eds. New York, Simon & Schuster, 2002. 949p. illus. maps. index. $45.00. ISBN 0-684-86350-2.

This is a significant and important new addition to the reference literature of the American Civil War. In terms of comprehensive treatment of the subject, it is as good as, and perhaps better than any this reviewer, a Civil War historian and former reference librarian, has had the pleasure of examining. This makes it an excellent companion for casual readers, students, and professional historians in need of further information regarding virtually all aspects of the pre-war period, the war years, and the Reconstruction era following the conflict, including military, political, social, economic, legal, medical, and other issues. This work was compiled under the editorial guidance of the respected Civil War historian Gary Gallagher, legal historian Paul Finkelman, and Margaret Wagner of the Library of Congress. Unfortunately, the actual writers are listed only by name, without data on their expertise in this area.

In 14 lengthy chapters that are both highly readable and informative, the editors present the story of the Civil War from its pre-war background through the war years and the Reconstruction era that followed. This is done primarily through narrative articles that are supplemented by numerous well-chosen photographs, maps, charts, statistics, biographical sketches, lists of supplemental readings, and the inclusion of many excerpts from letters and diaries of the men and women who lived through the conflict. Chapter 1 introduces users to the war by means of an excellent monthly timeline covering 1860-1865. The thing that makes this book particularly useful and readable is its expansion beyond the usual emphasis on campaigns, battles, and military and political leaders to include detailed information on the home front, army, life and activities of the common soldier, medicine and medical practice, battle tactics, mapping, telegraphy, side-by-side comparisons of the Confederate and Union constitutions, weapons and ammunition, political parties, elections, and other topics too numerous to mention. The two concluding chapters are particularly useful for their discussions of the Civil War in literature and the arts, and lists of museums, libraries, and other organizations as sources for further study on the war. Easy access to the contents is gained through a 49-page index and detailed table of contents.

The book, however, is not without criticism. The collaborative efforts provide some uneven coverage and varying quality in writing, which ranges from highly readable to adequate. The section on Reconstruction is not as well done as earlier sections. The failed military reconstruction of North Carolina in 1862-1863 under Lincoln appointee Edward Stanley is not mentioned. The fact that the impeachment of President Andrew Johnson was carried out as a political vendetta by one party against an unpopular president is also ignored. And the important presidential election of 1876 is inadequately treated and the term "Compromise of 1877," which is generally regarded as resulting in the conclusion of the military occupation of the Southern states, is nowhere used. These are minor criticisms. The low cost and superior treatment of its subject make this an outstanding reference work that should be considered for purchase by public, college, university, and other libraries as well as institutions and individuals with an interest in the American Civil War. [R: BL, 1 Jan 03, p. 940]—**Donald E. Collins**

S

162.   **Life & Times in 20th-Century America.** Westport, Conn., Greenwood Press, 2004. 5v. illus. index. $200.00/set. ISBN 0-313-32570-7.

Each of these five attractively bound volumes spans a 20-year period. The first, "Becoming a Modern Nation," begins at 1900 and its cover sports a photograph of a triumphant President Theodore Roosevelt; the last, "Promise and Change," ends at 2000 and its cover features a resigned-looking President Bill Clinton and wife Hillary. Sandwiched in between are "Boom Times, Hard Times, 1921-1940," "Hot and

Cold Wars, 1941-1960," and "Troubled Times at Home, 1961-1980." Each volume opens with an overview followed by chapters on subjects such as family life, social and political attitudes, religion, education, science and technology, entertainment, and fashions and fads. A bibliography points readers to other sources, and an index makes the material readily accessible. Numerous photographs, charts, and drawings interspersed throughout enhance the appeal.

Since this work is aimed at students from the sixth- to eighth-grade levels, the writing is simple and clear. And, importantly, the content for the most part is balanced and free of any obvious bias. Youngsters will find here an account of the nation's triumphs and failures, the rich and poor, the mainstream and the fringes. The chapters on religion, for instance, as readily call attention to the Pentecostal movement of the early 1900s and the origins of the Church of God in Christ, the large African American body, as to mainline Protestants, Catholics, and Jews. On the other hand, the treatment of labor unions struck this reviewer, at points, as not altogether fair, especially in light of the widening gap in American society between the rich and poor, the enormous loss of jobs to foreign countries, and corporate greed. Nonetheless, this is a fine work and middle school libraries should consider it for their reference collections.—**John W. Storey**

C, S

163.   **Our Documents: 100 Milestone Documents from the National Archives.** New York, Oxford University Press, 2003. 256p. illus. index. $40.00. ISBN 0-19-517206-X.

Primary sources are the backbone of history and crucial to secondary history telling. As history continues to be reworked, excerpts from primary sources are relied on heavily and tend to be regarded as the summation of the entire original document—definitely a mistake. This is why *Our Documents* is such a valuable source—it collects 100 of the most important documents in American history.

The selections are arranged in chronological order, beginning with the Lee Resolution of 1776 and ending with the Voting Rights Act of 1965. In between are 98 others, including the Declaration of Independence, Constitution of the United States, Missouri Compromise, Gettysburg Address, various U.S. Constitution amendments, National Industrial Recovery Act, Social Security Act of 1935, and Marshall Plan. Of course, there are thousands of U.S. documents from which to choose—it is reassuring to know that this selection was compiled by experts from National Archives and Records Administration. Each entry has a concise introduction that provides an overview of the document's content.

The book is also an attractive one, including heavy paper, good use of color, and a generous dose of illustrations, photographs, and reproductions of the documents themselves. Further, there is an extremely valuable "Further Reading" section that lists key sources that further examine the impact of these documents on American and world history.

Secondary treatments of original sources leave out a tremendous amount of detail. There is much to be learned by reading original documents in their entirety. *Our Documents* is an outstanding, fairly priced reference that allows students, teachers, and researchers of American history to do just that.—**Mark J. Crawford**

S

164.   **Primary Sources in American History Series.** New York, Rosen Publishing, 2003. 6v. illus. maps. index. $175.50/set; $29.25/vol. ISBN 0-8239-3681-3 (v.1); 0-8239-3680-5 (v.2); 0-8239-3682-1 (v.3); 0-8239-3683-X (v.4); 0-8239-3684-8 (v.5); 0-8239-3685-6 (v.6).

The Primary Sources in American History Series is a set of six volumes arranged alphabetically by title: that is, "The Alamo" is the first and "Women's Suffrage" is the last. A chronological arrangement would begin with "The Salem Witch Trials," by Jenny MacBain; followed by "The Erie Canal" and "The Alamo," both by Janey Levy; "The Gold Rush," by Kerri O'Donnell; "The Transcontinental Railroad," by Gillian Houghton; and "Women's Suffrage," by Colleen Adams.

Each volume has a pertinent picture on the front cover and includes many black-and-white and color illustrations; a table of contents; an introduction; a timeline; sidebars for each illustration; a list of primary sources; a glossary; and a bibliography. In addition to a "For Further Reading" section, each volume also directs the reader to the publisher's Website, which it states contains regularly updated links to other sites related to the book's topic.

The Primary Sources in American History Series, designed for the 8- to12-year-old student, is different from most juvenile history books. The use of primary sources and the reproduction of actual related documents, besides being sound scholarship, also offers readers a fascinating glimpse into the past. In some cases, original material has been "translated" into contemporary English (e.g., as in transcriptions of the Salem witch trials and Spanish-language documents relating to the Alamo). In other cases, newspaper pages and records make the point that American history is a collection of incidents concerning real people whose actions were important, not only in their own lifetimes, but even to us today. For opening a door to the past, the Primary Sources in American History Series should be a valuable addition to any elementary or middle school library.—**Kay O. Cornelius**

AFRICAN HISTORY

General Works

C

165.   **Encyclopedia of Twentieth-Century African History.** Paul Tiyambe Zeleza, ed. New York, Routledge, 2003. 652p. index. $150.00. ISBN 0-415-23479-4.

The *Encyclopedia*, which has more than 250 entries, explores the peoples of Africa, their politics, economic environments, cultures, and their history. The goals of this source are to provide comprehensive coverage of all aspects of African history and the African people.

The editors have put together an impressive list of contributors from Africa and the Diaspora, all experts in their own fields of study. This reviewer tried to understand why the editors decided to use only one volume for a topic so diverse and complex. One solution would be that users should not use it by itself, of course, because it should not be considered complete, but should instead be considered a complement to the previously published encyclopedic works on this same subject. One that comes to mind is the four-volume set *Encyclopedia of Africa South of the Sahara* by John Middleton (see ARBA 99, entry 100). A more recent source found in this reviewer's collection is *The Encyclopedia of African History and Culture* by Willie F. Page (see ARBA 2002, entry 446). These works will make up for whatever is not fully covered in this particular source.

Most of the articles in the *Encyclopedia of Twentieth-Century African History* are varied in length and have suggestions for further reading by the authors at the end of each entry. The article on environmental change (pp. 188-193), for instance, is very fascinating and quite lengthy as opposed to the articles on Eritrea and Dar es Salaam, Tanzania. The index in this source is an added feature that makes this a useful reference source for both undergraduate and graduate students in the area of African Studies. The index also provides the user with cross-references. This reviewer would recommend this tool as a must have in undergraduate and research libraries.—**Valentine K. Muyumba**

P, S

166.   **History of Africa Series.** By the Diagram Group. Tempe, Ariz., Facts on Demand Press, 2003. 6v. illus. maps. index. $180.00/set; $30.00/vol. ISBN 0-8160-5060-0.

In this six-volume set, covering all major geographical regions of the African continent, precise and consistent information is presented to the reader considering each of these regions. For example, in the volume subtitled, *History of Central Africa*, an in-depth synopsis of the region is presented including information about religion, land, climate, language, and cultural customs of the people of this region. Each volume of the set also highlights the impact of colonialism on the African continent and its peoples.

Through maps, charts, timelines, and pictures this series is able to convey to the reader a cultural snapshot of Africa which will further one's knowledge of this complex continent and its inhabitants. Also included in this series are short biographies of the most significant African leaders both past and present. Schools and public libraries will find this series a useful reference text to enhance their African studies collection. —**Patrick Hall**

ASIAN HISTORY

Dictionaries and Encyclopedias

C, P

167.   Edwards, Paul M. **Korean War: A Historical Dictionary.** Lanham, Md., Scarecrow, 2003. 367p. (Historical Dictionaries of War, Revolution, and Civil Unrest, no.23). $75.00. ISBN 0-8108-4479-6.

Korean War: A Historical Dictionary, by Dr. Paul M. Edwards, is the 23d addition to the Historical Dictionaries of War, Revolution, and Civil Unrest series, which uses an alphabetic format. The entries range from a few sentences to several paragraphs. This work deals with contributing factors, political and social, plus the military actions and individuals that the reader expects to find. The entries are crisply written and useful to all students of this subject.

The dictionary uses an alphabetic format, but the 281 pages of entries are not the entire dictionary. Included are several photographs, maps, a chronology, reader's notes, lists of abbreviations and acronyms, a glossary, an excellent introduction, a helpful bibliography, two appendixes (a list of American casualties broken down by unit and a list of United Nations commanders during the war), an extremely detailed 67-page bibliography, and a brief biography of the author. An example of a typical biographical entry is the entry on Robert A. McClure (1897-1957), who is described by his World War II exploits and his role as chief of the United States Army Psychological Warfare Division during the Korean War. The critical element that is discussed are the concerns he raised over the prisoners of war from the Republic of China and the issue of repatriation. Overall, this work is well done and is especially useful for anyone interested in the Korean War, from the novice just getting started to the scholar double-checking a date or fact. It should be included in all libraries.—**Scott R. DiMarco**

C, P

168.   Gutzman, Philip. **Vietnam: A Visual Encyclopedia.** New York, Sterling Publishing, 2002. 447p. illus. $24.95pa. ISBN 1-85648-639-7.

Gutzman's *Vietnam: A Visual Encyclopedia* is a unique addition to the literature on the Vietnam War that nicely complements Spencer Tucker's superb three-volume *Encyclopedia of the Vietnam War* (see ARBA 99, entry 527). Gutzman's coffee-table-size volume contains over 800 color and black-and-white pictures, hundreds of which have never been seen before, including that of a young, blindfolded Viet Cong prisoner of War; an exhausted Lyndon B. Johnson, head bowed down on his desk in the Oval Office; and a female North Vietnamese militia fighter escorting a downed American fighter pilot to prison. The entries, short and factual, are arranged alphabetically. Gutzman rarely passes judgment or criticizes policymakers, although he notes the failure of Westmoreland's "search and destroy" strategy and blames the media and President Johnson for perpetrating the idea that Tet was a military defeat. Compared to Tucker's *Encyclopedia of the Vietnam War*, the entries on important persons are insufficient, especially those on Presidents Nixon and Johnson and Generals Westmoreland and Abrams, as are those on larger historical events in general, like anti-war activities or Watergate. However, along with the fascinating pictures, the real strength of *Vietnam* lies in the extensive knowledge of military operations, machinery, and personnel it contains. Gutzman is especially good at identifying a dizzying number of obscure (and not-so-obscure) military campaigns and people (both civilian and military) from the United States and South and North Vietnam that make this volume an indispensable addition to all reference libraries and to everyone seriously interested in the Vietnam War. [R: LJ, Jan 03, p. 90]—**E. Wayne Carp**

C

169.   Kim, Ilpyong J. **Historical Dictionary of North Korea.** Lanham, Md., Scarecrow, 2003. 212p. (Asian/Oceanian Historical Dictionaries, no.40). $75.00. ISBN 0-8108-4331-5.

North Korea is a hot topic, but there are few good reference books for it. One thinks of the Library of Congress's *North Korea: A Country Study*, by Andrea Matles Savada (GPO, 1994), or *A Handbook on North Korea*, by Bong-uk Chong (Naewoe Press, 1998).

The introduction outlines the country's history, rulers, government structure, political ideology, economy and society, and speculates about the uncertain future. Coverage stopped with 2001, so the worrisome recent events are not mentioned. The alphabetically arranged entries are well written, and cover people, places, events, policies, and other miscellaneous items. They also contain many *see also* references and cross-references. The helpful prefatory material includes a short explanation of the Korean writing system and romanization practice, a list of abbreviations and acronyms, a chronology, and a map of the Korean peninsula (but not a more detailed one of the country itself, which would have been useful). The four appendixes contain the texts of the September 1998 Socialist Constitution, the July 1953 armistice agreement, the June 2000 North-South Joint Declaration, and the October 2000 US—DPRK Joint Declaration. There is a good 25-page bibliography of important source materials, many from the two Koreas, and is topically arranged. A short list of relevant Websites is also provided at the end. This is definitely a politically oriented reference work, with little information in regards to culture and society, as is expected with this closed nation. As with other Scarecrow titles, there are no photographs, nor is there an index. Users will have to access the subjects by entry headings, which are in heavy black type so that they are easier to read. This title is a series companion to Andrew C. Nahm's *Historical Dictionary of the Republic of Korea* (see ARBA 94, entry 117). Kim is professor emeritus at the University of Connecticut, Storrs (political science), and was the president of the International Council on Korean Studies (http://www.icks.org). If one cannot read the various Korean-language reference books on this country, then this volume is for you. The expensive item under review is recommended for all reference collections.—**Daniel K. Blewett**

AUSTRALIAN AND PACIFIC HISTORY

C, P

170.   Day, Alan. **Historical Dictionary of the Discovery and Exploration of Australia.** Lanham, Md., Scarecrow, 2003. 321p. (Historical Dictionaries of Discovery and Exploration). $77.00. ISBN 0-8108-4588-1.

What a treat to find a reference work so packed with tales of adventure! Alan Day, a professional librarian who researched the material for this book for decades in his native England, was himself inspired to take a trip of exploration to Australia in 2001, using resources in local research centers on the way. It was Day too who came up with the idea of a series of Historical Dictionaries of Discovery and Exploration, of which this is the first. The format of this book sets the pattern for those to follow: a chronology, general introduction, alphabetic entries on persons and places and events, and an extensive bibliography. The bibliography in this book covers 80 pages, arranged first by subject and then by geographical area.

In its early history, Australia proved an unpromising object of exploration: it was not located where it was supposed to be and was not as fertile as was hoped. Its rivers violated European norms by flowing inland, and its mountain areas were more fertile than its plains. Its inhabitants did not meet European standards of beauty or high culture. But the fact that its exploration was late (roughly two centuries after the Spanish conquest of South America) and beset by difficulties makes the stories even more exciting. As the series editor writes, "The material contained in many entries . . . is truly gripping," so that one is compelled to skip from entry to entry. Rarely has history proved so rewarding to both researcher and reader.—**John B. Beston**

EUROPEAN HISTORY

General Works

Biography

C, P
171.   **Industrialization and Imperialism 1800-1914: A Biographical Dictionary.** Jeffrey A. Bell, ed. Westport, Conn., Greenwood Press, 2002. 434p. index. (The Great Cultural Eras of the Western World). $99.95. ISBN 0-313-31451-9.

Industrialization and Imperialism 1800-1914: A Biographical Dictionary is the most recent installment in Greenwood Press's The Great Cultures of the Western World series, which begins chronologically with the ancient world. Written for the general reader, each entry provides basic information on the most important intellectual and cultural people of the time, along with a short bibliography for those interested in learning more. The volume includes entries on leading industrialists and nationalists of the age such as Cornelius Vanderbilt and French leader Napoleon Bonaparte, and cultural icons such as German author Johann Wolfgang Von Goethe and Russian composer PyotrIlich Tchaikovsky.

From the aftermath of the French Revolution to the beginning of World War I, Bell presents interesting information on each subject and notes cross-references with an asterisk where necessary. An extensive bibliography is included that covers general history, art and architecture, culture and economy, literature, military and politics, music, philosophy, and science and technology. The index is also cross-referenced, providing not only main entry information, but also indicating in which entry the subject is only mentioned. A chronology at the front of the book provides a quick overview of world events from 1800 to 1914. This is an excellent introductory reference work for the general reader or student interested in the major cultural figures of the era. It is highly readable and recommended for public and undergraduate libraries.—**Deborah L. Nicholl**

Dictionaries and Encyclopedias

C
172.   **Ancient Europe 8000 B.C. to A.D. 1000: Encyclopedia of the Barbarian World.** Peter Bogucki and Pam J. Crabtree, eds. New York, Charles Scribner's Sons/Gale Group, 2004. 2v. illus. index. $265.00/set. ISBN 0-684-80668-1.

Rarely does a reference work truly break new ground, but *Ancient Europe 8000 B.C. to A.D. 1000: Encyclopedia of the Barbarian World* does just that. The editors have tackled an enormous subject and have produced an excellent result. This *Encyclopedia* opens up the worlds beyond the splendors of the Mediterranean and shows that there was indeed civilization and culture in the hinterlands of Europe before the modern period.

After a series of articles introducing topics such as the origins and growth of European prehistory, the nature of archaeological data, trade and exchange, gender, and ritual and ideology, the remaining articles are arranged by loose time periods: postglacial foragers, 8000-4000 B.C.E., transition to agriculture, 7000-4000 B.C.E., consequences of agriculture, 5000-2000 B.C.E., masters of metal, 3000-1000 B.C.E., the European iron age, c. 800 B.C.E.-C.E. 400, and the early Middle Ages/migration period. Within each time period, various articles provide useful information on topics as varied as agriculture, dwellings, and social organization. Often, specific archaeological sites are highlighted to provide greater detail on the subject. The articles are accompanied by sharp, well-reproduced, black-and-white illustrations and photographs. Each volume also includes a set of good color illustrations as well as maps and timelines. The authors are experts in their respective fields. The volumes conclude with a helpful glossary of terms related to archaeology and a comprehensive index.

The only minor weakness of the work is in the arrangement of *see also* references that accompany the articles. The references point to a volume and part of the set by section number, not to a page number. Since the articles are not arranged alphabetically, the index must be used to find the actual page number for the referenced articles. With this small weakness noted, this set is a joy to read and a worthwhile purchase, especially for academic libraries and larger public libraries.—**Gregory A. Crawford**

C

173. **Europe 1450-1789: Encyclopedia of the Early Modern World.** Jonathan Dewald, ed. New York, Charles Scribner's Sons/Gale Group, 2004. 6v. illus. maps. index. $695.00/set. ISBN 0-684-31200-X.

With solid scholarship, wide-ranging scope, ease of use, and 567 contributors, this multivolume historical encyclopedia is a joy to read and a research tool any school or university would welcome to its shelves. Each entry is direct, factual, and individually intriguing. Editor Dewald has done a great favor to the academic community in producing this set.

In addition to instructions on how to use the encyclopedia, each volume contains a complete contents listing for the entire set with the specific in-hand number listed first. Also, a set of six historical maps covering the period is included within each book. Volume 1 has a well-conceived introduction and a 120-page chronology of the period. Volume 6 outlines and lists all the articles under more broad subject headings, including "Social History," "Concepts and Ideas," and "Biographies"; articles may be listed more than once. A 194-page index to the set ends this volume. Each essay has a *see also* section that refers to other entries within the set. Also, there is a bibliography divided into both primary and secondary sources following each article. There is a plethora of black-and-white, well-reproduced illustrations and each well-constructed volume contains a color plate section.

This encyclopedia covers from the revolution in print to the French Revolution, a busy, exciting, and an important historical time frame. What is heartening is that a confidently presented set of books is here that is as usable as the Web and has the expertise of the academy behind it.—**Kennith Slagle**

C, P

174. **The Oxford Dictionary of the Renaissance.** By Gordon Campbell. New York, Oxford University Press, 2003. 862p. illus. $150.00. ISBN 0-19-860175-1.

For libraries not wishing to purchase Grendler's six-volume *Encyclopedia of the Renaissance* (see ARBA 2001, entry 440), this dictionary is the best single-volume work on its subject. It supplants Thomas G. Bergin's *Encyclopedia of the Renaissance* (1987) by offering a wider variety of non-English listings and more extensive recommendations for further reading. Campbell defines his work as covering "a long Renaissance" (p. vii), generally extending from 1618 backwards to 1415, but varying according to national culture or topic (e.g., entries on "Dante in the Renaissance" and "Lope de Vega" who died in 1635). No one born after 1595 is included. Campbell, who wrote most of the 4,000 entries himself with the aid of specialists, diminishes the space given to English topics (these are addressed in other Oxford University Press volumes), favoring the relatively neglected Spanish, Scandinavian, and Dutch and Central European cultures. Most entries contain a brief reference for further reading, either to a larger biographical resource such as the *Dictionary of National Biography* or to recent secondary scholarship. Frequent black-and-white illustrations enliven the text. Entries are introduced by a thematic index. Four appendixes include "Tables of Ruling Houses"; "Place Names in Imprints"; "Dates at which Cities, States and Territories in Europe Adopted the Gregorian Calendar"; and "Ligatures and Contractions in Renaissance Greek." Until such time as a single-volume reference work on the Renaissance with the scope of the *Oxford Dictionary of the Christian Church* (see ARBA 98, entry 1389) is produced, Campbell's book will provide the most authoritative one-volume coverage of the period. [R: LJ, July 03, p. 71; AG, Dec 03-Jan 04, p. 63; Choice, Jan 04, p. 886]—**Christopher Baker**

P, S

175.   Streissguth, Thomas. **The Greenhaven Encyclopedia of the Middle Ages.** San Diego, Calif., Greenhaven Press/Gale, 2003. 332p. illus. index. (Greenhaven Encyclopedias). $74.95. ISBN 0-7377-0793-3.

     In *The Greenhaven Encyclopedia of the Middle Ages*, Streissguth provides an excellent resource for beginning an exploration of the Middle Ages. Beginning his coverage of the Middle Ages in Europe at 476 C.E., (the most generally accepted date for the fall of the Roman Empire) and ending with the beginning of the Renaissance in Italy, Streissguth discusses important concepts, people, kingdoms, and events in a manner that is designed for those unfamiliar with this historical period. His entries are informative, concise, and clearly written for a lay audience. The coverage is good, discussing concepts from this period in the Middle East and other parts of Eurasia as they pertain to developments in Europe. There are plenty of maps to assist in interpreting the text, and many black-and-white illustrations are provided where appropriate. Streissguth summarizes the main historical concepts and themes associated with the Middle Ages in the foreword to this book. In the appendix, he presents lists of rulers of important major countries and other geographic entities (e.g., England, France, the Holy Roman Empire), a complete list of medieval popes (including those of Avignon), and a concise timeline of major events.

     The quality of this encyclopedia is quite high, with a rugged library binding designed to stand up to much use. The layout and typeface make it easy to read, and the information seems authoritative. An index is included to assist users in locating specific entries. While the level of information provided is not in-depth enough to use in upper-level historical research, it is a great resource for beginning level college students, researchers from another field needing background information, high school students, and public library patrons with questions about the Middle Ages. It is highly recommended for college and public libraries as well as high school media centers. [R: SLJ, Oct 03, pp. 108-109]—**Mark T. Bay**

Handbooks and Yearbooks

C, P

176.   **The Longman Companion to Central and Eastern Europe Since 1919.** By Adrian Webb. White Plains, N.Y., Longman Group/Addison-Wesley, 2002. 329p. illus. index. $22.95pa. ISBN 0-582-43732-6.

     This *Companion* provides a panoramic view of post-Treaty of Versailles Central and Eastern Europe, defined as including the Balkan countries minus Greece, Austria, the Czech Republic, Slovakia, Hungary, and Poland, with mention of adjacent areas, such as East Germany and Ukraine. The book is systematic, starting with a guide to pronunciation (with some omissions), geographical names, and a general historical chronology. The topical parts have general introductions and commentaries for individual sections, followed by chronologies. Thus, the part on "Government and Politics" begins with an essay on "The Concept and History of Nationalism in Eastern Europe," followed by a commentary and chronology on "Authoritarianism, Fascism and the Problem of National Minorities from 1919 to 1939," then a section on "Anti-Semitism" (which omits Jewish cooperation with the organs of communist repression in 1939-1941 and during the Stalinist period that began in 1945), chronologies of World War II and of "Retribution and Revenge," short essays on "The Liberal Tradition" and "Marxism-Leninism," a commentary on "The Post-War Consolidation of Communist Power" followed by a commentary and chronology of "The Purges and Show Trials" and a chronology of "Orthodoxy and Reform 1953-90" (a section that should have included the formation of Poland's Solidarity movement), statistics on Communist Party membership, a chronology of "The Struggle Between Church and State," an essay on "Titoism," a commentary and chronology on "The Reformed Communist Parties since 1990," and a list of office holders since 1919. The above sample indicates the breadth of coverage of this sourcebook. Other parts, with similar subdivisions into sections, are "Foreign Policy," "The Economy," "The Environment," "Human Statistics," "Culture," "Biographies," "Glossary," and "Bibliographical Essay," the latter citing recent sources. Almost inevitably, there are some misspellings of names. The chronology of the consolidation of communist power omits Jan Masaryk's 1948 defenestration, while his short biography includes it. The author incorrectly writes that Poland sought accommodation with the Germans to pursue its "national ambitions," and in a curious contradiction, writes shortly afterward that Poland had "ceased to exist." The collapse of the communist system is incorrectly dated at 1990, instead of 1989. Despite such minor faults this *Companion* is useful for the general interested reader as well as for the researcher. It is highly recommended. [R: Choice, Jan 03, p. 810]—**Bogdan Mieczkowski**

German

P, S
177.   Hay, Jeff T. **A History of the Third Reich.** San Diego, Calif., Greenhaven Press/Gale, 2003. 2v. illus. index. $149.90/2-volume set; $299.80/set. ISBN 0-7377-1478-6.

P, S
178.   Hay, Jeff T. **A History of the Third Reich, Volume 3: Personalities.** San Diego, Calif., Greenhaven Press/Gale, 2003. 292p. illus. index. $74.95; $299.80/set. ISBN 0-7377-1120-5.

P, S
179.   Hay, Jeff T. **A History of the Third Reich, Volume 4: Primary Sources.** San Diego, Calif., Greenhaven Press/Gale, 2003. 292p. index. $74.95; $299.80/set. ISBN 0-7377-1477-8.

The four-volume set, *A History of the Third Reich*, written by Jeff Hay of San Diego State University in consultation with Christopher R. Browning of the University of North Carolina at Chapel Hill, was designed to teach young adults and undergraduate students about the rise and rule of the Nazi regime in World War II Germany. The first two volumes serve as an encyclopedia for topics covering events, places, battles, and policies of the Third Reich. It is careful to include the social policy and attitudes that lead to this shift in power and thinking. The expected topics are here as well as other less-researched topics, such as those on the roles of women, education, and film during World War II Germany. Volume 3 serves as a biography of key players in the Nazi party as well as in World War II in general. By separating biographies into their own volume researchers will more easily be able to focus on key players in the war. Volume 4, "Primary Sources," provides a bibliography of key sources on the war and the Third Reich in particular, including reports in newspapers and magazines, diaries, memoirs, government reports, and other key sources. It will be extremely helpful for students needing to conduct further research on the war. Cross-references between volumes are provided, which tie the volumes together and will help researchers quickly associate key points. The volumes are supplemented with a timeline of events, a list of key resources (both print and online), detailed maps, photographs, and sidebars providing succinct charts as well as excerpts from primary documents.

These volumes are highly recommended for high school libraries and undergraduate university libraries. The value is in the accuracy of information and the fact that so much information has been gathered in one place and in a format that will be easy to understand by young adults. This set is highly recommended.—**Shannon Graff Hysell**

Greek

C, S

180.   Konstam, Angus. **Historical Atlas of Ancient Greece.** New York, Checkmark Books/Facts on File, 2003. 192p. illus. maps. index. (Historical Atlas). $35.00. ISBN 1-8160-5220-4.

Although there is no lack of good atlases on ancient Greece, this one offers more than just maps. With its rich illustrations and excellent summaries of events, the work will fill a definite niche in the reference collections of many libraries.

Following in the mold of traditional atlases, the work does provide a wealth of useful color maps, yet it goes beyond those atlases as a result of its organization and breadth. The 15 chapters include those that would generally be expected, such as the war with Persia, the Peloponnesian War, and the conquests of Alexander the Great. Other chapters provide a greater understanding of the civilization that was ancient Greece, such as Greek mythology and religion, the thinking process, society and everyday life, recreation and religious festivals, art and architecture, and the world of Hellas (which examines the legacy of ancient Greece). Thus, in addition to providing well-drawn, useful maps, the book can serve as a general introduction to the study of the history and culture of the ancient Greek world.

Special note must be made of the illustrations, which are well chosen to supplement and complement the text and the maps. Frequently, details from works of art or vases are used to illustrate a specific point. Almost all the illustrations are reproduced with a clarity often lacking in other publications. The printing of the text itself is sharp and clear. The paper is acid-free, ensuring a long life to the work, and glare-free, providing an ease of reading that patrons will appreciate.

Of course, other books go into greater depth for the subjects covered and other atlases provide more maps, but this work presents the history and culture of Greece in an easy-to-understand manner that is suitable for high school and college students and for interested general readers. This resource is highly recommended. [R: Choice, Jan 04, p. 889]—**Gregory A. Crawford**

Russian

C, P

181.   **Encyclopedia of Russian History.** James R. Millar, ed. New York, Macmillan Reference USA/Gale Group, 2004. 4v. illus. maps. index. $475.00/set. ISBN 0-02-865693-8.

This four-volume encyclopedia meets the need for a thorough, up-to-date reference work on Russian history. None of the existing works brings together such breadth, currency, and depth of expertise. This durable, handsome, well-illustrated set provides nearly 1,600 entries written by over 500 scholars. The 250 to 5,000 word articles range from the Caucasian ethnic group "Abkhazians" to "Zyuganov," head of the revived Communist Party. The set is aimed at the general reader rather than the specialist.

The prefatory material includes a "List of Articles" and an "Outline of Contents." The former is useful for the casual reader who may be uncertain as to what heading he or she should consult; for example, while there is no entry for "Anti-Semitism," the articles on "Jews" or "Cosmopolitanism" may be helpful, as will the former's cross-references to "Tsarist Pale" and "Pogrom." The contents outline provides a broad listing of articles broken down 21 subject categories, some further subdivided by time periods. The reader can thus conveniently locate nearly all articles in a given subject area, such as Agriculture or Political Policy, although not all relevant entries are included (i.e., the writers Bunin and Bulgakov are not listed in the category "Literature," although they are the subjects of articles). Apart from "Historical Events and People," the largest subject categories are "Economics," "Military," and "Regions, Nations, and Nationalities," while cultural subjects receive less attention. Both the historical role and cultural achievements of the Russian emigration are underrepresented. Some of the gaps are offset by the final index, which directs the readers to topics scattered within other articles. The otherwise satisfactory index cites only page numbers, without volume numbers, leaving the reader to guess which of the consecutively page numbered volumes to consult.

The *Encyclopedia*'s greatest strength is the quality and timeliness of the articles, which include information as recent as 2003. Readers of the daily press will find succinct descriptions of the small ethnic groups and nationalities that have come into the news with the breakup of the Soviet Union. Up-to-date bibliographies are attached each entry, although they are restricted to English-language publications. Concern for nonspecialist readers is also shown in the transliteration of Russian names and terms as found in publications such as *The New York Times* rather than in arcane academic systems. Also useful is the short guide to Russian abbreviations and acronyms. The numerous illustrations are supplemented by sections of colored photographs in each volume devoted to "Architecture and Landscape," "Arts," "Peoples," and "Power and Technology."—**D. Barton Johnson**

MIDDLE EASTERN HISTORY

C, S

182. David, Rosalie. **Handbook to Life in Ancient Egypt.** rev. ed. New York, Facts on File, 2003. 417p. illus. maps. index. (Facts on File Library of World History). $50.00. ISBN 0-8160-5034-1.

The revised edition of this handbook adds a solid and extremely informative chapter to the earlier edition (see ARBA 99, entry 510), providing a lengthy and very informative discussion entitled "Egyptology, Archaeology, and Scientific Mummy Studies in Egypt." This addition greatly enhances the book's approach to Egyptian life by discussing how two of the three main sources available to investigators —monuments such as temples and tombs and objects and artifacts from archaeological sites—help them gain the raw material with which they work. (The third source is written materials from different times of history.) Thus, in this new chapter the author, a noted Egyptologist, describes briefly the development of Egyptology, its early history, how archaeological activities developed in Egypt, and recent scientific studies using mummies, including work on disease and chronic conditions (the author has done considerable work with mummies herself), concluding with short notes about some notable Egyptologists. Beyond this first chapter, the book's materials are essentially those of the 1st edition, providing 11 chapters presenting Egypt's historical background, geography, society and government, religion of the living, funeral beliefs and customs, architecture and building, written evidence, the army and navy, foreign trade and transport, economy and industry, and everyday life. Many photographs, line drawings, and maps support the text, drawn largely from the Manchester Museum at the University of Manchester, England, thus providing the audience less familiar but appropriate materials.

As in the earlier edition, each chapter includes references to other readings by topic, encouraging the reader to explore further. Many omissions and some misinformation of the earlier edition have been rectified, although not all. Nevertheless, this edition remains a valuable resource and, as with the earlier edition, belongs on the shelves of public and school libraries. The breadth and thoroughness of its coverage will serve the beginning student well, and there is still nothing else known to the reviewer quite like it.—**Susan Tower Hollis**

S

183. **The Greenhaven Encyclopedia of Ancient Egypt.** By Patricia D. Netzley. San Diego, Calif., Greenhaven Press/Gale, 2003. 336p. illus. index. (Greenhaven Encyclopedias). $74.95. ISBN 0-7377-1150-7.

This volume, designed for middle school ages and up, provides a broad spectrum of information about ancient Egypt. It is extremely thorough with excellent cross-referencing for virtually every entry. The entries cover people, places, deities, and other pertinent concerns such as stories, time periods, and the like. Its major flaw is the lack of maps showing the locations to which the entries refer. The three maps included serve the purpose each is intended to serve: to show where Tuthmosis III's influence lay; present the Nile; and show the different scope of the Old, Middle, and New Kingdoms. This last map is quite interesting and a highlight of the book, illustrating nicely the picture of the growth of Egypt's sphere of influence in its different floruit periods.

In addition, the volume concludes with three appendixes, one listing the dynasties with their dates, a second detailing the kings within their dynasties, and a third containing a list of the major deities. Two bibliographies are provided: one entitled "For Further Research" and a second entitled "Works Consulted." All these resources will be helpful for students, although the reviewer would recommend adding *KMT: A Modern Journal of Ancient Egypt*, a quarterly publication that is highly illustrated with very readable articles written by international scholars; it is readily available in major bookstores and some libraries. One of a number of recent publications on ancient Egypt and the ancient Near East, this volume will work well for middle and high school libraries as a complement to other works, particularly those dealing with the broader ancient Near Eastern scope.—**Susan Tower Hollis**

WORLD HISTORY

General Works

S

184. **Cold War: Almanac.** By Sharon M. Hanes and Richard C. Hanes. Farmington Hills, Mich., U*X*L/Gale, 2004. 2v. illus. index. (U*X*L Cold War Reference Library). $105.00/2-volume set; $250.00/set. ISBN 0-7876-9089-9.

S

185. **Cold War: Biographies.** By Sharon M. Hanes and Richard C. Hanes. Farmington Hills, Mich., U*X*L/Gale, 2004. 2v. illus. index. (U*X*L Cold War Reference Series). $105.00/2-volume set; $250.00/set. ISBN 0-7876-7663-2.

S

186. **Cold War: Primary Sources.** By Sharon M. Hanes and Richard C. Hanes. Farmington Hills, Mich., U*X*L/Gale, 2004. 355p. illus. index. (U*X*L Cold War Reference Library). $58.00/volume; $250.00/set. ISBN 0-7876-7666-7.

The U*X*L Cold War Reference Library provides a comprehensive overview of the Cold War period from 1945 through 1991 that is ideally suited for young adults at the middle to high school grade level. The series is divided into three separate titles: *Cold War: Almanac*, *Cold War: Biographies*, and *Cold War: Primary Sources*. All of these titles focus on the major causes of the war, including the mistrust between the communist USSR and the democratic United States, as well as the global confrontations that ensued, including the Korean and Vietnam Wars and the Cuban Missile Crisis.

Cold War: Almanac begins with introductory material needed for understanding the history of the Cold War, including an introduction, a reader's guide, a list of words to know, a list of key people, a timeline, and research and activity ideas. It then provides 15 overview chapters that discuss such topics as the origins of the war, key programs and treaties (e.g., the Marshall Plan, the Strategic Defense Initiative), and the fears of society during the Cold War.

Cold War: Biographies provides details on the lives and roles of 50 prominent individuals during the Cold War from 1945 to 1991. Persons from the United States, the Soviet Union, China, Great Britain, and other places affected are presented. *Biographies* includes the expected (e.g., Mikhail Gorbachev, Ronald Reagan, Joseph Stalin) as well as some that may be a surprise to some, such as Condoleezza Rice (U.S. advisor on the Soviet Union in 1990), Igor Kurchatov (developer of the first Soviet atomic bomb), and Kim Il Sung (dictator of North Korea). Biographies include a description of the role the person played in the Cold War, information on their political or professional career, black-and-white photographs, and a list of books and Websites for further research.

Cold War: Primary Sources provides 31 excerpted documents from both sides of the war. Excerpts are arranged by subject, such as "Communism Spreads" (which include Douglas MacArthur's speech "Old Soldiers Never Die; They Just Fade Away") , "Homeland Insecurities," "Cuban Missile Crisis" (which includes President Kennedy's speech on October 22, 1962), and "End of the Cold War" (with speeches from both Mikhail Gorbachev and former President Bush). This title concludes with a valuable bibliography of books, magazines, novels, and Websites where students can learn more about the subject. This set will be a valuable addition to middle and high school libraries.—**Shannon Graff Hysell**

Almanacs

P

187.   Vandiver, Frank E. **1001 Things Everyone Should Know About World War II.** New York, Random House, 2002. 260p. illus. index. $15.95pa. ISBN 0-7679-0584-9.

Along the lines of such commercially successful guides as the "For Dummies" series, we now have Frank E. Vandiver's *1001 Things Everyone Should Know About World War II*. Vandiver is the President Emeritus of Texas A&M University, a military historian, and author of several earlier books on the Civil War. The reader should not be misled by the sensational title and the bold cover art, for this is a serious reference work that will appeal to a broad audience. The $15.95 paperback price also makes the book extremely appealing.

A book with 1,001 entries arranged in order by year of the war (there are 6 separate chapters arranged by years: 1939-1940, 1941, 1942, 1943, 1944, 1945) invites the reader to begin with the first entry on page 1 and work their way through to the end. While this may seem a logical way to progress, it is not necessarily the most rewarding. This reviewer would suggest, instead, a grazing pattern in which you open the book randomly to a page in order to pick up whatever nugget of information that captures your fancy. Within the individual years, there are various subheadings, such as "Germany 1941" and "The Empire of Japan 1943," which will help orient someone looking for information on a general topic. There is a sustained narrative within each topic, with individual chunks of information separated in bold face by the lead sentence. Succinct answers are provided for such burning questions as: "What Texan Organized the U.S. Women's Army Corps" and "How Did Hitler Die?"

1001 Things Everyone Should Know About World War II is also a visually pleasing work, interspersed with sharp black-and-white photographs of villains and their villainous deeds as well as propaganda posters, cartoons, and pictures of allied military leaders. It was a pleasant surprise to discover a picture of Brigadier General Benjamin Oliver Davis, the first black soldier to hold the rank of general. Maps of the various theaters of operations complement the entries. Another interesting feature of this guide are the facts related to technological advances and military equipment innovations that occurred during World War II.

1001 Things Everyone Should Know About World War II concludes with a detailed index, which, in the case of a reference guide listing so many diverse facts, is an indispensable tool. This work, while not a scholarly treatise per se and targeting a general readership, will prove useful for a wide audience of World War II buffs, students, teachers, and amateur historians.—**John B. Romeiser**

Bibliography

C

188. ACLS History E-Book Project. http://www.historyebook.org/. [Website]. New York, ACLS History E-Book Project. $300.00-$1,300 based on size of institution. Date reviewed: Dec 03.

In September 2002 the American Council of Learned Societies launched the *ACLS History E-Book Project*. Funded by a grant from the Andrew W. Mellon Foundation, at that time the project provided 500 high quality e-books in the field of history. Today the project provides 750 e-books, with the intention of adding another 250 each year as well as 85 selected electronic titles. The goal of the ACLS is to encourage historians to write and use e-books (as that is the new direction publishing is taking), provide a way for historians to author books at a reduced cost, design an infrastructure for archiving scholarly historical texts, and to encourage libraries to purchase historical e-books and make them widely available to their clientele. The titles chosen for this reference are those that are of the highest quality and that have been painstakingly researched, often including an abundance of footnotes, bibliography, illustrations, maps, and indexes.

The *ACLS History E-Book Project* is very easy to use. Once logged in, users can search the site by a simple search (supplying a word or phrase), a Boolean search, a proximity search, or a bibliographic search. Users can also browse the book titles by author, title, or subject. When an e-book is selected, the user is given full bibliographic information (author, title, copyright date, copyright holder, and publisher name and location); the cover of the book; a list of the table of contents, which provides links to chapters and parts of the book; sample reviews (if available); and catalog record. Users can then go directly to chapters to read parts of the book or they can conduct a search within the book using selected terms. While conducting research the site allows users to create a list of relevant citations or review their search history.

This resource will be extremely useful to historians and scholars. The usefulness is limited, of course, by the titles available; however, the outlook for the site is very hopeful and title numbers will increase quickly. Subscription rates are reasonable (from $1,300 for the largest institutions to $300 for the smallest), especially considering how much it would cost a library to provide all of the titles available here. This site is recommended for academic and large public libraries.—**Shannon Graff Hysell**

Biography

C, P

189. Who's Who in World War Two. 2d ed. John Keegan, ed. New York, Routledge/Taylor & Francis Group, 2002. 182p. $14.95pa. ISBN 0-415-26033-7.

John Keegan is a preeminent military historian. His sterling reputation has been solidly established and maintained with such award-winning books as *A History of Warfare* (Knopf, 1994) and *The Face of Battle* (Penguin, 1983). Any new work appearing under his editorship must, therefore, command attention. His new reference guide, *Who's Who in World War Two*, is another such contribution to the field.

The beauty of this biographical guide is its succinctness and its affordability. While every serious scholar of World War II needs to own the magnificent *Oxford Companion to World War Two* (see ARBA 97, entry 571), not everyone can afford such a work. To his credit, Keegan has managed to pack in over 300 detailed, cross-referenced entries covering such dictators and demagogues as Stalin and Hitler, as well as proponents of national resistance and liberation like de Gaulle and Gandhi, in less than 200 pages. This reviewer would quibble only with the smallness of the typeface, a necessary evil in a reduced format publication.

It is rewarding to read these biographical entries for their factual content. It is also revealing to compare the length of the entries for the various World War II personalities. For instance, I was pleasantly surprised to find that General Francisco Franco's entry was several lines shorter than that of Anne Frank. Moreover, the fact that Anne Frank is even mentioned commends this work all the more, for we are not limited to the standard list of generals and politicians. For example, the Australian-born French Resistance leader Nancy Fiocca, someone whom I had never heard of, is listed along with scientists like the radar pioneer Sir Robert Watson-Watt.

This easy-to-use reference guide will attract the general reader as well as students from the middle school through university levels. It is both versatile and informative in all respects.—**John B. Romeiser**

Dictionaries and Encyclopedias

C

190. **Colonialism: An International Social, Cultural, and Political Encyclopedia.** Melvin E. Page and Penny M. Sonnenburg, eds. Santa Barbara, Calif., ABC-CLIO, 2003. 3v. illus. maps. index. $285.00/set; $310.00 (e-book). ISBN 1-57607-335-1; 1-57607-762-4 (e-book).

This well-designed, three-volume encyclopedia examines the nature of colonialism from 1400 to the present. The first 2 volumes provide A-Z entries, 15 maps, and 15 historical chronologies. The maps and chronologies do not cover the same subjects. The entry format includes *see also* references, a brief bibliography, and the name of the entry author. Volume 3 includes primary documents from 12 empires, as well as numerous documents under an international heading.

The preface clearly states the scope of this work and how the editors defined the idea of colonialism. Further, the editors correctly refer to this work as a valuable introduction. The strongest coverage in the first two volumes is the political dimension of colonialism, but the subtitle is accurate—social, cultural, and intellectual concepts are included and ably covered. The third volume is a collection of useful, relevant documents, each with a brief introduction. Some documents are in their entirety; others offer only a portion. The only limitation to this volume is the need for more. For example, no documents are included from the Portuguese Empire, and only one Russian Empire and two Dutch Empire documents appear. This superbly crafted encyclopedia would be useful for any academic institution. [R: LJ, 1 Feb 04, p. 72]—**Allen Reichert**

P, S

191. **Exploring Ancient Civilizations.** Tarrytown, N.Y., Marshall Cavendish, 2004. 11v. illus. maps. index. $329.95/set. ISBN 0-7614-7456-0.

This set of volumes, containing 249 articles and targeted at grades 5 and above, provides a solid presentation of ancient civilizations, permitting the young investigator to learn not only about the peoples and cultures of the ancient Near East and the Classical world but also a very wide variety of others, both prehistoric and early historic, from every continent of the world. It is heavily illustrated with color plates and line drawings, good maps, and timelines. To assist the reader, the table of contents not only lists the contents of each volume but also presents thematic contents as follows: cross-cultural entries; civilizations and peoples; biographies of people, legendary figures, and deities; places; philosophy, religion, and mythology; and writings. In addition, each article has a *see also* note at the end, thus helping the young researcher comprehend that one encyclopedia article does not provide all the information that is needed in learning about a topic. The set concludes with an eleventh volume that contains a comprehensive index, bringing together the indexes included in each individual volume; a set of timelines, which allows the reader to see the changes in each civilization against the other contemporaneous peoples; and a comprehensive glossary, again bringing together the helpful glossaries from the end of each individual volume; an annotated list of museums, both in the United States and abroad; a list of Internet resources (correct as of July 2003); and several other sets of resources, such as books, magazine and journals, CD-ROMs, and videos, including a special list of resources for younger readers. Finally, it provides an index of maps and sites to be found within the text and a thematic index to complement the comprehensive index.

Overall, this set of volumes belongs in every public library and in larger elementary and middle school libraries. Its comprehensiveness and approach will help students learn about the ancient history from all parts of the world, not just those thought to affect western civilization directly. It will represent a solid investment in learning possibilities for all.—**Susan Tower Hollis**

C, P, S

192.   **History Resource Center. http://infotrac.galenet.com.** [Website]. Farmington Hills, Mich., Gale. Price negotiated by site. Date reviewed: 2003.

History Resource Center is a Web-based database designed for historical research by students with specific features for instruction via distance education. The U.S. history module of the database combines documents from Primary Source Microfilms's digital archives; encyclopedic articles from Macmillan and Charles Scribner's reference works; full-text periodicals and journals; a historical bibliography; a research guide; and links to digitized special collections. There are five main search paths: person, time period, subject search, full-text, and custom search. The database blends different content by electronic searching and cross-linking. A chronology links a graphic timeline with significant events to relevant articles and shows the period in history from a world perspective. Documents, URLs, and bibliographic citations can be marked for remote access or on-site instruction. Users can e-mail search results to themselves or others and save results to a disk. There are links to special digitized collections outside the library system. Search results can be organized according to type of data such as: an annotated chronology; encyclopedic and critical articles, essays, and biographies; original documents (including 500 full-text history journals); bibliography, abstracts, and indexes; overview information by country, era, and topic; and unannotated Web links. *History Resource Center* provides integrated access to over 1,000 historical primary documents, more than 30,000 reference articles, and over 65 full-text journals covering themes, events, individuals, and periods in U.S. history from pre-Colonial times to the present. The material also includes access to the citations for over 189 additional history journals from the Institute for Scientific Information's *Arts and Humanities Citation Index*. The Website brings together a broad collection of facts, primary documents, and scholarly analysis with integrated access to all.—**Anna H. Perrault**

C, S

193.   Klein, Martin A. **Historical Dictionary of Slavery and Abolition.** Lanham, Md., Scarecrow, 2002. 348p. (Historical Dictionaries of Religions, Philosophies, & Movements). $55.00. ISBN 0-8108-4102-9.

To cover a topic so vast from the dawn of history to the present in 300 pages or so is comparable to reducing a 30-volume encyclopedia to a single volume; yet, that is exactly what this study does, and the result is a surprisingly useful overview of one of humanity's more enduring institutions. Martin A. Klein, a professor emeritus at the University of Toronto, is amply qualified for the task, having studied and written on slavery for some 30 years. He treats slavery as an economic institution, noting that for "almost 4,000 years" people of power "have figured out ways to get people to work for them" (p. 1). Although people of all races and from all parts of the globe have been slaves, Africans have been the principal victims over the last 500 years. However, whether the locale was ancient Athens, sixteenth-century Spain, or nineteenth-century America, three variables usually marked a slave: he or she was property that could be bought or sold, an outsider whose lack of kinship ties rendered him or her powerless, and they are a casualty of violence, first of the slave raider, later of the legal system. Abolitionists crusading against the institution emphasized its immorality and alleged inferiority to free labor, and by 1865 slavery was illegal in virtually all areas settled by Europeans. And when Saudi Arabia ended the practice in 1962, formal slavery no longer existed anywhere. Yet, as Klein shows, many people, especially women and children, are still held in slave-like conditions.

This is a book for a general audience. The chronology begins at 3200 B.C.E. and ends in 1993; the introductory essay is excellent; and the dictionary itself, comprising some 281 pages, features people, events, organizations, movements, and countries, and the entries are quite objective in tone. Absent here is the "preachiness" that sometimes pervades works dealing with emotional subjects. There is an adequate bibliography, but no index, which is an unfortunate omission. Even so, high school and college students will find this study helpful, and reference librarians should consider adding it to their collections.—**John W. Storey**

Handbooks and Yearbooks

P, S
194. Schneider, Carl J., and Dorothy Schneider. **World War II.** New York, Facts on File, 2003. 472p. illus. maps. index. (An Eyewitness History). $75.00. ISBN 0-8160-4484-8.

    Facts on File's *World War II*, part of An Eyewitness History series, is an outstanding resource for first-hand accounts of Americans who took part in the twentieth-century's bloodiest conflict. The book is divided into 11 chapters that each focus on a particular aspect of the American experience of the war on both the civilian and military fronts. This includes the isolationist/interventionist debates, government responses to events, the effects on civil liberties, reactions to victory, and the formation of the United Nations. Each chapter opens with an essay describing the historical context of the eyewitness accounts that follow. Some chapters include chronological listings and all include a generous amount of photographs. The larger purpose of the book, of course, is to provide first-hand testimonials and these are culled from an amazing variety of sources, ranging from letters sent by enlisted men to their parents, accounts from veteran Websites, and reminiscences featured in journals and popular magazines. The accounts are skillfully edited, with the date of the testimony and sometimes a brief explanation provided in italics at the close of the narrative. There are five appendixes included. The first includes excerpts from key documents of the war, the second consists of biographies of significant figures, the third provides several maps, the fourth is a glossary of terms, and the fifth is an article on refugees displaced by the war. The appendixes are followed by footnotes from the main text and are followed, in turn, by a comprehensive bibliography and a subject index.—**Philip G. Swan**

10 Law

GENERAL WORKS

Dictionaries and Encyclopedias

P

195. **1001 Legal Words You Need to Know.** Jay M. Feinman, ed. New York, Oxford University Press, 2003. 239p. $17.95. ISBN 0-19-516503-9.

Edited by Jay M. Feinman, a law professor at Rutgers University, *1001 Legal Words You Need to Know* is a quick guide to common legal terms used in the American legal system. All main entries appear alphabetically in boldface type, followed by pronunciation and the part of speech, and then a brief definition. Most entries include sample sentences using the term defined to provide users information about collocations and grammar associated with a particular term. Each entry also has a derivative and etymology section that can be used to find the linguistic origins of a term. One can also resolve the differences in U.S. and British spellings (license vs. licence), look up singular and plural forms of terms (dicta or dictums from dictum), correct choice of words (plead not guilty vs. plead innocent), and usage (guaranty vs. warranty).

Also included are 10 brief explanatory essays that answer commonly asked questions about power of attorney, understanding contracts, making wills, and choosing a lawyer. The appendixes at the end of the book include a directory of legal aid organizations across the United States and a selective bibliography of books on the American legal system.

The book is reasonably priced and is nicely bound in hardcover. It is ideal for students and general users who may need to look up the spelling, usage, or the definition of legal terms in plain English. [R: Choice, Jan 04, p. 883]—**Shikha Sharma**

C, P, S

196.   **The Supreme Court A to Z.** 3d ed. Kenneth Jost, ed. Washington, D.C., CQ Press, 2003. 576p. illus. index. (CQ's American Government A to Z Series). $125.00. ISBN 1-56802-802-4.

The 3d edition of *The Supreme Court A to Z* has updated its text to include information on events that have faced the Court since the last edition in 1998 (see ARBA 2000, entry 635). The article on impeachment now includes a discussion of the Clinton impeachment trial, the article entitled *Bush v. Gore* addresses the presidential election controversy of 2000, and passing mention is made of current laws relating to terrorism. Articles are arranged in alphabetic order and include discussions of general topics the Court has addressed, such as loyalty oaths and voting rights, biographies of individuals that include, but are not limited to, justices of the Court, as well as individual cases the Court has wrestled with. The text, which is written for the layperson, is clear, concise, includes cross-references, and is enlivened by photographs, illustrations, and political cartoons. After the main text, there is a multipart appendix. This includes a timeline of important dates in the history of the Court and a table listing the Supreme Court justices by the president who nominated them. There is a chart that illustrates the years various justices sat on the court, giving the reader a better idea of who were contemporaries in a given span of time. This is followed by the text of the United States Constitution, a list of online resources, and a guide to reading a Court citation. A bibliography and index close out the text of the book. This work is recommended for public and school libraries, high school and higher.—**Philip G. Swan**

C

197.   Vile, John R. **Encyclopedia of Constitutional Amendments, Proposed Amendments, and Amending Issues, 1789-2002.** 2d ed. Santa Barbara, Calif., ABC-CLIO, 2003. 635p. index. $85.00; $130.00 (w/e-book). ISBN 1-85109-428-8; 1-85109-433-4 (e-book).

Anyone whose knowledge of U.S. constitutional amendments is limited to a passing familiarity with the Bill of Rights and some of the more salient of the other 16 existing amendments (one has been repealed) may be stunned to learn the vast scope of this topic as expounded in Vile's compendious encyclopedia. To begin with, there have been approximately 11,500 proposed amendments that have either died on the vine or have not yet been acted upon. Vile's 500-plus entries (100 of which are new to this edition, and the majority of which have been revised since the 1st edition, according to the author) encompass not only existing and proposed amendments, but all manner of proposals for new or revised constitutions, and other "amending issues" (e.g., whether states can rescind ratification of pending amendments). Entry topics include amendment subjects (e.g., prayer in public schools), Supreme Court cases that have ruled on amendment issues, the existing amendments themselves, and numerous individuals ranging from famous statesmen to obscure critics or commentators who have proposed amendments or variant constitutions. An A-Z list of entries at the beginning, normally superfluous in an alphabetic encyclopedia, is in this case very useful for quickly scanning the wide variety of topics covered. The entries are well written and provide source references (collected in a substantial bibliography at the end). Appendixes include tabular data on number of amendments by decade, "most popular" amending proposals by year, as well as the text of the Constitution and its amendments. This work is highly recommended for academic libraries.—**Jack Ray**

Handbooks and Yearbooks

C, P

198.   Crooker, Constance Emerson. **Gun Control and Gun Rights.** Westport, Conn., Greenwood Press, 2003. 180p. illus. index. (Historical Guides to Controversial Issues in America). $50.00. ISBN 0-313-32174-4.

Crooker has written a concise, clear, and coherent introduction to the debate on gun control versus gun rights. For people with little or no background on the "facts" of the debate, this book not only dispels the myths that surround the debate but also guides novices in their research on the subject. The chapters, for the most part, are short and informative in nature. Chapter 1 provides some brief statistics on gun violence in America. Chapter 2 looks at whether guns should be controlled. Chapter 3 consists of a series of quotes from recognizable figures who have spoken on gun control as well as views on gun control from law enforcement. Chapter 4 is perhaps the most important chapter in that it focuses on the Second Amendment. Crooker not only gives a brief history of that amendment but also offers an insight into the nature and meaning of the words used in that amendment. The remaining chapters focus on the federal jurisdiction over firearms, the history of federal gun control laws, gun control, and gun rights organizations. The endnotes and bibliography are quite good and useful. As a follow-up to this general introduction, this reviewer recommends James B. Jacobs' *Can Gun Control Work?* (Oxford University Press, 2002).—**Michael A. Foley**

C, P

199.   Dirck, Brian R. **Waging War on Trial: A Handbook with Cases, Laws, and Documents.** Santa Barbara, Calif., ABC-CLIO, 2003. 342p. index. (ABC-CLIO's On Trial Series). $55.00; $85.00 (w/e-book). ISBN 1-57607-948-1.

This handbook explores the constitutional issues related to the waging of war by the United States. Dirck focuses on three broad areas: the war powers debate, civil liberties during war, and the military justice system. The Constitution grants Congress the power to declare war and designates the President as Commander in Chief of the military branches. In his historical overview Dirck shows that from the beginning it was recognized that not all military action required a declaration of war, but that there has been an inexorable shift toward presidential assumption of war-making powers without any declaration from Congress even for major engagements such as Korea and Vietnam. Indeed, there has been no declaration of war since World War II began in 1941. While the Supreme Court has largely treated this issue as a "political question" that makes its intervention inappropriate, it has taken a more active role in the questions of civil liberties and the constitutional limits of the military justice system. In a nonpartisan manner, Dirck explores these issues even up to the questions raised by President Bush's and Congress's actions in response to the terrorist attacks of 2001 and leading up to the 2003 invasion of Iraq. About half of the book is composed of primary document excerpts (e.g., the 1964 Gulf of Tonkin Resolution, Supreme Court decisions upholding the President's right to intern Japanese-Americans during World War II). This timely, well-written, and fair-minded compendium is aimed at college students, and is highly recommended for academic and public libraries.—**Jack Ray**

C, P, S

200.   Glenn, Richard A. **The Right to Privacy: Rights and Liberties Under the Law.** Santa Barbara, Calif., ABC-CLIO, 2003. 399p. index. (America's Freedoms). $55.00; $60.00 (e-book). ISBN 1-57607-716-0; 1-57607-717-9 (e-book).

This brilliantly written and eminently readable introduction to the right of privacy as guaranteed by the U.S. Constitution is written for upper-level high school and college students; however, its scholarly and well-balanced research penned in both legal terminology and everyday English translation make it a suitable vehicle for all but the most advanced students of the topic. Richard Glenn deftly explains the philosophical underpinnings of the U.S. Constitution and Bill of Rights, both of which were written by statesmen versed in Aristotle, Cicero, St. Thomas Aquinas, Hobbes, and Locke. It may comes as a surprise that is was not until 1965 that the U.S. Supreme Court held, under *Griswold v. Connecticut*, that persons have a fundamental right to privacy, a right not specifically enumerated by the Bill of Rights. Yet this right evolved out of that very Bill of Rights. Specific rights of privacy have been vastly expanded by succeeding U.S. Supreme Court decisions. Glenn quotes liberally from *Griswold vs. Connecticut* and the later twentieth-century decisions, giving majority opinions, concurring opinions, and dissenting opinions. In addition to explaining the relevance of each decision, Glenn gives the reader background information about each case and the circumstances that prompted the case to end up in the Court's lap.

Lawrence v. Texas was decided on June 26, 2003. This case extended "constitutional privacy [in private sexual relations] to include activities outside of the traditional categories of procreation, marriage, and family life." This landmark decision came too late to be incorporated into the body of the work so Glenn penned a 24-page prologue explaining its ramifications. The author provides references at the end of each chapter as well as an annotated bibliography at the end of the volume. Another useful feature is an A-Z background reference section, which covers "important people, laws, and concepts that are central to understanding the right of privacy." A chronology, full-text documents, table of cases, and index round out this work. *The Right to Privacy* is strongly recommended for all high school libraries, undergraduate college libraries, and all but the smallest public libraries.—**Dene L. Clark**

C, P

201.   Kersch, Ken I. **Freedom of Speech: Rights and Liberties under the Law.** Santa Barbara, Calif., ABC-CLIO, 2003. 395p. index. (America's Freedoms). $65.00. ISBN 1-57607-600-8.

Kersch's treatment of the topic of freedom of speech is at once sophisticated and nuanced, yet easily accessible to students and general readers. Approximately one-half of the books is a narrative that explores the conceptual foundations of freedom of speech and then traces its historical evolution from sixteenth-century England to twenty-first-century America. The way this right has been understood and interpreted over time has varied widely, and has often been more influenced by political and cultural factors than by constitutional considerations. Originally developing as a facet of the Protestant "freedom of conscience," freedom of speech came to be seen as a necessity for a democratic society by the founders of our nation. But it was often interpreted as a matter of common law by state courts in the nineteenth century; only with the enlargement of the national government in the twentieth century did it become a right that was primarily interpreted as a constitutional matter by the U.S. Supreme Court. And while the general trend has been toward an expansion of how the right is defined, historical and cultural forces such as September 11th continue to create tendencies in the opposite direction. Following the narrative there is a chapter of extended paragraphs on 89 "Key People, Cases, and Events" (references to these from their mention in the text would have been helpful), 69 excerpts from documents (ranging from court cases to legal treatises to speeches), a chronology, and a bibliography. This splendid book is thoughtful, well written, and informative. It is highly recommended for public and academic libraries.—**Jack Ray**

P

202.   Morton, David A., III. **Nolo's Guide to Social Security Disability: Getting and Keeping Your Benefits.** 2d ed. Berkeley, Calif., Nolo Press, 2003. 1v. (various paging). index. $29.99pa. ISBN 0-87337-914-4.

In the past 30 years Nolo Press has acquired a well-deserved reputation for producing high-quality self-help guides in various areas of law. This revision, coming two years after the first edition, is in keeping with Nolo's high standards. In spite of the ferocious complexity of Social Security disability law, Morton (a physician who served many years as a medical consultant for the Social Security Administration) succeeds in making the topic intelligible for the average person. He does this primarily by scrupulously organizing the material and then breaking it up into manageable chunks of information written in plain English. At the same time, there is no "dumbing down" here: the book's chapters are separately paged, but total 540 double-columned, $8\frac{1}{2}$-by-11-inch pages. There are numerous examples, definitions, and samples of filled-in forms. Topics covered include applying for benefits, proving disability, who decides claims and what standards they use, reasons benefits may be denied, and appealing adverse decisions. There are also individual chapters on various types of conditions (e.g., heart and blood vessel diseases, kidney diseases, mental disorders) that may be a basis for disability benefits. The rules on Social Security disability are constantly changing, so a revised edition after two years is justifiable; in addition Nolo has a Website on which it posts updates to the law for this book as well as for other titles it publishes. This guide will be especially useful for public libraries.—**Jack Ray**

P

203.   **Nolo's Encyclopedia of Everyday Law: Answers to Your Most Frequently Asked Legal Questions.** 4th ed. By Shae Irving. Berkeley, Calif., Nolo Press, 2002. 1v. (various paging). illus. index. $29.99pa. ISBN 0-87337-830-X.

Nolo Press aims to provide consumers with information on legal issues they are likely to encounter in language that is easy to understand. This book is organized around more than 100 frequently asked questions that have been arranged into 18 chapters on particular subjects. Individual chapters are written by Nolo staff members, most of whom have law degrees. Sample topics covered include houses, neighbors, landlords and tenants, workplace rights, small business, money, travel, and criminal law and procedure.

Practical as well as strictly legal advice is included, with emphasis on where to get more information, including on the Internet as well as other sources. The writing is clear and easy to understand, and the format works well. A glossary, index, and appendix on how to perform further legal research are included. This edition includes new information on homeowner's insurance, satellite and cable access for tenants, and finding and working with a lawyer. This is a practical book, very different from, for instance, Jay M. Friedman's *Law 101: Everything You Need to Know About the American Legal System* (Oxford University Press, 2000), which is intended to explain the general rules and principles that lawyers and judges use. Nolo's book will not give the user as much understanding of the underlying principles of our legal system, but it should be much more useful in providing practical information. Although no book can substitute for personalized advice from a lawyer, this one should provide useful information to people faced with a legal issue. Nolo also provides updates on its Website. This work is recommended for all types of libraries.

Nolo Press offers a free Website that provides much of the same information that can be found in this volume, although with less depth. *Nolo's Legal Encyclopedia* can be searched by subject with such broad topics as "Caring for Children," "Criminal Law," "Debt and Bankruptcy," "Employment Law," "Internet Law," "Real Estate," "Small Business," and more. Each topic is broken down into smaller sections and will answer users' most frequently asked questions. This site also offers a dictionary of key legal terms (which is continually being added to), as well as calculators that will help readers with real estate, tax, and retirement questions; a guide to conducting your own legal research by consulting cases and statutes; and a list of frequently asked questions. Since the site is sponsored by Nolo Press, Nolo print products are listed on the right-hand side and users are encouraged to purchase the books for more information. For users needing basic information on common legal problems, this site is a good place to start.—**Marit S. Taylor**

C

204. Smith, Christopher E. **Courts and Trials: A Reference Handbook.** Santa Barbara, Calif., ABC-CLIO, 2003. 263p. index. (Contemporary World Issues). $45.00; $70.00 (w/e-book). ISBN 1-57607-933-3.

Christopher E. Smith, a professor at Michigan State University, is the author of 20 books and over 80 journal articles. His Website (http://www.cj.msu.edu/~people/csmith/) includes information about his professional writings, including this newest offering. Smith has devoted his career to researching and writing about the judicial system and has a deep knowledge of the people, the history, and the evolving nature of our court systems in the United States. ABC-CLIO, the publisher of *Courts and Trials: A Reference Handbook*, includes this title in its Contemporary World Issues series. The series publishes overview treatments of a variety of contemporary issues, such as environmental activism, food safety, and healthcare reform in America. Books in the series target the general public as well as students and scholars.

Radio, television, the Internet, and other media outlets tend to simplify the workings of the courts. The reality of most court trials is hardly as exciting as the Kobe Bryant or Enron-type cases we see televised on an almost daily basis. The reality of the thousands of unsensationalized cases is much more mundane and might involve lawyers spending days or weeks studying reams of records, artifacts, or weapons to determine admissibility of evidence and formulating precise arguments based on legal precedent. Books such as this can disabuse us of misperceptions upon which most of us blithely operate—until, heaven forbid, we are called upon to participate in a trial, whether as plaintiffs on the accusing side or defendants trying to protect our own or our organizations' interests.

Smith describes, in an easy, comprehensible style, the courts, jurisdictions, and legal systems of the United States. He opens with introductory material on current issues and controversies, followed by a chapter on court history and landmark cases arranged chronologically. Next he furnishes a chapter of biographical information on a selection of important jurists. Another chapter treats "documents and statistics," including analysis of key decisions of the U.S. Supreme Court. The final chapters offer resources for further information (including print resources, films, and Internet sites) about relevant agencies and organizations. The text contains only a few charts and tables, and a glossary, which is, unfortunately, not very comprehensive. As if to compensate, it contains a carefully detailed back-of-the-book index.

Supplementary to this book, the World Wide Web is increasingly becoming a repository for legal documents such as court transcripts, much of it free. An excellent free site is http://findlaw.com, a popular legal portal. Researchers also rely upon the excellent National Center for State Court's Website at http://www.ncsconline.org/, probably the very best Website for information at the state level. For federal courts, http://www.uscourts.gov/ is outstanding.

Courts and Trials: A Reference Handbook would be valuable for those wishing an introduction and brief history of court systems in the United States. It provides a solid, although not too taxing, overview of the subject for patrons of public and community college libraries, or even advanced high school students.
—**Linda D. Tietjen**

C, P

205.   Stathis, Stephen W. **Landmark Legislation 1774-2002: Major U.S. Acts and Treaties.** Washington, D.C., CQ Press, 2003. 429p. index. $130.00. ISBN 1-56802-781-8.

As indicated in its press release, *Landmark Legislation 1774-2002* is intended to be a "treasure trove" of information about the most significant laws and treaties approved by Congress over 200 years. The author is a senior staff member at the Congressional Record Service who has spent many years studying numerous legislative sources to identify and put into context the most important actions taken by Congress from the Continental Congress in 1774 to the 107th Congress in 2002. This work has its genesis in an original list of bills prepared by the author in 1982 and clearly the amount of time and care taken in this effort is reflected in the fine quality of the resulting publication. The cover design, the binding, and the typeface and layout of the text contribute to the impression that this is a first-rate publication. In a world where most people perceive civics or political science texts to be dry, complex, or biased, *Landmark Legislation* is a welcome addition to the literature.

A typical entry in *Landmark Legislation* begins with the number and dates of the Congress, along with dates of individual sessions, the names of the sitting president, and the dates when he was in office. Several pages of historical essays follow, providing noteworthy background about the particular Congress and interweaving information about significant legislation with commentary on the social, political, and cultural events of the time. The essays are concise, well written, and informative. Each entry contains brief summaries of the major acts and treaties for that Congress. These brief summaries include the official title of the act or treaty, the date of approval, and public law and statute numbers. Although there have been nearly 44,000 public acts approved by Congress since 1774, this volume includes only about 1,300 that have been selected by the author for their enduring importance, their impact on society, and their reflection of the changing role of government and of the legislative process. Some of the entries contain bibliographic notes; however, there is an extensive bibliography at the end of the volume, arranged by broad subject headings. The most interesting entries in *Landmark Legislation*are in the front of the volume, because these entries contain the acts that cover specification of the flag, establishment of the postal service, authorization of the army and navy, and the admission of various states into the union.

There are many special features in *Landmark Legislation* that add to the value of this publication. There is a brief but helpful introduction on the role of Congress and the development of new legislation. The volume also has an extensive "Finder's Guide," with entries assigned to one or more subject categories, such as civil liberties, education, or foreign affairs. This is in addition to an extensive index at the back of the volume. There is a key to the "Finder's Guide," which indicates session of Congress, dates of the session, the name of the act or treaty, and the page number. There is also a table of contents arranged by Congress member.

Landmark Legislation 1774-2002 is an appropriate purchase for nearly any type of library. The book is particularly suited for public libraries, academic libraries, and for libraries that serve journalists and scholars in law and political science. It has be beautifully and thoughtfully produced to provide an overview of the most important legislation in the United States and will be useful as both a ready-reference tool and as a foundation for further study [R: Choice, Jan 04, p. 890]—**Sara Anne Hook**

P, S

206.   Uradnik, Kathleen. **Student's Guide to Landmark Congressional Laws on Youth.** Westport, Conn., Greenwood Press, 2002. 252p. index. (Student's Guide to Landmark Congressional Laws). $50.00. ISBN 0-313-31461-6.

For more than a century after its founding, the federal government paid very little attention to the welfare of children, which was considered to be a concern of state and local governments and private charities. In the Progressive and New Deal eras, and especially with the advent of the Great Society programs, that attitude changed considerably. However, as can be seen from perusing the selection of "Landmark Congressional Laws on Youth" that are explicated in this volume, the federal government's direct involvement with the concerns of children is still relatively limited. While some of the laws, such as the National School Lunch Act (1946), Head Start (1965), and the Elementary and Secondary Education Act (1965), have as their fundamental purpose the education and welfare of youth, quite a few others, such as the Social Security Act (1935), Food Quality Protection Act (1996), and the Americans with Disabilities Act (1990) are only partially or indirectly concerned with children. And amendments to the Constitution (the 14th and 26th are discussed) are not exactly "Congressional laws."

The text is pitched at the level of high school students, as is evidenced by an introduction that provides a very basic treatment of the formation and structure of the federal government, and phrases such as "young people should understand" and "today's young people . . . do not remember what it was like." However, the writing is very clear and informative, and salient texts of the laws are included at the end of each piece. The volume concludes with a useful bibliography. This source will be most appropriate for high school and public libraries.—**Jack Ray**

CRIMINOLOGY AND CRIMINAL JUSTICE

Dictionaries and Encyclopedias

C, P

207.   Bell, Suzanne. **Encyclopedia of Forensic Science.** New York, Facts on File, 2004. 350p. illus. index. (Facts on File Science Library). $75.00. ISBN 0-8160-4811-8.

Currently forensic science is the focus of considerable attention and public interest. In part this is a reflection of high-profile television shows such as *CSI*, and various best-selling works of fiction featuring forensic analysis. It is also a function of the critical role that fairly recent forensic science developments (e.g., DNA analysis) have played in establishing the innocence of individuals who have served many years on death row. As a consequence, criminal justice professors encounter growing numbers of students who express an interest in a career in forensic science. These students have to be apprised of the need to master some branches of hard science if they are to succeed in this field, as well as the finite number of openings for qualified applicants. All that said, forensic science is an important dimension of the current criminal justice response to crime, and is likely to play an expanding role in this response in the years ahead.

The encyclopedia under review has been authored by Suzanne Bell, a professor of chemistry at West Virginia University with some practical experience in forensic analysis. Although she indicates that she has consulted with some knowledgeable people in the field, and has had some specific assistance on some of the encyclopedia entries, she is nevertheless listed as the author of the work in its entirety. As encyclopedias of this type are typically overseen by a general editor, with individual entries produced by numerous specialists, the sole authorship of this encyclopedia is surely a remarkable achievement. The entries appear to be conscientiously researched and written. It is possible that specialists in the topics addressed might identify deficiencies and errors, but any such shortcomings are not readily apparent.

This encyclopedia is intended for use by a broad audience, ranging from interested members of the public to students to working professionals. The entries themselves include some that define basic concepts in fairly rudimentary terms and others that include rather technical and sometimes challenging details. The author informs us in a brief introductory essay that she has adopted the International System of Units (SI) conventions. The entries range from specific chemical terms (e.g., alkaloids) to sources of forensic analysis, such as fingernails (and fingerprinting), to biographical entries on key figures, such as Mathieu Orfila, founder of forensic toxicology. Altogether, the encyclopedia seems to be quite comprehensive in its coverage of all imaginable terms, cases, and techniques that are of significance in the forensic sciences. Entries range from a brief paragraph to several pages in length, commensurate with the importance (and complexity) of the topic addressed. Many cross-references are listed. For many entries between one and three sources for further reading are listed.

Perhaps unsurprisingly, in light of the author's standing as a chemistry professor, the entries relating to chemicals appear to be especially well developed, and often include instructive diagrams. Indeed, numerous tables, charts, and photographs, as well as such diagrams, can be found throughout this volume. A central section features color photographs of such phenomena as blood cell evidence, an atomic absorption spectrophotometer, gunshot residue patterns, and the bombed Murrah Federal building. A series of 14 feature essays are found throughout the encyclopedia as well, addressing topics ranging from "Forensic Science and History" to "Careers in Forensic Science: A Reality Check" to "The Future of Lie Detection." The three appendixes address "Bibliographies and Web Resources," "Common Abbreviations and Acronyms" and "Periodic Table of the Elements." An index is included as well.

Altogether, this handsome, polished reference work should prove useful to a wide range of constituencies, as suggested by the author, and in light of the high level of interest today in the subject matter should be among the more frequently consulted reference works in public and university libraries. It is significantly more comprehensive and sophisticated than another recently published reference work from Oryx Press, the *Encyclopedia of Forensic Science*, by B. G. Conklin, R. Gardner, and D. Shortelle (see ARBA 2003, entry 564). The present encyclopedia is accordingly more suitable for university libraries, or libraries serving professionals than is the earlier work, which is geared more toward secondary school students and the general public.—**David O. Friedrichs**

C, P

208.   **Encyclopedia of Juvenile Justice.** Marilyn D. McShane and Frank P. Williams III, eds. Thousand Oaks, Calif., Sage, 2003. 416p. illus. index. $99.95. ISBN 0-7619-2358-6.

The juvenile justice system in the United States has been in existence for over 100 years now. If the need for separate procedures and penal options for most juvenile offenders has been quite widely accepted, the specific policies and practices for addressing such offenders has been a topic of enduring controversy. The media coverage of juvenile justice cases tends to focus on especially sensational and atypical cases, which contributes to public misperceptions of the true nature of juvenile justice. Our society has much at stake in ensuring that the juvenile justice system operates as effectively and fairly as possible.

The co-editors of this encyclopedia, Marilyn D. McShane and Frank P. Williams III, are enterprising and well-known criminologists. In addition to their own scholarly work—including the highly regarded *Criminological Theory* (3d ed.; Pearson Education, 1998)—they have served as editors of monograph series and the *Encyclopedia of American Prisons* (see ARBA 97, entry 505). For the present work they commissioned over 200 entries from 140 contributors. The contributors include some of the best-known scholars in the field, including Frankie Bailey, Robert M. Bohm, Gilbert Geis, Don Gibbons, John Laub, Doris MacKenzie, Alida Merlo, Laura Moriarty, Frank Scarpitti, David Shichor, Austin Turk, and Neil Websdale. Of course, many other accomplished scholars, as well as some junior scholars, also contributed to this encyclopedia.

The encyclopedia articles are divided into the following categories: Delinquency Theories and Theorists (e.g., cycles of violence, Albert Cohen); Historical References: People and Projects (e.g., Augusta Bronner, Chicago Area Project); Delinquent Behavior (e.g., race and delinquency, status offenders);

Treatment and Interventions for Delinquency (e.g., boot camps, scared straight); Juvenile Law and Legislative Initiatives (e.g., Juvenile Justice and Delinquency Prevention Act, waivers to adult court); and Juvenile Issues and Public Policy (e.g., missing children, school responses to juvenile violence). Although anyone working in the field of juvenile justice is likely to find one or more favorite topics excluded, a good deal of thought seems to have gone into the selection of the topics covered, and certainly all of the key issues are addressed.

The entries typically run two or more pages; a few are more brief. They are broken up by appropriate subheadings. Cross-references are noted at the end of each entry; for example, at the end of the Child-Saving Movement users will find a *see also* reference to Courts, Juvenile-History; Female Delinquency—History; Law, Juvenile; Parens Patriae Doctrine; Reformatories and Reform Schools; and Status Offenders. A bibliography of typically between 5 and 10 sources can also be found at the end of each entry. A small handful of appropriate illustrations are scattered throughout this volume (e.g., Judge Lindsey Presides in the Chambers of His Juvenile Court; Elmira Reformatory). Appendix 1 lists print and online resources for juvenile justice, while appendix 2 lists Internet resources for juvenile justice. A fairly detailed index is included as well.

Altogether, the editors are to be commended for once again making a substantial contribution to criminological knowledge. This attractively produced encyclopedia, with many well-written and informative articles, will surely be a useful resource for any party seeking basic information on a range of topics related to juvenile delinquency and juvenile justice. It can be recommended for purchase by public libraries as well as college and university libraries and those serving a scholarly community with an interest in juvenile justice issues. [R: LJ, 1 April 03, p. 90; VOYA, June 03, pp. 165-166; SLJ, Aug 03, p. 111]—**David O. Friedrichs**

C, P

209.   Palmer, Louis J., Jr. **Encyclopedia of DNA and the United States Criminal Justice System.** Jefferson, N.C., McFarland, 2004. 464p. illus. maps. index. $95.00. ISBN 0-7864-1735-8.

The use of DNA analysis in criminal justice is recent, dating back to the mid-1980s. In the short period of time that it has been in use, DNA analysis has achieved a rather high profile, and has played a significant role in both establishing guilt in some cases and innocence in others. In quite a number of widely publicized cases DNA testing has demonstrated that individuals who had spent many years on death row could not be directly linked to the crime for which they were convicted, as blood and semen samples obtained in connection with the crime could not have come from them. In 2003 the House of Representatives passed a bill called Advancing Justice Through DNA Technology Act (HR-3214, S-1700), authorizing funding to provide a right to DNA testing. President Bush and other supporters of the "crime control" model supported this legislation on the premise that it would establish guilt more often than innocence, and would make appeals of convictions more difficult. Altogether, DNA testing could be expected to play an important role in especially serious crime cases in the years ahead. Accordingly, the production of an *Encyclopedia of DNA and the United States Criminal Justice System* would appear to be timely.

The author of this volume is a West Virginia attorney who has produced encyclopedias on abortion, capital punishment, the death penalty, and organ transplants from executed prisoners, all within the past five years. He is listed as the sole author of the present encyclopedia. This is certainly a remarkable achievement, although it is at odds with the more typical pattern of having specialists author individual entries in their areas of expertise. Nevertheless, this encyclopedia appears to be thoroughly researched and conscientiously produced. It incorporates a wealth of information relating to DNA testing, with much of this information inevitably of very recent vintage. First, it includes the full text of federal and state statutes pertaining to the use of DNA analysis in criminal cases, with the author's summaries of the key themes of these statutes. This growing body of law is a new and consequential element of our legal system. In addition to statutory laws, many entries provide excerpts from case law (or judge-made law) that address forensic DNA issues, again including the author's summaries. Inevitably, the use of DNA analysis has generated complex and challenging new issues for law. For example, rape shield laws are intended to prevent the defense in rape cases from exploring the alleged victim's past sexual history, but does this mean that defendant's are unable to introduce DNA evidence indicating that semen found on the alleged victim did not come from the defendant? An issue of this nature arose in the high profile rape case against basketball star Kobe Bryant. Issues relating to rights of defendants and self-incrimination arise in connection with whether those accused of crimes or convicted of crimes can be compelled to supply DNA samples.

Many cases where DNA evidence played a key role—especially in some dramatic cases where it established innocence after conviction on murder charges—are summarized in various entries. These entries are typically listed by the name of the key party in the case. Other entries define specific scientific terms or procedures relating to DNA analysis (e.g., Molecular Weight Size Marker and PCR cycles). Concepts such as "false positive" (when DNA testing "incorrectly includes a suspect sample as a source of a forensic sample") are concisely defined. A variety of federal and private organizations play an important role in the analysis of DNA evidence, or its dissemination. These organizations are described in a series of entries. Some entries address accreditation, certification, and scandalous applications as they apply to DNA testing.

Altogether, this volume should certainly prove useful to students, researchers, practitioners, and interested members of the lay public. It can be considered for acquisition by any library serving such diverse populations. In light of the recent development of DNA, its inherent complexity, and the single-authored character of the entries, it is possible that specialists will identify mistakes here and there. No such mistakes, if any, are readily apparent, however, and the author deserves commendation for his efforts in connection with this reference volume.—**David O. Friedrichs**

Directories

P

210.   Hinton, Derek. **The Criminal Records Book: The Complete Guide to the Legal Use of Criminal Records.** Tempe, Ariz., Facts on Demand Press/BRB, 2002. 317p. $19.95pa. ISBN 1-889150-28-2.

A Penn State University professor was recently discovered to have been the murderer of three people when he was a teenager, for which he had served many years in prison. He had also acquired two doctorates. When the Pennsylvania Parole Board learned of his presence in the state it informed him that he could not legally reside in the state. He resigned his position at Penn State, but when this story came out a job offer from a California university was rescinded. This incident generated considerable discussion within higher education of whether colleges and universities must engage in searches of criminal records for prospective academic employees, and whether in any case it is fair or unfair to those who have served their time to discriminate against them due to a criminal record.

The Criminal Records Book has been published, then, at a time when a range of information about individuals has become more widely available, but also in the context of on-going controversy over privacy rights. Derek Hinton, the author of this book, is Director of Communications and Legal Affairs for an employment screening company. The book begins with an account of two employers who were defrauded by an employee, who subsequently turned out to have a criminal record unknown to these employers. It is certainly a legitimate concern for employers that they have information relevant to the integrity and dependability of prospective employees. The balance of this book is devoted to systematically providing a wealth of information on criminal records, and how they can be obtained.

Chapter 2 provides users of this book with a review of some key terms and phrases relating to criminal records (e.g., the difference between felonies and misdemeanors). Chapter 3 identifies those who use such records, differentiating between criminal justice agencies (for whom such record use is standard) and noncriminal justice agencies and the general public. Some criteria for granting access to FBI records, for noncriminal justice agencies, are identified. A fourth chapter reviews the on-going debate about the appropriate use of criminal records, with special attention to the privacy objection, and to the use of such records as they relate to victimless and nonviolent crimes.

The second section of this book includes six chapters that quite exhaustively explore where criminal records are found. These chapters differentiate between criminal records on the county, state, and federal level, spelling out how these records are compiled and criteria for access on each level. Another chapter differentiates between various types of records, including military criminal records and state sexual offender records (with the latter being a special focus of concern in recent years). The remaining chapters in this section differentiate between obtaining criminal records on one's own or through a criminal record vendor.

A third section of this book includes six chapters providing detailed information on who should use criminal records, and how users can ensure that they are complying with various guidelines for the use of such records. For example, users of such records must ensure that they are in compliance with the Fair Credit Reporting Act and the EEOC guidelines called for by Title VII. Individual states also impose certain restrictions on the use of criminal records by prospective employers. A fourth section of this book is comprised of a state-by-state listing of specific information relating to the accessing of criminal records, and parallel information from federal records, divided by federal districts.

Finally, the book closes with several appendixes, including a chart for easy reference on state criminal records data (e.g., whether probation information is released), summaries of the relevant provisions of the Fair Credit Reporting Act and Title VII EEOC notices, and a "Quick-Find Index."

Altogether, this book should prove immensely useful to organizations and individuals undertaking criminal background checks, for whatever reason. The benefits and drawbacks to making such records widely available are likely to be a topic of on-going debate.—**David O. Friedrichs**

Handbooks and Yearbooks

C, P

211.   Hastedt, Glenn. **Espionage: A Reference Handbook.** Santa Barbara, Calif., ABC-CLIO, 2003. 225p. index. (Contemporary World Issues). $45.00; $50.00 (e-book). ISBN 1-57607-950-3; 1-57607-951-1 (e-book).

The term "espionage," to my mind, has an almost quaint ring to it, as it can be so thoroughly associated with the Cold War era, during which time the United States and the Soviet Union engaged in intense efforts to learn each other's secrets. These efforts were chronicled in countless news reports, nonfiction books, and some high-profile fiction works as well. But, of course, espionage has a long history, and is an on-going enterprise.

This book is yet another addition to the admirable Contemporary World Issues series published by ABC-CLIO. These books are all available in both print and e-book versions. They are organized in a uniform format, are attractively produced, and are filled with useful information for those interested in learning more about the issues addressed by each volume. Some closely related titles in this series include *Nuclear Weapons and Nonproliferation* by Sarah J. Diehl and James Clay Moltz (see ARBA 2003, entry 669), *U.S. National Security* by Cynthia Watson (see ARBA 2003, entry 730), and *War Crimes and Justice* by Howard Ball (see ARBA 2003, entry 584). The author of the present volume, Glenn Hastedt, is a professor of political science at Indiana University, who has published books on U.S. foreign policy and intelligence policy issues.

The first chapter of this book reviews the history of espionage in the United States, beginning with the American Revolution era, and concluding with the "Post-September 11, 2001" era. The "Cold War" era is appropriately addressed in the longest section of this chapter. But in the concluding section 9/11 is characterized as a "transformational event," in light of the extensive criticism directed at American intelligence services, for their failure to clearly anticipate this attack on America. In this section the author identifies some responses and initiatives following 9/11, although of course we are still too early in this era to determine the long-term and enduring impact on espionage as a consequence of this national trauma. A second chapter addresses the various contemporary espionage debates; for example, how espionage relates to national security threats, how an increasingly globalized economy impacts on espionage, and how counterespionage initiatives work. Again, 9/11 has generated some new challenges in this realm. The U.S. Patriot Act, adopted almost immediately in the wake of the 9/11 attacks, is currently a focus of considerable debate and concern, in terms of its effectiveness and its impact on privacy and human rights issues.

Chapter 3, titled "Espionage around the World," selectively reviews espionage issues relating to a number of countries, with the principal emphasis on Great Britain, Israel, China, and the Soviet Union/Russia. Following a brief review of the history of espionage in these countries, each section of this chapter also devotes attention to a high-profile intelligence agent who either stole secrets from the country featured, or provided the country with secrets. These featured individuals are Kim Philby (Great Britain), Jonathan Jay Pollard (Israel), Larry Wu-tai Chin (China), and Oleg Penkovsky (Soviet Union/Russia). In the case of Pollard, Israel (and American sympathizers) have campaigned for years for his release, on the basis that he was providing key information to an American ally, and does not deserve to serve out a life sentence in prison.

The fourth chapter of this volume is composed of 34 brief biographical sketches of individuals who have played some significant role in the history of espionage. These individuals include spies (e.g., Nathan Hale, Klaus Fuchs, John Walker, Aldrich Ames), heads of intelligence services or divisions (e.g., James Jesus Angleton, William Donovan, Felix Dzershinsky, George Tenet), and important political figures involved with espionage issues (e.g., Frank Church, Joseph McCarthy, A. Mitchell Palmer, Richard Nixon). Whittaker Chambers, who famously accused Alger Hiss of spying, is the subject of a sketch here (as is Hiss). These sketches include key dates, and essential information about the profiled individual.

Key documents pertaining to espionage are reprinted or excerpted in a fifth chapter. These documents begin with a 1941 Presidential, and include some very recent documents (e.g., the Homeland Security Act of 2002). This chapter is divided into sections on Organizational Procedures and Authorities, Law, and Evidence of Domestic Spying, with excerpts from the Economic Espionage Act of 1996 illustrative of the law section, and a 1975 statement by Senator Frank Church as one example of an evidentiary document. As the author notes, the very nature of espionage means that much of importance is not recorded in documents (or at least in nonclassified documents).

This volume concludes with a chronology on espionage, running from 1765 to 2003, and an annotated guide to relevant print and nonprint resources. The volume also includes a glossary and an index. Once again, ABC-CLIO has succeeded in contracting with a well-qualified scholar to produce a thoroughly useful reference volume on an important and interesting issue.—**David O. Friedrichs**

C, S

212.   Henderson, Harry. **Terrorist Challenge to America.** New York, Facts on File, 2003. 316p. index. (Library in a Book). $45.00. ISBN 0-8160-4975-0.

Whenever there is a crisis or an intervention of some sort involving multiple parties, the media are quick to remind us not to "rush to judgment." For the most part this is wise counsel, and book publishers would do well to remember it. All too often, before a hostage crisis is over or a natural disaster cleaned up, a book is out on the market and a made-for-television movie scheduled for the weekend. Happily, even though we are only knee-deep in the war on terrorism, Harry Henderson did not make this "rush-to-judgment" mistake. The race to be "first" has not spoiled what is an admirable survey of a difficult and most timely topic. Facts on File's Library in a Book series provides up-to-the-minute materials as the "first-stop research source" for important contemporary issues. One must surmise that since the Web has, mistakenly so, made many people think libraries are obsolete, Facts on File felt it could reduce a library to one book. Even so, the effect in the present case is satisfying.

Henderson provides chronologies, events, places, facts, figures, and all the rest in his survey of the war on terrorism. After a brief overview, he tackles in turn chapters on the law and the war on terrorism, its chronology, important (as well as infamous) biographical sketches, organizations, agencies, and more.

Henderson chronicles the evolution of the Homeland Security Office, the Patriot Act, and background materials on the war in Afghanistan.

While it was too early for the book to include current controversies about the Patriot Act (the chronology ends April 22, 2003), it does anticipate what some of these turned out to be. Because of the end date, little is included about the ongoing "clean-up" work in Baghdad. In an effort to cover all the bases, Henderson includes some who might otherwise have been left out. For example, just because Noam Chomsky made remarkable linguistic discoveries does not mean he necessarily has anything important to say on the "War on Terrorism." What Henderson includes here from Chomsky strongly supports this contention. On the balance, however, libraries will want to buy this book, especially for high school students and college freshmen. [R: SLJ, Aug 03, p. 110]—**Mark Y. Herring**

EMPLOYMENT LAW

P

213.   DelPo, Amy, and Lisa Guerin. **Federal Employment Laws: A Desk Reference.** Berkeley, Calif., Nolo Press, 2002. 1v. (various paging). index. $49.99pa. ISBN 0-87337-798-2.

This book is possibly the best popular current reference work summarizing federal employment law. The lawyer authors have written a practical and easy-to-use book on a major legal issue and Nolo Press has once again lived up to their motto of "putting the law into plain English." Managers, workers, and human resource directors can use this book to find the answers to their questions about federal employment laws: who do they protect, which employers are covered, what the laws require and what they prohibit, what obligations employers have, what rights employees have, and where to go for additional help.

The book is organized into chapters, with each chapter explaining one of the 19 major federal employment laws covered. The information synthesizes the text of each law, any regulations issued by the enforcing agencies, the major court cases that interpret the law, and a summary of state laws related to each federal law. The book is very easy to read and uses lay language for both the descriptions of the laws themselves and the explanations of their application and interpretation.

Some of the significant contributions of the book include: summaries of related state laws; contacts for additional information, with addresses, Websites, and telephone numbers; full text of the laws; and lay-language definitions of key terms at the front of each chapter. There are a couple of omissions, which the authors acknowledge: the two major amendments to the National Labor Relations Act (the Taft-Hartley Act and the Landrum-Griffin Act), both of which are important to an understanding of federal regulation of union activity are not covered. The book also does not cover federal regulation of government employers and employees of federal contractors. Nevertheless, this book is an important contribution to law by making employment laws understandable. It will supplement other popular Nolo Press titles, such as *Employment Law Made Easy, Your Rights in the Workplace* (6th ed., 2002), and *Employees Legal Handbook* (5th ed., 2002).—**Georgia Briscoe**

P

214.   Repa, Barbara Kate. **Your Rights in the Workplace.** 6th ed. Berkeley, Calif., Nolo Press, 2002. 1v. (various paging). index. $29.99pa. ISBN 0-87337-836-9.

Labor law is by its nature a complex subject. The 6th edition of this comprehensive guide helps make it less so by providing comprehensive information on all aspects of employees' workplace rights. The 17 chapters cover federal labor laws dealing with health and safety, civil rights, wages and hours, privacy, and unemployment. The information in each section is logically organized beginning with an overview of the law followed by subsections dealing with specific topics covered under legislation. A good example is the wage and hours chapter in which the Fair Labor Standards Act is explained in four succinct paragraphs. This is followed by subsections delineating how the law applies to various types of employees. Minimum wage requirements and all the exceptions appear in another subsection.

The impact of scientific and technological advances is reflected in the privacy chapter that discusses the implications of such things as genetic testing and e-mail privacy rights. The chapter covering FMLA gives an excellent explanation of the law and all its ramifications. State labor law information is covered in numerous charts. Using the charts one can quickly find a state's position on such things as overtime or time off for voting. Specific details are given to employees who might be considering filing a complaint. The importance of solid documentation is emphasized and advice is tempered with caution. Employees are encouraged to pursue arbitration or mediation before taking their employer to court. The appendix is a topical resource list of organizations related to specific workplace issues.

Other titles on employee's rights, including *Every Employee's Guide to the Law* (Pantheon Books, 2001) and *Your Workplace Rights* (AMACOM, 1999), cover most of the same material, but this guide stands out as the best. Its logical format, organization of information, and clearly written text will be a boon to employees seeking redress for workplace violations and to librarians seeking to assist them.—**Marlene M. Kuhl**

HUMAN RIGHTS

C, P, S

215.   **The Wilson Chronology of Human Rights.** David Levinson, ed. Bronx, N.Y., H. W. Wilson, 2003. 573p. index. $100.00. ISBN 0-8242-0972-9.

These briefly annotated events affecting groups usually considered protected under human rights laws—women, children, indigenous peoples, homosexuals, physically challenged people, ethnic and racial minorities, and aliens—are international in scope and span about 2,000 years. The two-page preface warns the unwary reader of the wide disagreement about how the term "human rights" should be defined. Indeed, human rights laws, often the result of mass sympathy for grossly abused groups of people, end up begging the question of what anyone means by human rights, in an objective sense. To appreciate these disturbing reminders of man's inhumanity to man, readers would do well first to study the debate and decide for themselves. Suitable works would include, Michael Arnheim's *A Handbook of Human Rights: An Accessible Approach to Issues and Principles* (Kogan Page, 2004), The United Nations' Universal Declaration of Human Rights, Jack Donnelly's *Universal Human Rights: Theory and Practice* (Cornell University Press, 2002), and Michael Ignatieff's *Human Rights as Politics and Idolatry* (Princeton University Press, 2001). The chronology could also use a glossary. However, its extensive index and bibliography of works focusing on specific rights are useful tools. Certainly the broad scope and nonjudgmental tenor of this work, as well as the lack of current chronologies on this topic, make this chronology a desirable addition to reference collections of high school, university, and public libraries.—**Nancy L. Van Atta**

IMMIGRATION LAW

P

216.   Canter, Laurence A., and Martha S. Siegel. **U.S. Immigration Made Easy.** Edited by Ilona Bray. 10th ed. Berkeley, Calif., Nolo Press, 2003. 1v. (various paging). index. $44.99pa. ISBN 0-87337-899-7. ISSN 1055-9647.

Nolo Press has long been known for its successful self-help law books and, in recent years, for its up-to-date legal information online. Although this immigration volume is in its 10th edition, the title now seems somewhat ironic since the view of the American public is generally that immigration should be made more difficult and the government also has moved in this direction. Still, this book continues to make the rules and procedures of immigration as clear and understandable as possible, including such topics as how to get a green card though various means, nonimmigrant and student visas, the naturalization process, and special rules for Canadians and Mexicans. The information is readily accessible through the clear chapter headings and subheading and a detailed index. The text is written in a no-nonsense, easy-to-read style, which usually includes helpful examples. Additionally, some 44 tear-out immigration forms are provided.

It is extremely important that users read the introductory chapter on how the text is to be used—particularly since this latest edition was published shortly before the Immigration and Naturalization Service (INS) became the Bureau of Citizenship and Immigration Services (BCIS) and thus has more than the usual number of changes. For example, 21 of the 44 forms included have been updated and, understandably, many of the fees have been increased. Nolo Press, however, has made the information concerning these changes quite easily accessible. In an insert on the first page of the text, specific information for finding the updates is given. Readers are reminded that the text is reliable up to the date of publication in February 2003, but it is necessary to check the Nolo Website for any updates. Under the section "Legal Updates" summaries of important changes and the date they are to take effect are listed, occasionally followed by links to the government agency involved. It is possible to go directly to the agencies, but without the simplified, step-by-step directions given in the Nolo volume, it would be very difficult to work through all the complicated processes involved.

Authored by 2 immigration attorneys who have had over 25 years of experience, this book provides information that is sorely needed by those hoping to qualify for immigration to the United States or to remain in the country through one of the various programs available. Not only informative, it also provides advice on the best steps to take in particular cases. For these reasons and for the fact that the updates are made easily available, this volume should be a useful addition to any academic and public library.—**Lucille Whalen**

INTELLECTUAL PROPERTY

P
217.   Elias, Stephen, and Richard Stim. **Patent, Copyright & Trademark: An Intellectual Property Desk Reference.** 6th ed. Berkeley, Calif., Nolo Press, 2003. 512p. $39.99pa. ISBN 0-87337-949-7.

Patent, Copyright & Trademark: An Intellectual Property Desk Reference is an excellent source of information on the four main components of intellectual property law: trade secret, copyright, patent, and trademark. Now in its 6th edition, the book offers a wealth of information that is presented in a concise, understandable, and easy-to-use format. The book is published by Nolo Press, an established resource of legal information for the layperson, and its authors are attorneys who have had considerable experience writing and editing for Nolo Press, particularly in the area of intellectual property law. Although the book is intended for the layperson, it will also be an excellent desk reference for attorneys who do not normally work in the intellectual property arena. While there are many books available on intellectual property law for the layperson as well as the practitioner, this book stands out for its clarity, its completeness, and its careful organization.

The organization of *Patent, Copyright & Trademark* is simple but effective. The book is divided into four major sections, one for each of the areas of intellectual property law. Then each part is subdivided into an overview section, a definitions section, a section with forms, and a final section on statutes. These sections are designated by printed tables, making it easy to find information quickly. The overview sections of the book are clearly written and thorough without being either boring or overwhelming to the reader. The use of subheadings, bullets, and lists of related terms throughout the overview are helpful in navigating complex issues. In the definitions section, a considerable number of terms are defined and cross-referenced. This section is more than a glossary; it really gives the reader a comprehensive grasp of the jargon and technical terms used in the field. There are a number of illustrations and examples provided in this section. Some definitions are extensive, encompassing more than a page of explanation, and contact information and Website addresses are provided where appropriate. Even a reader with expertise in their field will find freshness in the way that the material is presented in the definitions section, which reads more like a textbook than a glossary. The forms section for patents provides a directory of Patent and Trademark Depository Libraries and a sample patent application. Copyright and trademark applications are also included for those sections of the book. The final section on patents provides selected statutes from the Patent Act.

The introductory material for *Patent, Copyright & Trademark* is minimal but helpful. There is a brief overview of intellectual property, which includes a section on the intersection of these areas of law. There is also a very short explanation of how to use the book, a breakdown of what legal rights might apply to creative work, a chart of intellectual property law protection for various types of creative work, and a short bibliography of other sources of intellectual property information that are recommended for the layperson. The book has been attractively produced with typeface that is easy to read, and there is considerable use of bold typeface and a generous number of illustrations, particularly in the patent and trademark sections. The cover design is attractive and engaging.

Patent, Copyright & Trademark is highly recommended for public libraries that serve patrons interested in intellectual property pursuits. It would also be appropriate for academic libraries. It would be an excellent choice for law libraries to have on hand to use in advising and educating clients on intellectual property law matters. The book is interesting to read, easy to use, and would be an excellent choice for nearly any reference collection. It would also make an excellent text for courses and educational programs that include intellectual property law topics within the curriculum.—**Sara Anne Hook**

11 Library and Information Science and Publishing and Bookselling

LIBRARY AND INFORMATION SCIENCE

Reference Works

Bibliography

C

218.   ***Choice's* Outstanding Academic Titles 1998-2002: Reviews of Scholarly Titles That Every Library Should Own.** Rebecca Ann Bartlett, ed. Chicago, American Library Association, 2003. 642p. index. $90.00. ISBN 0-8389-8232-8.

This is the second installment of *Choice*'s five-year compilation of outstanding titles (see ARBA 2000, entry 551, for the first compilation). The volume features 3,181 reviews, and offers a valuable vantage point on what has been published in the academic market over the last five years. Although the social and behavioral sciences receive the bulk of the reviews, the work also has admirable breadth and sweep in terms of subject content. Indeed, the normal list of *Choice* subject parameters was expanded especially for this volume. One also notes a new emphasis on examining Websites and commercial databases.

The key issue at stake for any work that purports to represent the best in a field is how and why items are selected for inclusion. The editor of the volume indicates that the principal criteria for a work to be deemed outstanding are based upon the "usefulness of the title in an academic collection serving undergraduates." Choice editors are dependent on reviewers and their own knowledge of the discipline to select titles. In practice this comes down to an issue of the degree to which an individual review is favorable or otherwise. This leaves a lot of leeway, and to be fair the editors do not make any claim that their selections are "definitive and uncontestable." Checking against two major history book awards, the Bancroft Prize and the Herbert Baxter Adams Prize, reveals that only 3 of 13 titles and 2 of 5 titles respectively gained the distinction as outstanding titles. This is not meant to diminish the utility of the volume, but to simply point out how difficult it is to pinpoint what is truly outstanding. The volume remains an essential purchase for all academic libraries.—**Jim Millhorn**

Dictionaries and Encyclopedias

C, P

219.   **International Encyclopedia of Information and Library Science.** 2d ed. John Feather and Paul Sturges, eds. New York, Routledge/Taylor & Francis Group, 2003. 688p. index. $195.00. ISBN 0-415-25901-0.

The *International Encyclopedia of Information and Library Science* was originally published in 1997 and has since become a major reference work in the field (see ARBA 98, entry 571). The 2d edition has been fully revised and updated to reflect the many changes that have occurred in the field since the 1st edition was written.

The approximately 600 entries, which were written by an international team of over 150 specialists, are arranged alphabetically, with 12 conceptional topics judged by the editors to have been the most significant given the most space. These topics are: communication, economics of information, informatics, information management, information policy, information professions, information society, information systems, information theory, knowledge industries, knowledge management, and organization of knowledge. Each includes references, suggestions for further reading, and cross-references.

The shorter, topical entries cover more specific subjects that define the key terms in the field. Examples are barcode, databases, library associations, and library buildings. The biographical entries provide information on well-known figures in the field, among which are Tim Berners-Lee (inventor of the World Wide Web), Theodore Besterman, Andrew Carnegie, Melvil Dewey, and Sir Anthony Panizzi. The geographical topical entries cover descriptions of library services of defined international regions of the world. The topical entries include references, suggestions for further reading, and cross-references as well.

The *International Encyclopedia of Information and Library Science* includes illustrations and a substantial index. It is highly recommended for schools of information science and library science collections, as well as for large public and academic libraries.—**Rita Neri**

Directories

P, S

220.   **The Neal-Schuman Authoritative Guide to Kids' Search Engines, Subject Directories, and Portals.** By Ken Haycock, Michelle Dober, and Barbara Edwards. New York, Neal-Schuman, 2003. 234p. index. (Neal-Schuman NetGuide Series). $55.00pa. ISBN 1-55570-451-4.

This addition to the Neal-Schuman NetGuide Series addresses a neglected age range in children's Internet use: young people ages 9-14 or in grades 4-9. These middle-age children are too old for the young children's sites and too young for the adult sites. Designed to be a handbook for parents, teachers, and librarians, this title sheds light on Internet resources for these middle-age Internet users.

Introductory material explains what Internet search engines, subject directories, and portals do. Seven popular portals for younger and older children are listed on page 3. The main portion of the volume deals with evaluation of search engines for this age group. First the authors discuss the evaluation process, including an excellent form to use in assessing an engine. They then present detailed reports on the 20 top search engines they have chosen for recommendation. Each entry covers approximately six pages, ending with a chart detailing the various aspects of the engine and ranking it with a 1 through 4 star rating. Each report delineates the strong areas of the search engine as well as its weaknesses. The authors evaluated more than 60 search engines for this book, and have included some other locations that were not good enough to make the top 20 but deserved an honorable mention.

The book also contains a listing of recommended reference sites for children, which are grouped by subject areas. Several pages are devoted to the filtering issue and protection of a child's privacy on the Internet. Five appendixes provide additional information. This volume is a invaluable asset for anyone working with middle-age children who are beginning users of the Internet for information resources. This resource is highly recommended.—**Nancy P. Reed**

Handbooks and Yearbooks

S

221.   Johnson, Mary J. **Primary Sources in the Library: A Collaboration Guide for Library Media Specialists.** Worthington, Ohio, Linworth, 2003. 145p. index. $39.95pa. ISBN 1-58683-075-9.

Library media specialists looking for a new direction in their work will find this to be one of the most refreshing books on the recent lists. Johnson, according to the introduction, spent a week in 2000 at the Library of Congress learning how to integrate primary source materials into the curriculum, and her library life changed forever. She has written a very thorough guide to the use of primary materials. Johnson does not soft-pedal the difficulties of locating them (many are readily available) or of introducing a faculty and students to a new way of doing research projects. She introduces the subject thoroughly then includes guidelines, checklists, lesson plans, and reproducible pages for students at various grade levels. She suggests projects the entire school can work on. Print and the abundance of multimedia and electronic sources available in libraries today can be integrated into projects that make excellent use of the library media specialist's training and give high visibility to a sometimes low-profile professional. This work is highly recommended for the professional libraries of school library media specialists.—**Edna M. Boardman**

PUBLISHING AND BOOKSELLING

Directories

P

222.   **American Book Trade Directory 2003-2004.** 49th ed. Medford, N.J., Information Today, 2003. 1930p. index. $285.00. ISBN 1-57387-157-5. ISSN 0065-759X.

This 49th edition lists 28,640 retailers and wholesalers in the U.S. and Canada, with 1,844 new entries. E-mail addresses are included for 7,351 entries and Websites are included for 7,539 entries. The *American Book Trade Directory* is the only complete public source for bookseller standard address number (SAN). Following the preface is a statistical section based on compiled data from responses to a questionnaire mailed to all booksellers. Comparing the statistics in this edition with the statistics from previous editions will indicate industry trends. This edition is organized the same way as previous editions and provides the same basic information (48th ed., see ARBA 2003, entry 647; 45th ed., see ARBA 2000, entry 585; and 43d ed., see ARBA 98, entry 596). This book is an excellent standard reference for everyone involved in the industry and for all public and academic libraries.—**Ladyjane Hickey**

P

223.   **Directory of Small Press/Magazine Editors & Publishers, 2003-2004.** 34th ed. Len Fulton, ed. Paradise, Calif., Dustbooks, 2003. 324p. $23.95pa. ISBN 0-916685-99-3.

P

224.   **The International Directory of Little Magazines & Small Presses, 2003-04.** 39th ed. Len Fulton, ed. Paradise, Calif., Dustbooks, 2003. 761p. index. $55.00; $35.95pa. ISBN 0-916685-97-7; 0-916685-96-9pa.

Writers interested in submitting their work to small publishers or magazines have come to rely on these annual directories, as have many who work in the publishing and book-reviewing industry. *The International Directory* continues to list alphabetically both magazines and presses in entries that include publisher/editor name, contact information, date of founding, material published, editor's comments, circulation, annual number of books or issues, single-copy and subscription prices, magazine length or press run, percentage of manuscripts published, simultaneous submissions policy, payment arrangements, rights/copyright, subjects of interest, and advertising rates. A geographic index by state and country and a subject-area index help users narrow their focus. This year's edition has a convenient new addition: up to 10 subject-matter categories as found in the index are listed at the end of each entry, which means users need not flip to the subject index as frequently as before. The *Directory of Small Press/Magazine Editors & Publishers*, a companion to *The International Directory*, alphabetically lists all the editors and publishers found in the latter, plus a number of self-publishers not found there. Thus, if users have only the personal name of an editor or publisher, they can locate the publication or press name, its addresses, and telephone numbers for that person and then turn to the larger directory for more information.—**Lori D. Kranz**

P

225.   **Literary Market Place 2004: The Directory of the American Book Publishing Industry with Industry Yellow Pages.** Medford, N.J., Information Today, 2003. 2v. index. $299.00/set. ISBN 1-57387-178-8. ISSN 0000-1155.

The 2004 edition of *Literary Market Place* provides users with directory information for nearly 13,000 publishers, editorial services, associations, trade magazines, book marketing specialists, book manufacturing companies, sales and distributions companies, and services and suppliers. The number of companies listed is down 1,500 since the 2002 edition (see ARBA 2002, entry 672), perhaps an indication of the tough economic times the publishing world has faced in the last few years. Regardless, LMP boasts that 166 entries are new to this edition and thousands of updates have been made to the existing entries. Volume 1 provides information for publishers (including Canadian and small presses); editorial services and agents; associations, events, courses, and awards; and books and magazines for the trade. Volume 2 provides information on service providers to the book industry, including advertisers and marketing, book manufacturers, sales and distribution, and suppliers. Directory information includes the name of the company; address; telephone, fax, and toll-free numbers; e-mail and Website addresses; names of key personnel with titles; company reportage; branch offices; brief statistics; and a short description of the company. When appropriate Standard Address Numbers (SANs) and ISBN prefixes are provided. A variety of indexes will help users expedite their search. They include company and personnel indexes, a toll-free directory, an index to sections, and an index to advertisers.

The information provided in the print version of this directory is as accurate as one will find. The LMP staff contacts each publisher directly for updates on an annual basis and is continually researching to find new publishing or publishing-related companies. The directory also includes a six-page list of book trade acquisitions and mergers that occurred between June 2001 and July 2003. Those libraries considering this title should note that there is an online version available for an annual subscription rate of $399.00 per year, which includes access to the information in *International Literary Market Place* as well. Both are highly recommended for public and academic libraries.—**Shannon Graff Hysell**

Handbooks and Yearbooks

P

226.   **Book Industry Trends 2003: Covering the Years 1997-2007.** 26th ed. New York, Book Industry Study Group, 2003. 250p. $750.00pa.; $100.00pa. (BISG members). ISBN 0-940016-82-6.

The Book Industry Study Group is a not-for-profit research organization that provides a forum in which publishers, booksellers, librarians, wholesalers, and authors can interact and exchange ideas and needs. *Book Industry Trends* is a compilation of data from the Association of American Publishers that serves to provide those in the book industry with a review of book trends from the years 1997-2002 and a forecast of book trends for the years 2003-2007. The Association of American Publishers gathered their statistics from such sources as *ACRL Academic Library Trends and Statistics*, the *Bowker Annual Library & Book Trade Almanac*, *Publishers Marketing Association Industry Reports*, *Publishing Research Quarterly*, and *World Book Report*, just to name a few.

The work begins with an overview chapter discussing factors that are affecting the sales of books in the United States, including a flat or declining economy, the Internet boom, a refocus on education, and so on. It then offers short chapters on each of seven book markets and the key factors that are affecting each market's sales. These markets include adult trade publishing, juvenile trade publishing, religious book publishing, university press publishing, college publishing, Elhi publishing (e.g., books for schools), and library markets. The remainder of the volume provides detailed charts that give statistical information and projections that cover nearly all scenarios imaginable. The work concludes with a description of the methodology used to gather statistics and create projections as well as definitions of terms used within the text. This work will be an indispensable volume for professionals in the book industry, including those in the publishing industry, bookstore owners, wholesalers, and all types of libraries.—**Shannon Graff Hysell**

C, P

227.   **The Columbia Guide to Digital Publishing.** William E. Kasdorf, ed. New York, Columbia University Press, 2003. 750p. index. $65.00; $34.95pa. ISBN 0-231-12498-8; 0-231-12499-6pa.

C, P

228.   **The Columbia Guide to Digital Publishing Online. http://www.digitalpublishingguide.com.** [Website]. New York, Columbia University Press. Price negotiated by site. Date reviewed: April 03.

In a world where all things electronic have become dominant, this remarkable volume serves as a comprehensive handbook to every conceivable aspect of digital publishing. Topics covered include the necessary hardware and software infrastructure for the digital environment, markup languages, metadata and linking content, data capture and conversion, page composition and design, graphics and multimedia, access for the disabled, digital printing techniques, Web publishing, content management, electronic books, copyright, and archiving.

What one notices first about this book is its structure. Kasdorf has done a masterful job of organizing the readable text written by a team of subject experts into a volume that either can be read straight through or dipped into for background on specific questions. Since few are likely to read this book cover to cover, the wealth of interconnected entry points afforded here are most welcome. To begin, the detailed table of contents is 40 pages in length and directs the reader to specific chapter sections and subsections throughout the book. Second, there is an extensive glossary of digital publishing terminology that, in addition to defining these terms, is also keyed to specific chapter sections for further information. Third, the text itself is filled with cross-references. For example, in chapter 11 on electronic books there is a write-up on Unicode (11.6.V.6) that refers to the section on Markup (3.3.III.4.1) that discusses Unicode in a different context. Finally, there is a standard index. With this breadth of access, it is easy to get right to the most relevant information.

This valuable compendium is most highly recommended for all collections. There is also an online edition of this work available that includes this same written text and supplements it with regular updates, graphics, multimedia demonstrations, and hyperlinks.—**John Maxymuk**

12 Military Studies

GENERAL WORKS

Atlases

C, P

229.   **Atlas of American Military History.** James C. Bradford, ed. New York, Oxford University Press, 2003. 248p. illus. maps. index. $50.00. ISBN 0-19-521661-X.

American military history is replete with scores of excellent reference works. This is another. The 19 units, written by some of the nation's most noted military historians, treat every significant U.S. military campaign and war, from the colonial Indian conflicts through the beginning of warfare in Afghanistan. Since it does not include the whole of Operation Enduring Freedom or the liberation of Iraq in 2003, the book is dated upon publication. The text is brief but excellent. Division of each essay into subtopics allows for quick ready-reference use. However, the feature that makes this book among the top reference sources is the 143 specially commissioned colored maps and graphic reconstructions as well as reproductions of historical military cartography. Along with the numerous black-and-white pictures, the book is visually most impressive. The maps and cartography are worth the purchase price. [R: SLJ, Dec 03, p. 94]—**Joe P. Dunn**

Dictionaries and Encyclopedias

C, P, S

230.   **Encyclopedia of American Military History.** Spencer C. Tucker, ed. New York, Facts on File, 2003. 3v. illus. maps. index. (Facts on File Library of American History). $225.00/set. ISBN 0-8160-4355-8.

Tucker (Virginia Military Institute), editor of several reference works, including the *Encyclopedia of the Vietnam War* (see ARBA 99, entry 527) and the *Encyclopedia of the Korean War* (see ARBA 2001, entry 489), has prepared an excellent 3-volume encyclopedia on the topic of American military history. Like his previous efforts, this work is well organized, has an easy-to-use format, and presents clear and well-written entries. The encyclopedia covers American military history from the colonial period to the present day. The selection of entries is quite balanced and gives each era of American military history and individual conflict the appropriate level of coverage.

The over 1,000 entries, prepared by 215 contributors, are alphabetically arranged and range from 350 words to several thousand words in length. The wide-ranging coverage includes wars, campaigns and battles, military branches, weapons (e.g., machine guns), institutions (e.g., West Point), organizations (e.g., Office of Strategic Services), events (U-2 incident), and other topics (e.g., terrorism, logistics, intelligence, casualties in U.S. wars). Over 40 percent of the entries are biographical and include military officers, political leaders, famous soldiers, Indian leaders (e.g., Crazy Horse), and military theorists and educators (e.g., Alfred Thayer Mahan). The editor's stated intention of providing "due attention to minorities and women" is met by including such articles as "African Americans in the Military" and "Women in the Military."

Each entry is signed and concludes with *see also* references and a list of further readings. Access is provided by a comprehensive list of entries that appears at the start of each volume, as well as by internal cross-indexing within the entries and a detailed index at the end of the volume. Supporting materials include many photographs and maps, a glossary, and a selective bibliography. Librarians and patrons alike should find this encyclopedia extremely useful. [R: LJ, Aug 03, p. 70; SLJ, Oct 03, p. 109]—**Bradley P. Tolppanen**

C, P, S

231.   Gilbert, Adrian. **The Encyclopedia of Warfare: From Earliest Times to the Present Day.** Guilford, Conn., Lyons Press, 2002. 304p. illus. maps. index. $19.95pa. ISBN 1-59228-027-7.

This interesting volume traces warfare from ancient Sumeria in 2371 B.C.E. to the present War on Terrorism. Units treat the ancient world, the medieval and renaissance eras, the eighteenth century, the Napoleonic wars, the American Civil War (which receives an exceptional amount of coverage in the volume), other nineteenth-century conflicts, World Wars I and II, and the conflicts since 1945. Most of the topics are usually two pages of sharply honed text supported by abundant colored pictures and maps. The colors of these visuals are vibrant, which makes the volume stunningly attractive. Auxiliary features include a glossary, bibliography, and index. This is an excellent book. At its inexpensive price, it should be in all libraries. —**Joe P. Dunn**

C, P

232.   Sutherland, Jonathan D. **African Americans at War: An Encyclopedia.** Santa Barbara, Calif., ABC-CLIO, 2004. 2v. illus. index. $185.00/set; $280.00 (w/e-book). ISBN 1-57607-746-2; 1-85109-371-0 (e-book).

One of the best recently published reference books, *African Americans at War* is a comprehensive encyclopedia filling a major void for libraries. Designed for students and scholars, the volume includes 280 entries in an alphabetic arrangement covering blacks in combat from the colonial era to recent military activities in Afghanistan and Iraq. Entries run from lengthy descriptions of blacks in the American Revolution and the Civil War to shorter biographical entries. Each entry includes a source list and *see also* references. There are no cross-references within the text of the entries, such as bolding to indicate related material. The 35-page index is quite extensive and essential for efficient use of the book. A bibliography includes monographs and government publications but no articles. Volume 2 features several useful listings—an excellent chronology, records resembling an order of battle for black troop units, African American troop camps, and black Medal of Honor recipients. Also offered as an e-book, *African Americans at War* is a must for all libraries.

With all the plaudits the book deserves, there are a few minor criticisms. Black historian Benjamin Quarles deserves an entry for his landmark histories of blacks in war. The entry on the Tuskegee Airmen lacks a citation for the dissertation by Jeff Jakeman (1992). The inclusion of an entry on the Amistad Affair is curious, as it is not war-related, and similar cases involving the ships *Hermosa*, *Encomium*, *Creole*, and *Comet* are not included. Despite the minor flaws—ones which require extensive review to identify—Sutherland is to be applauded for this model reference work.—**Boyd Childress**

Handbooks and Yearbooks

P, S

233.   Henderson, C. J., and Jack Dolphin. **Career Opportunities in the Armed Forces.** New York, Facts on File, 2003. 282p. index. $49.50. ISBN 0-8160-4624-7.

Increasingly, recruitment efforts, and benefits (travel, technological training, and experience) call forth those interested in military serve. For career-seekers considering military opportunities, this volume describes 80 occupations in 10 industry sections, such as administration, construction, electronics, engineering, health care, media, and transportation. Each profile gives key information on duties and working conditions, requisite skills, education and training, salaries, career ladders, and advancement prospects. Extensive pay tables provide military pay scales by rank and differentials.

Uniquely, this guide applies the military experience to comparable industries and occupations in the civilian work, thus making explicit the usefulness of military service even for noncareer military. Each occupational profile gives civilian salaries and employment and advancement prospects. Appendixes provide resource directories of educational institutions and industry associations by field and Websites.

However, this guide is less comprehensive than *Military Careers: A Guide to Military Occupations* (Department of Defense, 2001), which lists 140 occupations with training, opportunities within the service, and the civilian counterparts. Selected occupations include detailed in-service career advancement paths. All occupations are correlated with codes and scores from the Armed Service Vocational Aptitude Battery (ASVAB) assessment often used for pre-service screening in high schools. Appendixes indicate occupations by Standard Occupational Classification (SOC) and the *Dictionary of Occupational Tiles* (DOT) for ease in using with other career tools.—**Barbara Conroy**

C, P, S

234.   Lanning, Michael Lee. **The Battle 100: The Stories Behind the Most Influential Battles of All Time.** Naperville, Ill., Sourcebooks, 2003. maps. index. $24.95. ISBN 1-57071-799-0.

This is a remarkable, useful, and delightful reference source. Lanning's 14 previous books on military history, the majority of them on the Vietnam War, have established him as one of the nation's outstanding military historians. His earlier contribution, *The Military 100: A Ranking of the Most Influential Military Leaders of All Time*, was the precursory model for this volume. In this latest book, he ranks world history's 100 greatest battles according to their immediate and long-term influence. Of course, such a subjective ranking is impossible, almost silly, and the author does not actually articulate arguments for the relative rank of the battles. However, this approach is a convenient gimmick for what the book's real contribution is: a short, three- to four-page description of these important battles and the historical significance of each of them. The entries, each with a useful map, are well written, precise, informative, and interesting—in sum, excellent contributions. The composite is extremely useful both as quick reference or simply fascinating reading from cover to cover. The table of contents listing the battles in order of his ranking and the index are extremely useful. A good bibliography is included. This inexpensive volume should be in all public, school, and even university libraries. [R: SLJ, Aug 03, p. 111]—**Joe P. Dunn**

C, S

235.   **Warfare in the 21st Century.** Jeremy K. Brown, ed. Bronx, N.Y., H. W. Wilson, 2003. 187p. illus. index. (The Reference Shelf, v.75, no.3). $45.00pa. ISBN 0-8242-1021-2.

This book, which consists of a collection of 23 previously published articles, is a further volume in the Reference Shelf series from the publisher H. W. Wilson. The book is divided into sections that are entitled "Theatres of Modern War," "Terrorism," "Chemical and Biological Weapons," "Nuclear and Radiological Weapons," "Non-lethal Weapons," and "The Future of Modern War." Each section is accompanied by a short introduction by the editor. The majority of the articles are reprinted from newspapers and popular magazines, such as the *Washington Post*, *Wall Street Journal*, *Business Week*, and *The*

New York Times. The articles range in length from 3 to 18 pages. The articles are all current, with most being published in 2002 and 2003. A brief bibliography that lists 33 books and a further 24 articles (with annotations), 7 photographs, and an index complete the volume. *Warfare in the 21st Century* presents a collection of clear and easy-to-read articles that provide a solid introduction to this important and topical subject. The general reader, high school student, and college freshman will find this volume to be very useful.
—Bradley P. Tolppanen

WEAPONS AND EQUIPMENT

C, P, S

236.   Mauroni, Al. **Chemical and Biological Warfare: A Reference Handbook.** Santa Barbara, Calif., ABC-CLIO, 2003. 243p. index. (Contemporary World Issues). $45.00; $70.00 (w/e-book). ISBN 1-85109-482-2; 1-85109-487-3 (e-book).

This volume provides a general-purpose introductory guide to its subject, written by a respected specialist with working experience in this field. The author focuses on operational considerations rather than the physical technologies or moral issues involved, taking a level-headed, common-sense approach.

While providing an authoritative fact base, the theme stressed throughout is: the readers should do the work and make up their own minds. The writing style is direct and accessible, with many complex concepts clearly rendered. While the history of current issues in chemical and biological warfare serves to inform the case studies and the discussion of means and motives, an annotated selection of organizations, agencies, and print and nonprint resources provide the pathways for additional research. The annotations are clearly written and provide an effective guide to selecting individual sources based on the particular direction one's research might take.

Apart from a misprint on page 50 and a hyphenation error on page 80, this book appears error-free. With only a few exceptions, the organizations and resources are located in the United States, and predominantly English-language in nature. The nonprint resources include Websites (a selection of these was tested, with a 5 percent error rate). Many of the Websites have an extensive menu of information and discussion items. Sturdily bound and clearly printed on acid-free paper, this title deserves consideration from school and public libraries seeking a handy starting handbook to the information base for this area of warfare.—**John Howard Oxley**

13 Political Science

GENERAL WORKS

Biography

C, P, S

237.   Fredriksen, John C. **Biographical Dictionary of Modern World Leaders: 1992 to the Present.** New York, Facts on File, 2003. 566p. illus. index. (Facts on File Library of World History). $65.00. ISBN 0-8160-4723-5.

This work contains some 400 biographies of world leaders (some with photographs) arranged in alphabetic order. Biographies range from 700 to 1,500 words. Every biography is attached with a list for further reading. Each biography lists name of biographee, year of birth and death (if known), and position. It would have been helpful if the years in term were given after the position title.

Although no guidelines for inclusion are given, the introduction states that "all 190 of the world's countries, ranging from newly constituted Afghanistan to newly independent East Timor and quasi-independent Kosovo, are represented." But there are omissions. For some countries, presidents are not given, such as Vanuatu and Vietnam. No biography of Ahmet Mesut Yilmaz, a three-time prime minister of Turkey, is given. Its coverage of country leaders also varies. Israel and Russia each have nine biographies, France and Italy each have eight, and Japan has seven. In contrast, the United States has only four. The book ends with a bibliography, an index by country, and a general index. The author uses the word "country" loosely. Readers will wonder why the United Nations and Tibet are considered nations in the index by country. In spite of many sources on world leaders (including the Internet), it is convenient to have a book that contains in one place many of them. Many libraries will find the book a useful addition to their reference sources. [R: Choice, Jan 04, p. 888]—**Tze-chung Li**

Dictionaries and Encyclopedias

C, P

238.   **Encyclopedia of Modern Ethnic Conflicts.** Joseph R. Rudolph Jr., ed. Westport, Conn., Greenwood Press, 2003. 375p. illus. index. $74.95. ISBN 0-313-31381-4.

Ethnic conflict has been around throughout history. Despite the huge importance of the two world wars, the Korean War and the Vietnam War, this type of conflict has had a major impact on the last century, and has seemed to multiply in number and intensity since 1945. It has certainly risen to global prominence since the end of the Cold War. The 29 contributors wrote 38 essays that cover ongoing controversies, most of which have important implications for the international relations system. Internal struggles for racial civil rights are also considered. The United States and the United Kingdom are both allocated four essays; their large and complicated multiethnic societies are able to encompass more than one large issue at a time. Some of these entries cover topics such as Basque and Quebec nationalism, the Lebanese civil war, foreign workers in Germany, and the peaceful breakup of Czechoslovakia. Essays on the roles of the various international organizations would have been a useful complement. The entries start out with a timeline, followed by a section on the historical background to the problem, a description of the conflict and the attempts to manage it, and a discussion of its significance. Reference notes and a short bibliography of suggested readings round out the essay. At the beginning of the book are five regional maps that indicate where the main conflicts are located. Perhaps there should have been more detailed maps of individual countries that were included with the essays as well. Something that is missing, although not absolutely necessary, is a list of acronyms and abbreviations. The appendix groups the book's contents by broad geographic region. The list of contributors actually provides more information about the individuals than just the usual institutional affiliation. The editor had previously written, with Robert J. Thompson, *Ethnoterritorial Politics, Policy, and the Western World* (Lynne Rienner, 1989).

The item under review is suitable for all reference collections, especially those that do not own the more expensive multivolume *World Conflicts and Confrontations* (see ARBA 2001, entry 696), the *Encyclopedia of Conflicts since World War II* (see ARBA 2000, entry 672), and the *Encyclopedia of Stateless Nations: Ethnic and National Groups Around the World* (see ARBA 2003, entry 677). [R: SLJ, Oct 03, p. 108]—**Daniel K. Blewett**

Handbooks and Yearbooks

C, S

239.   **Pro/Con 2.** Danbury, Conn., Grolier, 2003. 6v. illus. index. $309.00/set. ISBN 0-7172-5753-3.

Pro/Con 2 is a continuation of Grolier first six volumes of *Pro/Con*, which was favorably reviewed in ARBA 2003, entry 685. The original set featured such debate topics as "Economics," "Environment," "Media," and "Individuals and Society." This set adds to this series' theme by providing volumes on "The Constitution," "U.S. Foreign Policy," "Criminal Law and the Penal System," "Health," "Family and Society," and "Arts and Culture."

Each of the six volumes begins with its own preface and is then broken down into parts. For example, "The Constitution" contains three parts, which discuss the constitution, government and the rule of law, equal rights, and the protection of civil liberties. Under each part several debate topics are provided, which include both a pro and a con response. For example, under "Civil Liberties" the question "Is Internet Surveillance Constitutional?" is posed and both a pro and a con response are written. Each response is one to two pages in length and includes sidebars with additional information, explanations of related court cases, definitions of key terms, and a summary. The debates end with lists of resources for further information (e.g., books, Websites) and a chart that provides graph representation of the key points of the debate.

Both *Pro/Con* and *Pro/Con 2* will be valuable additions to high school and undergraduate collections. The debates are both articulate and the key points well documented.—**Shannon Graff Hysell**

POLITICS AND GOVERNMENT

United States

Biography

C, S

240.   Rummel, Jack. **African-American Social Leaders and Activists.** New York, Facts on File, 2003. 246p. illus. index. (A to Z of African Americans). $44.00. ISBN 0-8160-4840-1.

Containing 160 biographical profiles, this volume covers a wide range of community activists and political leaders from colonial times through the present. Arranged alphabetically by name, each entry highlights the person's political or community involvement. The entries range from several paragraphs to a few pages and conclude with a list of references, including print sources and Websites. The editor helpfully cites the date when the Website was last accessed. The work includes 50 black-and-white illustrations and contains a combined keyword and subject/name index. In addition, the volume contains an occupational chart and a helpful chronologically arranged list of biographees by decade of birth. In contrast to some other ethnic reference works that publish only positive essays on their biographees, this work offers honest assessments, noting both their accomplishments and negative aspects. The editor of this work should be especially commended for presenting a more balanced picture of the subjects (i.e., Jesse Jackson's Operation PUSH and its questionable relationships with major corporations; the criticism of the writings of Cornel West, the Princeton University scholar and activist).

Unfortunately (but understandably), some publishers are so eager to rectify the historical omission of minorities in their books that they seem extremely reticent to publish anything negative and thus compromise the reference value of their works. One hopes that this useful and informative work will spur other publishers to produce similar quality works on American minority groups. [R: SLJ, June 03, p. 87]—**Donald Altschiller**

Dictionaries and Encyclopedias

C, S

241.   **Current Issues.** New York, Macmillan Reference USA/Gale Group, 2002. 4v. illus. index. $475.00/set. ISBN 0-02-685744-6.

The use of debatable issues in writing assignments is pervasive throughout education. These topics, by their nature, should generate sufficient interest to motivate the student writer and provide enough depth for a well-focused and thoughtful paper. Unfortunately, some issues tend to be recycled endlessly by both the students selecting their topics and the teachers assigning them. A real strength of this 4-volume encyclopedia is the number (265) and range of issues that are presented. Not only are students presented with many ideas, but these are issues outside of the media bubble that most students are exposed to. This is particularly the case given the middle school to high school targeted audience. The value afforded by the wide range of topics, however, is offset by what is often a lack of depth. Articles provide a good overview, but except for the younger students, further research will be required. This shallow treatment is exasperated by the lack of bibliography for individual topics. The only bibliography is in the Additional Sources section at the end of the volume. The readings listed here are organized in very general subject categories and are too few given the number of issues covered. Neither are these readings referenced to any individual articles. A student searching for more information on controversies surrounding the World Trade Organization (WTO) would be hard pressed to find additional sources through this resource, even though the WTO is discussed or mentioned in a number of articles. It would have been advantageous to provide a short bibliography for each article, not only from a research perspective, but from a pedagogical one also.

Aside from these faults, *Current Issues* is well written and clear. Younger students will find enough depth on most issues for short research projects. High school and older students will need to use the encyclopedia primarily as a springboard for ideas and a source of background information. [R: SLJ, June 03, p. 88; VOYA, June 03, p. 165]—**Lorraine Evans**

C, S

242.   Djupe, Paul A., and Laura R. Olson. **Encyclopedia of American Religion and Politics.** New York, Facts on File, 2003. 512p. illus. index. (Facts on File Library of American History). $85.00. ISBN 0-8160-4582-8.

From the seventeenth-century Puritans to the twentieth-century Christian Coalition, religion and politics have always been intertwined to some extent in American society. Even the principle of church-state separation, a hallmark of the American Revolution, was never intended to effect an impenetrable division between the sacred and profane. But to what extent should religion influence affairs of state, and does the state have a right to encourage or proscribe certain religious practices? Such questions inevitably surfaced when Americans of the past pondered the issues of slavery, plural marriage and the Mormons, and national prohibition, and today they arise anew when Americans grapple with civil rights, abortion, and prayer in the public schools. This fine encyclopedia by two political scientists, Paul Djupe at Denison University and Laura Olson at Clemson University, is a worthy addition to a growing body of literature that attempts to sift through the tangled and complex terrain of religion and politics.

Spanning from the colonial era to the present, the 600 or so entries average one-to-two pages in length, are clearly written, fair-minded in tone, and focus on political and religious leaders, historical events, concepts, religious denominations, and court cases. Among the subjects included, for instance, are Cotton Mather, the abolitionist movement, home schooling, William Jefferson Clinton, Jehovah's Witnesses, the Ku Klux Klan, Pat Buchanan, polygamy, *Roe v. Wade*, the Shakers, and the Southern Baptist Convention. Admittedly, not everyone can be included in a study such as this, but people like Will Campbell and Cal Thomas deserved at least some mention. And Walter Rauchenbusch, although discussed in the piece on the social gospel, surely merited individual attention. But this is quibbling. This is an outstanding encyclopedia for a popular audience, and an exhaustive index makes the wealth of information readily accessible. High school and college students will find it useful. [R: LJ, Aug 03, p. 70; SLJ, Dec 03, p. 94]—**John W. Storey**

C, P

243.   **The Presidency A to Z.** 3d ed. Michael Nelson, ed. Washington, D.C., CQ Press, 2003. 603p. illus. index. (CQ's American Government A to Z Series). $125.00. ISBN 1-56802-803-2.

This is the 3d edition of the *Presidency A to Z*, ready-reference encyclopedia in the American Government A to Z Series from Congressional Quarterly. The 3d edition updates entries related to the Clinton Administration, including the impeachment process, the Gulf Wars, campaign finance reform, and an analysis of President Clinton's last days in office. The 3d edition also includes a number of new entries reflecting the first half of President George W. Bush's first term in office. There are entries about the controversies surrounding the 2000 presidential election, the effort to eradicate global terrorism, the establishment of the new Department of Homeland Security, and an analysis of President Bush's domestic and foreign policy initiatives. And, given their role in combating terrorism, the essays about the Federal Bureau of Investigation and the Central Intelligence Agency have also been updated. Finally, the 3d edition includes new biographical profiles of key leaders who have emerged during the last five years. These include President George W. Bush, First Lady Laura Bush, Vice President Richard B. Chaney, Senator Joseph Lieberman, and Defense Secretary Donald H. Rumsfeld.

As with the previous volume, the entries provide a brief but succinct description of key concepts and issues related to the Executive Branch of government; profile the accomplishments and impact of important political figures within the Office of the Presidency; and analyze relations with the other branches of government and the larger federal bureaucracy. Numerous photographs and reproductions can be found throughout the book. As with the 2d edition (see ARBA 2000, entry 634), only a selected number of essays, such as the entry on third parties, include a list of additional readings that could lead the user to more substantial information about a topic. However, this work continues to provide informative, introductory information on a broad spectrum of topics related to the American presidency and remains a recommended addition to any library collection.—**Robert V. Labaree**

Directories

P

244.   **Counties USA: A Directory of United States Counties.** 2d ed. Detroit, Omnigraphics, 2003. 672p. index. $120.00. ISBN 0-7808-0546-1.

Counties USA provides contact and statistical information for the 3,140 counties located in the 50 states. This 2d edition has improved in several ways when compared to the 1st edition (see ARBA 98, entry 662). Besides providing the standard contact information for each county seat (address, telephone and fax numbers, and Website), descriptions of the locations of the county, and how it got its name, it also provides the area in square miles, population (broken down by race and ethnicity), median age, state rank, population change since 1990, income, population below poverty level, unemployment rat, median home value, and median travel time to work. Statistics are taken from the U.S Bureau of the Census and the U.S. Bureau of Labor Statistics. The work is organized alphabetically first by state and then by county name. Each state features a map with the counties clearly outlined and state government contact information. Statistical tables on the back cover list counties ranked by population, counties ranked by population growth, counties ranked by percentage of population growth, counties ranked by per capita income, and counties ranked by total area in square miles. The work concludes with an index, which again lists county seat telephone numbers.

All of the information in this work can be found in various places on the World Wide Web by going to individual county Websites, the U.S. Bureau of the Census Website, or the U.S. Bureau of Labor Statistics Website; however, *Counties USA* provides all of the information in one easy-to-use resource. This work will be useful in all public libraries. [R: LJ, 1 Nov 03, p. 68; Choice, Jan 04, p. 887]—**Shannon Graff Hysell**

C, P

245.   Smith, Lori L., and others. **Tapping State Government Information Sources.** Westport, Conn., Greenwood Press, 2003. 477p. index. $64.00. ISBN 1-57356-387-0.

As almost any reference or government documents librarian will confirm, one of the trickiest domains in which to find specific information is that of state government information. With U.S. government information, there is only one government with which to deal; with the states, there are 50 (not counting U.S. territories and overseas possessions, tribal governments, and so on), each distinctly different and each having its own organization, philosophy of disseminating government information, and priorities. With *Tapping State Government Information Sources*, librarians and other information professionals finally have an outstanding guide for navigating the domains of all 50 state governments, all in one easy-to-use volume. Authored by a team of experienced government information librarians, this rare gem is a reference resource that will be useful for every type of library.

Tapping State Government Information Resources begins with a section covering general resources applicable to all 50 states. It discusses the most useful commercial print resources, along with several nongovernmental Internet sites that have general information and links for more specific sites. A very quick overview of useful federal government sites, like FirstGov.gov, which provide access to state sites is included as well. After this general section, each state is covered by a single chapter. Each of these chapters follows a similar format, discussing government publishing and the depository system, useful addresses and telephone numbers, indexes to state publications, and essential state publications. Within this section of each chapter, these essential publications are further divided into directories, financial and budget resources, legal resources, statistical resources, and other resources. Each state's Web page and electronic resources are mentioned, along with the most useful URLs for locating relevant information for the particular state. A final section on useful commercial publications and Websites is provided as well, along with a list of sources consulted for further research. An appendix is included as a quick reference guide to depository laws and coordinating agencies, including establishing legislation and Web addresses.

The organization of this book makes it particularly easy to use. After the section on general resources, each state is listed alphabetically in its own chapter. This obvious organizational system makes the book easy for even novices to use with little assistance. Within each chapter, the information is organized by information type, again making it easy to locate relevant information. Anyone looking for more in-depth information on a state can consult the bibliography at the end of each chapter or use the contact information provided to contact the state directly, and an exhaustive index is provided. *Tapping State Government Information Sources* is a must-have reference resource and is strongly recommended for all types of libraries and school media centers.—**Mark T. Bay**

Handbooks and Yearbooks

C, P

246.   **African Americans and Political Participation: A Reference Handbook.** Minion K. C. Morrison, ed. Santa Barbara, Calif., ABC-CLIO, 2003. 400p. index. (Political Participation in America). $55.00; $85.00 (w/e-book). ISBN 1-57607-837-X; 1-57607-838-8 (e-book).

This newest addition to ABC-CLIO's Political Participation in America handbook series examines in six chapters the history of African Americans both as voters and as elected officials and how this group impacts the overall electoral process. The six authors, including Hanes Walton Jr. and Minion K. C. Morrison (who wrote two articles and co-wrote another), are all professors of political science at U.S. universities and expert in this area. These well-written articles do not discover any new information so much as suggest how each aspect of the political arena, from civil rights organizations to protest politics and voting patterns of African Americans, falls on a continuum from the colonial days to the present. The articles are also free of polemic and are well researched, which should make them welcome reading for any U.S. history or political science class. Morrison's "Overview" introductory article is additionally handy for its broad coverage of racial demographics since the Depression Era. Each article concludes with an excellent three- to five-page bibliography, and the volume concludes with a series of appendixes on "key people, laws, and terms," an annotated list of current organizations and select Internet resources, a chronology of key dates (1492-2003), an annotated bibliography, and an index. The numerous charts will be of great help to students and researchers. *African Americans and Political Participation* is highly recommended as a basic introduction to the field, and as a complement to Barker's *African Americans and the American Political System* (Prentice-Hall, 1999).—**Anthony J. Adam**

S

247.   **American Presidents in World History.** Westport, Conn., Greenwood Press, 2003. 5v. illus. index. (Middle School Reference). $200.00/set. ISBN 0-313-32564-2.

American Presidents in World History is a five-volume series for middle school readers that concentrates on the foreign policy of presidents from George Washington to George W. Bush. Each presidential article includes a brief "Fact File" listing the president's date and place of birth, date of death, political party, vice presidents, and secretaries of state. Articles open with a brief summary of the individual's life before becoming president and give the necessary background on both foreign and domestic events during his time in office while exploring the administration's foreign policy in more detail. The articles are well written and comprehensive, with difficult words in italics defined in the glossary at the end of each volume. There are "Fast Facts" along the margins, giving the reader a summary of important events that occurred during the presidency that are not always related to foreign affairs. The margins also include information on famous figures of the age as well as quotes from important documents of the era. Each article has many black-and-white illustrations. The text is broken into sections that are clearly headed with a bold font title to help users find a particular topic. A bibliography and a list of relevant Websites can be found at the end of each volume in addition to a glossary and an index. The binding is very good and should be able to withstand repeated use. This will be an excellent resource for any middle school library. [R: SLJ, Dec 03, p. 93]—**Philip G. Swan**

C

248.   Frymier, Jack, and Arliss Roaden. **Cultures of the States: A Handbook on the Effectiveness of State Governments.** Lanham, Md., Scarecrow, 2003. 411p. index. $65.00. ISBN 0-8108-4768-X.

Cultures of the States: A Handbook on the Effectiveness of State Governments is a study of the efficacy of U.S. states in dealing with governance problems. It presents a summary ranking of all states, plus a database of more than 700 statistical tables on hundreds of variables over which state governments have either control or influence, with each table showing every state's ranking on each variable. Some data pertain to areas of governance in which states exercise direct control, such as crime, punishment, education, and highway construction. Other data pertain to areas in which states exercise minimal control or none at all, such as type of employment, income, procreation, value of a house, patents issued, or causes of death. Still other data pertain to areas that may be affected indirectly but significantly by state policies. In addition, a "Problems Profile" for each state shows that state's position relative to every other state.

The massive amount of data organized in a very accessible way is a treasure trove for policymakers, researchers, and administrators. It has a variety of uses. It presents a comprehensive overview of each state and the differences between states. It can also be used to locate specific information on hundreds of variables. The authors' analysis of the historical events that contributed to the differences is compelling and interesting. *Cultures of the States* is recommended for college libraries with statistical collections.—**George Thomas Kurian**

P, S

249.   Misiroglu, Gina. **The Handy Politics Answer Book.** Canton, Mich., Visible Ink Press; distr., Detroit, Omnigraphics, 2003. 607p. illus. index. $46.00. ISBN 0-7808-0726-X.

When you read the editorial page this morning, did you wonder about the difference between executive power and executive privilege? Where to go to answer this question? This reference tells you that executive powers are granted to the president in the Constitution and include such things as the power to enforce federal law and the power to nominate ambassadors, while executive privilege gives the president the right to withhold information. Written in a question and answer format, the author portrays the complexity of our government and how it operates.

The book begins by describing the current American political climate and moves on to civil liberties, our current party system, voting, the media and its role in politics, social policy, economic policy, foreign policy, and national defense. From there the author goes on to explain the executive, legislative, and judicial branches of our governing system. The book finishes with an interesting review of our colonial roots, the Revolution, and the first years of our republic. Along the way, readers will learn that in 1964 Margaret Chase Smith was the first woman to be nominated for president by a major national party. Judson Welliver, hired by President Coolidge, was the first official presidential speechwriter. The appendixes include the U.S. Constitution, the Declaration of Independence, references for further reading, and a list of politically active organizations with contact information. Interestingly, there is a who's who of political commentators illustrating the increasingly important role the media now plays in our political scene. The key to a strong democracy is an informed and participating citizenry. This reference is a meaningful addition to the educational tools available to junior and senior high school students as well as general political observers and voters who want to better understand the issues of the day.—**Adrienne Antink Bien**

P, S

250.   **World Almanac Library of American Government Series.** By Geoffrey M. Horn. New York, World Almanac Books, 2003. 4v. illus. index. $106.40/set; $26.60/vol.

This set from World Almanac Library provides students grades five through nine with concise, easy-to-read information on U.S. government. The four titles provide coverage of the presidency, Congress, the armed forces, and the Supreme Court. Each title in the series is arranged into 7 chapters (each about 5 to 10 pages in length). The writing is clear and succinct and is supplemented with plenty of photographs, sidebars, and charts to hold a young reader's attention. The volume on the presidency addresses such topics as the presidential inauguration, getting elected, presidential power, the first family, and leaving the White House. Historical facts about past presidents are provided as well as U.S. government procedures, such as the Electoral College and the process of impeachment. Each volume ends with a timeline of historical events, a glossary of terms used throughout the volume, a list of books and Internet sites to consult for more information, and an index.

School libraries will find this series extremely useful in their reference collection. The only drawback may be the price; the four-volume set is only 200 pages long and is priced at more than $100. —**Shannon Graff Hysell**

Asian

C

251. Stockwin, J. A. A. **Dictionary of the Modern Politics of Japan.** New York, Routledge/Taylor & Francis Group, 2003. 291p. index. $95.00. ISBN 0-415-15170-8.

J. A. A. Stockwin is Director of the Nissan Institute of Japanese Studies and Nissan Professor of Modern Japanese Studies at Oxford University. He is the author of *The Japanese Socialist Party and Neutralis* (Melbourne University Press, 1968), *Japan: Divided Politics on a Major Economy* (W. W. Norton, 1975), and other works. He wrote this *Dictionary* in response to his students' persistent demands for a book that would serve as a factual database of Japanese politics and related fields. The *Dictionary* contains the names of all prime ministers, important cabinet members, journalists, prominent political figures, all political parties, many labor organizations, all ministries, new religions, various social and political events, Japan's relations with other countries, and more. With few exceptions, all entries pertain to the post-1945 period. The author's explanations for each entry are comprehensive and accurate. In the preface and introductory parts of the *Dictionary*, he introduces the Japanese political systems and theories of Japanese politics, useful for readers to understand the complicated nature of Japanese politics. The "Bibliography" will direct readers to sources for more advanced study. The listing terms in the index is not done systematically: some terms are in Japanese with the English equivalent added, while some are listed only in English without the original Japanese. Were all terms listed in both Japanese and English equivalents, readers would find the *Dictionary* more helpful. The *Dictionary* is still very useful, especially for political science and history majors. It is recommended for college and university libraries.—**Seiko Mieczkowski**

European

C

252. Henig, Simon, and Lewis Baston. **The Political Map of Britain.** London, Politico's; distr., Portland, Oreg., International Specialized Book Services, 2002. 1011p. maps. index. $59.95pa. ISBN 1-84275-015-1.

Changing greatly since the arrival of "Thatcherism" in the 1980s, politics in the United Kingdom is now dominated by Tony Blair and his "New Labour" supermajority in Parliament, while the Conservatives struggle to define who they are, just as the Liberal Democrats emerge as a strong third party. Add to this the devolution of powers to Scotland and Wales, and the political scene looks remarkably different than just 20 years ago.

Henig (University of Sunderland) and Baston (Kingston University), along with an expert team of contributors, survey the political landscape of the United Kingdom by taking a look at the 659 constituencies that compose the British House of Commons. Arranged geographically, each entry includes a description of the constituency detailing geographic landmarks, historical facts, and socioeconomic information as well as election data from the last three general elections (1992-2001), broken down by political party and voter turnout. The Member of Parliament for each constituency is also listed.

The authors also describe the state of politics in the nation as a whole. A brief summary of each general election since 1945 provides voting data. This is followed by a thorough analysis of the political parties since the 2001 general election and a look at regional trends on issues such as devolution and the Euro. Included is a 24-by-16-inch map showing constituency boundaries color coded by political party.

At over 1,000 pages, it is one of the most comprehensive books ever compiled on British electoral politics. This readable and easy-to-use volume belongs in most academic libraries.—**Joe Hardenbrook**

INTERNATIONAL ORGANIZATIONS

C, P

253.   Osmanczyk, Edmund Jan. **Encyclopedia of the United Nations and International Agreements.** 3d ed. Edited by Anthony Mango. New York, Routledge/Taylor & Francis Group, 2003. 4v. index. $495.00/set. ISBN 0-415-93920-8.

The publication history of this encyclopedia is both interesting and unusual. The 1st edition was written by Osmanczyk in Polish in 1975. A year later a Spanish translation was published, and an English-language version finally appeared in 1985 (see ARBA 86, entry 715). A 2d revised English edition was published in 1990, but by this time Osmanczyk had died. Anthony Mango and his editorial team have now released a long-overdue, and significantly expanded, new edition of this important work. Now filling four large volumes, the *Encyclopedia* has not only been revised and updated, but has been refocused. There is more emphasis placed on the organization of the United Nations and the entire UN system, as well as major NGOs (nongovernmental organizations). Mango also emphasizes the United Nation's role in the codification of international law. He further explains this new focus in the introduction: "The focus in this third edition is on how the United Nations and its institutions work, and on the results of their work. The entries do not (in general) deal with the political disputes, bargaining, compromises, and quid pro quos that preceded the adoption of the various treaties, covenants, and declarations" (p. x).

There are more than 5,700 entries in this edition—on countries, regions, conferences, and topics—arranged in one alphabetic sequence with many cross-references. The cut-off date for preparation of the entries was, in most cases, December 31, 2001. A list of all the entries is provided in the first volume, and a single comprehensive index is found in volume 4. Most of the entries contain a short list of references to other works. Also, the full text of over 50 General Assembly Declarations can be found scattered throughout the *Encyclopedia*. A typical entry, such as "Aliens' Rights," will best illustrate the scope and arrangement of the *Encyclopedia*. Two-and-a-half pages are devoted to this topic, with cross-references to "dual nationality," "asylum for aliens," "extradition of aliens," "the Bolivar Congress in Caracas," and the "Inter-American Convention on the Status of Aliens." Other conferences and treaties are discussed, and the complete text of the 1985 "Declaration on the Human Rights of Individuals Who Are Not Nationals of the Country in Which They Live" is provided. The entry concludes with references to five publications, including the *Yearbook of the United Nations*. In the index, "Aliens' Rights" directs the user to five additional entries.

This is a very important reference source for all academic and most public libraries. Nothing comparable has been published on the United Nations recently that provides the same kind of thoroughness and level of detail. One minor complaint: this edition is classified in the fairly new KZ category of the Library of Congress classification system, which puts it far removed from most of the other United Nations resources in JX.—**Thomas A. Karel**

INTERNATIONAL RELATIONS

C

254. **American Foreign Relations Since 1600: A Guide to the Literature.** 2d ed. Robert L. Beisner and Kurt W. Hanson, eds. Santa Barbara, Calif., ABC-CLIO, 2003. 2v. index. $225.00/set; $340.00 (w/e-book). ISBN 1-57607-080-8; 1-57607-530-3 (e-book).

This is the latest installment of a venerable research guide. The original edition, compiled by Samuel Bemis and G. G. Griffin, was published under the title *Guide to the Diplomatic History of the United States, 1775-1921* (U.S. Government Printing Office, 1935). In 1983, Richard Dean Burns updated and revised the guide with a new title, *Guide to American Foreign Relations since 1700* (see ARBA 84, entry 472). Now, a massive new revision has been crafted by Beisner and Hanson that adds material in two chronological directions. This 2-volume set is almost twice as long as Burns' work and contains over 16,000 entries. Burns' work was organized into 40 sections, ranging from "Reference Aids" to "The Armed Forces, Strategy, and Foreign Policy," with a chronological and geographic treatment in between. The new edition follows a similar arrangement, but does so in just 32 chapters. There are some interesting differences. Now there are separate chapters devoted to the Korean War and the Vietnam War; previously, this material was contained within broader chapters on "The United States and East Asia" and "The United States, Southeast Asia, and the Indochina Wars." The final two chapters look at the "new Cold War" under Carter and Reagan, and the end of the Cold War. More importantly, the basic approach to the compilation of this guide is very different from that of Burns. Beisner recruited just one consultant (i.e., contributing editor) for each chapter and that person decided on the criteria for his or her section. Each chapter begins with a detailed table of contents and a brief introduction in which the selection criteria is defined. Burns had many more contributors involved in the project. Beisner also decided to eliminate the long bibliographic essays that introduced each of Burns' chapters, for reasons of space and redundancy. The annotations for each item remain brief but useful. Because this is primarily a bibliography of printed material, few Websites are included, but there are over 100 microform works listed. The cut-off date for the entries was generally 2001, although Beisner added some *see also* notes to annotations in order to include important publications from 2002. Some items are cited more than once—not unusual in a bibliography of this magnitude—although the text of the annotations differ. Finally, there are three comprehensive indexes appended to the bibliography: an index of authors and editors; an index of subjects, events, places, and areas; and an index of individuals. This is an essential work for all academic libraries, although it does not entirely replace Burns' compilation. [R: LJ, July 03, p. 71; AG, Nov 03, p. 60]—**Thomas A. Karel**

C, P

255. Anderson, Ewan W. **International Boundaries: A Geopolitical Atlas.** New York, Routledge/Taylor & Francis Group, 2003. 941p. maps. index. $175.00. ISBN 1-57958-375-X.

Observing that approximately 75 percent of conflicts throughout the world can be related to issues of boundaries between countries, this superb reference provides maps, descriptions, and assessments of national boundary vulnerability for all existing international land and maritime boundaries worldwide. There are 197 countries listed alphabetically—from Afghanistan to Zimbabwe—and for each one a great deal of information is clearly provided: its setting (synopsis of location, basic geography, and population), its land and/or maritime boundaries (contiguous countries are identified and the length of each shared boundary is given), and an assessment of the security of its borders concluding with assessment indexes of four critical matters (the country's potential geographical accessibility, its potential political instability, its geopolitical index, and its worst case boundary). A glossary of geographical terms, numerous maps specifically produced for this book, and a comprehensive index contribute to the excellence of this reference work, which belongs in all academic and public libraries dedicated to enhancing patrons' global awareness. —**G. Douglas Meyers**

PUBLIC POLICY AND ADMINISTRATION

C

256. **Encyclopedia of Public Administration and Public Policy.** Jack Rabin, ed. New York, Marcel Dekker, 2003. 2v. index. $420.00/set. ISBN 0-8247-4240-0.

C

257. **Encyclopedia of Public Administration and Public Policy. http://www.dekker.com.** [Website]. New York, Marcel Dekker. $158.00 (life of the edition); Free for one year with purchase of print edition. Date reviewed: July 03.

This encyclopedia is the first major reference work in the field of public administration since Jay Shafritz' massive *International Encyclopedia of Public Policy and Administration* in 1998 (see ARBA 99, entry 702). While the emphasis is on the practice of public administration in the United States, many of the entries reflect international or comparative issues. There are more than 300 alphabetically arranged entries, which range in length from two to nine pages. Each entry is signed and contains a list of references. The topics cover almost every conceivable aspect of public administration, including some unexpected areas. Here is a sample of some of the more interesting topics: Administrative Discretion, Appearance of Impropriety, Public Policy and Biomedical Ethics, Burnout in Public Agencies, Civil Disobedience, Constitutional Constraints on Administrative Behavior in the United States, Customer Service, Data Integrity, Diversity, Electronic Government, Federalism in Homeland Security and Crisis Management, Feminist Perspective on Ethics, Feminism and Chaos Theory, Global Ethics and Corruption, Linear Programming, Motivation, Newtonian Paradigm, Patronage and Spoils, Risk Pools, Seniority, Team Building, Watergate, and the Win-Win Approaches to Domestic Peace, Prosperity and Democracy. And, of course, many economic and management topics are included as well. Some of the entries contain statistical tables and flow charts. An online edition of this resource is also available from the publisher. The database version provides links to relevant bibliographic information and Web resources and quarterly updates; recent updates include new entries on capital purchases, environmental policy, and values and policy analysis, just to name a few. The Web edition is free for one year with purchase of the print edition.

This is a well-written compilation of timely and timeless articles. The *Encyclopedia* is highly recommended for all academic libraries that support coursework in public administration.—**Thomas A. Karel**

14 Psychology, Parapsychology, and Occultism

PSYCHOLOGY

Bibliography

P

258. Norcross, John C. **Authoritative Guide to Self-Help Resources in Mental Health.** rev. ed. New York, Guilford, 2003. 468p. index. $46.00; $26.50pa. ISBN 1-57230-896-6; 1-57230-839-7pa.

If there is a field that cries out for an authoritative voice to separate the wheat from the chaff, it is the field of self-help materials. Consumers are constantly bombarded via the media by self-help "experts" who promise us Nirvana on earth. However many of these "experts" have no more expertise in the areas of mental health than the average talk show or talk radio host. The purpose of this book is to guide the professional health care worker and the seeker of personal help in finding materials that are most effective to help alleviate their pain and aid in their recovery. This book offers 6 authoritative voices—6 professional psychologists who conducted 8 national studies, polling over 3,000 clinical and counseling psychologists. The result is a comprehensive, as "authoritative" as possible, list of the most valuable self-help materials: books (including autobiographies), films, Internet resources, and self-help support groups.

The editors did a masterful job in organizing their material. The book is divided into 36 different categories, beginning with Abuse, Addictive Disorders, Adult Development, and ending with Weight Management, Women's Issues, and Violent Youth. Each book or film under each category is rated via the star system (five stars being strongly recommended to a dagger symbol meaning strongly not recommended) and comes with a clear and concise commentary. The editors also did a splendid job in keeping out the psychological jargon, "pop," overtly scientifically arcane, or otherwise, and each commentary is easily readable and understandable by the layperson. The only objection this reviewer has to the book is the inclusion of mainstream movies under films. Although some may have a message that might help the wounded or troubled, the purpose of many of these movies is not to instruct, but to entertain. Giving Mel Brooks's 1977 "Hitchcockian" parody movie *High Anxiety* a "strongly not recommended" rating because it does not tackle the problems of anxiety disorder is similar to condemning *Casablanca* for not being an accurate documentary of a Moroccan city. However, this is a minor objection and does not in any way take away the value of the book as a whole. I give this book "five stars"—strongly recommended for both the layperson and the mental health professional.—**Glenn Masuchika**

Dictionaries and Encyclopedias

C

259.   **Dictionary of Cognitive Science: Neuroscience, Psychology, Artificial Intelligence, Linguistics, and Philosophy.** Olivier Houdé, ed. New York, Psychology Press/Taylor & Francis Group, 2004. 428p. index. $125.00. ISBN 1-57958-251-6.

Cognitive science is "a new field of knowledge in which experimentation, modeling, and state-of-the-art technology are combined . . . to uncover the mystery of the mind and how it is embodied in . . . the brain, the body, and the computer" (p. xvii). Describing the "key concepts in virtually all cognitive science" (p. x), this book, comprising 130 entries written by over 60 French scientists, is the English translation of *Vocabulaire de Sciences Cognitives* (Presses Universitaires de France, 1998), "updated and adapted for the American edition" (p. xv). Each entry falls into one of five major disciplines: Cognitive Neuroscience, Cognitive Psychology, Artificial Intelligence, Cognitive Linguistics, and Philosophy of Mind. Entries include such concepts as activation/inhibition; complexity; desire; dynamic system; infant cognition; lexicon; metacognition; neural network; problem solving: qualitative physics; subdoxastic; and turing machine. Some entries are defined by more than one discipline, such as *syntax*, where definitions are from the disciplines of philosophy and linguistics. Understanding the entries in this book requires prior knowledge in the field. One representative sentence in the entry for *cognitivism* states: "Cognitivism postulates the existence of symbolic mental representations [cross-reference *Symbol*] or statements in formal internal language [cross-reference *Language of Thought*]." Each entry is signed and many include cross-references as well as bibliographic references, mostly ranging from the 1990s to the present, depending on the topic. This is a constantly changing field; academic and reference collections in large public libraries lacking in current titles in the field will want to purchase it. It is an entirely different work from the 4-volume, $950.00 *Encyclopedia of Cognitive Science* (see ARBA 2004, entry 770), which includes 700 entries written on a variety of educational levels and covers disciplines outside the core area.—**Martha E. Stone**

C, P

260.   **Encyclopedia of Psychological Assessment.** Rocío Fernández-Ballesteros, ed. Thousand Oaks, Calif., Sage, 2003. 2v. index. $395.00/set. ISBN 0-7619-5494-5.

The *Encyclopedia of Psychological Assessment* seeks to present psychological assessment as an important discipline in psychology, and as an applied task. An international and cross-cultural perspective is attained, both in terms of the selected contributors and the nature of the individual entries. These are intended to inform the psychological community, consisting of academics, students, practitioners, and other professionals.

The 234 entries are classified, by a "Reader's Guide," into 9 subject categories, including "Personalities," "Intelligence," "Theory," and "Methodology." The list assists readers in locating related articles. Entries of various lengths are arranged alphabetically and illustrated with tables, figures, and exhibits. They include numerous references and a short list of "Related Entries." A helpful subject index completes the second volume.

The volumes expand our knowledge and understanding of the assessment involved in psychology. However, readers could also be further assisted in their research by expanding the article's brief "Related Entries" listing to include its "Reader's Guide" category.—**Anita Zutis**

C, P

261.   **Magill's Encyclopedia of Social Science: Psychology.** Nancy A. Piotrowski, ed. Hackensack, N.J., Salem Press, 2003. 4v. index. $385.00/set. ISBN 1-58765-130-0.

Psychology is a vast field, and no single encyclopedia can cover it fully or meet all readers' expectations. This four-volume work, a significant revision of *Survey of Social Science: Psychology Series* (see ARBA 95, entry 782), should, like its predecessor, be considered with the American Psychological Association's and Oxford University Press's *The Encyclopedia of Psychology* (see ARBA 2001, entry 765) and *The Corsini Encyclopedia of Psychology and Behavioral Science* (3d ed.; see ARBA 2002, entry 770) as

an important addition to many psychology collections. For its intended audience of high school and college students, and therapy clients and caregivers, it rivals and sometimes even surpasses *Corsini*. The most
serious scholars, however, should choose the APA/Oxford collaboration for its breadth and
authoritativeness.

This encyclopedia is clearly written and neatly organized. Its 452 articles contain well over half that
are new or updated and range from 1 to 8 pages. Entries are signed and comprise title, date (where relevant),
type of psychology, fields of study, key concepts, summary, text, current annotated bibliography, and
cross-references. Entries on clinical psychology reflect changes from the revised 3d edition of the Diagnostic
and Statistical Manual of Mental Disorders (1987, DSM-III-R) to the text revision of the 4th edition (2000,
DSM-IV-TR). The set is attractive, with more than 200 illustrations, graphs, tables, and sidebars.

Each volume has its own table of contents as well as lists of all entries in the set, including one by
categorical topic. Volume 4 contains an index, glossary, annotated bibliography, and several notable appendixes. These include a Website directory and list of support groups and organizations; an annotated list
of movies and television programs with psychological themes; an annotated list of major court cases in the
history of forensic psychology; information on psychopharmaceuticals; and additional biographies of
major psychologists.

Despite its overall value, there are some flaws in content and organization that can hinder readers'
efforts toward full understanding of a topic. For example, entries on "Diagnosis" and "Diagnostic and Statistical Manual of Mental Disorders (DSM)" discuss potential for cultural bias but ignore well-known criticism of reliability and validity. More thorough coverage of diagnostic issues is found in a sidebar to the
entry "Madness: Historical Concepts," but really belongs with the main entries. Information on family
therapy is also disorganized and is incomplete. There is no entry on the broad topic, just on one method,
with additional information in other entries. There are other smaller flaws, but on the whole, this is an excellent effort. [R: LJ, 15 June 03, pp. 60-64; SLJ, Aug 03, p. 112]—**Madeleine Nash**

Directories

C, P

262. **PsycCentral: Dr. Grohol's Mental Health Page. http://psychcentral.com/grohol.htm.**
[Website]. By John Grohol. 1994- . Free. Date reviewed: 2003.

Dr. John Grohol's Mental Health Page was first formed in 1994 when the Web began to rise in popularity. A note on the page describes itself as the "best annotated guides to the most useful Websites,
newsgroups, and mailing lists online today in mental health, psychology, social work, and psychiatry."
There are between 3,000 and 4,000 visitors a day and almost 2 million total visitors. The main "resources"
page is divided into more than 25 subject areas containing nearly 1,500 links. The site also lists online articles, book reviews, chats, and online forums. Although originally an academic, Grohol is now CEO of
HelpingHorizons.com, an online counseling firm that sponsors this site. Visitors are able to assign ratings
to the sites included, providing a convenient and fast assessment tool. This site has won a number of
Internet awards. Although the resources are great, the layout of the page contains a number of graphics to
other sites, making the resources on this site more difficult to find. Once users learn to navigate the site, the
resources are quite impressive.—**Diane Zabel**

C

263. **Tests: A Comprehensive Reference for Assessments in Psychology, Education, and Business.**
5th ed. Taddy Maddox, ed. Austin, Tex., Pro Ed; distr., Farmington Hills, Mich., Gale, 2003. 581p. index.
$96.00. ISBN 0-89079-897-4.

As does its predecessors, the 5th edition of *Tests* offers psychologists, educators, and human
resources personnel concise descriptions of assessment instruments. Its weaknesses as a test selection

resource remain apparent: while the editor clearly states that he does not intend, nor attempt, to review or evaluate the instruments, it is unlikely that any professional would purchase or administer a test without first considering its reliability and validity in addition to the information *Tests* provides. Also, nowhere does the editor advise the reader that many of the included instruments cannot be administered by anyone other than a licensed professional.

The organization of this edition remains the same as in previous editions: the three main sections ("Psychology," "Education," and "Business") are each divided into various subsections. Tests are listed alphabetically by title. New to this edition is the inclusion of test publishers' Websites (when applicable), and a new psychology subsection identifying test instruments that measure pathologies.

Tests could provide the layperson with insight into the range of available assessment instruments, but better sources for professionals include Test Corporation of America's Test Critiques series, *Tests in Print VI* (University of Nebraska Press, 2002), or *Mental Measurements Yearbook* (15th ed.; Buros Institute of Mental Measurements, 2003).—**Leanne M. VandeCreek**

OCCULTISM

P

264.   Buckland, Raymond. **The Witch Book: The Encyclopedia of Witchcraft, Wicca, and Neo-paganism.** Canton, Mich., Visible Ink Press; distr., Detroit, Omnigraphics, 2002. 602p. illus. index. $52.00. ISBN 0-7808-0718-9.

The Witch Book: The Encyclopedia of Witchcraft, Wicca, and Neo-paganism is one of over 30 books written by Buckland, which attempt to inform readers about the true basis of witchcraft as a religion and sort out the falsities he believes Christianity has spread. This work provides 560 entries—from the well-known term *Abracadabra* to the lesser-known *Zoomorphism*. Each of the entries runs from several paragraphs to several pages in length and provides in-depth discussion. The more substantial entries provide sources for further information and Buckland has provided useful cross-references for those unfamiliar with the topic. Entries include terms associated with witchcraft (e.g., *astral projection, channeling*), portrayals of witches (e.g., *Harry Potter, The Wizard of Oz*), and related topics (e.g., Voodoo, astrology). Buckland also includes many terms that are associated negatively with witchcraft that he states came from the Christian church. In these entries the term "witchcraft" is put in lower case letters; when dealing with terms that he feels portray the truth about witchcraft as a religion, the term is put in uppercase letters. The work is supplemented with more than 100 photographs, a list of resources for further study, and an index.

This work is an excellent reference source for those researching the historical and contemporary world of witchcraft. It would be a useful addition to public and academic libraries.—**Shannon Graff Hysell**

C, P

265.   Burns, William E. **Witch Hunts in Europe and America: An Encyclopedia.** Westport, Conn., Greenwood Press, 2003. 359p. illus. index. $75.00. ISBN 0-313-32142-6.

Too many books on witchcraft and the destruction of people accused of making a pact with the Devil dwell on the reality or nonreality of evil and the details of satanic rituals. What this title gives us in its encyclopedic entries are the facts of who did what to whom, where and how it happened, and the social and religious reasons as motives. To be sure, the belief in witchcraft is discussed, but the subject matter is rather defined by the real life facts of a world moving from medieval to enlightened thinking.

Each entry has its own references following the essay. Words in the text that are titles of separate entries are printed in bold to make the book easy to use for research. There is a good index that is, in reality, a listing of the entries with cross-references to other essays. What is of note is the excellent bibliography of both classic and contemporary books and essays on the subject. Of course, Websites are listed here too.

There is a black-and-white collection of the standard pictures and drawings found in titles on this subject. What is quite useful is a chronology listing major historical events from 1307 to 1793. This timeline starts with the political and economically motivated charges of witchcraft against the Knights Templar and ends with the "legally dubious executions" of two women in Poland. Also, there is an alphabetic list of the entries at the beginning of the book. Burns and Greenwood Press have done research in this area a great service by publishing this well-made book and giving historical context to what can be a misunderstood subject.—**Kennith Slagle**

P

266.   Greer, John Michael. **The New Encyclopedia of the Occult.** Saint Paul, Minn., Llewellyn, 2003. 555p. $29.95pa. ISBN 1-56718-336-0.

Reading or using material on the occult is fraught with pitfalls. Too many editors and authors trade on the gullibility, ignorance, and wishful thinking of their readers. It is refreshing to review a book that has useful information on this subject and is still mindful of the humbug that permeates many publications in this area. While admitting he is a pagan, Greer does not get caught up in justifying every detail as metaphysical truth. In many cases, he points out the historical inconsistencies and claims that are less than accurate.

Greer's encyclopedia has 531 pages of entries encompassing explanations of aspects of all the occult sciences, astrology, numerology, necromancy, and more, while other essays put the subjects in historical context and with biographical material on the major players in this arcane field. While there are no pictures of witches, there are diagrams and illustrations of pertinent symbols that explain pagan practices. Each essay has entries that reference the 22-page bibliography. If the user were to read the titles in this list, they would come away with a balanced view of modern occultism. There is no separate index, but there are *see* references to other essays within each section.

In fact, the only lacuna in this book is that it contains only modern, twentieth-century information on the occult. The bibliography has few entries from before 1900 and those are the standard classical works and the books written by the various members of the Golden Dawn group. However, for those wanting to know what is currently of interest to the modern pagan and how the occult is viewed, this is the book of choice. [R: LJ, 15 Nov 03, pp. 58-59]—**Kennith Slagle**

PARAPSYCHOLOGY

P

267.   **The Gale Encyclopedia of the Unusual and Unexplained.** By Brad Steiger and Sherry Hansen Steiger. Farmington Hills, Mich., Gale, 2003. 3v. illus. index. $175.00/set. ISBN 0-7876-5382-9.

As in many encyclopedic titles, each entry must be truncated to give breadth rather than depth to the overarching subject matter. In choosing the Steiger's to write, or, more accurately, to compile this 3-volume, 1,129-page tome, Gale chose authors with a wide reputation in this marginal field. The field is given good coverage. Users will find everything from ancient mystery schools to medieval witchcraft to UFO's, with ESP and urban legends added for good measure. What users will not find is a bibliography of any extent that leads to more specific titles or scholarly content. Yes, there are entries called "Delving Deeper" on every second or third page, but they contain references to other publications as surface as this title or are dated to the 1960s craze concerning the occult. Also, there are many references to Websites that might expand the subject where they are found. This type of citation reflects the change in how scholars do research, but it does not guarantee accurate information. Gale even says so on the copyright page.

Each of the 3 volumes has the same 20-page introduction and 42-page cumulative index that does make for ease of use. There are glossaries at the end of each major subject area that will clear up words or concepts that the beginner may not know. These smaller lists are combined at the end of each volume and contain the same material in each. The small, black-and-white illustrations are found in every book in the subject areas.

If the user looks up a bibliography of other books by the Steiger's, they will find that what they have already published on has the best coverage in this title. This is what led this reviewer to use the word "compiled" above. It seems that the essays are a "copy and paste" text from previous publications with an introduction and index reprinted three times for heft. This title will give its reader a good, popular, and surface introduction to its many subjects, but Hollywood films and actors who played occult figures and monsters keeps this publication from any deeper significance.—**Kennith Slagle**

15 Recreation and Sports

GENERAL WORKS

Biography

P, S

268.   Aaseng, Nathan. **African-American Athletes.** New York, Facts on File, 2003. 262p. illus. index. (A to Z of African Americans). $44.00. ISBN 0-8160-4805-3.

Another volume in Facts on File's A to Z of African Americans, this volumes focuses on 159 black athletes from a variety of sports, although the vast majority represent baseball, basketball, football, and track and field. Included are 28 women (such as the tennis playing Williams sisters) and about 30 active sports stars. The entries vary in length—longer entries are reserved for figures who have had a greater impact on sports. Lesser sports (one entry per sport) included are horse racing, skating, cycling, wrestling, soccer, auto racing, volleyball, weightlifting, and gymnastics. There are three golfers (including the incomparable Tiger Woods), five tennis stars, and a handful of boxers included. Some would question the inclusion of controversial athletes such as Allen Iverson, Jack Johnson, and especially Mike Tyson, but the emphasis is on sports, not societal role models. This reviewer questions entrants such as Hakeem Olajuwon and Rod Carew, not as sportsmen but as African Americans (neither was born in the United States). Entries are well written and include a brief list of suggested readings. A breakdown of those included by their sport and an index conclude the volume. It is refreshing to see several players from baseball's old Negro Leagues included but the entry on O. J. Simpson raises a red flag. His legal battles over the murder of his wife are treated in one paragraph yet all five of the suggested readings surround his murder trials. Overall, this is a good book that has a few flaws but that is still a solid addition to the Facts on File library of biographical volumes. [R: SLJ, June 03, p. 87]—**Boyd Childress**

C, P

269.   **Notable Sports Figures.** Dana Barnes, ed. Farmington Hills, Mich., Gale, 2004. 4v. illus. index. $350.00/set. ISBN 0-7876-6628-9.

This 4-volume set contains more than 600 entries about sports figures from the last 100-plus years. As would be expected, there are entries on baseball, football, basketball and hockey players; boxers; track athletes; and Olympians. In addition, there are entries on cricket players, X game athletes, yachtsmen, Norwegian skiers, Russian figure skaters, Mexican soccer players, Canadian curlers, and American dogsledders, not to mention coaches, sports officials, and even a few teams. Criteria for the selections include those who achieved notable firsts, those who had a strong impact on sport or society, record-setters, and those principally involved in on- or off-field controversies. Most entries run three to four pages and contain a photograph of the individual. The biographical essays detail the life and sports achievements of the person and are written in an even-handed style that covers such difficult subjects as Tonya Harding and O. J. Simpson without falsification or sentiment. Each essay is complemented by relevant statistics, a personal chronology, a listing of awards and honors won, and bibliographic information on materials by and about the person. Many entries also include a "Where Is He Now" feature to bring the entry up to date. A number of entries are supplemented further with sidebar biographies of people significant to the topic. For example, the entry on baseball pitcher Grover Cleveland Alexander has a sidebar biography of his personal catcher "Reindeer" Bill Killefer. That entry also features a sidebar on *The Winning Team*, a biographical movie about Alexander starring Ronald Reagan. Finally, the set contains a brief sports timeline from the first Olympic Games in 776 B.C.E. to the present and indexes by geography, occupation, and subject.

As with most Gale resources, this set is well done, expensive, and expansive. Because there are probably 10 times as many reasonable entry subjects as the ones that are included here, one can easily envision supplemental volumes being produced in the future, particularly if this set sells well. This is an excellent source for a quick biography on important people from the realm of sports and is recommended for any library with a sports collection. [R: LJ, Jan 04, p. 92]—**John Maxymuk**

Dictionaries and Encyclopedias

C, P, S

270.   Bell, Daniel. **Encyclopedia of International Games.** Jefferson, N.C., McFarland, 2003. 591p. index. $75.00. ISBN 0-7864-1026-4.

The *Encyclopedia of International Games* focuses on international multisport competitions held since 1896 that are based on the model of the modern Olympic Games. The 163 entries chronicle 1,220 instances of games held from 1896 (when the first modern Olympic Games was held) until the end of 2000. The featured games range from the familiar (the Olympic Games) to the not-so-familiar (the Renaissance Games), as well as from older games that are no longer held (the Tailteann Games) to newer games that are still held (the X Games). Games for particular populations (the Special Olympics and the North American Indigenous Games), particular professions (the World Police and Fire Games and the Journalists World Games), and particular regions (the Central American and Caribbean Games) are also featured.

The entries are arranged alphabetically by name, and entries span in length from less than one full page to over 40 pages. Each entry provides a written history of that particular game. These histories are footnoted and range from a paragraph to 14 pages in length. As available, entries provide the dates of each games as well as the number of participants, nations, and sports. In addition, 343 medal tables are included to compare medal totals for particular games by country.

The introduction provides a good general history of the development of the modern Olympic Games and other games, and is extensively footnoted. Additional access is provided by an index, and the eight useful and interesting appendixes include lists of "Games by Year," "Games by Nation," "Games by Host City," and "100 Largest Games by Number of Participants." The book is well footnoted, and also contains an extensive bibliography. The bibliography is arranged alphabetically by each Game's name, and includes references to Websites as well as books and articles.

The author's preface details how difficult all of this information was to collect, thus proving the value of this particular compilation. Indeed, the author is continuing his research and posts updated information to a Website (www.internationalgames.net) listed in the preface. The Website did indeed contain updated information as of late May 2003.

This book is thorough, well researched, and well documented, yet interesting, appealing, and easy to read. In addition, it is well organized and compiles information that is difficult to find. For these reasons, this book is highly recommended for middle school and high school libraries, public libraries, and any library that collects sports-related materials.—**Karen Selden**

Handbooks and Yearbooks

P
271.   Giordano, Ralph G. **Fun and Games in Twentieth-Century America: A Historical Guide to Leisure.** Westport, Conn., Greenwood Press, 2003. 304p. illus. index. $49.95. ISBN 0-313-32216-3.

As income and consumer buying power grew during the twentieth century, Americans enjoyed more leisure time and activities. More free time meant more time for fun and games, and corporate America marketed a vast range of leisure activities, from board games to movies, from radio and television programming to music, and from vacation opportunities to participatory games. This is a fun book, documenting a history of American leisure since 1900. In nine chronological chapters (e.g., Progressive era, New Deal, Generation X), American entertainment is viewed in brief sections on games, travel, movies, media, theater, music, dance, travel, play, hobbies, and fads. Each chapter opens with a general chronology followed by a narrative. There is a bibliography and very good index. Most of us remember *Star Wars*, break dancing, baseball cards, and Elvis. But how many recall the era of mah-jongg, flappers, bocce, and "talkies"? All are here, although curious omissions include the nerf ball, backpacking, white water rafting, and flea markets. A useful addition to public and academic libraries, the strength of the book is how the author relates leisure activities to the larger social fabric of America.—**Boyd Childress**

P
272.   Postman, Andrew, and Larry Stone. **The Ultimate Book of Sports Lists.** New York, Black Dog & Leventhal Publishers, 2003. 432p. index. $14.99. ISBN 1-57912-277-9.

Ultimate no, but unique, entertaining, fun, and void of boring statistics, this book is ideal for collections featuring sports trivia and oddities. Arranged into 16 sections such as personalities, extremes, curiosities, and off-the-field activities, the volume is 400-plus pages of interesting facts and figures. Examples are athletes who enjoyed short-lived success, great substitutes, freak injuries and deaths, ugly scenes in sports, frustrated athletes and teams, and great choke acts. The index is quite good, especially in identifying players. No sport is spared, all periods are mentioned, and women are prominent. Yet there are odd omissions in a book of sports oddities. For example, few athletes share in a more frustrating moment than University of Alabama linebacker Tommy Lewis, who came off the sidelines in the 1954 Cotton Bowl to tackle Rice's Dickie Moegel after he had broken loose for an obvious touchdown. Moegel was awarded a touchdown and Lewis won his place in the hall of shame. Far more useful than a 1998 statistically based book of the same title (see ARBA 98, entry 727), this ultimate book is a tribute to compilers Postman (sports books author) and Stone (*Seattle Times* baseball writer).—**Boyd Childress**

BASEBALL

Almanacs

P
273.   **Baseball Almanac: The Official Baseball History Site. http://baseball-almanac.com/.** [Website]. Free. Date reviewed: Dec 03.

This remarkable free site is entirely the work of one person, Sean Holtz, who runs this as a hobby and part-time business. The level of depth is stunning as the site consists of over 30,000 Web pages as well as an infinite number of dynamic search links. The Website colors of tan and green are reminiscent of a baseball field, and the basic arrangement of the site is set up for ease of access. Along the left side of every page is a navigation bar with an alphabetic list of general topics, each providing a different view of the history of major league baseball (future plans call for sections on the Negro Leagues, the women's league, and college baseball).

Among those topics are All-Star Games and World Series providing capsules and statistics for those games, Awards, Year in Review histories for each season, the Hall of Fame, Hitting and Pitching Charts of remarkable achievements, Record Books, Rules, Fabulous Feats, Famous Firsts, and Ballparks. Broader topics include Book Shelf, Movie Time, Poetry & Song, and Humor & Jokes. The Team by Team topic provides year-by-year rosters with uniform numbers, a list of results for every game played with the box scores of most available to be ordered for a fee, team vs. team wins and losses, standings, managers, attendance, and so on. Complete registers are accessible for managers, umpires, and, of course, players. The player stats register is the centerpiece of the site, and it is arranged by pull-down menus for each letter of the alphabet. For each player entry the user will find biographical facts, such birth and death dates and places, college attended, height and weight, right or left handed, and, in many cases, a representative quote by or about the player. This brief data sometimes misses things; it was curious, for example, that the entry for Pete Gray does not note that he was a one-armed outfielder. Year-by-year hitting, fielding, and pitching statistics include all standard statistical measures and more. Uniform numbers worn are usually given, and salary figures are sometimes listed as well. Links are provided to team statistics and to other players who were rookies the same year as the player being viewed.

The search engine for the site is a primitive word search type that could be improved upon. The pop-up ads that help pay for the site can be annoying, so it would be nice to see someone from Major League Baseball provide some financial support for this unique and wonderful baseball site. All reference librarians should be aware of this resource.—**John Maxymuk**

Biography

P

274.   Boyle, Timm. **The Most Valuable Players in Baseball, 1931-2001.** Jefferson, N.C., McFarland, 2003. 340p. illus. index. $45.00. ISBN 0-7864-1029-9.

Working chronologically, Boyle packs considerable information into the two pages that he devotes to each MVP. Each entry begins with highlights from around the league for the year. An overview of the player's career follows, although Boyle sometimes fails to place enough emphasis on the player's MVP season. Nevertheless, the attentive reader will come to appreciate Bob Gibson's 13 shutout season, Yogi Berra's leadership qualities, and the multiple ways that Joe Morgan could beat a team. Boyle even almost convinced this reviewer that shortstop Zoilo Versalles deserved the award in1965, despite hitting only .273 and committing 39 errors. Apart from listing the top five MVP vote-getters of each league for each year, Boyle gives very little information about the runners-up. As in the case with Versalles, the reader may often question whether another player should have won the award.

Two appendixes make some comparisons possible. One allows readers to compare a player's MVP season statistics with other seasons. Phil Rizzuto's .324 average was indeed an aberration, whereas Yogi Berra's 1950 statistics were superior to any of his three MVP years. A listing of MVPs by team indicates that Yankees players dominated the award in the 1950s, whereas a Cincinnati Reds player won more often than not in the 1970s. Numerous black-and-white photographs and an excellent index further enhance the volume. On the whole, Boyle does a fine job of summing up the accomplishments and personal qualities of more than 140 MVPs. No other source, in print or online, comes close to the depth that he provides.—**Ken Middleton**

P

275.   Marazzi, Rich, and Len Fiorito. **Baseball Players of the 1950s: A Biographical Dictionary of All 1,560 Major Leaguers.** Jefferson, N.C., McFarland, 2004. 450p. illus. $55.00. ISBN 0-7864-1281-X.

There have been a number of biographical dictionaries of baseball figures published in the last 15 years. David L. Porter's three-volume *Biographical Dictionary of American Sports: Baseball* (see ARBA

2001, entry 790) has been revised and expanded over the years and now includes over 1,400 profiles of baseball's most famous and significant players, managers, and executives. Dewey and Acocella's *The Biographical History of Baseball* (Triumph, 2003) is in its 2d edition and includes over 1,500 summaries of celebrated people associated with the sport. Best of all, Total Baseball brought out *Baseball: The Biographical Encyclopedia* in 2000 (see ARBA 2001, entry 793), and that volume includes 2,000 biographical essays on the most talented and influential people in baseball history. Illustrations and brief statistics are provided for each entry in that volume. *Baseball Players of the 1950s*, however, offers a more pointed and detailed approach.

Twenty years ago, Marazzi and Fiorito wrote a similar book, *From Aaron to Zuverink* (Stein & Day, 1982), that also covered all the players from the 1950s. However, this updated volume is in a much larger format and incorporates much longer entries, while still concentrating on the 1,560 players who appeared in one decade of baseball history. The entries range from 2 paragraphs for many of the lesser lights to close to 100 for Ted Williams, and are drawn from over 20 years of research and writing for *Sports Collectors' Digest* by the two authors. By narrowing the frame of reference, the authors are much more able to provide great depth in their text.

Entries are strong on narrative, stories, and anecdotes and generally short on statistics. The focus is on these players as people both on and off the field. By including all players from the decade, the authors have gained a wealth of stories from the silenced majority of non-stars who are not profiled in any of the biographical sources noted above. Indeed, many of the most interesting, entertaining, and telling tales spun here come from those whose time in the big leagues was neither long nor spectacular. This book also serves as a great source for the "whatever happened to" questions that arise periodically.

There are several illustrations and a brief bibliography is included, but there is no index. An index would have been a nice feature in tracking how different players turn up in various stories throughout the book. While some may question the need for a volume devoted to a single decade of players, this book is very well done, covers a large number of names not found elsewhere, and is recommended for all libraries.
—**John Maxymuk**

Dictionaries and Encyclopedias

P

276.   Loverro, Thom. **The Encyclopedia of Negro League Baseball.** New York, Facts on File, 2003. 368p. illus. index. (Facts on File Sports Library). $75.00. ISBN 0-8160-4430-9.

In the first half of the twentieth century, major league baseball was another instance of so-called separate-but-equal treatment for African Americans. Because blacks were barred by an unwritten agreement from participating in the American and National Leagues, blacks formed their own teams and leagues, known collectively as the Negro Leagues. Aside from a very few larger-than-life characters, the players of the Negro Leagues were ignored and largely unknown outside of the black community at the time. Due to the efforts of a cadre of dedicated researchers over the past 35 years, that lack of renown has changed, and the public now knows more about these players than when they were playing. Through interviews of countless former players and officials as well as assiduous study of primary newspaper resources on microfilm by amateur and professional scholars, a whole literature of the Negro Leagues has emerged.

One of the leading historians has been James A. Riley who has published half a dozen books on the topic. His most important work is the essential reference *The Biographical Encyclopedia of the Negro Baseball Leagues* (2d ed.; Carroll & Graf, 2002). Covering nearly 1,000 pages, that volume consists of an alphabetic arrangement of approximately 4,000 entries on players, officials, and teams, and it has been widely hailed as the classic work on the subject.

With all of that said, we come to Loverro's book, his first on the Negro Leagues. It features the same alphabetic arrangement of entries on players, officials, and teams as Riley. There are roughly 1,000 fewer entries and less than half as many pages, however. The entries themselves convey less detail, relay fewer statistics, and reveal less insight than Riley's. Moreover, this book has no new features or significant data updates compared to Riley. Strangest of all is the fact that none of Riley's books, let alone the one this one mirrors, is included in the bibliography; Riley is mentioned once in the text according to the index, and his Website (www.blackbaseball.com) is noted in the bibliography.

On its own, this book is a serviceable work that provides an introduction to the faces of black baseball in the first half of the twentieth century. However, Riley's work is definitive and costs about the same as the paperback edition of Loverro and much less than the hardback. This is an optional purchase at best. [R: LJ, Aug 03, p. 72]—**John Maxymuk**

Handbooks and Yearbooks

P

277.   Friend, Luke, and Don Zminda, with John Mehno. **The Best Book of Baseball Facts & Stats.** New York, Firefly Books, 2003. 304p. $14.95pa. ISBN 1-55297-667-X.

This book attempts the impossible: cramming the entire history of Major League baseball, everything from legendary players to statistics, into 300 pages. Surprisingly, compilers Luke Friend, Don Zminda, and John Mehno achieve this daunting task. The result is an attractive, well-designed, useful, and entertaining overview of the sport.

There are 1-page histories of the current 30 teams, with chronologies of the highlights of each franchise. There are profiles, also a page each, of 79 notable past and present players (including several who played in the Negro leagues), 15 managers, 16 famous ballparks (including many that have been demolished), and 40 famous games, from the Boston Pilgrims (later Red Sox) winning the first World Series in 1903 to the Arizona Diamondbacks' last-inning victory in the seventh game of the 2001 Series. In addition to the obvious choices, the famous games include a few little-known facts to the casual fan, such as the 21 strikeouts in 16 innings by the otherwise obscure Tom Cheney of the Washington Senators in 1962.

The profiles of the players and managers include not only career statistics and summaries of their achievements but telling quotations from or about them. Al Kaline, the Hall of Fame outfielder from the Detroit Tigers, admits that without baseball he would probably have worked in a broom factory like his father. Oddly, Casey Stengel, the second most quotable character in baseball history, after Yogi Berra, is represented not by his own words but Sparky Anderson's assessment of the colorful manager.

The statistics section includes career, season, and single-game records; World Series records and results; standings for all seasons through 2002; All-Star Game results; post-season awards; and members of the Hall of Fame. There is even a glossary of baseball terms. While many libraries will have sources offering this information, this book presents it all in an easily accessible format.—**Michael Adams**

BASKETBALL

P

278.   Marcus, Jeff. **Biographical Directory of Professional Basketball Coaches.** Lanham, Md., Scarecrow, 2003. 443p. (American Sports History Series, no.23). $79.95. ISBN 0-8108-4007-3.

What do Magic Johnson, George Halas, and Dink Alter have in common? Who in the world is Dink Alter? If you guessed all were once professional basketball coaches, you still might want to consult this volume in Scarecrow Press's American Sports History Series. Marcus, an actor in New York, covers professional basketball league coaches and their records from the American Basketball League to the modern day NBA, including the colorful and often zany American Basketball Association (1967-1976). In all, there are 439 coaches, from those like Boston's Red Auerbach whose career spanned three decades, to unrecognizable names like Gene Latham, who was 0-6 with the Evansville Agogans of the NPBL from 1950 through 1951. Most biographies are a page or less and feature the coach's coaching career and overall team record, with a brief player summary where appropriate. There are a great many men (like Latham and Alter) as well as teams (like the Toledo Red Man Tobacco club) that readers will not recognize, making for an intriguing collection of pro basketball trivia. There is no index and a list of teams by franchise or city would have greatly enhanced the volume. Yet, the book is packed with coaches and their records and will find a place in many sports collections.—**Boyd Childress**

HOCKEY

P

279.   Weber, Dan. **The Best Book of Hockey Facts & Stats.** New York, Firefly Books, 2002. 304p. $14.95pa. ISBN 1-55297-660-2.

The Best Book of Hockey Facts is a decent overview of NHL history contained within a small single volume. The book opens with franchise histories for all current NHL teams. Each history opens with a one-page overview of the team that skims over such entertaining topics as the choice of team colors. The regular season, playoff and Stanley Cups records of the franchise, as well as a list of milestones for the team. Short biographies of important players, arranged by position, make up the second section of the book, followed by brief biographies of the greatest coaches. "Key Games" are listed in the fourth section of the text, ranging from game four of the 1927 Stanley Cup finals to game five of the 2002 finals. The latter half of the book covers career regular season, career playoff, and individual single-season statistics for players, as well as NHL season standings starting in 1917, Stanley Cup results, All Star results, Hall of Fame inductees, and winners of the various NHL trophies. The book is well bound and printed on acid free paper, which is a refreshing change from most books of its ilk. Unfortunately, the writing, for the most part, is awkward, amateurish, cliché ridden, and in need of an attentive editor. Taken as an easily accessible compendium of hockey history and numbers, and not as an outstanding study of the sport, it would be a reasonable addition to a public library.—**Philip G. Swan**

SCUBA DIVING

P

280.   **Dive Atlas of the World: An Illustrated Reference to the Best Sites.** Jack Jackson, ed. Guilford, Conn., Lyons Press, 2003. 300p. illus. maps. index. $39.95. ISBN 1-59228-206-7.

This atlas-sized armchair diver's wish book is loaded with numerous color photographs of underwater life, plus maps, charts, and graphs. There is also a British edition of this book. The general editor is Jack Jackson, a diver, expedition leader, author, and photographer. He has been a member of the Royal Geographical Society since 1970, and has published numerous articles, relating to diving, in newspapers and magazines. He gathered 19 experts to contribute to the book. The book is organized according to oceans and regions within those oceans, beginning with the Atlantic and working west to east and north to south. The work contains comments about various diving environments, with tips and suggestions that stress safety. The Atlantic Ocean gets 17 pages, the Mediterranean 12 pages, the Red Sea 23 pages, the Indian Ocean 53 pages, the Pacific Ocean 89 pages, and the Caribbean Sea 41 pages. An appendix contains information about various areas, which include brief paragraphs headed "Climate," "Best Time to Go," "Getting There," "Water Temperature," "Visibility," "Quality of Marine Life," "Depth of Dives," "Recompression Chambers," and more. There is an index and a glossary of terms. This is a nicely produced and sturdily bound resource.—**Frank J. Anderson**

SKIING

P

281.   Holyoak, David. **Ski North America: The Ultimate Travel Guide.** New York, Firefly Books, 2003. illus. maps. index. $29.95pa. ISBN 1-55297-828-1.

This is a fairly inclusive sourcebook for 40 of the biggest and best ski resorts in the United States and Canada. An introductory section includes very useful data in the form of charts on "Mountain Facts" (i.e., the base and summit elevations of each of the 40 resorts covered; longest vertical drop; longest trail; annual average snowfall; total skiable area; area covered with snowmaking; percentages of easy, intermediate, and advanced trails; and number of lifts). These charts are followed by brief sections on climate and avalanche safety. The main part of the book is devoted to the 40 individual resorts: one resort each for Oregon, Maine, New Mexico, Wyoming, Idaho, and Quebec; two each for Alberta and Montana; three for Vermont; four in British Columbia; six in Utah; seven in California; and ten in Colorado. Each listing covers directions on how to get there; the lodging, dining, and night life scene; descriptions of the terrain available; numbers and types of lifts (e.g., gondolas, high speed, surface); lift ticket prices and multi-day prices; ski schools; heli-skiing and guiding if available; related activities such as Nordic skiing, sleigh rides, snowshoeing, dog sledding, and ice skating; and alternate activities such as tennis, fishing, museums, performing arts, concerts, and shopping. Very brief, cursory coverage of snowboarding and freestyle opportunities are provided. Excellent color photographs complement the text. Central reservations telephone numbers are provided for each area. A brief index is included.

This 1st edition of this guide will benefit from continuing editing and updating. There are numerous factual errors—some obvious, some not so obvious. A perhaps more serious error includes showing that Mammoth Lakes, California, can be reached through Yosemite National Park when in fact the road is closed all winter; and mentioning the availability of indoor tennis at Copper Mountain and Keystone, Colorado, when in fact the indoor courts have been closed for a year at Copper Mountain and six months at Keystone. Therefore, if planning to use this guide for anything more than an overview to help with the initial decision on a ski trip destination, the reader should take care to check other guidebooks, maps, and contact the resorts for detailed information.—**Thomas K. Fry**

WRESTLING

P

282.   Lentz, Harris M., III. **Biographical Dictionary of Professional Wrestling.** 2d ed. Jefferson, N.C., McFarland, 2003. 395p. $45.00pa. ISBN 0-7864-1754-4.

The popularity of professional wrestling has flourished since the 1st edition of this work was published in 1997 (see ARBA 98, entry 752). Although often ignored by sportswriters and journalists, this sport and form of entertainment is hugely popular among young fans, who, as the author of this work points out, are rarely concerned with whether the sport is "legitimate." Lentz has updated this edition with the latest stars of wrestling as well as added new information discovered about older stars and athletes. The entries are arranged in alphabetic order and include athletes and managers in the sport. For each athlete the author provides as much information as he could find on each individual, often including full name and stage name, date of birth and death, height and weight, and a short history of their time in the ring. Cross-references are made between entries of the wrestler's stage name with their real name. Those who competed as a team are listed under the team name as well as individual names.

This work will be popular among those interested in the most popular names in wrestling, such as The Rock (Duane Johnson), Jesse Ventura, and Stone Cold Steve Austin, but will also provide historical data on those famous in the sport in the early twentieth century. Although biographies on the most popular individuals in the sport abound, there is a shortage of comprehensive biographical resources for the sport of wrestling. This work fits this need nicely and can be recommended for public library collections. —**Shannon Graff Hysell**

16 Sociology

GENERAL WORKS

C, P, S
283. Miller, Julia R., Richard M. Lerner, Lawrence B. Schiamberg, and Pamela M. Anderson, eds. **The Encyclopedia of Human Ecology.** Santa Barbara, Calif., ABC-CLIO, 2003. 2v. illus. index. $285.00/set; $430.00 (w/e-book). ISBN 1-57607-852-3; 1-57607-853-1 (e-book).

The *Encyclopedia of Human Ecology* seeks to be the "single authoritative source" (p. ix) in the field, and it succeeds in doing so without the use of technical prose and jargon. Human ecology focuses on the study of individuals and groups and the relationships with and interactions between the physical and social environments that surround them. It also encompasses various interdisciplinary fields, such as home economics, agriculture, anthropology, and sociology.

The *Encyclopedia* begins with a concise yet in-depth summary on the evolution of human ecology and briefly discusses the issues currently being studied. The resource also places an emphasis on human ecological topics surrounding race, gender, ethnicity, age, and culture. All of the over 250 entries within this 2-volume set are written by human ecology professionals or specialists, and depending on the term, most entries are at least 1 page or more in length. Each term includes *see also* references and a short bibliography for further reading. Black-and-white illustrations accompany some of the terms.

Examples of entries featured in this resource include key words used in human ecology (e.g., indoor air pollution, elder abuse in the family), organizations and associations (e.g., UNICEF), and people who have made noteworthy and influential contributions to the field (e.g., Anna Freud). Although a bit high in price for its size and content (no special appendixes or sidebars and charts highlighting major issues are provided) people of all intellectual levels may find *The Encyclopedia of Human Ecology* to be a useful resource. It would be a welcome addition to middle school, high school, and undergraduate libraries. [R: Choice, Jan 04, p. 882]—**Maris L. Hayashi**

ABORTION

C, P, S
284. Palmer, Louis J., Jr. **Encyclopedia of Abortion in the United States.** Jefferson, N.C., McFarland, 2002. 420p. index. $75.00. ISBN 0-7864-1386-7.

In an alphabetic listing, attorney Palmer offers a thorough overview of abortion as the issue has played itself out in the United States. His book deals thoroughly with historical matters. It reviews all abortion-related Supreme Court decisions and how each justice voted on them, and gives the rationale behind both concurring and dissenting opinions. The work provides charts that trace the numbers since 1990. The text of each state's abortion laws appears in its alphabetic position. The author includes the names of organizations that have weighed in on the issue, biographical sketches of key people, relevant laws, and related items (e.g., buffer zones at abortion facilities, wrongful birth lawsuits, abortion violence). He provides a review of both the male and female reproductive apparatus, fetal development, complications of pregnancy, abortion methods, and sexually transmitted diseases (including HIV/AIDS). Separate entries describe major genetic disorders. The *Encyclopedia of Abortion in the United States* is an excellent general reference source. [R: LJ, 1 Nov 02, pp. 80-82]—**Edna M. Boardman**

AGING

P
285.   Sharpe, Charles C. **Online Resources for Senior Citizens.** Jefferson, N.C., McFarland, 2003. 183p. index. $32.00pa. ISBN 0-7864-1600-9.

This is an excellent ready-reference source that provides a comprehensive look at Internet resources for this age group. Ranging from the general to the specific, the coverage begins with federal government sources, which also often have links to state offices providing local level services. Next there is a compilation of general Websites of interest to senior citizens, including private and commercial organizations, educational institutions, and professional organizations. Some of the topic areas that follow the general Website area include sections on "Computers and the Internet," "Death and Dying," "Employment and Volunteering," "Genealogy," "Healthcare," "and "Diseases and Medical Conditions." The final section offers subscription information for a selected list of free online publications, again providing enough information for the reader to determine if the focus of this publication would be of interest.

All sections have Websites listed alphabetically, with an explanatory description of each site included, which is often derived from the organization's information. One commendable feature of this resource is that the user will find listings for the same site in more than one area, making this useful as a ready-reference source. An alphabetized index of Websites is included. Public libraries and as well as academic libraries that support social sciences and medical programs should acquire this valuable resource. —**Marianne B. Eimer**

DEATH

C, P
286.   **Handbook of Death & Dying.** Clifton D. Bryant, ed. Thousand Oaks, Calif., Sage, 2003. 2v. index. $295.00/set. ISBN 0-7619-2514-7.

This *Handbook* has two volumes. The first is titled "The Presence of Death," and the second, "The Response to Death." Each volume is divided into 10 parts, which are broad subject areas. These are further subdivided by topics and then into specific issue-oriented chapters. The 103 chapters are all signed essays written by academics and researchers, primarily faculty members of universities from across the country. The entries all have significant references, some with an additional readings list and, when appropriate, footnotes. The volumes have the table of contents of both volumes, and the second volume contains an excellent index. Controversial topics such as capital punishment, abortion, and euthanasia are discussed in a fair and balanced manner covering all of the perspectives. Specific chapters on individual ethnic and religious groups provide a wealth of information on little-known facts about these groups' beliefs and practices surrounding death and dying. The focus of this set is primarily the sociological, cultural, and historical experience of death and its related topics and issues.

The audience is students and scholars in the multiple academic disciplines addressed, and educated laypersons. This set will also be a useful tool for librarians in academic libraries. This is a well-researched and truly scholarly work that will be a classic in thanatology, the study of death and dying, for years to come. The *Handbook of Death & Dying* is highly recommended for public, academic, undergraduate, graduate, and medical libraries. [R: LJ, Jan 04, p. 90]—**Lynn M. McMain**

FAMILY, MARRIAGE, AND DIVORCE

C, P

287.   Derks, Scott. **Working Americans 1880-1999. Volume IV: Their Children.** Millerton, N.Y., Grey House Publishing, 2002. 579p. illus. index. $135.00. ISBN 1-930956-35-5.

   Working Americans 1880-1999. Volume IV: Their Children is one of a new five-volume series. Volumes 1 through 3 have been reviewed in *American Reference Books Annual* (see ARBA 2003, entry 218; ARBA 2002, entry 203; and ARBA 2001, entry 193). Another volume, subtitled "Americans At War," is newly available (see ARBA 2004, entry 199). The author has a B.A. in journalism, is a freelance writer, and, according to a quick Google search, is director of the division of marketing of the State of South Carolina's Department of Commerce. He is editor of two editions of *The Value of the Dollar: Prices and Incomes in the United States, 1860-1999*, published by Gale in 1994 and Grey House in 1999 (see ARBA 2000, entry 139).

   Volume IV is a captivating volume with its black-and-white photographs, personal profiles, historical snapshots, and economic profiles of American children by decade. For each 10-year period 3 profiles accompanied by photographs describe the home, school, and community lives of a child of elementary age through college freshman year somewhere in the United States in a particular socioeconomic and ethnic situation, in a series of bullet points. Whereas previous volumes in the series focused on separate socioeconomic classes, this volume mixes them all together. The reader must gather from the reading which class the child belongs to. It is fascinating to read about the typical home, school, and community life of one's own childhood decades and those of one's parents. The book could be highly useful to those wanting or needing to grow their empathy for their parents and vice-versa. A major flaw, which ought to be remedied in succeeding editions, is the absence of specific documentation—there are no footnotes, no bibliography, and no credits for the illustrations. There is scant discussion, even, of the source materials used. Academics expect this information to be present in quality reference works. The introduction tells readers the basis of the profiles are diaries, private print books, personal interviews, family histories, estate documents, high school annuals, and magazine articles. Additional information from other relevant primary sources "beefs up" the real lives to make them fuller incarnations of the decades. Along with changed names, this preserves the anonymity of the people profiled; but it gives them no credit for allowing their personal story to appear in print. The economic profiles' purposes are to put the profiled children's lifestyles into perspective. Most likely government statistical information is used, which is in the public domain, and so it does not have to be credited. Yet, students need to learn where such information comes from and how to cite it properly, especially if they have an assignment to create a similar profile. Historical snapshots, news profiles, articles from the local media where the subject lived, and illustrations from printed popular culture of the day complete the personal profiles by setting them in historical context. The historical snapshots provide short information on notable events, by year, in the decades. Again there is no documentation, save that numerous magazine articles have the date of issue in the illustration itself. There is a good index.

   There are no other works in the reviewer's reference department that include both personal profiles and organization by decade. Numerous traditionally organized, one-volume and multivolume dictionaries and encyclopedias of American life emphasizing cultural and socioeconomic information have appeared in recent years. Among them are the American Eras series (Gale Group); ABC-CLIO Companion to 1960s Counter Culture in America (see ARBA 98, entry 437); *Columbia Chronicles of American Life, 1910-1992* (Columbia University Press, 1995); *Gay Nineties in America* (Greenwood Press, 1992); *American Decades* (Gale Group); and *Encyclopedia of American Cultural and Intellectual History* (see ARBA 2002, entry 913). All of these appear to have better documentation, but cannot necessarily be approached so easily by time period. Superb coffee-table books usually have somewhat fewer pages of text or more than one volume, provide at least some bibliographic information, and employ credited color illustration. Superb academic reference works provide documentation for factual information in the text, often provide extensive bibliographies citing the works used, describe both primary and secondary sources, and discuss the sources used for the edification of the reader. Revision of this work in both directions would likely be quite successful and would make wonderful contributions to our understanding of American childhoods in the late nineteenth and twentieth centuries.—**Agnes H. Widder**

HOME ECONOMICS

P

288.   Emery, Carla. **The Encyclopedia of Country Living: An Old Fashioned Recipe Book.** 9th ed. Seattle, Wash., Sasquatch Books, 2003. 885p. illus. index. $29.95pa. ISBN 1-57061-377-X.

From the time Emery began compiling the information for this substantial book 32 years ago, it has proved a popular source for "from scratch" living. (The cover states that "over 600,000 have been sold.") With every updating, she has corrected and expanded it, responding to reader request/demand and the growth of technology. This edition contains Website addresses, many of which probably will have a very brief life, but which will expand its immediate usefulness until the next edition comes along. The book is filled with information that used to be common knowledge, but which has been largely lost with the growth of urban living. The title suggests a country, even pioneering audience, but the recipes and instructions will serve persons with a desire to "do it themselves" wherever they live. Emery explains such processes as fencing, cheese making, vegetable growing, saving seeds, serving up wildlife for dinner, canning, brooding and raising chickens, insect eradication, sausage making, cooking without electricity, and so on. She has inserted a scattering of personal stories and experiences, letting the book grow along with her own life and family, which is a nice, authentic touch. Libraries will find it an excellent source for the frequent questions about how to do once everyday things. [R: LJ, 1 June 03, p. 105]—**Edna M. Boardman**

MEN'S STUDIES

C, P

289.   **American Masculinities: A Historical Encyclopedia.** Bret E. Carroll, ed. Thousand Oaks, Calif., Sage, 2003. 562p. illus. index. $150.00. ISBN 0-7619-2540-6.

American Masculinities is the first historical encyclopedia to explore the multiple ways that American men have experienced and imagined male identity. Its strength lies in the broad range of topics that are covered in over 250 signed entries. Readers can explore such familiar historical topics as "Manifest Destiny" and "Cold War" from new perspectives. The 45 biographical profiles provide new insights into the lives and influence of writers, actors, activists, and politicians. About 50 entries, including "Breadwinner Role," "Men's Movements," and "Sensitive Male," reflect new scholarship in the field and are not covered in other historical encyclopedias. Indeed, *American Masculinities* should prove to be a valuable source for answering a multitude of reference questions, from the origin of the term "confidence man" to an overview of the relationship between masculinity and war.

Several features improve access to appropriate entries and additional information sources. Most entries include cross-references. The three-page entry on ethnicity concludes by referring readers to entries about seven specific ethnic groups. The "Reader's Guide" lists entries under 14 broad headings (e.g., "Body and Health," "Family and Fatherhood," "Sexual Identities and Sexuality") . An excellent index, well-chosen photographs and illustrations, and an extensive bibliography add further value. *American*

Masculinities is well worth what would otherwise be too hefty a price for many libraries because no other encyclopedia comes close to covering this growing field so well.—**Ken Middleton**

PHILANTHROPY

P
290.   **The International Foundation Directory 2003.** 12th ed. Florence, Ky., Europa Publications/Taylor & Francis Group, 2003. 656p. index. $300.00. ISBN 1-857-43140-5. ISSN 1366-8048.

     Now in its 12th edition, this work has been updated annually for the past 3 years. This directory contains 2,300 entries on nonprofit institutions and organizations from over 100 countries. Included are charitable and grant-making NGO's, including foundations and both private and corporate trusts. Governmental bodies are only included if they are independent of political control. To be included, a foundation must be international or have a widespread impact; have charitable or public benefit status; and either have significant funds available, make charitable donations, or run its own projects. Arrangement is alphabetical by country, then by name of foundation under the categories "Foundation Centers and Coordinating Bodies" and "Foundations, Trusts, and Non-profit Organizations." Entries feature the date of origin and purpose; a brief description of activities; geographical area of activity; restrictions; a list of publications; finance information (such as assets and grants); key board and staff members; and contact information, including a URL.

     Three introductory essays precede the main section. Topics discuss the development and current state of foundations, the impact of global change, and the process of researching and applying to foundations. Directory entries are followed by a select bibliography and three indexes: a foundations name index, a "main activity" index, and a geographical index. The latter two indexes are too broad to be of much use, as for example wanting the topic of AIDS and getting only as close as "Medicine and Health" or looking for a particular city and having to sort through all entries under "USA and Canada." *The International Foundation Directory* lacks the specific application information for grant-seekers found in *The Annual Register of Grant Support* (35th ed.; see ARBA 2003, entry 827), which also covers grants funded by the government but is less global in scope. It appears that the 2-volume, lesser-known, German-published *World Guide to Foundations*, covering 115 countries, offers a similar arrangement and scope. Large academic and public libraries will benefit from this directory, but there is probably not enough new material to justify updating it every single year.—**Susan J. Gardner**

C, P
291.   Miner, Jeremy T., and Lynn E. Miner. **Funding Sources for Community and Economic Development 2003/2004: A Guide to Current Sources for Local Programs and Projects.** 9th ed. Westport, Conn., Oryx Press/Greenwood Publishing Group, 2003. 727p. index. $64.95paa. ISBN 1-57356-593-8.

     Funding Sources for Community and Economic Development draws on the GrantSelect database to provide an easy tool for locating funding sources for community development projects. Over 3,000 sources are included in the latest edition (see ARBA 2003, entry 829, for a review of the previous edition), each containing the following standard information: "Grant Title," "Accession Number," a narrative "Grant Description," "Requirements," "Restrictions," "Sample Award(s)," "Funding Amount," "Contact Information," "Internet Address," and "Sponsor Information." Those sources that have geographical limitations are clearly marked at the top of the entry.

     The book includes a subject index, a sponsoring organizations index, a grants by program type index (which includes 38 categories), and a geographic index for those sources that impose a geographic restriction. A section on "Proposal Planning and Writing" provides useful advice to those new to grant writing. This is a useful resource with a reasonable price. It should be a part of all public and academic reference collections.—**Michael Levine-Clark**

SEX STUDIES

C, S

292.   Turner, Jeffrey S. **Dating and Sexuality in America: A Reference Handbook.** Santa Barbara, Calif., ABC-CLIO, 2003. 287p. index. (Contemporary World Issues). $45.00; $50.00 (e-book). ISBN 1-85109-584-5; 1-85109-589-6 (e-book).

The Contemporary World Issues series is designed to provide accurate, unbiased reference books on critical topics of the day. Each follows a similar format: there is an introductory essay, a chronology of events, biographies of people in the field, some statistical tables, a directory of organizations and agencies, annotated lists of print and nonprint resources (including Web resources), a glossary, and a comprehensive index. This particular work follows that pattern exactly. The sources used to compile this volume are dated generally from 2000 forward, so the research is current. The list of organizations is current, although at least one of the links to a Website went to a page that could no longer be found due to a reorganization of the Website.

The second chapter identifies 13 areas of dating that are of concern, such as dating and sexual values, media impact on dating, Internet romance, dating and club drugs, date rape, and several other topics. Each area is briefly discussed with many references. Subsequent chapters, one of organizations, associations, and agencies and a second on selected resources that are available, are divided into the same subject areas. The writing is solid and the list of resources is impressive. This should be used as a very good starting point for the discussion of dating in America.—**Robert L. Turner Jr.**

SOCIAL WELFARE AND SOCIAL WORK

P

293.   Dumouchel, J. Robert. **Government Assistance Almanac 2003-2004.** 17th ed. Detroit, Omnigraphics, 2003. 962p. index. $235.00. ISBN 0-7808-0650-6.

Traditionally, U.S. government documents have been a mixed blessing to the average user. The exhaustive nature of their coverage is a tremendous asset, yet due to the volume of these materials, most individuals are overwhelmed. The U.S. General Services Administration's *Catalog of Federal Domestic Assistance* (CFDA) has presented programs that represent over $1.5 trillion worth of government assistance in a massive document. The *Government Assistance Almanac* (GAA) has served as an interpreter of the CFDA, attempting to condense 2,500 pages into a tool for those looking for government assistance programs.

GAA offers unique features over CFDA, including a section on program funding levels, an extensive master index, and a streamlined listing of all U.S. programs. However, where CFDA excels is in the exhaustive detail of programs, unique indexes (including functional, applicant, and deadline), and appendixes on the developing and writing of grant proposals and an authorization appendix. Although GAA simplifies using the full catalog, one would still need CFDA to go beyond an initial search after a program has been identified.

What makes the *Government Assistance Almanac* a less desirable purchase is the availability of the free online *Catalog of Federal Domestic Assistance* (www.cfda.gov). A search using the term "libraries" results in 28 programs from the paper copy of CFDA, 60 programs from GAA's master index, and 96 programs from CFDA Online. The annual updating of the *Government Assistance Almanac* also pales in comparison to the CFDA Online's bi-weekly updates.

Overall, although well organized, user friendly, and useful for a quick perusal of government programs offering assistance, the *Government Assistance Almanac* has been eclipsed by the online version of the *Catalog of Federal Domestic Assistance*.—**Rob Laurich**

SUBSTANCE ABUSE

C, P, S

294.   Miller, Richard Lawrence. **The Encyclopedia of Addictive Drugs.** Westport, Conn., Greenwood Press, 2002. 491p. index. $75.00. ISBN 0-313-31807-7.

    Miller, an independent scholar, has written a volume that is objective, scientifically rigorous, and somewhat nontraditional. Contending that facts take a back seat to personal and moral values, fear, and other strong emotions in most discussions about drug abuse, the author synthesizes research from several scientific fields and presents comprehensive information that many readers may find mind opening. A reference guide on more than 130 pharmaceutical and naturally occurring drugs, it does not present Miller's personal views, just his encyclopedic knowledge of the issues. For his personal views readers can look to Miller's works titled *Drug Warriors and Their Prey* (Praeger, 1996) and *The Case for Legalizing Drugs* (Praeger, 1991).

    The book begins with a discussion of chemical, psychological, sociological, and legal aspects of addiction, including "scheduling," the federal law that ranks drugs by their potential for abuse. The second chapter is an overview on drug types and their subclasses. The core of the book is an alphabetic listing of substances, whose descriptions comprise correct pronunciation, formal and street names, drug type, Chemical Abstracts Service registry number, federal schedule listing, U.S. availability information, and risk of birth defects if the substance is used by a pregnant woman. Entries range from 2 to 9 pages and also contain historical and current uses and misuses, abuse factors, drug interactions, and footnotes. The book ends with a chapter on additional information sources representing a wide range of views, and good indexes by subject and drug names (formal and street). It is recommended for academic, public, and special libraries in areas like journalism, government, and public policy. [R: SLJ, Aug 03, pp. 111-112]—**Madeleine Nash**

YOUTH AND CHILD DEVELOPMENT

C

295.   **Encyclopedia of Children and Childhood in History and Society.** Paula S. Fass, ed. New York, Macmillan Reference USA/Gale Group, 2004. 3v. illus. index. $360.00/set. ISBN 0-02-865714-4.

    If childhood seems to be a floating and ill-defined construct in our current society, history will at least give us a context for understanding why. This encyclopedia will serve as a reference tool for those interested in the historical, anthropological, or wide-ranging sociocultural study of children, childhood, and youth. The 3 volumes and 445 articles provide a wealth of interesting material for the student or professional looking for information on childhood. The encyclopedia should be of particular interest to those in education or professions that involve an interaction with young people. The historical scholarship inherent in the articles is an important feature of this work. In articles on toys, disease, work, war, education, and play, for example, the reader will see a treatment of the historical elements that we may take for granted as either a part of childhood or something to protect children against. Images of the social and historical context of children are further and powerfully represented by examples of art from the era. Many articles feature an important artwork or image, enhancing not only the aesthetic of the volumes but the information provided and its presentation. These images are typically annotated with a short comment on the significance or message conveyed in the work.

    The organization of the encyclopedia provides efficient access to the content. Articles are in alphabetic order and cross-reference other related articles. An "Outline of Contents" provided in the first volume, groups articles by topic. This will be helpful for readers needing all articles that fit in a general category. A comprehensive and detailed index in volume 3 provides further access to the article content.

Of particular note, is a section of the encyclopedia devoted to primary sources. This is not simply a bibliography of important works, but lengthy excerpts or entire reproductions of the works. In this section one can read letters from Theodore Roosevelt; poetry from Robert Louis Stevenson; excerpts or reprinted case law; The United Nations Declarations of the Rights of the Child, 1959; and sections of important papers from Sigmund Freud, G. Stanley Hall, Emile Zola, and others.

This encyclopedia is both engaging to read and an excellent source for the professional or student. It is appropriate for all academic and large public libraries. [R: LJ, 1 Feb 04, p. 74]—**Lorraine Evans**

17 Statistics, Demography, and Urban Studies

DEMOGRAPHY

General Works

C

296.   **Encyclopedia of Population.** Paul Demeny and Geoffrey McNicoll, eds. New York, Macmillan Reference USA/Gale Group, 2003. 2v. index. $265.00/set. ISBN 0-02-865677-6.

It would be difficult to find a more comprehensive, accessible, or readable treatment of population and demographics than that provided in *Encyclopedia of Population*, edited by Paul Demeny and Geoffrey McNicoll (both with the Population Council). Some 336 articles, alphabetically arranged by subject, were submitted by 278 authors, each an authority in his or her field of submission. Of particular importance is the attention given to recent trends and developments; for example, the impact of AIDS and other life-threatening diseases, the problems resulting from longevity and aging populations, the expanding populations in lesser-developed countries, the problems created by dense populations, and the pressures arising from migration and refugee location. Entries include 60 biographies of persons who have made notable contributions to the study of population.

To assist readers in locating specific information, a list of articles by topic with authors' names, a list of contributors with affiliations and entries contributed to the encyclopedia, a comprehensive index, and a topical outline are included. The articles are generally nontechnical and each is followed by references to other related entries as well as a bibliography for further reading. Summary tables are presented that provide rankings of countries with 10 million or more persons by selected demographic indicators and characteristics. This set is recommended for a broad range of readers. [R: Choice, Jan 04, p. 888]—**William C. Struning**

United States

P

297.   **Access to Money Income in the United States: 2002 Annual Demographic Supplement to the Current Population Survey on the Characteristics and Incomes of Americans.** By the Editors of New Strategist Publications. Ithaca, N.Y., New Strategist, 2003. 386p. index. $89.95pa. ISBN 1-885070-55-1.

Access to Money Income in the United States offers detailed tables of socioeconomic data related to money income in the United States provided by the Census Bureau. There is a companion report titled *Access to Poverty in the United States* (see entry 298).

The income statistics in this report are for 2001 and the demographic information is for 2002. A total of 36 detailed tables are provided and include: "Median Income of Households by Selected Characteristics, Race, and Hispanic Origin of Householder"; "Marital Status: People Aged 18 or Older by Total

Money Income"; "Educational Attainment and Age: People Aged 25 or Older by Total Money Earnings"; and "Total Money Earnings by Occupation of Longest Job in 2001: People Aged 15 or Older by Sex and Work Experience in 2001." The report also contains a glossary of terms and definitions, source and accuracy of CPS estimates, and the Census Bureau's document "Money Income in the United States: 2001." It includes a detailed index, which is not a part of the original CPS.

Although the Bureau provides the same data on its Website, the number of the data sets and their organization may be overwhelming to the average person and this publication serves as a quick reference. This work is recommended for researchers who prefer neatly packaged and readily accessible money income information.—**Mihoko Hosoi**

P

298. **Access to Poverty in the United States: 2002 Annual Demographic Supplement to the Current Population Survey on the Poverty Status, Health Insurance Coverage, and Pension Plan Participation of Americans.** By the Editors of New Strategist Publications. Ithaca, N.Y., New Strategist, 2003. 387p. index. $89.95pa. ISBN 1-885070-56-X.

Access to Poverty in the United States offers detailed tables of socioeconomic data related to poverty in the United States provided by the Census Bureau. There is a companion report titled *Access to Money Income in the United States* (see entry 297).

The poverty, health insurance, and pension statistics in this report are for 2001 and the demographic information is for 2002. A total of 26 detailed tables such as the following are included: "Poverty Status of People by Race, Hispanic Origin, and Family Relationship, 1959-2001"; "Poverty Status of People Aged 25 or Older by Educational Attainment, Sex, Age, Nativity, Household Relationship, Race, and Hispanic Origin, 2001"; and "Health Insurance Coverage Status of People by Poverty Status, Race, Hispanic Origin, Sex, Age, Region, Metropolitan Residence, Household Relationship, and Work Experience, 2001." The report also contains a glossary of terms and definitions, source and accuracy of CPS estimates, and the Census Bureau's document "Poverty in the United States: 2001." It includes a detailed index, which is not a part of the original CPS.

Although the Bureau provides the same data on its Website, the number of the data sets and their organization may be overwhelming to the average person and this publication serves as a quick reference. This resource is recommended for researchers who prefer neatly packaged and readily accessible poverty information.—**Mihoko Hosoi**

C, P

299. **The American Marketplace: Demographics and Spending Patterns.** 6th ed. By the Editors of New Strategist Publications. Ithaca, N.Y., New Strategist, 2003. 533p. index. $89.95. ISBN 1-885070-49-7.

The American Marketplace: Demographics and Spending Patterns is an outstanding resource for anyone conducting demographic research about the American population, particularly in the area of business and marketing. While most of the data included in the book are freely available from a variety of other sources, the chief value of the book is that all of this information is provided in a single, easy-to-use volume. The book is divided into nine main chapters: "Education Trends," "Health Trends," "Housing Trends," "Income Trends," "Labor Force Trends," "Living Arrangement Trends," "Population Trends," "Spending Trends," and "Wealth Trends." Within each chapter are statements about the population (for example, "Income Inequality is on the Rise," "Many Workers Drive to Work Alone") , with a short narrative summary and graphs and tables to back up the statement. Each chapter has a "Highlights" page, with a bulleted summary of each of the statements about the trends in the chapter. The information provided is authoritative, with sources clearly indicated, and unbiased. The book is as up to date as possible for a print publication, including information from the 2000 Census and a good deal of data from sources as recent as 2002.

The organization of the book is straightforward, and the index makes it easy for the user to locate needed data quickly. The type is clear and easy to read, and the charts and tables are well constructed for data clarity. It has a stout binding, making it able to stand up to much use and abuse. Its price is relatively low, making it accessible for most libraries. This book is highly recommended for public and academic libraries, and might be useful in a high school media center reference collection.—**Mark T. Bay**

C, P

300.   **Ancestry in America: A Comparative City-by-City Guide to over 200 Ethnic Backgrounds—with Rankings.** Millerton, N.Y., Grey House Publishing, 2003. 3045p. index. $225.00pa. (w/CD-ROM). ISBN 1-59237-029-2.

This is the 1st edition of a new reference that quantifies the ethnic and racial composition of U.S. cities and towns. Census data from 2000 is broken down into 217 categories. In addition to the customary racial designations, more difficult to find heritages are given, such as Houma American Indians, Assyrians/Chaldeans, Maltese, and more. In the first section, data are provided by state for 4,206 cities with over 10,000 inhabitants. Each entry includes the county, total population, and a listing of all ethnic and racial designations with the actual number of people reporting that descent as well as that segment as a percentage of the total population. For example, Deming, New Mexico has 14,116 people. Some 180 are American Indians (designated by tribe), 159 are of Dutch ancestry, 211 have a French background, and 97 have a Norwegian descent.

The second part of the book provides comparative rankings for a larger universe of 33,150 locations. For each category, the top 150 cities or towns with individuals reporting a specific ancestry are listed in 3 tables: total number regardless of size of the city, locations in which that category make up the largest percentage of the population of any size locale, and the percentage of total population in cities over 10,000. For example, Seattle has the largest total number of Icelanders with 906. Mountain, North Dakota has the largest percentage of Icelanders by total population for all size locations. Spanish Fort, Utah has the largest percentage of Icelanders as a percentage of total population in cities over 10,000. The publisher also includes a CD-ROM version of the data. This book is a practical market research tool. It can be used to identify new markets and to more effectively promote to existing markets by creating targeted campaigns building on cultural preferences. [R: LJ, 1 Sept 03, p. 151]—**Adrienne Antink Bien**

C, P

301.   Russell, Cheryl. **Demographics of the U.S.: Trends and Projections.** 2d ed. Ithaca, N.Y., New Strategist, 2003. 452p. index. $89.95. ISBN 1-885070-48-9.

For those who have ever wondered what our census found in the rate of interracial marriages, or of confidence in the Supreme Court, or the homeownership rate in different cities, this book can answer these and many other questions found in the 2000 census that are rarely published. In this single volume are tables covering many variants on current American life. The broad sections deal with attitudes and behavior, education, health, housing, income, labor force, living arrangements, population, spending, and wealth, but within each section, alongside the usual divisions by race, national origin, age, and gender, are fascinating bits of other subjects. Individually and collectively these tables can spark the interest of most any student with an interest in sociological topics. (One further example: one cannot obtain the 2000 data for U.S. metropolitan areas from the census Web page, but here they all appear in tables ordered by size and growth rate over the 1990s as well as alphabetically.) In this vein this book is recommended for individuals and for libraries serving all age and educational groups.—**Arthur R. Upgren**

P

302.   **The Who, What, and Where of America: Understanding the Census Results.** Martha Farnsworth Riche and Deirdre A. Gaquin, eds. Lanham, Md., Bernan Associates, 2003. 1123p. maps. $95.00. ISBN 0-89059-763-4.

Every 10 years the United States conducts a Census of Population and Housing. A sample of the total population fills out a long form, while almost all housing units complete a short form. As there were more than 280 million persons living in some 105 million households in 2000, the year of the most recent census, a massive quantity of data resulted. That mass of data had to be organized and formatted in order to provide useful information. That is the function of *The Who, What, and Where of America: Understanding the Census Results*, edited by Martha Farnsworth Riche (former Director of the U.S. Census Bureau) and Deirdre A. Gaquin (consultant on federal statistics). Significant changes and major trends in U.S. population are highlighted, followed by rankings of states, counties, metropolitan areas, and cities by selected demographic characteristics. The bulk of the volume is composed of three sections, each containing more detailed tables and summary graphics. The first includes information related to age, race, origin, household structure, ancestry, and language. The second offers data on education, labor, and income. The third is devoted to migration patterns, housing, and transportation to work. Access to specific information is facilitated by providing column headings of the detailed tables in an introductory location. Appendixes contain helpful insights into geographical concepts as well as source notes and definitions. The book is a convenient and accessible guide to and source of authoritative and recent information on the population of the United States. [R: AG, Dec 03-Jan 04, p. 64]—**William C. Struning**

STATISTICS

United States

P

303.   **CQ's State Fact Finder 2003: Rankings Across America.** By Kendra A. Hovey and Harold A. Hovey. Washington, D.C., CQ Press, 2003. 418p. index. $99.00; $55.00pa. ISBN 1-56802-810-5; 1-56802-309-1pa.

First published in 1993, *CQ's State Fact Finder* includes tables and profiles for the United States' 50 states and the District of Columbia. The 2003 edition provides new data for more than 90 percent of the statistics covered in the 2002 edition.

There are three major sections: "Finding Information Users Want to Know," "Subject Rankings," and "State Rankings." The section titled "Finding Information Users Want to Know" uses a question-and-answer format and is divided into three parts: "About Personal Decisions on Where to Live or Visit," "About Business Decisions on Where to Locate and Expand," and "About Government and Public Policy." The "Subject Rankings" section is the heart of the publication and includes 13 subject areas: population, economics, geography, government, federal impacts, taxes, revenues and finances, education, health, crime and law enforcement, transportation, welfare, and technology. The "State Rankings" section provides a quick summary of each state's position in each subject area. There is also a comprehensive index at the end of the publication.

This resource differs considerably from ordinary statistical resources: it includes many statistics that are not contained in standard government reports; information from other sources is converted to makes comparisons meaningful; each table provides a ranking of the states; it begins with an essay describing the use of the information; each chapter in the subject rankings section begins with an outlook brief; and it offers carefully documented source notes. This resource is a valuable source for anyone interested in trends in the states.—**Mihoko Hosoi**

C, P

304.   **Fedstats. http://www.fedstats.gov/.** [Website]. Free. Date reviewed: 2003.

Fedstats is a Web-based portal and search engine for statistical information available from federal agencies reporting expenditures of more than $500,000 per year in statistical activities (e.g., surveys, forecasts, data analysis). Users search for statistics through an A to Z topic list (from "Acute Conditions: Common Cold" to "Weekly Earnings") , through a list of agencies with statistical programs, statistics available by geographic areas, press releases (including links to agency press release sites), or a search across agency Websites. Other features include links to kids' sites on agency Web pages and statistical profiles of states, counties, and congressional districts.—**Christine A. Whittington**

P

305.   **Social Change in America: The Historical Handbook 2004.** Patricia C. Becker, ed. Lanham, Md., Bernan Associates, 2003. 146p. index. $49.00pa. ISBN 0-89059-897-5.

The explosion of statistical information on the Internet has made this once difficult-to-locate resource much more easily accessible. What is more difficult to find is a way to help users understand statistics once found and to place them in context. *Social Change in America* aims to provide this context for high school and college students.

The handbook consists of 12 thematic chapters, ranging from population to health to leisure. Each 8-15 page chapter offers a narrative summary and analysis of historical and contemporary trends in each area and various related subtopics, as well as an overview of issues affecting statistical data gathering or interpretation in that specific area. Interspersed with the densely packed text are numerous graphs, charts, and tables. Most of the tables and charts are reproduced directly from U.S. federal government agency Websites or publications, supplemented with data from private publications and custom charts providing time-series data. A brief bibliography ends each section, with resources for locating further reading or more detailed statistics in print and on the Internet.

This book covers a lot of ground in terms of subject matter and time. Its analyzes and overviews present complex issues (social and statistical) in a clear, concise fashion, but does not provide much depth. Most charts and tables provide data for multiple time periods, supporting the work's aim of placing contemporary developments in context. However, time periods and intervals in the tables and narrative are not consistent between chapters, or even within chapters. This accurately reflects the vagaries of statistical data gathering and publication, but makes this publication less suitable as a reference work for those seeking specific statistical information. Rather, this work should be seen as an introduction to issues of social change in the United States and a resource for locating further information on each topic. *Social Change in America* is recommended for public libraries.—**Hui Hua Chua**

URBAN STUDIES

P

306.   **The American Tally, 2003: Statistics & Comparative Rankings for US Cities with Populations over 10,000.** 2d ed. Millerton, N.Y., Grey House Publishing, 2003. 807p. $125.00pa. ISBN 1-930956-29-0.

This volume is designed to serve a single purpose—to provide a comparison of various kinds of data for all of the 3,761 cities, towns, villages, boroughs, and CDP (census designated places) with populations over 10,000 in the United States, using the 2000 census figures. This is the second such volume in the series. The first, published in 1993, does the same for the 1990 census. The book is divided into broad categories that include distributions by age, educational attainment, languages spoken in the home, immigration and ancestry, income, employment, and housing. In each category the pattern is the same; the tables are arranged alphabetically by state and community, followed by another list giving the 100 places in the country ranking highest and the 100 ranking the lowest in the percentages of the data under consideration. Much can be inferred by the cities found in each of these lists of rankings. For this reason, the book is recommended as a source for all libraries with an interest in social demographics. [R: LJ, 1 June 03, p. 105]—**Arthur R. Upgren**

P

307. **America's Top-Rated Cities, 2003: A Statistical Handbook.** 10th ed. Millerton, N.Y., Grey House Publishing, 2003. 4v. $195.00pa./set; $59.95pa./vol. ISBN 1-891482-79-3.

This is a set of four volumes that cover America's top-rated cities as the title proclaims. Each volume covers about one-fourth of the United States. Together they are divided by geographical section: East, Central, South, and West. Each volume covers 25 cities, for a total of 100 cities. In truth, and the better for it, each extends in most categories to the Metropolitan Statistical Area (MSA) surrounding the core city or cities. In a few cases two cities within a single MSA, such as Fort Worth and Dallas, and Minneapolis and Saint Paul, are covered separately. When all is said and done, the places included adhere very closely to a list of the top 100 MSA's by total population. Almost no places with metropolitan areas less than about 200,000 people are included. Thus as a ranking between the largest cities, the books have merit, as they include almost all of the larger cities. But, with a few exceptions, the smaller places with perhaps 50,000 to 200,000 inhabitants, do not appear. Lovely university towns like Charlottesville, Virginia, and a few northeastern cities, large and small (e.g., Hartford, Connecticut; Portland, Maine), are curiously missing from the count. This work is recommended with this caveat in mind.—**Arthur R. Upgren**

P

308. **Moving & Relocation Directory 2004.** 4th ed. Nancy V. Kniskern, ed. Detroit, Omnigraphics, 2004. 1204p. index. $225.00. ISBN 0-7808-0662-X.

The *Moving & Relocation Directory 2004* is basically designed to provide essential information to those considering relocating to any one of the 121 U.S. cities profiled in the directory. However, the availability of wide-ranging local data in a single convenient location extends the usefulness of the book to others, including travelers and employers, as well as anyone who has need for local information. The cities profiled in the directory are major population centers and smaller cities that are most likely to attract those contemplating relocation. While the cities selected should fulfill the needs of most readers, it was obviously impossible to include every potential destination for relocation in the United States. The data provided for each city are comprehensive and include location, climate, history, government, realtors' associations, nearby communities (suburbs), economy, quality of life indications (e.g., crime statistics, cost of living, average home prices), educational facilities, hospitals, transportation, utilities, banks, shopping, media, cultural/recreational attractions, sports facilities, and special events. Also provided are U.S. time zone maps, lists of moving companies and associations, chambers of commerce, realtor associations, area codes, and a chart showing distances between major cities. Wherever feasible, mailing addresses, telephone numbers, fax numbers, and Internet addresses are given for each entry to facilitate contacts. Sources for obtaining further information are included for each city. The cities are arranged alphabetically and are listed separately in alphabetic order as well as by state. A table of contents enables easy access to broad sections and special features. An introduction offers brief descriptions of the topics discussed for each city. The directory provides the basics to facilitate relocation and a platform to secure further details. —**William C. Struning**

18 Women's Studies

BIBLIOGRAPHY

C, P

309. **Women's Studies Online Resources. http://research.umbc.edu/~korenman/wmst/.** [Website]. Free. Date reviewed: Dec 03.

Women's Studies Online Resources is a project of Dr. Joan Korenman, Director of the Center for Women and Information Technology, Professor of English and Affiliate Professor of Women's Studies at the University of Maryland, Baltimore County. Korenman is a recognized expert in this field, founder of the Center (in 1998) and of WMST-L (in 1991), the largest women-related academic e-mail forum in the world. She is also author of *Internet Resources on Women* (1997), and has received several awards for her work in this field.

The Website is a valuable tool for students, scholars, and researchers in the field of women's studies. It aims to help the user find "information rich, high quality web sites focusing on women's studies or women's issues." It also includes women- or gender-related e-mail lists, links to women's studies programs, financial aid and job opportunities for women, and updates to Internet resources on women.

The listing of 600 links to Websites offering resources and information about women's studies and women's issues can be accessed by broad subject area. Dates in which the links have last been updated are included. The design and presentation of the site is attractive, clear, and easy to read and use. The site has received 34 awards, commendations, or special recognitions during the period from 1996 to 2003. *Women's Studies Online Resources* is an important, useful reference tool that should be highlighted and made accessible to library users in all types of libraries, particularly academic libraries.—**Susan J. Freiband**

DICTIONARIES AND ENCYCLOPEDIAS

C, P, S

310.   Harper, Judith E. **Women During the Civil War: An Encyclopedia.** New York, Routledge/Taylor & Francis Group, 2004. 472p. illus. index. $95.00. ISBN 0-415-93723-X.

Harper's work will be a welcome addition to reference collections because so many important topics about women are left out of even the best general encyclopedias about the war. More than half of the 120 entries in Harper's work do not appear in the award-winning *Encyclopedia of the American Civil War* (see ARBA 2001, entry 410). The topical entries are the most valuable because very few of these are covered in other encyclopedias. For instance, readers can learn about Catholic Nuns as nurses, the anger that sparked the Bread Rebellions, and the activities of Western women during the Civil War era. Even familiar topics like "Fort Sumter" and "Gettysburg, Battle of" are unique because the author approached them from the perspective of women. Although information about most of the women profiled in the biographical entries can be found elsewhere, having them compiled in a single volume is a big plus. Researchers will have to consult state biographical dictionaries for profiles of numerous additional women who played important roles in the conflict. A short glossary, bibliography (which is not comprehensive), and an excellent index round out the volume. The illustrations are well chosen. Harper, an independent scholar and the author of *Susan B. Anthony: A Biographical Companion* (see ARBA 99, entry 800), has written an enjoyable and usable work that is most suitable for high school students, undergraduates, and the general public. [R: LJ, Jan 04, p. 90]—**Ken Middleton**

HANDBOOKS AND YEARBOOKS

C, P

311.   Kuersten, Ashlyn K. **Women and the Law: Leaders, Cases, and Documents.** Santa Barbara, Calif., ABC-CLIO, 2003. 256p. illus. index. $85.00; $90.00 (e-book). ISBN 0-87436-878-2; 0-57607-700-4 (e-book).

This work claims to give a broad overview of the legal rights of women in the United States from the Revolutionary War to the present day, as well as provide a solid understanding of gender discrimination and inequality. Happily, this well-organized, interesting, and easy-to-read encyclopedia accomplishes these goals.

The work begins with a thorough introductory essay about the history of gender equity in the United States. Like all information in this volume, this essay is written for the layperson and is very informative and interesting. The bulk of the volume consists of over 200 entries divided into 8 topical chapters: "Key Historical Concepts and Pioneers"; "Constitutional Equality"; "Education"; "Family Law"; "Reproductive Rights"; "Violence Against Women"; "Workplace Rights"; and "Documents." These entries include brief biographies of nearly 50 contemporary and historical women, analysis of nearly 80 key court cases, and the text of 21 important documents. The topics covered by these entries range from familiar to lesser known. For example, biographical entries cover such well-known figures as Susan B. Anthony and Harriet Tubman, as well as less widely known women such as Alice Paul and Lucy Stone. Similarly, court cases range from the well-known *Roe v. Wade* to *Fullilove v. Klutznick*, a case dealing with workplace rights. The documents range from speeches and declarations in support of women's right to vote to the text of important legislation, such as the Nineteenth Amendment to the Constitution and the Civil Rights Act. The entries range in length from one-half page to several pages, and are arranged alphabetically within each chapter, with the exception of the entries in the "Documents" chapter, which are arranged chronologically. Almost every entry provides references to related entries or references to other resources on the topic. In addition, each chapter ends with a substantial list of references and suggested readings about the general topic. The work also contains an interesting chronology, a table of cases (which provides the citation to each court case as well as the year it was decided), and an extremely detailed and useful index. Black-and-white illustrations, many of which are portraits that accompany many of the biographies, are found throughout the volume.

Because this work provides a wealth of information on an important topic, is well-organized, and contains well-written entries that are detailed, provide good historical context, and clearly explain the significance of the topics, it is a highly recommended purchase for public, high school, and undergraduate libraries.—**Karen Selden**

C, S

312.   Strom, Sharon Hartman. **Women's Rights.** Westport, Conn., Greenwood Press, 2003. 353p. index. (Major Issues in American History). $55.00. ISBN 0-313-31135-8.

Favoring an issues-centered approach to the study of the past, books in the Major Issues in American History series attempt to frame the historical record around selected themes and problems that have shaped the American experience. Each book in the series includes 10 to 15 case studies of pivotal events that define a given issues. For each entry there is a brief overview that explains and interprets the event, followed by a selection of contemporary documents that present opposing views about the topic under discussion. Each volume concludes with a general bibliography of key works on the subject. The most recent volume in this series published by Greenwood Press traces the issue of women's rights across the sweep of American history.

Although the "Chronology of Events" section and the overview to the first chapter provide late-eighteenth-century material, the documents in the opening three chapters that cover the antebellum era date only to the 1830s. Consequently, students interested in studying women's rights in colonial, revolutionary, and early national America may be disappointed by the selections. However, students with particular interest in late-nineteenth-century and twentieth-century women's history will find this book a rewarding volume. Contemporary America is particularly well covered with such diverse modern topics as "The Right to Privacy, Abortion, and the Debate of *Roe v. Wade*" "'The Personal is Political' and Its Aftermath: Addressing Sexual Liberation and Sexual Violence," and "Title IX and Women in Sport."

Throughout the 15 chapter volume the primary documents are short (generally less than 1,500 words each), easy to understand, and pertinent to the topic. Likewise, the chapter overviews (each approximately 3,000 words) contain constructive information that enables readers to place the sources into their historic context. Also useful are the annotated reading guides that accompany each chapter, and the complete 13-page index. Students who enjoy a problem-solving approach to history will enjoy this sourcebook on women's rights in American history.—**Terry D. Bilhartz**

C, S
313.   Whaley, Leigh Ann. **Women's History as Scientists: A Guide to the Debates.** Santa Barbara, Calif., ABC-CLIO, 2003. 252p. illus. index. (Controversies in Science). $85.00; $130.00 w/e-book. ISBN 1-57607-230-4; 1-57607-742-X (e-book).

This book belongs in most library collections—academic and public. It is essential to understanding the exclusion of women throughout most of history from science, and the reluctance of women to enter science programs, engineering studies, and computer fields today. It will help readers understand the contributions made by women to science through the ages. Footnotes lead the reader to extensive bibliographies, chapter by chapter, at the back of the book, and many black-and-white illustrations are used to spark interest. This lively, well-written, solidly researched volume is helpful to anyone studying women in most facets of science and in many areas of women's studies. Educators and admissions representatives considering the lack of women in scientifically charged programs will find the book enlightening.
—**Adalyn Smith Watts**

Part III
HUMANITIES

19 Humanities in General

HUMANITIES IN GENERAL

C, P, S

314.   **Art and Culture. http://www.artandculture.com/.** [Website]. New York, Art and Culture Network. Free. Date reviewed: Dec 03.

The *Art and Culture* Website is sponsored by The Art Council, a nonprofit organization whose stated mission is "supporting arts education in primary and secondary schools." The site offers information on important people and artistic movements within the categories of design arts, film, literature, music, performing arts, and visual arts. Users can search the entire site by artist name, movement, or keyword, or explore each category individually. Categories are subdivided into several more specific areas. Each subcategory offers a brief essay about that particular type of art and biographical information on selected artists. While rather sophisticated art terminology is used in some of the essays, many are written in a more folksy style. Artists' names can be listed alphabetically, geographically, or by time period.

An annotated list of recommended links to related Websites is displayed at the bottom of each biography. Each entry is also accompanied by a useful list of linked cross-references—"Related Artists," "Movements," and "Keywords." Perhaps the most unusual feature of the site is the "cloud" that appears at the top of each page. Centered in the cloud is the name of the selected artist, and floating around it are the hyperlinked related keywords, movements, and artists' names.

Navigation is easy within this useful site, and the cross-referencing system is helpful for making connections between artists and artistic styles. One criticism of the site is that none of the biographies is signed, so the user does not know the authority of the source. This seems an important omission.—**Janet Dagenais Brown**

C, P

315.   **Directory of Grants in the Humanities 2003/2004.** 17th ed. Jeremy T. Miner and Lynn E. Miner, eds. Westport, Conn., Oryx Press/Greenwood Publishing Group, 2003. 586p. index. $84.95pa. ISBN 1-57356-592-X.

The format of this annual guide to grant-funding opportunities in the arts and humanities has remained unchanged since last year's edition (see ARBA 2003, entry 879). As with earlier editions (see ARBA 99, entry 812; ARBA 95, entry 931; ARBA 93, entry 946; ARBA 90, entry 883; and ARBA 87, entry 348), an alphabetic list of public and private funding programs continues to make up the majority of the volume. Although the focus is on programs in the United States, a small portion of the list refers to programs in Canada and several other countries. Each entry includes: name and description of the grant; requirements and restrictions for application; examples of previous awards; typical funding amounts; application deadline; contact telephone number, fax number, and e-mail address; Internet address (if available); and sponsor contact information. The program number entry for grants that are also listed in the *Catalog of Federal Domestic Assistance* is provided. Four indexes offer useful access points—a subject index, a sponsoring organization index, a program type index (which arranges grants into 37 broad categories), and a geographic index for grants that focus on a particular locale. Useful introductory sections provide guidance on efficient use of the volume, helpful information on grant writing, and a directory of sponsors with Internet sites (URLs are included). While even more up-to-date information can be obtained for a fee through the *GRANTS Database*, this annual volume remains a valuable resource for both academic and public libraries of all sizes.—**Janet Dagenais Brown**

20 Communication and Mass Media

GENERAL WORKS

C
316.   **ComAbstracts. http://www.cios.org/www/abstract.htm.** [Website]. By the Communication Institute for Online Scholarship. Rotterdam Junction, N.Y., Communication Institute for Online Scholarship, 1997- . Price negotiated by site. Date reviewed: 2003.

C
317.   **ComIndex. http://www.cios.org/www/comindex.htm.** [Website]. By the Communication Institute for Online Scholarship. Rotterdam Junction, N.Y., Communication Institute for Online Scholarship, 1993- . Price negotiated by site. Date reviewed: 2003.

     ComIndex uses menu-driven software to provide bibliographic citations to articles in 74 journals from the core literature of the communication field (journalism, speech, communication studies, rhetoric, and mass communication). The time period covered is from the initial publication date of the journal or 1970; whichever date is later. *ComIndex* provides bibliographic citations, but not abstracts or full-text articles. This is an inexpensive ($100 for individuals and $1,000 annually for campus-wide access) and critical source for libraries that support communication programs.

     ComAbstracts provides indexing and abstracts for 53 communication journals. Chronological coverage varies from journal to journal; coverage of *Public Opinion Quarterly* begins with volume 30 (1966), for example, but coverage of *Research on Language and Social Interactions* begins with volume 33 (2000).

     Author, wild card, and Boolean searching are available in both *ComIndex* and *ComAbstracts*. Words in abstracts are searchable, and the abstracts are enriched with additional key words to increase the likelihood of success.—**Christine A. Whittington**

AUTHORSHIP

General Works

P
318.   **Children's Writer's & Illustrator's Market, 2004: 1000+ Editors, Agents and Art Directors Who Want Your Work.** Alice Pope and Mona Michael, eds. Cincinnati, Ohio, Writer's Digest Books/F & W Publications, 2003. 394p. index. $24.99pa. ISBN 1-58297-191-9. ISSN 0897-9790.

     The 16th edition of this annual directory is more than just a "how to" source for creating plots, characters, or illustrations for children's books. It also includes such business principles as promotion and marketing. Experts in children's literature offer advice on such varied topics as creating Websites, creating promotional materials, converting books to film, co-editing anthologies, and more. The "Markets" section of the book includes insider reports from editors, authors, and illustrators. Markets highlighted are for U.S. book publishers; international book publishers; publishers of greeting cards, puzzles, and games; play publishers and producers; and young writer's and illustrator's markets.

The "Resources" section contains not just a helpful list of books and publications, but also information about agents and representatives; clubs; regional and national conferences and workshops; contests, awards, and grants; and online resources. A glossary and five indexes complete the work. The indexes are by age-level, subject, poetry, photography, and a general index. The authors suggest beginning with the indexes to determine which companies buy the type of manuscript one might be interested in submitting for publication. Listings are very concise; many of them begin with one or more symbols to avoid repetition and to save space. This is a must-have resource for those who wish to specialize in writing or illustrating for the children's market. The price makes it affordable for individuals and the smallest of public and academic libraries.—**Lois Gilmer**

P

319.   **Novel & Short Story Writer's Market, 2004: 2,000+ Places to Get Your Fiction into Print.** Anne Bowling, Michael Schweer, and Vanessa Lyman, eds. Cincinnati, Ohio, Writer's Digest Books/F & W Publications, 2003. 680p. index. $24.99pa. ISBN 1-58297-193-5. ISSN 0897-9812.

This latest edition of *Novel & Short Story Writer's Market* has been expanded to include information on the emerging graphic novel art form, as well as an extended listing of literary agents (up from 50 to more than 200). Serving not only as a listing of contacts and available resources, it also provides helpful guidelines and suggestions on both the art of writing and the business of getting published. Interspersed throughout are commentaries ranging in length from single quotes to essays of several pages by writers and individuals in the publishing industry. The information is arranged into categories so that a particular area or format of interest can be easily located. There are guidelines in the beginning pages that explain the format of each entry and the meanings of symbols and abbreviations. A typical entry will indicate a publication's particular focus, the conditions of consideration or acceptance of a submission, contact information, payment terms, and pertinent notes from the editors or publishers. There is also a listing of conferences, writing programs, contests, definitions of terms, and other valuable information.

The entries are concise and the commentaries and helpful and interesting. This is not only a source of extensive, useful information, it is also an entertaining read for those interested in writing and publishing. —**Martha Lawler**

P

320.   **Writer's Market, 2003: 3,100+ Book and Magazine Editors Who Buy What You Write.** Kathryn Struckel Brogan and Robert Lee Brewer, eds. Cincinnati, Ohio, Writer's Digest Books/F & W Publications, 2002. 1112p. index. $29.99pa. ISBN 1-58297-120-X. ISSN 0084-2729.

The 82d annual edition of the *Writer's Market*, praised as the number one resource for writers, now describes over 3,800 markets, of which more than 350 are new to this edition. This work opens with five sections of general essays addressing issues of the business of writing and of getting published. The largest part of the work consists of listings of literary agents, markets (i.e., book publishers and producers, consumer, trade, technical and professional periodicals as well as scriptwriting, syndicates, and contests and awards), and resources (publications, Websites, and organizations). The book publishing market reflected herein is predominantly American, although there is a 25-page section devoted to Canadian and international publishers. Consumer magazines are categorized under 50 headings from "Animal" to "Women's," and journals are listed under 57 categories, from "Advertising" to "Veterinary." Two extensive indexes close the work: a book publisher subject index (divided by subject headings under fiction and nonfiction groupings) and a general index.

General text material and market entries appear in one-column paragraph style in Roman typeface. Headings (chapter titles, subheadings, running headers, and entry names) appear in bold typeface. The mix of typefaces works well. The overall appearance is neat, clean, and easy to read. The work is printed on newsprint paper and bound in paper covers.

One glaring discrepancy needs to be noted. The cover and title-page subtitles differ: where as "8,000+" book and magazine editors are proclaimed on the cover, the figure is only "3,100+" on the title page.—**Glenn R. Wittig**

Style Manuals

C

321.   Gibaldi, Joseph. **MLA Handbook for Writers of Research Papers.** 6th ed. New York, Modern Language Association of America, 2003. 293p. index. $17.00pa.; $25.00pa. (large print edition). ISBN 0-87352-986-3; 0-87352-987-1 (large print edition).

Librarians, students and researchers will probably be most interested in learning what changes have been made in the new 6th edition of the *MLA Handbook*. First, no modifications were made to the MLA documentation formats. The arrangement of this new edition is nearly identical to that of the 5th edition (see ARBA 2000, entry 819). Although some additions have been made to the text, overall, much of the wording duplicates that found in the previous edition. In a number of chapters, section headings and bullets have been introduced, breaking up longer passages of text and making it easier to find needed information. The new edition has been expanded in several areas, and many sections now offer a short "Summing Up" segment that pulls together the information presented. The most notable additions to the 6th edition include: an entire chapter devoted to plagiarism (the previous edition offered about four pages on this topic); new sections on "Library Research Sources" and "Full-Text Databases"; and expanded sections on "Reference Works" and "Internet Sources." The segment on citing electronic publications has been enhanced with graphics from Web pages, and includes additional and updated sample citations. Other additions include a new entry in the "Punctuation" section related to updated rules for spacing at the end of a sentence, and the inclusion of examples for citing comic strips and patents in the "Citing Miscellaneous Print and Nonprint Sources" section. All academic, high school, and public libraries will want to acquire this new edition. [R: LJ, 1 Sept 03, p. 152]—**Janet Dagenais Brown**

C, P, S

322.   **The Oxford Style Manual.** R. M. Ritter, ed. New York, Oxford University Press, 2003. 1033p. index. $45.00. ISBN 0-19-860564-1.

The Oxford Style Manual, which combines two classic writers' references (*The Oxford Dictionary for Writers and Editors* and *Hart's Rules*), is an essential tool for anyone who needs expert advice on the proper use of the written English word. Students, professionals, and even people who write as a hobby will find this resource indispensable for improving the quality and clarity of their work. *The Oxford Style Manual* provides clear and concise instructions for the use of English grammar and syntax, punctuation, capitalization, abbreviations, and many other aspects of the written language. In addition, the resource has in-depth instructions for the use of mathematical and scientific symbology as well as foreign-language constructions. It clearly explains the proper treatment of quotations, tables, notes, references, and illustrations. Extremely useful are its instructions for using and citing electronic media, writing for electronic publication, and an overview of current copyright law. Approximately one-half of the book is taken up by a mini-dictionary of words that usually give writers trouble due to spelling, hyphenation, punctuation, or differences between American and British English usage.

This resource is extremely well executed, as is expected from Oxford University Press. It is authoritative, easy to read and use, and has an outstanding index that allows users to quickly find answers to their questions. *The Oxford Style Manual* is an essential reference resource, and belongs in the ready-reference section of any academic, public, corporate, or school library.—**Mark T. Bay**

RADIO, TELEVISION, AUDIO, AND VIDEO

C

323. Casey, Bernadette, and others. **Television Studies: The Key Concepts.** New York, Routledge/Taylor & Francis Group, 2002. 291p. index. (Routledge Key Guides). $60.00; $17.95pa. ISBN 0-415-17236-5; 0-415-17237-3pa.

This collection of 76 alphabetically arranged essays on television was written by 5 British academics who are involved in media studies. The subtitle, "The Key Concepts," aptly defines the parameters and limitations of this work. Instead of factual material on television's history, development, stars, and series, this volume explores the theoretical and conceptual principles of the nature and study of television. These aspects include: influential background perspectives like semiology and feminism; concepts that underlie television presentation (e.g., narrative); research methods (including content analysis and audience research); background phenomena like ownership and culture; and various television genres, including soap opera and science fiction. (Sitcoms are discussed under the general heading of "Humor.") The average length of each essay is 3-4 pages during which the concept and its elements are explained, their evolution traced, current thinking and developments outlined, and salient research studies reported on. These studies are predominantly British in origin, and the references to past and present trends and actual television shows also show a British emphasis. Access to the text is helped by *see also* references at the end of each chapter and a thorough subject index. A 14-page bibliography lists all the studies referred to in the text. The coverage is scholarly, sometimes opinionated, and highly theoretical. Therefore, the audience will probably be confined to serious students of media who have some knowledge of communication theory and can cope with the often-convoluted text. This work is recommended for academic and large public libraries.—**John T. Gillespie**

C

324. Sies, Leora M., and Luther F. Sies. **The Encyclopedia of Women in Radio, 1920-1960.** Jefferson, N.C., McFarland, 2003. 407p. illus. index. $95.00. ISBN 0-7864-1476-6.

In the first encyclopedia to concentrate on chronicling the contributions of women who worked in and on radio, Luther Sies and his wife Leora have filled a large gap in the coverage of the history of radio. Sies is a respected scholar and collector who's audio research materials have been preserved as the Luther F. Sies Radio Collection in the Rogers and Hammerstein Archive of recorded sound at the New York Library of the Performing Arts at Lincoln Center.

Covering the "Golden Age" of radio prior to the emergence of television, the author concedes the entries included are only a representative sample of the women who helped shape American broadcasting since much of the original record has been lost. Nevertheless, the 10,500 alphabetically arranged entries offer a valuable look at the impact women had on the radio industry. Although many of the entries consist simply of the name of the performer, the call letters of the station they are associated with and dates/locations of appearances, some entries also supply additional information. Entries for performers are not biographical and focus only on verifiable professional broadcasting appearances. Especially valuable are the nine extended entries that describe women's special contributions to American radio, including topics such as gender discrimination, pioneers, and comediennes. These generally run 5 to 10 pages and include black-and-white illustrations.

The entries covering earlier time periods use individual broadcasters as entries, while later entries use programs with the individuals who appeared and the length of time the programs were broadcast when available. When original sources were in conflict about name entries and no definitive verification was available, possible variations are provided that could be extremely helpful to researchers.

The authors provide an introduction that serves as a brief yet concise overview of the place of women in radio history. Also included is a section on how to use the book, a bibliography, and indexing by both program names and performers names. There is also an appendix with broadcasters listed by category, although this would be more useful if the categories were listed at the beginning to give the reader an idea of what categories to consider while looking for entries. While more narrowly focused than Sies more comprehensive *Encyclopedia of American Radio* (see ARBA 2001, entry 948), this is an important resource for anyone looking for information about this overlooked facet of radio broadcast history. [R: Choice, Jan 04, pp. 878-879]—**Patrick J. Reakes**

C

325.   Terrace, Vincent. **Radio Program Openings and Closings, 1931-1972.** Jefferson, N.C., McFarland, 2003. 278p. index. $45.00. ISBN 0-7864-1485-5.

While reviewing this book, two thoughts (actually one wish and one question) kept coming to mind: how delightful it would be to have more than just the openings and closings of so many radio shows recalled from my childhood, and of what reference value is this listing? Of course, Vincent Terrace never intended this volume to go beyond openings and closings, but the question of research usefulness of such abstracts is still unanswered. Nevertheless, a perusal of the 516 opening and closing themes of 444 numbered entries does evoke reminisces and uncover some interesting data. It includes titles such as *I Want a Divorce*, *I Was a Communist for the FBI*, *Coast-to-Coast on a Bus*, *Candid Microphone* (predecessor to television's *Candid Camera*), *It Pays To Be Ignorant*, and *It Pays To Be Married*. It also includes a number of already famous movie and stage (and later television) stars who performed in radio.

Terrace includes all types of programs, beginning in 1931 with the earliest theme that could be found (*The Vaughn DeLeath Show*) and ending with the final broadcast of *The Devil and Mr. O*. Each entry has a brief introduction with storyline, principal cast, sponsors, and air dates, and each theme is reproduced with music, sound effects, and announcer's plugs for the sponsor and cast. This volume is recommended for mass communications libraries and collections.—**John A. Lent**

P

326.   **The Video Source Book: A Guide to Programs Currently Available on Video ....** 30th ed. Farmington Hills, Mich., Gale, 2003. 2v. index. $395.00/set. ISBN 0-7876-7067-7. ISSN 0748-0881.

The *Video Source Book* (VSB) provides one of the largest collections of video program listings in one source. Delivering access to over 126,000 listings of more than 165,000 programs, the resource includes materials in a variety of formats from 8 mm to VHS and DVD. Divided into seven sections in a two-volume set, the sections include: "Video Program Listings," "Alternate Title Index," "Subject Index," "Credits Index," "Awards Index," "Special Formats Index," and "Program Distributor Index." Each program listing comprises multiple classification points that aid in describing the item, such as title, year of release, synopsis, running time, audience level, subject category, and many other classification points. Prices are also included when available for most entertainment-related programs and more recent non-entertainment releases.

Although the VSB is similar to *Bowker's Complete Video Directory* in providing access to a comprehensive listing of video titles, there are some differences between the two sources. The VSB compiles all the titles in one alphabetic listing and then provides subject indexes of titles, while *Bowker's* divides the listings into entertainment, education, and special interest. Depending upon the user's preference, the division or separation of titles can help or hinder searching. The VSB includes larger font for title listings, which allows for easier browsing. On the other hand, the Bowker source does list ISBN numbers or order numbers for each entry that facilitates ordering of the materials. Well designed and formatted, this is a valuable tool for constructing video collections or locating a video program listing.—**Glenn S. McGuigan**

21 Decorative Arts

COLLECTING

General Works

P
327. Miller, Judith, with Mark Hill. **Collectibles Price Guide 2004.** New York, DK Publishing, 2003. 600p. illus. index. $25.00pa. ISBN 0-7894-9657-7.

Lavishly illustrated with more than 5,000 illustrations, this work by the author of over 80 books on antiques and collectibles is currently in a 2d annual edition. Judith Miller has consulted with a number of experts in writing this book: Glen Hart and Mitch Michener for Americana; Noel Barrett for toys; Hugo Lee Jones for computer games; Dudley Brown for glass; Roxanne Stuart for costume jewelry; Christina Bertrand for sewing; and David Hunt for sporting. The volume is divided into broad subject classes such as: "Wine & Drinking"; "Toys & Games"; "Smoking Accessories"; "Marine Collectibles"; "Kichenalia & Domestic"; "Dinseyana"; "Dolls, Fifties, Sixties and Seventies"; "Books"; "Cameras"; and "Glass." Some sections feature additional information ("Collectors' Notes") , which help provide basic information on the topic, while in other cases the author had provided "a closer look" for items, which helps to further identify a specific item illustrated. Additional resources can be found at the end: a glossary, a key to illustration abbreviations, a directory of specialists, a directory of auctioneers (by state), clubs and societies, Internet resources (e.g., eBay), and an index.

With over 5,000 illustrations, each entry is rather small, making it difficult to see the item in detail. Since condition is a major factor in price, this lack of detail can lead the readers to assume a higher value than the item may be worth. Often mint in box prices are given for items, but the item is shown out of box. Some prices are somewhat optimistic, such as the $30-50 for a Motorola flip phone, and $100-150 for an Ericofon. At times the indexing is sloppy. For example, under "Telephone: Phone Cards" in the index, page 248 is referenced. Two "Dr. Who" British Telecom phone cards are shown on page 249, but no other types of phone cards are shown on page 248 or any other page. Western jewelry is located in the "Americana—Native Americans" section, and only indexed under "Native American Collectibles" with no cross-reference to either jewelry or Western jewelry. The selections for some entries are somewhat puzzling; for example, one page is devoted to radios, while there are six pages of "Scottie Dog Collectibles." There is a similar unbalanced effect in the doll section where there is a huge section for the Mobilitie (Annalee) dolls and just a few entries for other doll types (e.g., composition, bisque). "The Fonz" button, which features prominently on the back cover, is not in the index, but is buried in an inside spot on the next to last double-page spread of the "Film & Television" collectibles section. Some areas, such as railroad and train, fountain pens, and African American collectibles, are not even mentioned in the book. In fairness, there are small sections entitled "Americana—Black Souvenir Dolls" and "Tribal Art," but the bulk of the African American collectibles market is ignored.

Overall, the work is attractive and fun to look at. It is an inexpensive paperback that according to the front cover blurb is "the best all-color, all-new guide to over 5,000 collectibles." Well it is in color and it is new, but the illustrations are small and the prices somewhat optimistic. In short, this guide is fun to look at, but this reviewer would not take it to the bank. It is recommended, with the above caution about the prices, for general reference collections in most libraries.—**Ralph Lee Scott**

Antiques

P

328.   Miller, Judith. **Antiques Price Guide 2004.** New York, DK Publishing, 2003. 752p. illus. index. $35.00. ISBN 0-7894-9550-3.

This work is designed with convenience of use in mind. Color-coded, top-of-the-page tabs identify main category headings. Each category and subcategory (for example, subcategories of ceramics are porcelain, pottery, and oriental) has an introduction with key facts about factories, makers, styles, and identification points. Advice on fakes is also offered. Over 8,500 high-quality, full-color photographs illustrate items along with a generalized price guide. Of note is a very complete section of American furniture. This is one of the few price guides with illustrations and prices for commemorative ceramics featuring British royalty. Noteworthy are the numerous fine examples of china commemoratives of the coronation of Edward VII and Alexandra. Some of the many overlooked areas of coverage in most guides are featured in this work. There are sections on American and Canadian folk art, bronzes, art deco ceramics, and silhouettes and miniatures. Thoroughness of this guide may be seen in that the usual section of clocks and watches also includes scientific, surveying, microscopic, and medical and telescopic instruments. A whole new trend in collecting objects made and manufactured within the lifetime of our senior citizens is well represented in a section of "modern classics." Illustrations here include modern furniture, lighting, and ceramics. A brief section on posters reflects ships, trains, and tourist travel destinations. One surprise is that musical instruments, including phonographs, are not in this guide. A directory of auctioneers that conduct regular sales is a useful inclusion. The work is well indexed by subject including subheading entries. This annual guide should be a part of the fine arts reference collection in public libraries and in appropriate special collection libraries.—**Louis G. Zelenka**

Books

P

329.   **Antique Trader Book Collector's Price Guide.** By Richard Russell. Iola, Wis., Krause Publications, 2003. 448p. illus. $24.99pa. ISBN 0-87349-607-8.

This price guide by an experienced American bookseller gives current market values for some 5,000 English-language books of the 19th and 20th centuries. The books are arranged in 12 categories, of which 6 are literary: fantasy, horror, and science fiction; literature in translation; modern first editions; mystery; poetry; and vintage fiction (mostly nineteenth century). The other categories are: Americana, art, and illustrated books; banned books; biographies; occult and paranormal; and philosophy and religion. For each book there is basic publication information followed by two prices: the average current market value of copies in near fine and fine condition, and the average current price of copies in good or very good condition. There are small black-and-white photographs of the dust jackets of many of the listed books. An introductory section provides helpful information on the methods used by various publishers to identify their first editions; the pseudonyms used by various authors; examples of the signatures of some well-known authors; a short glossary of book terms; and discussions of pricing, grading used books, and vanity presses.

Those interested in the current market value of books often turn first to the Internet, particularly Abebooks.com or Bookfinder.com. But this can be very time consuming when there are a large number of copies in varying condition for sale. And while there are other price guides of this type such as the more comprehensive *Collected Books* by Allen and Patricia Ahearn (2002 ed.; see ARBA 2003, entry 906), Russell's price guide has a number of unique features, such as its topical organization, a list of 10 classic rarities in each topic area, pictures of dust jackets, and a two-tier pricing system that make it a useful supplement to previously published works. Anyone desiring an informative overview of collectable books, especially literary ones, will find this nicely executed and inexpensive work a useful starting point. —**Joseph Cataio**

Ceramics

P

330.   Florence, Gene, and Cathy Florence. **Collector's Encyclopedia of Depression Glass.** 16th ed. Paducah, Ky., Collector Books, 2004. 253p. illus. $19.95. ISBN 1-57432-353-9.

A guide to collectible, machine-made glass made from the late 1920s to 1940, this encyclopedia is published regularly in new editions in order to add more glass patterns and pieces, and keep up to date on retail sales prices. Arranged alphabetically by pattern name, most of the more than 160 entries are 1 to 2 pages long. The heading notes name, alternate names, company name, date range, and colors. Descriptive text outlines points of interest, such as the history of the pattern or company, different styles of pieces such as pitchers or plates, relative scarcity of items and where the "finds" have been found, and trends in the popularity of colors and patterns. Beautiful full-color photographs are the real attraction here. Each entry shows a variety of pieces, often in several colors, such as the bowl, candy dish, plate, vase, tumbler, cheese and cracker plate, salt and pepper set, and candlestick. Finally, known pieces are listed with identifying measurements and prices with shaded columns that make it easy to read prices for different colors. All the usual American companies are represented here—Anchor Hocking, Paden City, Indiana Glass, to name a few—but there is no index in which one can look up patterns by manufacturer. Reproductions of several popular patterns are listed at the end, along with hints and photographs on how to identify them. This is a good addition to reference or the stacks for any library catering to patrons interested in "old stuff."—**Deborah V. Rollins**

Coins (and Paper Money)

P

331.   Friedberg, Arthur L., and Ira S. Friedberg. **Gold Coins of the World: From Ancient Times to the Present.** 7th ed. Clifton, N.J., Coin & Currency Institute, 2003. 732p. illus. index. $75.00. ISBN 0-87184-307-2.

Gold coins have been around since about 700 B.C.E. Their significance has moved beyond the precious metal content to the artistic and historic realms. Thus they have become desirable to collectors, historians, and museums alike. *Gold Coins of the World* is now in its 7th edition. A venerable resource, it was first published in 1958. Then, it was a mere 348 pages. It has since more than doubled to a hefty size of 732 pages. As the title implies, this resource endeavors to be comprehensive not only in its geographical coverage but also chronologically, from ancient times to the present.

The catalog is divided into three chronological parts. Part 1 is the ancient world till about C.E. 600, part 2 covers world coins C.E. 600 to 1950, and the last part covers the world output from 1950 to the present. By far the bulk of the book (over 500 pages) falls within part 2. Each part is subdivided geographically by country. Each coin entry has a half-tone photograph of the obverse and reverse, with minimal description, date, and denomination. Also included are estimated prices for "very fine" and "extremely fine" conditions, while for a few there are values for other grades. It should be noted that these prices are just guidelines of value and are not meant as a statement of fact for buying or selling coins. Value is based on condition, rarity, and market demand, which can fluctuate.

Completing the book are several tables of such data as weights and measures, foreign-language numerals, and the Mohammedan Calendar, followed a list of references and a geographical index. It would have been a genuine pleasure had the photographs of gold coins been in color, but that would have put this reasonably priced resource out of reach for most collectors, if not libraries. The photographs are as sharp and as detailed as the condition of the original allows and, therefore, are quite adequate for most identification purposes. *Gold Coins of the World* has stayed true to its predecessors and the original work of Robert Friedberg. This title is recommended for public library collections and large academic collections serving history, anthropological, or archaeological programs.—**Margaret F. Dominy**

P

332.   **Standard Catalog of World Paper Money. Volume 3: Modern Issues 1961-Date.** 9th ed. Neil Shafer and George S. Cuhaj, eds. Iola, Wis., Krause Publications, 2003. 924p. illus. $45.00pa. ISBN 0-87349-591-8.

The 9th edition of the *Standard Catalog of World Paper Money* covers modern issues from 1961 to the present. It is arranged in alphabetic order by country, and within a country by the political or bank issuer in chronological order, and then by denomination of the note. In cases where there has been a change in country name during this time range, both names are listed. There are also about 45 pages of supplementary material at the beginning of the catalog. Some of this information found here is a user's guide, issuer and bank index, a table of standard international numerical systems, security devices, a beautiful set of color photographs displaying the "color of money," Hejira date chart, and banknote printers. For each currency listing the obverse and reverse of the first issue of the series is depicted, including any specific description and valuation according to grade. This catalog is the standard for the currency enthusiast. This work is suitable for public library collections.—**Margaret F. Dominy**

Firearms

P

333.   **Shooter's Bible.** 2004 ed. Accokeek, Md., Stoeger Publishing, 2003. 576p. illus. index. $23.95pa. ISBN 0-88317-244-5.

This ready-reference annual for civilian handguns, rifles, shotguns, and supporting equipment comes from a major publishing house specializing in shooting sports. Although its parent company manufactures products covered by the book, treatment is completely even-handed. Nearly 20 percent of this volume comprises articles on hunting techniques, military and civilian arms history, and gun collecting, giving it permanent value. The articles are well illustrated and clearly written. Providing highlights on new items and custom gunmakers adds welcome focus, and a directory provides contact information (including Websites) for all manufacturers listed.

The heart of this reference is the listing of firearms and equipment, broken down into firearm type, sights, ammunition, and handloading supplies, and alphabetically arranged by manufacturer within section. Almost all items specified in each section are illustrated by crisp photographs, with tabulated data and pricing information. Whether one is looking for a Pedersoli replica 1875 Sharps Cavalry Carbine, a Bushnell HOLOsight, or the ballistics of a 6x50 Japanese rifle cartridge, it is all here. With a sturdy, lay-flat perfect binding and clear printing on high-quality newsprint stock, any library serving a clientele interested in shooting sports will want to consider this volume.—**John Howard Oxley**

Militaria

P

334. Graf, John F. **Warman's Civil War Collectibles.** Iola, Wis., Krause Publications, 2003. 517p. illus. index. $24.95pa. ISBN 0-87349-437-7.

Like so many price guides, this is a straightforward listing of collectibles with prices. There are 18 categories of material offered, culled from the author's personal collection, catalogs, auction records, sales results, and dealer interviews. Topics are: accoutrements, artillery, bayonets, belts, bullets, buttons, carbines, ephemera, flags and musical equipment, groupings (i.e., collection of miscellaneous artifacts from one person or event), insignia, medical, personal items (i.e., toiletries, watches, and mirrors), photographs (including carte de vistes), revolvers, swords, and uniforms. Some books are included, but Tom Broadfoot's *Civil War Books: A Priced Checklist* (Broadfoot, 2000) is the best price list for Civil War books. Civilian goods are not covered, nor are commemorative or veteran items. Beyond a short introduction and an adequate index, the data are complemented by a truly fine, up-to-date, seven-page, annotated bibliography of books on nineteenth-century military collectibles, which identifies hard-to-find items from obscure publishers. Serious collectors will find this bibliography invaluable. For each of the 18 categories, he offers a very useful, 1- to 5-star rating system and description of availability, price, and reproduction alert. Items can range in price from a few dollars to tens of thousands. Over 1,000 mostly black-and-white images are included for the 3,000-plus price listings. Individual entries include name, production date and producer (if known), description of the item, its use, and physical condition. Entries can run to over half a page, while multiple entries for the same item show variants and price ranges. The nearest competitor is the *Official Price Guide to Civil War Collectibles* (2d ed.; Random House, 1999), which has about the same number of entries and is also reasonably priced, but has shorter descriptions, fewer illustrations, and price ranges rather than realized prices. It also includes more supplementary material, such as re-enactor data, but that appears to be filler.

Of the two, *Warman's* would be a first choice and is clearly one of the better executed of all price guides. Its descriptive value will be useful for material culture collections and collectors long past the time when prices are out of date. This guide is very highly recommended for public libraries serving Civil War clients and for colleges with civil war archaeology or material culture interest.—**Patrick J. Brunet**

CRAFTS

S

335. **Crafts for Kids.** Danbury, Conn., Grolier, 2003. 16v. illus. index. $339.00/set. ISBN 0-7172-5760-6.

This 16-volume set from Grolier provides a wealth of craft ideas that are ideal for elementary-aged children. Each volume in the set focuses on a different event, celebration, or theme, including birthdays, myths and tales, the back-to-school season, vacations, and backyard crafts. The volumes begin with an introduction that focuses on the importance of following instructions, gathering materials, clean up, and safety. Following this are the crafts. Each craft is presented in a two-page spread and includes a list of supplies, numbered instructions, and ideas for what to do with the finished product. Clear color photographs will help children better follow the easy instructions. The crafts are designed to do more than just keep children busy; they are arranged to encourage specific educational and motor skills. Many of the crafts teach very basic math and science skills, introduce art concepts, and stimulate cooperation as well as self-reliant thinking. This set will be most useful in school library media centers with elementary-aged students.—**Shannon Graff Hysell**

FASHION AND COSTUME

P, S

336.   Pendergast, Sara, and Tom Pendergast. **Fashion, Costume, and Culture: Clothing, Headwear, Body Decorations, and Footwear Through the Ages.** Farmington Hills, Mich., U*X*L/Gale, 2004. 5v. illus. index. $275.00/set. ISBN 0-7876-5417-5.

This five-volume set from U*X*L provides a broad overview of how clothing and fashion represent our cultural, religious, and societal beliefs, both now and in centuries past. The set is arranged chronologically into 25 chapters that focus on either a specific time period or a specific cultural tradition. Each chapter is arranged in the same format. They begin with an overview that discusses the historical time period and major cultural and economic factors of the time. Following this are four sections on clothing, headwear, body decoration, and footwear. For example, in volume 1, "The Ancient World," users learn about the significance of the clothing in Ancient Egyptian life, including the use of wigs, headdresses, fragrant oils, and sandals. In the fourth volume, " Modern World Part I: 1900-1945," users learn how economic and social hardships have affected clothing and style—how short hair and short flapper dresses represented wealth and freedom for women in the 1920s and how the Depression and World War II sent hem lines down and made simple clothing fashionable. The work is supplemented by more than 330 color and black-and-white photographs, which will aid the reader substantially. Other supplementary material include a timeline, a glossary, "For More Information" sections at the end of each entry, and a "Where to Learn More" section that offers lists of books and Websites students can consult for more information.

This set does an excellent job of describing the changes and significance of clothing and fashion in relation to society's cultural and societal beliefs. The photographs add significantly to the text and create a work that is fun to use for both research and for browsing. *Fashion, Costume, and Culture* is highly recommended for school libraries and the children's reference collections of large public libraries.—**Shannon Graff Hysell**

INTERIOR DESIGN

P

337.   Miller, Judith. **The Style Sourcebook: The Definitive Illustrated Directory of Fabrics, Wallpapers, Paints, Flooring, Tiles.** rev. ed. New York, Firefly Books, 2003. 416p. illus. index. $59.95. ISBN 1-55297-791-9.

This is a revised edition of the 1998 book of the same name. Researched to cover fashionable styles of decoration from the Middle Ages to the present, this reference work for design professionals contains over 2,300 detailed color photographs. The book is divided into six encyclopedic sections: a style guide that contains a historical overview of interior design styles for the past 500 years; fabrics categorized by design, pattern type, and historical period; wallpapers divided into design type and then historical period; paints and finishes, with detail provided on the composition and finish of each paint sample along with the evolution of paint pigments; tiles categorized by mediums, such as ceramic, stone, clay, and marble; and flooring divided into mediums, such as rubber, vinyl, linoleum, carpet, matting, and wooden.

Symbols are used throughout the book to assist the reader in determining cost factors and appropriate application and usage of materials; the key to the symbols is provided in the introduction. An up-to-date directory of international manufacturers and distributors is included, along with a glossary of design terms and an index. For those interested in interior design and remodeling, this is a wonderful book full of suggestions; contact information; and prices on fabrics, wallpapers, paints, flooring, and tiles. —**Bradford Lee Eden**

22 Fine Arts

GENERAL WORKS

Biography

P
338.   **American Abstract Expressionism of the 1950s: An Illustrated Survey with Artists' Statements, Artwork and Biographies.** Marika Herskovic, ed. Franklin Lakes, N.J., New York School Press, 2003. 372p. illus. index. $95.00; $57.00 (institutions). ISBN 0-9677994-1-4.

Politics, popularity, or hype tend to bring certain artists to the forefront of the movement with which they are associated. Warhol is the poster boy for pop art, and Dali can be considered the elder statesman of surrealism. However, there are often a number of overlooked artists who work within a given style. This publication attempts to bring some of abstract expressionism's lesser-known, but equally competent, artists to the forefront. Well-known individuals (De Kooning, Gottlieb, and Mitchell) are included, but many of the individuals are not easily recognizable names. Some 88 artists are included and are listed alphabetically by last name. Entries for each artist are four pages in length and consist of two full-page reproductions (almost all are in color), a statement from the artist including the citation for the source, biographical information, and a list of selected solo and group exhibitions. For the biographical information, birth and death dates, education, and teaching experience are listed. If applicable, military and Federal Art Project participation are given. Criteria for inclusion are that all artists were born before 1927 and worked during the height of American abstract expressionism (1950-1959). No geographical, racial, or gender boundaries restrict inclusion. The introductory essay provides good background information and offers the methodology behind the publication. An index is provided, but no bibliography or selected reading list is offered, which would be a useful addition particularly for the lesser-known artists. This is a gorgeous publication and is highly recommended for all art collections.—**Terrie L. Wilson**

C, P, S
339.   **AskART. http://askart.com.** [Website]. Free access to site; membership service $19.50/month. Date reviewed: Nov 03.

AskART is intended to be a comprehensive database on American artists. It contains images, biographies, bibliographies, information on museum holdings of artwork, and auction data for hundreds of artists, chiefly from the nineteenth and twentieth centuries. Much of this information is available free, but auction data, archives of reproductions from magazines from the last 20 years, and most of the images are available only to subscribers.

Much of the free information is of limited use. Biographies are submitted by database users or are "from the archives of AskART.com." They vary widely in level of detail and in quality of information. Some artists have no biographical information listed. The bibliographic information is separated into

"Books on this Artist" and "Periodical Articles," but the citations are not complete and in the books section there is no distinction drawn between monographs, encyclopedia entries, or mention of the artist in books on otherwise unrelated topics. Museum listings for the artists display in random order. While obscure artists have reproductions of their artwork available, the free version gives only limited background data and displays no more than five artworks per artist. Images are slightly larger than thumbnail size and vary in quality. Altogether, *AskART* is not very valuable as a free site.

For subscribers, the site may be more useful. In some cases images of hundreds of artworks are displayed, along with their most recent sales information. This information would make the site useful for museums and galleries and possibly for art libraries supporting advanced degree programs. *AskART* will not, however, replace the *Grove Dictionary of Art Online* (see ARBA 2002, entry 993).—**Amy K. Weiss**

P, S

340.   Otfinoski, Steven. **African Americans in the Visual Arts.** New York, Facts on File, 2003. 262p. illus. index. (A to Z of African Americans). $44.00. ISBN 0-8160-4880-0.

A significant work providing insight and background on a subject area in art passed over or superficially covered in the past, this volume is 1 of 10 in the new series by Facts on File entitled A to Z of African Americans. The series covers fields such as the performing arts (see entry 430); sports; math, science, and invention (see entry 457); and social activism (see entry 240). The current work includes over 180 individuals who have influenced the direction of the visual arts, including painters, sculptors, illustrators, installation artists, performance artists, film and video artists, mixed-media artists, and other visual formats. The work is arranged alphabetically with entries ranging from one-half to one page in length. Each entry begins with the standard birth and death dates where applicable. The entry also references media types or activities associated with the artist. An interesting departure from many biographical works on artist is that a great deal of personal information or life history is included in each entry. This inclusion is perhaps due to these artists being overlooked in the past with some of their exhibitions being outside the traditional art world. Each entry also includes a brief bibliography featuring Websites of interest and a filmography for viewing the artist's works and life. Indexes at the end of the work include medium or area of activity, artistic style, and year of birth, as well as the traditional subject format. The work is illustrated with portraits of many of the artists. The only complaint is the captions under the illustrations add little to the understanding of the portrait or of the artist. This is a minor complaint in an otherwise interesting and valuable addition to the subject. This work is well worth the purchase price, especially due to the quality of the library binding and the reputation of the publisher for producing noteworthy reference materials.—**Gregory Curtis**

Dictionaries and Encyclopedias

C, P, S

341.   **ArtCyclopedia. http://www.artcyclopedia.com/.** [Website]. Free. Date reviewed: Dec 03.

For free online information about artists, *ArtCyclopedia* is an excellent starting point and provides basic facts about select artists and access to images of their work. The site was launched in 1999 and supplies information by listing artists that are represented in fine art museums and galleries that have an online presence. The site can be searched by artist's name, title of work, or by art museum (name or location). Also, users can browse artists by name, movement, media, subject, or nationality. Information listed in the search results includes birth and death dates, nationality, movement, alternate names or spelling variations, significant relationships with other artists (i.e., "student of") , and the list of works in museums and galleries represented through the site. The 8,000 artists featured on the site are primarily painters and sculptors and are well known, as are the museums and galleries represented through the site that house major collections. If applicable, auction record sites are listed, as are online image archives, online articles, and "other links," which might include multimedia applications or miscellaneous Websites. As with any portal that links to external sites, the user frequently will have to click the "back" button to return to

ArtCyclopedia. A glossary of art terms, list of saints, and glossary of Greek and Roman mythological terms is provided. This reviewer used both Internet Explorer 6.0 and Netscape 7.1 to access the site and found it easy to navigate in both browsers. *ArtCyclopedia* will prove useful and interesting to a variety of patrons. It is recommended to any library that has a need to provide online fine arts information.—**Terrie L. Wilson**

C, P

342.   **The Concise Oxford Dictionary of Art and Artists.** 3d ed. Ian Chilvers, ed. New York, Oxford University Press, 2003. 653p. $14.95pa. ISBN 0-19-860477-7.

The *Concise Oxford Dictionary of Art and Artists* is an abbreviated lexicon based on *The Oxford Dictionary of Art.* Its scope remains the same. It includes western art from the fifth century B.C.E., but has been expanded to include more recent artists born prior to 1965 instead of 1945. Entries include biographies of artists, sculptors, writers, leading collectors and dealers, materials and techniques, and galleries and museums. It only excludes architects, architecture, and Oriental art. There are exceptions to every rule, however, as the editor includes "Ukiyo-e, as the subject of Japanese prints occurs so frequently in the discussion of late 19th century French painting" (preface).

In the preface Chilvers goes into great detail about how entries and cross-references are listed. He then lists a few abbreviations. The length of the entry is generally based on the significance of the subject. Where necessary, entries have been paraphrased or eliminated. Surprisingly, this concise dictionary is longer than its parent volume by 203 pages. It only has 2,500 entries as compared to 3,000 in the *Oxford Dictionary of Art.* Although the 1988 and 1997 editions of the *Oxford Dictionary of Art* included "a chronology, an index of galleries and museums (with Web site addresses), and, in the case of the 1988 edition, a selected list of Christian and classical themes in painting and sculpture," these have been eliminated. One wonders why. The text does include bibliographic information when needed. Art historians, gallery patrons, students, and educators will find this mini-tome a portable wealth of information. —**Nadine Salmons**

Handbooks and Yearbooks

C, P, S

343.   Ross, Leslie. **Artists of the Middle Ages.** Westport, Conn., Greenwood Press, 2003. 182p. illus. index. (Artists of an Era). $59.95. ISBN 0-313-31903-0.

Artists of the Middle Ages is the first volume in a new art history series where each book is devoted to artists of a specific era. After a two-page timeline highlighting important developments in medieval art there is an introduction that presents a thought-provoking examination of why so few medieval artists are known by the public today. Each of the subsequent 10 chapters are fully annotated, with endnotes and a bibliography. Chapters focus on a particular practitioner of a significant area of specialization, such as sculpture, metalworking, architecture, mural painting, or stained glass. Thus, in the chapter on scribes, Eadwine is discussed in detail, while Andrei Rublev heads the chapter on icon painters. Artists such as Herrad and Hildegard are discussed in a chapter devoted to women artists, and the Limbourg brothers come under scrutiny in the chapter on court artists. The chapters are largely anecdotal, focusing on a particular work of art or a problem the artist in question had to overcome, while skillfully tying the life of the individual to the larger societal issues of the time. The text is presumably written for an undergraduate audience, although it would also be appropriate for high school upperclassmen. There is an eight-page insert in the middle of the book with excellent color illustrations that supplements the black-and-white illustrations throughout the text. The book closes with a list of additional resources, a general index, and an index of artists and architects.—**Philip G. Swan**

P

344.   **Women Artists of the American West.** Susan R. Ressler, ed. Jefferson, N.C., McFarland, 2003. 357p. illus. index. $75.00. ISBN 0-7864-1054-X.

This volume grows out of an Internet archive project of the same name (http://www.sla.purdue.edu/waaw/), founded by the title's editor, Susan R. Ressler (Purdue University), who is also a contributor to the work. Organized in two parts, the work covers more than 150 artists working in a wide range of media including quiltmaking, clay art, and digital art. The work "addresses significant topics in American history through the lens of women's history art" (p. 5). Ressler's introduction discusses the attempts of women to fit into the male-dominated art landscape of the early twentieth century.

The first part reads much like an art history textbook with 15 analytical essays focusing on the themes of community, identity, spirituality, and locality in women's artwork from the nineteenth and twentieth centuries. The essays are contributed by a wide variety authors (most notably Peter E. Palmquist), including artists, art historians and faculty, a gallery director, and a psychotherapist.

The second section is an invaluable biographical dictionary. The entries are brief but still manage to include a description of the artist's work, education and training, influences, recent exhibitions, and awards. This title is well illustrated with color and black-and-white reproductions. Although not as comprehensive as the *A to Z of American Women in Visual Arts* (see ARBA 2003, entry 864), the narrow regional scope of this work allows for more focused discussions of theme and experience. It is recommended for any library with a modern or contemporary art collection. [R: LJ, 15 Sept 03, p. 50]—**Paolina Taglienti**

ARCHITECTURE

C, P

345.   Arnold, Dieter. **The Encyclopedia of Ancient Egyptian Architecture.** Princeton, N.J., Princeton University Press, 2003. 274p. illus. $39.95. ISBN 0-691-11488-9.

This volume, a translation and updating of the author's *Lexikon der ägyptischen Baukunst* (1994, 1997), provides much information for the general reader as well as for the Egyptologist and historian of architecture and art. More than 600 entries and over 300 illustrations comprise its contents, making it a virtually unsurpassed compact resource on the topic in English. The solid and extensive bibliographic entries included with virtually every entry (updated for this edition), enhance its value for all readers. In addition, the author includes maps, a glossary of concepts peculiar to Egyptology, and a timeline of ancient Egypt's history. As a result, the volume provides an extremely valuable resource for anyone interested in Egyptology or the study of ancient architecture.

Entries range from quite brief to fairly extensive, each with appropriate and helpful cross-references and definitions of technical architectural terms as needed. Among the topics treated extensively are the expected ones, such as tombs, temples, pyramids, mastabas, columns, palaces, and houses. Perhaps less expected are the lengthy entries on bricks and brick construction, stone construction and quarrying, towns, and symbolism. This last provides a wonderful link between the architecture, particularly of temple and tomb, and the pervasive mythological meanings present in the world of the ancient Egyptians.

In sum, due to the expansiveness and depth of its contents, this modestly priced volume belongs in every university and art library and most public libraries of any size. It should also be on the shelves of serious students of ancient Egypt and architectural history. [R: LJ, 15 Feb 03, p. 126; SLJ, Oct 03, p. 103]—**Susan Tower Hollis**

P

346.   Burden, Ernest. **Illustrated Dictionary of Architectural Preservation.** New York, McGraw-Hill, 2004. 280p. illus. $34.95pa. ISBN 0-07-142838-0.

This volume is a delight to look at. It is well laid out and has a number of black-and-white illustrations on each page to complement the terms being defined. Organized in a handy A to Z format, entries include not only information about well-known architects, but also illustrated examples of major buildings. Users can find small architectural features, such as *haunched beam*, defined, as well as essays on major firms, such as Herbert S. Newman Associates. Novices will find in topics such as *arcade* a basic definition of the term along with several informative illustrations. This volume is a handy compendium of architectural terms, building code nomenclature, material and construction jargon, and general building restoration terms. The emphasis is on "restoration, rehabilitation, renovation and adaptive use." Many significant examples are given with most text entries. The work bills itself as "a treasury of images, ideas, and answers" in architectural preservation. It lives up to its claimed reputation. In fact it was hard to put down and can provide the reader with a comprehensive introduction and review of the field.

The volume claims to make use of "extensive cross-referencing" but this reviewer could find only one cross-reference in the book: "Adaptive reuse" refers users to "Adaptive use." There are a few examples of careless proofreading: for the text on page 245 and on page 270 the illustrations are reversed. Some terms, such as *bonds*, could be expanded upon and illustrated a little better. Photograph credits appear at the end of the volume on pages 278-279. The work ends with a small section entitled "About the Author" on the final page. Overall, this is a very attractive, handy, easy-to-use compendium. Readers should compare this work with its companion also published by McGraw-Hill, *Historic Preservation Handbook*, written by J. Kirk Irwin (see ARBA 2004, entry 937). Patrons will find this work useful in most reference collections.—**Ralph Lee Scott**

P

347.   **The Houses We Live In: An Identification Guide to the History and Style of American Domestic Architecture.** Jeffery Howe, ed. Berkeley, Calif., Thunder Bay Press/Publishers Group West, 2002. 448p. illus. index. $24.98. ISBN 1-57145-855-7.

The author of this book contends that houses, besides providing shelter, also reflect cultural norms, values, and preferences to others. It is an often overlooked art form embedded in American society. This book provides a history of the development of the American house, from Native American homes of pre-contact times to the present. This book will assist the novice in the identification of various styles and building types. While the primary focus of the work is style, it also provides a travel guide to examples of regional architecture and a mental guide to the possibilities architecture offers.

Some 600 photographs and approximately 600 drawings by the editor illustrate the key features under discussion. Individual chapters cover Native American and early colonial houses, seventeenth- and eighteenth-century styles, European revival (chiefly nineteenth century), Victorian, eclectic revivals (nineteenth and twentieth centuries), and modern housing. The development of construction elements for different styles (windows, roofs, and so on) is discussed throughout the book. A list of one-paragraph biographies of important people in the history of American architecture follows chapter 6. Listings are in alphabetic order and describe the work each architect is best known for. An illustrated glossary and an index complete the work.

The majority of the photographs depict houses in New England, where so many architectural styles mix. The photographs are beautifully reproduced, as are the drawings. This is important, as the written descriptions are fairly limited. The reader will easily understand the differences in styles and how they came to exist, at least on a basic level. This book does its job both efficiently and beautifully. It is recommended for all collections.—**Joanna M. Burkhardt**

PHOTOGRAPHY

C, P

348.   Ang, Tom. **Dictionary of Photography and Digital Imaging: The Essential Reference for the Modern Photographer.** New York, Watson-Guptill, 2001. 383p. $21.95pa. ISBN 0-8174-3789-4.

This is an interesting dictionary of all things photographic and digital. The author has provided a good balance between traditional photographic terms and more modern digital ones. The entries are arranged alphabetically and are pleasant, attractive, clear, and easy to read. Billed as "the essential reference for the modern photographer" the volume covers everything from large format plate cameras to tools used in Adobe Photoshop. There are no illustrations of any of the terms used. There is a bibliography of additional resources of photographic and digital terms and conventions. Some pages have sidebars covering photographic topics and aphorisms, an example of which is "Road Rage" on page 105, which discusses device conflict control. Some others are entitled "Keeping a watchful Eye," "Querying the Pitch," "No noise can be bad news," "Once were uncorrected," "Smug and Play," "Gamut, match and set," "Waving good bye to Fourier," and "Patently stupid things to do." Unfortunately, these sidebars are not indexed, so the user will just have to hunt to find their favorites again. The volume is an attractive, modestly priced paperback.

There are some odd errors and omissions. Ang mentions in the introduction the term "bucket as in Bucket Tools," but bucket is not included in the dictionary. Other photographic favorites are also missing: fixer, splice, paper, close-up, bulb, stamp, cables, tray, date and time-stamp, and Polaroid. In general, brand names are not mentioned. The sidebar on the page with "Tongue," entitled "Tongue in Cheek," does mention how Leica and Nikon cameras briefly used a film tongue. Some but not all Photoshop tools are mentioned. For example, the brush is mentioned, but the lasso, spray, and eraser tools are not. Some other terms such as "Brownout" and "UPS" while containing interesting commentary, actually have primary uses outside the photography and digital imaging arena and thus their inclusion is puzzling.

Most libraries having general readers interested in photography and digital imaging will want to purchase this dictionary. As mentioned, the main drawback of the work is the lack of a single illustration.
—**Ralph Lee Scott**

P

349.   **Photographer's Market, 2004: 2,000 Places to Sell Your Photographs.** Donna Poehner and Erin Nevius, eds. Cincinnati, Ohio, Writer's Digest Books/F & W Publications, 2003. 633p. index. $24.99pa. ISBN 1-58297-186-2. ISSN 0147-247X.

This is the 27th edition of an essential reference book that began publication with the 1st edition coming out in 1978. The volume is divided into a number of resource intensive sections: "Just Getting Started"; "Getting Down to Business"; "Portfolio Review Events"; "Making It in Niche Stock Photography"; "The Markets" (publications, consumer publications, newspapers and newsletters, trade publications, book publishers, greeting cards, posters and related products, stock photo agencies, advertising, design and related markets, and galleries and contests). At the end of the volume there are a series of appendixes (called "Resources") : "Photo Representatives"; "Workshops & Photo Tours"; "Professional Organizations"; "Publications"; "Websites"; "Portfolio Review Events"; "Glossary"; and geographic, international, subject, and general indexes.

A typical entry in "The Markets" section includes the name of the publication or agency, contact person (including postal and e-mail address), and a brief description of the publication including circulation numbers. Next is a section that describes the needs of the publication in terms of photographs (e.g., "We often use photos tied to the season, a holiday or an upcoming event of general interest.") . This is followed by a "Specs" section (e.g., "Uses 5 x 7, 8 x 10 glossy, b&w and/or color prints. Accepts images in digital format for Mac. Zip and TIFF, JPEG at 180dpi.") , and a "Making Contact & Terms" section (e.g., "Send unsolicited photos by mail for consideration. SASE.") . The entries conclude with a "Tips" section.

The most frequent tip is to read the publication and become familiar with the type of photographs the company uses.

Photographers wanting to enter the professional market will find this volume hard to beat. It is a comprehensive introductory review of the field, yet it is also a timely update for current professionals. It is on the bookshelf of all professional photographers. It is paperbound, has a few black-and-white photographs, and costs only $24.99. Most libraries will want to add this volume to their general reference collections. —**Ralph Lee Scott**

SCULPTURE

C

350.   **The Encyclopedia of Sculpture.** Antonia Boström, ed. New York, Routledge/Taylor & Francis Group, 2004. 3v. illus. index. $375.00/set. ISBN 1-57958-248-6.

Filling a gap in art reference sources, *The Encyclopedia of Sculpture* is the first major encyclopedia devoted solely to the medium. The three volume set is a compilation of essay-style entries contributed by experts in the field, including art historians, curators, and independent scholars. Finding aids included in the set are an index, an alphabetic list of entries, and a thematic list of entries. Categories in the thematic list include, but are not limited to, artist biographies, styles and periods, and materials, forms, and techniques. Entries reflect sculpture of all time periods in Europe, the Americas, Asia, and Africa. *The Encyclopedia of Sculpture* is illustrated with small (quarter page or less) black-and-white reproductions.

There are 763 essays included in the set. Essays are no less than a page in length, with many consisting of numerous pages of text; for example, the essay on African sculpture is approximately 10 pages long. All have a "Further Reading" list at the end that points the reader toward additional information on the topic. Entries for individual artists include the artist's name, birth and death dates, the essay, a separate biography, and a list of selected works. Entries on well-known artists often are followed by entries on one or more of their major works; for example, the entry on Rodin is followed by entries on *The Gates of Hell* and the *Monument to Honoré de Balzac*. Entries for individual works and monuments include the artist, birth and death dates, date of execution of the piece, medium, dimensions (height only), and present location. Entries that are more thematic, such as "Academies and Associations" consist of the essay, *see also* references, and the list of further readings.

Overall, *The Encyclopedia of Sculpture* is an excellent resource for basic information and a springboard for further research in the subject. Most essays cover topics sufficiently, but for certain subject areas (e.g., Romanesque sculpture), other resources will offer good if not better coverage of the topic. This reviewer compared the entry on Romanesque sculpture with the one found in the *Grove Dictionary of Art*, and found the *Grove* entry not only longer (53 pages compared to 4 pages) but, not surprisingly, more comprehensive. That said, it is often more convenient and timesaving for the librarian or the patron to go directly to a resource specifically geared toward the subject of their inquiry. Academic, museum, and larger public libraries will want to include *The Encyclopedia of Sculpture* in their art reference collections. [R: LJ, Dec 03, p. 94]—**Terrie L. Wilson**

23 Language and Linguistics

GENERAL WORKS

Dictionaries and Encyclopedias

C

351.   **The Linguistics Encyclopedia.** 2d ed. Kirsten Malmkjaer, ed. New York, Routledge/Taylor & Francis Group, 2002. 643p. index. $150.00. ISBN 0-415-22209-5.

The fact that there is a 2d edition of this *Encyclopedia* testifies to the positive response of the profession to the 1st edition. This new edition will have the same success, I believe, as the first. It is well positioned between the four volumes of the *International Encyclopedia of Linguistics* edited by William J. Frawley (2d ed.; see ARBA 2004, entry 945), and David Crystal's *Cambridge Encyclopedia of Language* (2d ed.; see ARBA 98, entry 989). These two encyclopedias do contain articles on the linguistic methods and schools of thought, and beyond that they offer a plethora of data about natural and artificial languages, and similar information. In contrast to this, the encyclopedia under review concentrates on methods and theories, prevalently those from the later twentieth century. Indeed, I think that something like "Encyclopedia of Theoretical Linguistics" would be a possible title for this book.

The single articles, each written by a specialist on the given topic, are comprehensive, so that the user sometimes must find the location of the information sought in the topical index; for instance, various forms of structuralism are discussed in one comprehensive article. Modern schools of thought that have a methodology of their own are treated in their own articles (e.g., stratificational grammar). Most attention is given to the various approaches within generative linguistics, so in this area users get single articles for generative grammar, generative phonology, generative semantics, and so on. The distribution of topics into single articles is adroit. The *Encyclopedia* has a historical dimension, hence there are articles dealing with history of grammar, Port-Royal grammar, and traditional grammar.

As already said, the articles are written by highly competent specialists within each area, so that one can rely on the information offered. On the whole, this is a highly useful book for any library, public or private, that is interested in linguistics.—**L. Zgusta**

ENGLISH-LANGUAGE DICTIONARIES

General Usage

C, P, S

352.   **The American Heritage Desk Dictionary.** 4th ed. New York, Houghton Mifflin, 2003. 950p. illus. $12.95. ISBN 0-618-11772-5.

The American Heritage Desk Dictionary is one of the most efficient desk dictionaries to use. Bolded entries are followed by clear, concise definitions. This small desk dictionary offers the etymology, pronunciation, parts of speech, singular and plural forms of words, and related synonyms. Comparable desk dictionaries, such as those from Oxford University Press and Chambers, do not offer these elements of etymology and the inflection of terms. Some of the entries are illustrated by black-and-white drawings or photographs. New contemporary words (e.g., *ezine, email, Y2K*) are among the entries. Biographical entries have a photograph, the person's birth and death dates, and a biographical description.

The low price and added features (such as etymologies) that other desk dictionaries do not include, make this 4th edition of *The American Heritage Desk Dictionary* a highly recommended purchase for all ready-reference shelves in public, school, and academic collections.—**Kay M. Stebbins**

C, P, S

353.   **The Chambers Dictionary.** 9th ed. New York, Houghton Mifflin, 2003. 1825p. $40.00. ISBN 0-550-10105-5.

Although precise numbers are unavailable and are ultimately meaningless, the 9th edition of *The Chambers Dictionary* defines several hundred thousand words, terms, and abbreviations. More than 6,000 references and more than 10,000 new definitions were added to this dictionary, including a number of words one associates with computers and technology (e.g., *hypertext, dotcom, cybercafe*) as well as a definition of the *mullet* hairstyle. Definitions provide pronunciation in the international phonetic alphabet, the part of speech, and the plural form(s); usage examples are occasionally given, but neither syllabifications nor date of origin are given. The volume concludes with a wonderful miscellany of appendixes listing, among other things, some first names, phrases in foreign languages, a few alphabets and numbers, Internet suffixes, the books of the Bible, the plays of Shakespeare, the chemical elements, conversion tables, the sizes of wine bottles, and international paper sizes; none, however, is cross-referenced in the body of the book, and it will be the exceptional user who locates them. (Indeed, cross-references as a whole are weak, and it will be the fortunate user who stumbles on the relationship between metonymy and synecdoche.) One may cavil at some of the definitions: *science fiction* and *fantasy* are not as well defined as they might be, and such relevant related terms as *Lovecraftian* and *muggle* are not mentioned. But *The Chambers Dictionary* is not *The Oxford English Dictionary* and does not try to be, and one of its virtues is that it is frequently quite witty. One simply cannot object to a work that defines the aforementioned *mullet* as "a hairstyle that is short at the front, long at the back, and ridiculous all around."—**Richard Bleiler**

C, P

354.   **Webster's New Explorer College Dictionary.** Darien, Conn., Federal Street Press, 2003. 1098p. illus. $14.98. ISBN 1-892859-42-4.

This volume contains most of the standard features one expects from a dictionary aimed at college students—instructions for effective use, a table of standard abbreviations and chemical element symbols, a table of general symbols and signs, a guide to proper use of punctuation, and, of course, the word definitions. Definitions include information on proper hyphenation and pronunciation, parts of speech, word forms (e.g., plurals, tenses), the definition, cross-references to synonyms, examples of how words might commonly be used, and etymological information. Very simple black-and-white line drawings illustrate one or two of the definitions on the majority of pages.

While *Webster's New Explorer College Dictionary* has few features that distinguish it from other similar dictionaries, it does provide a handy pronunciation guide at the bottom of every other page. Also, 200 of the definitions include more in-depth information about word origin and development. Having the name "Webster" in the title likely lends an air of authority to this work, but it is surprising that no editors or editorial boards are listed. Only the statement "Created in Cooperation with the Editors of Merriam-Webster" offers insight into the developers of this work. The newsprint-colored paper on which the book is printed makes the entries difficult to read. A whiter, crisper paper color would improve usability. Also, the addition of thumbnail access to each letter of the alphabet would provide for speedier use of the contents. This dictionary is recommended only for libraries that wish to supplement their existing dictionary collections. [R: LJ, Dec 03, p. 102; Choice, Jan 04, p. 874]—**Janet Dagenais Brown**

Juvenile

P, S
355.   **The American Heritage Children's Dictionary.** New York, Houghton Mifflin, 2003. 856p. illus. maps. $17.95. ISBN 0-618-28002-2.

The American Heritage Children's Dictionary contains many features that make it easier to use than the average children's dictionary. It begins with an easy-to-understand "How to Use Your Dictionary" section, followed by two annotated sample pages and a full pronunciation key. Among the features covered for many words are sidebars for word history (etymology), language detective (regional dialectical variants), vocabulary builder (prefixes and suffixes), and synonyms.

Each of the 34,000 main entry words is written in blue, followed by the part of speech label and primary and other definitions. The word is then rewritten in black, showing the syllabication and then, in parentheses, the pronunciation. The latter is made easier by the inclusion of a pronunciation key at the bottom of each right-facing page. Illustrations, both drawings and photographs, are in color and large enough to show detail. Other material follows the main entries: a six-page mini-thesaurus; eight pages devoted to phonics and spelling; one page of measurement information; one page of homonyms; seven pages of geographical names; a 1996 map of the world; and a United States map showing capitals and some large cities.

The American Heritage Children's Dictionary has much to offer for the price, but its hefty weight could keep younger children from using it if they have to carry it very far. While it is labeled as a children's dictionary, this volume would also be a great help to those adults for whom English is a second language. —**Kay O. Cornelius**

S
356.   **The American Heritage Student Dictionary.** New York, Houghton Mifflin, 2003. 1068p. illus. $19.95. ISBN 0-618-25619-9.

This visually pleasing, completely revised version of *The American Heritage Student Dictionary* offers the user many more features than the alphabetic listing of 65,000 entries as reported by the publisher. Intended for middle school and lower-level high school students, it continues as a user-friendly reference tool (see ARBA 95, entry 1047, for a review of the previous edition), offering both clear definitions, and a chance to discover additional information about the term, located in the margins. Revised to include full-color images of approximately 2,000 entries, this edition has added approximately 3,000 new terms, such as *dark matter*, *hyperlink*, and *instant messaging*. Each page consists of two wide columns of terms defined, along with a third column that is devoted to color images, proper usage of the term in context, pronunciation and style manual guides, and biographical and geographical entries. Additional features include cross-references to further information, word history, and variant spellings of terms.

There is a "Guide to Using the Dictionary" at the beginning of the book, which provides detailed explanations for the various notes provided for each term. The user will also find a "Capitalization, Punctuation and Style Guide," which provides basic term paper help for this grade level. The table of contents lists the various charts and tables included, such as the periodic table of elements and the solar system. Once again, this reasonably priced dictionary is highly recommended for the intended audience, and can be considered for acquisition by school media centers, public libraries serving this level, and for home use. —**Marianne B. Eimer**

Slang

C, P

357.   Ostler, Rosemarie. **Dewdroppers, Waldos, and Slackers: A Decade-by-Decade Guide to the Vanishing Vocabulary of the Twentieth Century.** New York, Oxford University Press, 2003. 239p. illus. index. $25.00. ISBN 0-19-516146-7.

   Dewdroppers, Waldos, and Slackers: A Decade-by-Decade Guide to the Vanishing Vocabulary of the Twentieth Century attempts to "give yesterday's words another chance to sparkle before they retire to the archives for good." While it does not claim to be comprehensive, this volume is an attempt to gather words and terms that served a purpose in their time and then were largely (perhaps mercifully) forgotten. Arranged by decades beginning with the 1900-1919 era, each chapter contains an essay on cultural history punctuated with definitions of that era's catchwords. Sidebars offer more detail on terms like *twenty-three skidoo* and *tin lizzie*, and each chapter contains a few black-and-white photographs. End material includes a bibliography and an index with entries from "AA" to "zot."

   The title, *Dewdroppers, Waldos, and Slackers*, derives from three defined words. A *dewdropper* is a 1920s jobless youngster who slept all day; *Waldo* is a 1980s homeless wimp, from the picture book series *Where's Waldo*; and *Slackers* are Generation X persons who are marginally employed by choice. Some words and phrases in this work, such as *G.I.*, *H-bomb*, and *Battle of Britain* are already a part of the lexicon, and it would be a mistake to assume all of the terms defined were in wide use at any particular time, or that all face certain linguistic death. With that caveat, *Dewdroppers, Waldos, and Slackers: A Decade-by-Decade Guide to the Vanishing Vocabulary of the Twentieth Century* should be of interest to cultural historians as well as trivia and slang aficionados. [R: LJ, 1 Feb 04, p. 78]—**Kay O. Cornelius**

Terms and Phrases

C, P, S

358.   **The Facts on File Encyclopedia of Word and Phrase Origins.** 3d ed. By Robert Hendrickson. New York, Facts on File, 2004. 822p. index. (Facts on File Library of Language and Literature). $82.50. ISBN 0-8160-4813-4.

   This marvelous reference has grown by about a third from its predecessor, which was published six years ago (see ARBA 98, entry 1001). The grand total now exceeds 12,500 letters, words, and expressions, all alphabetized, defined, and traced to their most likely provenance(s). Here one can find slang expressions like "It's the pits," foreign terms like "fatwa," abbreviations and acronyms like "AWOL," euphemisms like "gee!," terms from Classical literature like "Sisyphean," pop culture items like "smiley face," place-names (including all 50 states), homonyms like "quail," and so on. Drawing from both historical and contemporary sources, Hendrickson's book will appeal to researchers, and with its broad range and scope, word lovers are likely to become addicted—it is hard to read just one! Of course, this information can be found in *The Oxford English Dictionary* and in the works of Bartlett, Brewer, Mencken, Partridge, Pepys, and sundry other well-established authorities, but having it in one book is hard to beat. An index of proper names mentioned in the entries adds to its value.—**Lori D. Kranz**

C, P

359.   **The Oxford Dictionary of Catchphrases.** Anna Farkas, comp. New York, Oxford University Press, 2002. 357p. index. $25.00. ISBN 0-19-866280-7.

   Although this dictionary does not have a subtitle the news release accompanying it provides a good one: " A Guide to Popular Modern Expressions and Sayings, from Old Chestnuts to Current Jargon." Included are over 800 twentieth-century phrases culled mostly from television, radio, films, and books. There seem to be as many British as American phrases included, not surprising, perhaps, since the editor is an American who has lived in the United Kingdom for over 10 years and because the publisher is the Oxford University Press.

A typical entry includes an extended definition, information about the origin or presumed origin, and a documented example or a plausible made-up example of usage with occasional cross-references. A catchphrase is understood to be one that is "catchy" or memorable because it has resonance with the public. The first catchphrases, according to John Ayto who introduces this book (and who is a noted authority on neologisms), were mostly nineteenth-century hucksterish slogans. But the term catchphrase as it is now used has lost a lot of its original pejorative connotations.

Some of the entries here provide historical detail about frequently misunderstood catchphrases. For instance, Humphrey Bogart's character Rick Blaine never said "play it again, Sam" in the movie *Casablanca*. He actually said "Sing it, Sam. Sam, Sam, play that song for me again, will you?" But, never mind, the catchphrase has become "play it again, Sam." Other entries began as advertising slogans and made their way into other contexts, such as "I'd walk a mile for a camel." Some entries have mostly nostalgic value and will not be understood in a few years without the help of dictionaries like this, such as "have gun, will travel." If you do not watch television you will be clueless about recent catchphrases such as "yadda, yadda, yadda."

Catchphrases are often related to a number of similar and sometimes overlapping verbal categories such as clichés, metaphors, idioms, slogans, quotations, sayings, and proverbs. Since there are numerous specialized dictionaries for each of these categories there is inevitable double coverage between entries in this dictionary and these others. But there is one very similar dictionary, compiled by the Englishman Nigel Rees, which seems to include more British than American phrases titled the *Dictionary of Catchphrases* (see ARBA 96, entry 1084). There is little overlap between these two books. This dictionary is fun to browse as well as potentially quite useful for reference.—**David Isaacson**

Thesauri

C, P

360.   Kipfer, Barbara Ann. **Roget's Descriptive Word Finder: A Dictionary/Thesaurus of Adjectives.** Cincinnati, Ohio, Writer's Digest Books/F & W Publications, 2003. 457p. $24.99. ISBN 1-58297-170-6.

People typically turn to a thesaurus to find a substitute for a word that they feel is a cliché or that does not express their meaning as precisely as they would like. It is a safe guess there are many more people in the first category than the second. Discriminating writers know that most thesauri must be taken not simply with a grain of salt, but also with a granular saline substance. Actually, what I have just demonstrated is the error undiscriminating synonym finders make when they are not attentive to the nuances between words and expressions that are only nominally similar. You just cannot willy-nilly substitute the pompous mouthful "granular saline substance" for the cliché "grain of salt."

This thesaurus claims to solve this problem for the user because of two features: it is arranged not arbitrarily by the alphabet but sensibly by conceptual category, and it includes brief definitions of the synonymous words so that discriminations are easier to make. This is fine if the user chooses the right category to begin with. But there is still a problem with this book: the reader uncertain of the context needs to be cautioned to consult a good dictionary for further information about the word he or she is thinking of using as a synonym. For instance, under the category of "Receptacle - Receiving" some of the choices are common words like "given: presented as a gift," "unbestowed: not given," and "secondhand: received after use by another." But some of the other choices would only be viable alternatives in very rare contexts: "camerated: provided with chambers," "polygastric: provided with many stomachs," and "suscipient: receiving as an effect or influence." This book needs to be used with caution, if not also considerable solicitude. [R: LJ, 1 June 03, p. 106]—**David Isaacson**

C, P, S

361.   **Webster's New Explorer Dictionary of Synonyms & Antonyms.** Darien, Conn., Federal Street Press, 2003. 443p. $8.98. ISBN 1-892859-47-5.

Webster's New Explorer Dictionary of Synonyms & Antonyms joins a long line of thesaurus-like references with the specific aim of providing users with the "precisely suitable word for a particular purpose." Containing more than 4,800 entries, this volume lists a word, then either lists and describes the meaning of its synonyms or refers the reader to another main entry word. For example, the word "bewitch" is followed by "SEE attract." The entry for "attract" lists "allure, charm, captivate, fascinate, bewitch, enchant." Each word is further defined and an example of its use is given, along with its antonym, if any. The entry for "bewitch" reads: "implies exertion of an overwhelming power of attraction *bewitched by the promise of great wealth*." The book also contains thousands of cross-reference entries.

One possible problem with *Webster's New Explorer Dictionary of Synonyms & Antonyms* is its general lack of part-of-speech labels. The book jacket claims "Part of speech labels help with word selection," but they are few and far between. One single-word entry, "bough," refers the user to "shoot," which is defined as a part of a plant. There is no synonym for "shoot" as a verb. Most of the entries are nouns, but some adjectives ("sharp, keen, acute") and verbs ("jerk, snap, twitch, yank") are also defined.

Webster's New Explorer Dictionary of Synonyms & Antonyms is printed on pulp-like paper, thus making it light to carry and relatively inexpensive. Its emphasis on shadings of meanings would probably be more valuable to native English speakers who need something more than a dictionary to help them find a precise word.—**Kay O. Cornelius**

Visual

P

362.   **5 Language Visual Dictionary.** New York, DK Publishing, 2003. 400p. illus. index. $30.00. ISBN 0-7894-8439-0.

In many ways, this is a very impressive publication. It is produced along the lines of the famous Duden pictorial dictionaries. Lavishly illustrated, printed on heavy coated stock, it covers a lot of ground. There is hardly any activity or area of endeavor that is not covered. A general (illustrated, of course) index in the front of the book directs the user to each specific section. A five-language index in the back of the book (arranged in the following order: English, French, German, Spanish, Italian) lets the user find a specific word and its place in the dictionary. A glue gun, for instance, can be found on page 78 and its Spanish equivalent is "la pistola per colla." There are many advantages for the students of foreign languages in this volume, but there is one glaring omission: lack of pronunciation. I spent quite a while wondering who this book would be useful for. It is a heavy book, so a salesman dealing with foreign countries would probably not choose to have it in his or her suitcase. Would it be useful as an aide-memoire for people already proficient in five languages or as a quick look-up for radio and television announcers? Whatever its usefulness, it is a delightful browse through hundreds (1,600, to be exact) colorful images and their meanings.—**Koraljka Lockhart**

NON-ENGLISH-LANGUAGE DICTIONARIES

Arabic

C, P

363.   Bateson, Mary Catherine. **Arabic Language Handbook.** Washington, D.C., Georgetown University Press, 2003. 127p. (Georgetown Classics in Arabic Language and Linguistics). $22.50pa. ISBN 0-87840-386-8.

First published in 1967, Bateson's classic work has been reprinted to fill a gap in currently available materials on analysis of Arabic language and linguistics. This streamlined resource is broad in scope, covering basic structure of Arabic as well as linguistic topics. Short sections on historical and current forms of classical and colloquial Arabic, dialects, and literature and writing systems are illustrative of the numerous subjects covered. The reprinted volume includes some supplemental updates, such as a new introduction, a map of Arabic-speaking counties in Africa and the Middle East, and additional bibliographic entries. Students and researchers with a need for a basic handbook on the foundations of Arabic will appreciate the thoroughness and extensive coverage provided.—**Ahmad Gamaluddin**

German

P

364. Jelden, Michael. **German-English, English-German Concise Dictionary.** New York, Hippocrene Books, 2003. 522p. $14.95. ISBN 0-7818-0857-X.

Michael Jelden is a linguist and the author of two earlier dictionaries. This dictionary, with a total of 14,000 entries, is compact yet informative. Its limited size leads to some omissions of terms in both languages, while many identical words (Japan, Luxemburg, computer, protest, menstruation) are included, presumably to confirm their commonness. The *Dictionary* provides a good basic introduction on grammar, the use of pronouns, nouns, verbs, and their conjugation, and sentence syntax, to mention only its main features. This gives the *Dictionary* a secondary but important role of teaching German as a language, especially so with its addition of simple information on the alphabet and pronunciation. Judicious use of abbreviations adds to the usefulness of this volume, while saving space. British and American terminologies are provided (lift, elevator; flat, apartment), and many geographical names are provided in the appendixes (not as "comprehensive" as claimed) for each of the languages, German and English. Flipping through the *Dictionary*, one cannot help but notice the large number of words that are similar or identical in both languages due to the original Saxon-derived content of the English language and to the contemporary trend toward international acceptance of many modern terms, mostly from English. The *Dictionary* is portable and easy to use by students of German, travelers, and business people.—**Bogdan Mieczkowski**

Spanish

C, P, S

365. **The Oxford Spanish Dictionary.** 3d ed. Beatriz Galimberti Jarman, Roy Russell, Carol Styles Carvajal, and Jane Horwood, eds. New York, Oxford University Press, 2003. 1977p. $49.95. ISBN 0-19-860475-0.

The most recent successor to the revised 2d edition (1998) of this standard reference work, this massive yet affordable volume is quite probably the most clearly laid out and comprehensive Spanish dictionary currently available, containing some 300,000 words and phrases and 500,000 translations. Nearly 10,000 new terms have been added, selected through a search of the Internet for new words and terms not included in previous editions, as well as via input from a team of readers in both Spanish- and English-speaking countries. All 24 varieties of spoken Spanish are covered, with information in each entry indicating the country or region where the term is commonly used, making it easy for readers to identify the context of a term that may have several local meanings in addition to its standard definition. Content emphasis is on modern idioms and colloquial usage. The new color layout is easily navigated, with opening sections presenting the structure of the entries outlining how the volume's coverage of individual terms is to be read and guides to the pronunciation of both English and Spanish for native speakers of other languages. Interspersed throughout the text are cultural notes providing background to augment the basic dictionary entry as needed. An unusual feature is the guide to correspondence, which offers sample letters in a range of contexts from professional business writing to travel. The final section of the dictionary offers tables of Spanish verbs and *los verbos irregulars ingleses*, together with an index to the boxes on grammatical topics and details of daily life, such as forms of address and telephone use distributed through the dictionary. This work is recommended for all libraries.—**Robert B. Marks Ridinger**

24 Literature

GENERAL WORKS

Bio-bibliography

C

366. Dean, Katharine A., Miriam Conteh-Morgan, and James K. Bracken. **The Undergraduate's Companion to Women Writers and Their Web Sites.** Westview, Conn., Libraries Unlimited/Greenwood Publishing Group, 2002. 182p. index. (Undergraduate Companion Series). $29.95pa. ISBN 1-56308-935-1.

This bibliographic volume contains references to both print and free electronic resources and provides a rich source of information that undergraduates may use to write reports on women writers associated with the fields of women's studies, African American studies, comparative studies, history, and literature. Sources often include brief annotations.

The 180 women selected for inclusion wrote in English from medieval to modern times. They reflect diverse social, cultural, religious, and ethnic experiences. Included are writers featured in some standard literary reference works and other genre-based titles and series found in academic and large public libraries and for whom at least one Website exists.

The names of authors are arranged in alphabetic order. A list of names, including birth and death dates, is placed before the main body of the work, as are lists of frequently cited Websites and frequently cited references. The body of the work contains listings of available sources in the categories of Websites; biography and criticism; dictionaries, encyclopedias, and handbooks; journals; and bibliographies. Depending on the amount of information available, individual entries vary from less than a half page to approximately two pages. An index to authors concludes the work.

Strategies for research based on the guidelines adapted from the Association of College and Research Libraries (ACRL) document "Information Literacy Competency Standards for Higher Education" are provided by the authors. That the authors tried to think like undergraduates as they compiled this volume is evident by the types of sources included, and even in the arrangement of the sources. Listed first, for example, are Websites, because of the tendency that young researchers have to search the Web first. Sites were carefully selected for relevancy and also, apparently, for some degree of permanence. Sites listed for an author studied in some depth by this reviewer are all still active. This valuable resource is very modestly priced and should be widely available in academic and public libraries.—**Lois Gilmer**

Biography

C, P

367.   Sharrock, Alison, and Rhiannon Ash. **Fifty Key Classical Authors.** New York, Routledge/Taylor & Francis Group, 2002. 421p. index. (Routledge Key Guides). $60.00; $19.95pa. ISBN 0-415-16510-5; 0-415-16511-3pa.

General surveys of classical literature are rare. Most collections speak to an academic audience and focus on one theme, such as cross-cultural stories or imagery. This reference work, in contrast, not only educates lay readers, but also entertains them. Most of the popular authors are included. However, a few authors (such as Marcus Aurelius) often found in anthologies have been omitted, and one unusual entry, a brief discussion of the half dozen poems—and the disputed gender—of Sulpicia, is included. Reading lists, a timeline, and a detailed subject index also make this reference useful for the high school or undergraduate student. Each short chapter (2 to 15 pages) combines biography and literary criticism, with much terminology, such as "epigram," defined within the text. Little text itself appears in the discussion, although the reading lists do name the collections (in Greek, Latin, or translation) available for each author. Readers who wish to avoid trekking to the reference shelves for the lengthier discussions of the Dictionary of Literary Biography's series *Ancient Roman Writers* and *Ancient Greek Authors* will enjoy this accessible and portable encyclopedia of classical writers. This work is recommended for public, school, and academic libraries.—**Nancy L. Van Atta**

C

368.   **Who's Who in Contemporary Women's Writing.** 2d ed. Jane Eldridge Miller, ed. New York, Routledge/Taylor & Francis Group, 2002. 385p. (Routledge Who's Who Series). $14.95pa. ISBN 0-415-15981-4.

This is a compact guide to hundreds of international women writers. Most of the world's countries are represented. Most of the entries are for fiction, drama, and poetry writers but some are writers of literary nonfiction and critics. Some writers of popular fiction, such as romance and thrillers, are included but most of the entries are for literary fiction. The editor defines contemporary as writers who (usually) began their careers in the 1960s or later.

Many writers will be little known to American or British readers. With a few exceptions, each writer had to have at least one book translated into English. Selection criteria were broader for women in countries other than the United States, Britain, and Canada because one of the major purposes of this guide is to represent writers from less-developed countries.

The alphabetic entries are brief and non-evaluative, usually about 200 words, combining key biographical facts with descriptions of major works and themes. Such evaluation as exists is mostly implicit rather than explicit: the fact that a writer has been selected for inclusion constitutes a recommendation. The book is intended only an introduction; a bibliography lists sources for further study. An appendix groups writers by nationality.

As long as the reader knows there are more extensive biographical and literary reference sources for more information, at least about the canonical writers covered here, this volume serves its purpose of acting as a brief introduction to many perhaps otherwise neglected contemporary women writers all over the world.—**David Isaacson**

C, P

369.   **The Writers Directory 2004.** 19th ed. Miranda H. Ferrara, ed. Farmington Hills, Mich., St. James Press/Gale Group, 2003. 2v. index. $215.00/set. ISBN 1-55862-487-2. ISSN 0084-2699.

The Writers Directory 2004 is the 19th edition of a 2-volume set designed to provide information about writers from all countries of the world who have had at least one work published in English. The current version lists over 19,700 writers writing under over 21,000 names. The chosen writers range from best-selling fiction authors and prominent nonfiction writers to some just beginning their career. This section includes nearly 1,200 writers whose listings are new to this edition. In addition, an "Obituaries" section lists 230 formerly included writers who are no longer living.

Each entry in *The Writers Directory 2004* contains some or all of the following information: the writer's name and pseudonyms; birthplace and nationality; birth year; genres; career information; publications (title, year of publication, if a pseudonym is used, special awards); and address, e-mail, and Website. The methods used to determine who should be listed are not disclosed, but suggestions for writers to be included in future editions are invited to be sent to the editors, who are the final arbiters.

Casual readers are more likely to find their favorite authors in *Current Biography* than *The Writers Directory 2004*. However, serious researchers should welcome the wealth of information in these volumes. —**Kay O. Cornelius**

Chronology

C, P
370.   Kurian, George Thomas. **Timetables of World Literature.** New York, Facts on File, 2003. 457p. index. (Facts on File Library of World Literature). $65.00. ISBN 0-8160-4197-0.

This book is a collection of tables of names providing both general readers and scholars with a quick way to place literary authors and works in time. Seven large time periods are included, beginning with the Classical Age (up to 100 C.E.) and continuing through the year 2000. Some 12,000 works of literature by 9,800 authors from 58 countries in 41 languages are included. Besides the major genres—fiction, drama, poetry, and essays—there are ballads, autobiography, romance, science fiction, and other less major genres represented.

A work like this has to be selective, but some lesser-known works and authors are included besides the canonical ones. Each section begins with a brief overview of important literary developments in that age, followed by capsule biographies of major writers. Instead of being arranged alphabetically, Kurian lists these writers "in order of prominence." This reader would have appreciated a rationale for this order. One can only guess why, for instance, the list for the twentieth century, has the following as its top 10, in descending order of importance: Joyce, Kafka, Eliot, Yeats, Mann, Shaw, Hemingway, O'Neill, Tagore, and Brecht.

Notable literary events are listed for individual years after 1500. Each year includes a list of births and deaths of authors followed by a list of important literary events, such as the founding of significant literary magazines and significant awards, such as the Nobel, Pulitzer, and Booker Prizes. Each section also lists prominent publications for each year arranged alphabetically by the language in which the work was originally published, followed by another list of publications by nationality. In some cases, language and nationality overlap, but a writer like Nabokov is hard to classify because he published works in both Russian and English.

For precise known-item searching there are four indexes. Authors are listed both by name and by nationality. Publications are indexed by title, language, and also grouped by genre. [R: LJ, 1 June 03, p. 106; SLJ, Dec 03, p. 96]—**David Isaacson**

Dictionaries and Encyclopedias

C
371.   **Cyclopedia of Literary Places.** R. Kent Rasmussen, ed. Hackensack, N.J., Salem Press, 2003. 3v. index. $290.00/set. ISBN 1-58765-094-0.

While many literary reference works provide critical summaries, analyses of characters, and overviews of writers, this is the first devoted to the role of place in literature. It covers approximately 6,000 places in 1,304 novels, short stories, plays, and poems selected from the titles in Salem Press's *Masterplots* (2d ed.; see ARBA 97, entry 906), with the entries ranging from 300 to 1,000 words.

The goal of the 311 contributors is not to describe the places but to show how place matters within a work and how it functions as literary device. Thus Robin Hill in *The Forsyte Saga* represents Soames Forsyte's inability to exert control over all aspects of his life, and Pamplona in *The Sun Also Rises* is significant as the place where all the novel's elements reach a crisis. The places discussed range from countries, regions, states, cities, and towns to neighborhoods, buildings, and rooms. In addition to New York City and Newport, settings for *The Age of Innocence* include the homes of the major characters. The places under discussion may be real (indicated by an asterisk) or imaginary, as with Toad Hall and the unnamed river in *The Wind in the Willows*.

Each entry includes the type of work, type and time of plot, publication date, and a two-sentence overview followed by the analysis. The three volumes also include "An Introduction to Place in Literature" by Brian Stableford of King Alfred's College; a key to pronunciation; and title, author, and place-name indexes. The index entry for London includes Blackfriars Bridge, Blackfriars Bridge Road, Bloomsbury, and Bloomsbury Street. Each of these locations is also listed separately in the index.

This unique work is valuable for those researching the roles played by literary places and for those simply interested in a guide to these locations, and it also complements the other titles in the Masterplots series. [R: LJ, 15 June 03, p. 60; SLJ, Oct 03, p. 108]—**Michael Adams**

C, P

372.   **Encyclopedia of World Writers: 19th and 20th Centuries.** Marie Josephine Diamond, ed. New York, Facts on File, 2003. 512p. index. (Facts on File Library of World Literature). $75.00. ISBN 0-8160-4675-1.

For libraries that already have a wide variety of bio-bibliographic dictionaries and encyclopedias about world authors, such as *Encyclopedia of Continental Women Writers* (see ARBA 92, entry 1232), *Encyclopedia of World Literature in the Twentieth Century* (see ARBA 2000, entry 932), *Nineteenth Century Literature Criticism* (Gale Group), *Contemporary Authors* (Gale Group), *Contemporary Literary Criticism* (Gale Group), and *Twentieth-Century Literary Criticism* (Gale Group), this volume is an optional purchase. However, it is a nice one-volume survey of world authors, intended for "young readers" of high school and college age. It covers several hundred authors from all over the world, and is most useful for its coverage of third world authors. The focus is on authors who lived or worked during the previous two centuries.

Length of entries varies with the importance of the author, but even the most important receive little more than a page. Entries contain a biographical sketch and sometimes a "critical analysis." One or two works of the author and one work about the author are cited. There are occasional topical entries on subjects like "Aboriginal movement" and "classicism." In addition to a list of authors with their birth and death dates, there is also a list by geographical area, an 18-page selected bibliography, and a 29-page index by subject that is very helpful in getting at authors from a specific location, or by specific written works.

The print here is quite readable and the appearance of the page is pleasant. This is not an in-depth, scholarly work, but for a quick overview of world authors from K. A. Abbas (India) to Emile Zola (France). This is a handy volume and makes for enjoyable and informative reading. Its price will limit its accessibility almost exclusively to libraries.—**Bill Miller**

C

373.   **Holocaust Literature: An Encyclopedia of Writers and Their Works.** S. Lillian Kremer, ed. New York, Routledge, 2003. 2v. index. $250.00/set. ISBN 0-415-92985-7.

Making sense of the Holocaust is a difficult task. Literature of all types written by those who were involved as victims or survivors or by second and third generation descendants is an attempt to come to terms with the horrible events of 1933-1945. This new encyclopedia examines the work of more than 300 memoirists, poets, novelists, dramatists, philosophers, and theorists. Over 120 contributors from 60 universities in North and South America, Europe, Israel, and Australia, interpreting the literature from different points of view, have written essays for the set. The interdisciplinary approach seeks to understand the historical events and comment on the specific cultural contexts of the writing as well as the critical reception of the authors' works.

The encyclopedia begins with an overview essay that discusses the critical and theoretical aspects of Holocaust literature and its cultural themes. The alphabetic author entries that follow include brief biographical information as well as an examination of the writer's history and interest, the major themes in his or her work, how the work contributes to the understanding of the Holocaust, and the stylistic representations. Each entry has a bibliography of primary and selected secondary sources. The authors included are diverse: Hannah Arendt, Yehudah Amichai, Saul Bellow, Gerda Weissmann Klein, Gunter Grass, Nelly Sachs, Franz Werfel, and Rajzel Zychlinsky are examples. They represent all literary genres and come from a variety of cultures and nationalities. Their writing represents the literature of witness, mourning, mediating trauma, and the implications of the Holocaust on post-war thought.

A series of appendices offers lists of ghettoes, concentration camps, historical figures, and key events that appear in the literature. There are also indexes by authors' birthplaces and language of composition as well as a comprehensive general index. *Holocaust Literature* is more comprehensive and has more detailed coverage than the *Encyclopedia of Holocaust Literature* (see ARBA 2003, entry 520). It is an excellent source for academic libraries supporting Holocaust studies and comparative literature programs. [R: LJ, 15 April 03, p. 72; AG, June 03, p. 64]—**Barbara M. Bibel**

Directories

P
374.　**The Europa Directory of Literary Awards and Prizes.** Florence, Ky., Europa Publications/Taylor & Francis Group, 2002. 518p. index. $225.00. ISBN 1-85743-146-4.

Current reference works on literary awards found in libraries today usually concentrate on individual awards, such as the Newbery Medal award or Caldecott Medal award. Others will specify categories, such as children's literature of genres such as science fiction. Now, thanks to Europa Publications, we have the first international directory of just about all literary awards and prizes in existence. Since there are so many, the editors have decided to exclude small local awards, specialized awards, and awards for journalism.

This work lists more than 1,000 awards, some of which are brand new, from 70 countries. Prior to the actual entries, there is a list of abbreviations used and a table of currencies and exchange rates. Each main entry contains the same categories of information. After a short description of each award, there are sections for eligibility and restriction, how to apply for the award, recent winners of the award, the sponsoring organization, and contact information (including fax numbers and Websites and e-mail addresses when available). The awards are listed alphabetically, but any award named after a person will be listed alphabetically by surname. This means you will find the Coretta Scott King Award under "K." The main body of entries is followed by a number of indexes. The index of awards this time will list surnames first, with *see* references. This is followed by an index of awarding organizations, an index of awards by country, and finally, an index of awards by subject.

Normally, I would enthusiastically recommend any reference book that was as well organized as this one, and covered new territory as well. The prohibitive cost of this work, however, may make reference librarians think twice in these times of budget cuts.—**Richard Slapsys**

Handbooks and Yearbooks

P, S
375.　Galens, Judy. **Experiencing the Holocaust: Novels, Nonfiction Books, Short Stories, Poems, Plays, Films & Music.** Edited by Sarah Hermsen. Farmington Hills, Mich., U*X*L/Gale, 2003. 2v. illus. index. (Experiencing Eras and Events). $95.00/set. ISBN 0-7876-5414-0.

Teaching junior high and high school age students to appreciate history is not easy due to the overwhelming need to relay facets of these events other than just dates and facts. History is a story, a series of interlinked pieces of a social framework coming together to form a story and its ongoing interpretation. In this regard, Judy Galens and Sarah Hermsen have provided us with a suitable guide to the history of the Holocaust in their work *Experiencing the Holocaust.*

This work's coverage lends itself well to the study of this period. The editors arrange their coverage by specific literary type—novels, nonfiction books, short stories, poems, plays, films, and music. Within each section, they have selected leading sources for consideration and analyzed them for background and social context. Each essay has a works cited list for further reading. In addition, the introduction provides a good background for the events described in the literary works discussed later. The absence of the works within the text is troubling. In this regard, the teacher will want the students to read the original works as well. That word of caution aside, this is a great work for introducing students to Holocaust studies. It also sets students up for the right method of historical analysis and research. The author did a great job of incorporating those elements into this text. Hopefully, other texts like this one will soon follow. This work is recommended for high school, public, and community colleges libraries.—**David J. Duncan**

C

376.   **Women in Literature: Reading Through the Lens of Gender.** Jerilyn Fisher and Ellen S. Silber, eds. Westport, Conn., Greenwood Press, 2003. 358p. illus. $65.00. ISBN 0-313-31346-6.

Women in Literature makes feminist literary criticism accessible to teachers who want to include gender issues in their classroom discussions. Essays, 3 pages in length, examine a total of 96 literary works and provide references for further reading. Most of the works are novels, but plays by Sophocles, Shakespeare, Shaw, and Miller and Anne Frank's *Diary of a Young Girl* are included. Diverse works by male and female authors from world and American literatures span the centuries from Homer's *Odyssey* to Morrison's *Beloved.*

One or more of the female characters in each work are examined to show their place in society and how they relate to the male characters. Practical suggestions follow to help students compare and reflect on the relevance of such literature to their own lives. Contributing authors are well-credentialed teachers and scholars. The editors' resulting list of titles chosen from high school reading lists, college syllabi, and recommendations from teacher's and women's studies scholars is a worthy contribution to the much debated "what should be read by students today?" One source, "The P.A.C.T. Program—Reading List" from McREL is no longer available at the URL listed (p. xxvii).

The arrangement is alphabetical by titles of the works, followed by an author index and a very useful, detailed subject index. A "Thematic List of Books" groups each of the titles into one or more of 30 different themes, such as "Young Boys and Adolescents" or "Female Characters that Challenge Gender Stereotypes." This unique book will be a valuable addition to libraries supporting secondary school teachers, college literature professors, student teachers, and librarians building a collection of feminist criticism. [R: LJ, 1 Oct 03, p. 66]—**Patricia Rothermich**

CHILDREN'S AND YOUNG ADULT LITERATURE

Bibliography

P, S

377.   **Awards and Prizes Online. http://awardsandprizes.org.** [Website]. New York, Children's Book Council. Price negotiated by site. Date reviewed: Oct 03.

This Website from Children's Book Council features winners of nearly 300 literary awards from the award's inception to 2003 winners. The latest update as of October 2003 provided awards for 70 new awards, which increased the size of the database by 20 percent. The site currently features over 6,500 books, nearly 5,000 authors, and over 700 publishers. The site features well-known, annual awards, such as the Caldecott Medal and the Coretta Scott King Awards, as well as literary awards that have been discontinued.

The site is searchable with a basic search function and an advanced search function. The basic search feature allows the user to put in the name of the award they would like to research or browse through all awards. Awards have been grouped under one of four headings: Adult-Selected Awards; Young-Reader-Selected or Children's Choice Awards; Australia, Canadian, New Zealand, and United Kingdom Awards; and International Awards. The advanced search feature allows users to narrow their search or to search for awards or award winners they may be unfamiliar with. This feature allows the user to search by author, award title, book title, compiler, editor, illustrator, publisher, year, age group, and/or keyword. For each award the following information is provided: a description of the award, the name of the award sponsor, address of the award sponsor, contact name, a complete list of winners, publisher and publication date of title, and publisher information.

The site is updated on a quarterly basis, which allows the Children's Book Council to update it with the latest winners as well as update it with newly found literary awards. This is truly a convenient, comprehensive source for information about children's literary awards. It is recommended for any library needing this type of information—public, academic, and school media centers.—**Shannon Graff Hysell**

P, S
378. Bodart, Joni Richards. **Radical Reads: 101 YA Novels on the Edge.** Lanham, Md., Scarecrow, 2002. 376p. index. $34.95pa. ISBN 0-8108-4287-4.

As a source for the analysis of young adult literature, *Radical Reads*, edited by Joni Richards Bodart, brings together a series of book reviews on controversial subjects that are germane to the lives of teenagers. Substance abuse, abortion, sexual abuse, and gender issues are just a few of the topics that are contained in this review of more than 101 young adult titles. Reviews are arranged alphabetically by title followed by a concise yet thorough overview of the young adult literature in question. Although the target audience of this one-volume handbook is teachers and librarians, this work also contains tips for students on how to do an effective book report or booktalk. *Radical Reads* also provides valuable information on such issues as censorship and dealing with any book challenges that may arise from the presence of these books on your shelves. Of the many bibliographic resource tools that anyone can have, this work is a must for librarians, teachers, and the general public who wish to promote the best in young adult literature.
—**Patrick Hall**

P, S
379. Gillespie, John T., and Catherine Barr. **Best Books for Children: Preschool Through Grade 6. Supplement to the Seventh Edition.** Westport, Conn., Libraries Unlimited/Greenwood Publishing Group, 2003. 509p. index. $35.00. ISBN 1-59158-082-X.

Catherine Barr joins John Gillespie as coauthor/editor of this extensive work (first published in 1978), which is intended to be used as a selection tool, collection evaluation tool, to give guidance to children, and as a resource for the preparation of bibliographies. Editions are normally published at four-year intervals (7th ed.; see ARBA 2002, entry 1063), but the authors have produced this supplement listing 5,662 entries and an additional 430 cited titles to cover the two years since the 7th edition, in response to customers' suggestions. This supplement is organized in the same way as the 7th edition and uses the same subject headings. Major sections include "Literature," "Biography," "The Arts and Language," "History and Geography," "Social Institutions and Issues," "Personal Development," "Physical and Applied Sciences," and "Recreation." "Major Subjects Arranged Alphabetically" lists the ranges of entry numbers for 59 subject areas. Author/illustrator, title, and subject/grade level indexes are provided. Each entry includes author or editor, title, grade levels, adapter or translator, illustrator or indication of illustrations, series title, date of publication, publisher, price, ISBN, a short annotation, review citations, and Dewey classification. The preface lists the review sources from which titles are chosen and the criteria used for selection. Extensive and well organized, this title is the best current children's literature bibliography this reviewer has seen. Every edition should be considered an essential purchase for elementary school libraries and children's departments of public libraries.—**Rosanne M. Cordell**

P, S

380.   Herald, Diana Tixier. **Teen Genreflecting: A Guide to Reading Interests.** 2d ed. Westport, Conn., Libraries Unlimited/Greenwood Publishing Group, 2003. 251p. index. (Genreflecting Advisory Series). $40.00. ISBN 1-56308-996-3.

The 2d edition of *Teen Genreflecting* differs from the 1st edition (see ARBA 98, entry 1096) in several respects. Publication dates, reading levels, and awards are noted; more explanation of the various genres is included; and books may be cross-referenced under more than one genre. Several changes were made in the way the genres are delineated. Romance is no longer treated as a separate genre, but romance novels are included under all genres. The author considers "Issues" (novels having to do with themes such as teenage pregnancy, racism, and disabilities) as distinct from "Contemporary Life" (novels dealing with themes such as coming of age, romance, and sports). A separate category now exists for "Multicultural Fiction," including both works about characters from ethnic minority groups and books about clashing cultures. Christian fiction, encompassing works from other genres, such as "Adventure," "Mystery," and "Contemporary Life," is a category used for books that carry a Christian orientation and message. Finally, a new category, "Alternative Formats," was added to cover nontraditional formats, such as novels in verse, graphic novels, and fictional diaries.

This edition takes into account both the changes in the publishing industry and in the reading preferences of the teenage audience. It is valuable both for the professionals who select books for teenagers and for teenagers who might be looking for certain types of books. As in the case of the previous edition, this book would be more useful if publisher and price information were included.—**Jeanne D. Galvin**

P, S

381.   **Horn Book Guide Online. http://gem.greenwood.com.** [Website]. Westport, Conn., Greenwood Press. $150.00-$300.00. Date reviewed: Dec 03.

Horn Book Guide Online provides a clean and easy transformation of the venerable print publication into electronic format. In the transfer all the reviews from 1989 forward were compiled (over 51,000), more entry points for searching were added, and, sadly, images were removed. The online entries are exact translations of those brief annotations in the paper format and include the same rating system. The database, like the print version, is updated twice a year, in the Spring and Fall.

Searching is offered in both basic and advanced formats. A basic search includes keyword (titles, subject, and reviews), author/illustrator, title, series (mostly juvenile nonfiction), publisher, rating, and grade level. The grade level choices may be a bit frustrating to some as they are set and cannot be adapted to meet local norms. Advanced searching expands upon basic search to allow an author search limited by editor, reteller, illustrator, photographer, or translator. Reviews can be searched by title or subject, which is accessed via a hyperlink. In addition, searches can be constructed to include ISBN, genre, year of the publication of the review, and either fiction or nonfiction. The database can also be browsed in an A-Z format by author, illustrator, or subject. Author and illustrator links go to the same book entry. Subjects can be a bit idiosyncratic but are easily searched; for example, World War II is under history rather than its own entry.

The power and options of the search engine makes the *Horn Book Guide Online* useful as a selection and readers' advisory tool. Search results can be saved in lists that include title information only or title and review information so that librarians can build both reading lists (based on a host of the search options) or selection lists. New to the online version is a list of Caldecott winners (from 1989 onward) and Newbery winners (from 1990 onward).

For those that use the print version of *The Horn Book Guide* infrequently and have other ways of building selection and reading lists, the online version will offer very little that cannot be obtained by thumbing through the print version. However, for those that use the print version extensively or need access to readers' advisory and selection tools for youth material, the electronic version should be a welcomed and much-used resource. [R: SLJ, May 02, p. 100; BR, Sept/Oct 02, p. 82]—**Neal Wyatt**

P, S

382.   LiBretto, Ellen V., and Catherine Barr. **High/Low Handbook: Best Books and Web Sites for Reluctant Teen Readers.** 4th ed. Greenwood Village, Colo., Libraries Unlimited/Greenwood Publishing Group, 2002. 231p. index. $48.00. ISBN 0-313-32276-7.

The 4th edition of this title presents over 500 of the best new titles for teens aged 12-18 who read below grade level or who are reluctant readers. High/low is defined as reading levels at the grades 1 to 5 levels. Section 1 provides a core collection of 426 high/low fiction and nonfiction books and Websites with an additional 100 titles mentioned within the main entries. These titles are arranged alphabetically by author under topics such as dating, friendship, gangs, and biographies. The numbered entries include standard bibliographic information such as author, title, publisher, copyright date, number of pages, paperback or hardcover, price, ISBN, fiction or nonfiction, reading level, interest level, and accelerated reader status as well as a paragraph-length annotation. The copyright dates cluster between the late 1990s through 2002, although some titles are earlier. Publishers include Perfection Learning, Capstone, Globe Fearon, Rosen, and Morning Glory Press. Most titles run 25 to 75 pages in length, but some longer titles are also suggested. Section 2, arranged alphabetically by author, offers a list of "mainstream" young adult books and periodicals that would also appeal to the book's intended audience and supplement the core list. These titles receive only brief one- to two-sentence summaries. One appendix lists Web-based resources; the other, a high/low publishers list. There are separate author, title, and subject indexes. This is an excellent resource for readers' advisory and collection development.—**Esther R. Sinofsky**

P, S

383.   Stan, Susan. **The World Through Children's Books.** Lanham, Md., Scarecrow, 2002. 324p. index. $27.95pa. ISBN 0-8108-4198-3.

The first part of this book is composed of two chapters: "An Overview of International Children's Literature" and "Books as Bridges." The second chapter explains how to connect international books with children. Books written or set in other countries convey the culture of the author to children of a different culture. Written for educators to teach children about children from other countries, this chapter concludes with action programs, learning sites, and references. Part 2, the larger part of the book, is an annotated bibliography of titles from many different countries. In addition to the usual publishing information, the bibliography includes the age range of the target reader and awards received by the book. Annotations describing the works are followed by the initials of the annotators. A list of annotators is provided.

Books are not always published in the country in which an author lives, nor are the settings of books always in the country where the author lives. Entries, therefore, are generally listed under the author's home country and cross-listed in the appropriate places in the bibliography. The purpose of this book is to bring to the attention of America's children some of the best books from other parts of the world. American authors are not listed in a separate section of the book, but they may be listed under another country if they have written books with settings in other countries. According to the editor, in some instances the only books available in some countries were written by American authors. Listings in the bibliography are from Latin America and the Caribbean, Canada and the Far North, Asia, North Africa and the Middle East, Africa South of the Sahara, Australia and New Zealand, and Europe. Some books that are global in scope are also included.

Part 3, titled "Resources," contains children's book awards arranged by years the awards were presented, organizations that work on behalf of international literacy and children's literature, North American publishers with an international focus, and sources for foreign languages and bilingual books. These sources are useful in finding books that have not been published in the United States, as well as in locating the original language edition of a book published in translation or other books published by the same author or illustrator. The book concludes with an author/illustrator/translator index, a title index, a subject guide, and information about the editor. Librarians and teachers who work with children will find this book a valuable guide to the literature of different cultures.—**Lois Gilmer**

S

384.   Wright, Cora M. **More Hot Links: Linking Literature with the Middle School Curriculum.** Westport, Conn., Libraries Unlimited/Greenwood Publishing Group, 2002. 212p. index. $32.00pa. ISBN 1-56308-942-4.

Useful for teachers, parents, and media specialists alike, *More Hot Links* adds more than 300 informative annotations for fiction and nonfiction books to the earlier 300 Hot Links by the same author. Included are both contemporary and classic titles that support and enhance the middle school curriculum. Wright divides the publication into 18 chapters—with categories from English classics and fine arts to humor and sports and games. Her ties to children's literature (she is a middle school librarian and also teaches children's literature) are evident in the choices she includes. Titles chosen represent top-quality literature that ties into all areas of the curriculum, with a thematic arrangement. Selections are geared specifically for grades 5 through 9, but special categories actually encompass grades 4 through 10.

The books were chosen for the quality of writing, interest level, appropriateness of illustrations, and current availability. In addition, the book includes a chapter highlighting the best of newly published materials and a chapter featuring titles that are presented in a unique and creative manner. A "Literature Links" section in the back of the book offers an easy-to-read chart that explains exactly in which curricular areas a book can be used.

Standard subjects such as science, mathematics, social studies, and biographies are covered, as are more unique topics such as "Greatest of the Latest," "Picture Books for All Ages," "Multicultural," and "Series." Many of the books are multifaceted, allowing them to fit into more than one category, and when this occurs, the "most appropriate" category includes the main annotation, but a brief summary is also included in the other category as well. Wright provides fully annotated current titles with complete bibliographic information and cross-references, making this a valuable collection development tool. She includes a handy chart at the back of the book listing each title and its corresponding subject areas along with a detailed author/title index.—**Jill Rooker**

Bio-Bibliography

P, S

385.   Drew, Bernard A. **100 More Popular Young Adult Authors: Biographical Sketches and Bibliographies.** Westport, Conn., Libraries Unlimited/Greenwood Publishing Group, 2002. 379p. illus. index. (Popular Authors Series). $60.00. ISBN 1-56308-920-3.

This is a companion volume to the *100 Most Popular Young Adult Authors* published in 1996 (see ARBA 97, entry 941) with a revised edition in 1997 (see ARBA 98, entry 1102). Somewhat broader in scope than its predecessor, this volume features many less-well-known authors but also includes some older standard favorites, from Robert Louis Stevenson to the more recent Mary O'Hara and Laura Ingalls Wilder. It also adds some newly published authors, including perhaps the current most popular young people's writer, J. K. Rowling. None of the writers in this volume were covered in its predecessor. Readers are recommended to use the two volumes together. The entries, in alphabetic order, follow the same pattern as

Drew's earlier publications: for each author there is a brief biography, short summaries and critiques of major works, a list of all works by the author, and bibliographies of other sources of information.

The main stated purpose of this series is as a reference tool for teenagers looking for information about their favorite authors. Both teens and their educators were consulted in the series planning. The text has a very readable style with comments by the writers themselves about their experiences and their writing processes. However, as a previous reviewer observes, the main use will probably be by librarians and teachers as a selection aid rather than use by the young people themselves.

This series is recommended as a welcome addition to a young adult collection, although probably not the first choice for libraries with limited funds. The reviewer of the revised edition concludes that a more comprehensive selection may be the Something About the Author series from the Gale Group.—**Patricia A. Eskoz**

P, S
386.   Schon, Isabel. **The Best of Latino Heritage 1996-2002: A Guide to the Best Juvenile Books About Latino People and Cultures.** Lanham, Md., Scarecrow, 2003. 269p. index. $37.50. ISBN 0-8108-4669-1.

A straightforward guide to good reading, Schon's book is a boon to librarians, parents, and teachers who want to increase cultural awareness for readers. The insightful text is beautifully organized, beginning with an introduction explaining methods of inclusion and evaluation. A country-by-country method of arrangement presents works by author along with the essentials (size, ISBN, price, and grade level). The author specifies enough details to characterize each work, such as facts about Texas heroes in *Three Roads to the Alamo* and the particulars of folklore in *The Legend of Lord Eight Deer*.

Following the listings for 20 countries are a survey on series (e. g., Latinos in Baseball), and listings by author, title, subject, and grade level. Titles extend from reference works on female artists and biographies of sports figures to delightful works on food, entertainment, and family life. Subject areas are generous, including missing persons, alcoholism, dining, motorcycling, jungles, and Native Americans. Age categories begin with preschool and continue through high school and adult levels. Schon, an expert in her field, presents material with confidence in her selections. Book buyers can share her confidence in choosing the best in Latino literature.—**Mary Ellen Snodgrass**

DRAMA

C, S
387.   Abbotson, Susan C. W. **Thematic Guide to Modern Drama.** Westport, Conn., Greenwood Press, 2003. 292p. index. $50.00. ISBN 0-313-31950-2.

This is a thematic guide to 99 plays that range from the most commonly studied titles to those by more recent and multicultural dramatists. Modern drama began with the form breaking work of Ibsen, Shaw, and Strindberg who rejected the tidy package of the "well-made play" in favor of the more open-ended and participatory "discussion play." Plays discussed in this work range from *Death of a Salesman* to *Waiting for Godot* and from *The Diary of Anne Frank* to *Barefoot in the Park*. Writers span the age of Ibsen and Odets to Neil Simon and David Mamet. The work is arranged alphabetically based on 33 different themes, such as aging, courtship, death, growing up, war, and substance abuse. Each chapter addresses one theme as illuminated by three different plays. A basic introduction to the theme is included as is a list of further readings. An integrated index rounds out the work.

This is a very unique and useful approach to studying plays as it both illuminates a text and provides students with new ways of thinking about the play. The title is part of a series by Greenwood Press. Other subjects in the series include British and American poetry, popular short stories, the American novel, and Shakespeare's plays.—**Neal Wyatt**

C, P, S

388. **The Facts on File Companion to American Drama.** Jackson R. Bryer and Mary C. Hartig, eds. New York, Facts on File, 2004. 562p. index. (Facts on File Library of American Literature). $71.50. ISBN 0-8160-4665-4.

Alphabetically arranged, this outstanding handbook covers American plays and playwrights from the earliest years (Thomas Godfrey's *The Prince of Parthia* [1767] and Royall Tyler's *The Contrast* [1787]) to the most recently acclaimed (Tony Kushner's *Angels in America* [1990-1991] and Terrence McNally's *Love! Valor! Compassion!* [1994]). Each of the 600-plus entries, contributed by academic scholars, ranges from 500 to 1,500 words and gives a nicely balanced view of its subject. Important movements (e.g., African American drama, Asian American drama, group theater, performance art) and theater companies (e.g., The Theater Guild, Actors Studio, Circle Repertory Theater Company) are also treated, some with individual entries, others mentioned in context. The 10-page introduction is an excellent essay on the history of American drama. Two appendixes—"Winners of Major Drama Prizes" and a selected bibliography—are included, as well as a comprehensive index. This attractively formatted companion will be useful in academic, public, and high school libraries.—**Charles R. Andrews**

FICTION

General Works

Bibliography

P

389. **What Do I Read Next? A Reader's Guide to Current Genre Fiction. Volume 1.** 2003 ed. Farmington Hills, Mich., Gale, 2003. 699p. index. $145.00. ISBN 0-7876-6181-3. ISSN 1032-2212.

Begun in 1991, this annual publication is, since 2000, issued in two volumes per year. Volume 1 appears mid-year and volume 2 in October. The present volume (volume 1 of the 2003 edition) covers books published during the last half of 2002; volume 2 covers the first half of 2003. The main body of this over-sized book gives details on 1,245 adult-level titles and is divided into 9 sections, each edited by a subject expert and each dealing with a different genre in fiction. In order of the size of coverage, the genres are: mystery (92 pages), romance (66 pages), popular fiction (52 pages), historical fiction (50 pages), horror (32 pages), inspirational fiction (30 pages), westerns (30 pages), science fiction (28 pages), and fantasy (28 pages). Each section is preceded by a well-written, informative overview of publishing in that genre with material on trends, important reference works, awards and prizes, and a list of the 25 top books published in this 6 month period. Each book entry includes a brief plot summary, plus material on subjects, major characters, locales, review citations, other books by the same author, and an unannotated listing of four or five similar books by different authors. A special feature is the extensive indexing. The author and title indexes include both the main entry books as well as authors and titles listed within entries. The main entry titles are also indexed by subject, series, genre, time period, geographic setting, and character name and description (e.g., accountant, actor, alien). Like previous volumes, this current edition is an interesting, well-edited volume that is highly recommended for all public libraries that do extensive readers' advisory work and can afford the cost. A CD-ROM version and online edition are also available.—**John T. Gillespie**

Handbooks and Yearbooks

C, P

390.   Burt, Daniel S. **The Novel 100: A Ranking of the Greatest Novels of All Time.** New York, Facts on File, 2004. 468p. index. (Facts on File Library of World Literature). $45.00. ISBN 0-8160-4557-7.

This work, written by a university professor of English, serves as a suitable companion to the author's earlier *The Literary 100: A Ranking of the Most Influential Novelists, Playwrights, and Poets of All Time* (see ARBA 2002, entry 1050). In the present volume, he fearlessly chooses and annotates what he believes to be "the most significant novels of all time" (introduction). The novels are entered in order of importance and the choices are both judicious and fairly predictable. For example, the top five are, in order, *Don Quixote*, *War and Peace*, *Ulysses*, *In Search of Lost Time*, and *The Brothers Karamazov*; *Gone with the Wind* squeaks in as number 100. There are a few surprises, however, like Alfred Doblin's *Berlin Alexanerplatz* in 70th place and Andrey Bely's *Petersburg* at 55. About one-half of the novels are twentieth-century works. Each entry is accompanied by an interesting, nontechnical essay of four or five pages that usually contains some biographical facts about the author, information on the genesis of the novel and its critical reception, a brief plot summary, and material on stylistic qualities and reasons for the work's lasting importance. Appendixes include the novels arranged chronologically, and a section on "also rans" (a list of 100 additional novels of quality, which are arranged by author not rank). There is also an author/title index, but no bibliographies.

For more in-depth material including full plots and character analyses for many of the same titles at a fraction of the cost ($9.95) consult W. John Campbell's *The Book of Great Books: A Guide to 100 World Classics* (Barnes and Noble, 2000). Burt's volume, however, provides interesting introductions to these great works and will be of some value in readers' advisory situations and in collections in academic, public, and a few high school libraries.—**John T. Gillespie**

Crime and Mystery

P

391.   Niebuhr, Gary Warren. **Make Mine a Mystery: A Reader's Guide to Mystery and Detective Fiction.** Westport, Conn., Libraries Unlimited/Greenwood Publishing Group, 2003. 605p. index. (Genreflecting Advisory Series). $65.00. ISBN 1-56308-784-7.

Gary Niebuhr, who is an avid mystery reader, has written a guide that is meant to serve as an introduction to mysteries with an emphasis on series detectives. He has included titles from the entire history of the genre from the late 1880s to 2002. The introduction outlines the subgenres of mystery fiction, and describes the appeal of series and of their protagonists. Chapters on readers' advisory services and on building a mystery collection follow. Also included is information on awards and a history of the mystery.

The bulk of the book is devoted to the literature itself. Niebuhr divides mysteries into types of detectives (e.g., amateur, eccentric). He further subdivides types into "historical founding members," "golden agers and beyond," and "modern practitioners." Each of the 2,500 entries includes bibliographic information, a brief summary of the plot, and its geographic location. The work's appendixes cover bibliographies, book review sources, conventions, encyclopedias, filmography, guides, history and criticism, mystery bookstores, journals, online resources, organizations, and publishers. Authors, titles, characters, subjects, and locations are all indexed.

Although readers' guides are always welcome in the growing field of mystery literature, readers should keep in mind that this work has a narrow focus. The book also contains some minor errors in the descriptions of the characters. The work would have been strengthened by including birth and death dates with the authors and by listing all series under the authors. Additionally, reducing the number of subdivisions within the text would have made the guide easier to use. This book should be purchased where demand warrants.—**January Adams**

Horror

P

392.   Fonseca, Anthony J., and June Michele Pulliam. **Hooked on Horror: A Guide to Reading Interests in Horror Fiction.** 2d ed. Westport, Conn., Libraries Unlimited/Greenwood Publishing Group, 2003. 464p. index. (Genreflecting Advisory Series). $55.00. ISBN 1-56308-904-1.

Everything you ever wanted to know about horror fiction can be found in this book. Fonseca and Pulliam provide concise, lively descriptions of approximately 1,000 contemporary and classic titles of this fascinating and popular genre. In addition, they give extensive background information on the history, trends, and appeal of the genre. Focusing on titles that are either in print or widely available in library collections, Fonseca and Pulliam classify works into 13 subgenres. Keywords (subjects) are listed with each entry to lead users to related titles. They also cite titles that have won awards. A final section includes bibliographies in the areas of history and criticism, periodicals and magazines, and ready-reference sources. Lists of organizations, conferences, awards, and publishers complete the work. A must-have for readers advisory and collection development specialists, this book will also be of interest to those covering the horror genre in English literature classes, as well as to bookstore personnel, writers, and horror fans.—**Denise A. Garofalo**

Science Fiction and Fantasy

P

393.   Burgess, Michael, and Lisa R. Bartle. **Reference Guide to Science Fiction, Fantasy, and Horror.** 2d ed. Westport, Conn., Libraries Unlimited/Greenwood Publishing Group, 2002. 605p. index. (Reference Sources in the Humanities Series). $75.00. ISBN 1-56308-548-8.

Bartle joins Burgess in a timely update to this standard one-volume source (see ARBA 93, entry 1155, for a review of the 1st edition). Some 148 entries have been added to this edition, and a significant number of entries from the 1st edition have been revised. As expected, some of these revisions are second or third editions. Others have been revised to flush out the scope and usefulness of the resource further. The resource-focused structure of the publication continues to be one of its strengths. Sections include "Encyclopedias and Dictionaries," "Guides to Secondary Sources," and "Artist Bibliographies." New sections include "Major Online Resources," providing a selected list of reference guide Websites; and "Printed Guides to the Internet," which only lists one resource. Burgess and Bartle do a good job of balancing the selection of Websites for what could be an overwhelming section. Libraries who purchased the 1992 edition will want to add the 2002 edition to their collections. This resource is recommended for all library collections.—**Courtney L. Young**

NATIONAL LITERATURE

American Literature

General Works

Bio-bibliography

C, P

394.   **American Writers: A Collection of Literary Biographies. Supplement XIII.** Jay Parini, ed. New York, Charles Scribner's Sons/Gale Group, 2003. 617p. index. $135.00. ISBN 0-684-31233-6.

This volume continues the American Writers Series, which is devoted to extensive essays providing a critical and biographical perspective on major literary writers in the United States and Canada from earliest time to the present. Supplement XIII focuses on 18 mostly contemporary writers, a few of whom, like Margaret Atwood and Tillie Olsen, already have firmly established reputations, while others, like Terry McMillan and Octavia Butler, are just beginning to develop a critical as well as popular following. Each signed essay weaves together biography, literary analysis, and cultural commentary. Each essay also includes a selected unannotated primary and secondary bibliography.

Jay Parini, the editor of this volume, is a well-regarded poet, novelist, critic, and teacher. He has held the authors of these critical essays to a high standard of clear, almost completely jargon-free writing for a general audience. Some of these critics, like Christopher Buckley and Sanford Pinsker have established a considerable reputation themselves and are thus candidates for inclusion in a subsequent volume in this series.

The poets in this volume are Stephen Dobyns, Yusef Komunyakaa, Lucy Larcom (who goes back to the nineteenth century), Luis Omar Salinas, William Jay Smith, Pat Mora, and Naomi Shihab Nye (these last three are also children's writers). The fiction writers are Margaret Atwood, Tillie Olsen, John Nichols, Nicholson Baker, Terry McMillan, Walter Mosely, Horace McCoy, and Octavia Butler. Also included are the playwright, Terrence McNally, the literary critic Leslie Fiedler, and the nature writer Edward Abbey. Actually, Nicholson Baker is perhaps as well known for his critical essays about libraries as he is for his fiction; the essay about his work makes a persuasive argument that Baker's extraordinary attention to minute detail is the common concern of his essays as well as his seemingly offbeat fiction.

While some biographical and critical information about these authors can be found in other reference sources directed to a general audience, such as the Dictionary of Literary Biography series, this will be a valuable addition to both academic and public libraries. It is a stand-alone volume; it is not necessary to own the previous volumes of the series to get the full benefit of this one.—**David Isaacson**

Dictionaries and Encyclopedias

C, S

395.   Aberjhani, and Sandra L. West. **Encyclopedia of the Harlem Renaissance.** New York, Facts on File, 2003. 424p. illus. index. (Facts on File Library of American History). $65.00. ISBN 0-8160-4539-9.

The *Encyclopedia of the Harlem Renaissance* provides a wealth of information in minute detail on a literary and cultural time period significant not only for Americans generally but for African Americans specifically. The entries are clear, concise, and alphabetized, thereby making this reference source easy to use. Additionally, this is a thorough and rigorously comprehensive work that constitutes an eclectic selection of elements spanning the entire spectrum of contributions made by intellectuals, artists, critics, and musicians in New York City during the 1920s and 1930s. For example, Aberjhani and Sandra L. West include surprising and refreshing details concerning such cities as Philadelphia and its pivotal connection to the black renaissance. In fact, West asserts, "With its cultured black writers, artists, educators, and publications, Philadelphia added important talent and creative substance to the Harlem Renaissance" (p. 263). Further, scholars, students, and members of the general public who are either seeking a deeper understanding of the literary history of the Harlem Renaissance or who are unfamiliar with the era will discover many helpful sources at the end of each entry. This useful text also contains several appendixes that include items such as a four-page list of additional resources, a chronology to keep the literary history in perspective, and a glossary of slang from the period. The in-depth discussion of the personalities as well as the events that ushered in the Harlem Renaissance reveals an important and an intricate part of the African American literary canon. This book is an enjoyable read. [R: LJ, Dec 03, p. 94; AG, Dec 03-Jan 04, p. 62; Choice, Jan 04, p. 874]—**Charmaine Ijeoma**

C, P, S
396.   **The Continuum Encyclopedia of American Literature.** Steven R. Serafin and Alfred Bendixen, eds. New York, Continuum Publishing, 2003. 1305p. index. $49.95. ISBN 0-8264-1517-2.

This massive compilation might well be one of the best buys a reference department could want. Relatively inexpensive, well bound, and sensibly conceived, this alphabetically arranged encyclopedia provides biographical information on American writers from Colonial times to the present. Some 1,100 entries from 300 contributors focus not only upon well-selected biographical elements but also upon 70 topical articles, among them transcendentalism, science fiction, the detective story, humor, utopia, the orient, and war. For each figure birth dates and birthplaces as well as dates and places of death are listed. Each entry—biographical and topical—concludes with a brief bibliography. The scope is well balanced from the historical (Melville, Emerson, Faulkner, Wharton, Welty, Phillis Wheatley) to the contemporary (Robert Creeley, Richard Wilbur, Rita Dove, Allison Lurie, Michael Crichton, Mary Gordon, and Elmore Leonard). The topical articles are nicely balanced essays. Physically the volume can be praised for its handsome jacket art and design (a John Singer Sargent painting) and criticized for its minuscule font of text throughout.—**Charles R. Andrews**

Individual Authors

Mark Twain

C, P
397.   **The Oxford Companion to Mark Twain.** By Gregg Camfield. New York, Oxford University Press, 2003. 767p. illus. index. $75.00. ISBN 0-19-510710-1.

Unlike its Cantabrigian cousin—*The Cambridge Guide to Mark Twain*, edited by Forrest G. Robinson (Cambridge University Press1995)—which is but a compilation of 11 scholarly essays by as many contributors, this work is a comprehensive 1-volume encyclopedia of some 300 article entries, nearly all of which have been composed by University of the Pacific Professor of English Gregg Camfield. Interspersed throughout the text are extended essays by other Twain experts, focusing on the topics of "Censorship," "Critical Reception," "The Dream of Domesticity," "Etiquette," "Performance," "Realism," "Mark Twain's Reputation," and "Technology." Nearly a quarter of the entries in this compendium are biographical profiles of friends, family, writers, or business associates known to have influenced Twain. Place-names and names of periodicals and literary genres and techniques make up a significant number of other entries. A random perusal through the pages of this resource turns up entries on "Alcohol," "Canada," "Tricksters," "Dialect," "Museums," "Seventieth Birthday Dinner," "Fashion," and "Reading,

Clemens's." Entry length also varies widely, ranging from pieces in the 75-150 word range (e.g., the entries on "Freud" and "Slang") to those that extend to 5-7 pages in length (i.e., the entries on "William Dean Howells," "Work Habits," and "Roughing It") . As noted in the preface, by casting such a wide net, Camfield is able "to show interconnections" between innumerable elements of Twain's works, life, and times. Various aspects of culture, commerce, and literature commingle in the pages of this volume. For example, under "Telephone" users discover that Twain was possibly the first person to have a telephone installed in his private residence. And under the entry for the Reverend Joseph Hopkins Twichell, we learn that this virtually forgotten figure may well have been Twain's closest friend throughout his life. Camfield's straightforward expression and candor are refreshing throughout, as exemplified by his plain admission of the difficulties he shares with other literary historians, critics, and biographers in trying to establish any line of demarcation between the personas of Clemens and Twain.

One of this reference's most useful features is its "Thematic List of Entries," which subsumes titles of entries and back matter essays under more than 30 subcategories (e.g., "Travel Narratives," "Professional Associates," "Science and Technology") . These, in turn, have been grouped under the categories "Works," "Life," and "Times." Also helpful to both the scholar and general reader are the 14 pages of timetables in the "Chronology" section, which pertain to these same 3 headings. Nearly 50 black-and-white illustrations are dispersed throughout this book, with 16 of these gathered as a section of glossy photographs that feature Twain with family, friends, and business associates. Other renderings include a facsimile of Twain's riverboat pilot's license and a map of Virginia City, Nevada.

Factual errors appear to be few in this book, the most egregious of which being the misstating of Clemens' death year as 1909, rather than 1910 (p. 112). Occasional pagination gaffes mar this resource. Judith Martin's etiquette essay begins on page 197, rather on page 187 as claimed in the table of contents. Also, the citation for "Daily Press (Worcester)" is a blind one, because there is no reference nor illustration that corresponds to this publication on the page to which one is directed (p. 383). Although boldface page number citations in the index are intended to signify pages containing an illustration, at least 13 such citations misdirect the user to pages devoid of illustrations. The impact of the death of loved ones upon Twain's psychological makeup is alluded to throughout several article entries, rather than being addressed directly under an appropriate heading such as "Psychological Forces Upon Twain's Writings" or "Depression and Twain." Camfield's articles "Health and Disease" and "Association" do not sufficiently address the multiple traumas endured by Twain during his life. Similarly, Arthur Miller's essay titled "Performance" merely touches on the many forms of emotional anguish that Twain battled throughout his writing career. (Through the years, Twain was affected by the premature deaths of his father, wife, two daughters, son, younger brother, and sister. His bankruptcy contributed to his advancing years' depressed state, as well.)

Broadly speaking, cross-references have been adequately and appropriately provided by Camfield. Asterisked terms within articles refer the user to other article entries under those terms. Cross-referenced citations sporadically appear at the end of articles. However, there is no mention of the entry on social Darwinist Herbert Spencer within the article on Darwin. Similarly, there is no mention of the "Collaborations" entry under the entry on Charles Dudley Warner. Nor is there a cross-reference from "Posthumous Publications" to "Unfinished Works," nor from "False Attributions" to "Maxims," nor from "Celebrity" to "Public Image." These shortcomings notwithstanding, Camfield's volume is a balanced and insightful distillation of Twain scholarship, highlighted by its unparalleled annotated bibliography, which lists more than 1,700 writings attributed to Twain. This companion merits inclusion within most academic and public library collections. [R: LJ, Jan 03, p. 96]—**Jeffrey E. Long**

British Literature

General Works

Dictionaries and Encyclopedias

C, P, S

398.   **The Continuum Encyclopedia of British Literature.** Steven R. Serafin and Valerie Grosvenor Myer, eds. New York, Continuum Publishing, 2003. 1184p. index. $175.00. ISBN 0-8264-1456-7.

American academic, Steven R. Serafin, who edited this weighty volume (over five pounds) with Cambridge-based Valerie Grosvenor Myer, also edited the equally impressive *The Continuum Encyclopedia of American Literature* (see entry 396). The present volume contains about 1,200 biographical entries and 70 survey articles in a single alphabetic listing. Each entry is signed. The distinguished contributors are listed in an appendix with their affiliations. The biographies are of important authors who were born or resided for some time in Great Britain (like American T. S. Eliot) or Ireland. Depending on the importance of the subject, these articles range in length from a single paragraph to three double-column pages. As an exception, Shakespeare gets four pages. Each article supplies biographical material plus a critical survey of the author's work. All but the shortest entries end with a brief bibliography of a few books and articles about the subject. The choice of authors is extensive and judicious and shows particular strength with contemporary writers. Even current *wunderkinder* like playwright Martin McDonagh and novelist Zadie Smith are included. The topical articles are about four pages each and are of three types: articles on specific genres (e.g., humor, fairy tales, gay male literature), specific time periods (e.g., Old English, Restoration Drama), or specific countries. The latter gives concise and fascinating historical overviews of the literature of countries in the Commonwealth or the former British Empire including Australia, Canada, India, New Zealand, and South Africa. Appendixes include a timeline, which lists chronologically in two parallel columns important historical and literary events, and also a section on about 20 literary prizes and their winners. A single index includes the name of all of the authors mentioned in the text. Other one-volume literary handbooks on this subject like *The Oxford Companion to English Literature* (see ARBA 2001, entry 1121) and *The Cambridge Guide to Literature in English* (see ARBA 95, entry 1103) use shorter entries to cover a broader field (e.g., entries for individual works, printers, literary societies, movements) but the material is usually basic and the treatment, of necessity, superficial. The *Continuum* volume, however, gives greater depth and detail both in factual material and critical judgments. It is highly recommended for adult or young adult library collections. [R: LJ, 1 May 03, p. 102; SLJ, Oct 03, p. 108]—**John T. Gillespie**

P, S

399.   **Encyclopedia of British Writers.** Christine L. Krueger, George Stade, and Karen Karbiener, eds. New York, Facts on File, 2003. 2v. index. (Facts on File Library of World Literature). $150.00/set. ISBN 0-8160-4670-0.

Unlike most literary reference works, these two volumes devoted to nineteenth- and twentieth-century writers are not aimed primarily at the student but at the general reader. The editors hope to encourage informed reading of 799 writers from Edmund Burke to Zadie Smith. The format includes brief biographies, overviews of the writers' careers, analyses of their most important works, and a bibliography of recommended biographies or critical studies. The entries range from a few hundred to over 1,000 words, and there are also bibliographies of general studies of the periods and detailed indexes in each volume. The overviews and analyses often quote from experts on the writers under discussion.

The *Encyclopedia* covers not only novelists, poets, and playwrights but critics and nonfiction writers. There are entries for Isabella Beeton, author of the best-selling Victorian cookbook, and Florence Nightingale, who, in addition to her nursing career, wrote 16 nonfiction books. The entries generally achieve the goals of the editors, but there are some odd omissions. There is no mention of novelist Simon Raven's adapting Anthony Trollope's novels for the popular miniseries *The Pallisers*, and the entries on John and Penelope Mortimer mention their 1949 marriage but not their divorce, a significant influence on her fiction. Such flaws, however, are rare.

This *Encyclopedia* is especially useful for calling to the attention of potential readers once-famous writers who have faded into obscurity. As such, it is more valuable for public and school libraries than academic libraries. [R: Choice, Jan 04, p. 876]—**Michael Adams**

Handbooks and Yearbooks

C, S

400. **British Writers Classics. Volume II.** Jay Parini, ed. New York, Charles Scribner's Sons/Gale Group, 2004. 368p. index. $135.00. ISBN 0-684-31269-7. ISSN 1541-8995.

In Volume II of the British Writers Classics series, essays on 19 individual works arranged alphabetically from *Bleak House* to *Wasteland* contain biographical information, discussion of texts, and the critical reception they received. Included are 12 nineteenth- and twentieth-century novels, the earliest being Mary Shelley's *Frankenstein* (1816) and the most current being A. S. Byatt's *Possession* (1990); 4 poems ranging from seventeenth-century *Hesperides* to twentieth-century *Crow* by Ted Hughes; 2 modern dramas ranging from Beckett's *Waiting for Godot* and Michael Frayn's recent hit play *Copenhagen*; and a collection of tales by Kipling. The selections are rather idiosyncratic; along with such acknowledged classics as *Mrs. Dalloway* and *The Mayor of Casterbridge* are works such as *Things Fall Apart* by the Nigerian writer Chinua Achebe, whose work is deliberately not British in either style or content. Although the essays are uneven in writing and interpretation, they all contain useful information and follow the same format.

Each of the 14- to 22-page essays has a shaded box column containing a chronology of the author's life. After a general introduction to the author and their times, the essay is divided under pertinent topics ending with the importance and influence of the work, followed by a lengthy selected bibliography of both primary and secondary sources. A comprehensive index covers both volumes 1 and 2. Because the essays are written in a simple style and the terminology is designed for high school students and college undergraduates, the general reader will also find the volume easy and enjoyable to use.—**Charlotte Lindgren**

C, P

401. Merz, Caroline, and Patrick Lee-Browne. **Post-War Literature: 1945 to the Present.** New York, Facts on File, 2003. 96p. illus. index. (Backgrounds to English Literature). $30.00. ISBN 0-8160-5130-5.

This well written and carefully organized work aims to set the literature of England after World War II in its historical, political, and economic context, with a chapter dedicated to each decade beginning with the 1940s. It is an especially useful reference source for anyone living outside Britain, since English political, social, and economic history of that period are not well known in other countries.

Contrary to the authors' claims, Britain did not win the war: it was merely on the winning side, and took years to recover from the devastation. Dean Acheson was correct in observing that Britain lost an Empire in the post-war years without finding a role, and he could have maintained further that it also lost a high culture, replacing it with a popular culture of only mild and sporadic interest. Countries and cultures in decline do not invite one's continued interest, and that is why we are so unaware of recent English history and literature—an unawareness that this book does much to dispel.

There are a number of useful appendixes: a list of books and Websites for further reading, good definitions of literary terms like *Modernism* and *Post-Modernism*, and some biographies of writers. Particularly good is the parallel timeline in three columns: science and technology and the arts, literature, and history.—**John B. Beston**

Individual Authors

J. K. Rowling

P, S

402.   Kirk, Connie Ann. **J. K. Rowling: A Biography.** Westport, Conn., Greenwood Press, 2003. 141p. illus. index. (Greenwood Biographies Series). $27.50. ISBN 0-313-32205-8.

Greenwood Press's handsome addition to its biography series is a must-have for school and public libraries. Kirk has written an appealing and highly readable introduction to the publishing phenomenon known as Harry Potter. The relaxed tone and diction spare young readers the scholarly hauteur and dictatorial interpretations that stymie personal assessment of good books. The organization of text carefully separates the most important considerations as it examines Rowling from a number of perspectives.

Kirk makes a particularly clever tutorial of chapter 6, which allies the controversies over Rowling's sources with age-old questions about who wrote Shakespeare's plays. The comparison is a worthy link to classic literature. Subsequent commentary on the types of agencies and institutions that ban and burn books rightfully places the emphasis on the censor's motivation rather on Rowling's harmless layering of magic and fantasy.

The book's shortcomings are few. Illustration is mixed, beginning with a beautiful cover portrait and dwindling to a few grainy photographs that add little to the book. Movie stills might be more successful in this type of critical volume. Overall, Kirk earns points from teachers, librarians, students, and parents for five excellent appendixes that structure important data about this imaginative author. The publisher and author are to be commended on a job well done!—**Mary Ellen Snodgrass**

African Literature

C, P

403.   **Encyclopedia of African Literature.** Simon Gikandi, ed. New York, Routledge, 2003. 629p. index. $150.00. ISBN 0-415-23019-5.

This book attempts to survey the vast field of African literature from the nineteenth century to the present, including native African literature translated into English as well works originally written in English, French, and other European languages. Because another volume by Routledge, the *Encyclopedia of Arabic Literature* (1998), covers the ancient and classic Arabic traditions, this volume only covers the modern period of Arabic literature. There are more than 700 entries, most of them briefly discussing particular authors. Major authors, like Alan Paton and Chinua Achebe, get longer entries than less well-known authors. There are a number of entries on themes and subjects, such as the novel, oral literature and performance, literary criticism, and apartheid.

Although intended for a general audience, some of the entries (this is an edited volume with essays by many contributors) are decidedly not written for this audience. A long article on apartheid and post-apartheid, for instance, begins "If, as Bertrand Russell said, war banishes ambiguity, then presumably demobilization restores it." Nowhere in the first and second paragraph of this meditation beginning so beguilingly is the word "apartheid" defined. Fortunately, most of the other articles sampled by this reviewer are in fact written for a general reader.

The author entries sometimes conclude with a short list of further reading recommendations. Numerous cross-references are provided as well as a name and topical index. It is curious that a book with a 2003 copyright provides only a 1994 map of Africa. Scribner's *African Writers*, edited by C. Brian Cox (see ARBA 98, entry 1167), is a much more extensive encyclopedia that focuses on major writers and should be used in tandem with this new source. [R: LJ, 1 Feb 03, p. 74]—**David Isaacson**

Asian Literature

C
404.   **Asian American Short Story Writers.** Guiyou Huang, ed. Westport, Conn., Greenwood Press, 2003. 359p. index. $94.95. ISBN 0-313-32229-5.

This guide to Asian American short story writers in the twentieth century is well timed and valuable. The genre is a particularly fruitful one for Asian American writers and bringing the data together in one volume will increase their individual exposure. Almost 50 writers are arranged alphabetically in this reference. A biography, discussion of major works and themes, and a sampling of the critical reception the author received are compiled by an expert on the subject. This is followed by a primary and secondary bibliography. Of notable importance is the introductory essay, which sets the stage and contextualizes the works to follow. Students of Asian studies, Asian history and culture, as well as curious and general readers will benefit from this book. [R: LJ, 15 Oct 03, p. 57]—**Linda L. Lam-Easton**

Eastern European Literature

C
405.   **The Columbia Guide to the Literatures of Eastern Europe Since 1945.** By Harold B. Segel. New York, Columbia University Press, 2003. 641p. index. (The Columbia Guides to Literatures Since 1945). $95.00. ISBN 0-231-11404-4.

Since the countries of Central and Eastern Europe have emerged from the Soviet Bloc and are moving toward the European Union, publishing and literature are undergoing a renaissance in many countries and drawing attention from the rest of the world. Two of the last eight winners of the Nobel Prize in literature have been from Central and Eastern Europe. This superb guide to authors and their works fills a much-needed gap in reference works on literature. Emphasis is placed on authors whose works have been translated into English, but this emphasis does not limit the book; there are more than 700 entries from 13 countries. Authors include novelists, poets, playwrights, and short story writers. Each entry not only gives a brief biographical and literary overview of the author, but also references to literature about the author and English-language translations of each work. Poetry and short stories in translated anthologies are included as well. A most helpful alphabetic index lists authors by country, and other added features such as a list of literary journals published in each country make this a wonderful tool for bibliographers. Segel's book does not cover every country of Central and Eastern Europe; countries of the Former Soviet Union are not part of this guide. While the *Guide* does not have the lengthy entries of the The Dictionary of Literary Biography's three volumes of *Twentieth-Century Eastern European Writers* (DLB vols. 215, 220, and 232), Segel's work covers many more authors, including younger authors who are making an impact on their national literatures and world literature as a whole. [R: LJ, 15 May 03, p. 82]—**Terri Tickle Miller**

Italian Literature

C
406.   **The Oxford Companion to Italian Literature.** Peter Hainsworth and David Robey, eds. New York, Oxford University Press, 2002. 644p. $75.00. ISBN 0-19-818332-1.

Covering Italian literature from its beginnings (ca. 1200 to 2000), the nearly 2,400 alphabetically arranged entries in this volume include authors, important individual works, literary periodicals, and a wide range of topics (even some not often treated in literary handbooks, such as comics and cookery books). Italians who wrote in languages other than Italian (e.g., Latin, Provencal) are also covered. Entries vary in length from a short paragraph to several pages. The authors of each entry are identified, with most being scholars at European universities. There are abundant cross-references in the text, doing away with the need for an index. Selective bibliographies accompany most major articles, but there is no general bibliography. Preceding the alphabetic listings are a useful chronology and four maps showing political units in Italy at different time periods. Comprehensive, up-to-date, and authoritative, this will be an essential resource in any library where there is an interest in Italian literature.—**Paul B. Cors**

Latin American Literature

C, P

407.   **Latino and Latina Writers.** Alan West-Durán, María Herrera-Sobek, and César A. Salgado, eds. New York, Charles Scribner's Sons/Gale Group, 2004. 2v. index. (The Scribner Writers Series). $265.00/set. ISBN 0-684-31293-X.

Carlos Solé's *Latin American Writers* (see ARBA 90, entry 1208) was a useful addition to the Scribner Writers Series when first published in 1989. The work under review proves itself a worthy companion to its predecessor within the same series. *Latino and Latina Writers* features bio-critical essays on 57 writers of Hispanic origin, including Oscar Hijuelos and Sandra Cisneros, whose writings have been published since 1960. In addition, there are five valuable thematic essays: "Chicana Feminist Criticism"; "Crossing Borders, Creative Disorders: Latino Identities and Writing"; "Historical Origins of U.S. Latino Literature"; "The Latino Autobiography"; and "Performance Art and Theater." These serve to put the writers into context with one another.

One common thread between the authors selected for inclusion is that they write predominantly in English. This work could have been improved immensely through the addition of prominent authors who choose to write in Spanish. The editors of this volume should strongly consider publishing a supplement to address this serious shortcoming. Still, this is a valuable reference tool for English-speaking readers and should be highly considered for purchase by academic and public libraries.—**John R. Burch Jr.**

NONFICTION

C, S

408.   **Nonfiction Classics for Students: Presenting Analysis, Context, and Criticism on Nonfiction Works. Volume 5.** David Galens, ed. Farmington Hills, Mich., Gale, 2003. 344p. illus. index. $80.00. ISBN 0-7876-6034-5. ISSN 1533-7561.

Designed specifically for high school and college undergraduates, much attention has been paid to the visual design of this volume. Icons introduce blocks of "Compare and Contrast," "Topics for Further Study," "What Do I Read Next?," and "Quotations" (introduced with giant quotation marks interspersed in the midst of text). All but 4 of the 14 nonfiction works discussed are illustrated including two pictures of Leonardo Di Caprio from the film version of Jim Carroll's *The Basketball Diaries* and 2 of Abbie Hoffman in the section on *Steal This Book*.

As in previous volumes, the contributors follow a designated format that is less suitable for nonfiction than fiction. "Plot Summary" might better have been labeled "Content." Key figures are often little more than a brief reference. Each essay also contains sections on themes, style, historical context, critical overviews, criticism, sources, and a list for further reading. In addition to the major essays, the volume contains a foreword on "Literature, Conversation, Communication, Idea, Emotion" by Carol Dell'Amico and an introduction explaining the purpose and criteria used. A "Literary Chronology" of the writers included in the volume ranges from 1842, the birth of William James, to 2001, the year E. H. Gombrich died, followed by acknowledgments and contributor's credentials. The book concludes with a 33-page "Glossary of Literary Terms" and 3 cumulative indexes covering all 5 volumes by author/title, nationality/ethnicity, and subject/theme. In spite of some oversimplification of "Compare and Contrast," the summaries, critical overviews, criticism, and suggestions for further readings offer students helpful information and direction.—**Charlotte Lindgren**

POETRY

Dictionaries and Encyclopedias

C

409.   Myers, Jack, and Don Charles Wukasch. **Dictionary of Poetic Terms.** College Station, Tex., Texas A&M University Press, 2003. 434p. $22.95pa. ISBN 1-57441-166-7.

This easy-to-use, alphabetically arranged handbook is a thorough guide for both the serious reader of poetry and the poet. For the student it is a useful catalog of definitions and a companion reader to traditional and contemporary poetry. For the poet it can ignite his or her interest in ancient, modern, and contemporary ideas about poetry. The definitions are comprehensive and clearly presented, and in some instances are little essays in themselves. The entries *myth* and *metaphor*, for example, two terms many students have difficulty in grappling with, are seven and eight pages in length and are as thorough and lucidly presented as could be desired. Ample cross-references are included in each entry, and parts of poems are included where necessary as examples of the term. Entries can be as basic as *sonnet* and as esoteric as *epistrophe*. Three appendixes are included. The first, "Selected Topics," under which the appropriate dictionary terms are grouped, such as *cinematic terms, criticism,* and *imagery,* is particularly helpful and should, perhaps, be looked at before perusing the handbook.

This excellent dictionary will easily find a place among the various poetry handbooks and guides in most academic and public libraries. After using this very reasonably priced guide once or twice, the English major may well wish to add it to his or her personal library. [R: LJ, Aug 03, p. 74; Choice, Jan 04, p. 878]—**Charles R. Andrews**

Indexes

C

410.   **Bibliographical Catalogue and First-Line Index of Printed Anthologies of English Poetry to 1640.** Frederic William Baue, comp. Lanham, Md., Scarecrow, 2002. 281p. $75.00. ISBN 0-8108-4464-8.

The compiler of this descriptive bibliography has succeeded in making a unique contribution to the study of early English poetry anthologies. His aim is to provide additions and corrections to a landmark work in this area, Arthur E. Case's *Bibliography of English Poetical Miscellanies, 1521-1750* (Oxford, 1935), by listing and describing additional works falling within Case's scope that appear in A. W. Pollard and G. W. Redgrave's *Short-Title Catalogue of Books Printed in England, Scotland, and Ireland and of English Books Printed Abroad, 1475-1640* (2d ed.; The Bibliographical Society, 1976-1991). In addition, Baue offers a first-line index to all the poems in the 53 anthologies he describes. His bibliography entries, arranged in the order they appear in the *Short-Title Catalogue* (STC), describe the first edition of each anthology, and give short-title descriptions of subsequent editions, the corresponding STC item numbers, and the University Microfilms International (UMI) reference number. The first-line index is linked to the bibliography by STC item and folio numbers. As Baue points out in his introductory comments, the combination of scope, description, and indexing of first lines to be found here represents an enlargement of coverage and an improvement of access for the scholar or bibliophile with an interest in this area. Libraries supporting advanced studies in early English lyric poetry and literary taste will find this a worthwhile purchase.—**Gregory M. Toth**

25 Music

GENERAL WORKS

Biography

P
411.   **Women and Music in America Since 1900: An Encyclopedia.** Kristine H. Burns, ed. Westport, Conn., Greenwood Press, 2002. 2v. illus. index. $150.00/set. ISBN 1-57356-267-X.

This two-volume encyclopedia is arranged alphabetically and has entries on women whom, according to the advisory and editorial board members listed in the preface, have made significant contributions that "have advanced the role of women in music" since 1900. Each volume begins with the same chronology of events from 1900 to 2000 and also includes a "Guide to Related Topics," which lists in broad outline the topics and women covered in the set. Researchers interested in gender issues in music will find articles on theories of female inferiority, feminist music criticism, feminist music history, feminist music theory, gender coding, and gender in music analysis, among others.

The text includes more than 400 entries and 100 photographs. The articles are signed and include short bibliographies, which are referred to as sources "for further reading." The articles are written in an uncritical, laudatory style and do not offer in-depth scholarly treatment of the subject. The utility of this encyclopedia for serious music research is limited, but for the music fan interested in biographical information on women involved in music across a broad spectrum of genres, this encyclopedia will be a valuable source. [R: LJ, Dec 02, p. 112]—**Alan Asher**

Directories

P
412.   Pruett, Jon, and Mike McGuirk. **The Music Festival Guide: For Music Lovers and Musicians.** Chicago, Chicago Review Press; distr., Chicago, Independent Publishers Group, 2004. 461p. index. $18.95pa. ISBN 1-55652-515-X.

The Music Festival Guide provides information on more than 600 music festivals worldwide. It is clear from the amount of festivals covered as well as the amount of information provided that the authors have done their research. Festivals are organized first into chapters by genre of music (e.g., blues, classical and chamber, electronic, rock and indie rock, world) and then alphabetically by festival name within each chapter. A typical entry includes the month, location, and general cost of the festival; one paragraph describing what one can expect; information on camping and hotels; and contact information for more information (including telephone and e-mail and Website addresses). Interspersed throughout the chapters are excerpts from interviews of festival-goers, festival planners, and musicians, which provide an "insider's view" of what goes on behind the scenes. Supplementary material include a list of 12 things one needs to know before going to a festival (e.g., what to bring or not bring, how to volunteer); a list of the authors' top 10 festivals; a list of further resources (including both books and Websites); and indexes arranged by genre, location, month held, and alphabetical.

This book is ideal for the music-lover looking for information on where to hear live music or the band looking to get into the festival circuit. Unfortunately, because of the nature of the business, much of the information presented here will change quickly, such as dates of performances, cost of festivals, and location of festivals. This guide can therefore only be used as a starting point; users will most likely have more research to do after finding the festival they are looking for. This book is recommended for large public libraries.—**Shannon Graff Hysell**

P

413.   **Song Writer's Market, 2004: 1,700 Places to Market Your Songs.** Ian Bessler, ed. Cincinnati, Ohio, Writer's Digest Books/F & W Publications, 2003. 520p. index. $24.99pa. ISBN 1-58297-188-9. ISSN 0161-5971.

This latest version of the *Song Writer's Market* has several short (1 to 3 page) articles that provide answers to the types of questions most frequently asked by beginning songwriters, such as "where do I send my songs," "how do I submit a demo," and "how do I avoid getting ripped off." There are also some articles written by music industry professionals that provide advice to more experienced songwriters. The heart of this reference work can be found in the listings of music publishers, record companies, record producers, managers, and booking agents. The book has several useful indexes, including an index of record companies by category of music sold, and a very useful index of companies that accept submissions from beginners. Although mainly a resource for the popular music industry, there is a section devoted to classical performing arts organizations that accept submissions of musical works. The *Song Writer's Market* is an important reference work valuable to all who work or wish to work in the music business.—**Alan Asher**

Handbooks and Yearbooks

C, P

414.   **Encyclopedia of National Anthems.** Xing Hang, ed. Lanham, Md., Scarecrow, 2003. 704p. $125.00. ISBN 0-8108-4847-3.

This handy reference work is a social studies or world geography teacher's dream. There are entries for most of the sovereign nations of the world. Each entry contains a small fact box that gives geographic location and statistics, such as land area, population estimates as of 2002, official languages, Gross Domestic Product, monetary unit, and the name of the capital city. When known, the names and dates of the composers and lyricists for the anthems are given. When possible, the lyrics of the anthems are printed in the original language of the country along with an English transliteration and then a translation into English. With just a few exceptions, such as Afghanistan, each entry has sheet music in piano score format for users to play and sing. Many entries also contain short historical notes about the composition of the anthems. The *Encyclopedia of National Anthems* is an invaluable reference work for teachers and students and should be included in every library collection.—**Alan Asher**

INDIVIDUAL COMPOSERS AND MUSICIANS

C, P

415.   **From Convent to Concert Hall: A Guide to Women Composers.** Sylvia Glickman and Martha Furman Schleifer, eds. Westport, Conn., Greenwood Press, 2003. 403p. illus. index. $75.00. ISBN 1-57356-411-7.

The publisher of this volume is known as a source for reference books, and this is certainly a worthy addition to that list, but it may also serve as a serious textbook. Implicit in its coverage is the arduous task of major musicological research and confrontation with past comments ("There never have been women composers," conductor Sir Thomas Beecham remarked, "and there never will be.") A search of the literature will show three waves—one at the end of the nineteenth century, another following World War I, and now this flourish that began in the 1970s and has since only intensified. The treatment here is chronological, with each of its six chapters providing an introduction, coverage by country, an interdisciplinary timeline, bibliography, discography, and lists of modern editions (these last three in splendid detail, organized by the composer). The appendixes offer further aid: a chronological listing of the composers (starting in 800), a geographical index, and even a syllabus. The didactic orientation is given additional focus by the glossary, not a critical matter for the music major but something that would be very helpful for the humanities student (who is also spared the inclusion of musical examples or technical analyses). This will be a major aid for the scholar and provide a strong challenge for the curriculum.—**Dominique-René de Lerma**

MUSICAL FORMS

Classical

P

416.   **Classical Music: The Listener's Companion.** Alexander J. Morin, ed. San Francisco, Calif., Backbeat Books, 2002. 1201p. index. (Third Ear). $29.95pa. ISBN 0-87930-638-6.

It indicates something about the world of classical music recording that, despite all the prophecies of doom over the past decades, this guide with very brief discussions of recordings requires 1,163 pages of text with tiny type and double columns to cover part of the field. More than 50 contributors review the records. Many of them will be familiar to readers of reviews from their contributions to *Farfare*, *American Record Guide*, and *The New York Times*. They all review specific types of music, such as vocal music, or orchestral music, and all entries are signed. These are reviewers that can be trusted to help prospective buyers through the maze of multiple recorded versions of the same work.

The major parts of the entries are by composers with internal breakdowns by type of music, such as choral, piano, and so on. The entries are very concise and written in narrative form with proper names of artists in very bold type. Some of the entries are out of date and there are often specific clues that some were written some years ago. The section on Wagner's *Tristen und Isolde* reports, "The Met hasn't put it on for nearly twenty years . . ." well predates the company's new production in the fall of 1997. Carelessness occurs too. In the discussion on the recordings of the great Friedrich Schorr's scenes from *Die Meistersinger*, the conductor is given as Bohm who conducted none of them. The conductors included Blech, Coates, Heger, and Barbirolli.

The second part is devoted to musical genres such as Christmas, Jewish, and electronic music; medieval and renaissance music; and music for children. The discussions are short but thorough, and the recorded recommendations are reliable. Part 3 has sections on instrumentalists and singers. Major recording artists past and present get thumbnail sketches and CD recitals are recommended.

The coverage throughout the guide is broad, with many of the reviewers giving consideration to classic recorded performances of the past and to recordings on small and special interest labels. Some even give space to performances of great value that have never made it from LP to CD or have otherwise been unavailable but which should become available.

The index is of poor quality and seems to omit more than it indicates. Many more of the many recordings of artists, such as Renée Fleming and Ben Heppner, are reviewed than are indexed. [R: LJ, 1 Nov 02, p. 76]—**George Louis Mayer**

Operatic

P
417.   **The New Penguin Opera Guide.** rev. ed. Amanda Holden, ed. New York, Penguin Books, 2002. 1142p. illus. index. $30.00pa. ISBN 0-140-51475-9.

This "fully revised and updated edition of the most comprehensive single-volume opera encyclopedia ever published" more than lives up to its promise. It covers nearly 850 composers and around 2,000 works in concise, informative articles filled with relevant and interesting facts about the composer, the opera, its performance history, and at least one recording. Not only is every opera ever seen included, but rarely performed and obscure operas, such as Shostakovich's *Lady Macbeth of the Mtensk District* and Handel's *Agrippina* are covered well enough to help this reviewer decide if I want to go to San Francisco and Santa Fe to see them. This is one encyclopedia that is so well written it is actually fun to just pick up and read. [R: LJ, Dec 02, pp. 110-112]—**Anthony Gottlieb**

Popular

General Works

Biography

C, P
418.   **Baker's Biographical Dictionary of Popular Musicians Since 1990.** New York, Schirmer Books/Gale Group, 2004. 2v. illus. index. $195.00/set. ISBN 0-02-865799-3.

Baker's Biographical Dictionary of Popular Musicians Since 1990, a 2-volume set, includes more than 600 of the most popular artists from rock, pop, hip-hop, blues, electronica, musical theater, soundtrack, classical country, R&B, jazz, folk, Latin, and world music, with the bulk of the set devoted to rock, pop, country, R&B, and hip-hop. For the editors to determine inclusion, popular is defined differently for the different genres. For example, rock and R&B artists have to have shown consistent relevance from a commercial perspective, whereas with the other genres commercial success was a factor for inclusion, but also a "crossover" factor was included as well as critical acclaim. Ultimately, for inclusion, all artists needed to have wide appeal.

Alphabetic entries note name; birth and death dates; genre; best-selling album since 1990; hit songs since 1990; history; a selective discography; and in many cases a bibliography, selective filmography, and Website. The entries discuss the history of the artist or group, the impact the artists have made on the genre, their performance during the 1990s, and how the artists were influenced by and have influenced others. For many of the artists a "Spot Light" section is included magnifying a recording, event, or movement. This highly informative and fun two-volume set would make a splendid addition to any general reference collection.—**Linda W. Hacker**

Dictionaries and Encyclopedias

P
419.   Jeffries, Stan. **Encyclopedia of World Pop Music, 1980-2001.** Westport, Conn., Greenwood Press, 2003. 277p. illus. index. $54.95. ISBN 0-313-31547-7.

The author, a pop music critic and radio show host, has written a single-volume biographical encyclopedia of pop music acts that were visible on the international music scene from 1980-2001. Criteria for selection was based upon sales figures from the weekly music charts compiled from national record store chains. Eschewing groups that were popular in the United States, the author has focused on acts that achieved success in their native countries but were not commercially viable in the United States. Readers who are familiar with late twentieth-century pop music may recognize a few names such as A-Ha, Roxette, and Split Enz as one-hit wonders in America. Acts from 43 countries are represented and include styles such as electronica, grunge, rock, and metal. Each entry contains basic personal information about band members, a brief history of the formation of the group, and the career highlights of the band. Entries conclude with a reference heading (usually a Web address) where more information can be found. By no means exhaustive, this work does serve as a useful introduction to some of the important artists working in the pop music genre in the late twentieth century. [R: LJ, 1 Oct 03, pp. 62-64; Choice, Jan 04, p. 878]—**Alan Asher**

Country

P
420.   Carlin, Richard. **Country Music: A Biographical Dictionary.** New York, Routledge, 2003. 497p. illus. index. $125.00. ISBN 0-415-93802-3.

If you are a country music fan, you will want to have *Country Music: A Biographical Dictionary*. Author Richard Carlin, who has written frequently on a variety of music subjects over the years, has put together an interesting and comprehensive 497-page, A-Z source on country music.

A short but informative history of country music serves as an introduction to over 700 entries. Each entry provides a chronological history of the artist, usually followed by a selected discography (complete with the record numbers). More extensive entries describe general aspects of country music (e.g., record labels, railroad songs, minstrel shows); subgenres (e.g., bluegrass); and different instruments. The text is concise and well written; occasionally the author's opinion sneaks in, which adds a little zest to the entries. The larger 8½-by-11-inch format of the book makes the text easier to read. There are an adequate amount of black-and-white photographs. The backmatter consists of a selected bibliography, appendixes of artists according to their genre and musical instrument, and a name index.

This *Dictionary* should be especially enjoyable for younger fans who are not familiar with bands and performers from earlier generations, such as the Hi Flyers (1930s), Carl Story (1940s), or the Wilburn Brothers (1950s). *Country Music: A Biographical Dictionary* is an excellent purchase for any serious country music fan or libraries with an interest in music. [R: LJ, 1 Feb 03, p. 72]—**Mark J. Crawford**

Jazz

P
421.   **All Music Guide to Jazz: The Definitive Guide to Jazz Music.** 4th ed. Vladimir Bogdanov, Chris Woodstra, and Stephen Thomas Erlewine, eds. San Francisco, Calif., Backbeat Books, 2002. 1472p. index. $32.95pa. ISBN 0-87930-717-X.

Keeping track of players and styles in any musical genre is difficult at best, but in jazz, this difficulty reaches its highest levels. In the improvising spirit of the genre, musicians go solo, switch groups, and get together for impromptu "jam" sessions more than in any other category of music. Combined with the long history of jazz, this makes developing any type of useable guide extremely tough. However, with the *All Music Guide to Jazz*, Backbeat Books has come up with one of the most useful jazz reference resources available. Going back to the beginning of the twentieth century, the *All Music Guide to Jazz* provides brief, yet useful, biographical and album information to help users find out more about a newly discovered or favorite artist. Dates and album labels are provided to assist in locating albums, and ratings have been assigned by experts to help the novice explore the best jazz recordings available. Scattered throughout the book are inset "maps," which detail some aspect of the genre, such as the development of the use of bass clarinets in jazz ensembles. At the end of the book is a section on the history of jazz and its different subgenres, again using maps to chart different developments.

This resource is extremely well executed, expertly prepared, and put together to be user-friendly. A thorough index of names and titles is provided to help the user locate wanted information quickly. At $32.95, the price is well within the reach of most libraries. This essential resource for an overview of jazz is most suited for public libraries, particularly those with large audio collections or a diverse listening clientele. Academic libraries will find it useful with undergraduates who need background information or who are beginning research on a jazz-related topic. The *All Music Guide to Jazz* is highly recommended. [R: LJ, 15 Mar 03, p. 74]—**Mark T. Bay**

Rock

P

422.   **The Billboard Illustrated Encyclopedia of Rock.** New York, Watson-Guptill, 2002. 400p. illus. $35.00pa. ISBN 0-8230-7701-2.

The text for this *Encyclopedia* is distilled from Colin Larkin's definitive 8-volume *Encyclopedia of Popular Music* (see ARBA 2001, entry 1178). To fit the demands of the one-volume format, many entries were dropped and those that remain have been edited significantly. What the larger set provides in detail, this single volume makes up in appearance. The layout of this book is first rate. There are more than 600 color illustrations imaginatively arranged within the text of this book, and they make it a joy to flip through. Although it is not always clear exactly who is pictured since no captions have been included. Entries are arranged alphabetically, and while these edited narratives are not as comprehensive as the originals from which they are derived, they do cover the most important material in a sharp, opinionated fashion. Each entry is supplemented by the sidebars located on each page margin that provide information on the artist in up to five categories: Albums (up to three of the artist's key albums are listed and awarded from one to five stars); Collaborators (other performers who have worked with this artist); Connections (bands with whom the artist has previously worked or has been associated); Influences (musicians, writers, or events); and Further References (books, films or videos by or about the artist). For example, the two-paragraph entry on Steve Winwood is accompanied by a sidebar that lists two four-star albums ("Arc of a Diver" and "Back in the High Life") , collaborators Jim Capaldi from Traffic and lyricist Vivian Stanshall, connections to the Spencer Davis Group and Traffic, and two biographies for further reference. The reference to Vivian Stanshall as a collaborator is a bit mysterious, however, since he is not mentioned in the edited text and has no individual entry in this book. The relationship with Stanshall is spelled out in the multivolume work by Larkin, however. Finally, more complete discographies, bibliographies, videographies, and filmographies for each artist are featured at the end of the book.

There seems to be a slight UK bias in the selections themselves. One is more likely to find an obscure Brit band like Inspiral Carpets than an American one like the Georgia Satellites. However, this is a very enjoyable compilation and will appeal to both libraries and the general public. It is recommended for any library.—**John Maxymuk**

26 Mythology, Folklore, and Popular Culture

FOLKLORE

C, P

423.   **South Asian Folklore: An Encyclopedia.** Margaret A. Mills, Peter J. Claus, and Sarah Diamond, eds. New York, Routledge/Taylor & Francis Group, 2003. 710p. illus. index. $175.00. ISBN 0-415-98919-4.

The editors of this encyclopedia are very upfront and informative regarding the construction of this volume. First of all, they indicate that, for the purposes of the book, the term "South Asia" is defined as the nation states of Afghanistan, Bangladesh, India, Nepal, Pakistan, and Sri Lanka. Second, they do not deal with South Asian folk musical forms, as Garland has already issued a separate encyclopedia on this topic (see ARBA 2001, entry 1142). In the introduction, other constraints and current issues regarding this topic are discussed and iterated.

Over 500 articles by more than 250 authors are represented in this reference work. There are general concept articles, case study articles, and short definitional articles. A set of maps showing the regions referenced in the articles is included, as well as an index. This book fills a current gap in the literature on the topic of South Asian folklore, and while the editors realize that it is not comprehensive, they have done a good job of tackling this topic and beginning the move toward more scholarly work in this area. [R: LJ, 15 April 03, p. 76]—**Bradford Lee Eden**

MYTHOLOGY

P, S

424.   Daly, Kathleen N. **Greek and Roman Mythology A to Z.** rev. ed. Revised by Marian Rengel. New York, Facts on File, 2004. 146p. illus. index. (Mythology A to Z). $35.00. ISBN 0-8160-5155-0.

Originally published in 1992, the current volume has new entries and an updated bibliography. A six-page introduction gives a brief history and explains the differences between Greek mythology and the Roman borrowings. Roman and Greek counterparts are paired, then followed by a descriptive listing of Greek Gods and their Roman equivalents in parenthesis. It would have been helpful to also have lists of the Muses and Fates since their individual names appear in the main text and index only under the generic term; thus, to find a name such as Clotho one would have to be already aware that she is one of the Fates.

The book contains 45 black-and-white illustrations and 2 full-page maps—the Greek World (1600-323 B.C.E.) and Rome and its Environs (500-200 B.C.E.) with major sites indicated. The alphabetically listed subjects include not only mythological figures, but also major writers from Hessiod and Homer to Virgil, and places from Delos to Thessaly and Troy. While each definition is succinct, the user can easily navigate the maze of complex mythologies by following the cross-references marked by small capital letters. For example, Earth Mother as "creator of new life" references Zeus also. The index then provides over 50 references to Zeus broken down by topics, such as children, lovers, wars, and those he punished.

Although this rather slim volume is written and organized simply enough for young readers it is complete enough to be a useful reference for serious scholars.—**Charlotte Lindgren**

C, P

425.   **The Oxford Dictionary of Classical Myth and Religion.** Simon Price and Emily Kearns, eds. New York, Oxford University Press, 2003. 599p. maps. $39.95. ISBN 0-19-280288-7.

This volume, derived from the 3d edition of *The Oxford Classical Dictionary* (3d rev. ed.; see ARBA 2004, entry 477) by the two area advisors for that volume, provides a reasonably priced and accessible reference work that interested nonspecialists and specialists in related fields will surely find useful. It opens with a brief discussion of mythology as interpreted by classicists and then follows with short discussions of religious pluralism and the reception of myths. After another short section on how to use the book, the editors provide an extremely brief bibliography followed by a most useful thematic index. This last resource makes it easy for the user to see the volume's entries on particular topics, including different types of ancient authors, different kinds of religions, and various types of deities. As a tool to make using the dictionary easier, this thematic index proves to be invaluable.

The dictionary entries not only include mythological references but also topics such as religious places, officials, organizations, and rituals. In addition, among the entries, one finds discussions of "regional religions and 'mystery cults' " along with entries related to "Judaism and Christianity in the Hellenistic and Roman periods" (p. xvii). Many of the entries also provide cross-references as well as include references to appropriate primary texts. The volume concludes with three related maps and six genealogies, including one outlining the deities in Hesiod's Theogony. The modest price of this volume along with its extensive coverage makes it an appropriate acquisition for every college and high school library as well as most public libraries and many private collections.—**Susan Tower Hollis**

P

426.   Sherman, Josepha. **Mythology for Storytellers: Themes and Tales from Around the World.** Armonk, N.Y., M. E. Sharpe, 2003. 369p. illus. index. $85.00. ISBN 0-7656-8056-4.

Josepha Sherman's introduction defines myths as having the purpose of offering explanations of major life questions and teaching cultural behaviors and the meanings behind various rituals. She then follows myths through history demonstrating how myths live on and are being created even in American life today by the likes of *Star Wars*, *Lassie*, and Billy the Kid.

The myriad of myths collected here represent all cultures on all continents and are arranged thematically by such topics as creation and heroes. Each retelling is preceded by a brief paragraph that identifies the major themes and shows the specific myth's interrelation to similar myths in other cultures. Photographs of relevant artifacts enliven the pages. The retellings themselves are classic storytelling and can be read as they are to audiences of all ages. Sherman warns against altering them through reinterpretation or omission. A general index, name index, and culture index make the myths easily accessible.—**Deborah Hammer**

POPULAR CULTURE

Dictionaries and Encyclopedias

P, S

427.   **Bowling, Beatniks, and Bell-Bottoms: Pop Culture of 20th-Century America.** Sara Pendergast and Tom Pendergast, eds. Farmington Hills, Mich., U*X*L/Gale, 2002. 5v. illus. index. $215.00/set. ISBN 0-7876-5675-5.

This beguiling and well-organized multivolume set presents short essays (150-1,000 words) on some 750 popular culture topics. One of the best organized books of this type this reviewer has seen, *Bowling, Beatniks, and Bell-Bottoms* provides set-wide listings of entries in alphabetic order, listings by category, a timeline, and a complete index in each volume, such that finding information in any of the five volumes is simple. The decision to reproduce all of the organizational material in every volume certainly swells the size and cost of the set but is a good educational strategy. The entries are written so that preteen readers can make sense of them and older children will stay engaged by the lively style. Although this source is certainly a homage to popular culture, the contributors are careful to acknowledge their viewpoints. Topics are grouped by decade under headings such as "Commerce," "Fashion," "Film and Theater," "Music," "Print Culture," and "The Way We Lived," with overviews preceding individual essays. In general, personalities are dealt with as part of a movement or context rather than by biography, but pop icons are readily found and adequately discussed. Each entry mentions additional sources, including books and the World Wide Web. The entries cross-reference each other and black-and-white illustrations complement the text. The contributors seem very knowledgeable and their coverage of the culture is comprehensive if not encyclopedic. While the entries and opinions are inclusive, the focus, as stated in the title, is definitely on mainstream American popular culture. This set will be a helpful reference for young people, trivia buffs, and general readers alike. [R: LJ, 15 Nov 02, p. 60]—**R. K. Dickson**

P, S
428.   **Holiday Symbols and Customs.** 3d ed. Sue Ellen Thompson, ed. Detroit, Omnigraphics, 2003. 895p. index. $68.00. ISBN 0-7808-0501-1.

The 3d edition of this title updates the two earlier publications by the addition of 100 holidays (2d ed., see ARBA 2000, entry 1200; and 1st ed., see ARBA 99, entry 1189). In total, 274 special days and their related symbols and customs are included. Entries that appeared in earlier editions are unchanged, with the exception of the addition of Web addresses for additional information.

The book's format remains the same. Entries are listed alphabetically with a snapshot of the holiday, giving its type, date, and place of celebration preceding the descriptive section. The entries run from 2 to 14 pages. The origin, meaning, and development of each holiday are given along with a description and explanation of related symbols and customs. Suggestions for further reading are provided. The addition of Websites as a source of information is of limited value. Some offer substantive information while others do not. For example, the site given for the Tibetan festival, Dosmoche, gives lots of detail about customs. The site provided for the African holiday Aboakyer, leads to an article on biodiversity that is only marginally relevant. The majority of the holidays are religious. Many are Christian, but non-Christian traditions are well represented. New to this edition are more African and Native American celebrations. In addition, symbols unique to immigrant groups in the United States are included. Many of the new additions are technically not holidays but events. Among them are the Kentucky Derby, the Daytona 500, and the Westminster Dog Show. These are among the shorter entries since there is not a lot to say about them in terms of customs and symbols and their inclusion is puzzling. The target audiences for the book are students and the general reader. These groups will find good information on a wide range of special days important to a diverse population. [R: Choice, Jan 04, p. 874]—**Marlene M. Kuhl**

Handbooks and Yearbooks

P
429.   Sperling, Joy. **Famous Works of Art in Popular Culture: A Reference Guide.** Westport, Conn., Greenwood Press, 2003. 277p. illus. index. $54.95. ISBN 0-313-31808-5.

In this remarkable and overdue reference guide, Joy Sperling, Associate Professor of Art at Denison University, has assembled examples of art and architecture that have bridged the gap between high art and popular culture and entered our "collective visual memory." Each work presented here is notable not only

because it has become famous, but also because its meaning is constantly evolving with the times. There are 29 works examined, including the Taj Mahal, da Vinci's *Mona Lisa*, the Eiffel Tower, van Gogh's *Starry Night*, Monet's *Nymphéas (Waterlilies)*, Dali's *Persistence of Memory*, and Warhol's *Marilyn*. While readers will likely question the inclusion or exclusion of some works, Sperling clearly explains her criteria in the introduction to each chapter. Chapters are arranged by historical period, from antiquity to the twentieth century, and include a discussion of the influences, such as tourism, scholarship, or publicity, which made the chosen works famous and transformed them from high art to popular culture. The sections on individual works include a picture; conditions under which it was originally created; description (including appearance, dimensions, and material and techniques); biography of the artist or architect (if known); and discussion of the original and changing meaning of the work. Extensive bibliographies also accompanying each entry, but no works newer than 2000 are listed. The carefully designed index includes authors and titles noted in the text, as well as the expected artists and works of art. This clearly written, well-organized, and extensively researched book will make a welcome addition to any reference collection.
—**Erica L. Coe**

27 Performing Arts

GENERAL WORKS

Biography

C, P

430. Otfinoski, Steven. **African Americans in the Performing Arts.** New York, Facts on File, 2003. 276p. illus. index. (A to Z of African Americans). $44.00. ISBN 0-8160-4807-X.

This volume in Facts on File's biographical series on African Americans draws together historical and contemporary figures in the performing arts. As defined by the editor, "performing artists" includes actors, singers, musicians, comedians, dancers, composers, and choreographers, but the last two are present only when they were performers as well as creators of works. The 190 individuals in the collection were chosen on the basis of the editor's personal preference, historical importance, variety, and level of importance, which leaves the range open to include everyone from Louis Armstrong to tap dancer Peg Leg Bates. Most figures are historical, although Otfinoski features those contemporary performers who either are unique among their peers or who have already made a substantial contribution to their discipline. One could argue for inclusion of performers who did not make the cut, such as Audra McDonald and "Bronze Buckaroo" Herb Jeffries, but overall Otfinoski's choices are reasoned. Each one-page entry features biographical information, significance as a performer, a brief bibliography, and "further viewing/listening" titles. No entry is written in great detail, but readers will get a basic knowledge of performers. Also, photographs are sporadic and do not accompany every entry. Lists of performers by "activity" and year of birth conclude the volume. Useful in conjunction with the standard *African American Almanac* (8th ed.; see ARBA 2002, entry 303) and *Contemporary Black Biography* (Gale). This work is most suitable for undergraduate and public library collections. [R: LJ, 1 June 03, pp. 106-108; SLJ, June 03, p. 87]—**Anthony J. Adam**

FILM, TELEVISION, AND VIDEO

Bio-bibliography

C, P

431. Hannsberry, Karen Burroughs. **Bad Boys: The Actors of Film Noir.** Jefferson, N.C., McFarland, 2003. 780p. illus. index. $75.00. ISBN 0-7864-1484-7.

The term *film noir* ("black cinema") was coined by French critics in 1946 to describe an emblematic type of Hollywood film produced in the early 1940s that portrayed a gritty and violent world of urban crime. Often filmed in heavy shadow, *film noir*'s signature cinematic style features sharp contrasts of light and dark. Character types include world weary, cynical private eyes, vicious gangsters, scheming dames, and corrupt civil servants. Notable examples of the genre are *Double Idemnity* (1944) and *White Heat* (1949). Hannsberry, a frequent contributor to *Classic Images* and *Films of the Golden Age*, covered the female side of the *film noir* street in 1998 with *Femme Noir: Bad Girls of Film* (McFarland). In this companion to the actresses of the genre, she examines the lives and careers of 104 actors who have become well-known *film noir* stars during the genre's heyday of 1940-1959. In addition to cinema greats like John Garfield, Edward G. Robinson, and Humphrey Bogart, are lesser-known stars like Steve Cochran and Ralph Meeker. Each entry contains a wonderfully detailed biography of the star, a filmography with production credits of the actor's work in the genre, and a bibliography. Photographs accompany each entry, a real plus to fans of the films. An appendix covers an additional 25 character actors (in much less detail) who are genre regulars. Also included are notable quotes from the films. This is a very well-researched and well-written companion study to Hannsberry's earlier volume that is likewise both entertaining and informative. This title is highly recommended for public and academic libraries.—**David K. Frasier**

Catalogs

P

432.   Stevens, Michael G. **Reel Portrayals: The Lives of 640 Historical Persons on Film, 1929 Through 2001.** Edited by R. Thompson. Jefferson, N.C., McFarland, 2003. 421p. illus. index. $39.95pa. ISBN 0-7864-1461-8.

Stevens sadly died before completely this work himself, but Thompson has done a splendid job finishing this guide to 569 real people of historical or social importance—George Adamson to Emile Zola—who have been portrayed in at least two international full-length feature films from 1921 to 2001. The entries, alphabetically arranged by person, provide brief biographies, lists of each relevant film, country of production, release year, running time, whether in color or black and white, director, source (e.g., novel, play), awards, alternate titles, and brief cast credits. Boldface cross-references are available, as are a few black-and-white stills. Separate appendixes list U.S. presidents, British and French monarchs, Russian rulers, Kaiser Wilhelm II, and Western series for Billy the Kid and Wild Bill Hickok. The authors also note nonfeature film appearances (television movies, serials) in the brief introductions. A short secondary bibliography and name/title index conclude the volume. Readers will also note the numerous biblical figures (e.g., Moses, David) included. The sole complaint might be the presidents appendix, which does not include major presidents (they are listed in the main section). The Internet Movie Database (www.IMDB.com) occasionally features additional minor portrayals, but for the most part Stevens' work is comprehensive and an excellent guide for teachers and historians. An updated silent companion volume would be an excellent project, as the authors commence with "talkies." A welcome and highly recommended update to Pickard's *Who Played Who on the Screen* (see ARBA 90, entry 1324) and Karsten's *From Real Life to Reel Life* (see ARBA 94, entry 1442).—**Anthony J. Adam**

Chronology

P

433.   **Cinema Year by Year 1894-2003.** Robyn Karney and Joel W. Finler, eds. New York, DK Publishing, 2003. 1005p. illus. index. $50.00. ISBN 0-7894-9946-0.

This latest edition of what began as *Chronicle of Cinema* in 1995 (see ARBA 96, entry 1371), and which has grown through several editions since that time, covers the period 1894 through the first three months of 2003. It is a remarkable coffee-table book about film, organized by year. Each year contains a one-page chronology of important events in the industry for that year, and a list of births of important figures. For instance, in the page for 1941, there is an entry for "Paris, 30 June" which states that "Abel Gance, who has been accused of being Jewish, is required by the Vichy Government to provide his 'Aryan' origins to the head of the cinema industry." The births section for 1941 records the birth of Julie Christie in India on 14 April, and of Ryan O'Neal in Los Angeles on 20 April.

The book contains thousands of short entry articles about particular films, or about events of film-related interest (for instance, a one-paragraph entry for 31 October, 1968, with the headline "Hollywood," records the murder of Ramon Novarro in his home). Most of the entries are short reviews or discussions of films that are quite literate and evaluative. There are also occasional long thematic entries, such as "Color and Widescreen," which covers two pages, although the text would have covered just one. The rest of the article consists of color illustrations, a great strength of this large-format book, which contains more than 3,000 illustrations, many of them in color, and some of these full-page posters for films, smaller-sized stills from films, and photographs of individuals or events (such as Marilyn Monroe's funeral).

Each entry is given a location and date, and the entries are in rough chronological order. So, for instance, in the pages for the year 1950, there is an entry with the headline "Gabin and Carné are back together again" with the dateline "Paris, 25 February," and this is followed by "Film turns spotlight on the racist South" with the dateline "Los Angeles, 3 February." Because virtually every entry has a photograph or illustration, it may be that the size of these illustrations sometimes affected the order of items on a page.

The entries are written as though they are newspaper articles, in quite a lively style, but none are signed, and it is not clear who the authors are. However, the title page mentions editor-in-chief Robyn Karney, associate editor Joel W. Finler, and "contributors" Ronald Bergan, Josephine Carter, Robin Cross, Angie Errigo, and Clive Hirschorn, so these are presumably the writers of the entries.

The volume contains a fine 33-page general index, in small type, consisting chiefly of personal names but not film titles because they are in a separate index of their own, both for films with text and illustration, and for films represented by an illustration but not a text entry. The book indexes approximately 5,000 films. There is also a four-page list of picture credits.

The serious film researcher will still want to rely on *The New York Times Film Reviews*, *The American Film Institute Catalog*, *Variety Film Reviews*, and other major sources of information about film. The entries in this volume give one only a brief taste of each film, clearly not enough for scholarly research. Still, as a one-volume overview of the whole history of film, including a full representation of its non-U.S. aspects, this is a remarkable work, and a great value at $50.

Libraries will want to own this volume, and many individuals will want it on their coffee tables.
—**Bill Miller**

Dictionaries and Encyclopedias

C, P

434.   LoBrutto, Vincent. **The Encyclopedia of American Independent Filmmaking.** Westport, Conn., Greenwood Press, 2002. 566p. illus. index. $74.95. ISBN 0-313-30199-9.

The increasing popularity of independent films in the last decade is one measure of the decline of the Hollywood studio system. Audiences no longer require the validation bestowed by the film having been produced by a major studio with a huge budget, and off-beat, often controversial independent films have never been more in vogue among discriminating filmgoers. Accordingly, as LoBrutto (instructor of cinema at the School of Visual Arts) points out, every major studio has created a small "indie boutique" (p. 14) division to make films in imitation of authentically independent films.

But the film industry has always been enriched by eccentric outsiders who prefer artistic freedom without the constraints imposed by studio executives, and the present work acknowledges this by providing retrospective coverage all the way back to the genre's pioneers, including Buster Keaton, who eventually established his own studio. The alphabetic entries tend to focus more on the industry (producers, directors, companies) than the films themselves. While some are included, notable films such as *Fargo* and *The Killing of Sister George* are absent, although they are discussed in the entries for their filmmakers.

Independent production companies (e.g., BBS, The Cannon Group) are well covered, and a wide net is cast for filmmakers considered independent. Not only present are the familiar names of John Sayles, Kenneth Anger, Jonas Mekas, and Andy Warhol, but also included are John Lennon and Yoko Ono, Jack Kerouac, and Clint Eastwood. There are entries for beat films, gay cinema, and feminist filmmaking. Generous coverage of Gerald Damiano and Behind the Green Door identifies the seventies porno chic movement as an indie phenomenon. The essays are consistently well researched and authoritative, demonstrating a firm command of this emerging field of cinema study.

For purely reference functionality, this fine compilation supersedes *VideoHound's Independent Film Guide* (see ARBA 2000, entry 1169), whose A-Z format by film title is muddled by the excessive use of sidebars profiling indie filmmakers, although it does include many more separate entries for individual films than the present work. Both are highly recommended, given the meager amount of reference material on this new and important topic, as is the good but now dated *Off-Hollywood Movies: A Film Lover's Guide* (see ARBA 90, entry 1334), which provides thoughtful reviews for more than 400 independent films. [R: LJ, 15 May 03, p. 80]—**Richard W. Grefrath**

Handbooks and Yearbooks

P

435.   Ash, Russell. **The Top 10 of Film.** New York, DK Publishing, 2003. 208p. illus. index. $19.00pa. ISBN 0-7894-9640-2.

Ash, who for the last 15 years has put out *The Top Ten of Everything* (see entry 27), has expanded the chapter on film from that work. This is the result. The "Top 10" does not necessarily refer to the best, but rather rates the films according to the income that the film produced, unless otherwise stated. What a smorgasbord of film facts and figures! The work is divided into six color-coded sections: the film industry; box office hits and misses; the stars; directors and writers; film genres; and awards, polls, best, and worst. The top 10 lists cover a multitude of interesting facts about the film industry, including: extensive lists of award winners (both U.S. and foreign); lists of losers (those nominated, but not winning); top films in different genres and countries; the top actors, actresses, directors, and studios; and more. There are often very interesting footnotes to the tables that give some of the behind the scenes information. There are many stills throughout the book. This will be useful as a reference source, even though the index is not extensive. For example, from the index one would never realize that *Singin' in the Rain* was on the American Film Institutes "Top 10 Greatest Films" list since the film itself is not indexed. However, this book will most likely be used for browsing. It is a great source for movie information as well as trivia, and should be in all film collections and many general collections.—**Robert L. Turner Jr.**

P

436.   **British Film Institute Film Classics.** Edward Buscombe and Rob White, eds. New York, Routledge/Taylor & Francis Group, 2003. 2v. illus. $250.00/set. ISBN 1-57958-328-8.

Often a "best of" compilation, loaded with photographs, scanty on text, and highly suitable for the proverbial cocktail table, film books invite endless browsing and little serious study. This is hardly the case with the essays on the more than 50 films that have been spotlighted here by the distinguished British Film Institute. Technical, academic, and lengthy, these analyses cover all aspects of the films, from camera angles to historical context.

The essay on Leni Riefenstahl's famous, or to some, infamous film *Olympia* (1938) is typical of the prevailing high level of cinema scholarship throughout. The extent to which Riefenstahl used innovative filmmaking techniques in this documentary of the 1936 Berlin Olympic games is described in detail, from the panning wide shots used in covering the 100 KM cycling road race, to a photograph of a cameraman in a rubber dinghy filming a close-up of a swimmer. Cinema being a visual medium, the language of film, the edits, angles, shots, and lighting are all crucial to whether a motion picture successfully communicates with the audience. In addition, the history of this controversial film and its role in Nazi propaganda is explored, and there is a detailed chronicle of Riefenstahl's life, and her relationships with Hitler and the German high command, during and after the making of the film. The mere inclusion of this film here, judged "One of the best, if not the best, sports film ever made" (p. 400), attests to the primacy of the films themselves in singling out those judged to be classics.

If each essay appears to be a book in itself there is good reason, since this compendium is actually an anthology of previously published monographs, namely the acclaimed BFI Film Classics series, which commenced publication in 1992. These essays are definitely worth an encore, and the increased accessibility for libraries in having them collected in two reference volumes is appealing. A wide variety of authors are featured, their diversity reflecting the cinema audience itself: critics, novelists, filmmakers, broadcasters, and even a member of Parliament. Accordingly, the perspective varies from essay to essay, a virtue to the editors, who preferred that to a mediocre consistency in outlook and orientation. The essays are classics in themselves, stimulating and engrossing, making it difficult to single any out in particular, although prominent authors featured include Salman Rushdie on *The Wizard of Oz*, Camille Paglia on *The Birds*, and Richard Schickel on *Double Indemnity*. Foreign films (*L'Avventura*, *Wild Strawberries*) and silent films (*Sunrise*, *Greed*) are covered. Most selections could be anticipated by knowledgeable students of cinema, but there are a few surprises, including films that are not widely considered enduring classics, such as *Performance* and *Meet Me in St. Louis*. The authors convincingly elevate these from the realm of the neglected.

While each essay includes detailed film credits, notes, and a bibliography, there are no indexes, either for the individual essays or the set overall, which would have to be seen as a shortcoming in a reference work. Since the essays are arranged chronologically rather than alphabetically, a format reflected in the table of contents, the lack of an index can be irksome when looking for a particular film title, the approach likely to be taken by many readers. The heavy, glossy paper allows for excellent reproduction of the photographs and stills, although all of the illustrations in the original monograph series are not included, probably owing to considerations of space.

This work is highly recommended for cinema collections. Libraries that already have most of the monograph series may want to pause before purchasing this rather expensive set, although in terms of quality, it is well worth it.—**Richard W. Grefrath**

Videography

P

437. **VideoHound's Golden Movie Retriever.** 2004 ed. Jim Craddock, ed. Farmington Hills, Mich., Gale, 2003. 1577p. index. $24.95pa. ISBN 0-7876-7312-9. ISSN 1095-371X.

The 13th edition of *VideoHound* is a solid, reliable reference source on cinema. Like its predecessors, it follows the established succinct format, offering a series of one to four dog bones as rewards for quality (e.g., two for *The House of the Spirits*, three for *Out of Africa*, and four for *Road to Perdition*). Careful abbreviation compresses such data as rating, length, songs, cast and voiceovers, writer, narrator, and names major awards. In addition to 855 pages of entries, the text offers alternate titles, adaptations, awards and nominations, and indexing of cast, director, writer, cinematographer, composer, video sources, and Websites pertinent to films and their evaluation. One of the most useful of *VideoHound* indexes is the category listing, which places titles under such headings as historical detectives, period pieces by century, and scams, stings, and cons.

One of the benefits of using *VideoHound* for general film research is the inclusion of side issues on major movies. In the discussion of *A Beautiful Mind*, the editor comments on public controversy over accuracy of biographical elements about mathematician John Nash. For *Philadelphia*, the entry summarizes theme criticism by gay activists. Occasionally, as with the entry on *O Brother Where Art Thou?*, the analysis becomes snide and cynical, as with the editor's insider sneer about "Coenesque situations and characters." [R: LJ, 1 Feb 04, p. 76]—**Mary Ellen Snodgrass**

THEATER

Dictionaries and Encyclopedias

C, P
438.   Bloom, Ken. **Broadway: Its History, People, and Places: An Encyclopedia.** 2d ed. New York, Routledge/Taylor & Francis Group, 2004. 679p. illus. index. $95.00. ISBN 0-415-93704-3.

Bloom, who has well established himself as a source of information on popular entertainment with such titles as *American Song* (see ARBA 86, entry 1359), gives us a new edition of his Broadway encyclopedia (1st ed.; see ARBA 92, entry 467). This edition, half as long as the 1st, includes 276 articles (some quite substantial essays), with 16 new entries. It follows the format of the first: entries are alphabetically arranged with numerous illustrations and a lengthy index (plenty of cross-references, including entries to items not meriting separate articles).

Right off, this is a very personal document, reflecting the interests and views of the author. Bloom also admits it is selective. But it is a wonderful reference work. It is an excellent source for history of Broadway theaters (well complementing the information in Louis Botto's *At this Theatre* [Applause, 2002] and Nicholas van Hoogstraten's *Lost Broadway Theatres* [expanded ed.; Princeton Architectural Press, 1997]). But it lacks maps of the New York theater district, showing locations of buildings discussed. It provides selective coverage of playwrights (O'Neill, Williams, and Miller but not Anderson or Odets); musical teams (Rodgers and Hart and Lerner and Loewe but not Kander and Ebb or Adler and Ross); performers (Cohan, Merman, and Martin but not Bobby Clark or Ed Wynn); and shows (*Annie Get Your Gun* and *Cats* but no *Oklahoma!* or *Life with Father*). But why quibble? There are so many riches, including individual articles on many producers (Belasco, Ziegfeld), critics (Atkinson, Barnes), columnists (Winchell, Sullivan), restaurants (Automat, Sardi's), organizations (ASCAP, Theatre Guild), buildings (Brill), hotels (Astor, Knickerbocker), awards (Tonys), press agents, theater slang, Times Square signage, and the actors' strike of 1919, just to name a few. This work does restrict itself to the commercial theater in the Times Square area, thus there is no recognition of off Broadway. Most illustrations are different from those in the earlier edition. (Overall, the illustrations in the 1st edition are superior.) Bibliographic references following the articles would have enhanced this work. An essential addition for all performing arts collections, this work will also be very useful in larger public and academic libraries. Libraries with shelf space should keep the 1st edition.—**Richard D. Johnson**

Handbooks and Yearbooks

P
439.   *The New York Times* **Theater Reviews.** New York, Times Books and New York, Routledge/Taylor & Francis Group, 2002. 625p. index. $240.00. ISBN 0-415-93697-7.

Compilations of theater reviews from *The New York Times* have been available dating back to 1870. The present volume updates this collection by adding all of its reviews published in 1999-2000. Included are cabarets and one-person shows as well as plays and musicals.

Entries are arranged chronologically, first by year and then by date of review. The main section is followed by several articles about shows that won awards, and a listing of Tony Awards winners for 1999 and 2000. The comprehensive indexes cover all reviews in this volume and begin with the 1997 index, which was not included in the previous volume. Indexes are divided by year, and each by three sections —titles, personal names, and corporate names. The latter two include the function of the entry. All refer to the date of the review. *The New York Times Theater Reviews* are relied upon to keep the public abreast of what is happening in New York's theaters. May this tradition continue!—**Anita Zutis**

28 Philosophy and Religion

PHILOSOPHY

Dictionaries and Encyclopedias

C

440.   **The Continuum Encyclopedia of Modern Criticism and Theory.** Julian Wolfreys and others, eds. New York, Continuum Publishing, 2002. 882p. index. $175.00. ISBN 0-8264-1414-1.

At first glance, seeing a book on literary theory might cause the hair to raise and the lip to twitch. Literary theory of the last three decades is not known for its sanity so much as for its willingness to entertain "flapdoodle." Happily, this volume of more than 100 essays on modern literary criticism offers students and faculty a lantern for the dark land of the history and development of literary and cultural criticism. Included here are theorists, philosophers, literary critics, schools of thought, and more. The volume "aims at inter- and trans-disciplinary criticism," limiting the coverage to the beginning of the twenty-first century. It does this exceedingly well. Thus, for example, Descartes, Spinoza, Marx, Kant, Husserl, Derrida, and others are treated. Also included are essays on phenomenology, French structuralism, and the periodical *Tel Quel*. Essays on African American studies, lesbian and gay studies, postmodernism, and the like are proffered to the reader as well.

The volume falls into three neat divisions: criticism in Europe; in North America; and in England, Ireland, Scotland, and Wales. The essays are all signed and include some of the best minds writing on the topic today: Veronique M. Foti, Mitchell R. Lewis, Stephen Shapiro, Martin McQuillan, Stephen Womack, and ore than three dozen more. While other encyclopedias offer some overlap, this volume is so specific as to be *sui generis*. It appears a must buy for those interested in its subject matter. [R: LJ, 15 June 02, p. 56]—**Mark Y. Herring**

P

441.   Grenz, Stanley J., and Jay T. Smith. **Pocket Dictionary of Ethics.** Downers Grove, Ill., InterVarsity Press, 2003. 128p. $7.00pa. ISBN 0-8308-1468-X.

Coming in at 4-by-7-inches and 128 pages, the A to Z *Pocket Dictionary of Ethics* is a useful tool for students of any age, especially at the college and seminary levels. With nearly 400 clearly written entries focusing on Greek, Western, and Christian ethical traditions, this volume will be useful for the study of history, the social sciences, philosophy, and religion. Students will benefit from its thorough yet brief treatment of topics that will enliven and give meaning to the many abstract concepts they will encounter in their studies. The layperson who has an interest in studying ethics will also benefit from this handy tool, which can be carried in a pocket or a purse with ease. The dictionary coverage is wide and diverse. It includes both secular, analytic, applied, and religious ethics and takes the reader from the obvious (e.g., *abortion*, *character*) to the obscure (e.g., *eugenics*, *Hindu ethics*, *zygote*). It provides a quick reference tool on concepts that frame much wider ethical discussions. To this end, the authors have achieved their purpose.

Because of the events stemming from the terrorist attacks on September 11, 2001, the inclusion of *Islamic ethics* is a wise choice, but because of the close relationship between Judaism, Christianity, and Islam, perhaps a few more topics in this general area—such as the Islamic ideas associated with medical ethics, health policy, sex education, death and dying, and religion and science—would have been useful. Overall, as a general reference tool for ethical discussion, this *Pocket Dictionary* will serve as a valuable resource for both the novice and the ethicist seeking understanding and knowledge in a difficult and changing ethical environment.—**Joseph P. Hester**

RELIGION

General Works

Dictionaries and Encyclopedias

C, P

442. **Encyclopedia of Religious Freedom.** Catharine Cookson, ed. New York, Routledge/Taylor & Francis Group, 2003. 555p. illus. index. (Routledge Encyclopedias of Religion and Society). $125.00. ISBN 0-415-94181-4.

Polls have consistently shown that the United States is the most religious of the western industrialized nations, and so studies treating religion and politics have considerable appeal to the American public. This work, the fourth volume in the Routledge Encyclopedias of Religion and Society series, is no exception. Editor Catharine Cookson, director of the Center for the Study of Religious Freedom at Virginia Wesleyan College, wisely aims at a popular audience. Although religious freedom in the United States is the primary focus, the volume's 140 articles span the globe, offering insights on everything from the Falun Gong, the medieval Islamic empire, and the Middle East to the Reformation in early modern Europe, Shintoism, and Vatican II. Often running three to five pages, the entries, drawing largely upon scholars from the fields of law, religious studies, history, philosophy, theology, and political science, are clearly written and accompanied by a list of suggested readings. Frequently photographs and relevant documents, as in the Gobitas letter in the article on Jehovah's Witnesses, or the Requermiento, a classic example of Spanish legalism, in the feature on the Spanish Empire, are included.

Such material is made readily accessible by a sensible organization. The entries are subsumed under seven major topics: key concepts, such as civil religion and religious tolerance; U.S. history, featuring such subjects as the Great Awakening and Pledge of Allegiance; world history, treating matters like Augustine on religious freedom and witch hunts; world religions, from Baha'i to Sikhism; major issues, such as brainwashing and religious terrorist groups; minority groups and their rights, highlighting Jews in Europe and the U.S. and nineteenth-century American colonial Catholics; and key documents, exemplified by the Fourteenth Amendment and the Virginia Declaration of Rights. The index is adequate, but unfortunately not exhaustive. Even so, the work will be useful to anyone interested in the subject of religious freedom. [R: LJ, Aug 03, pp. 70-71]—**John W. Storey**

C, P

443. **Encyclopedia of Science and Religion.** J. Wentzel Vrede van Huyssteen, ed. New York, Macmillan Reference USA/Gale Group, 2003. 2v. index. $240.00/set. ISBN 0-02-865704-7.

The *Encyclopedia of Science and Religion* is a great reference resource that addresses a wide variety of topics in religion, science, and the intersection between the two. The resource addresses obvious topics like abortion and creationism, along with less-well-known concepts, such as pneumatology and logical positivism. In its most valuable feature, the *Encyclopedia* gives brief overviews of the religion v. science issues in the major world religions as well as in the various streams of Christianity (e.g., Catholicism, Lutheranism, Calvinism, Evangelicalism). The entries are written for nonprofessionals in both religion and science, and are balanced and without obvious bias.

Each article is signed by an authoritative author, whose qualifications are specified in the preface of volume 1. A synoptic outline of the contents is provided, allowing the user to look at a classified topic list under general headings like "Technology," "Cosmology," and "Method." This makes this easy-to-use resource even more useful. An excellent index assists users in finding topics of interest quickly and efficiently. One weakness of this resource is its lack of illustrations. This is not a major problem, although some graphs, photographs, or plates of symbols would greatly enhance the *Encyclopedia*'s value as a research tool. Still, even without illustrations, the *Encyclopedia of Science and Religion* is very useful and is recommended for academic and public libraries. School libraries, if their budgets allow, might even find this resource useful for older students. [R: LJ, Aug 03, p. 71]—**Mark T. Bay**

C, S
444.   **Religion and American Cultures: An Encyclopedia of Traditions, Diversity, and Popular Expressions.** Gary Laderman and Luis León, eds. Santa Barbara, Calif., ABC-CLIO, 2003. 3v. illus. index. $285.00/set; $430.00 (w/e-book). ISBN 1-57607-238-X; 1-57607-854-X (e-book).

This work's revisionist tone would have been in order 20 or 30 years ago, for studies then often overemphasized the Protestant character and uniformity of this nation's religious heritage. That changed dramatically with Will Herberg's *Protestant, Catholic, Jew* (1955). Since then numerous scholars have probed America's religious and ethic pluralism, following its roots to at least the late 1600s. But even if this treatment is not as unique as it purports to be, it is nevertheless a useful contribution to religious scholarship, one that will be most helpful to a general audience. Editors Gary Laderman, a professor of American religious history and culture at Emory University, and Luis D. Léon, a professor of Latino and religious studies at the University of California, Berkeley, take a sociological and anthropological approach, meaning they define religion as "an ultimate belief and value system, a 'worldview,' understood through and constituted by various types of symbols, rituals, myths, and other cultural forms of expression" (p. xviii). This fusion of religion and culture allows for considerable latitude.

Included are almost 200 entries and over 75 documents. Beginning with African American religions, volume 1 moves alphabetically from Buddhism, Islam, and Judaism in America to Native American religions and politics, New Age, and Protestantism in America. Introducing each major topic is a clearly written five- to seven-page overview, followed by briefer treatments of specific aspects of the subject. Subsumed under "New Religious Traditions," for instance, are entries on such things as Christian Science, Mind Cure, Mormonism, and Vampire Culture. Volume 2 attempts to explain where Americans actually get their beliefs about God, ethics, and death, and how they develop spiritual practices. Among the subjects covered here are Public Theologies and Political Culture, Sacred Space, and Sexuality. Documents from the late fifteenth century to the present comprise volume 3, and they touch on everything from the Half-Way Covenant (1662) and Lincoln's Emancipation Proclamation to Martin Luther King's "I Have a Dream" and George Bush's proclamation following the September 11th terrorist attacks. Photographs and an extensive bibliography enhance this work, while a thorough index affords easy access to its wealth of information. This is a must for high school and university libraries.—**John W. Storey**

Handbooks and Yearbooks

P

445.   **How to be a Perfect Stranger: The Essential Religious Etiquette Handbook.** 3d ed. Stuart M. Matlins and Arthur J. Magida, eds. Woodstock, Vt., SkyLight Paths, 2003. 399p. $19.95pa. ISBN 1-893361-67-5.

The editors of this 3d edition have produced a helpful and reasonably priced handbook for church-goers in the United States. This volume includes 29 religious organizations/denominations, a glossary of common religious terms and names, a calendar of religious holidays and festivals, and a summary of proper forms for addressing leaders of various faiths. The book's consistent organization, comprehensiveness, and simplicity of writing make it a reference tool worth owning by the average layperson as well as religious leaders.

The entries each follow the same easy-to-use, organizational pattern. They begin with the organization's title and affiliation, followed by a section on history and beliefs, which includes information on membership numbers, U.S. membership, and contact information (address, telephone number, and e-mail address). Information on a basic service is provided that includes information on proper attire, the layout of the sanctuary and its nomenclature, the organization of the service and how guests are to enter and exit, the major officiants, rituals, books used during the service, and the order of the service. The information on guest behavior during the service is a major entry and is a helpful inclusion for the uninitiated guest. Information on what, when, and what not to do will save guests from embarrassment when visiting an unfamiliar church. Information is included about what occurs after a service, special vocabulary used by the denomination, and significant beliefs (dogma and ideology). This section also includes general guidelines and advice for preventing mistakes during such rituals as Holy Communion. A section of special vocabulary includes key words or phrases that might be helpful for a visitor to know, such as *Torah*, *Simcha*, *Eucharist*, and *Ardas*. "Holy Days and Festivals" includes dates and explanations of such events as Christmas, Pentecost Sunday, Yom Kippur, Ramadan, and so on. The section titled "Life Cycle Events" covers such details as birth ceremonies, initiation ceremonies, marriage ceremonies, and funerals and mourning. This section provides needed information about appropriate attire, gifts, and ceremonies themselves, and appropriate behaviors before and after each kind of ceremony. A section on "Home Celebrations" concludes each section where applicable. For example, it includes in the Jewish section detailed explanations about Passover Seder commemorating the Jewish people's liberation from slavery in Egypt, and the Shabbat Dinner, which commemorates the day on which God rested after creating the world.

This reference book will make a handy guide for people of all faiths and all backgrounds. It provides the well-meaning guest a manual of attire and behavior, of information and explanation, that allows each to comfortably participate in the religious ceremonies of other faiths while uplifting their own spiritual sensitivity and awareness.—**Joseph P. Hester**

Bible Studies

Bibliography

C, P

446.   **The Unbound Bible. http://unbound.biola.edu/.** [Website]. Free. Date reviewed: Dec 03.

The Unbound Bible's stated purpose is "to provide the Bible to the nations of the world," and it has done an admirable job of beginning that task. In addition to nine English versions, *Unbound* provides multiple original-language versions (6 Greek New Testaments, 3 Hebrew Old Testaments), 6 ancient translations (including the Latin Vulgate and the Greek Septuagint), and 37 versions of all or part of the Judeo-Christian Bible in 30 languages. Links are provided for downloading fonts. The site supports word searches of individual books, portions, or the whole Bible in the various languages. Both language and portion of scripture to be searched must be selected, provided for through drop-down boxes. Non-English word searches are facilitated by a point and click method in which characters are selected from a menu in a pop-up window and then pasted into the search box. Boolean searches are supported as are parallel searches, wherein the search is done and results are shown for up to three versions simultaneously.

In addition to the Bible translations, *The Unbound Bible* provides several useful public domain research tools (Bible dictionary, commentary, lexicon, and more). For the user to make the greatest use of the site, registration (free with password and optional e-mail) gives access to a clipboard to which passages may be attached and deleted, and to a "Notes" function in which the searcher may make personal comments. The "Notes" feature is searchable by keywords, which are selected by the user at the time the notes are made. Both the "Clipboard" and the "Notes" contents are retained between sessions until deleted by the user.

Little negative can be said about the site. The site is not as intuitive as one might prefer, thus the wise searcher will begin by reading the useful "Help" section found under the heading "Using this Site." In addition, pop-ups must be allowed for the system to work properly, so utilities that prevent them must be adjusted to account for this. The final negative comment is that the site uses frames and does not offer a "no frames" option. On the positive side, once understood, searching is powerful, quick, and easy. The research tools add value to the student who wants more than just the source document, and the "Clipboard" and "Notes" functions provide tools that will enhance study. This site is highly recommended for public and academic libraries for religious studies in both Jewish and Christian disciplines.—**Jeannie Colson**

Biography

C, P
447.   Tischler, Nancy M. **Men and Women of the Bible: A Reader's Guide.** Westport, Conn., Greenwood Press, 2002. 267p. illus. index. $59.95. ISBN 0-313-31714-3.

Biblical reference books have large academic and popular audiences. Tischler, a retired university English professor, aims at both sets of readers by providing biographical and literary information on more than 100 characters from the Bible. Aimed at students and general readers, this volume offers not only a description of the characters' exploits in the biblical texts, but also several additional features: the historical context of the original stories; archaeological evidence supporting the biographical information or, if that is unavailable, its cultural context; references to the characters in later literary works; and a brief bibliography after each entry. The entries vary from one to four pages in length, depending on the relative importance of the characters in the literature. Supplemental materials include an index that picks up most of the names and places from the articles, nicely reproduced black-and-white art, and a general bibliography.

The text is clearly and engagingly written, and will be accessible to a wide range of readers. The consistency and breadth of treatment for each entry distinguish this volume from other similar sources. However, there is not great depth here. It does not have the detailed treatment of textual issues or historical problems, such as those found in many other specialized reference books on biblical and literary studies. While it would serve well in a small religious reference collection and it is an excellent browsing book for general readers, it is not an important addition for larger collections.—**Christopher W. Nolan**

Dictionaries and Encyclopedias

C, P
448.   **The Basic IVP Reference Collection.** [CD-ROM]. Downers Grove, Ill., InterVarsity Press, 2003. Minimum system requirements: Pentium 133MHz. CD-ROM drive. Windows 98 or later. 64MB RAM. 60MB hard disk space. 800x600 screen resolution. $50.00. ISBN 0-8308-1457-4.

The Basic InterVarsity Press (IVP) Reference Collection contains a wealth of IVP reference resources including the *Dictionary of Biblical Imagery*, the *Dictionary of Jesus and the Gospels*, the *Dictionary of New Testament Background*, the *Dictionary of Paul and His Letters*, the *Dictionary of the Later New Testament and Its Developments, Hard Sayings of the Bible, The IVP Bible Background Commentaries of the Old and New Testaments*, the *New Dictionary of Biblical Theology*, the *New Dictionary of Theology*, the *Pocket Dictionary of the Study of New Testament Greek*, the *Pocket Dictionary of Apologetics and Philosophy of Religion*, and the Pocket Dictionary of Biblical Studies, and the King James Version of the Bible.

This CD-ROM features the new Libronix Digital Library System (DLS) technology, which allows the user to search, parallel scroll the footnotes with the text, integrate Internet resources, and is designed to work with scalable language support. Unlike the Libronix DLS predecessor, Logos Libronix DLS is designed to work with Arabic and Asian scripts. Libronix DLS can work with user interfaces even if they have only been partially translated, and defaults to English when something is not available in a particular language. The Libronix DLS supports localized user interfaces and electronic books in hundreds of languages and includes languages that are not provided in Microsoft Windows.

An excellent tutorial, extensive help screens, and zoom options for low vision are included. The ease of loading, accessibility, comprehensive information, and links make this a must-purchase for any collection. One of the only disadvantages is that the software only contains the King James Version of the Bible. However, other versions may be used simultaneously.—**Ravonne A. Green**

Handbooks and Yearbooks

P
449.   **Eerdmans Commentary on the Bible.** James D. G. Dunn and John W. Rogerson, eds. Grand Rapids, Mich., William B. Eerdmans, 2003. 1629p. index. $75.00. ISBN 0-8028-3711-5.

Founded in 1911, the independently owned William B. Eerdmans publishing company has long been known for publishing a wide range of religious books, from academic works in theology to books for pastors and general audiences. The *Eerdmans Commentary on the Bible* (ECB) is a general and introductory Bible handbook in a single volume of 1,629 pages, which lays open easily for study and research. The editors have brought together 67 academics who encapsulate both modern and international biblical scholarship. ECB includes general introductions to both the Old and New Testaments, the Apocrypha, Pseudepigrapha, I Enoch (a part of the canon of Scriptures in the Ethiopian Orthodox church and sometimes referred to as the "Ethiopic Enoch" since it survives only in that language), the New Testament Apocrypha, and the Dead Sea Scrolls.

ECB's primary objective is to clarify the meaning of each section of the Bible, focusing on large themes and highlighting their interconnections with the rest of the biblical text. Although general and introductory in nature, ECB does provide a reader-friendly commentary on biblical history and biblical texts with wide-ranging foundational articles. The scholarship is solid, up to date, and points the serious student of the Bible in the direction of problematic areas that require more in-depth reading for more than a cursory understanding. By being comprehensive, the volume addresses and answers major issues, including many possible interpretations, and points the reader to more comprehensive, engaging material.

ECB is a solid, general reference on the Bible, but is not intended for serious biblical scholarship and textual evaluations. This is evident by the cursory treatment given to the New Testament Apocrypha material. Only 2 of the 30 to 40 manuscripts of the Nag Hammadi literature was treated—*The Gospel of Thomas* and *The Gospel of Peter*—with the summative remark that on the whole the New Testament Apocrypha is "a mixture of orthodoxy and heterodoxy" and that "that is important to realize because the predominant stance of the Great Church has been that these works are heretical." This in no way provides the serious reader with any clue about the debates over the contour of the New Testament canon that were long, hard, and sometimes harsh, the theological issues of the first and second centuries, and the role of Mary Magdalene in the early development of Christianity.—**Joseph P. Hester**

Buddhism

C, P
450.   **Encyclopedia of Buddhism.** Robert E. Buswell Jr., ed. New York, Macmillan Reference USA/Gale Group, 2004. 2v. illus. index. $265.00/set. ISBN 0-02-865718-7.

The two-volume *Encyclopedia of Buddhism* offers a comprehensive view of the topic with a generalist Western audience in mind. The preface makes the case for a resource that helps Westerners relate Buddhism to the larger cultures of its diverse adherents, and the encyclopedia does this job admirably. Signed articles, written by over 200 scholars in the field, are arranged alphabetically by subject and include individual bibliographies as well as cross-references. Articles vary from half-column biographies to discussions of topics like the "Four Noble Truths" that range over several pages. The articles do not avoid controversial issues, such as Buddhism's sometimes contradictory stance on war and sexuality, and this gives the work a compellingly nuanced tone that is in keeping with such a complex topic. Each volume includes illustrations in an eight-page color insert and numerous black-and-white illustrations scattered throughout the text. Following the preface in volume 1 is an alphabetic list of article topics along with their authors, who have their names and credentials listed in a separate list of contributors. Volume 1 also includes an excellent synoptic outline of articles, which helps with cursory cross-referencing. Maps of Asia follow this outline, which illustrate the spread of Buddhism from India to the rest of the region. There is a timeline of Buddhist history at the close of volume 2 covering the major regions of Asia, and this is followed by a tremendously detailed subject index. This is an appropriate addition to public or undergraduate libraries.—**Philip G. Swan**

Christianity

Biography

P
451.   **Biographical Dictionary of Evangelicals.** Timothy Larsen, ed. Downers Grove, Ill., InterVarsity Press, 2003. 789p. index. $45.00. ISBN 0-8308-2925-3.

"Evangelical" as a subcategory of "Protestant" is both widely misunderstood and at times contested, so editor Larsen wisely introduces this volume by explicating his definition. This conjoins approaches borrowed from his two consulting editors, eminent church historians David Bebbington and Mark Noll. Larsen embraces Bebbington's widely accepted characterization incorporating four criteria—conversionism, activism, biblicism, and crucicentrism—but also Noll's more descriptive approach that looks to an identifiable network of institutions and individuals. The latter influence contributes to a stated bias toward figures "who have had a substantial impact in the wider evangelical movement (cross-denominationally) and away from those whose influence was contained within denominational, ethnic, theological, or regional subcultures" (introduction). Thus constructed, Larsen's definition covers a remarkable diversity of individuals whose wider persuasions often clash as profoundly as their core Evangelical convictions may mesh. Anglican John Stott, Pentecostal Oral Roberts, abolitionist Harriet Beecher Stowe, fundamentalist Bob Jones, Methodist ecumenist Lesslie Newbigin, faith healer Katherine Kuhlman, British feminist Christabel Pankhurst, Republican Mark Hatfield, and Democrat Jimmy Carter all find places here, along with some 400 others as famous as Billy Graham and as obscure (to most) as a Canadian missionary couple with the fitting name Goforth. Excluded are persons born after 1935. At the other end of the timescale, the 1730s are accepted as the beginning of a recognizable Evangelical movement, but there is room for those considered its major progenitors: Wyclif, Luther, Calvin, Menno Simons, Puritans (such as Cotton Mather), and a handful of others. Coverage is generally limited to the English-speaking world, but does encompass some figures outside that orbit who achieved significant influence within it, such as Dutch statesman-theologian Abraham Kuyper and Chinese Local Church Movement founder Watchman Nee. Contributors comprise a large international cast of scholars whose own Evangelical sympathies are frequently evident. Scholarly but accessible, this work is suitable for both academic and public libraries. [R: Choice, Jan 04, p. 874]—**Hans E. Bynagle**

Dictionaries and Encyclopedias

C, P

452.   Day, Peter. **A Dictionary of Christian Denominations.** New York, Continuum Publishing, 2003. 516p. $115.00. ISBN 0-8264-5745-2.

For the average person trying to understand the diversity of Christian denominations and sects, Peter Day's *A Dictionary of Christian Denominations* provides a comprehensive overview of these groups. Day's text also gives a short background on each group, including the parent denomination and its individual development. These entries include important dates, texts, and events. Other names for the sects are included at the bottom of each entry. Other church groups that come into contact with a group in question are set in all upper-case letters. The coverage spans the entire Christian era, granting equal coverage to Arianism and Albigensians as it does to Estonian Evangelical Lutheran Church and the Fellowship of Christian Pilgrims. Day gives attention to discontinued sects as well as current groups.

Day's only potential oversight comes with the lack of *see also* references in this text. For example, if someone is looking for Cathars, they have to know that the editor put them under "Albigensians." A listing for "Cathars: *see* Albigensians" would help the reader to find the information much easier. While he does list alternate names for each sect at the entry's end, this cross-referencing would be extremely helpful. This work is recommended for public, community college, college, and university libraries.—**David J. Duncan**

P

453.   **The New Westminster Dictionary of Liturgy and Worship.** Paul Bradshaw, ed. Westminster, Colo., Westminster Publishing, 2002. 493p. $44.95. ISBN 0-664-22655-8.

In this revision of the earlier work of the same name (see ARBA 88, entry 1426), Bradshaw recognizes the interdenominational, not to mention interreligious, nature of his subject. Contributors are drawn from all across mainline Christianity, as well those at the margin of the tradition (e.g., Mormons, Quakers, Shakers) and those of non-Christian bodies (e.g., Hinduism, Islam, Judaism, Rastafarianism). For topics that traverse denominational boundaries (e.g., funerals, marriage, ordination), the sizeable articles are divided into various sections that explore the topic's development, as well as the current attitudes and practices of various ecclesial families.

Full and well-balanced coverage is provided on controversial topics, such as "Inclusive Language" or the "Ordination of Women" (although the Anglican author of the latter article can be faulted for not adopting the cross-denominational perspective found elsewhere in the work). Many articles include short bibliographies that permit the reader to explore the topic in more depth, although these are not as universal as one might wish. For example, patrons exploring such topics as "Blind Persons" will find no references for further reading. Finally, given the interreligious nature of the work, it should be noted that topics with obvious parallels in non-Christian traditions (e.g., funerals, marriage) have no articles that address those topics in any of the non-Christian contexts represented elsewhere in the work. Of course, to do so the resulting product would have to be considerably larger than the present work, but by the same token some explanation of why some elements of non-Christian practice were included but not others might have been desirable. Still, for researchers requiring information on all aspects of Christian worship this work will be useful.—**Christopher Brennan**

Hinduism

C, P

454.   Dallapiccola, Anna L. **Dictionary of Hindu Lore and Legend.** New York, W. W. Norton, 2002. 224p. illus. maps. $31.95. ISBN 0-500-51088-1.

This delightful dictionary is a pleasure to read and browse through as well as a useful reference. Amply illustrated and carefully prepared by an eminent art historian, the book serves to educate and entertain. More than 1,000 topics of myths, legends, festivals, temple architecture, rituals, religion, Ayurvedic medicine, and astrology are defined and described. Cultural and religious background, Sanskrit equivalents, and chronologies help to conceptualize the data. The introduction provides a concise and helpful overview of the subcontinent and its peoples. The index is particularly useful because it serves in part as a small English-Sanskrit dictionary. This is a highly recommended dictionary and will be of use to scholars as well as general readers interested in India. [R: LJ, 1 Feb 03, p. 72]—**Linda L. Lam-Easton**

Islam

P

455.   **Encyclopedia of Islam and the Muslim World.** Richard C. Martin, ed. New York, Macmillan Reference USA/Gale Group, 2004. 2v. illus. maps. index. $265.00/set. ISBN 0-02-865603-2.

Can there be a more necessary reference source in these troubled times such as this? With the memories of the terrorist attacks of September 11th still vivid in our minds and the American invasions of Afghanistan and Iraq, the Islamic world has been falsely demonized as a cult of murderous, religious fanatics. So many people, Americans in general, know next to nothing about a faith that is over 15 centuries old and is a guiding force in the lives of over a billion people. Perhaps a well-argued narrative would have a stronger impact to enlighten the masses; however, there is nothing better than an encyclopedia to serve as a repository of authoritative information, especially one written as a general reference tool for the lay reader and the student. Macmillan Reference has produced a two-volume work that covers many facets of Islam and the Muslim world from antiquity to the present time. It is edited by the eminent Islamic scholar and historian Richard C. Martin of Emory University, and he has gathered together over 200 scholars who have produced 515 entries. Each entry is signed and contains its own bibliography for further study. There has been a major attempt to keep the work easily accessible and understandable for the lay reader and the student. The articles are not weighed down by academic jargon and the size of the individual articles is limited not to exceed a maximum count of 5,000 words—quite a task for both writer and editor when dealing with broad theological and cultural concepts. Also included is a comprehensive index, timelines, genealogical charts, maps, and numerous illustrations. This set is recommended for all public libraries.—**Glenn Masuchika**

C, S

456.   **The Muslim World.** Geoffrey Orens, ed. Bronx, N.Y., H. W. Wilson, 2003. 199p. index. (The Reference Shelf, v.75, no.1). $45.00pa. ISBN 0-8242-1019-0.

This book, like others in The Reference Shelf series, is a collection of articles from both scholarly and popular publications. Each section consists of three to five articles on a particular aspect of Islam, including beliefs and practices, women, democracy, other Abrahamic traditions, and western interpretations of Islam. The introduction to each section gives an overview of the issues considered and a summary of each article included in that section. The index is very helpful. The well-prepared bibliography provides the reader with many additional sources.

The purpose of the book is to educate the reader about the various aspects of Islam at a time when Islam is more feared than understood. The articles are carefully selected to inform, but not to proselytize or dwell on political controversies. The customs that are most likely to offend western readers, such as female circumcision, are dismissed as part of a culture, but not essentially part of the religion. Most of the articles were written after the terrorist attacks of September 11th and some of the authors are members of the Islam religion. The desire to explain the difference between Islam and terrorism is evident.

The concept of a collection of articles seems, at first glance, to be outdated in this age when full-text databases make so many articles available. However, the quality of the selections and the excellent introductions unify the articles. This book would make a useful addition to many collections, especially for high schools and community colleges.—**Jeanne D. Galvin**

Part IV
SCIENCE AND TECHNOLOGY

BIOGRAPHY

P, S

457.   Spangenburg, Ray, and Kit Moser. **African Americans in Science, Math, and Invention.** New York, Facts on File, 2003. 254p. illus. index. (A to Z of African Americans). $44.00. ISBN 0-8160-4806-1.

This is a collection of short biographies of Americans whose roots began in Africa, and who have distinguished themselves in science and technology. Aside from that ancestral root, this is a very diverse group; there is no commonality of background, upbringing, advantage, or lack of advantage. Benjamin Banneker, born free in 1731, did have the advantage of a short attendance at a Quaker school. John Parker, born a slave in 1827, purchased his freedom, established his own foundry, and was granted several industrial patents. Ronald McNair came from a more conventional middle class background and earned a MIT doctorate and qualified as an astronaut before perishing in the *Challenger* disaster. This book belongs in every high school library. It is interesting to read, and is dramatic proof that all people can triumph. [R: SLJ, June 03, p. 87]—**Robert B. McKee**

P, S

458.   **World Book's Biographical Encyclopedia of Scientists.** Chicago, World Book, 2003. 8v. illus. index. $289.00/set. ISBN 0-7166-76001.

This 8-volume set provides extensive biographical information on approximately 1,300 scientists in the fields of agriculture, astronomy, biology, chemistry, engineering, geology, mathematics, meteorology, medicine, and physics. Inventors and individuals who made major contributions to later inventions and discoveries are also included. The set is alphabetically arranged with each slim volume having approximately 184 pages. Each page is in a two-column layout. A fact box containing the name of the scientist, birth and death dates, nationality, and occupation introduces each article. The opening sentence of each article repeats the individual's name and gives their nationality and their most noted accomplishment. The biographies are well written and vary in length from one column to two pages. A chronology is provided for the longer articles. Also included are 48 special reports on significant discoveries and developments. Each special report is distinguished by cream-colored paper and follows the biography of the scientist whose work was in this area of research (i.e., "Island Universes" follows the biography of Edwin Powell Hubble). These reports also note the contributions and efforts of others who contributed to the topic. Those individuals whose names appear in bold within an article or report have their own biography. Each volume contains a table of contents for that specific volume and a cumulative index. The set is illustrated with more than 750 photographs and illustrations. Volume 8 contains a glossary, list of other reference sources arranged by scientific field, a list of Nobel Prize winners, index by occupation, index by nationality and ethnicity, and an index by century. The 146-word glossary provides pronunciation and a definition; however, there is no cross-reference to the biography or article containing that term. Some of the entries in the glossary are included in the comprehensive index. This source is highly recommended for middle school, junior high school, and high school libraries, as well as public libraries. [R: SLJ, Aug 03, p. 112]—**Elaine Ezell**

CHRONOLOGY

P, S

459.   Fernández-Armesto, Felipe. **Ideas that Changed the World.** New York, DK Publishing, 2003. 400p. illus. index. $30.00. ISBN 0-7894-9609-7.

The London-based publishing giant Dorling Kindersley has long produced colorful pictorial information books for children such as the 3-volume *Illustrated Family Encyclopedia* (2002) edited by Karen O'Brien. With John B. Teeple's *Timelines of World History* (see ARBA 2003, entry 517), and now *Ideas That Changed the World*, the publisher is clearly moving into the adult field of reference books with the same style that relies heavily on short, high-interest, reader-friendly textual materials amplified with an abundance of related visual information. Brevity is actually a necessity in this case. How else can a distinguished historian distill more than 175 of the most dominant ideas to be formed by humankind across approximately 30,000 years in less than 400 pages?

The format used here blurs the lines between print and electronic media. The printed material mimics well-designed Internet Web pages. There is a dominant heading, attention getting, tantalizing information, plenty of art, photographs, symbols, artifact representations, and pithy quotations combined with connections (links) to other relevant pages (sites). This description accurately describes Fernández-Armesto's double-page treatments of the 175 dominant ideas of humankind he has chosen.

The spread on "Inalienable Rights: The Idea of Human Rights" (pp. 264-65), for example, consists of 2 pages dominated not by text but by a sepia-tone photograph of a suburban home and car, circa 1950, with the caption, "An American Dream." A cameo painting of Rousseau identifies him as one of the thinkers who formulated the concept of inalienable rights, and this is accompanied by a list of four recommended books for further reading by Rousseau and others, including, curiously, Harper Lee's 1960 novel, *To Kill A Mockingbird*. A brief quotation is from the U.S. Declaration of Independence (1776), and a short text box directs readers to four other connecting ideas discussed elsewhere in the book. Fascinating as all this accompanying visual and boxed information is, it leaves the author just four paragraphs of text space to introduce, explain, and consider the lasting influence of the Idea of "Inalienable Rights."

To his considerable credit, Fernández-Armesto, who holds history faculty positions at both Oxford and the University of London, executes his task with considerable dash. Each entry is both fascinating and provocative. The range of ideas the historian introduces is simply staggering whether he is describing the ideas of an orderly universe or measuring time or introducing Islam and predestination.

There is something completely fascinating to learn on every page. For example, The Great Pyramid of Cheops, built around 2500 B.C.E. (pp. 92-93) remains even today the largest human-made structure ever built. All of the 175 ideas are not equally agreeable just as not all have had equal influence. Cannibalism and incest are far more disturbing than Zen or sacred art. The ideas of slavery, massacre, terrorism, and anti-Semitism have been greatly more harmful to the welfare of the world than the ideas of human rights, representative democracy, and universal love.

Fernández-Armesto acknowledges that the selection of the ideas was entirely his own and that his primary criteria was the influence and relevance of each idea. He also states that he eschewed developments such as inventions that primarily have had their influence outside the mind of man in favor of thinking that has constituted new ways of humans contemplating both themselves and the cosmos. For each of the 175 ideas, he provides a definition or description of the idea, how it arose, its context, and its influence on society.

The author draws his collection of ideas from the vast time expanse of 30,000 years. He berates contemporary intellectuals who believe the notions of thinking beings and the production of ideas are modern phenomena. He cites the achievements of Paleolithic art as but one piece of evidence that there were many who enjoyed the luxury of "Stone Age" affluence, blessed as they were with abundant game, excellent nutrition, leisure time, and hence the conditions for thinking about and making observations of their world. He argues that most of the world's history is indeed prehistory since writing is a relatively recent invention. He argues that those who want a true picture of the vast intellectual riches of the ancient past need to turn to the expertise of archaeologists and anthropologists for help in deciphering and interpreting the past.

Even while the author makes his strong case of the beginning of ideas in prehistoric times, the weight of the book definitely tilts toward modernity. For example, his opening chapter, "The Mind of the Hunger," surveys 23 ideas of humankind that he believes evolved up to 30,000 years ago from 30,000 to 10,000 B.C.E., while his final chapter examines exactly the same number of ideas (23) that evolved in the mere 10 years from 1990 to 2000 C.E.—**Jerry D. Flack**

DICTIONARIES AND ENCYCLOPEDIAS

C, P

460.   Cole, David J., Eve Browning, and Fred E. H. Schroeder. **Encyclopedia of Modern Everyday Inventions.** Westport, Conn., Greenwood Press, 2003. 285p. illus. index. $49.95. ISBN 0-313-31345-8.

The 42 alphabetically arranged sections in this book cover almost four times as many separate products, since many inventions are overlapping and several are treated in each section. Thus, "Adhesive Tapes" includes band-aids, masking tape, cellophane tape, and duct tape. The treatment is historical and aimed at the general reader. The writing is lively. References at the end of each section are chiefly print sources, but include a few Websites. A useful timeline of inventions follows the introduction. There is a very good index and *see* references are bolded within the text.

A similar recent book by Stephen van Dulken titled *Inventing the 20th Century* (New York University Press, 2000) has some overlap, but the approaches differ making the overlap less than one might expect. The two works are rather complementary. The emphasis in this encyclopedia is on "everyday," as in "found in homes, offices, etc."; for example, the zipper is included, but not the airplane. Each book includes some playful inventions, such as the Slinky (van Dulken) and pinball machines (Cole). As with van Dulken's book, this is fun reading as well as a useful source of reference information for general collections. [R: SLJ, Oct 03, pp. 103-104]—**Robert Michaelson**

C

461.   **McGraw-Hill Dictionary of Scientific and Technical Terms.** 6th ed. New York, McGraw-Hill, 2003. 2380p. illus. $150.00. ISBN 0-07-042313-X.

This large tome is the latest edition of the *McGraw-Hill Dictionary of Scientific and Technical Terms* that has evolved over the past 30 years. The 1st edition was intended for the communities of scientists, engineers, and researchers. This 6th edition supports nonscientists as well. It covers the language of science to include words that have permeated our culture in our endeavor to answer questions about the environment and our world.

Each of the 110,000 terms has a pronunciation guide and the 125,000 definitions include synonyms, acronyms, and abbreviations. The chosen pronunciation scheme is thoroughly explained in the preface, showing why all American dialects are not represented. Each entry falls into one of 104 listed fields, the abbreviation of which is included immediately after the item name. The scope of each field is defined, giving the reader needed context and explanation of the publisher's placement of included items.

This edition also features 3,000 black-and-white illustrations located on the outside margin of the appropriate term. There is a "How to Use this Dictionary" page, as well as a 35-page appendix that includes chemical nomenclature, mathematical signs and symbols, the periodic table of elements, and biographical listings, plus 12 more sections of scientific information.

As the *Dictionary* continues to grow, the editors of future editions may want to break it up into multiple volumes to facilitate use. The telephone book style (i.e., A-K and L-Z) would work well, or perhaps dividing the book into the physical and life sciences would be another possibility.

This dictionary is an excellent reference tool for most libraries. It is especially recommended for academic and large public libraries.—**Laura J. Bender**

S

462.   **The New Book of Popular Science.** Danbury, Conn., Grolier, 2003. 6v. illus. maps. index. $269.00/set. ISBN 0-7172-1223-8.

The New Book of Popular Science is a six-volume science encyclopedia appropriate for students in junior high and above. Its arrangement is not that of a traditional encyclopedia; it is arranged by theme, with 6 volumes covering 13 different sections of science (astronomy and space science, mathematics, earth sciences, energy, environmental sciences, chemistry, physics, biology, plant life, animal life, mammals, human sciences, and technology). Within each section, there are individual articles written on topics specific to that section, providing 400 articles in all.

Most articles are signed, and range from 6-8 pages in length. Articles touch on the history and background related to the topic presented, and then cover general information on that topic. There are bountiful images, photographs, and diagrams to accompany and illustrate the articles, and most pictures have descriptive, stand-alone captions. Stand-alone shaded text offers supplemental information within an article topic. At the end of each volume, a list of annotated books ("Selected Readings") will guide curious students to additional sources of information. It appears the bibliographies have been updated and newer titles have been added. Also at the end of each volume is an alphabetic index to the entire six-volume set, with reference to specific topics, keywords, and notable scientists.

Specific sections have been revised over the past few editions (plant life and animal life were updated in 1998 and chemistry and physics were updated in 2000, for example). For the 2002 edition, biology was re-written and reorganized. Also new to the 2002 edition are several new career articles (for both geographers and engineers) and an article on science fairs and projects. New to the appendix in volume six is a listing of manned space flights by date and manned space shuttle flights by date.

The New Book of Popular Science offers quality, thematically arranged science reference information, and this series continues to be valuable to students as well as educators. An online version is also available, but not seen for this review.—**Caroline L. Gilson**

C, P

463.   **The Oxford Companion to the History of Modern Science.** J. L. Heilbron and others, eds. New York, Oxford University Press, 2003. 941p. illus. index. $110.00. ISBN 0-19-511229-6.

This volume is designed to set the context for appreciating the ramifications of modern science, from the Renaissance to the present, in such diverse areas as industry, literature, religion, war, and entertainment (including television and film). More than 200 scholarly authorities have contributed to make this a very readable and informative volume. It covers historiography, major time periods, institutions, philosophy of science, epistemology, methods, theories, apparatus, and computers among the more than 600 entries it provides. The only aspect of the history of science not covered in detail is the section on biographies. Some 100 scientists are included, making it a complement to the very useful *Dictionary of Scientific Biography* (DSB), which is beginning to show its age. *The Oxford Companion*, when it includes biographies, seeks to provide coverage that goes beyond what may be found in the DSB, although the omissions in the *Oxford Companion* are at times surprising; there is a biography of Newton for example, but none for Leibniz. Another omission concerns the coverage of academies, which includes the major Italian, French, and British societies, but not the Leopoldina, The German Academy of Natural Scientists, the oldest in continuous existence in Europe (and which includes an active section for History of Science). Photographs help enliven the text. The extensive cross-references are useful and extensive lists of works of "further reading" are also included with each article. This is ready-reference work for anyone interested in knowing the major implications of modern science for world history. It will serve as an invaluable source of concise but detailed information. [R: LJ, 1 June 03, p. 108; AG, June 03, p. 66]—**Joseph W. Dauben**

DIRECTORIES

S

464.   **Educators Guide to Free Science Materials, 2003-2004.** 44th ed. Kathleen Suttles Nehmer, ed. Randolph, Wis., Educators Progress Service, 2003. 216p. index. $35.95pa. ISBN 0-87708-385-1.

Given today's constraints on school budgets, free is good. This paperback guide gives information on more than 1,000 free educational aids in the sciences, including free Websites and VHS videotapes on just about every topic. The latter are usually lent by mail, and the borrower pays either postage both ways or return postage only. There are also some free printed materials—pamphlets, articles, and workbooks. Sources are varied, both in type and in reliability. Many of the best sources are government and university departments. There are also items from trade associations (e.g., the American Petroleum Institute) and companies (e.g., Pendleton Woolen Mills).

All entries give a brief description of the material, the date of production, suggested audience, and who may order it. Many sources will ship to homeschoolers as well as public and private schools, although sometimes the geographic area is limited. An interesting inclusion is numerous captioned videotapes available only to educators and parents of the deaf. Entries are arranged in broad subject areas, then indexed by title, specific topics, and sources. As with most such guides, this one will gradually go out of date. Luckily, the publisher updates this publication annually.—**Carol L. Noll**

HANDBOOKS AND YEARBOOKS

P, S

465.   Krebs, Robert E., and Carolyn A. Krebs. **Groundbreaking Scientific Experiments, Inventions, and Discoveries of the Ancient World.** Westport, Conn., Greenwood Press, 2003. 376p. index. (Groundbreaking Scientific Experiments, Inventions, and Discoveries Through the Ages). $65.00. ISBN 0-313-31342-3.

This volume represents one entry in Greenwood's series Groundbreaking Scientific Experiments, Inventions, and Discoveries Through the Ages. The stated purpose of the authors is to bring the vast field of science alive and make it exciting for high school students, college undergraduates, and the general public.

Following the format of volumes in the series that address the seventeenth, eighteenth, and nineteenth centuries, Krebs and Krebs cast their spotlight on science in the long ago past of the ancient world. They begin with the invention of agriculture and domestication of animals and proceed through such diverse subjects as the invention of writing, medicine, metallurgy, timekeeping, weapons, transportation, trade, and navigation. The orientation of the book is decidedly scientific and the aim of the authors is to make the sciences both comprehensible and accessible for readers who lack vast scientific background knowledge. The science categories of astronomy, biology, botany, zoology, engineering, medicine, and the role of mathematics in the sciences are the foci of this volume. While there is brief mention of agricultural developments in North America around 5000 B.C.E., the book is almost exclusively devoted to science, invention, and technology in Mesopotamia, Egypt, China, the Indus Civilization, Ancient Greece, and the Roman Empire.

There is much to delight and fascinate the reader in these pages. The greatest structure ever built, the Great Pyramid of Khufu (Cheops), was built with only four simple machines: the lever, the inclined plane, the wedge, and the pulley. Dogs were most likely the first domesticated animals, while cats were the last creatures of the wild to become tame. Discussions of timekeeping are fascinating, especially the evolution of calendars, the days of the weeks, and the months of the years. Equally intriguing is the fact that preventative medicine is not new; it originated with Hebrew priest-physicians in ancient times.

While most of the writing is fluid and enjoyable to read, there are passages that some readers will find more challenging. Comprehending ancient Chinese mathematical equations, for example, is much more of an ordeal than learning that the first postal system consisted of clay tablets and clay envelopes created by the Assyrian and Babylonian civilizations. The authors provide a comprehensive glossary, selected bibliography, and both name and subject indexes. Krebs and Krebs provide a lens that helps people of today learn more about the past and how the world they take for granted came to be. It is no small accomplishment. Their book is especially inviting to readers without strong scientific credentials.—**Jerry D. Flack**

P, S

466.   **The Young Oxford Library of Science.** New York, Oxford University Press, 2002. 11v. illus. maps. index. $250.00/set. ISBN 0-19-521906-6.

Ten of the eleven volumes in this set each addresses a different subject area: "Mind and Body," "Plants and Animals," "Land, Sea and Air," "Atoms and Elements," "Materials," "Light and Sound," "Electricity and Electronics," "Energy and Forces," "Science in Action," and "Stars and Planets." Volume 11 is a reference volume and comprehensive index. Each individually authored, 48-page volume contains a table of contents, a 1-page glossary, and a 2-page volume-specific index. Each entry includes a short introduction and one to three pages of text. Within the text are a short list of "key words, boxes containing detailed information about an inventor or an item of interest (e.g., "Portable Power" [about batteries] contains an information box with biographical information about Luigi Galvani and Alessandro Volta and another about types of batteries), and occasionally a small, shaded area highlighting a piece of subject-related trivia, such as "When there is a current of 1 ampere in a circuit, more than 1,000,000,000,000,000,000 electrons flow through it in a second."

Volume 11 contains a variety of supplemental materials: diagrams and tables of various specific subjects, a table of inventors and discoverers, "Further Reading" sections (3-5 text resources for more information about each volume), a 1-page list of Websites for the set, and a comprehensive full-set index. Volume 11 provides specific supporting materials for volumes 1, 3, 4, 5, and 10. Unfortunately, the material contained is not referenced in the original volume so its utility may be minimal. Each volume is well illustrated with color photographs, drawings, diagrams, tables, and charts. The illustrations are a strength of the set. Many diagrams will be extremely useful to students trying to comprehend complicated systems such as digestion (volume 1), plant or animal cells (volume 2), or operation of an electrostatic copier (volume 7). Many articles include references to environmental affects of the entry, such as mining, plastics, or electrical generation.

The volume glossary may not be as useful as one would like. The publisher writes it "provides simple explanations of difficult words or technical terms that readers might be unfamiliar with." Yet in volume 1, for instance, the glossary contains entries for "artery," "skeleton," and "vitamin," but not entries for "autoclave" or "macrophages." Each subject entry contains a list of key words of several important words used within that entry: sometimes they are in the glossary, sometimes they are not. Units are usually provided in the English system, with metric (S.I.) units in parentheses. Occasionally, however, they may only be given in the English system.

Although other grade levels could certainly gain some information from this set, it would be most useful to students in upper primary and secondary grades. This set is a British production so the authors and publisher may be forgiven some "Anglo-centric" emphasis. For instance, radio telescopes are illustrated with the Lovell Telescope in England, rather than the much larger Arecibo Telescope in Puerto Rico. The sea transpiration timeline contains an illustration of the 1907 Blue Riband holder, *Mauretania*, rather than the fastest ocean liner ever build, the *United States*. This is not intended as any criticism of the British, but merely an observation so that a reader looking for American examples may avoid disappointment. [R: SLJ, April 03, p. 101]—**Craig A. Munsart**

30 Agricultural Sciences

FOOD SCIENCES AND TECHNOLOGY

Dictionaries and Encyclopedias

P

467. Margen, Sheldon, with the editors of the *UC Berkeley Wellness Letter*. **Wellness Foods A-Z: An Indispensable Guide for Health-Conscious Food Lovers.** New York, Rebus, 2002. 640p. illus. index. $39.95. ISBN 0-929661-70-2.

There is no question that our society is bombarded with information about nutrition and diet. Unfortunately, this leaves most people with more questions than answers. This volume is a straightforward guide to eating nutritionally, eating moderately, and eating for wellness. This book focuses on nutritional facts, skipping fad diets and trends. The book begins with a chapter titled "Eating for Optimal Health," which addresses 12 "wellness eating strategies" (e.g., eat a varied diet, moderate fat intake, get vitamins chiefly from foods); discusses the role of carbohydrates, protein, fat, fiber, and cholesterol in the diet; and provides a chart of phytochemicals and how to naturally consume them. It then presents an A to Z listing of vitamins and minerals that provides information on what each one does, health benefits, and foods for consumption. Following this is a short chapter on wellness foods, including vegetables, meat, fish, grains, milk, and eggs. The largest section of this book is a listing of 500 fresh foods. Each food is given a two-page spread and includes a description, a nutritional profile, how to find them in the market, how to prepare it (with a suggested serving table), and a vitamin and mineral guide. Nearly all natural foods are presented here, including fruits, vegetables, herbs, meats, grains, and nuts. The work concludes with sections on how to read a food label, the importance of water, a food preparation glossary, and an index.

This work provides a no-nonsense approach to nutrition that easily explains the link between good nutrition and good health. Nearly everyone will walk away from this guide with new information on at least one topic, whether it be how to prepare vegetables to get the key nutrients, learning what phytochemicals are and their benefits, or learning the latest on disease-fighting antioxidants. This guide is highly recommended for academic and public libraries.—**Shannon Graff Hysell**

C, P

468. **The Oxford Book of Health Foods.** By J. G. Vaughan and P. A. Judd. New York, Oxford University Press, 2003. 188p. illus. index. $27.95. ISBN 0-19-850459-4.

Written by a botanist and a nutritionist, *The Oxford Book of Health Foods* provides an overview of a variety of herbs, supplements, and traditional food products popularly regarded to have special health benefits. The book begins with a 21-page introduction on nutrition and herbal medicine. It contains over 110 entries, which typically include information on the origin and description of the food or product, its culinary and nutritional value, health claims and folklore, and evidence to support or refute those claims. Most entries are accompanied by attractive color illustrations. Other features of the book include a list of recommended readings on nutrition, a glossary of terms, and an index.

As one might expect, this book provides authoritative information with a balanced approach to a very popular and often controversial topic. Given its high quality and affordability, *The Oxford Book of Health Foods* is highly recommended for public and academic libraries.—**Martha Tarlton**

Handbooks and Yearbooks

P

469.   Shulman, Martha Rose. **The Foodlover's Atlas of the World.** New York, Firefly Books, 2002. 288p. illus. index. $35.00. ISBN 1-55297-571-1.

Food is more than a necessity for survival. It is also a symbol of hospitality and social status. It often has religious significance as well. Noted cookbook author Martha Rose Shulman examines the foods of the world to see how migrations have influenced the evolution of cuisines. The result is a beautifully illustrated book that takes readers on a journey through 90 countries and 43 regions of Europe, Africa, the Middle East, Asia, Australasia, and the Americas. Since political borders rarely coincide with cultural boundaries, the regional approach makes sense.

The book has four sections: Europe, Africa and the Middle East, Asia and Australasia, and the Americas. Each section has chapters on specific countries and regions. These chapters contain a brief food history of the region, a list of traditional staples, signature dishes and national drinks, local customs and lore, and sample menus. Shulman notes the influence of migration and trade on cuisines. Merchants and explorers brought hot peppers to China and tomatoes to the Mediterranean from the New World during the Age of Discovery. Religion plays a role also. The prevalence of vegetarian dishes in Hindu and Buddhist cultures and the absence of pork in Jewish and Muslim regions are examples of this. The book contains more than 300 color photographs that take readers to the farms, markets, and festivals of each region. A section of recipes offers examples of various culinary traditions with dishes such as pho, piperade, spanakopitta, crab cakes, and Scandinavian fruit soup. A bibliography and index complete the work. Despite the absence of maps, *The Foodlover's Atlas of the World* is a useful addition to reference collections in public and academic libraries. It supplements works such as *The Encyclopedia of Food and Culture* (see ARBA 2003, entry 1307). [R: SLJ, July 03, p. 153]—**Barbara M. Bibel**

HORTICULTURE

Dictionaries and Encyclopedias

P

470.   **The Complete Encyclopedia of Garden Flowers.** Berkeley, Calif., Thunder Bay Press/Publishers Group West, 2003. 703p. illus. index. $24.98. ISBN 1-59223-056-3.

From its striking title page to the entry for Zinnia this book is a visual delight. Some 1,400 brilliant color photographs and illustrations show both well-known and less common annual and perennial flowering plants, shrubs, and trees in their natural habitats and in selected garden settings. The "Colorful Garden" introductory section outlines the many different groups of flowering plants available to gardeners and yields basic guidance on plant selection, U.S. Plant Hardiness Zones, and garden design. Profusely illustrated A-Z entries for individual flowering plants extend to more than 500 oversized pages. Each entry describes plant characteristics; suggests appropriate cultivation methods; offers a helpful "Top Tip" for successful growing; and presents a very useful table of favorite varieties identified by scientific name, flower color, blooming season, fragrance, size, hardiness zone, and frost tolerance.

Additional features of the book, including a glossary of common gardening and plant terms, assist novice and experienced gardeners alike. The keys, the seasonal calendars, and the cultivation guidelines permit readers to select desirable plants by type, size, and flowering season to place selected plants in proper soil and light conditions, and to protect and maintain or propagate each plant correctly. The substantial index, unfortunately, omits some common names, but includes all scientific names cited in the text. Two more expensive and comprehensive American Horticultural Society books, the *Encyclopedia of Plants and Flowers* (see ARBA 2003, entry 1316) and *A-Z Encyclopedia of Garden Plants* (see ARBA 98, entry 1432), remain definitive, but many public and academic libraries will want to own this beautiful, well-designed volume devoted to flowering plants.—**Julienne L. Wood**

P

471. **The Complete Gardening Encyclopedia.** Berkeley, Calif., Thunder Bay Press/Publishers Group West, 2002. 349p. illus. index. $19.98. ISBN 1-57145-841-7.

As a gardening encyclopedia, this work makes a great coffee-table book. The pictures are beautiful, the prose fun and inspirational, but in no way can this be looked at as a comprehensive guide to all or even most aspects of gardening. Rather than the exhaustive alphabetic listing of topics that one would expect of an encyclopedia, this book is a series of 17 articles on various broad topics in gardening, each article by one of several contributors. The index consists almost entirely of plant varieties, so it helps little in locating information on specific questions or problems. A few articles treat basic aspects of gardening, such as cultivation, soil preparation, garden planning, and different types of plants (e.g., perennials, bulbs, herbs). Here the presentation is colorful, with wonderful pictures of various plants, but the information given is sometimes superficial. An exception is the chapter on pruning and training shrubs and trees, which is very thorough and makes a confusing subject understandable. Many of the chapters consist of a series of fun projects—building one's own containers for patio and window box gardening, building a garden bench, and making a bog garden. These chapters, while not what one expects in a gardening encyclopedia, are worthwhile on their own.

The publisher seems to have a somewhat naïve view of the potential problems of the typical garden project. Maybe they all live somewhere in the world with perfect soil, plenty of water, and no insect pests. Only a few pages are devoted to pests and diseases, while in the real world most gardeners fight a constant battle with the two. There is also very little here on two of the most popular current trends in gardening —the use of native plants and "xeriscaping," or planning gardens for minimal water use. Carol L. Noll—**Carol L. Noll**

P

472. **Rodale's Illustrated Encyclopedia of Organic Gardening.** Pauline Pears, ed. New York, DK Publishing, 2002. 416p. illus. maps. index. $40.00. ISBN 0-7894-8908-2.

The definition of "encyclopedia" usually includes an alphabetic arrangement of articles, covering every aspect of an area of knowledge. This is the second gardening book to be published in 2002 that does not fit that definition. *The Complete Gardening Encyclopedia*, by Thunder Bay Press was not even close to complete (see entry 471). This Rodale Press offering is much more comprehensive, and is sort of a hybrid between a well-illustrated text on organic gardening and an encyclopedia. The main body of the book consists of long articles (15-30 pages) on organic gardening topics, from the basics, including weed and pest control, plant propagation, and soil preparation, to more advanced topics such as growing fruit trees, gardening in containers and greenhouses, organic lawn care, and water-saving landscaping. Throughout the book, there are wonderful color pictures illustrating techniques, garden types, and recommended plants. Important concepts are summarized in many charts and sidebars.

The last 60 pages of the book are two short-entry alphabetic reference sections. The first is titled "Vegetable and Salad Crops," which gives specific information on growing these edibles. The second such section is "Plant Problems," which offers tips on identification, prevention, and control of pests and diseases. While the information in this latter section is brief, it does introduce the reader to organic, rather than chemical warfare approaches to treating gardening problems.

The last few pages of the book include a plant hardiness map for the United States, an index, a list of suppliers, a bibliography, and a copy of the H.D.R.A. Organic Guidelines for Gardeners. This latter is an interesting summary of best practices, acceptable practices, and gardening practices that are definitely frowned upon. Overall, this text is a well-organized and reader-friendly introduction to gardening the organic way.—**Carol L. Noll**

Handbooks and Yearbooks

P

473.   DiSabato-Aust, Tracy. **The Well-Designed Mixed Garden: Building Beds and Borders with Trees, Shrubs, Perennials, Annuals, and Bulbs.** Portland, Oreg., Timber Press, 2003. 460p. illus. index. $39.95. ISBN 0-88192-559-4.

Tracy DiSabato-Aust, a nationally recognized horticultural author, speaker, and consultant, has over 15 years of experience with designing mixed gardens. The knowledge that she has accumulated is beautifully and artfully displayed in this comprehensive work that far exceeds the author's goal of providing practical, "fairly in-depth" information about garden design. DiSabato-Aust skillfully guides the reader through the steps of creating borders, island beds, or mixed gardens. The process unfolds through her explanations of site selection and evaluation, how to set realistic design goals, and how to select plants. Information on color and composition, the design process and how to draw a garden design complete this section. The encyclopedia of plant combinations features 27 plant combinations as they might appear in small, medium, and large gardens. Each of these includes a color photograph, and notes on design considerations and maintenance. Three appendixes follow. Appendix A contains scientific and common plant names. Appendix B lists plants by design characteristics, arranged by color schemes, blooming seasons, textures, forms, heights, winter interest, fruits and seed heads, evergreen foliage, cut flowers, fragrances, and by those plants known to attract songbirds, butterflies, and hummingbirds. Appendix C includes a culture chart, followed by lists of plants arranged by light, moisture, and maintenance requirements. The book concludes with a Plant Hardiness Zone Map, a metric conversion chart, a glossary, a bibliography, a list of sources, and an index. Readers will gain a greater appreciation of the role of color and the principles of design, and will be able either to design a mixed garden or to work effectively with a garden design professional. All libraries should purchase this extraordinary work.—**January Adams**

P

474.   Lord, Tony. **The Encyclopedia of Planting Combinations.** New York, Firefly Books, 2002. 416p. illus. index. $59.95. ISBN 1-55209-623-8.

This book is a visual delight. The color photography alone makes it a worthwhile purchase. The author describes his work as "a menu of suggestions from which readers can choose or reject, revise or augment combinations to suit their own tastes and conditions" as they combine plants to achieve personal works of art in the garden. There are over 4,000 color photographs of plants in lovely color, and more than 1,000 plant descriptions, offering cultural and descriptive notes. The first section of the book is called "The Art of Combining Plants." It looks at assessing the garden site, choosing plants, harmonious form and texture, pleasing color combinations, and the overall affect of a planted border. The largest section of the book provides individual plant descriptions divided by plant types such as shrubs, climbers, bulbs, perennials, annuals, and so on. The section on roses is especially detailed with descriptions of types and individual varieties. The author asserts that roses are the most versatile of all garden plants. What makes this book quite different from numerous plant books with descriptions of plants and their culture is that the author comments on what other plants go well with the plant to achieve pleasing combinations, based on color, texture, and growing conditions. He succeeds, as the results pictured are quite beautiful. There is a brief glossary of common plant names with their scientific counterparts, and a full index, with each plant and variety fully listed.

While the author, Lord, is well qualified, special recognition also should be given to the photographer, Andrew Lawson, who has been named "Garden Photographer of the Year" and certainly deserves any and all accolades. As with many garden books on the market today, this is a British publication, subsequently published in Canada, and then in this U.S. edition. It has hardiness zones listed for Europe, North America, and Australia. This reviewer recognizes many of the plant varieties as available in the United States, and certainly the combination advice transcends continental borders. The only criticism is that the cultivators described are those that grow in a temperate climate with moisture, either rain or irrigation. The desert southwest of the United States is not addressed here, nor is the now very popular and often necessary xeriscaping garden plan.

This book is recommended for libraries, although not necessarily for the reference collection. It is beautiful to look at, informative to read, and offers first-rate suggestions for making one's garden truly a work of art. [R: LJ, 15 Oct 02, p. 62]—**Paul A. Mogren**

VETERINARY SCIENCE

P

475.   Bleby, John, and Gerald Bishop. **The Dog's Health from A-Z: A Canine Veterinary Dictionary.** rev. ed. United Kingdom, David & Charles Book; distr., Cincinnati, Ohio, F & W Publications, 2003. 288p. illus. $24.99pa. ISBN 0-7153-1602-8.

This veterinary dictionary is designed to fill a very specific perceived gap in the literature: "Not much is at hand on how to *prevent* ill-health, accidents, injuries … due to the dog being 'out of condition' ". It is also intended to fill two other gaps: not much is written on combined actions by the veterinarian and dog owner, and basic anatomy and physiology written for the layperson. It should be noted that there have been dog health guides for the general public (see ARBA 72, entry 1697, and ARBA 77, entries 1532 and 1533); however, these may not exactly fill in the gaps discussed in the introduction to this guide. This is a small paperback dictionary illustrated with black-and-white drawings. The headings for the terms are placed in the margins. An entry can be just a definition, or a definition followed by a lengthy text. The dictionary has a two-page introduction, and at the end a brief list of important associations and kennel clubs. A very brief half page bibliography is included. Major topics include diseases, accidents, outdoor hazards, safety precautions, behavior, anatomy, general hygiene, exercise, and mating and breeding.

The writing is clear and authoritative, and the coverage for all the pitfalls a dog can run into is thorough. Having the entry headings in the margins is a considerable convenience. The black-and-white illustrations are basic and serve their purpose, although they are not a substitute for a dog anatomy text. This dictionary will be very useful in the home of a dog owner (its primary purpose), and of some use in a library collection as well.—**John Laurence Kelland**

31 Biological Sciences

BIOLOGY

Biography

C, S
476.   Yount, Lisa. **A to Z of Biologists.** New York, Facts on File, 2003. 390p. illus. index. (Notable Scientists). $45.00. ISBN 0-8160-4541-0.

Facts on File has published a Notable Scientists series of biographical reference volumes titled "A to Z of …" that provides general biographies of women, African Americans, and Native Americans in various professions, and, most recently, scientists in selected specializations. Users should not confuse these publications with the well-reviewed *Notable Scientists from 1900 to the Present* from the Gale Group (2d ed.; see ARBA 2002, entry 1304) as well as Gale's biographical titles on women and African Americans.

Earlier volumes in the Notable Scientists series include *A to Z of Chemists* (see ARBA 2002, entry 1508), *A to Z of Earth Scientists* (see ARBA 2002, entry 1516), and the *A to Z of STS Scientists* (see ARBA 2002, entry 1273). In each review, the reviewer has noted the fact that any compilation that dates back to the beginning of the history of a field will have to omit hundreds if not thousands of individuals. This is especially true in the volume of biologists since only 184 are selected for inclusion beginning with Hippocrates, Aristotle, Theophrastus, and Galen and ultimately citing several contemporary "biologists" such as JoAnn Marie Burkholder (b. 1953), Robert Weinberg (b. 1942), David Ho (b. 1952), and Lap-Chee Tsui (b. 1950). Moreover, the term biologist is defined quite broadly in that it includes not only "pure" biologists, if such exist, but biochemists, biophysicists, pharmacologists, pathologists, economists (e.g., Thomas Robert Malthus), geneticists, chemists, surgeons, naturalists, paleontologists, physicists, and a small host of other areas that have some claim to a significant contribution to the field of biology. A comparison of this volume to *Notable Scientists from 1900 to the Present* contrasts some 80 entries in this volume for individuals born after 1900 to 1,600 scholarly entries in the Gale publication; there are numerous omissions for this century of unique contributions to biology.

Lisa Yount has been well received for her writing directed to secondary school students, college-level readers, and the general public; she "presents the stories of 184 biologists from a wide range of countries, time periods, backgrounds and fields" (p. viii). There is an illustration for many of the entries and each biography is 1 to 2 pages long (500 to 1,500 words). The articles, in addition to basic data, provide an assessment of the biographee's contribution to biology, and each also cites at least one major source.

Several useful appendixes are included: "Entries by Country of Birth" (with Great Britain and the United States dominating in coverage); "Entries by Country of Major Scientific Activity"; "Entries by Year of Birth" (which clearly shows that over 40 percent of the biologists selected were born after 1900); a "Chronology" of events in the field of biology (which justifies the inclusion of a given individual regardless of how professionally classified); a glossary; and an index.

The volume does reflect the editor's selective vision with the upshot that numerous key figures for whom one searches will not, of course, be found among the 184 individuals chosen to represent all of biological history. However, the coverage of women, races, and international history in general make it a good source for exploring the many faces of biologists and points to the remarkable scientific discoveries related to the biology of the entire animal kingdom. [R: SLJ, Oct 03, p. 109]—**Laurel Grotzinger**

Handbooks and Yearbooks

C, S

477.   **Human Physiology on File.** new ed. By the Diagram Group. New York, Facts on File, 2003. 1v. (various paging). illus. index. (Facts on File Science Library). $185.00 looseleaf w/binder. ISBN 0-8160-5104-6.

Human Physiology on File is a one-volume reference source aimed toward high school, public, and academic library users. Like other titles published by Facts on File, the content is presented on cardstock pages within a three-ring binder, to facilitate multiple handlings of individual pages for photocopying. Over 1,500 black-and-white illustrations, charts, and graphs cover the physiological processes of the human body in 16 sections, including a combined glossary/index.

The first section provides an overview of all the components of the human body. Sections 2 and 3 cover the cell and cell division. The fourth section provides information on genetics and DNA. The remaining sections review specific body systems, such as digestive, reproductive, circulatory, and respiratory. Every section begins with a summary review of the topic or body system, and then offers more detailed information in a logical sequence. A typical page in *Human Physiology on File* has the appropriate section name and page number, with a subtopic heading and accompanying labeled drawings or graphics illustrating the topic. Sections range in length from 15 to 34 pages. The 26-page glossary offers basic definitions to medical terms; the 10-page index includes cross-references.

The appeal of this source includes the ability to remove and photocopy pages (either for personal reference use or for use in a classroom setting) as well as the quality of the diagrams and drawings that reproduce clearly. Academic libraries will want this source for physiology courses and school and public libraries may want this source to supplement their health and medical reference sources.—**Caroline L. Gilson**

ANATOMY

C, P, S

478.   Abrahams, Peter. **The Atlas of the Human Body.** Berkeley, Calif., Thunder Bay Press/Publishers Group West, 2002. 256p. illus. index. $24.98. ISBN 1-57145-860-3.

This is a classic table-top description of the anatomy of the human body. Colorful with glossy pages, the short descriptions of the structures of the body are well marked. The volume starts at the head and works down while covering the various system organs in that same sequence. The pages are marked with the area covered as a header for the page. The index is complete. *The Atlas of the Human Body* is recommended primarily for the public library, high school library, and perhaps an academic library.—**James W. Oliver**

BOTANY

General Works

Dictionaries and Encyclopedias

C, P

479.   **Magill's Encyclopedia of Science: Plant Life.** Bryan D. Ness, ed. Hackensack, N.J., Salem Press, 2003. 4v. illus. index. $435.00/set. ISBN 1-58765-084-3.

Designed for the use of high school and undergraduate students, this encyclopedia contains 379 essays, about half of them taken from other Salem publications such as *Magill's Survey of Science: Life Science* (see ARBA 92, entry 1522) or *Encyclopedia of Genetics* (see ARBA 2000, entry 1321). The *Encyclopedia* covers the "true" members of the plant kingdom as well as other organisms such as archaea, bacteria, algae, and fungi that are often studied in botany classes. Topics covered range from molecular biology and physiology to taxonomy, environmental issues, and economic botany. Each signed entry includes a list of broad categories or scientific fields related to the topic (such as anatomy or biomes), a short overview or definition of the topic, a discussion, cross-references, and an annotated list of sources for further study. There are many tables and other illustrations, which are listed in the front of each volume for easy access. The *Encyclopedia* also contains several appendixes, including biographies of 134 botanists, a plant classification table, a list of scientific names for common plants, a timeline, a glossary, and a bibliography. In addition, the *Encyclopedia* has a list of about 100 major Websites with a well-chosen selection of associations, botanical gardens, taxonomic resources, and other sites. Separate indexes cover biographies (including individuals named in the text but not in the biographical appendix), broad categories, and subjects.

Articles in the *Encyclopedia* are written at a fairly technical level but are appropriate for the intended audience of high school and undergraduate students. Its nearest competitor is probably the four-volume encyclopedia *Plant Sciences* published by Macmillan, which appears to be aimed at a lower grade level (see ARBA 2002, entry 1385). The *Encyclopedia* will also be useful for nonspecialists looking for a good description of both technical and popular botanical topics. The annotated bibliography, index of categories, and list of Websites are particularly useful. This *Encyclopedia* is highly recommended for high school, public, and undergraduate academic libraries. [R: LJ, July 03, p. 73; SLJ, Aug 03, p. 112]—**Diane Schmidt**

Handbooks and Yearbooks

P

480.   Phillips, Roger, and Martyn Rix. **The Botanical Garden I: Trees and Shrubs.** New York, Firefly Books, 2002. 491p. illus. index. $75.00. ISBN 1-55297-591-6.

P

481.   Phillips, Roger, and Martyn Rix. **The Botanical Garden II: Perennials and Annuals.** New York, Firefly Books, 2002. 539p. illus. index. $75.00. ISBN 1-55297-592-4.

This large two-volume work incorporates some of the new knowledge of plant ancestry gained through DNA technology, providing up-to-date identifications and relationships between plant groups. Botanist Martyn Rix begins both volumes with an introduction to each plant group included in that volume. Following are the encyclopedic entries, organized first by group, then broken down into family, and finally genus and species. Each entry consists of data on physical description, identifying features, evolution and relationships, geography and ecology, and then comments on plant use (as medicine, timber, fruit, ornamental, and so on).

Rix and Phillips intend their book for gardeners, not just botanists, however. This is evident in Phillips's open design and his splendid full-color detail photographs make these books a true feast for the eyes. No square snapshots here; instead cuttings-leaves, flowers, stems, twigs, seeds, and nuts are set against the white background of the page, allowing the viewer to discern forms. The scale of reproduction and time of year taken appear below each photograph to show seasonal variation. Each genus takes up at least a half page; larger or more diverse genera may span one or two two-page spreads. A glossary, bibliography, and name index (for both volumes) are included at the end of each book. The use of capital letters and italics differentiates between families, genera, and species in the latter. [R: LJ, 15 Oct 02, p. 64]—**Lori D. Kranz**

Flowering Plants

Dictionaries and Encyclopedias

P

482. **Flora: A Gardener's Encyclopedia.** Portland, Oreg., Timber Press, 2003. 2v. illus. index. $99.95/set (w/CD-ROM). ISBN 0-8812-538-1.

P

483. **Flora's Plant Names.** Portland, Oreg., Timber Press, 2003. 376p. $14.95pa. ISBN 0-88192-605-1.

Lovely to behold and guaranteed to give gardeners far more ideas than they can implement, *Flora* is a worthy successor to such classic horticultural encyclopedias as *Hortus Third* and *Exotica*. The encyclopedia includes over 20,000 plants. Entries are arranged in alphabetic order by genus, and include a description of the genus along with paragraph long species accounts with both botanical and horticultural information. Most entries are illustrated with one or more color photographs, including many popular cultivars. The species chosen include trees, garden plants, some food plants (such as peppers or wheat), and "newsworthy" plants (such as the gigantic Titan Arum). The encyclopedia also includes gardener-oriented descriptions of each of the world's 12 hardiness zones as well as information on plant classification. In several cases the hardiness zones listed for plants are incorrect or misleading; for instance, corn (*Zea mays*) is listed as zone 8-10, which would surprise the many zone 3-4 farmers who grow it annually. The encyclopedia comes with a CD-ROM containing a number of plant selection tools allowing users to narrow choices by plant type, hardiness zone, season, color, and so on. The CD-ROM also has several other tools including a list of Web links, a glossary, and a botanical spell checker for Word.

The associated gardener's dictionary *Flora's Plant Names* contains the common names found in *Flora*. Common names are listed in a single register by both standard and inverted forms (e.g., plains acacia and acacia, plains) along with their scientific name, allowing users to glance at a list of all lilies or proteas. It can also be used as a supplemental index for *Flora*, since the encyclopedia's index does not include inverted forms of common names. For quick background information on the plants most likely to be of interest to gardeners, *Flora* and *Flora's Plant Names* are ideal purchases for horticultural, academic, and public libraries. [R: LJ, Jan 04, p. 88]—**Diane Schmidt**

P

484. Quest-Ritson, Charles, and Brigid Quest-Ritson. **The American Rose Society Encyclopedia of Roses.** New York, DK Publishing, 2003. 448p. illus. $40.00. ISBN 0-7890-9675-5.

A bargain in the reference book world is a rarity, especially a profuse melange of the world's roses. Dorling Kindersley's encyclopedia offers concise, easy-to-read entries on some 2,000 varieties in myriad colors. Tucked into each of the four columns per page are delicious photographs of blossoms with their centers open to the sun. Pinks, creams, and reds come close to nature, lacking only fragrance for perfection.

The front matter includes a two-page tutorial on how to read entries to learn code names, classification, size and spread, awards, and hardiness. Special features include sidebars on hybridizers (Jackson and Perkins, William Paul), mutations (Mary Rose), and famous rose gardens (Westfalenpark). Generous cross-referencing simplifies the search for just the right plant. A planting and cultivation guide at the back pictures gardeners performing the staking, pruning, suckering, and winterizing necessary to produce the best from each plant. Contributing to the grandeur of the text are photographs of roses in action, such as the two-page spread of a courtyard garden in Christchurch, New Zealand, and another of Mottisfont Abbey in Hampshire, England. The triumph of this book is its suitability for reference shelves in libraries, schools, landscaping services, and greenhouses and as a gift book or coffee-table book for the rose lover. Do not miss out on this one.—**Mary Ellen Snodgrass**

Trees and Shrubs

Dictionaries and Encyclopedias

P

485.   **The Complete Encyclopedia of Trees and Shrubs.** Berkeley, Calif., Thunder Bay Press/Publishers Group West, 2003. 816p. illus. index. $24.98. ISBN 1-59223-055-5.

Plants with woody parts that winter above ground and yield green growth in spring are trees or shrubs, even if they are prostrate or small. This volume describes 8,500 species of trees and shrubs, or about 1 in 18 extant kinds. Emphasized are plants that flora lovers see frequently in the world's gardens and parks. Cacti are included. Roses (Rosa) get 45 pages of coverage. Generic names provide the entryway to the A to Z (Abelia to Ziziphus) list of species (and cultivars). Photographs accompany approximately half of the entries. The short introduction to plants is lucid and accurate. A hardiness zone map deserves high marks for being fully intelligible. Aside from a jarring use of "classed" for "classified" (page 18), the volume is a model of excellence. It offers economy of scale and price. Even insect pests, such as rasping thrips that damage rhododendron leaves, get sufficient mention to be understood. The index includes common names. Well-chosen fruit, flower, and leaf illustrations amplify words used in the text. Most entries for genera include notes on cultivation, geographic range, size of the genera, and discussion of etymology. Gardeners of all sorts will want to get their hands on this book. [R: Choice, Jan 04, pp. 880-882]—**Diane M. Calabrese**

P

486.   More, David, and John White. **The Illustrated Encyclopedia of Trees.** Portland, Oreg., Timber Press, 2002. 800p. illus. index. $79.95. ISBN 0-88192-520-9.

This 800-page hard cover book, in excess of 6 pounds, is not a "field guide to trees." It is an outstanding assembly of well-executed, full-color drawings of trees with associated text. This includes a silhouette of the tree and its botanical parts, thus providing sure-fire help in identification of the species. The book was originally intended as a catalog of British and European trees. With the thought that a great deal of these plants originated in North America, some "adjustments" in content were made to make the book of value to an additional population. Its prime value appears to be as an adjunct to U.S. and Canadian Province tree books that list primarily native species. The immense listing of ornamental trees that find their way into our landscapes are illustrated and described in great detail. Unfortunately, the book does not list all of the trees of North America and should not be considered a checklist of U.S. and Canadian trees. Trees from tropical climates were not intended to be included. The title could have been a bit more descriptive of the geographic coverage. Taxonomically, attempts were obviously made to update the scientific names of the trees, often a difficult process because of their ever-changing nature, but a few may have an obsolete name such as *Cupressus glabra* that is now a synonym of *C. arizonica*. This book is a valuable addition to the reference material to landscape planners and gardeners, and the plant illustrations are an exceptional tool for both the amateur and professional. [R: LJ, 15 Mar 03, p. 78]—**James H. Flynn Jr.**

GENETICS

C

487.   Rédei, George P. **Encyclopedic Dictionary of Genetics, Genomics, and Proteomics.** 2d ed. New York, John Wiley, 2003. 1379p. illus. $179.00. ISBN 0-471-26821-6.

To create a tool that is both a comprehensive dictionary and a useful single-volume encyclopedia is a difficult task, perhaps particularly in an area of science that is changing rapidly. Most tools with such a goal become, in the end, a dictionary with little context to guide the student into a fuller understanding of a topic. Rédei provides in the 2d edition of this publication an excellent example of what can be achieved if the author is a first-rate scholar. Rédei, a retired professor of genetics, has created a tool that is both readable and scholarly. The user will find a significant expansion over the earlier edition, at nearly 25,000 entries. Most entries are 10 to 20 well-chosen words. Others can range from several hundred to 1,000 words, complete with simple black-and-white diagrams, photographs, or tables. Acronyms and initialisms are alphabetized as words, with the definition given for the form most commonly used in the literature. All are tied together with cross-references. Many have bibliographic references to the essential works. A 34-page topical monographic bibliography is appended. This work is highly recommended. [R: Choice, Jan 04, pp. 882-883]—**John M. Robson**

NATURAL HISTORY

C, P

488.   **Ecology Basics.** By the Editors of Salem Press. Hackensack, N.J., Salem Press, 2004. 2v. illus. index. (Magill's Choice). $104.00/set. ISBN 1-58765-174-2.

Science is an endeavor to understand the universe through the increasingly intractable disciplines of mathematics, physics, chemistry, and biology. The latter encompasses ecology. "Ecology is the study of the relationships of organisms to their environments" (p. 171) and is arguably the most unruly discipline in all of science because organisms change through time. The 132 short essays by 105 authors present brief well-referenced and well-illustrated insights into select aspects of ecology from the balance of nature (p. 28) to punctuated equilibrium (p. 543). The basics of ecology are presented either by subject (e.g., extinction, predation) or accessible through the index (e.g., K/T boundary, parasitism). The strength of this work is in providing a crisp synopsis of the selected subject. The occasional weakness is that a subject of interest may not be addressed (e.g., Occam's Razor, masting, Malthus). Teachers seeking material to bolster lectures will find this work very useful. A glossary, list of Websites, and subject indexes are also provided. —**Marvin K. Harris**

C

489.   Groombridge, Brian, and Martin D. Jenkins. **World Atlas of Biodiversity: Earth's Living Resources in the 21st Century.** Berkeley, Calif., University of California Press, 2002. 340p. illus. maps. index. $54.95. ISBN 0-520-23668-8.

The *World Atlas of Biodiversity* is chronicled from the inception of the biosphere to the present in a lucid, succinct, and entertaining manner. Insights are provided into fascinating subjects of biology, systematics, paleontology, biogeography, evolution, ecology, natural resources, agriculture, and politics, providing a prodigious database for the concluding chapter on human endeavors to respond to changing biodiversity. Color illustrations, including pictures, maps, graphs, and tables, allow easy comprehension of sometimes difficult concepts. Original works are referenced in the text with unobtrusive superscripts. The discussion of science, policy issues, and proposed solutions endeavor to objectively inform the reader on the current status. The passive documentation of the propensity of humans to first understand and then to exploit the biosphere is thorough. Most biologists agree every species follows a biological imperative to increase density until the carrying capacity of the environment externally exerts limits. Are humans different? This book aids the understanding of our place in the biosphere and describes efforts to redirect exploitation. This is an excellent reference for those unafraid of jeopardizing their views with facts on this complex and often contentious subject. The attractive appearance qualifies the book for display purposes, and the academic rigor commends it for the college classroom and reference shelf. [R: LJ, Dec 02, pp. 106-108]—**Marvin K. Harris**

C, S

490.   **Wildlife Reference Center. http://www.marshallcavendish.com.** [Website]. Tarrytown, N.Y., Marshall Cavendish. Price negotiated by site. Date reviewed: Sept 03.

Following the success of Marshall Cavendish's two other online resources (see ARBA 2003, entry 300 and ARBA 2002, entry 1321), the publisher and EBSCO Publishing have now introduced *Wildlife Reference Center*. The database is set up much like the other two resources. It provides articles from other Marshall Cavendish encyclopedias that contain information on animals, plants, and dinosaurs. The majority of this work's material comes from *Dinosaurs of the World* (1999), *Encyclopedia of Mammals* (see ARBA 98, entry 1469), and *Endangered Wildlife and Plants of the World* (see ARBA 2002, entry 1593), with supplemental material from EBSCO's periodical database. The site currently features 1,600 core articles and more than 5,000 supplementary articles. The periodical database is updated monthly and one would hope that forthcoming articles from relevant Marshall Cavendish publications will be added in the future as well.

The site features EBSCO's point-and-click interface, making the product easy to use for both older and younger students. Users can search by subject, encyclopedia entry, or category. Once information is found it can be printed, saved, or e-mailed. Pictures are embedded periodically within the text.

This resource is most appropriate for young adult researchers and interested laypersons. The information is easy to read and even entertaining, but will be too elementary for undergraduates and scholars. School libraries will benefit the most from this resource. A 30-day free trial is available from the publisher for those needing to try before they buy.—**Shannon Graff Hysell**

ZOOLOGY

General Works

C, P

491.   **Oxford Dictionary of Zoology.** rev. ed. By Michael Allaby. New York, Oxford University Press, 2003. 597p. $16.95pa. ISBN 0-19-860758-X.

Consisting of more than 5,000 terms, this dictionary defines, describes, and explains terminology in all major areas of zoology. The lengths of the explanations vary, depending upon the entry. In addition to terminology in the various fields of zoology, this work also provides information on each of the major taxonomic groups from phylum to families. Sponges to mammals are included in this taxonomic endeavor. In addition to taxonomic terminology, entries from animal behavior, ecology, physiology, genetics, cytology, evolution, earth history, and zoogeography are included. Line drawings are interspersed among the pages of the dictionary in order to enhance explanations.

According to the preface to the second edition, the revised edition takes into account extremophile organisms, new animals that have been recently discovered, and relationships revealed by genetic studies that have caused some species to be reclassified. In addition, a number of new entries in genetics and evolutionary studies have been added. A list of endangered animals, the universal genetic code, geologic code, geologic time scale, and derived SI units complete the reference. This work is recommended for all university and college libraries having programs in the biological sciences.—**George H. Bell**

Birds

C, P

492.   **Firefly Encyclopedia of Birds.** Christopher Perrins, ed. New York, Firefly Books, 2003. 656p. illus. maps. index. $59.95. ISBN 1-55297-777-3.

Noted ornithologist Christopher Perrins has coordinated writings from more than 100 bird experts from around the world. The product is this truly authoritative, but very readable, review of the more than 9,800 bird species on our planet, organized by the natural groups of families (e.g., parrots, waterfowl, owls, warblers, penguins). Each of the 172 families is reviewed in a dual format: there is a concise "fact file" that briefly summarizes distinctive features of the group (number of species and genera; world distribution with maps; basic details of plumage, size, voice, nest, and eggs; diet; and conservation status), and a more lengthy discussion of noteworthy species and biological highlights of the group (e.g., specialized migrations, feeding methods, courtship behavior). Throughout there are a great many excellent illustrations and color photographs showing selected species in their natural habitats. The text has given particular attention to recent ornithological discoveries and to important environmental/conservation issues. This well-done reference should be useful for the academic library but also for general public with its easy-to-read text. Indeed, many serious birders may well want to have this hefty volume on their home shelves. [R: LJ, 1 Oct 03, p. 62]—**Charles Leck**

P, S

493.   **World of Animals: Birds.** Danbury, Conn., Grolier, 2003. 10v. illus. maps. index. (World of Animals, v.11-20). $419.00/set. ISBN 0-7172-5731-2.

These 10 books are only volumes 11-20 of a planned 50-volume set covering the entire animal kingdom. The first 10 volumes are on mammals (see ARBA 2003, entry 1389); future offerings will be on reptiles, amphibians, insects, and one-celled animals. The format, large-size pages with numerous outstanding color photographs and well-organized text, works perfectly for the subject of birds. Birds are so omnipresent in our environment, whether we live in the city, suburbs, or rural areas, and being mostly diurnal, we cannot help but notice them. Yet few people appreciate the intricacies of their adaptations to their habitats. These volumes are full with those details, and make fascinating reading.

The set covers birds of the entire world, divided into volumes based on a combination of taxonomy and lifestyle. For instance, the first book is entitled "Ground Birds," and includes both the closely related flightless birds, and a variety of birds from other orders (Northern Bobwhite and Jungle Fowl, for instance) who spend most of their time foraging for food on the ground. This arrangement can be a bit confusing if one is used to the typical taxonomic arrangement of bird field guides, but since this is an encyclopedia, the reader can just consult the set index (printed in all volumes) to locate the desired bird species or group. A handy chart in a section labeled "Find the Animal," also printed in each volume also helps with locating birds in the 10 volumes.

Within each book, around 30 entries discuss either an entire order of family of birds, or an individual species. Species to discuss are chosen both for their interest (weird and wonderful behavior or appearance, for instance), or their economic importance. Entries are 2 to 5 pages long, with magnificent color pictures of birds in their natural habitats. Every entry is full of amazing details. The entry on puffins describes sharp spines inside their mouths, the better to hold a mouthful of struggling fish. The chapter on bower birds explains how their court-building behavior enables them to attract a mate without the conspicuous (and risky) colorful plumage of the closely related birds of paradise. And the entry on our familiar jays and crows describes the mysterious behavior called "anting" in which the birds crush ants and smear them onto their feathers, possibly as a self-medicating form of parasite prevention. One could go on and on, but it is safe to say that this set does justice to the world of birds in an accessible and captivating manner.—**Carol L. Noll**

Domestic Animals

P
494.   Fogle, Bruce. **Dog Owner's Manual.** New York, DK Publishing, 2003. 288p. illus. index. $25.00pa. ISBN 0-7894-9321-7.

This guide is ideal for dog owners needing basic information about how to best care for their pet as well as those looking to adopt a dog and looking for specific qualities in a pet. The author is a well-respected veterinarian and has written several books on the topics of both dogs and cats.

This volume begins with a chapter on dog anatomy, which explains the canine skeleton and movement, brain and mind, senses, and communication. It then discusses 50 dog breeds in depth, which are arranged by small, medium, large, and extra large sized dogs. For each breed the following information is provided: personality type, history of the breed, life expectancy, temperament (including if they are good with children and other dogs), information about exercise and dietary needs, and physical characteristics. Clear, color photographs are provided for each breed. The remaining chapters discuss dog behavior (e.g., pack mentality, mating, birth, socialization, grooming, aging), living with a dog (e.g., equipment needed for dog care, training, grooming, nutrition), and health concerns (e.g., parasite control, dental care, conditions and disorders, emotional disorders). The work concludes with a glossary of terms, a page of useful contacts (including veterinary associations, breed registries, and dog training associations), and an index.

The easy-to-read style of writing and colorful photographs will make this guide appealing to the general public seeking information on dog breeds and dog ownership. This guide will be a useful addition to public libraries.—**Shannon Graff Hysell**

Insects

C, P, S
495.   **Firefly Encyclopedia of Insects and Spiders.** Christopher O'Toole, ed. New York, Firefly Books, 2002. 240p. illus. index. $40.00. ISBN 1-55297-612-2.

This book covers insects, chelicerates (spiders, mites and ticks, and scorpions and their relatives), and myriapoda (centipedes, millipedes, and related groups). Christopher O'Toole, a bee specialist at Oxford University's Museum of Natural History, and a distinguished group of mostly British contributors very successfully provide an overview of insect natural history. There is a chapter on each order; for example, the entry on beetles provides information on phylogeny, body plan, and other general characteristics, concentrating on ecology, behavior, and conservation rather than anatomy and systematics. Each chapter has a "Factfile" box that gives numbers of species, families and suborders, a range map, and basic biological data. The numerous photographs and paintings are splendid. The organization is very clear and the writing is highly readable and accurate. There is a glossary, short bibliography, and index. The bibliography seems rather slapdash. Especially for more general books, early editions are listed where recent ones are available, and there are more recent treatments of several of the subjects included. This is a fine book and an excellent purchase for high school, college, and public libraries. [R: LJ, Jan 03, p. 88]—**Frederic F. Burchsted**

Mammals

C, P, S
496.   **Mammal.** Don E. Wilson, ed. New York, DK Publishing, 2003. 216p. illus. index. $30.00. ISBN 0-7894-9972-X.

This fine new book on mammals was produced in association with the Smithsonian Institution. It is unusual in its geographical arrangement, presenting the mammals continent by continent rather than in taxonomic order. After an introduction on definition, evolution, human influences, and classification, it is divided into sections on the continents (plus one on the oceans), and within each section into subsections on grassland, desert, mountains, wetlands, and forest. Brief section introductions include a geological history and a map showing the distribution of the major habitats. The subsections give overviews of the mammals of each habitat, splendidly illustrated with photographs. Conservation problems are discussed.

This books nicely complements reference books arranged by taxonomy, such as Facts on File's *The Encyclopedia of Mammals* (see ARBA 2002, entry 1438) and several other books. The habitat-based organization scheme works less well for Africa where savannas show largely as forest on the section map but are discussed in the grassland subsection.

The organization of *Mammals* gives students a better grasp of the basics of mammalian distribution and habitat relations than does the usual taxonomic arrangement. The book is a fine choice for school, college, and public libraries.—**Frederic F. Burchsted**

Marine Animals

C, P, S
497.   **Interdisciplinary Encyclopedia of Marine Sciences.** James W. Nybakken, William W. Broenkow, and Tracy L. Vallier, eds. Danbury, Conn., Grolier, 2003. 3v. illus. maps. index. $349.00/set. ISBN 0-7172-5946-3.

This three-volume encyclopedia is truly interdisciplinary, as should be any resource on marine sciences. The fields covered range from chemical oceanography, through geography, economics, marine life, people, and environmental issues to geological and physical oceanography. There are over 800 entries, each written by a specialist. The entries range from a couple of paragraphs to several pages in length and each is followed by a further reading list and references to related articles. The appendixes include a very thorough directory of marine research institutions, which includes detailed information about missions and facilities along with Web pages. There are also short bibliographies for each covered field, a synoptic outline, an alphabetic list of topics, and an extensive index.

The prose style of this encyclopedia is "nontechnical" and designed for high school and college students. Sometimes this simplification goes too far; for example, there are relatively few equations and few graphs. Students will be able to receive a good summary of a particular topic with this set, but for more information they will have to find other references. It is a surprise that there are not more illustrations considering this intended audience. All the figures are in black and white, and the choice of what topics to illustrate appears to have been haphazard. Researchers could use more diagrams to support the plate tectonics section, for example, instead of a supposed portrait of Ptolemy. (And where, for that matter, are Galileo and Copernicus?)

This will be a useful encyclopedia set for high school and college students interested in oceanography and other marine sciences. A primary and growing concern with all such volumes, however, is how quickly Web resources are supplanting them. A library may invest several hundred dollars in such paper books only to find that most students no longer consider them relevant. That is unfortunate because today the Web still cannot provide the kind of consistent information found in encyclopedias like this. [R: SLJ, Aug 03, p. 112]—**Mark A. Wilson**

Reptiles

C, P, S

498.   **Firefly Encyclopedia of Reptiles and Amphibians.** Tim Halliday and Kraig Adler, eds. New York, Firefly Books, 2002. 240p. illus. maps. index. $40.00. ISBN 1-55297-613-0.

Editors Tim Halliday and Kraig Adler utilized the artwork of David M. Dennis and Denys Overden and the writings of 38 specialists to achieve a superbly attractive, authoritative, and highly informative sourcebook on amphibians and reptiles. The volume is presented as a 1st edition. Although ignored, the obvious progenitor was a 1986 book with a similar title by the same editors titled *The Encyclopedia of Amphibians and Reptiles* (Facts on File and Equinox). The 16 contributors produced works for both books and much artwork and a number of photographs are repeated. The *Firefly Encyclopedia*, however, is updated, greatly expanded, and much more attractive. It is organized into a preface; major units titled "Amphibians," "Reptiles," "Pollution and Hormone Mimics," and "Unisexuality: The Redundant Male?"; and a glossary, bibliography, and index. "Amphibians" has a series of general topics on amphibian biology, natural history, and conservation followed by subunits on caecilians, salamanders and newts, and frogs and toads. Each subunit covers introductory systematics, natural history, and distribution of included taxa. The "Reptiles" section begins with fossils and reptilian history and continues with general information on the group as a whole. Included subunits follow on turtles and tortoises, lizards, worm-lizards, snakes, tuatara, and crocodilians, with systematics, natural history, distribution, and interesting aspects covered on each. A chapter on pollution and hormones and another on unisexuality complete the narrative. "Factfile" panels with summaries and distribution maps are provided for many taxa. Discussions throughout are supported by superb color photographs and vividly rendered artwork. Technical terminology is minimal and the text can be easily comprehended by anyone with a high school education. This work is highly recommended for general purchase by high school, municipal, and college and university libraries. [R: LJ, Jan 03, p. 88]—**Edmund D. Keiser Jr.**

32 Engineering

GENERAL WORKS

C, P

499.   **Plunkett's Engineering and Research Industry Almanac 2003-2004.** Jack W. Plunkett, ed. Houston, Tex., Plunkett Research, 2003. 635p. index. $249.99pa. (w/CD-ROM). ISBN 1-891775-24-3.

This 635-page, 2d edition of Plunkett's engineering and research reference almanac offers an in-depth look at "The Engineering 500." This is a group of 468 companies chosen specifically for their prominence and leadership in engineering- and research-related segments: design and development, technology-based research and development, and manufacturing. Only publicly traded companies are featured because of the editorial requirement that each firm have "sufficient objective data" (i.e., financial data and vital statistics to facilitate broad-based comparisons).

The almanac is written in lay terms to help the general reader compare financial records, company growth statistics, employment opportunities, and investment possibilities. The six industries represented are energy, entertainment and hospitality, health care, information technology, manufacturing, and services. The accompanying CD-ROM could be very valuable for creating prospect or personal contact lists. Installation of the CD-ROM requires a key number obtainable by calling the telephone number listed on the front of the disk.

Although these industry and company profiles will provide an excellent overview for students, researchers, and executives, a caveat must be stated: this volume, as are all print volumes that include corporate data, is a snapshot in time. Changes occur rapidly in the corporate arena—financials change daily, and mergers and acquisitions, downsizing, and division elimination occur every year. It may behoove the reader to delve more deeply into a given industry by contacting specific companies, industry associations, key individuals, and some government agencies to garner the most current information. Perhaps more valuable for planning purposes are the chapters devoted to major trends and industry outlooks. For example, some major trends to watch include rapid growth in the biotech sector, continued growth in research partnerships between corporations and universities, and emphasis in research and development in nanotechnology. The glossary of engineering and research industry terms on pages i-xix should help clarify the concepts presented in those chapters. Indexes appear on pages 603-635, beginning with an index of 161 firms noted as "Hot Spots for Advancement for Women and Minorities." Also included is an index of subsidiaries, brand names, and affiliations.

The content of this reference resource will provide many answers for researchers, students, and general information seekers. It is recommended for reference collections in public and academic libraries.

—**Laura J. Bender**

CIVIL ENGINEERING

C, P

500.   **Sweet's Directory 2002.** New York, McGraw-Hill, 2002. 1596p. index. $69.95pa. ISBN 0-07-138689-0.

   Providing information on 61,300 products from 10,700 manufactures (with expanded coverage of 1,900 products and over 1,500 color photographs), as well as 15,000 trade names, the 6th edition of this directory is an excellent reference source for anyone in the business of building, construction, landscaping, interior design, and architecture. The product classification index in the front of the directory explains how the listings are organized numerically according to the CSI MasterFormat developed by Sweet's. The majority of the manufacturer entries list the address, telephone and fax numbers, e-mail address, and Website, plus brief explanations of the product, its applications, features, and benefits. This source will help interior designers, architects, builders, and landscapers find everything from acrylics to furnishings to woven wire. If this directory is not comprehensive enough, the consumer can look at the multivolume set of *Sweet's Catalog Files* normally found in larger libraries. What makes this directory so valuable is that it pulls together thousands of manufacturer listings in one reasonably priced source. Individuals in any field listed could afford to have this in their personal or business libraries to make informed decisions about products they need to succeed.—**Diane J. Turner**

ELECTRICAL ENGINEERING

C

501.   **Reference Data for Engineers: Radio, Electronics, Computer, and Communications.** 9th ed. Wendy M. Middleton, ed. Woburn, Mass., Newnes/Butterworth-Heinemann, 2002. 1v. (various paging). illus. index. $149.95. ISBN 0-7506-7291-9.

   For 60 years *Reference Data for Engineers* has been the standard reference work of quality for students and professionals in the field. Now in the 9th edition, it remains a basic source for succinct explanations and illustrations of all aspects of electrical engineering, electronics, and communications. Since the 8th edition of 1998, the editors have substantially incorporated the evolving topics of such areas as satellite technology, global positioning, telecommunications, and frequency data. They have substantively updated most sections, including integrated circuits, power electronics, intellectual property, properties of materials, and DSP. The chapters are individually or collectively authored, chiefly by field practitioners, not academics. Each of the 46 begins with a detailed table of contents and ends with a highly selective and useful list of references. In between the user will find carefully composed technical text, which is clear and understandable. The black-and-white tables and figures are abundant and of great simplicity. Only the essential math is provided. The index is good but a bit short on cross-references. The practice of separately paginating each section leads to some confusing page references. As a result of this practice, the table of contents provides the user with no specific location for the start of a needed chapter. It compares well to its chief American competitors—*Standard Handbook for Electrical Engineers* (McGraw-Hill, 2000) and *Electronics' Engineers Handbook* (McGraw-Hill, 1997). To provide users with a choice in explaining difficult concepts, libraries should consider owning all three.—**John M. Robson**

33 Health Sciences

GENERAL WORKS

Bibliography

P

502. **Consumer Health Information Source Book.** 7th ed. Alan M. Rees, ed. Westport, Conn., Oryx Press/Greenwood Publishing Group, 2003. 325p. index. $65.00pa. ISBN 1-57356-609-1.

Much has changed in the last 20 years in consumer health. The Internet has changed how people look for health information, patients have become greater consumers of health care information, and a greater emphasis has been placed on taking responsibility for one's own health. The 7th edition of this volume includes a discussion on the trends in health care—an honors list of consumer health information (CHI) books. There is a chapter dealing with clearinghouses and other health-related associations, a chapter on computer-based resources (including CD-ROMs and the Internet), chapters covering mainstream books, pamphlets in both Spanish and English, and a chapter focusing on 12 CHI libraries considered to be models of excellence. The book is well indexed by author, title, and subject, a must for a book of this nature. This book is a valuable resource for all libraries providing consumer health information and for professionals with an interest in CHI, including health professionals. The one caveat with this book as with all books with Internet resources is that Internet resources are very fluid and often disappear. This book is a must for any library with any focus on consumer health information.—**Leslie M. Behm**

Dictionaries and Encyclopedias

P, S

503. Ronzio, Robert. **The Encyclopedia of Nutrition and Good Health.** 2d ed. New York, Facts on File, 2003. 726p. index. (Facts on File Library of Health and Living). $71.50. ISBN 0-8160-4966-1.

This 2d edition reflects the growth in health and nutritional knowledge and awareness that has occurred since the publication of the 1st edition in 1997 (see ARBA 98, entry 1520, for a review of the 1st edition). Updated and new entries add greatly to the depth of coverage in this edition. Entry types include, among others, specific herbs, disease syndromes, vitamins and minerals, weight loss diets, foods, federal nutritional entitlement programs, spices, and human anatomical structures, along with discussions of common health issues. The *Encyclopedia* avoids the topic of communicable or infectious diseases and focuses on those disease syndromes resulting from nutritional deficiencies or disorders within the digestive system. There are *see* and *see also* references, and some entries end with specific citations to articles and books. A minimal glossary and a very useful index complete the book. This *Encyclopedia* is recommended for technical schools, secondary schools, public, community, and undergraduate libraries.—**Lynn M. McMain**

Directories

C, P

504.   **Health World Online. http://www.healthy.net/.** [Website]. Free. Date reviewed: Nov 03.

The vision and mission page of *Health World Online* states " . . . the only Internet health network that integrates both alternative and conventional health information into a synergistic whole," but in reality the primary focus of this site is alternative/complementary not conventional health information. However, this does not detract from the value of the Website; it contains a tremendous amount of knowledge ranging from everything about the uses and significance of a specific herb, to detailed descriptions and discussions of a particular alternative/complimentary treatment. The president and co-founder of *Health World Online* is James Strohecker, the author of 25 books, most of which are on natural healing and alternative/complimentary medicine. The advisors and contributors are all educated, respected professionals in various alternative health disciplines.

The opening page contains a graphic site map, a drawing of pathways connecting buildings labeled as "Marketplace," "University," "Health News," "Nutrition Center," and so on. To the left is a topic index, which contains, among others, a link to MEDLINE, the National Library of Medicine's enormous medical database of journal articles. To the right are drop-down menus for "Health Conditions," "Key Health Centers," "Alter. Therapies," and "Product Categories." Most of this is repeated in a text-only index that follows at the bottom portion of this opening page. It is apparent that much time and attention went into designing this Website, resulting in each page being consistent, functional, and easy to navigate.

Each page of a topic (disease, disorder, condition, or treatment) provides information primarily in the form of signed essays or chapters, and although most information on alternative/complementary medicine and treatments is anecdotal, there is some scientific research and more is ongoing in many areas of alternative/complementary medicine. A great many of the articles listed as the "Conventional Medicine" perspective are reprints from the American Institute of Preventive Medicine's *Healthy Self: The Guide to Self-Care and Wise Consumerism*, which severely limits the scope and depth of the conventional medicine point of view and treatment options listed.

Since the primary audience is consumers, there is a significant amount of advertising. The bottom of each page has a "Featured Products" list of products. As previously mentioned there is a "Market Place" area offering products on the site map, and additional advertisements appear between the drop-down menus on the right of the initial page. This Website will be most beneficial to those consumers already interested in alternative/complimentary health information, and as a resource for public and academic libraries.—**Lynn M. McMain**

Handbooks and Yearbooks

S

505.   **The Human Body & the Environment: How Our Surroundings Affect Our Health.** Westport, Conn., Greenwood Press, 2003. 4v. illus. index. (Middle School Reference). $160.00. ISBN 0-313-32558-8.

Despite the title of this set, this is really a reference set on the general subject of human health, suitable for middle and elementary school students. While there is some focus on environmental heath issues, all aspects of human anatomy, physiology, disease, and health are included. Once these basics are covered, there is very little room for discussion of the difficult issues involved in environmental health—trade-offs between economic progress and environmental protection, the difficulties of detecting and proving the effects of pollutants, the interactions between environmental factors and genetic predispositions.

The set includes four volumes: "The Circulatory & Respiratory Systems," "The Muscular & Skeletal Systems," "The Reproductive & Nervous Systems," and "The Digestive & Urinary Systems." Each volume, for each body system, includes a chapter on the basic biology of the system, a chapter on disorders affecting the system, and then a chapter on how factors in the environment may affect organs in the system. The term "environment" is taken very broadly here to include disease causing organisms, risky human behaviors, genetic disorders, and poor nutrition, as well as more obvious environmental factors such as toxic chemicals, radiation, and poor air and water quality.

The writing in these volumes is very clear, and suitable for most middle school and older elementary school students. All unfamiliar terms are defined and phonetic pronunciations given. Simplified diagrams, and black-and white photographs augment the text. No topic is treated in depth, but there are short discussions of contemporary issues such as AIDS, Mad Cow Disease, and hearing loss due to loud music, which are sure to spark students' interest. Each volume includes a glossary, a bibliography (giving both printed and Internet sources), and an index.

While this is a good, well-written basic middle school health course reference set, two other recent, larger (eight rather than four volume) sets should also be considered: *Health Matters!* (see ARBA 2003, entry 1427) and *Diseases* (see ARBA 2003, entry 1436). Both are more in-depth resources for human health aimed at the middle school audience and cover environmental health issues along with other human health topics. [R: SLJ, Dec 03, p. 96]—**Carol L. Noll**

S

506.   **Sexual Health Information for Teens: Health Tips About Sexual Development, Human Reproduction, and Sexually Transmitted Diseases.** Deborah A. Stanley, ed. Detroit, Omnigraphics, 2003. 391p. index. (Teen Health Series). $58.00. ISBN 0-7808-0445-7.

This title, one in the Teen Health Series from Omnigraphics, addresses health and hygiene issues that teens face during the adolescent years. Much like Omnigraphics' Health Reference Series, this series pulls together excerpts from government organizations such as the Centers for Disease Control and Prevention, the Department of Health Abstinence Education Program (State of Florida), and the National Institute on Drug Abuse as well as public organizations such as the Center for Young Women's Health and the National Campaign to Prevent Teen Pregnancy. The articles selected will specifically appeal to young adults and are designed to answer their most common questions.

Part 1 is a short section discussing the physical and emotional changes that occur in young men and women during puberty. Parts 2 and 3 are a bit longer and discuss reproductive health, addressing such issues as trips to the gynecologist, menstrual cramps, and toxic shock syndromes for girls and circumcision and testicular exams for boys. Part 4 discusses sexuality and social issues, including sexual orientation, date rape, and the debate over sex education in schools. Parts 5 and 6 discuss preventing pregnancy and avoiding sexually transmitted diseases. Because these two topics tend to make young adults the most uncomfortable, the chapters within these sections may be the most valuable in the book. The work concludes with Websites that discuss teen sexuality, contact information for relevant organizations, and an index.

This work should be included in all high school libraries and many larger public libraries. Because the majority of the material comes from governmental agencies it is accurate and non-offensive. This title is highly recommended.—**Shannon Graff Hysell**

MEDICINE

General Works

Dictionaries and Encyclopedias

P

507. **American Medical Association Complete Medical Encyclopedia.** Jerrold B. Leikin and Martin S. Lipsky, eds. New York, Random House, 2003. 1408p. illus. index. $45.00. ISBN 0-8129-9100-1.

This single-volume encyclopedia provides information on many medical topics, including diseases, medical terminology, types of drugs, functions of the body, and medical procedures. The entries are usually several paragraphs long and explain basic information on the topic. There are many clear diagrams and illustrations, ranging from how to burp a baby to the structure of the hand. The bulk of the book is the alphabetic encyclopedia, but the book also includes symptom charts that will help the user get an idea of a diagnosis for such symptoms as breast pain, vision loss, and depression. In addition, there is an atlas of the body with a page devoted to each of the major systems of the body that includes an explanation and diagram. There is also an essay on twenty-first-century medicine. The back of the book includes first aid instructions, a sample legal form, and an important section on the new HIPAA privacy laws that affects patients. This volume is a good first resource for finding information on a wide variety of medical and health topics. It is recommended for consumer health sections of any type of library. [R: LJ, 1 Oct 03, p. 62]—**Elaine Lasda**

C, P

508. Turkington, Carol, and Bonnie Lee Ashby. **The Encyclopedia of Infectious Diseases.** 2d ed. New York, Facts on File, 2003. 397p. index. (Facts on File Library of Health and Living). $71.50. ISBN 0-8160-4775-8.

With the advent of SARS, any book on infectious disease is going to be out-of-date by the time it is published. Yet the 2d edition of this encyclopedia could be useful for an undergraduate doing a paper or for any person who wants a better understanding of established and emerging infections. Diseases and conditions are listed alphabetically and usually include a basic description, symptoms, diagnosis, treatment, and prevention. The text is easy to understand and the authors do not talk down to the reader, which often happens in publications geared for the consumer. Most of the entries have been updated since the previous edition and there are many new entries, such as West Nile virus or pneumococcal vaccine.

The book contains several useful appendixes including information on drugs used to treat infectious diseases, guidelines on disinfecting a home, organizations, health publications, and a glossary. The main drawback to this book is that although an extensive bibliography is included after the appendices, the individual entries do not indicate which citations in the bibliography provide further information on the condition being discussed. This means the reader must look through seven pages of references. This resource is recommended for undergraduate collections as well as medical and public libraries with a consumer health collection.—**Natalie Kupferberg**

Handbooks and Yearbooks

P
509.   **Johns Hopkins Symptoms and Remedies: The Complete Home Medical Reference.** Simeon Margolis, ed., with the editors of *The Johns Hopkins Medical Letter Health After 50.* New York, Rebus, 2003. 736p. illus. index. $39.95. ISBN 0-929661-79-6.

It is no surprise that the more informed the patient the better medical care they receive. This guide, edited by Dr. Simeon Margolis and the editors of *The John Hopkins Medical Letter Health After 50*, will provide users with authoritative answers to most if not all of their medical questions. The work is divided into two sections—"Symptoms" and "Disorders." The first half of the volume provides users with an A to Z listing of 150 common symptoms, including such problems as abdominal pain, bad breath, fatigue, indigestion, muscle spasms, sweating, and weight gain and loss. For each symptom there are several possible diagnoses listed that provide additional information and distinguishing features of the diagnosis. For example, the user can look up "Joint Pain" and read about 29 possible diagnoses. The 29 diagnoses are then broken down into 14 that are not accompanied by a fever and 15 that are accompanied with a fever. The distinguishing features listed help the reader further decide which diagnosis is most appropriate for their problem. From here the reader can look to the second half of the volume to discover more about the disorder they are researching. The disorders are listed alphabetically and each includes a description of the disorder, causes, prevention, diagnosis, how it can be treated, and if and when a doctor needs to be consulted. The descriptions are written in an easy-to-comprehend style designed for the layperson and often include bulleted lists for clarification. Simple line drawings accompany some of the entries but in general the work is not well illustrated. A subject index concludes the volume.

This volume should be in all public and consumer health care libraries. It is designed for quick reference look up and provides authoritative answers to many questions.—**Shannon Graff Hysell**

P
510.   **Merck Manual of Medical Information.** 2d home ed. Mark H. Beers and others, eds. Whitehouse Station, N.J., Merck & Company; distr., New York, Simon & Schuster, 2003. 1907p. illus. index. $37.50pa. ISBN 0-911910-35-2.

Reviews of the first *Merck Manual* home edition are found in ARBA 1998 (see entry 1580) and 2000 (see entry 1406). Each review begins by noting the special professional value of the *Merck Manual of Diagnosis and Therapy* (17th ed.; see 2002, entry 1440). Both also point out that the original diagnostic title uses sophisticated medical terminology and illustrations, and that lay readers will find the new home edition of medical information highly useful and much more comprehensible. Such a conclusion is equally true of the 2d edition.

The format is still enough larger than the original *Manual* to make its physical handling easy and the larger print and highlighted charts, along with what editors claim to be a complete rewrite, make it a "highly detailed, complete, authoritative (compilation of) medical information" (p. v). Also apparently valid is the claim that this *Manual* "covers more topics in greater detail than all other home medical books. The book explains what a disorder is, who is likely to get it, what its symptoms are, how it is diagnosed, how it might be prevented, and how it can be treated. Information about prognosis . . . is given when possible" (p. v).

"A Guide for Readers" describes the book's organization including sections (25 in total); chapters; cross-references; medical terms; illustrations; sidebars, and tables (in color); drug information; diagnostic tests; and special subjects. Four standard appendixes ("Weights and Measures," "Common Medical Tests," "Drug Names: Generic and Trade," and "Resources for Help and Information") are followed by a very detailed index from page 1769 to page 1907.

There are numerous changes and updates from the first home edition, but the basic emphasis on a readable, easily searchable text are still paramount. The information is as current as a print source can be.

This *Manual* is undoubtedly a must have addition for public, health-related, and even academic libraries that typically serve patrons with a multitude of health needs and complexity. For the majority of concerns, the patron will find the right answer for, or explanation of, his or her medical education or query in the *Merck Manual of Medical Information*. [R: LJ, 15 June 03, p. 64]—**Laurel Grotzinger**

Alternative Medicine

P

511.   **The ABC Clinical Guide to Herbs.** Mark Blumenthal and others, eds. Binghamton, N.Y., Haworth Press, 2003. 480p. illus. index. $49.95. ISBN 1-58890-157-2.

Eastern cultures have a long history of using herbal remedies. Western medicine, however, has long been skeptical of their value. That attitude is changing as more and more patients cite herbal products in their medication list. As a result, health care providers need to be aware of the benefits and dangers of medicinal plants. This textbook is designed as a continuing education module for physicians, nurses, pharmacists, and dieticians. It covers the history of medicinal herbs in North America and discusses their clinical, legal, and regulatory status.

Some 29 herbs were selected for inclusion in the text based on their consistently high retail sales; 12 multi-herb products are also included. Each entry consists of three parts. The first is a clinical overview that provides at-a-glance information regarding a herb's use, dosage, and any possible adverse effects and contraindications. A one-page patient information sheet that can be reproduced for distribution follows this. In-depth clinical and pharmacological information is covered in a two-page monograph. This document reviews the history of the herb's use, pharmacological details (e.g., dosage, preparation options), clinical studies, physiological effects, interactions, and brand name products. Monographs have undergone peer review and reviewers' names are given in an appendix. This is a meticulously referenced work that not only cites textual sources but also provides a detailed chart of clinical studies. Appendixes include an extensive chart of commercial products used in clinical studies and contact information for the producing companies. There is also a supplemental list of recent clinical studies and a glossary. A post-test, continuing education credit application and a course evaluation form are provided.

This is an important, authoritative work that will be useful in health science libraries. Public library staff and users will find the *PDR for Herbal Medicines* (2d ed.; see ARBA 2001, entry 1483) or the mainstream *Encyclopedia of Medicinal Plants* (see ARBA 97, entry 1343) to be more accessible for the nonprofessional.—**Marlene M. Kuhl**

Dentistry

P

512.   **Dental Care and Oral Health Sourcebook.** 2d ed. Amy L. Sutton, ed. Detroit, Omnigraphics, 2003. 586p. index. (Health Reference Series). $78.00. ISBN 0-7808-0634-4.

It has been documented that dentists, as a profession, have a high suicide rate—some theorize it is due to continually treating overanxious and stressed patients. There are few people who do not cringe at the thought of a dental drill, but few who understand basic dental care and are willing to take preventative measures to pre-empt problems. This book could serve as turning point in the battle to educate consumers in issues concerning oral health.

Tightly written in terms the average person can understand, yet comprehensive in scope and authoritative in tone, it is another excellent sourcebook in the Health Reference Series. This book has an informative style yet its material has not been overly simplified. Many of the entries are reprinted from national associations and federal organizations (e.g., American Academy of Periodontology, American Dental Hygienist Association, Center for Disease Control, National Center for Dental and Craniofacial Research).

The editor has compiled information on topics in dental care important for infants to the aged, dental concerns from caries to Temporomandibular Dysfunction, and dental procedures from brushing and flossing to oral surgery. Controversial subjects like holistic dentistry and mercury toxicity from amalgam fillings are also covered. True to its name, this volume contains contact information to help the needy and those with special needs find appropriate dental care. A few well-chosen illustrations clarify salient points. This book should be in the reference department of all public libraries, and in academic libraries that have a public constituency.—**Susan K. Setterlund**

Pediatrics

P
513.   **Childhood Diseases and Disorders Sourcebook.** Chad T. Kimball, ed. Detroit, Omnigraphics, 2003. 637p. index. (Health Reference Series). $78.00. ISBN 0-7808-0458-9.

The editor's state that "this book was written to provide parents and caregivers with information about some of the most commonly encountered childhood ailments . . . .." It not only covers the common diseases associated with childhood, it also covers chronic conditions such as sickle cell and diabetes. The book is divided into nine parts that are broad general topics. Each part is divided into chapters that cover a specific disease. Each topic includes a general description of the disease or condition, when to seek medical help, the different treatments available, and whether to try treating the condition with over-the-counter pharmaceuticals. The medical tests used to diagnose a disease and therapies for treatment are discussed. Entries covering chronic disease also include the names, addresses, telephone numbers, and Websites for agencies that are specific to the disease. The entries are easy to read and understand. A glossary of terms is included as well as a bibliography for additional information and reading, a list of government and professional agencies that deal with childhood diseases, and an extensive index. This is an excellent book for new parents and should be included in all health care and public libraries.—**Betsy J. Kraus**

P
514.   **Healthy Children Sourcebook.** Chad T. Kimball, ed. Detroit, Omnigraphics, 2003. 624p. index. (Health Reference Series). $78.00. ISBN 0-7808-0247-0.

A child who has grown and developed within an environment of healthy behaviors is likely to become a healthy adult. It is hard to imagine that any other single resource exists that would provide such a comprehensive guide of timely information on health promotion and disease prevention for children aged 3 to 12. This book is an addition to the well-known Health Reference Series, which has a consistent style and format. Short excerpts from reliable resources are reprinted in over 53 chapters. The focus is on health promotion rather than illness care, although chapters on selecting a pediatrician and basic first aid are included. A major section of over 17 chapters discuss safety in regard to sports, cars, school buses, water, and play in general—an important emphasis since injury is a major cause of mortality in this age group. The current concern about obesity in American children is addressed, with entries on nutrition, fitness, school lunches, and eating disorders. Unique entries include the use of alternative medicine with children, how to work with children to use the Internet responsibly, and how to talk with children about the news and war. Information that might be predicted to change, like the immunization schedule, are so noted with resources as to where to obtain updated advice. An extensive directory of additional resources concludes the book. This volume is highly recommended for general libraries, primary schools, agencies serving school-aged children, and parents.—**Mary Ann Thompson**

Specific Diseases and Conditions

AIDS

C, P

515.   Watstein, Sarah Barbara, and Stephen E. Stratton. **Encyclopedia of HIV and AIDS.** 2d ed. New York, Facts on File, 2003. 660p. index. (Facts on File Library of Health and Living). $71.50. ISBN 0-8160-4808-8.

This updated and expanded edition of *The AIDS Dictionary* (see ARBA 99, entry 1470) provides hundreds of entries representing a wide range of topics and issues associated with AIDS including: biological and medical terminology concerning transmission, prevention, pathology, and treatment of the disease; psychological and sociological impact of the pandemic including cultural and political ramifications; and terms pertinent to financial considerations, government, activism, policy, and law. Terms are indexed and cross-referenced throughout. The appendixes offer a guide to common abbreviations; current statistical information; an updated bibliography; and telephone numbers and Websites for selected organizations and other resources.

Due to the swiftly changing nature of any disease and medical research, any such volume can be quickly out of date. However, a wide audience of professionals, researchers, and lay people will appreciate the comprehensive nature and clarity of this work. The *Encyclopedia of HIV and AIDS* is appropriate for public and all academic libraries.—**Leanne M. VandeCreek**

Alzheimer's Disease

P

516.   Molloy, William, and Paul Caldwell. **Alzheimer's Disease: Everything You Need to Know.** rev. ed. New York, Firefly Books, 2003. 220p. index. (Your Personal Health Series). $14.95pa. ISBN 1-55297-737-4.

A great deal of information is packed into this small book, for the stated audience of clinicians, caregivers, and other interested laypersons. Divided into 10 chapters, the book addresses topics such as the history of Alzheimer's, human brain anatomy, possible causes, common signs and symptoms, diagnosis, the diverse reactions to diagnosis, care and treatment, other dementias, and legal issues. Throughout the chapters helpful insets define words or explain concepts with headings such as "Alzheimer's and Education," "Dignity and Alzheimer's Disease," "Memory Changes in Normal Aging," "Common Sleep Changes," "Standardized Mini-Mental State Examination (SMMSE)," and "Stages in Alzheimer's Disease." The book ends with a chart of medications currently used to treat the various symptoms of Alzheimer's, a glossary, an index, and a short list of resources. Unfortunately for U.S. readers the resource organizations listed are Canadian, as are the physician authors, with only one U.S. organization, the Alzheimer's Association, listed. However, the readability, compassion, and quality of the information overshadow any minor shortcomings. This book is heartily recommended as a useful resource for physician's offices, public libraries, and high school and community college libraries.—**Lynn M. McMain**

Cancer

P

517.   **Cancer Sourcebook.** 4th ed. Karen Bellenir, ed. Detroit, Omnigraphics, 2003. 1096p. index. (Health Reference Series). $78.00. ISBN 0-7808-0633-9.

The Center for Disease Control and Prevention's statistics attribute 25 percent of all deaths in the United States to cancer. Only heart disease kills more Americans. It is not surprising that many library patrons need information about cancer. The 4th edition of Omnigraphic's *Cancer Sourcebook* is a good place to start. Like the other volumes in this series, this one provides basic information collected from government agencies, nonprofit organizations, and periodicals. It provides an overview that includes: statistics; information about cancer risks and prevention; chapters on specific cancers; and treatments, therapies, and coping with their side effects. The book also has a glossary, information about obtaining support, and dealing with end-of-life issues. The chapters on finding cancer information in both English and Spanish and on locating community resources are very helpful. Advice about explaining cancer to children is useful as well.

Although this book covers most of the major cancers, patrons seeking information about breast cancer, childhood cancers, gynecological cancers, leukemia, or prostate cancer should consult the volumes in this series devoted specifically to these cancers. The *Cancer Sourcebook* is a good introduction, but those in need of in-depth information will need to supplement it with medical textbooks, Medline searches, and books such as Ernest Rosenbaum's *Supportive Cancer Care* (Sourcebooks, 2001). [R: Choice, Jan 04, p. 880]—**Barbara M. Bibel**

Diabetes

P

518. **Diabetes Sourcebook.** 3d ed. Dawn D. Matthews, ed. Detroit, Omnigraphics, 2003. 597p. index. (Health Reference Series). $78.00. ISBN 0-7808-0629-8.

The 3d edition of *Diabetes Sourcebook* includes a substantial amount of new material while retaining many of the positive features of earlier editions. For example, the chapter subheadings make the book very usable as a consumer reference tool.

This edition contains more detailed descriptions of various types of diabetes, including impaired glucose tolerance and insulin resistance. More information is provided about the various kinds of tests for diabetes. A section on exercise and nutrition furnishes the reader with diabetic exchange lists, information about carbohydrate counting, and specific solutions to problems arising around eating for diabetics. In addition to a well-written section on the complications of diabetes, the book includes a comprehensive section on end stage renal disease, dialysis, and kidney transplantation. The section on research and statistics contains information about diabetes in specific groups, such as African Americans, American Indians, and children. Supplementary material consists of a helpful glossary, sources for recipes and cookbooks, information about organizations and financial help, and a first-rate index.

This edition is even more helpful than earlier versions in that it gives direct instructions for specific situations, such as gestational diabetes, dialysis, and other conditions. It is a truly valuable tool for anyone seeking readable and authoritative information on diabetes.—**Jeanne D. Galvin**

Sexually Transmitted Disease

C, P

519. Shoquist, Jennifer, and Diane Stafford. **The Encyclopedia of Sexually Transmitted Diseases.** New York, Facts on File, 2004. 326p. index. (Facts on File Library of Health and Living). $65.00. ISBN 0-8160-4881-9.

The latest volume in Facts on File's Library of Health and Living series proves to be a valuable one. Following the series' standard arrangement, this volume includes an introduction, guide to commonly used abbreviations, the entries, extensive appendixes, a bibliography, and a cross-reference index.

The introduction alone makes this work worthwhile. It delves into the current statistics and demographics surrounding sexually transmitted diseases (STDs), being careful to acknowledge that the numbers are not frequently reported to the CDC and why this is. It further highlights past and current trends and the significant changes. A brief mention of why public awareness and education are so important in the treatment and prevention of STDs and a thorough recounting of recent research findings round out the introductory chapter. The body of the volume includes more than 300 entries that identify the different types of STDs, symptoms, modes of transmission, treatment options, at-risk populations, and how to lower the risk of infection.

Exhaustive appendixes include Websites and contact information for STD information and education hotlines, organizations, and advocacy groups; state-by-state requirements on STD/HIV/AIDS education in public schools; concise summaries of STDs in an "at-a-glance" format; and home care advice for HIV/AIDS patients and their caregivers. Aimed at lay and professional audiences alike, this tool is appropriate for reference collections in medical, public, and academic libraries.—**Leanne M. VandeCreek**

Surgery

P

520.   **The Gale Encyclopedia of Surgery: A Guide for Patients and Caregivers.** Anthony J. Senagore, executive advisor. Farmington Hills, Mich., Gale, 2004. 3v. illus. index. $350.00. ISBN 0-7876-7721-3.

Anyone facing surgery may feel overwhelmed. Understanding exactly what will happen lessens anxiety and speeds recovery because informed patients participate actively in their care. *The Gale Encyclopedia of Surgery* will help patients and their families by showing them what happens during the diagnosis, surgical procedure, and aftercare. Anthony J. Senagore, M.D., F.A.C.S. of the Cleveland Clinic, is the executive advisor for this encyclopedia. He assembled a team of health care professionals and medical writers to prepare the 465 entries in this set. They cover 265 surgical procedures as well as diagnostic tests, drugs, medical devices, and related material.

Entries on surgeries include a definition of the procedure, its purpose, demographics, description, diagnosis and preparation, aftercare, risks, normal results, morbidity and mortality rates, alternatives, and resources. Many of these articles also have color illustrations of the procedure. Other entries cover important subjects such as anesthesia, hospital admission procedures, obtaining a second opinion, and communicating with medical personnel. Shaded sidebars contain definitions of key terms, who performs the procedure, and questions to ask the doctor. All articles are signed and all have resource lists. Ample cross-references lead users to relevant material in other articles. A glossary, list of organizations, and an index complete the work.

Although there is some overlap with *The Gale Encyclopedia of Medicine* (2d ed.; see ARBA 2003, entry 1437), *The Gale Encyclopedia of Surgery* provides more extensive coverage of surgical procedures. It is very up-to-date, offering information on new techniques such as virtual colonoscopy, and will be accessible to lay readers with high school literacy levels. It is an excellent addition to public and consumer health libraries.—**Barbara M. Bibel**

NURSING

P

521.   Mandleco, Barbara L. **Growth & Development Handbook: Newborn Through Adolescent.** Clifton Park, N.Y., Delmar, 2004. 262p. illus. index. $28.95 spiralbound. ISBN 1-4018-1013-6.

The *Growth & Development Handbook: Newborn Through Adolescent* was written for undergraduate nursing students and practicing nurses, and it covers the early stages of human development from a holistic and family-oriented perspective. The work emphasizes normal developmental milestones, health and health promotion, anticipatory guidance, and the education of families about home care, and it provides and easy-to-use, succinct summary of human development that can be used on clinical units as well as a supplement to the student's textbook.

The first chapter contains information and guides for communicating with children and families as well as physical, nutritional, developmental, and family assessment, and the second chapter reviews theories of development. The remaining chapters encompass the growth and development of children during various stages of development. Each chapter has summary tables of important developmental indicators, as well as a discussion of the physiological, psychosexual, cognitive, psychosocial, moral, and spiritual development that occur during the particular stages.

The *Growth & Development Handbook* contains nine appendixes, which include normal vital signs, growth charts, laboratory values, the Denver II developmental test, a family assessment model, the recommended childhood immunization schedule, recommended dietary allowances, sexual maturity ratings, and a resource of Websites relating to pediatrics. Each chapter is followed by references, and an index is included. This title is recommended for nursing schools, hospitals, and academic institutions that offer psychology programs.—**Rita Neri**

PHARMACY AND PHARMACEUTICAL SCIENCES

Directories

P

522.   **Rx List: The Internet Drug Index. http://www.rxlist.com/.** [Website]. Free. Date reviewed: Dec 03.

Rx List is an online Website for drug information. There is no general information on the Website explaining what is covered and what is not covered by the Website content. One must click on all the different links to find out what is covered. The home page is cluttered with advertisements and the day this reviewer chose to search it there were falling snowflakes down the page. This was extremely irritating and did not enhance the Websites information. The opening page starts with the topics "Top 200 Drugs of 2002," "Rx List Advanced Search," "Top 100 Searches," "Rx Laughs a Dose of Karma," and six boxes linking to major topics such as Alzheimer's disease, allergies, kids asthma, and more. The next section of the home page is "Recent Additions to Rx List Monographs," followed by "Top 100 Searches on Rx List," which brings one to the last item on the home page, "RxList Disease Index." The home page covers over three printed pages. The home page should be shortened to one screen for easier use rather than having all these topics, which keeps the user scrolling through to find what is there.

The advanced search is the only useful way to search this site. On this page there are five different ways to search for drug information. These include keyword with Boolean abilities, imprint code identification, NDC search code, and drug FAQ/patient monograph. Only the keyword search has any explanation of how to use it. The drug entry gives a brief description of the type of delivery, such as capsule or liquid, which is followed by the diseases or infections that the drug is used to treat, the dosage and administration, indications, how supplied, and references. There is also a date noting when the page was last revised. At the top of each drug entry is a tool bar covering the topics of description/brand, clinical pharmacology, indications and dosage, side affects/drug interactions, warnings and precautions, over dosage contradictions, and patient information. Each entry also has cross-references for more information on the disease being treated by the drug or the specific bacteria the drug is used against. There is a link to *Taber's Medical Encyclopedia*. Despite the cumbersome home page, this site does have a wealth of information especially for people having Internet access and no library close by to visit. It also refers users to

their local pharmacists for more complete information and any other questions not answered by this site.
—**Betsy J. Kraus**

Handbooks and Yearbooks

P

523.   **Physicians' Desk Reference for Nonprescription Drugs and Dietary Supplements, 2002.** 23d ed. Montvale, N.J., Medical Economics Data, 2002. 855p. index. $55.95. ISBN 1-56363-417-1.

This volume is divided into two sections. One section covers the over-the-counter medicines covered under the CFR labeling requirements. The second section covers herbal remedies and dietary supplements covered under the Dietary Supplement Health and Education Act of 1994. This is an annual publication that compiles the manufacturers information on their products. The information is strictly what the manufacturer has released. There are no independent evaluations of the products listed.

The over-the-counter drugs are the majority of those listed in the volume and indexed by manufacturer's name, product name, subject categories, active ingredients, over-the-counter drugs that work with prescription drugs, colored identification plates, and over-the-counter drug information and home testing kits by name. The last index covers the dietary supplement information consisting of natural remedies, vitamins, minerals, herbs, amino acids, metabolites, and combinations of these and other botanicals. Lastly there is a section on popular herbs and their use in addition to lists of drug information centers and poison control centers in the United States. Due to the information provided being strictly the manufacturer's information, this reviewer recommends having either *Mosby's OTC Drugs: An Over-the-counter Drug Resource for Health Professionals* (Mosby's, 1999) by Richard P. Donjon and Bryon J. Goeckner or the *Complete Guide to Prescription & Nonprescription Drugs* (Berkley Publishing Group, 2002) by H. Winter Griffith, Stephen W. Moore, and William N. Jones on hand to be used with this title. Every medical library and public library should have at least one volume covering this segment of drugs that are so heavily used by people in the United States.—**Betsy J. Kraus**

34 High Technology

COMPUTING

C, P, S
524.   Reilly, Edwin D. **Milestones in Computer Science and Information Technology.** Westport, Conn., Greenwood Press, 2003. 380p. illus. index. $70.00. ISBN 1-57356-521-0.

Not an encyclopedia, this work is a selective historical dictionary in which "topics were declared to be milestones by the selective opinion of the author." The 671 articles are arranged alphabetically from Abacus to Zuse computers. Each boldfaced entry is assigned one subject classification but may be listed more than once in the "Classification of Articles." Any term within the article that has its own separate article is also set in boldface. The articles that are not merely definitions conclude with a suggestion for additional reading. In addition to a "Listing of Cited References," the author also lists sources consulted but not actually cited.

The many helpful indexes not only help to locate information but also to place information within a context. The personal name index lists all people cited in articles with their birth and death dates and countries of birth and accomplishments. The geographical index classifies milestones by their associated countries. The chronological index lists significant dates in the articles, from natural language in 20,000 B.C.E. to wireless connectivity in 2002. There is even a "Top Ten" list of milestones.

Extremely readable and insightful, this book explains complicated concepts in straightforward language and sometimes provides a bit of humor. It is highly recommended for academic, public, and high school library collections.—**Deborah Sharp**

TELECOMMUNICATIONS

C, P
525.   Botto, Francis. **Encyclopedia of Wireless Telecommunications.** New York, McGraw-Hill, 2002. 1v. (various paging). illus. index. $59.95pa. ISBN 0-07-139025-1.

This volume is a sort of companion volume to *McGraw-Hill's Encyclopedia of Networking and Telecommunications* (McGraw-Hill, 2001). Botto's *Encyclopedia* will be used by some students as a textbook for wireless networking. The work covers technologies such as 1G, 2G, 2.5G, and 3G wireless architectures with regard to devices, globalization, service, standards, and protocols. The size of the articles varies from the 10 words for Seymour Cray to several pages for Bluetooth. The arrangement is initially confusing with each letter of the alphabet further broken up into topical sections, such as "General topics," "Computer/Software," "Acronyms," and "Miscellaneous." For example, the letter "M" has general articles, such as "Macromedia Flash Player," "Microwave Radio," "Mobile Networking," "Mobile Satellite Service

(MSS)," "MPEG," and "Multimedia Messaging Service (MSS)" at the beginning, followed by computer/software articles on "Macro," "Mainframe," "Meta Data," "Microwave Radio," "Middleware," "Mirror Site," and so on. Next comes the "Miscellaneous" section with articles on "Mbone,""MIME," "M-JPEG," "MP3," and "Multiplexing." In addition to the alphabet section, there is a numerals section before the letter "A" for articles like 2.5G networks, 900 MHz, 1024, 3D Vector coordinates. The numerals section is also divided up into "General," "Data Rates," "Display Technology," "Frequencies," "Miscellaneous," "Signification Dates," "Symbols," and "Common Syntax." Each numeral and alphabet section begins with a classed table of contents. There is a general table of contents at the front of the volumes listing the larger topics (such as Bluetooth), and there is an index at the end of the volume.

The work is illustrated with black-and-white line drawings and diagrams. The articles are for the most part well written, although some are written to convey only the most basic of information (e.g., "Telephone," "120mm") . Given the wide range of technical topics covered, the author tries to appeal to a wide range of readers. Some cross-references are hard to fathom. A few pages seem to suffer from printing flaws, with a black smudge running along the left margin of the page.

There are some electronic books covering similar topics that can be obtained online through NetLibrary (OCLC), including *The Wireless Technician's Handbook*, *The Complete Guide for Wireless Communications Professionals: A Guide for Engineers and Managers*, and *A Manager's Guide to Wireless Telecommunications*. A number of academic libraries may have these NetLibrary works already available for their online patrons. Reference collections wanting a traditional paper encyclopedia covering wireless technologies will find Botto's volume hard to beat. [R: Choice, Jan 03, p. 800]—**Ralph Lee Scott**

35 Physical Sciences and Mathematics

GENERAL WORKS

C

526.   **The Cambridge History of Science, Volume 5: The Modern Physical and Mathematical Sciences.** Mary Jo Nye, ed. New York, Cambridge University Press, 2003. 678p. index. $95.00. ISBN 0-521-57199-5.

The Cambridge History of Science is a landmark in history of science publishing. It reflects a shift in the discipline over the last 30 years or so away from narratives of discovery to specialized studies on the workings of scientific communities. Rather than relying on a unitary scientific method for a unifying theme, a wide variety of analytical approaches are applied. This volume on physical sciences in the nineteenth and twentieth centuries offers analyses drawn from intellectual and social history, cultural studies, and other perspectives. Constructionism and Kuhn's concept of scientific revolutions are themes in many of the essays. The volume begins with a section on science in public culture (relations to philosophy, religion, literature, popularization, and participation by women), followed by one on discipline building (five essays). About half the book (parts 3 and 4) consists of chapters on particular disciplines. These typically begin with a historiographical introduction on current debates among historians, followed by an overview of the field's history or a treatment from a particular perspective (e.g., the increasing dominance of geophysicists over field geologists in the earth sciences). The final section comprises essays on the role of science in war, national ideology, medicine, computers, and climate change.

This volume is a superb overview of current thinking in the history of physical science. The sciences are treated selectively; topology, algebra, oceanography (apart from plate tectonics) and some other fields are omitted. It may be used as a supplement with more traditional narrative histories, such as P. J. Bowler's *Norton History of the Environmental Sciences* (W. W. Norton, 1993), W. H. Brock's *Norton History of Chemistry* (W. W. Norton, 1993), I. Grattan-Guinness's *Norton History of the Mathematical Sciences* (W. W. Norton, 1998), H. Kragh's *Quantum Generations* (Princeton University Press, 1999), and J. D. North's *Norton History of Astronomy and Cosmology* (W. W. Norton, 1994). This book is essential for most academic and large public libraries.—**Frederic F. Burchsted**

PHYSICAL SCIENCES

Chemistry

Dictionaries and Encyclopedias

S

527.   **The Facts on File Dictionary of Inorganic Chemistry.** John Daintith, ed. New York, Facts on File, 2004. 248p. (Facts on File Science Library). $49.50. ISBN 0-8160-4926-2.

The target audience for *The Facts on File Dictionary of Inorganic Chemistry* is described as AP high school students, undergraduate college students in chemistry, and undergraduates in allied fields like materials science and earth sciences. The definitions are at about the level of a general chemistry course and should be readily understandable for a reader with some scientific background, including those in the target audiences. The use of cross-references and several appendixes with information regarding the chemical elements help to make the book more useful. On the other hand, advanced students will probably look for more in-depth definitions, and since the references provided for further reading are limited to a few standard textbooks and Websites, this book will probably not be especially helpful for them. The main listing includes brief biographies of some scientists who have made contributions to inorganic chemistry, but many individuals who helped define modern inorganic chemistry are omitted. This book seems to be a useful reference for the intended audience.—**Harry E. Pence**

S

528.   **The Facts on File Dictionary of Organic Chemistry.** John Daintith, ed. New York, Facts on File, 2004. 247p. (Facts on File Science Library). $49.50. ISBN 0-8160-4928-9.

This dictionary's roughly 2,000 definitions range in length from a couple of sentences to several paragraphs; some include diagrams. Entries are on technical terms, classes of compounds and specific compounds, reactions and reaction types, experimental techniques, and distinguished chemists. There are many *see* references. *See also* references are usually indicated by upper-case words in entries, although, confusingly, sometimes by italics; the phrase is also used. Appendixes include lists of carboxylic acids, amino acids, simple sugars, nucleosides, the elements, and a periodic table. There is a brief bibliography of textbooks, and a small list of useful Web pages.

Also edited by Daintith are *The Facts on File Dictionary of Biochemistry* (see ARBA 2003, entry 1339), *The Facts on File Dictionary of Chemistry* (3d ed.; see ARBA 2000, entry 1479), and *The Facts on File Dictionary of Inorganic Chemistry* (see entry 527). There is some overlap (e.g., *Biochemistry* has the same entry for "aerobic respiration" and nearly the same entry for "isomerism" as does this work).

Intended for students in high school advanced placement courses and introductory college courses, the entries are simply written but most avoid oversimplification. This could be a useful supplementary reference for high schools, colleges, and public libraries.—**Robert Michaelson**

Earth and Planetary Sciences

General Works

C, P

529.   **Earth.** James F. Luhr, ed. New York, DK Publishing, 2003. 520p. illus. maps. index. $50.00. ISBN 0-7894-9643-7.

This book is difficult to typify as it has aspects of a text, a dictionary, and a coffee-table extravaganza. The basic premise is a summary of all of the major physical, biological, and even human features of Earth. The contents fall into two broad categories. A substantial portion of the volume is given to concise descriptions of the important processes that have shaped Earth from its origin to the present day. These include things like the formation of rocks and of continents, the actions of plate tectonics, climate, weathering, erosion, and more. In many respects this information is an abstract of that normally found in a text. The second contribution of the book is as a visual dictionary of the major features of Earth. Thus, following four pages summarizing the form and function of volcanoes are 18 pages listing the important volcanoes of the world. Each is briefly described, located on an index map, and illustrated with one or more photographs. This approach is then carried through mountains, rivers, lakes, deserts, glaciers, major vegetation zones, meteorite impacts, and human land use. While the choice of some examples and exclusion of others is occasionally puzzling, on the whole the coverage is global and educational. The index is good, allowing the user to find particular topics. This is necessary as the overall organization is topical, not alphabetical.

As is typical of a DK Publishing product, the book is a clearly written, well researched, beautifully illustrated, and compelling volume that is easy to pick up and hard to put down. While it is not a text per se, if one assimilated all the material contained in these 520 pages, one would have the equivalent of several introductory university courses in the natural sciences. Yes, there are places where the quality falls (i.e., to read [yet again] that reptiles evolved into mammals is discouraging), but such complaints are minor relative to the scope and clarity of the whole. The audience level is young adult to adult, and this work will be of value in public and university collections. [R: LJ, 1 Nov 03, p. 72]—**Bruce H. Tiffney**

Astronomy and Space Sciences

Dictionaries and Encyclopedias

C, P, S
530.   **A Dictionary of Astronomy.** rev. ed. Ian Ridpath, ed. New York, Oxford University Press, 2003. 518p. $15.95pa. ISBN 0-19-860513-7.

A Dictionary of Astronomy (written by a team of over 20 contributors and edited by Ian Ridpath) contains over 4,000 entries, addressing topics such as objects in the solar system, astronomy and physics terms, and principle entries for stars and galaxies. This revised edition also provides up-to-date coverage of recent space exploration and discoveries. There are no photographs; over 40 illustrations highlight individual entries. Brief biographical sketches of major astronomers are also included.

Most individual entries are 35 to 75 words in length. Longer entries cover the planets and broader topics (such as asteroids, comets, supernovas, the Sun, and time). The alphabetic order of headwords is letter by letter up to the first comma (i.e., Brown, Ernest William, brown dwarf, B star, Bubble Nebula). Headwords with numbers are ordered as if the number was spelled out. Cross-references are used to direct users to the main entry, and cross-references within an entry are indicated with an asterisk. Multiple definitions of the same headword are numbered. Abbreviations (in conjunction with names of observatories, organizations, and telescopes) are written out in full in the main headword, with cross-references given from the abbreviated form. Guide words are printed on the top outer page corners to aid users in finding their word or term. A brief but detailed appendix includes data on the Apollo lunar landing missions, satellites of the planets, the constellations, the brightest and nearest stars, the Messier objects, and the local group of galaxies.

Overall, this is an excellent, affordable dictionary for advanced high school users and academic researchers. Ridpath is a known editor for other high-quality astronomy resources, including *Norton's Star Atlas* (1998) and the *Illustrated Encyclopedia of the Universe* (see ARBA 2002, entry 1556). *A Dictionary of Astronomy* is a valuable reference source for astronomy-related information seekers.—**Caroline L. Gilson**

Handbooks and Yearbooks

C, P, S
531.   **The Solar System: A Firefly Guide.** Giovanni Caprara, ed. New York, Firefly Books, 2003. 255p. illus. index. $24.95pa. ISBN 1-55297-679-3.

This guide is the latest in a flood of books on the solar system that have appeared on the scene in the last six months. With the overwhelming quantity of images provided by NASA from the orbiting Hubble telescope, numerous flyby missions, and satellites and landers, it is not surprising they can be repackaged so many ways. This particular version is more like condensed soup. The information is presented in visual and written "bytes." Each page is packed with stunning photographs, illustrative insets, with concise text—a visual feast. Designed more for random study than for straight-through reading, this guide will provide a basic understanding of the formation, evolution, and current knowledge of the solar system.

The arrangement of the guide is typical of books of this type. It begins with the Sun and then progresses through the solar system outward. The appendixes include a brief glossary, a very brief index, bibliography, and a sample list of Websites (most of which are NASA sites). More content than a dictionary but more connected than an encyclopedia, this guide could be a useful resource for a small reference collection with limited astronomy sources. This book is appropriate for school, public, and general academic collections.—**Margaret F. Dominy**

Climatology and Meteorology

C, P

532.   Newton, David E. **Encyclopedia of Air.** Westport, Conn., Greenwood Press, 2003. 252p. illus. index. $79.95. ISBN 1-57356-564-4.

This exciting book of more than 250 pages brings "air" into focus from a multidisciplinary perspective. Great breadth of the subject is achieved by alphabetic arrangement of entries within broader categories. This creates a more comprehensive depth than might otherwise have been achieved.

The categories, such as "Biographies," "Elements," "Meteorology," "Mythology," "Organizations," and "Transportation" (half of the dozen available), each have multiple alphabetically listed entries (over 125 total). A good selection of illustrations and photographs enrich the text, as do appropriate tables and formulas. Many of the entries end with "Further Readings" listed. Throughout the book *see* and *see also* references extend the value of many entries.

"Oxygen," an entry of about two pages, has the subheadings "Physical and Chemical Properties" (with formulas), "Discovery and Naming," "Biological Functions," and "Production and Uses." Another more tangible example, "Hovercraft," is about a page and a half and has the subheadings "Invention" (with a photograph); "Specifications, Operation, and Uses"; and "Hydrofoils." Both of these entries are followed by "Further Reading" citations, while some entries, such as "Parachute," include "Further Information" (about a parachute association).

Many specialized terms are used and clearly explained. The book is relatively easy to use, and is a very creative encyclopedic look at the rather nebulous topic "air." This encyclopedia has few if any competitors and is strongly recommended for all academic libraries, including many high school libraries. It should also be selected for library collections that support a science program, and included in all medium-to large-sized public libraries.—**James W. Agee Jr.**

Ecology

C, P, S

533.   **The Facts on File Dictionary of Ecology and the Environment.** Jill Bailey, ed. New York, Facts on File, 2004. 248p. (Facts on File Science Library). $49.50. ISBN 0-8160-4922-X.

This is another volume in the Facts on File Science Library series. As indicated by the title, it is an alphabetic arrangement of over 2,000 topics and terms associated with environmental science. The topics covered range from the common ones of *acid rain*, *smog*, and *acre* to more specialized terms such as *podzol* and *prokaryote*. Programs and organizations such as the International Biological Program and the EPA are included, as well as familiar individuals associated with the field. These biographical entries are very brief and few in number. Major legislative acts that directly relate to environmental issues are listed with the date of the act and its aims. Approximately 30 black-and-white line drawings illustrate the food chain, water cycle, and other key processes. The definitions range in length from a sentence to one page; most entries have less than 200 words. Cross-references are provided. Two appendixes supplement the volume: SI Units and Web pages covering universities, museums, and agencies. There is a short bibliography of recent resources. The intended audience is high school students, especially those enrolled in advanced placement classes. Besides high school libraries, this book will be useful in public and academic libraries.—**Elaine Ezell**

S

534. Nardi, James B. **The World Beneath Our Feet: A Guide to Life in the Soil.** New York, Oxford University Press, 2003. 223p. illus. index. $35.00. ISBN 0-19-513990-9.

This book examines the relationships among soils, plants, and creatures that live in or contribute to the soil. Soil is defined as: "A dynamic natural medium in which plants grow made up of both mineral and organic materials as well as living forms."

Divided into three parts, the first, "Working Partnerships," explains how the organisms in the soil interact with the mineral world and the organic world. Diagrams and photographs enhance text to describe processes and concepts such as how soil is formed, the elements of plant growth, how creatures give soil its fertility, and how plants and animals affect the layers of soil. Part 2, "Members of the Soil Community," highlights individual inhabitants of the soil—microbes, invertebrates, and vertebrates—and explains how particular groups contribute to the soil environment. A fact box is included with each entry in this section, giving the name of the organism, its classification, its place in the food web, its size, and the number of species. Fact boxes for vertebrates also include life span and gestation period. Drawings and photographs of the creatures accompany the text. Part 3, "The Gift Good Earth," provides discussions of erosion, the effects of excessive use of fertilizers, acid rain, and loss of soil structure. There are also a discussion of the benefits of composting and instructions for preparing compost. Other features of the book include a glossary; a topical bibliography for further reading; an annotated bibliography of Websites; and a comprehensive index.

The format of the book is very pleasing, with a beautiful cover depicting a myriad collection of life in the soil, glossy paper with wide margins and generous type size, guide words at the top of each page, captioned illustrations and diagrams, and color photographs. The text would be easily understood by middle grade students, yet does not talk down to older users. There is hardly a page without a diagram, drawing, or photograph, making this book a feast for the eyes as well as the mind. [R: SLJ, Oct 03, p. 106]—**Dana McDougald**

Geology

C, P

535. Rosi, Mauro, Paulo Papale, Luca Lupi, and Marco Stoppato. **Volcanoes.** New York, Firefly Books, 2003. 334p. illus. maps. index. $24.95pa. ISBN 1-55297-683-1.

Volcanoes, the newest field guide published by Firefly Books, is a comprehensive handbook outlining the origins, nature, and physical mechanics of volcanic activity. Throughout the edition, the reader is provided with a thorough explanation regarding the internal structure of volcanoes as well as related geodynamic structures. The book also explores the climatological impact of volcanoes on the ecosystem, which until the late twentieth century was not conspicuously discussed in earth science literature. Well illustrated with spectacular color photographs, maps, and charts, this work also defines for the reader the different types of volcanoes. Island arc, hot-spot, ocean ridge, and continental margin are just a few of the categories in the nomenclature of volcanic structures. This guide also discusses factors that cause volcanic eruptions, along with geologic formations such as volcanic cones, craters, and calderas. Researched and compiled by expert volcanologists, *Volcanoes* is a must resource that can aid both the novice geology buff and the serious graduate student in their understanding of this natural phenomenon.—**Patrick Hall**

Oceanography

P, S

536.   Day, Trevor. **Exploring the Ocean.** New York, Oxford University Press, 2003. 4v. illus. maps. index. $100.00/set. ISBN 0-19-515738-9.

This four-volume resource focuses on the study of oceanography. The format of the volumes is standardized with the first 3 volumes each having 29 topics, which are presented in 2-page spreads, and all 4 volumes having 64 pages each. Each topic is enhanced with three to five photographs, diagrams, or drawings all of which are in color. Sidebars of paragraph length are used to explain topics such as red tide, tidal basins, and salt. Cross-references are consistently placed at the bottom of each left hand page. Each volume is indexed individually and a comprehensive index is included in volume 4. Each of the first three volumes has a different theme: the physical ocean, ocean life, and uses of the ocean. Among the topics included in the volume on physical features are the ocean floor, coastlines, rocky and sandy seashores, wetlands, currents, and tides. Animals in various ocean environments from the deep sea to rocky shores are presented in the second volume. Man's many uses for the oceans from exploration to farming and mining are covered, as well as myths, pollution, and renewable energy sources. The impact of humans is also addressed in each book. The last volume serves as a reference for the set. The five oceans have in-depth coverage with sidebar data and maps. Timelines of the Earth, surface exploration, and undersea exploration are included with short descriptions. The biography section highlights 38 well-known scientists, navigators, and explorers. The information is two to three paragraphs in length. The bibliography is divided by volume topic followed by recommended Websites and a list of aquariums, museums, and parks to visit. The text is engaging and informative without being overly technical. This resource will be useful to middle school and high school students as well as public libraries.—**Elaine Ezell**

Paleontology

P, S

537.   **Firefly Guide to Fossils.** New York, Firefly Books, 2003. 192p. illus. maps. index. $14.95pa. ISBN 1-55297-812-5.

The subtitle on the cover of the *Firefly Guide to Fossils* is *A Practical Guide to the Identification and Hunting of Fossils* and it sums this book up nicely. For novice or moderately experienced fossil-hounds this book is a well-presented guide to major types of fossils, their context in the rock record, and means to collect and enjoy them. Particularly helpful is a brief section on the ethical codes of collecting. Color illustrations, line drawings, and concise descriptions provide information about specific fossils, while an accessibly written summary of geologic history (with schematic maps) provides the framework for understanding Earth's changes over time and how they have affected life. The table of contents and index function well together to help the reader find entries of particular interest. There is a glossary and maps of notable fossil locations, but no references for further reading. Experienced fossil collectors may find this book a useful quick reference but its greatest value is for the less-experienced readers from middle school onward.—**R. K. Dickson**

Physics

C

538. **Elemental Data Index. http://physics.nist.gov/PhysRefData/Elements/cover.html.** [Website]. Free. Date reviewed: Feb 03.

The *Elemental Data Index* from the National Institute of Standards and Technology (NIST) Physics Laboratory, Physical Reference Data is a Web database that accesses the holdings of the NIST Physics Laboratory, from which users may obtain the following values for any specific element: atomic weight, ionization energy, ground-state level, and ground-state configuration. The information is developed from a variety of other NIST databases, which include: Atomic Spectral Data, X-ray and Gamma Ray Data, Radiation Dosimetry Data, Nuclear Physics Data, and Condensed Physics Data. The true beauty of this Website is the organization of the data into a Web page that searches the information by means of a displayed table. The creators of the file anticipated the different access methods that all users might have, so they offer three avenues for browsers to access the data—frames, no frames, and text-only—and all are superb. They even explain that they used style sheets in the creation of the output and how to turn these sheets off if you wish not to use them.

The database version history indicates that it first came online in September 1999 and that this (current) revision is August 2001. So the files have been around for some time now. The data, regardless of the version one chooses to use, presents an index to the material in the form of a periodic table. If one uses any version other than the text it will add color to show the physical state that the element exists in: solid, liquid, or gas.

When one clicks on an element to see the data, they will see a menu selection of retrieving the Atomic Spectra Database, X-ray and Gamma Ray Database, Radiation Dosimetry, Nuclear Physics Data, or Condensed Matter Physics Data. At this page they also have the atomic weight, ionization energy, ground-state level, and configuration. For any element the user sees the properties listed or charted as the information can be best presented.

The data and presentation are so useful that it would be wise to create links to the site on your library's public computers so that library patrons may locate the information quickly. Users will not even need the specific data that is found in the files, even the general information found at the site, such as atomic weights and so on, is very useful.—**James W. Oliver**

S

539. **Physics Experiments on File.** By the Diagram Group. New York, Facts on File, 2003. 1v. (various paging). illus. index. (Facts on File Science Library). $185.00 looseleaf w/binder. ISBN 0-8160-5043-0.

Facts on File has produced another quality resource for the science classroom. The heavy-duty, three-ring binder with cardstock pages follows the publisher's standard physical format used for its On File volumes. Permission is given for reproduction for use in nonprofit educational settings. The volume is arranged into 10 sections, which cover the principle areas of physics: "Forces," "Materials," "Heat," "Light," "Energy," "Wave Motion and Sound," "Electricity," "Magnetic Effects," "Electronics," and "Our Findings." The last section reviews the findings of each experiment, provides answers posed in the analysis portions, gives information of the underlying principles, and presents ideas to assist students who want or need to locate more information on the topic.

The arrangement of each of the approximate 60 experiments follows a standard format: topic, introduction, time required, materials, safety notes, procedures, data table, and analysis. It concludes with a section for those who want to know more about the topic. Each section of the experiment is clearly labeled. There are approximately 300 line drawings and illustrations that are titled and labeled. Data tables provide students with a convenient means of note taking. The experiments vary in level of difficulty.

The extensive appendixes enhance the usefulness of this resource. Internet resources are divided into two sections: educational resources and suppliers of equipment. The eight-page glossary italicizes terms that have their own entry. This is followed by guides to the appropriate grade level of the experiment, the amount of adult supervision needed, suitability of school or home setting, the suggested number of participants in an experiment, and a list of experiments that can be completed in an hour or less. A topical index concludes the book. Safety is stressed throughout the volume. Two pages of special safety notes precede the experiments, each experiment has a section of safety notes in bold, and supervision and safety are repeated within the appendixes.

The experiments are easy to read with very clear directions and illustrations. Teachers can easily remove an experiment for reproduction and replace it in its numbered sequence. This reference will be a valuable resource in middle and high school classrooms.—**Elaine Ezell**

MATHEMATICS

Handbooks and Yearbooks

S

540.   **The Facts on File Algebra Handbook.** By Deborah Todd. New York, Facts on File, 2003. 164p. illus. index. (Facts on File Science Library). $35.00. ISBN 0-8160-4703-0.

A volume in the Facts on File Science Library series, which is designed to enable students to compare information across subject areas, place each subject in context, and shows the close connections among all the sciences, this volume seeks to give students a broad understanding of the basics of algebra. It consists of a glossary of more than 350 entries, with 85 diagrams and line drawings to help clarify the definitions; brief biographies (including 15 black-and-white photographs of more than 100 mathematicians from ancient times to the present who have dedicated a portion of their lives to enrich others with a better understanding of mathematics and whose discoveries pushed forward the world's understanding and appreciation of algebra); a chronology that spans nearly 4,000 years of algebra history; a section of basic charts and tables with in-depth examples (including measurements and their equivalents, theorems and formulas, and mathematical symbols); and a list of recommended reading and useful Websites.

As can be seen from the contents and their arrangement, this volume is a source for reference to specific facts rather than a book to read. Because of its content and arrangement, this reviewer fails to see its usefulness to a student in an algebra course but does considerate a useful reference book for libraries who serve these students. Libraries will find the volume useful for looking up facts about algebra as well as its concepts, its history, its chronology, its practitioners, and recommended reading.—**Janet Mongan**

36 Resource Sciences

CHRONOLOGY

C, P, S

541. Wright, Russell O. **Chronology of Energy in the United States.** Jefferson, N.C., McFarland, 2003. 120p. index. $30.00pa. ISBN 0-7864-1642-4.

This compact source provides a chronology of energy events such as Ben Franklin's kite experiment in 1752, the first licensed radio broadcast in 1920, the first atomic bomb detonated in 1945, President Carter's creation of the Department of Energy in 1977, and a discussion of new types of vehicles and fuel systems. The 27-page introduction piques the reader's interest for the chronology that follows. From this easy-to-read book with interesting facts and statistics one gets a basic understanding of the enormous variety of energy issues humans have faced in the past and will be facing for years to come. There are some problems—the charts in the appendixes could use better bibliographic citations and the index provides dates instead of page numbers, which makes it harder to find information within the book. This source can encourage further research on inventors and a wide variety of energy topics, and would be a nice supplement to the *Macmillan Encyclopedia of Energy* (see ARBA 2002, entry 1589). This titled is recommended for high school, academic, and larger public libraries.—**Diane J. Turner**

DICTIONARIES AND ENCYCLOPEDIAS

C, P

542. **Encyclopedia of World Environmental History.** Shepard Drech III, J. R. McNeill, and Carolyn Merchant, eds. New York, Routledge/Taylor & Francis Group, 2004. 3v. illus. index. $345.00/set. ISBN 0-415-93732-9.

Encyclopedia of World Environmental History is a three-volume set written by international scholars, including founders of the field of environmental history and prominent scientists in associated fields. Content is arranged alphabetically from "acid rain" to "zoos," and includes events, people, natural resources, and aspects of human culture and natural history. A convenient list of entries is found at the beginning of volume 1, and an index is contained in volume 3 that will allow readers to cross-reference among entries. A set of world maps showing country boundaries at the beginning of volume 1 will orient the reader to the ever-changing political world. Articles end in a list of literature sources for further reading.

Coverage truly concerns the history of the topics, rather than a scientific treatment, meaning other sources will have to be sought for technical discussions of the many entries. However, technical topics are briefly defined before the historical coverage begins. Somewhat surprising entries are included, such as "Catholicism." Subheadings in this entry are "Christian and Catholic Beliefs," "Sacramentality and Ecology," and "Church Statements on Faith and the Environment," so the author does indeed tie Catholicism to environmental history.

This encyclopedia should be useful not only to those wanting a first-source reference for environmental history research, but can also be useful to researchers needing more technical information and wishing to begin their research with a historical perspective. Therefore, this encyclopedia is highly recommended for the reference section of all libraries. [R: LJ, Dec 03, pp. 94-96; AG, Dec 03-Jan 04, p. 63]—**Michael G. Messina**

C, P

543.   **Water: Science and Issues.** E. Julius Dasch, ed. New York, Macmillan Reference USA/Gale Group, 2003. 4v. illus. index. $395.00/set. ISBN 0-02-865611-3.

Water: Science and Issues is a 4-volume encyclopedia containing just over 300 entries dealing with almost every aspect of fresh water, marine water, and water policy and management. Entries range in length from 500 to 2,500 words, and the encyclopedia contains more than 575 color photographs and illustrations. The volumes are replete with glossary definitions, sidebars, and cross-references, all of which greatly enhance the readability and usefulness of the encyclopedia. In each entry, technical words are bolded and then defined in the outer margin. Entries are also followed by a short bibliography, and includes Internet resources. Sidebars are sometimes included to treat interesting related topics. A glossary and a cumulative index for the encyclopedia are repeated in each volume.

Written by water scientists, professors, educators and professional communicators, the encyclopedia displays a breadth and depth of coverage that makes it valuable to both nonspecialists and those knowledgeable about water science and policy. Although the intended audience is high school students and general readers, the editor claims that the encyclopedia will be of use to undergraduates and water resource professionals. However, the depth of treatment of each topic limits this encyclopedia from being an exhaustive research tool, but will instead make it a first-source reference. Nevertheless, the sheer breadth of coverage of important water issues means this encyclopedia should be contained in the reference section of all libraries. [R: Choice, Jan 04, p. 882]—**Michael G. Messina**

HANDBOOKS AND YEARBOOKS

C, P

544.   **The Little Green Data Book 2002.** Washington, D.C., World Bank, 2002. 239p. $15.00pa. ISBN 0-8213-5103-6.

The information in this book, published by the World Bank, is taken from the 2002 World Development Indicators. The data are from between 1997 and 2000. Tables for more than 200 countries provide information on agriculture, forests, biodiversity, energy, emissions and pollution, water and sanitation, and national accounting aggregates (such as gross national savings, education expenditure, and net forest depletion). Comparing statistics such as the under 5-mortality rate (per 1,000 births) of 4 in Sweden to 279 in Afghanistan, makes it clear where the wealth and resources are and where they are not. There are gaps in the information for some countries because the statistics are unavailable from those governments. The wealth of information in this small book will help students, researchers, and decision-makers see the vast differences in the plight of humankind. The 2003 edition of this source has already been published and the information in the book is also available on the Web. Still, it is nice to have all this information in a compact, inexpensive, easy-to-use book. The newest edition available is recommended for academic and public libraries.—**Diane J. Turner**

P, S

545.   **Riches of the Earth.** Danbury, Conn., Grolier, 2003. 16v. illus. maps. index. $269.00/set. ISBN 0-7172-5730-4.

Each volume of this 16-volume set focuses on one of the many natural materials that are valuable to humans—both monetarily and for survival. The set focuses on naturally grown foods (e.g., apples, potatoes, rice, wheat), fuel (e.g., oil), gems (e.g., diamonds, pearls), or textiles (e.g., wool, cotton). Each of these materials is discussed in its own volume, covering such topics as where it is found, how it was discovered, and how its uses have evolved over time. For example, the volume discussing apples includes information on where and how they are grown and how they are eaten and fuel the human body. The volume on diamonds discusses how diamonds are made, diamonds throughout history, and the dangers of mining for diamonds. Each volume concludes with a one-page glossary of "Words to Know," a list of resources for further study (both Websites and print publications), and a short index.

This set will be of interest to young children because of its colorful photographs and its ability to answer many common questions. It can also help teachers with elementary lessons on agriculture, environment, nutrition, and mining. Because it provides descriptions and histories of only 16 of the world's riches and because of its high price tag, this set is limited in its teaching value and can only be recommended for children's collections in public libraries and school libraries that afford it.—**Shannon Graff Hysell**

37 Transportation

AIR

C, P
546.   Dick, Ron, and Dan Patterson. **Aviation Century: The Early Years.** New York, Firefly Books, 2003. 240p. illus. index. $39.95. ISBN 1-55046-407-8.

Aviation Century: The Early Years is the first in a set of five volumes. This is a large format book of 240, 9-by-12-inch pages with good general and subject indexes and a valuable bibliography. It is divided into four chapters in loose chronological order, although the fourth, "Great Names," contains alphabetically arranged biographical sketches of aviation pioneers such as Walter Beech, William Boeing, Clyde Cessna, James McDonnell, Igor Sikorsky, and about 35 more.

This comprehensive look at aviation from 1900 to 1939 draws on early aviators' family information, museum collections, and a variety of other fascinating information sources. The narrative takes the novice or professional through logical steps of aviation's beginnings. Detailed explanations of early aircraft construction methods describe individual attempts to solve aerodynamic challenges.

The excellent and knowledgeable narrative is matched by a truly exceptional collection and arrangement of art, including photographs, drawings, museum pieces, travel posters, family memorabilia, and more. A variety of black-and-white, color, cameo, full-page, close-up, and collage images bring the excitement of aviation history to life.

The successful layout of this beautiful and informative book draws its strength from the collaboration between author and illustrator. Ron Dick, a pilot with thousands of flight hours, nearly four decades of Royal Air Force service, and avid aviation lecturer and author has co-authored this project with Dan Patterson, a leader in aviation photography. Patterson's images have been featured in a dozen books, and this is the sixth book he and Dick have co-authored. The narrative and visual content are well balanced, visually appealing, and very informative.

Perhaps it is authorial knowledge and experience that causes this book to be a powerful celebration of flight. It is not, however, alone in this category. While others may compare, such as *Flight and Flying: A Chronology* (see ARBA 95, entry 1787); have a more strict chronological arrangement, such as *Chronology of Flight c. 843 B.C. – 1939* (see ARBA 2001, entry 1556); be focused on one source of information, such as *The Smithsonian National Air and Space Museum Book of Flight* (see ARBA 2002, entry 1612); or be composed of essays, such as *Encyclopedia of Flight* (see ARBA 2003, entry 1558) the category is still far from being crowded. This is an excellent general history of aviation that is highly recommended for public and academic libraries, especially those supporting transportation or aviation programs.—**James W. Agee Jr.**

P
547.   Smith, Myron J., Jr. **The Airline Encyclopedia: 1909-2000.** Lanham, Md., Scarecrow, 2003. 3v. illus. index. $695.00/set. ISBN 0-8108-3790-0.

This massive 3-volume set of more than 3,000 pages and 6,000 entries provides a prodigious amount of information about world airlines. It is truly encyclopedic in both arrangement and content. This is not a general encyclopedia of aviation. There are no entries for manufacturers or airports; it is tightly focused on airlines. *The Airline Encyclopedia: 1909-2000* is an excellent in-depth resource for anyone seeking airline information from aviation, business, or history perspectives. Airlines that existed during the twentieth century are included, regardless of their flag of registry.

Each entry is a concise narrative in chronological sequence. Main entry headings, years, and cross-indexed airline entries are shown in bold typeface. A few short paragraphs describe some smaller airlines, while larger airline entries fill many pages because of their constantly changing organizational histories. Fleet size, composition, and changes are detailed. Noteworthy business mergers, organizational changes, or airplane crashes are also included.

A postscript and two appendixes follow the final entry in volume 3. These are followed by more than 350 pages of indexes. The regional index and the name and subject index are well organized, detailed, and contain extensive alphabetic entries that include individuals, events, and organizations. The main index entry for "Skyjacking" has several pages of chronological sub-entries. Many chronological index entries are also listed under another main entry: "Strikes and Miscellaneous Job Actions." These two varied topics evidence the depth, breadth, and meticulous organization found in this set.

The many valuable details in these volumes make them exceptional resources in the scant published literature for aviation research. In 1998, Voyageur Press produced the directory-like *Airlines Worldwide* (see ARBA 99, entry 1573). The geographically specific *Encyclopedia of African Airlines* (see ARBA 99, entry 1574) by Ben R. Guttery and McFarland Press also became available that year. Nothing in recent years has begun to detail the airline industry as comprehensively as *The Airline Encyclopedia: 1909-2000*, the new airline reference standard. This set is highly recommended for large public libraries and academic or research libraries. It is a must for libraries supporting academic programs in aviation, business, or history.

Myron J. Smith Jr. compiled this valuable collection of international aviation information. The three-volume set builds on his previous works from Locust Hill Press, *Airline Bibliography, Volume 1, 1986* (see ARBA 87, entry 1732) and *Airline Bibliography, Volume 2, 1988* (see ARBA 89, entry 1684). His skillful librarianship and professional knowledge of aviation are combined in this rigorously constructed and much-needed aviation reference.—**James W. Agee Jr.**

GROUND

P

548.   Haajanen, Lennart W. **Illustrated Dictionary of Automobile Body Styles.** Illustrated by Bertil Nydén. Jefferson, N.C., McFarland, 2003. 165p. illus. $35.00. ISBN 0-7864-1276-3.

Beginning with the earliest nomenclature on coach building and bodywork growing out of carriage and wagon building, this work covers the various styles and terms used in describing the automobile design—sedan, coupe, and station wagon. The work includes the wider variety of vehicles commonly used as automobiles: minivans, sport utility vehicles, and so on. It is arranged alphabetically by term, each with a one- to two-paragraph definition. In addition, each entry has language variations for the term (where appropriate) as well as cross-references and important time periods for use of the term. A large number of line drawings illustrate the volume and add to the definitions and descriptions of the body types. An appendix showing the evolution of some of the more important automobile body styles, from horse-drawn vehicles to those of current day, and a brief bibliography for further reference complete the volume.

The *Illustrated Dictionary of Automobile Body Styles* is well worth including on the shelf for collections devoted to transportation, engineering design, or social and technological history. The library binding will stand up to years of research and reference activity.—**Gregory Curtis**

Author/Title Index

Reference is to entry number.

Subject Index

Reference is to entry number.

ABOLITIONISTS
Historical dict of slavery & abolition, 193

ABORTION
Encyclopedia of abortion in the US, 284

ACTORS. *See also* **MOTION PICTURES**
African Americans in the performing arts, 430
Bad boys, 431

ADVERTISING
Encyclopedia of advertising, 90

AERONAUTICS
Airline ency: 1909-2000, 547
Aviation century, 546

AFGHANISTAN
Conflict in Afghanistan, 54

AFRICA
African studies companion, 3d rev ed, 42
History of Africa series, 166

AFRICAN AMERICAN ACTORS
African Americans in the performing arts, 430

AFRICAN AMERICAN ARTISTS
African Americans in the visual arts, 340

AFRICAN AMERICAN LITERATURE
Encyclopedia of the Harlem Renaissance, 395

AFRICAN AMERICAN SCIENTISTS
African Americans in sci, math, & invention, 457

AFRICAN AMERICAN SOLDIERS
African Americans at war, 232

AFRICAN AMERICANS - POLITICS & GOVERNMENT
African Americans & pol participation, 246

AFRICAN AUTHORS
Encyclopedia of African lit, 403

AFRO-AMERICANS
African-American athletes, 268

African-American social leaders & activists, 240
Black firsts, 2d ed, 118
Black genesis, 2d ed, 137
Encyclopedia of Negro league baseball, 276
Encyclopedia of 20th-century African hist, 165

AGED
Online resources for senior citizens, 285

AIDS (DISEASE)
Encyclopedia of HIV & AIDS, 2d ed, 515

AIRLINES
Airline ency: 1909-2000, 547
Aviation century, 546

ALMANACS
Chase's calendar of events 2004, 1
New view almanac, 3d ed, 2

ALTERNATIVE MEDICINE
ABC clinical gd to herbs, 511

ALZHEIMER'S DISEASE
Alzheimer's disease sourcebk, 3d ed, 516

AMERICAN LITERATURE. *See also* **AUTHORS, AMERICAN**
Continuum ency of American lit, 396
Encyclopedia of the Harlem Renaissance, 395

ANATOMY
Atlas of the human body, 478

ANCIENT HISTORY
Ancient Europe 8000 BC to AD 1000, 172
Exploring ancient civilizations, 191
Greenhaven ency of ancient Egypt, 183
Handbook to life in ancient Egypt, rev ed, 182
Historical atlas of ancient Greece, 180

ANIMALS
Mammal, 496
Oxford dict of zoology, rev ed, 491
Wildlife ref center [Website], 490

ANTARCTICA
Exploring polar frontiers, 43